NATURAL COGNITIVE THEOLOGY

by Lorin Friesen

ISBN: 978-0-9879785-1-6

Published by Lorin Friesen

First Printing, 2015

http://www.mentalsymmetry.com

Contents

Thanks to Angelina Van Dyke for help with editing.

❋ Introduction

What is religion? Let us open this book by examining some of the answers that have been proposed to this fundamental question.

The 2006 Encyclopedia Britannica, for instance, defines religion as "Human beings' relation to that which they regard as holy, sacred, spiritual, or divine." This appears to be saying that religion deals with aspects of existence that would be regarded as *unusual*. The word 'holy' means 'set apart'. The sacred is 'set apart' because it deals with topics that have deeper significance than normal existence, the spiritual is 'set apart' because it involves realms that are non-material, and the divine is 'set apart' because it interacts with beings who are non-human.

Bertrand Russell defined religion as the *absence* of reason and scientific thought: "Religion is something left over from the infancy of our intelligence; it will fade away as we adopt reason and science as our guidelines." Here we see that normal, human, material existence is guided by rational scientific thought. Religion, in contrast, is something different that involves *irrational thinking*.

Karl Marx described religion as something that fills a *hole* in normal existence: "Religion is the sigh of the oppressed creature, the heart of a heartless world, just as it is the spirit of a spiritless situation. It is the opiate of the people." Russell viewed normal life as the *presence* of reason and science, while Marx portrayed it as the *absence* of meaning. Modern technology has provided us with an existence that is guided by rational scientific thought, but for many people this is also a world of oppression that lacks heart and spirit. And so the oppressed masses reach out to religion, hoping to find something more than just normal existence. Marx was not convinced that anything more exists, and so he described religion as an opiate, a way of artificially generating a sense of meaning while emotionally dulling a person to the pain of normal human existence.

Sigmund Freud, in his *New Introductory Lectures on Psychoanalysis*, also viewed religion as a sort of opiate: "Religion is an illusion and it derives its strength from the fact that it falls in with our instinctual desires." On the one hand, we are driven to search for something more. On the other hand, says Freud, there is nothing more.

One sees this same juxtaposition in atheism, a belief in the nonexistence of God. If God does not exist, then why is it necessary to assert his nonexistence? People do not call themselves a-Trekkies and insist that the world of Star Trek does not exist, because we all know that Kirk and Spock are merely figments of the imagination. And yet, when it comes to God, something is *inserting* the idea of God into our minds, while something *else* is causing us to reject this idea.

Wikipedia defines religion as "an organized collection of beliefs, cultural systems, and worldviews that relate humanity to an order of existence." In other words, religion gives us the 'big picture'. It ties everything together. Wikipedia adds that "Many religions have narratives, symbols, and sacred histories that are intended to explain the meaning of life and/or to explain the origin of life or the Universe. From their beliefs about the cosmos and human nature, people derive morality, ethics, religious laws or a preferred lifestyle." This is quite different than what we have seen so far. All of the other definitions regard religion as something that lies *outside* of normal life which *violates* scientific thought. Wikipedia, in contrast, defines religion as something that is *larger* than normal life, which goes *beyond* scientific thought.

This is the definition of religion we will be using in this book. First, I suggest religion provides a grand explanation, a reason for everything. Second, religion places us within this grand explanation and tells us how to act and think. But we can also see why religion is often defined as something outside of normal existence that violates scientific thought. Stated simply, we are caught in a dilemma. On the one hand, there is a deep desire for a grand explanation that ties everything together. This desire leads to the concept of God—a universal being who ties everything together. But on the other hand, our personal existence is incomplete, because we all live for a few decades and then... Well, we do not know. All we really know is the material world that science studies because it defines normal existence. And because normal material existence is all that we know, we are driven to reject the idea of a transcendent, universal being who exists beyond the material realm. Thus, we want to believe in God but do not know how to approach the subject in a rational, scientific manner. One sees this struggle in atheism.

> Religion addresses two related questions:
> 1) What is the grand explanation?
> 2) What is my place in this explanation?

However, the existence of God is not just a theoretical, philosophical dilemma. It is also an inescapable, personal plight. Is death the end, or does human existence continue after death? But even asking this question poses the dilemma of human existence merely as a theoretical search for a grand explanation. The real question is whether *my* death is the end of *my* awareness, and whether *my* human existence continues after death. And I am using the first-person pronoun deliberately because this is not a question that can be transferred to any other individual or group. Science does a marvelous job of describing physical existence. But when a person dies, then wherever he goes, if he still is, then he has *left* the realm of science. Russell said that religion is something left over from infancy that will fade away as we adopt reason and science, but Russell neglected to mention that religion *returns* to center stage as *we* fade away. The dying man may pretend that religion is not important, but death occurs inexorably, whether acknowledged or not.

If religion is such an important topic, then how should it be approached? Should one merely adopt the beliefs and practices of some existing religion? If so, which religion? They cannot all be right, which means one must *choose* between one religion and another. Does one merely embrace the religion of one's culture? That seems to be a rather risky way of addressing the topic of personal existence. Because of this uncertainty, it is rather important to *study* the topic of religion. We may succumb to impulse shopping when buying clothes and candy, but when purchasing large items such as cars and houses, then we shop around before making a decision. One should take even more care when addressing questions of cosmic import and personal existence.

But how does one study religion? If religion provides a grand explanation, then I suggest that it does not make sense to use a scientific approach that *begins* by limiting analysis to the purely material. If one wishes to explore an unknown world, one does not start by insisting it does not exist. Similarly, if religion places *us* within a grand explanation, then it also does not make sense to adopt the *objectivity* which science advocates. If I wish to explore my place within an unknown world, I do not start by *ignoring* myself.

But one also does not want to reject scientific thought because it has succeeded in giving us an understanding of the material, objective world. Therefore, what is needed is a form of scientific-like thought that includes the subjective and extends beyond the material. I suggest that a study of *cognition* provides this combination.

First, cognition can be studied in a scientific-like manner. Science is based upon *repeatability*. Cognitive science examines the thinking of many people and looks for underlying patterns. Science is a search for *general hypotheses*. Cognitive science comes up with cognitive models that explain underlying patterns of thought. Science wants *predictions*. A cognitive model allows one to predict that if a person develops his mind in a specific manner, then there will be certain cognitive results.

Second, studying cognition combines objective and subjective, because the mind is studying itself. The researcher doing the examining is using the same kind of mind as the individuals who are being examined. This automatically combines the two questions of religion. A cognitive theory is a grand explanation in the sense that it applies to all of human thought, and a cognitive theory determines a person's place within this grand explanation because it also applies to the thinking of the researcher.

Third, cognition is a hybrid of material and immaterial. Neurology tells us a lot about the physical basis for cognition from its study of the material brain—and neurology is discussed in detail in the final chapter of this book. However, neurology has not solved the problem of 'hard consciousness'. It can explain in great detail how information is internally processed but it cannot explain how everything comes together. Using an analogy, neurology tells us a lot about the engine, the controls, and the gauges of a car, but it cannot explain the driver who views the gauges and operates the controls in order to drive the car. Thus, I suggest that cognition gives us a window into the immaterial.

If the answer lies in studying cognition, then how does one do so in a manner that goes beyond the material and includes the subjective *while remaining rigorous*? The methodology that I have adopted is that of correlation guided by a cognitive model. Back in the 1980s, my older brother and I encountered a system of cognitive styles that divided people into seven different categories. My brother, Lane Friesen, fleshed out these seven categories by analyzing 200 biographies, which resulted in a detailed list of traits for each of the seven cognitive styles (Friesen, 1986). Notice the combination of correlation and cognitive model. The starting point was the cognitive *model* of a system of cognitive styles. This model was then made more rigorous by *correlating* the descriptions of 200 different individuals.

This combination of correlation and cognitive model then reoccurred at a higher level. As we examined these seven lists of traits, we noticed underlying fundamental characteristics. We realized that each cognitive style is not just a haphazard collection of personality traits but rather describes the functioning of a cognitive module that processes a certain form of information in a certain manner. This led to a refined cognitive model, which I call the *diagram of mental symmetry*. This model was then made more rigorous by correlating the functioning of these seven cognitive modules with the findings of psychology and neurology.

This combination of correlation and cognitive model then reoccurred—yet again—at a higher level. As I examined the diagram of mental symmetry, I noticed that it could be viewed as a sort of computer and that one could work out the steps that needed to be taken to program this mental computer. This led to a refined understanding of the cognitive model, now focusing upon the topic of cognitive *development*. As before, this research was then made more rigorous by correlating my cognitive analysis with the research of others.

When one approaches the topic of cognitive development guided by a cognitive model, then what gradually emerges is a *grand explanation*. Obviously, Jean Piaget's work on cognitive development is foundational. But, one can also explain the philosophy of science and its analysis of how the mind studies the natural world. Here, Thomas Kuhn's description of paradigms and paradigm shifts comes into focus. More pragmatic fields also become unified. For instance, I have recently been focusing upon TESOL, which teaches people new languages and helps them to acquire new identities as they move between cultures. Finally, religion emerges from the shadows as one repeatedly sees that there is a correlation (that word again) between cognitive mechanisms and religious beliefs. However, instead of debating the existence of God, one can now focus upon how the mind forms an image of God and how this mental concept affects personal identity.

In other words, one returns by a back door to the two major questions of religion posed earlier. Religion provides a grand explanation for everything, while a cognitive model provides a grand explanation for how the mind comes up with grand explanations. Religion describes my place within this grand explanation, while a cognitive model analyzes the relationship between my mental concept of personal identity and my mental concept of God.

This is the sort of 'thinking about thinking' that postmodern thought aims for, but seldom achieves. Many authors have come up with approaches that analyze the thinking behind the thinking of *others*, but these schemes often run into problems when applied to the thinking of the researchers *themselves*. In contrast, I have found that the theory of mental symmetry works well when applied to itself. It can explain how the *mind* functions, and it can also explain what is happening within the mind of the *researcher* who is attempting to explain how the mind functions. Going further, it can be viewed either as a *description* of how everyone's mind works, or as a *prescription* of the steps that need to be taken to get the mind to work.

By returning to religion through a cognitive backdoor, topics that are often regarded as a matter of faith or tradition become rational and discussable. For instance, choosing between the God of one religion and the God of another is a matter of faith and debate, while one can observe and analyze the type of concept of God that emerges when all of the mind is functioning.

Again, I suggest that it is possible to use a combination of cognitive model and correlation to add rigor to this analysis. How can one tell that a mental concept of God based in a cognitive model has any relationship to a real God? By correlating the attributes of a mental concept of God with the descriptions of God given by actual religions. If a major religion says the same thing—in detail—about the grand explanation and my place within that explanation, then this correlation adds rigor to the doctrines and practices of that religion as well as providing corroborative evidence for the cognitive model.

But why add the cognitive element to an existing religion? Because it is *already* present. As Immanuel Kant first asked, does the physical world have the form that it does because it actually *exists* that way or because human minds are *imposing* their structure upon their perception of reality? For instance, we all know that we live in a space-time universe, but is that because the universe is really composed of space and time or because our minds are only capable of thinking in terms of space and time? This is not an easy question to answer. Kant's dilemma reflects the hardware of the mind, the way in which it is wired. Thomas Kuhn described a similar predicament involving the software of the mind, noting that every scientist observes the world through the 'lenses' of some paradigm or grand explanation. While the average person may not have an *explicit* grand explanation, reality is still being viewed through some *implicit* worldview.

These are deeply personal problems and not just philosophical questions. That is because the thinking of my mind is being shaped by its structure no matter where I go and no attempt to remain objective is capable of bypassing this inherent limitation. Similarly, I am always viewing the world through some set of lenses and the only way to evaluate these lenses is by putting on a set of glasses.

As before, I suggest that the solution lies in the combination of cognitive model and correlation. In simple terms, I put on some set of lenses and see if the picture is clear or fuzzy. If my lenses are inconsistent with the structure of the mind and the nature of the world, then my picture of thought and reality will end up being hazy. In contrast, if my paradigm matches the structure of the mind and the nature of reality, then the picture will be clear. In order to make this a valid test, I must look at many parts of the picture and not just some specialization or small fragment of existence. That is where the correlation comes in: comparing the view of one aspect of the picture with the view of another. Almost any set of lenses will give me a clear view of some aspect of the picture; however, only a good set of lenses will put the entire picture into focus. Any valid model will have to include cognition, because I am looking at the world *through* the lenses of my paradigm, and I am using my *mind* to interact with reality. Notice again the combination of personal and universal. On the one hand, one is not just checking facts in an objective manner but rather wearing a set of metaphysical glasses and viewing reality through these glasses. On the other hand, because everyone has similar minds and lives in the same physical world, glasses that work well for one individual should also be suitable for other individuals.

Using another analogy, an inadequate explanation is like a set of clothes that do not fit properly. Parts of existence will be left uncovered by the cloth of explanation while other aspects of existence will have to be squeezed to fit. In contrast, a paradigm that is consistent with mental and physical structure will fit like a tailor-made garment, covering all of the body in a graceful manner.

The thesis of this book is that the theory of mental symmetry is tailor-made to cover both the human mind and the findings of neurology. In addition, I suggest that its cut and fit match the garment of scientific thought as well as the grand explanation provided by the religion of Christianity. I propose to demonstrate this by using mental symmetry to provide a clear, un-blurred picture of these various fields, focusing primarily upon theology—which is why this book is entitled *Natural Cognitive Theology*.

The word 'theology', by its very nature, is related to the religion of Christianity, because theology presupposes that it is possible to speak and reason about the nature of God. For Buddhism and Hinduism, what matters is naturalism, a study of the nature of the world. Theology (called Kalam) exists within Islam, but it plays a much lesser role than theology does in Christianity. Likewise, the primary focus in Judaism is on the relationship between God and the Jewish community as revealed in Torah. Thus, while Jewish theology exists, it takes a more pragmatic and communal form.

If we are going to use a combination of cognitive modeling and correlation to analyze religion, then we must begin by introducing the cognitive model of mental symmetry.

❋ 1. Mental Symmetry

I should start by confessing that we cheated. My brother and I did not come up with the system of cognitive styles upon which the theory of mental symmetry is based. Instead, we stole it—from the Bible. In the 12th chapter of Romans, the apostle Paul presents a list of seven 'spiritual gifts'.

> Therefore I urge you, brethren, by the mercies of God, to present your bodies a living and holy sacrifice, acceptable to God, which is your spiritual service of worship. And do not be conformed to this world, but be transformed by the re-newing of your mind, so that you may prove what the will of God is, that which is good and acceptable and perfect. For through the grace given to me I say to everyone among you not to think more highly of himself than he ought to think; but to think so as to have sound judgment, as God has allotted to each a measure of faith. For just as we have many members in one body and all the members do not have the same function, so we, who are many, are one body in Christ, and individually members one of another. Since we have gifts that differ according to the grace given to us, each of us is to exercise them accordingly: if *prophecy*, ac-cording to the proportion of his faith; if *service*, in his serving; or he who *teaches*, in his teaching; or he who *exhorts*, in his exhortation; he who *gives*, with liberal-ity; he who *leads*, with diligence; he who shows *mercy*, with cheerfulness (Ro-mans 12:1-8).

The list of seven cognitive styles occurs at the end of this quote and the seven names have been italicized. Some of the specific terms are slightly different, but that is a matter of translation because this passage was originally written in Koine Greek. I should also mention that my brother was not the one who originally interpreted this list as a system of cognitive styles. Instead, Don Pickerell was the first to gather lists of traits based upon questionnaires handed out in his church. This initial history is described in more detail in a 1976 article in Vision magazine (Harvey, 1976).

Looking at this passage in more detail, one notices the following characteristics. First, it is talking about cognitive development: 'Be transformed by the renewing of your mind'. Second, it says that cognitive development means transcending the content that was acquired through embodiment and culture: 'Present your bodies a living and holy sacri-fice... and do not be conformed to this world'. Third, it is referring to cognition. One is 'not to think more highly of himself than he ought to think; but to think so as to have sound judgment'. Fourth, it states that each cognitive style emphasizes one aspect of integrated thought: 'For just as we have many members in one body and all the members do not have the same function, so we, who are many, are one body'.

It does not make sense that a book written in the Roman era would contain a neurologically and psychologically accurate summary of human cognition and that this description would only be deciphered 1900 years after it had been written. But that is what I propose. The standard theory of personality used in Roman (and medieval) times was the four temperaments of sanguine, choleric, melancholic, and phlegmatic, which the Greek physician Hippocrates related to the four body fluids of blood, yellow bile, black bile, and phlegm. This may be an interesting observation of how people appear as well as a description of the fluids that they excrete, but it is rather inadequate as a cognitive model. As for the early church leaders, Augustine declared at the beginning of the fifth century that spiritual gifts were only valid during the time of Jesus and the apostles, and so the very concept of spiritual gifts was dropped.

Does this mean that I am following circular reasoning by using Christianity to prove Christianity? I suggest not. That is because extensive research was required to transform the biblical list of seven gifts into a cognitively based system of natural theology, and it is possible to place this model upon a solid, research-based foundation. However, the starting point was a passage from the Bible, and without that starting point it is doubtful that the cognitive model would have emerged.

The normal practice is to hide the ancestry of scientific theories that have non-rigorous parentage. After all, one would not want to appear unscientific. For instance, MBTI, the most widely used system of cognitive styles, has the rather dubious foundation of Karl Jung's Red Book, which Jung's heirs literally kept hidden from others until 2001. That is because "Its pages are made from thick cream-colored parchment and filled with paintings of otherworldly creatures and handwritten dialogues with gods and devils. If you didn't know the book's vintage, you might confuse it for a lost medieval tome" (Corbett, 2009).

For science, the source of information is very important, because all facts must be based in careful observation. But we are not dealing here with data but rather with the set of glasses that one puts on to examine this data. When one is wearing an inadequate pair of glasses, then many items will look fuzzy, distorted, or disappear from view, including *other pairs of glasses*. Wearing the wrong set of lenses can make me mentally blind to seeing the right set of glasses. The only solution is to have somebody else *give* me the right set of glasses and *tell* me to put them on.

This is what happens in education. Adults send children to school and teach them how to view the world through 'the correct' set of glasses. Of course, the educators themselves can also be mistaken. That is why *rote learning* needs to be followed by *critical thinking*. Rote learning puts on a set of glasses. Critical thinking evaluates these glasses. If teachers tell their students that they must not question the set of lenses that they have been given, or that these glasses are not meant to view certain topics, then this usually means that these glasses are inadequate.

If educators are giving inadequate glasses to their students, then how will the educators discover the right set of lenses? The only solution is for some *outside source* to reveal an adequate set of lenses, which is what happened in the case of spiritual gifts and the theory of mental symmetry. However, it was only in the 1970s that someone actually *put on* these glasses and started to view the world of people through these lenses. I suggest that this is because of the spread of psychology and the personal computer. Psychology made it possible to think about cognition, whereas the personal computer uses a primitive form of machine cognition. In other words, learning about psychology and using the personal computer gave people a set of glasses that made it possible to see the glasses of 'spiritual gifts'. I suggest that this is also a general principle. Religious believers often think that a holy book gives them inside access to absolute truth, but even if a holy book contains the very words of God, the human ability to *rationally comprehend* these words still depends upon the current level of scientific and social development.

The Diagram of Mental Symmetry

We have talked a lot about looking through glasses. Let me introduce you now to the pair of glasses through which I have been viewing my world, glasses which I have been using for about thirty years.

We will start by examining the *diagram of mental symmetry,* the general framework for these glasses. This diagram provides the basic framework for the theory of mental symmetry. It is fairly simple, composed of seven names tied together by some lines and arrows, a horizontal axis, a vertical axis, and a diagonal axis. While this diagram is straightforward, I have discovered many details and subtleties over the years that add to its explaining power. The seven names come from the list of seven 'spiritual gifts' mentioned earlier: Perceiver, Server, Teacher, Exhorter, Contributor, Facilitator, and Mercy. Those who are encountering these labels for the first time sometimes complain that the term 'Mercy' is grammatically inconsistent with the other six terms and they are technically right. However, as I pointed out, my brother initially acquired these names from others, and it is too late to change basic terms now. And these seven labels have the advantage of each starting with a different letter of the alphabet, so if one wants to conserve space one can speak of P, S, T, E, C, F, and M. I should also mention that the word 'teacher' in lower case will refer to the occupation or task of teaching while the capitalized word 'Teacher' will refer to the cognitive style or cognitive module.

Look first at the three axes. The *vertical* axes are labeled *analytical* and *associative*. This describes two different ways of thinking. *Analytical* thought deals with time and sequence and tends to focus upon order and structure. It is placed on the left side of the diagram because it corresponds to the processing of the left hemisphere of the brain. Analytical thought could be compared to a train switching yard, where individual cars are connected together to form trains. The sequence of cars in a train can be altered by adding or removing cars, or by rearranging the order of the cars. *Associative* thought deals with space and connections and tends to focus upon the individual item and its place in the overall picture. It is placed on the right side of the diagram because it corresponds to right hemisphere processing. Associative thought could be compared to a map containing locations and connections between these locations.

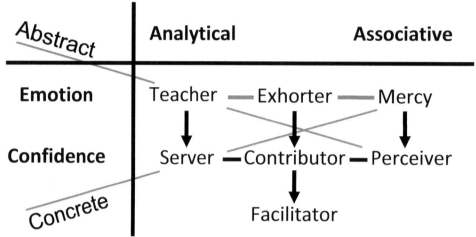

The diagonal axes are labeled *abstract* and *concrete*. Concrete thought deals directly with the physical world, whereas abstract thought lives in the 'abstract world' of words and ideas. The Teacher is abstract analytical, dealing with sequences of words. The Server is concrete analytical, working with sequences of actions. The Mercy is concrete associative, building connections between experiences, while the Perceiver is abstract associative, building connections between facts.

Finally, the horizontal axes are labeled *emotion* and *confidence*. These are two ways of evaluating information. Emotion is, well...emotion. We all know what emotions feel like. If one wished to get more technical, one could say that emotions add physical sensation to mental processing. For instance, we speak of 'butterflies in the stomach', a 'gut feeling', 'goose bumps', or 'feeling tingly all over'. In each case, physical sensation is being added to thinking. Is all emotion based in physical sensation? In order to answer that question fully one must know where the brain stops and the mind starts, which is rather difficult to do. One can say that physical sensation is a major *aspect* of emotion, and that physical sensation provides the *starting point* for emotion. But I suggest that emotion is *more* than just a physical sensation. For instance, a child will go on a camping trip and feel miserable because it is raining and the mosquitoes are biting, whereas an adult may go on the same trip and feel enjoyment rather than misery. Thus, what for the child is primarily physical sensation is something more for the adult.

Notice that both Mercy and Teacher use emotion. Everyone is familiar with *Mercy* emotion because physical sensation naturally causes *experiences* to acquire emotional labels. Using psychological language, Mercy emotion is based in embodiment. However, the

Teacher is also emotional. When many items fit together, then Teacher thought feels good. When there is chaos, or when an item is out of place, then Teacher thought feels bad. In simple terms, Teacher emotion comes from *order-within-complexity*. Notice that both order and complexity are required. One could compare Teacher emotion to the rule of a monarch. The status of the ruler depends upon the number of his subjects and how well they submit to his edicts. A monarch with no subjects has no status. Neither does a monarch whose subjects ignore his wishes. What is needed is a ruler with obedient subjects—order-within-complexity. I have mentioned that the Teacher works with sequences of words. Teacher emotion drives the Teacher to come up with general theories, simple word-based statements that can explain many situations. For instance, my older brother is a Teacher person. When we were working together he would often say, "Let me explain it to you in a single sentence", illustrating the desire to explain many concepts using a single sequence of words.

The label 'confidence' also needs some explaining, because I am defining it in a way that is somewhat unusual. In simple terms, it refers to a sense of *knowing* or *certainty*. Perceiver works with facts, and the Perceiver assigns a label of certainty (or confidence) to each fact. For instance, one can know for certain that the War of 1812 started in—you guessed it—1812. However, one cannot say for certain when this war finished, because the final major battle was fought in New Orleans after the peace treaty was signed in Ghent. Perceiver confidence can be increased by repeating connections. The more times a fact is heard or encountered, the more confident Perceiver will be that this fact is correct. In a similar way, the Server assigns a label of certainty (or confidence) to sequences. It is possible to build confidence in a sequence of actions by practicing that action. The first time a sequence of actions is carried out, Server confidence in performing this sequence will be fairly low. Repeating this sequence will build confidence. Thus, in the same way that repetition builds Perceiver confidence, so repetition builds Server confidence. However, notice that Perceiver and Server confidence can have different *sources*. Perceiver confidence is based upon facts and connections that are *observed*. Similarly, *observing* sequences being repeated will also lead to greater Server confidence. But it is also possible for me to build Server confidence by using my physical body to repeat an action. In other words, while Perceiver confidence can only come from *elsewhere*, Server confidence can come both from elsewhere *and* from myself. This distinction has several implications, which will be discussed later on.

The label 'confidence' also describes the ability to handle emotional pressure without falling apart. For instance, I may have sufficient Server confidence to walk on a log when it is lying on the ground while lacking the Server confidence to walk on that same log if it crosses a deep gully. The sequence of actions is precisely the same, but the level of confidence required is massively different. Similarly, I may have sufficient Perceiver confidence to know that there is a connection between eating too many sweets and getting fat, while lacking the Perceiver confidence to know this fact when I am staring at a slice of decadent chocolate cheesecake, iced with a rich layer of bittersweet dark Belgian chocolate, drizzled with crushed almonds and a dollop of fresh whipped cream. As the writers of restaurant menus have learned, adjectives sell food. Add enough emotions and facts go out the window. Of course, the facts themselves do not change, instead what changes is the Perceiver's ability to believe in these facts.

Let us turn now to the lines and arrows. Teacher, Exhorter, and Mercy are connected with a *gray* line. This means that the Exhorter can be viewed as a combination of Teacher and Mercy. The Teacher lives in abstract words and theories while the Mercy lives in concrete experiences. The Exhorter combines these two by connecting words with experiences. The Exhorter speaks a lot, but his speech is based in experience. The Exhorter thrives on experience, but these experiences are guided by abstract theories. The line connecting these three is *gray* because the connections between words and experiences are somewhat vague; what matters to the Exhorter is not precision but rather general effect. Teacher and Mercy function emotionally. The Exhorter, in contrast, is driven by excitement, which is based upon emotion but subtly different. First, emotion wants to feel good and does not like to feel bad. Excitement, in contrast, focuses upon emotional intensity. Riding a roller coaster, or seeing a scary movie, is emotionally unpleasant. However, it is exciting because the emotions are intense. Second, emotion is for always while excitement requires novelty. The Mercy may say 'Let us go to our familiar restaurant', while the Exhorter is more likely to say, 'I am tired of that restaurant, let us go somewhere else.' Once the Exhorter has eaten at the new restaurant, then he may be willing to go *back* to the familiar restaurant, because it has now regained some novelty. Neurologically speaking, it appears that the Exhorter is related to the brain chemical dopamine. Summarizing, the Exhorter *accesses* the same information as the Teacher and the Mercy, but *uses* this information in a different way.

Server, Contributor, and Perceiver are connected by a *black* line. Just as the Exhorter can be viewed as a combination of Teacher and Mercy, so the Contributor can be viewed as a combination of Server and Perceiver. The Server lives in sequences and actions, the Perceiver lives in facts and connections. What matters to the Contributor is the relationship between sequences and facts. The Server is often satisfied with performing actions, but what matters to the Contributor is carrying out a plan—a combination of facts and actions. The Perceiver is often satisfied with gathering facts. The Contributor, in contrast, wants facts that are applied, 'What can I do with this information?' The line connecting these three is black because the Contributor builds *precise* connections between facts and sequences; each fact is connected with a specific sequence. Contributor confidence is also subtly different than Perceiver and Server confidence. For the Perceiver and Server, confidence is a label that is attached to information. Each fact or sequence is known with a certain level of confidence. For the Contributor, confidence describes the ability to stay in control without falling apart. The Contributor who has confidence oozes certainty, and gives off an aura that is unmistakable when encountered. The Contributor who lacks confidence will 'become rattled' or 'lose his cool'. Like a defeated dog, he metaphorically cowers 'with his tail between his legs'.

Moving on, the diagram contains two sets of arrows. First, an arrow leads from Teacher to Server and from Mercy to Perceiver. This indicates that Perceiver builds upon Mercy and Server upon Teacher. The Mercy deals with experiences, such as a fragrant red rose, a friendly cat, George the nosy next-door neighbor, and the vacation in Hawaii where the passports got stolen. Notice how the Mercy focuses upon emotional labels and identifying features. The Perceiver, in contrast, looks at connections between Mercy experiences. What matters to Perceiver thought is not the emotional label but rather the similarities and differences between experiences—the connections that do and do not exist. For instance, how can one distinguish between roses and carnations, that cat seems to be appearing in the backyard quite often, George is quite knowledgeable about flowers, how common is passport theft in Hawaii?

Similarly, Server gives stability to Teacher by looking for sequences that are repeated. The Teacher deals with words and theories, such as the article on global warming, the recent conversation about local politics, the looming financial debt crisis, or the theory of relativity. The Server, in contrast, focuses upon actions and routine: Let me tell you what I did today. When company comes over I usually make chicken casserole because I know that recipe works. I will be in the garage working on the car.

Because both Mercy and Perceiver are interpreting the *same* world of experiences, they often *clash* over how to approach experiences. The Mercy feels that the focus should be upon emotions, while the Perceiver thinks that the focus should be upon facts. In contrast, Teacher and Server tend to operate in parallel *independently* of one another, because each is *capable* of functioning independently of the other. The Teacher can talk and the Server can do. Thus, the typical Teacher lives in words, while the average Server lives in actions. However, like the cat that remains nearby while 'doing its own thing', Teacher theorizing often accompanies Server routine. The Teacher likes to think in surroundings that are characterized by Server routine, and the Server will often perform repetitive actions in an environment that is guided by Teacher understanding and structure.

Moving on, a set of arrows leads from *Exhorter* to *Contributor* to *Facilitator*. The four 'simple styles' of Teacher, Server, Mercy, and Perceiver focus upon the content of thought and action, whereas the three 'composite styles' of Exhorter, Contributor, and Facilitator use this content to formulate and implement plans. The Exhorter provides the starting point by coming up with ideas and visions backed up by energy, motivation, and excitement. The Exhorter is good at starting a project, proposing a theory, and coming up with a vision, but the details are often absent (remember the gray line). The Exhorter typically lacks follow-through, starting projects without finishing them, instead moving on to something more exciting when it comes time to add details to the initial ideas and visions.

The *second* stage is provided by the Contributor who adds specific details to the ideas and visions of the Exhorter (remember the black line). The typical Contributor is not an original thinker, but instead gets his ideas and visions from others. However, the Contributor is superb at turning ideas into detailed plans and excels at optimization—taking an existing plan and improving it. The Contributor is also the decision-maker who chooses which plan will be followed and then ignores what lies outside of the context of this plan. While the Exhorter is tempted to move on when things get too complicated, the Contributor has the opposite tendency of tending to reject ideas that are too simplistic or insufficiently rigorous.

The *final* stage is provided by the Facilitator who uses adjusting and mixing to round the rough edges off the plans of the Contributor, fine-tuning to make allowances for specific situations and individual abilities. Saying this another way, the Facilitator is aware of everything—within the current context. When the context is unclear then the Facilitator feels muddled. When no adjustments are possible within the current context, then the Facilitator feels restricted. And when the current context has been fully explored, then the Facilitator moves on to a new context. The Contributor executive often has a Facilitator secretary who 'facilitates' the Contributor plans, adjusting them to meet the needs of real people in real situations and keeping 'plan B' and 'plan C' going just in case the plan that the Contributor has chosen fails to work. The Exhorter makes large changes, guided by energy, excitement, and novelty. The Facilitator prefers to make small adjustments, guided by circumstances and a desire to experiment.

I should emphasize that everything that has been said so far can apply either to *people* or to *brain regions*. The label Teacher, for instance, can describe either the cognitive *style* of Teacher, a person who emphasizes a certain kind of thinking, or the cognitive *module* of Teacher, a form of thought that is present in all individuals. From now on, whenever I am referring to the cognitive *style* of Teacher, I will use the term Teacher *person*, while Teacher *thought* will refer to the cognitive *module* of Teacher.

> Everyone has a brain composed of seven interacting cognitive modules.
> Each cognitive style is conscious in one of these cognitive modules.

This double meaning was originally developed to solve a problem. I mentioned earlier that the list of personality characteristics for each of the seven cognitive styles can be summarized by basic traits. When we compared these basic traits with neurology, we discovered that the fundamental thinking of each cognitive style corresponds to the function of a major brain region. For instance, the Perceiver person thinks in terms of connections and maps. Neurology has discovered that there is a specific region of the brain (the right parietal lobe) that handles physical maps, temporal maps, and social maps (Parkinson & Liu, 2014). But everyone has an *entire* brain. The brain of the Perceiver person, for instance, does not just consist of the right parietal lobe. This led us to conclude that each cognitive style is *conscious* in a different region of the brain. In other words, it appears that the relationship between mind and brain is not the same for everyone. Everyone has a right parietal lobe, but the Perceiver person appears to be conscious in this region of the brain in a way that other cognitive styles are not.

Because everyone possesses a *complete* brain while only conscious in *part* of the brain, cognitive development requires social interaction. For example, I am a Perceiver person. Because I am aware of Perceiver thought and can control Perceiver thought, it is obvious to me that information should be organized into internal maps, and easy for me to see the relationship between different pieces of information. But for a Server person it is equally obvious that information should be organized into sequences and that these sequences should be carried out one step at a time. That is because the Server person is aware of Server thought and can control Server thought. My brain is more than just Perceiver thought. Rather, it is composed of all seven cognitive modules. I may not be consciously aware of the other six cognitive modules, but they exist subconsciously under the surface. If I want Server thought to function within my own mind, then one of the most effective ways is for me to spend time with a Server person.

Notice that I said effective and not pleasant. If I want to find fulfillment, then I must eventually function in a way that expresses my cognitive style. However, if I refuse to learn from others and focus only upon using 'my way' of thinking, then I will end up using my cognitive style at a fairly low level. In contrast, if I spend time with other cognitive styles and learn from their way of thinking, then this will help to develop those modes of thought within my own mind, and I will find that I function at a much higher level when using my own way of thinking. Stated simply, if I want to be more effective, then I need to learn how others think, even when I do not find this pleasant.

For instance, I mentioned my brother is a Teacher person. Because I worked with him for several years, Teacher thought now functions within my own mind, even though it is not conscious. My mother is a Mercy person, and when I was growing up she made certain that Mercy thought was working: 'Don't just mumble thank you. Look in their eyes and say it as if you mean it!' Because these two forms of emotional thought are both functioning within my mind, my natural Perceiver ability to look for connections has become expanded into an ability to look for connections involving emotional structures such as paradigms, cultures, identities, and 'pairs of glasses'.

Are different cognitive styles really conscious in different parts of the brain? After studying neurological literature for thirty years, I have yet to come across definitive *neurological* evidence for this suggestion. But if consciousness is a property of the mind and not the brain, then one would not expect to find neurological evidence for differences in consciousness. When I *observe* people and how they think and behave, then the situation is quite different. I keep finding that other people really seem to be totally oblivious to facts and concepts that appear to me as obvious as the nose on my face. And when I attempt to put myself in other people's shoes and look at the world through their eyes, then I conclude that others appear to be deeply, effortlessly, and naturally aware of features of which I am only dimly cognisant.

✳ 2. Mental Networks

Albert Einstein married his first wife Mileva in 1903. By 1914, their marriage was in the process of unraveling and Einstein sent his wife a written contract (Isaacson, 2007). She actually agreed to this contract and lived under it for several months before taking their sons and moving to Zürich. It reads as follows:

Conditions.

A. You will make sure

1. that my clothes and laundry are kept in good order;

2. that I will receive my three meals regularly in my room;

3. that my bedroom and study are kept neat, and especially that my desk is left for my use only.

B. You will renounce all personal relations with me insofar as they are not completely necessary for social reasons. Specifically, you will forego

1. my sitting at home with you;

2. my going out or traveling with you.

C. You will obey the following points in your relations with me:

1. you will not expect any intimacy from me, nor will you reproach me in any way;

2. you will stop talking to me if I request it;

3. you will leave my bedroom or study immediately without protest if I request it.

D. You will undertake not to belittle me in front of the children, either through words or behavior.

Einstein was a Teacher person who developed the world's most famous general theory—the theory of relativity. I suggest that this 'contract' illustrates how Teacher thought often regards the rest of society. First, Einstein's wife is expected to carry out the routine actions of washing, cooking, and cleaning that make it possible for Einstein to continue living in the realm of words and theories. Thus, Einstein will live within Teacher thought using words to build general theories, while those around him will perform the Server actions necessary to bring practical order to his environment. Notice the sanctity of Einstein's desk, the place where he does his theorizing. Second, Einstein and his wife will live parallel lives, he in the realm of words and she in the realm of actions. Third, he will protect himself emotionally from her. He does not want to be troubled by Mercy emotions of love and intimacy, and he does not want his Teacher emotions to be influenced either by her words or by her presence. (Einstein's first wife was a Contributor person, and the final point is probably Einstein's reaction to the Contributor's tendency to belittle others.)

Compare this domestic arrangement with the *informal* contract that exists between the ivory tower of academia and 'normal' human society: Society shall provide for the physical needs of academia. Society should not expect any meaningful interaction from academia. Society must not trouble academia with personal issues or intrude upon the inner sanctum of academia. And society will respect academia. Thus, I suggest that we are dealing here not just with a marital squabble, but rather with an illustration of how Teacher thought tends to regard the rest the world.

I suggested at the beginning of this book that religion looks for a grand explanation and determines my place within that explanation. As Einstein illustrates, coming up with a grand explanation means using Teacher thought. But how can a person determine his place within that grand explanation when Teacher thought regards those who live within normal concrete thought as housekeepers who are unworthy of personal interaction? This is not just a domestic quarrel but rather a dilemma that reaches to the heart of religious thought.

I suggest that it is possible to explore this issue by looking at the relationship between *Teacher* thought, the cognitive module that comes up with general theories, and *Mercy* thought, the cognitive module that deals with personal identity. That means introducing the idea of *mental networks*.

One can find aspects of the concept of mental networks in the work of many others, such as the schemata of Piaget, cognitive science's Theory of Mind, Jonathan Edwards' affections, Swedenborg's ruling loves, or the Agency Detector described by the cognitive science of religion. A mental network ties together these various aspects and provides a cognitive explanation for these descriptions.

> A mental network is a collection of similar emotional memories that function as a unit.

A mental network is simply a collection of similar emotional memories that have joined together to form a network. One does not choose to create a mental network, rather it forms automatically. Once a mental network has formed, then triggering any memory within that mental network will bring to mind the entire network, which will then use emotional pressure to impose its structure upon the rest of the mind. A triggered mental network will generate positive emotion as long as it receives input that is compatible with its structure, and a person may not even realize that a mental network is present. Instead, a person will just find that he naturally thinks and behaves in a certain manner.

The presence of a mental network generally becomes apparent only when it experiences input that is *inconsistent* with its structure. A person will then feel a sense of unease, as well as an emotional drive to carry out the familiar pattern.

For instance, one couple that I know visited Japan for several months. When they returned to Canada, he cut the legs off their dining room table so that they could sit on the floor and eat dinner in Japanese fashion. In other words, visiting Japan caused a mental network to form involving the routine of dining. Because Canadian dining customs were inconsistent with this mental network, it created an urge to continue eating in the Japanese manner. When this couple was in Japan, they did not know that a mental network had formed. They only discovered its existence when they returned to Canada and the mental network was no longer satisfied.

When a person chooses to respond in a manner that is consistent with the structure of an unsatisfied mental network, then the sense of unease being generated by that mental network will instantly vanish. However, if the mental network continues to experience inconsistent input, then the feeling of unease will also continue to grow. Eventually, though, the mental network will fall apart and revert to being merely a collection of emotional memories. One can see this process in the breaking of a habit. While it is being broken, it is always present in the background, re-emerging with its emotional discomfort whenever triggered by some thought, word, or situation. When it is finally broken, the person may wake up and go through normal activity for several hours before suddenly realizing that the suppressed desire is no longer there. A suppressed mental network is easy to identify because one is using conscious effort to decide not to carry it out. When a mental network is not being triggered then it may feel as if that mental network is gone, but it still remains present under the surface ready to re-emerge when it is triggered. When a mental network fragments, then there is nothing left to trigger, and the urge to think or behave in a certain manner will be gone.

Tourette syndrome illustrates the behavior of a mental network. While the precise cause of Tourette 'tics' is still unknown, they express themselves in a manner that is consistent with the concept of mental networks.

> Tics are temporarily suppressible and often, but not always, preceded by a premonitory urge which is similar to the need to sneeze or scratch an itch. Individuals describe the need to tic as the buildup of tension in a particular body location. Depending on the intensity of the urge the individual may consciously decide to tic or not to tic. However, if the urge is very strong, it can be impossible to resist... The actual tic may be felt as relieving this tension or sensation, similar to scratching an itch. After the tic is done, there is often a fleeting and incomplete sense of relief... Almost everyone with Tourette can suppress their tics for brief periods of time... We have also met adults who were truly amazing in their ability to hold back their tics, hours at a time. Then in some cases, especially when the person is alone, the tics can "rebound" and erupt with great intensity (Leckman, et al., 2012).

A mental network acts like a living being. Once it is 'born' it must be treated as an integrated unit. It has likes and dislikes and expects to be 'fed' an appropriate diet. If it is not fed, then it will get hungry and start to 'scream' for food. If it does not receive food, then it will eventually 'starve' and 'die'. Going the other way, experiences with living beings naturally lead to the formation of mental networks. That is because living beings generate experiences that are similar and full of emotion. Think, for instance, of the dog that joyfully welcomes its owner home. The dog responds in this manner because the sight or smell of the owner triggers a mental network within the mind of the dog that is composed of experiences of being fed and petted. Similarly, emotional experiences such as being joyfully welcomed by the dog will cause memories involving the dog to form a mental network within the mind of the owner.

This means that much, and possibly most, of what a person regards as social interaction is not happening *externally* between that person and other individuals but rather *internally* within that person's mind between the mental networks that represent self and the mental networks that represent other individuals. For instance, how many times have we fooled ourselves into thinking that we are doing something for someone else when we are actually trying to satisfy our mental concept of that person? One can see this distinction in the relationship between a dog and its owner. The behavior of a dog demonstrates that its limited brain is capable of forming mental networks and being driven by them. But a dog is not capable of thinking or acting in a human fashion. Despite this, dog owners often treat their pets as if they are human, showing that the interaction is being driven primarily by the mental network that represents the dog within the mind of the owner rather than by the actual mental capabilities of the dog. This distinction becomes even more obvious when a child plays with a doll. Even though a doll is an inanimate object, the child acts as if the doll is alive. That is because the doll lives within the mind of the child in the form of a mental network, and that mental network is driving the 'social interaction'.

> Most social interaction occurs within people's minds guided by mental networks.

Looking at this from a different angle, I cannot tell what another person is thinking. However, observing the other person will provide cues, these cues will trigger mental networks in my mind, and these mental networks will predict what the other person is thinking. Cognitive science refers to this as *Theory of Mind*, using my mind to guess what another person is thinking. Researchers have discovered that Theory of Mind has both a cognitive and an affective (or emotional) side (Abu-Akel & Shamay-Tsoory, 2011). Cognitive Theory of Mind attempts to determine the *content* of another person's mind, whereas affective Theory of Mind guesses what another person is *feeling*. Both of these aspects are present within a mental network. It responds emotionally when it is triggered but it uses emotional pressure to impose content.

One can see this combination of content and emotion in *culture*. A culture is simply a group of people with similar mental networks. If everyone has similar mental networks, then everyone will be driven by their mental networks to act and think in similar ways, and everyone will observe behavior that is consistent with their mental networks. The result will be a set of unspoken rules implicitly enforced by mental networks, and anyone who violates the norms of a culture will experience emotional pressure from the other members of that culture to conform.

In a similar vein, I suggest that *personal identity* is simply the set of mental networks that cannot be ignored. For instance, my physical body follows me around wherever I go. Therefore, the mental network that represents my physical body is part of my personal identity. Personal identity begins with the mental network that represents the physical body, and it grows to include mental networks that represent my experiences, my knowledge, and my skills, because these also follow me around inescapably. We saw this transition in the example about going camping. For the young child, physical sensation plays a dominant role in determining personal identity, while personal identity for the adult includes many other mental networks as well.

> Culture is the set of mental networks that a group of people have in common.
> Personal identity is the collection of mental networks that cannot be ignored.

A mental network usually becomes obvious when it is violated. Similarly, the potency of cultural mental networks becomes most apparent when a person attempts to live in a different culture. Initially, the exotic experiences may bring excitement and energy to Exhorter thought. Eventually, the continued experience of doing things differently will threaten the integrity of cultural mental networks, leading to *culture shock*. The person who is in culture shock will feel strongly motivated to *retreat* away from the unfamiliar back to the familiar. However, if a person goes *through* culture shock, then his existing cultural mental networks will fall apart and be replaced by new cultural mental networks.

As Jonathan Edwards' concept of *affections* suggests, mental networks do not just motivate Theory of Mind and culture, they drive a person's deepest thoughts and desires. Saying this another way, if one could examine the very core of a person's mind, one would discover mental networks, which I will refer to as *core* mental networks. Saying this another way, I suggest that a person's core mental networks determine the *spectacles* through which the world is observed. As with all mental networks, one only realizes that one is ultimately driven by core mental networks when one attempts to *change* these mental networks, and it is much easier to see the core mental networks that drive a person of a different culture or religion than to see the core mental networks that drive my culture and my religion. I suggest that Jonathan Edwards *recognized* the existence of core mental networks because his focus was upon *changing* these mental networks.

Swedenborg mentions another important feature of mental networks, which is that they form an *emotional hierarchy*. When two mental networks are simultaneously triggered, then each will attempt to impose its structure upon the other. The mental network with the strongest emotions will succeed, forcing the mental network with the weaker emotions to conform to the structure of the winning mental network. As this jockeying for emotional dominance continues, mental networks will gradually arrange themselves into a hierarchy dominated by core mental networks.

Cognitive Science of Religion

The cognitive science of religion also attempts to understand the cognitive mechanisms driving religious thought, which it does primarily by using what it calls the *Agency Detector* to explain how a person forms a mental concept of God. We will start by looking at what the cognitive science of religion says, and then we will use mental networks to explain this and suggest how one can go further.

Suppose that I am sleeping at night and everything is quiet, and then suddenly I hear a scratching sound. It only lasts for a moment but it wakes me up. A few seconds later I hear the scratching sound again. Now I am totally awake and straining my senses to listen to hear if the sound repeats. Is it the neighbor's cat? Is it a branch that is rubbing against the side of the building? Or is it a burglar, creeping through the house? The part of my mind that does this questioning is known as the Agency Detector, because it assumes that events are caused by agents, and when some event occurs, it tries to guess which agent is responsible. It is fairly easy to see how mental networks would lead to an Agency Detector. The neighbor's cat is represented within my mind as a mental network, as is a burglar. The sound of scratching will trigger both of these mental networks and each will attempt to impose its pattern upon my thought. I may start to imagine a cat slinking across the roof, or possibly a cat burglar slinking across the hallway. If I just read a vivid story about household theft, then the mental network that represents the burglar will probably grab my attention.

Now suppose that an event occurs that does not match the structure of any *existing* mental network. For instance, Justin Barrett, in *Why Would Anyone Believe in God?* gives the example of a friend of his working in a grain silo when a leaking propane tank exploded. The initial blast jammed the door so that he could not get out, but before the second blast occurred that leveled the silo, he felt himself being lifted up and out of the building through a second-floor window (Barrett, 2004, p. 34). Barrett suggests that the Agency Detector will respond to such a situation by concluding that some supernatural person, such as an angel, performed the rescue. Similarly, when a jungle native sees lightning, he will conclude that some supernatural being is wielding the thunderbolt as a weapon. Lightning plays a role in many mythologies. For instance, in Greek mythology the thunderbolt is the weapon of Zeus, in Germanic mythology Thor is the God of thunder, and in Celtic mythology it is Taranis. Similarly, many North American natives thought that thunder was created by a Thunderbird, often portrayed at the top of totem poles.

The other key idea proposed by the cognitive science of religion is the *minimally counterintuitive* concept, originally suggested by Justin Barrett (2000). This sounds complicated, but the idea can be illustrated with a simple example. Suppose that I see some person walking down the street. Because I am *used* to seeing humans, my mind will naturally accept the sight of a human as intuitively normal. In contrast, the sight of a blob oozing down the street will naturally be regarded as *counter*-intuitive, and stories involving blobs oozing down streets will be rejected as physically impossible. However, a person who appears *slightly* abnormal, such as a very large person or a person with one eye, will be regarded as *minimally* counterintuitive. The cognitive science of religion suggests that the mind finds minimally counterintuitive concepts *appealing*, which explains myths about superhuman beings wielding thunderbolts, or angelic beings with wings rescuing humans. In each case, the mental network representing some real person has been modified in a minimally counterintuitive way.

Mental symmetry suggests that this natural attraction can be explained as an interaction between *Exhorter* excitement and *Facilitator* filtering. Exhorter thought finds unusual emotional experiences exciting. However, Facilitator thought will naturally reject concepts that deviate too much from the norm. When a concept is *minimally* counterintuitive, then the counterintuitiveness will make it *exciting* to Exhorter thought, while the minimal counterintuitiveness will allow it to *pass* the Facilitator filter.

If mental networks can cause a child to treat a doll as a living creature, then one can see how mental networks could also cause traumatic events, such as lightning bolts, tornadoes, volcanoes, and earthquakes to be interpreted in personal terms that are minimally counterintuitive. Even today we refer to events such as these as 'acts of God'. But the average person today no longer views lightning as a weapon hurled by Zeus. Does this mean that the Agency Detector is no longer functioning? I suggest not. Instead, I suggest that most natural events now trigger a different *kind* of mental network, one that is not based in emotional *experiences*.

If a general theory continues to be used, a Teacher mental network (TMN) will form.

All the mental networks that we have discussed so far involve the *Mercy* realm of emotional experiences. But we began this chapter by looking at a different kind of emotion: *Teacher* emotion. This implies that there are actually two different kinds of mental networks, Mercy mental networks (which we will refer to as MMNs) and Teacher mental networks (TMNs). An MMN forms out of similar emotional experiences. A TMN forms when a person continues to use a theory or work within some system of order-within-complexity. The distinction between a theory and a theory that has turned into a TMN became apparent to me when I was studying the traits of the Perceiver person back in the 1980s. Initially, it felt as if I was building a theory (together with my brother) of cognitive styles. I was active and the theory was passive. But then a mental threshold was crossed where the theory became the active participant and I was being dragged along passively. That was because the theory had turned into a mental network. Whenever it was triggered, it attempted to impose its explanation upon the situation. When a theory that explains conscious thought turns into a TMN, the results can be rather dramatic. Everything that I thought and did was followed a second or two later by an internal voice that explained why I was thinking or acting in such a fashion. I should mention in passing that we often found during our initial research that people would get very excited about cognitive styles and then a few months later drop the subject like a hot potato. I suspect that the theory was starting to form a TMN leading to an internal struggle with other mental networks, and this internal conflict was being 'resolved' by dropping the topic to ensure that the TMN of mental symmetry would no longer be triggered.

Having a theory turn into a mental network may sound rather unsettling. However, we have just seen that everyone's mind is *already* driven by core mental networks. But because we are surrounded by individuals who share the same core mental networks, we do not realize that they are present. Instead, they become apparent when we try to live in another culture, when we attempt to swim against the stream of our own culture, or when we try to change who we are. Thus, I suggest that the real question is not *whether* mental networks will drive us or not, but rather *which* mental networks will drive us.

Thomas Kuhn and Paradigms

Going further, I suggest that science *itself* is driven by individuals who have acquired theories that have turned into TMNs. One can see this by analyzing Thomas Kuhn's description of scientific thought in *The Structure of Scientific Revolutions,* the book that introduced the concept of the *paradigm shift* (Kuhn, 1970).

Kuhn begins by describing how pre-scientific thought works in the absence of a general Teacher theory.

> No period between remote antiquity and the end of the seventeenth century exhibited a single generally accepted view about the nature of light. Instead there were a number of competing schools and sub-schools, most of them espousing one variant or another of Epicurean, Aristotelian, or Platonic theory... Anyone examining a survey of physical optics before Newton may well conclude that, though the field's practitioners were scientists, the net result of their activity was something less than science. Being able to take no common body of belief for granted, each writer of physical optics felt forced to build his field anew from its foundations (p.12).

I have suggested that the mind is built upon core mental networks and that a culture is composed of individuals with similar mental networks. Kuhn tells us that pre-scientific thought was not held together by the TMN of a common theory. Researchers 'could take no common body of belief for granted.' Instead, thinking was held together by MMNs representing people with emotional status, such as Epicurus, Aristotle, or Plato.

When a TMN emerges, then it will impose its explanation upon situations when it is triggered. Saying this another way, everything will be interpreted through the lenses of the current paradigm, including previous scientific thought.

> Partly by selection and partly by distortion, the scientists of earlier ages are implicitly represented as having worked upon the same set of fixed problems and in accordance with the same set of fixed canons that the most recent revolution in scientific theory and method has made seem scientific (p.138).

A TMN will continue to impose its explanation upon situations even when the facts contradict this explanation. Kuhn describes

> what scientists never do when confronted by even severe and prolonged anomalies. Though they may begin to lose faith and then to consider alternatives, they do not renounce the paradigm that has led them into crisis. They do not, that is, treat anomalies as counterinstances, though in the vocabulary of philosophy of science that is what they are (p.77).

> By themselves, [counterexamples] cannot and will not falsify that philosophical theory, for its defenders will do what we have already seen scientists doing when confronted by anomaly. They will devise numerous articulations and ad hoc modifications of their theory in order to eliminate any apparent conflict (p.78).

Being guided by a TMN is a fundamental aspect of science, and the only way to change the TMN of a scientist is to *replace* it with another TMN.

> Once a first paradigm through which to view nature has been found, there is no such thing as research in the absence of any paradigm. To reject one paradigm without simultaneously substituting another is to reject science itself (p.79).

A new general theory does not change the underlying Perceiver facts, but rather places the same facts within the package of a different Teacher understanding.

> One perceptive historian, viewing a classic case of a science's reorientation by paradigm change, recently described it as "picking up the other end of the stick," a process that involves "handling the same bundle of data as before, but placing them in a new system of relations within one another by giving them a different framework" (p.85).

Replacing one TMN with another through a 'paradigm shift' is a deeply emotional process.

> Wolfgang Pauli, in the months before Heisenberg's paper on matrix mechanics pointed the way to a new quantum theory, wrote to a friend, "At the moment physics is again terribly confused. In any case, it is too difficult for me, and I wish I had been a movie comedian or something of the sort and had never heard of physics." That testimony is particularly impressive if contrasted with Pauli's words less than five months later: "Heisenberg's type of mechanics has again given me hope and joy in life" (p.83).

Choosing a new theory is often guided by Teacher emotions of elegance and order-within-complexity.

> Something must make at least a few scientists feel that the new proposal is on the right track, and sometimes it is only personal and inarticulate aesthetic considerations that can do that. Men have been converted by them at times when most of the articulable technical arguments pointed the other way (p.155).

> There is also another sort of consideration that can lead scientists to reject an old paradigm in favor of a new. These are the arguments, rarely made entirely explicit, that appeal to the individual's sense of the appropriate or the aesthetic—the new theory is said to be 'neater,' 'more suitable,' or 'simpler' than the old (p.155).

When a new TMN is adopted, then it will impose its structure upon thought, causing everything to be *reinterpreted* in the light of the new Teacher theory.

> Textbooks, however, being pedagogic vehicles for the perpetuation of normal science, have to be rewritten in whole or in part whenever the language, problem-structure, or standards of normal science change. In short, they have to be rewritten in the aftermath of each scientific revolution, and, once rewritten, they inevitably disguise not only the role but the very existence of the revolutions that produced them (p.137).

Even the physical world itself will be viewed in a different light.

> The historian of science may be tempted to exclaim that when paradigms change, the world itself changes with them. Led by a new paradigm, scientists adopt new instruments and look in new places. Even more important, during revolutions scientists see new and different things when looking with familiar instruments in places they have looked before. It is rather as if the professional community had been suddenly transported to another planet where familiar objects are seen in a different light and are joined by unfamiliar ones as well (p.111).

Competing theories will also be viewed through the spectacles of the current TMN.

> When paradigms enter, as they must, into a debate about paradigm choice, their role is necessarily circular. Each group uses its own paradigm to argue in that paradigm's defense... The status of the circular argument is only that of persuasion. It cannot be made logically or even probabilistically compelling for those who refuse to step into the circle (p.94).

This may give the impression that scientific thought is deeply unscientific, and that is how some people interpret Thomas Kuhn. However, I suggest that this is not the case. That is because a mental network only becomes obvious when it is *violated*. As we shall see later when discussing technical thought, the scientist is capable of highly rational thinking—when interacting with colleagues who share the same TMNs. The emotional response emerges primarily when the existing paradigm is *challenged*, usually by some outsider coming in with a strange new theory. Kuhn's book triggered a firestorm of response. Similarly, I have learned through personal experience that a rational scientist can respond with intense emotional belittling when exposed to a competing theory. And this emotional reaction will usually be phrased in the personal language of mental networks. The response will not be "your theory has some flaws". Rather, it will be "You have wasted your life. You do not know how to think rationally. You need to stop what you are doing. Your theory deeply offends me."

But according to Kuhn, a new theory generally comes from the outsider, because most scientists who work within a field have become so emotionally trapped by their TMN that they are literally incapable of changing.

> Scientific training is not well designed to produce the man who will easily discover a fresh approach. But so long as somebody appears with a new candidate for paradigm – usually a young man or one new to the field – the loss due to rigidity accrues only to the individual. Given a generation in which to effect the change, individual rigidity is compatible with a community that can switch from paradigm to paradigm as the situation demands (p.166).

Kuhn wrote back in the 1960s. However, his statements are backed up by more recent findings. For instance, Bilalić (2010) writes that

> Tetlock found that expert political scientists do not change their theories when events prove their predictions wrong; they keep the theories and discount the evidence. Similarly Gould showed that scientists can be so strongly influenced by the theory they already hold that they do not interpret new data objectively. The experts' theories were originally based on an accumulation of evidence, so it is not that they cannot absorb new information. The question is: Why, once a point of view has been formed, do people find it difficult to assimilate new information if it is not consistent with the view already held? The answer is suggested by recent studies of the Einstellung (mental set) effect – the fixation of thought produced by prior experience - which demonstrate its power and reveal its mechanism.

I am not suggesting scientists are *incapable* of changing theories or that they *ignore* evidence. But I am suggesting that it takes a lot of contradictory evidence to overturn an established theory. If one wishes to successfully challenge an existing theory, one must point out *critical* flaws in the existing explanation and provide an *alternative* theory. Unfortunately, by pointing out such critical flaws one runs the risk of offending the reader.

A Concept of God

Now that we understand how a TMN behaves, let us return to the concept of the Agency Detector. The cognitive science of religion says that a concept of God emerges when the Agency Detector *misfires* by concluding that unexplained events are being caused by supernatural agents. For instance, thunderbolts are caused by the god Thor. This may be able to explain why a scratching sound in the middle of the night is interpreted as a cat or a burglar, but what about interpreting the sound as a branch being blown by the wind. What cognitive mechanism is responsible for that conclusion?

This is where the concept of a TMN comes into play. The average modern citizen may not live within the world of TMNs as the scientist does, but he has received enough of a scientific education to develop a TMN based in common sense or what some refer to as 'folk science'. Thus, the scratching noise in our example is actually triggering three competing mental networks: an MMN that represents the neighboring cat, an MMN that represents a burglar, and a TMN that provides a natural explanation. A pre-scientific society lacks the TMNs of rational understanding, therefore situations that are now interpreted using the TMN of folk science *used* to be interpreted using the MMNs of supernatural agents. For instance, instead of viewing lightning as the weapon of some god, lightning will now be seen as the flow of electrical current.

Does this mean that science has replaced the concept of God? It depends on how one defines the word 'God'. Paul Dirac, the famous physicist, was well-known for his atheistic views. As Wolfgang Pauli, another famous physicist, said: "Well, our friend Dirac, too, has a religion, and its guiding principle is 'God does not exist and Dirac is His prophet'" (Heisenberg, 1971).

Dirac explained at a scientific conference in 1927 that

> If we are honest — and scientists have to be — we must admit that religion is a jumble of false assertions, with no basis in reality. The very idea of God is a product of the human imagination. It is quite understandable why primitive people, who were so much more exposed to the overpowering forces of nature than we are today, should have personified these forces in fear and trembling. But nowadays, when we understand so many natural processes, we have no need for such solutions. I can't for the life of me see how the postulate of an Almighty God helps us in any way (Heisenberg, 1971).

Notice that Dirac is viewing God from the *Mercy* perspective of an MMN. Primitive people personified natural forces in 'fear and trembling'. Using the language of mental symmetry, emotional experiences from the natural world caused MMNs to form within the minds of primitive people, who then interpreted these experiences in personal terms. In contrast, scientific thought does not need to stoop to the personal level of MMNs because it is now guided by the TMN of rational understanding. Because mental networks are driving people to interpret the world in a certain fashion, Dirac concludes that 'the very idea of God is a product of the human imagination'.

However, in 1963, Dirac said that

> It seems to be one of the fundamental features of nature that fundamental physical laws are described in terms of a mathematical theory of great beauty and power, needing quite a high standard of mathematics for one to understand it. You may wonder: Why is nature constructed along these lines? One can only answer that our present knowledge seems to show that nature is so constructed. We simply have to accept it. One could perhaps describe the situation by saying that God is a mathematician of a very high order, and He used very advanced mathematics in constructing the universe (Dirac, 1963).

Here Dirac is viewing God from the Teacher perspective of a TMN. Dirac notices the order-within-complexity of the natural universe and concludes that some agent is responsible for this 'great beauty and power'.

I have mentioned that the mind can use mental networks to represent people because a mental network behaves like a living being. But that principle applies to *MMNs*. People are composed of finite bits of matter placed in a finite package; an MMN is formed out of a group of similar emotional experiences. A person always occupies some specific location; an MMN also occupies a mental 'location' because it is only activated when it is triggered by specific experiences. The world is full of distinct living beings; Mercy thought is full of distinct MMNs that represent these distinct living beings.

Now suppose that one views a TMN in personal terms. What type of 'being' would this represent? Think, for instance, of the law of gravity. It does not make sense to say that the law of gravity lives in a specific location. Instead, it exists everywhere, independent of space and time. It is not formed out of a specific collection of experiences, but rather defines a pattern of behavior that applies universally. One can locate a person or animal by pointing out its physical body. The law of gravity, in contrast, is defined verbally, using a mathematical equation such as $F = mg$. People have limited awareness, limited knowledge, and limited power. Gravity always applies, it never fails to apply, and its power can grow so strong that nothing can escape, even light.

Interpreting this personally, a TMN leads to the concept of a universal being who lives outside of space and time who has total awareness, universal knowledge, and irresistible power. While such a being is not restricted to any physical location, it is possible to determine the character of such a being through the use of words. Thus, just as the mind uses MMNs to represent people, so the mind will believe that a TMN represents God.

I am not trying to prove that God exists, because I do not think that it is really necessary. Strictly speaking, *all* social interaction is based upon hunches guided by Theory of Mind. As Justin Barrett says,

> Belief in neither God nor other minds arises from measurable, physical proof. Neither God nor minds are physical objects that can be directly observed. Rather, only the consequences of their activities on the physical, material world service evidence for their existence (Barrett, 2004, p. 98).

I can only see the bodies of other people; I cannot see their minds. Therefore, I must use MMNs to *guess* what is happening within the minds of other individuals. Similarly, no one can 'see' God. Instead, interaction with 'God' is based upon hunches guided by a TMN. As Dirac said, "Our present knowledge seems to show that nature is so constructed... One could perhaps describe the situation by saying that God is a mathematician of a very high order."

And we saw from our look at Thomas Kuhn the emotional power that is exerted by a TMN. It imposes its explanation upon situations. It causes a person to ignore contradictory facts and reinterpret history. It determines the way that a person views the world. A person who acquires a TMN is incapable of existing without it, and the average scientist who follows a TMN will die without abandoning it. In other words, whether a TMN represents an actual God or not, the individual who is driven by a TMN *acts as if* his

TMN represents God. As Thomas Kuhn says, the study of science "is a narrow and rigid education, probably more so than any other except perhaps in orthodox theology" (p.166).

If this is the case, then why are so many scientists atheists? Part of the answer is that many scientists are probably Dirac-like atheists. As Kuhn has pointed out, a scientist cannot exist without a paradigm; he cannot function without a general theory. Thus, he is understandably incensed when the religious believer 'explains' something by saying, "God did it. I believe it. I do not understand it. God is transcendent and incomprehensible. End of discussion." This type of 'answer' shuts down Teacher thought because it replaces a TMN with...nothing. (More accurately, it replaces a TMN with the MMN of some authority figure.) As Galileo Galilei said in a letter to the Grand Duchess Christina in 1615, "I do not feel obliged to believe that the same God who has endowed us with sense, reason, and intellect has intended us to forgo their use."

> A concept of God forms when a general theory applies to personal identity.

Another reason why many scientists are atheists is because of the *objective* nature of science. We have seen that whenever more than one mental network is triggered at the same time, then each will attempt to impose its structure upon the other. This makes it difficult to perform rational thought in the presence of MMNs. The easiest solution is to prevent MMNs from being triggered by being objective. After all, if MMNs introduce personal bias, then personal bias can be eliminated by avoiding MMNs. This may win the battle but it loses the war, because the scientist does not realize that thinking rationally will lead eventually to the formation of a TMN. And we just saw from Kuhn that a TMN is just as emotionally entrapping as an MMN. Obviously, if a researcher gathers data by avoiding personal emotions, then any resulting theory will also avoid personal emotions. Thus, a TMN that is based upon objective thought will not lead to a mental concept of God because the very concept of personal involvement is being suppressed.

Summarizing, I offer the following formal definition: A mental concept of God emerges whenever a sufficiently general theory applies to personal identity. Notice that this definition of God automatically includes the two questions of religion posed at the beginning of this book. A sufficiently general theory is by definition a 'grand explanation'. And if this general theory applies to personal identity, then a person will naturally know his place within this grand explanation.

Evolution and a Mental Concept of God

The cognitive naturalness of a concept of God can be illustrated by the history of the theory of evolution. Willard Quine explains in *The Web of Belief* that the theory of evolution was initially developed to *avoid* the concept of a superhuman agent.

One proposed solution has been to assume Someone whose purpose was at work at the beginning of all causal chains. Here is a grand hypothesis, calculated to personalize the impersonal teleological explanations and so to accommodate them under the head of efficient cause after all. It is one of the classical arguments for the existence of God, and is known as the argument from design... Charles Darwin, then, to the rescue, with his abundantly documented hypothesis of natural selection. The seeing eye can evolve in the vertebrate, and hydrotropism in the willow, with never the intervention of purpose human or divine... [This] reduces the teleological explanations of biology sweepingly to explanations in the proper causal sense. Easy answers like 'To see with' and 'So that their seeds will float away' become, thanks to Darwin, interpretable as shorthand allusions to long causal chains of natural selection (Quine, 1978).

Quine says that the traditional approach was to 'assume Someone whose purpose was at work at the beginning of all causal chains', leading to the belief that mechanisms such as 'seeing eyes in the vertebrate' and 'hydrotropism in the willow' were *designed* by God. But this belief in a superhuman agent is not necessary because 'Charles Darwin to the rescue with his abundantly documented hypothesis of natural selection'. There is no longer any need to believe in a divine agent because 'The seeing eye can evolve in the vertebrate, and hydrotropism in the willow, with never the intervention of purpose human or divine'.

Unfortunately, that is not how the mind works. As David Hanke complains in a chapter entitled *Teleology: the explanation that bedevils biology* that begins with the sentence 'Biology is sick',

It is no longer acceptable to think of biological objects as having any purpose because the overwhelming consensus of scientific opinion is that they were not designed and built by a Creator (a mental construct necessary to inject a human sense of purpose into existence) with purposes in mind for them. Instead, we believe (I'll put that as strongly as I can) they are products of Darwinian evolution. Now this ought to mean that we can turn with some relief to the scientists who study the mechanism of evolution for an alternative, new way of thinking rigorously about biology that does not fall back on subjective modes of thinking. Er is... not so. Bizarrely, evolutionists lead the world in substituting teleology for objectivity. How so? One major reason is the manner in which natural selection slipped seamlessly into the place of the Creator: the Natural Selector as the acceptable new face of the Great Designer (Hanke, 2004).

In other words, evolutionists are not following Quine's advice by using the theory of evolution to avoid the concept of a supernatural agent. Instead, 'evolutionists lead the world in substituting teleology for objectivity'. Far from avoiding the concept of God, natural selection is viewed 'as the acceptable new face of the Great Designer'. Thus, even when one explicitly attempts to come up with a general theory of biology that *avoids* the concept of God, this general theory will end up *creating* a mental concept of

God. When something happens within the mind despite attempting to do the precise opposite, then this indicates that one is dealing with an underlying cognitive mechanism.

As we have seen, the cognitive science of religion is attempting to analyze this underlying cognitive mechanism, and it explains the concept of God in terms of the Agency Detector. As Tremlin explains in *Minds and Gods*,

> The question, however, is what ADD [Agency Detector Device] and ToMM [Theory of Mind Mechanism] have to do with gods. The promise was not simply to introduce new mental mechanisms but to directly link them with religious thought and behavior... First, of all the objects in the environment, agents matter most. The connection?—gods are agents. Second, humans understand the world, and particularly agents, in light of minds. The connection?—gods have minds. These facts are exceedingly trivial, but they are also exceedingly explicative. They tell us exactly what kind of things gods are and how we think about them (Tremlin, 2006, p. 86).

This *hyperactive* Agency Detector (as Barrett calls it) is suggested to be the result of evolutionary adaptation. Tremlin states in a more recent book that

> The capacity to quickly and accurately distinguish between objects and agents in the environment is clearly crucial to survival. An animal that fails to recognize a spotted form as a cheetah or a buzzing coil as a snake is unlikely to fare well or long. An animal that preys on rodents but habitually attacks trees is equally unfit for life. Even though the world of objects is important, agents deserve special attention... Because agents are the most relevant things in the environment, evolution has tuned the brain to quickly spot them, or to suspect their presence based on signs and traces... Cognitive psychologists have begun to call the mental mechanism responsible for recognizing agents the Agency Detection Device (Tremlin, 2013, p. 76).

I have suggested that a concept of God emerges when a sufficiently general theory applies to personal identity. It appears that this cognitive mechanism will continue to function even when one is explicitly analyzing how the mind forms a concept of God. One sees this illustrated by Tremlin's 2006 book on the cognitive science of religion. Tremlin's general theory is easy to identify because a description of the theory of evolution takes up the first quarter of his book. Tremlin regards evolution as a *general* theory.

> The fundamental premise of evolutionary psychology is that the complex design of the modern brain evolved through natural selection. Understanding the processes and products of the mind therefore requires close attention to their evolutionary background. As Robert Wright says, "if the theory of natural selection is correct, then essentially everything about the human mind should be intelligible in these terms" (Tremlin, 2006, p. 44) .

And he believes that the theory of evolution applies to *personal identity*.

> At first glance there may seem to be little point of contact between evolutionary history and the thoughts you are entertaining at this very moment. Even if the ins and outs of natural selection are accepted, it remains hard to see how ideas we humans ponder here in the twenty-first century have anything to do with the thoughts of strange hominids eking out a living millions of years ago. Likewise, it is difficult to clearly relate the physical structures and functions of the brains that we carry around inside our heads with the amorphous ideas that spring so naturally from them. Yet the connections between ancient past and present day, and between gray matter and invisible thought, are direct and paramount (p.74).

The end result is that Tremlin ends up implicitly treating the theory of evolution as a concept of God. The word 'design' implies an intelligent agent, and Tremlin uses the word 'design' to describe the 'work' of evolution about fifty times in his book. For instance, notice in the following quote how evolution 'designed' the Agency Detector and Nature 'provided' Theory of Mind.

> Evolution has designed a mental mechanism, ADD, to quickly detect and respond to agents. Of the kinds of agents that exist in the world, other humans are of special importance. As species-dependent animals, humans rely heavily on one another throughout the course of their lives. But constant interaction with others carries challenges and risks as well as opportunities and benefits. Social life is give and take, cooperation and competition, and it is crucial that individuals have a way to understand and predict the complex behaviors of those with whom they have contact. Nature's provision in this case is ToMM (p.85).

However, even though Tremlin analyzes extensively how a mental concept of God forms within the mind, he does not appear to recognize that the theory of evolution has formed a mental concept of God within his *own* mind. And even if one uses the attributes of a concept of God that Tremlin mentions within his book, the way that Tremlin treats the theory of evolution in that same book still qualifies as a concept of God.

Barrett has carried out experiments comparing a person's *explicit* and *implicit* concept of God. The explicit concept is based upon what a person says about God, while the implicit concept is based upon what a person actually regards as a universal agent. Tremlin describes these experiments in his book.

> In keeping with the mind's natural categories of thought, Barrett and Keil found an overwhelming tendency for subjects to think of 'God' as exhibiting Person-like characteristics rather than theological attributes... the participants agreed that God is all knowing, omnipresent, and atemporal, yet when reasoning about situations within individual stories they represented God with physical and psychological limitations. Participants readily characterized God as having to accomplish one task at a time, having a limited focus of attention, having fallible perception, and having a single location in space and time (Tremlin, 2006, p. 97).

In other words, subjects *explicitly* described God using the universal language of a TMN, but they *implicitly* regarded God as some sort of Superman based in an MMN. Tremlin appears to be doing the opposite, because he explicitly describes God as some sort of Superman based in an MMN, while implicitly regarding God as a universal being based in the TMN of the theory of evolution.

I suggested earlier that if one wishes to successfully challenge an existing theory, then one must point out *critical* flaws in the existing explanation and provide an *alternative* theory, and that doing so runs the risk of offending the reader. My goal is not to question the research being done by the cognitive science of religion, because I think that significant facts are being uncovered regarding religious thought and experience. Instead, I am trying to point out that there is a critical flaw in using the theory of evolution to explain these facts. At the specific level this combination works fairly well. One can see that proto-humans without functioning agency detectors would tend to get eaten by wild animals, while those with hyperactive agency detectors would tend to survive and pass on their genes. However, at a more general level, there is a major problem. The theory of evolution was originally designed to avoid the concept of supernatural agents. But evolution is now being used by the cognitive science of religion to explain why the mind naturally comes up with the concept of a supernatural agent. If the mind naturally forms a mental concept of God, as the cognitive science of religion claims, then this means that it is cognitively unnatural to believe in the theory of evolution—the theoretical basis for the cognitive science of religion. The end result of using evolution to explain the findings of the cognitive science of religion appears to be the cognitive disconnect of analyzing how a concept of God forms within the minds of *other* individuals while *not* analyzing how a mental concept of God forms within the mind of the researcher *himself*. This, I suggest, is a critical flaw, and this book presents mental symmetry as an *alternative* theory for explaining the findings of the cognitive science of religion.

✳ 3. Piaget and Childish Thought

We have seen that the mind can be guided by two kinds of mental networks: MMNs that form out of emotional experiences or TMNs based in general theories. In this chapter we will examine how mental networks *develop*. If one wishes to discuss cognitive development, then the obvious starting point is Jean Piaget and his theory of child development (Piaget, 1936). Piaget said that the growing child goes through four major development stages:

1) Sensorimotor stage (birth – 2): The childish mind acquires its initial content from movement and the five physical senses.

2) Preoperational stage (2 – 7): The child uses language, lives in concrete thought, and is not capable of understanding logic.

3) Concrete Operational stage (7 – 11): The child can use logic with concrete experiences and is capable of seeing situations from the viewpoint of others.

4) Formal Operational stage (12 – adult): The child becomes capable of using abstract logical thought.

Translating this into the language of mental symmetry, experiences from the physical body lead to the development of MMNs during the sensorimotor stage, the preoperational child lives in these MMNs, the concrete operational child builds TMNs upon this foundation of MMNs, while the formal operational stage child constructs TMNs that are independent of MMNs.

Saying this more simply, the sensorimotor child's mind is a creature of its environment, the preoperational child's mind approaches everything in personal terms, the concrete operational child needs concrete examples, while the formal operational child can use abstract thought. Using math as an illustration, the sensorimotor child reaches for the apple because it tastes good, the preoperational child knows that apples grow on trees tended by farmers, the concrete operational child can add two apples + three apples, while the formal operational child can use the variable 'X' to represent apples.

Every human starts with a mind that is ruled by MMNs.

Summarizing, embodiment comes first, then MMNs, then TMNs based upon MMNs, and then independent TMNs. Notice that *every* human starts with a mind that is ruled by MMNs. This is an inevitable result of growing up in a physical body that inhabits a physical world. In this chapter, we will learn what it means to have a mind ruled by MMNs by looking more closely at Piaget's *preoperational* stage.

Piaget says that the preoperational child exhibits the following traits:

Transductive reasoning: If two experiences occur together, then the child will assume that they are related. For instance, if the child hears a dog bark and then sees a balloon pop, the child may think that the barking dog caused the balloon to pop. In other words, emotional experiences that occur together will form MMNs and these will impose their patterns upon future experiences.

Animism: The child will treat inanimate objects as if they are alive. For instance, a child might think that the stars are twinkling because they are happy. Or as we saw in the previous chapter, a child may have social interaction with a doll or beloved teddy bear. This is because emotional experiences with inanimate objects are causing MMNs to form which cause the child to treat these objects as if they are people.

Artificialism: The child will believe that everything is made and controlled by people. For instance, the clouds are white because someone painted them that color, or it is windy because someone is blowing very hard. This indicates that MMNs are also viewed as the source of external reality.

Magical Thinking: The child will confuse imagination with reality. For instance, if a video shows the picture of an egg breaking, then a child may grab a paper towel to wipe it up. Or a child may think that 'the monster under the bed' really exists. This tells us that the child cannot step back from MMNs in order to evaluate them. When an MMN is triggered, then that defines reality for the child.

Centrating: The child will focus attention upon the current situation and ignore other situations. This tells us that the MMN that is currently active is controlling the entire mind. This MMN may temporarily determine personal identity, causing the child, for instance, to pretend to be an airplane or a fireman.

Egocentrism: The child has no concept of other people, but will assume that the world revolves around him. A child will think that everyone else shares his personal feelings and desires, such as assuming that daddy likes Sesame Street because the child likes Sesame Street. That is because personal identity is composed of MMNs and the MMN that is currently active is controlling the mind.

These traits can be cute when seen in the small child, but now let us translate them into adult terms.

Transductive reasoning: Suppose that I meet a movie star, win some prestigious event, appear on television, jump into bed with someone for 'a one night stand', or have a transcendental mystical experience. In each case, the strong emotions of some isolated experience will lead to the formation of an MMN, which will then be used to interpret subsequent experiences. This is an example of transductive reasoning, because *isolated incidents* are guiding thought and behavior, rather than long-term connections that are *repeated*.

Animism: When I pursue money or seek physical possessions, then I am mentally confusing inanimate physical objects with MMNs. Ludwig von Mises, the famous economist, said in *Theory and History,* "Value is not intrinsic. It is not in things and conditions but in the valuing subject." In other words, the real bottom line is personal happiness, generated by mental networks, and not money or physical possessions. And yet instead of seeking internal value and personal fulfillment, we typically focus upon the external 'things and conditions' that represent value. For instance, just as the small girl plays with her dolls and pretends that she is having meaningful social interaction, so the grown man roars around town in his pickup truck and pretends that he is having meaningful social interaction.

Artificialism: The child thinks that everything is governed by people. The adult swallows truth blindly from chosen authority figures. In both cases, MMNs are acting as the source of truth. "If it is on CNN news, it must be true." "Republicans are always right." "It must be absolute truth because it is written in my holy book." Similarly, how often do we blame the messenger instead of focusing on the problem? That too is a form of artificialism.

Magical thinking: Children have difficulties distinguishing reality from imagination. The adult confuses truth with belief. Instead of looking for facts, we say "That may be true for you but it is not true for me." We use spin and marketing to try to alter the appearance of facts, hoping that people will confuse imagination with reality. In some areas it is no longer possible to determine what is or is not the truth. Instead, all we see is imagination, and reality becomes redefined as imagination imposed by political and social power. "Who shot John F. Kennedy?" "What really happened on 9/11?" "Is there global warming?" Simply posing questions such as these is enough to trigger potent MMNs of imagination that reflect either 'official versions' or 'conspiracy theories'.

Centrating: The child fixates on the current situation. Similarly, hedonism allows thought and action to be guided fully by the MMN that is currently active. All that matters is the pleasure of the moment. Going the other way, 'out of sight is out of mind'. Therefore, we 'move on' in order to avoid triggering unpleasant MMNs, assuming that centrating will allow us to ignore the unpleasant MMN. *Specialization* is a more subtle way of centrating. For instance, the professional may focus upon his job and ignore personal shortcomings, or the businessman may devote his energy to his company while his marriage falls apart.

Egocentrism: The child has no concept of other people. Similarly, the adult who has never traveled has no concept of other cultures. We divide ourselves into tribes, believing that we are special. We treat our region, country, culture, religion, occupation, or special-interest group as if it is the center of the universe around which everything else revolves.

Summarizing, the adult mind may be capable of abstract thought, but if one looks below the surface, one notices that childish thought lingers on in major ways, especially when dealing with core mental networks. Because of brain development, the childish mind is *incapable* of going beyond MMNs. However, when one examines the adult mind, one sees that it is *also* trapped by MMNs. Unfortunately, adults with childish minds are capable of inflicting far more harm than children with childish minds. Childish egocentrism leads to temper tantrums; adult egocentrism starts wars. Childish artificialism blames the sidewalk for making me trip; adult artificialism drives fundamentalist religion and enables demagoguery. Childish animism plays with dolls; adult animism drives the consumer society. Childish magical thinking enables fantasy; adult magical thinking destroys democracy.

Embodiment leads naturally and inevitably to a mind controlled by inadequate MMNs.

Stating this in religious terms, one concludes that we are all 'born in sin', because living in a physical body leads to the formation of MMNs that cause us to think and behave in ways that are fundamentally inadequate. Notice that the problem is not with the structure of the mind, but rather with the *content* that the mind acquires through embodiment. Using computer language, the problem lies with mental software, not in mental hardware.

Teacher Thought and Childish MMNs

We have looked at the kind of MMNs that naturally emerge in the mind of the child. Let us turn our attention now to Teacher thought and the realm of TMNs. Teacher thought wants general theories that apply without exception. How will this desire for universal understanding view childish MMNs? We can answer this question by going again through our list of six characteristics.

Transductive reasoning: The childish mind jumps directly from specific to universal, because a *single* emotional experience is being used to interpret *many* subsequent experiences. For instance, transductive reasoning concludes that if one dog bit me, then all dogs always bite. Obviously, this type of 'reasoning' will lead to faulty general theories. The Exhorter person, who combines Mercy thought and Teacher thought, often uses this kind of reasoning, which one could refer to as 'proof by example'. It may be a good starting point for coming up with a general hypothesis, but a single juxtaposition is not the same as a universal law.

Animism: Teacher thought builds general theories by focusing upon *fundamental* relationships while ignoring what is secondary and peripheral. When one focuses upon the external objects that represent internal mental networks, then one is pursuing what is secondary while ignoring what is fundamental. For instance, a lot of current research is being devoted to 'social interaction'. This provides useful information, but we saw that most social interaction is actually happening *internally* within the minds of individuals between mental networks that represent people. Stated more simply, people can exist without social interaction, but social interaction cannot exist without people. Because social interaction is a *secondary* expression of personal mental content, any general theory that is based upon social interaction will end up being inadequate and incomplete.

Artificialism: Teacher thought wants general theories that do not change. Artificialism replaces universal facts that do not change with personal opinion which does change. For instance, Norman Fairclough says in *Language and Power* (1989) that all 'truth' is being imposed upon society by power groups, and Fairclough's approach guides the postmodern approach of deconstructionism. Nowhere in *Language and Power* does Fairclough acknowledge the existence of independent scientific facts. Instead, he concludes that medical facts are suspect because they are interpreted by doctors, and that the news is unreliable because it is being presented by broadcasters with an agenda, which is like concluding that reality does not exist because my glasses are making it look fuzzy. Mental networks do give a distorted view of reality, but one examines the spectacles that one is wearing in order to see more clearly and not to ignore reality. For instance, my glasses may give me a fuzzy picture of an oncoming train, but this picture is still clear enough to allow me to step off the tracks so that I do not get run over.

Magical thinking: Magical thinking confuses reality with illusion. Fairclough says in *Language and Power* that universality is merely an illusion reached through the process of 'naturalization'. For example, if some product, such as Coca-Cola, is present universally, then this is because the Coca-Cola Company has used its economic power to dominate the opposition and ensure that Coke is everywhere. Obviously, Teacher thought will not be pleased with a mindset that concludes that Teacher thought itself is an illusion. However, let us step back for a moment to apply Fairclough's thinking about thinking to Fairclough himself. If all truth is based in personal opinion, and if all general theories are illusion, then Fairclough's theory is itself an illusion based merely in personal opinion. Thus, Fairclough's theory breaks down when applied to itself.

Centrating: Teacher thought wants general theories that apply to *many* different contexts. Centrating focuses upon a *specific* context. Maslow summarized the resulting problem in *The Psychology of Science* (1966), "If all you have is a hammer, everything looks like a nail." In other words, the understanding of some specialization will be overgeneralized to apply to *all* fields. We live today in a world of specialists who are experts in some specific field but who lack the big picture. When general understanding is lacking, then the tendency will be to solve the immediate crisis while perpetuating or aggravating the overall problem.

Egocentrism: This regards me and my culture as the center of the universe. In contrast, Teacher thought wants general theories that relate to everyone and not just to me. When I regard myself as the center of existence, then the TMNs of general theory are being ruled by MMNs of personal identity. One of the first steps in gaining a general understanding is the realization that the world does not revolve around me. For instance, one of the initial breakthroughs of the scientific revolution was the recognition by Copernicus that the universe does not revolve around the earth. This was followed by

Newton's discovery that a single general theory can be used to describe both movement on Earth and the 'heavenly movement' of the planets and stars.

Summarizing, we see that childish MMNs deceive Teacher thought, misdirect its attention, feed it faulty information, conclude that it is an illusion, give it only part of the picture, and treat it as a servant. Saying this in a more structured way, childish MMNs give Teacher thought specific facts, the wrong facts, facts that change, a restricted set of facts, and they try to control Teacher thought and act as if Teacher thought does not exist. Stated simply, childish MMNs are the enemy of Teacher thought.

Immanuel Kant, the famous philosopher, came to the same conclusion back in 1785 with his concept of the *categorical imperative*, first mentioned in *Grounding for the Metaphysics of Morals*. This imperative is best known in its first formulation: "Act only according to that maxim whereby you can, at the same time, will that it should become a universal law." For instance, what would happen if everybody lied? It would no longer be possible to lie because nobody would believe anything that anybody said. Similarly, what would happen if everybody stole? It would no longer be possible to steal because everything would be locked up. Using the language of mental symmetry, an action is morally good if it can be stated within Teacher thought as a universal theory. Lying works best if *some* people lie within a society that *assumes* that people are telling the truth. Similarly, stealing works best if some people steal within a society that assumes that people do not steal. When a person chooses to act within the context of a universal law in such a way that violates that universal law, then Kant refers to this as *radical evil*. Notice the juxtaposition. A person *lives* within a realm governed by a universal law and then chooses to *violate* that universal law.

Childish MMNs versus Teacher Thought

I suggest that this inherent contradiction is implicitly present in childish MMNs. We have seen that childish MMNs are by their very nature destructive of Teacher thought. However, they also assume the presence of Teacher thought. Using the language of Kant, they are expressions of radical evil. Let us go through our list one more time with this in mind.

Transductive reasoning: Transductive reasoning occurs within a context that uses normal reasoning. For instance, my conclusion that 'all dogs bite' may be based upon an MMN that formed as a result of a single traumatic experience involving some particular dog, but the only reason that I can overgeneralize from this specific experience is because I have learned through repetition to recognize dogs. If I had a traumatic midnight encounter with some unknown entity, then it would not be possible to generalize this fear into a specific phobia. Similarly, the reason that appearing on TV feels special is because of the general knowledge that I have about television. I may only have appeared on TV once for a few minutes, but I have watched TV for many hours in many locations. In contrast, it would not feel special to have an encounter with Joe Schlabotnik from the small town of Wymark in southern Saskatchewan.

Animism: Focusing upon secondary external attributes is only possible as long as primary internal characteristics continue to function. For instance, economics analyzes the external relationship between supply and demand. But this assumes that people are mentally *capable* of evaluating different options. The relationship between supply and demand breaks down when people lose the internal ability to determine value. Similarly, communism assumed that everyone would become wealthy if the laborer 'gained control of the means of production'—if factory workers took ownership of the factories. But history shows us that this redistribution of wealth failed because the new owners did not have an internal understanding of what it means to own and run a factory.

Artificialism: The person who believes that truth is based in people thinks that his authorities are experts *in something*. If that 'something' did not exist, then there would be no need for experts. For instance, one does not generally inquire about the qualifications of a barber, because a bad haircut may make a person look bad, but there are no lasting consequences. In contrast, one does worry about the expertise of a surgeon, because the physical body generates long-term personal consequences.

Magical thinking: Magical thinking confuses imagination with reality. However, when one examines those who are trying to fool others, one notices that this fooling only goes one way. A spy agency may spread disinformation in order to prevent *others* from distinguishing imagination from reality, but that same agency will do its best to ensure that *it* is able to tell truth from fiction. And a group or individual will only go to the effort of spreading disinformation about topics and items that have *real* significance. For instance, nobody will counterfeit monopoly money. Instead, one counterfeits American hundred dollar bills.

Centrating: Specialization is only possible when *many* people interact in a *general* way. For instance, it is not possible for everyone in town to be a butcher. Instead, the butcher has his shop next door to the barber and the grocer. Individuals can only specialize when *everyone* has access to *all* of the specializations. One can see the inherent relationship between specialization and the larger picture in the American military policy of 'need to know'. The goal of this policy is to prevent secrets from being leaked by telling each individual only what he 'needs to know'. This may succeed in preventing leaks but it also stops an organization from functioning. This leads to a continual struggle between *sharing* information in order to function effectively and *restricting* information in order to stop leaks.

Egocentrism: The individual who acts as if he is the center of the universe is assuming that others will meet his needs. For instance, Louis XIV, the Sun King famously stated that *l'état, c'est moi*. (I am the state.) But maintaining this attitude required an army of courtiers and servants. Without this societal structure, Louis would have discovered very quickly that the natural world does not revolve around him.

Concluding, we notice that in each case childish MMNs function within a larger context that assumes order, structure, and stability, the hallmarks of a general Teacher theory.

Childish MMNs and a Concept of God

We have been looking at the relationship between childish MMNs and Teacher thought. I have suggested that a mental concept of God emerges when a general understanding applies to personal identity. If all childish minds are governed by childish MMNs, and if MMNs inevitably distort Teacher thought, then this implies that the childish mind will naturally come up with distorted ideas about the nature of God. Therefore, we will go through our list of six traits one last time, this time noting the flawed concept of God that emerges.

Transductive reasoning: This leads to the assumption that God—a *universal* being—can be grasped through a *single* emotional experience, which is the 'logic' behind *mysticism*. The mystic talks about having emotional encounters with God, but if one examines the life of the typical mystic, then one discovers that his concept of God is usually based in a mere handful of transcendental religious experiences. A similar mindset exists in the individual who believes that he is a Christian because of some defining conversion experience that he had at some religious meeting. In both cases, the mind is leaping from specific to universal.

Animism: This leads to the feeling that inanimate external objects have religious significance, a form of thinking that is common in many religions, including Christianity. In the extreme, this expresses itself through idolatry, which treats holy objects as if they are living and divine. Cognitively speaking, what difference is there between a child who acts as if a doll is alive and a religious worshiper who bows to a carved object or prays to a statue? More subtly, the religious believer may think that encountering God means entering a certain physical building at a certain time of the week. This too is a form of animism. Physical objects can act as symbols that represent religious concepts, but just as the meaning in a child's interaction with a doll comes from what is happening in the mind and not from the physical doll itself, so I suggest that the meaning in religious ritual is being generated by the mind and not by the holy objects and events themselves.

Artificialism: This leads to the assumption that one learns about God by believing the right religious sources and following the right religious experts. A person will feel that religious truth must be *proclaimed* by people, or that one must *convince* or *coerce* people into accepting a religion. But let us step back for a moment and examine what is being implied. If an all-powerful being really exists, then surely *he* has sufficient power to convince people to believe in Him. If *I* have to use force to convince someone else to 'believe in the most powerful being in the entire universe', then either he does not exist and I am merely pretending, or else if he does exist then I am belittling him in front of others by suggesting that he needs *me* to defend him. As I write this book, ISIS (a fundamentalist Islamic group) is in control of major parts of Iraq and is forcing people to convert en-masse to Islam or be killed. If God exists and is all-present and all-powerful, then all one has to do is point out this universal presence and power when it is encountered. Anything more would be a deep insult to God.

Magical thinking: The tendency here is to confuse belief with reality. Religious believers often feel that believing in God somehow makes him exist, or that God ceases to exist when one stops believing in him. Belief and existence are two separate qualities, one based in imagination and the other in reality. However, I suggest that there are cognitive principles that run deeper than belief and reality. That is because a person who constructs a sufficiently general theory that applies to personal identity *will* create a mental concept of God and *will* end up being driven by the resulting TMN to act as if this God exists. For instance, 90% of the British population in 1914 confessed a belief in Christianity, and the Bishop of London Arthur Winnington-Ingram called the war against the Germans "a great crusade – we cannot deny it – to kill Germans. To kill them, not for the sake of killing but to save the world …" However, every Prussian soldier, whom British soldiers were killing in the name of God, wore a belt buckle on which the words were stamped "Gott mit uns!" (God with us.) Obviously, the *same* God could not be helping *both* sides of The Great War. And yet, millions of Germans and Brits went to their death convinced that the God of Christianity was guiding them, telling us that a mental concept of God will motivate entire societies to act *as if* this God exists, even to the point of dying (Sharp).

Centrating: The assumption here is that some specific religion or denomination has a total knowledge of God. I am not suggesting that all religions are equal or that all religious truth is equally valid. I think that almost everyone would agree that the beliefs of ISIS regarding conversion are not valid. Similarly, if one compares different specializations, we would all agree that the specialization of physician is more fundamental than the specialization of hairdresser. But while all religions are not equally valid, I suggest that all contain at least some truth and are meeting some legitimate needs. I have repeatedly discovered nuggets of truth by examining the beliefs of groups or religions with which I would not normally associate.

Egocentrism: The tendency here is to create a God in my own image. Instead of submitting personal identity to the TMN of universal understanding, I extrapolate from my personal experiences, making universal understanding a servant of the MMNs of personal identity. Religiously speaking, I am regarding myself as the center of the universe. For many New Age religions, the concept that I am God is a fundamental doctrine. I am not suggesting that one should not practice self-reflection, but rather that one combine an examination of self with studying others and learning from others, because it is this *combination* that provides the larger picture.

Concluding, we see that a number of religious beliefs can be explained as expressions of childish thought. Because childish MMNs distort Teacher thought, and because a general theory within Teacher thought leads to the concept of a universal Godlike being, we can conclude that these religious beliefs are cognitively invalid. That is because they are all the result of Teacher thought being *deceived* or *controlled* by Mercy thought.

We have gone through Piaget's traits five times. Let us summarize what we have learned. First, the childish mind is governed by MMNs. Second, the adult mind is still ruled in fundamental ways by MMNs, and the results are not nice. Third, the childish mind which is ruled by MMNs naturally acts in ways that are destructive to Teacher thought. Fourth, the childish mind that attacks Teacher thought is operating within a larger context that assumes the existence of Teacher thought. Fifth, the childish mind naturally forms mistaken concepts about God. Stating these conclusions in religious terms, we are all born in sin, sin causes us to form faulty concepts of God, and we naturally hate God while simultaneously depending upon God for existence.

And yet one can also speak of the childish mind as being *innocent*. This may seem like a contradiction, but it makes sense if one recognizes the difference between mental *software* and mental *hardware*. Everything that has been discussed in this chapter involves mental software—the initial programming of the childish mind. This software may be flawed, but as far as I can tell there is no inherent flaw in the structure of the mind. Childish software is flawed because it causes the child to think and behave in ways that violate mental hardware. For instance, this chapter examined the conflict between Mercy thought and Teacher thought that results from childish MMNs. Instead of cooperating with Teacher thought, Mercy thought functions in a way that is harmful to Teacher thought. That is an example of behaving in a way that violates mental hardware.

A young child appears innocent because the hardware can be glimpsed through the software. The adult mind filters speech and activity through a thick web of mental networks. Thus, the software often *hides* the hardware; the adult is so busy putting on a façade that one does not know who the real person is. In contrast, a child has not yet learned how to hide his thoughts from others; it is this appearance of raw unfiltered thought that makes the child appear innocent.

❉ 4. Belief, Science, and Religion

What is truth? Whenever the topic of God and religion comes up, then the question of truth inevitably becomes part of the discussion. In this chapter we will be addressing this question from a cognitive perspective. Instead of asking "What is truth?" we will attempt to determine the nature of *belief*. Truth has to do with reality whereas belief describes *my view* of reality. Truth describes what is really out there, while belief refers to what *I* see through *my* glasses. For instance, the typical teenager often thinks that his parents know *nothing*. When the teenager was a child, he thought that his parents knew *everything* and in a few years he will realize that his parents know *something*. Obviously, parents do not turn instantly into doddering idiots on their child's 13th birthday. Instead, what changes is the belief of the child. A young child believes that parents are omniscient, a teenager (often) believes that parents are ignorant, and an adult believes that parents have limited but valid knowledge.

The previous chapter looked at Piaget's preoperational stage of cognitive development. This chapter will begin by examining Piaget's *concrete operational stage,* which starts about the time that a child enters school. By comparing these two stages, we can see how belief changes in the mind of the developing child. Looking at this in more detail, let us see how the six fundamental traits of the preoperational child change when a child enters the concrete operational stage:

Inductive logic replaces *transductive reasoning*. Instead of *leaping* from specific to general, the child can use inductive logic to *step* from specific to general. Concrete logic replaces *animism*. Instead of viewing everything in personal terms, the child is capable of thinking logically about concrete events. Comparing and arranging replaces *artificialism*. The preoperational child looks to people for truth. The concrete operational child is able to determine truth by arranging and comparing concrete objects. For example, the child can arrange a set of blocks from smallest to largest, realize that pouring liquid from one container to another does not change the amount of liquid, and recognize that a poodle is a dog and a dog is an animal. The concrete operational child is also capable of building mental maps of physical neighborhoods, making it possible to work out new ways of getting from home to school, for instance, without having to ask adults. This leads to a sense of reasonableness that will limit *magical thinking*. For instance, a child will realize that Santa Claus cannot exist because no one could carry everyone's toys in a single bag and deliver them all in a single night. The child no longer *centrates* but becomes capable of decentering, focusing upon several aspects of the problem at once. Finally, socio-centrism replaces *egocentrism*. The child realizes that other people exist with different perspectives.

I suggest that these new traits are not just a random combination. Instead, they all describe attributes of *Perceiver* thought. On the diagram of mental symmetry, one can see that there is an arrow leading from Mercy thought to Perceiver thought. This arrow indicates that information *travels* from Mercy to Perceiver, allowing Perceiver thought to *process* Mercy experiences. Thus, I suggest that the concrete operational stage emerges when Perceiver thought becomes *capable* of processing Mercy experiences.

Mercy thought remembers *specific* experiences and their emotional labels, such as the ugly green beater of a car that broke down on the trip to California forcing the family to wait in the hot sun for a tow truck, or the leafy tree in the backyard that provides lovely shade in the summer but drops many leaves in the fall. Perceiver thought examines Mercy experiences for *connections,* leading to a knowledge of *facts*. For instance, a car is a box of metal and glass with a motor that rests upon four wheels. These various elements combine to form a car. Similarly, a tree is a combination of trunk, branches, leaves, and roots. Perceiver thought then uses these connections to *compare* one item or fact with another. For example, whenever one sees the combination of 'box of metal and glass', 'motor', and 'four wheels', then one knows that one is dealing with a car. Likewise, any object that contains branches, leaves, and roots attached to a trunk will be identified as a tree. The result of all this comparing is a mental map of facts, a set of connections that relates many different kinds of objects and experiences.

> A fact is a set of solid connections in Perceiver thought.

Returning to the traits of the concrete operational child, notice how the child is *comparing* blocks in order to organize them by size, recognizing that all dogs have *similar* characteristics, and using the *connections* between objects to build mental maps of the neighborhood. These are all examples of Perceiver processing. When one is using Perceiver thought to build connections between specific Mercy experiences, then one is using a form of *inductive logic* to step from specific to general. The stepping of inductive logic is quite different than the leaping of transductive reasoning. Transductive reasoning is driven by MMNs. For instance, the unpleasant experience of waiting in the hot sun in a broken-down vehicle will create an MMN and this mental network will then be used to evaluate all subsequent experiences involving old cars. Inductive logic uses Perceiver thought. For example, Perceiver thought compares cars to look for common features and then comes up with general conclusions based upon these common elements. Continuing with Piaget's list of traits, Mercy thought is driven by MMNs which the mind uses to represent people, whereas Perceiver thought looks for connections that are *independent* of people. Perceiver connections *tie together* MMNs, allowing the mind to think of several aspects of a problem at the same time. Perceiver connections *compare* MMNs, making it possible to notice the similarities and differences between various

MMNs, leading to socio-centrism. And Perceiver connections *question* MMNs, limiting magical thinking that is not based upon realistic connections.

Summarizing, what characterizes the concrete operational child is the emergence of Perceiver thought. We saw in the last chapter that the mind of the preoperational child is governed by MMNs. In contrast, the concrete operational child acquires the ability to use Perceiver thought independently of MMNs.

> Independent Perceiver thought emerges during the concrete operational stage.

Two Kinds of Belief

This suggests that belief can operate in one of two primary ways. Either MMNs *impose* belief upon the mind or else Perceiver thought *evaluates* belief. Piaget discovered these two forms of belief by examining the thinking of the developing *child*. However, this distinction does not just apply to the mind of the child. Instead, it is also possible for a group of *adults* to emphasize one of these two forms of belief. This is what Jürgen Habermas describes in *The Structural Transformation of the Public Sphere* (1962), where he noted that European *society* has passed through three stages. We will be looking here at the first two stages.

Europe from the Middle Ages to the 18th century was characterized by what Habermas calls *representative publicity*. The king or noble would display his political power to the people by presenting himself before an audience as an embodiment of some 'higher power'. A ruler tried to create an aura of authority by his personal appearance, through the clothes that he wore, the insignia on these clothes, his demeanor, and the manner in which he spoke. Words such as excellence, highness, majesty, fame, dignity, and honor were used to describe eminent individuals. For instance, the following passage gives a flavor of what life was like under Louis XIV, the Sun King of France.

> "Sire, it is time", the first Valet de Chambre awakens the King. The First Levee begins. Doctors, familiars and a few favourites who enjoyed the privilege of the Grand Entries followed in succession into the bedchamber of the King who was washed, combed and shaved (every other day). The officers of the Chamber and the Wardrobe then entered for the Grand Levee during which the King was dressed and breakfasted on a bowl of broth. Only the most important personalities in the kingdom were admitted to observe this ritual. The number of attendants is estimated at around a hundred, all male. As they left the King's apartment, a procession formed in the Hall of Mirrors. Followed by his courtiers, the King crossed the whole breadth of the Grand Apartment. This was the moment when the crowd gathered along the passage of the royal cortège was at last able to catch a glimpse of the monarch. Some were even able to speak to him briefly or pass him a written request (Chateauversailles).

We see here a mindset dominated by the MMNs that represent important people. But what is being described is not a group of preschool children but rather the *adult* rulers of an entire nation. And yet the fundamental mindset in both cases is the same. Childish MMNs are in charge.

Habermas says that the *bourgeois public sphere* emerged during the 18th century. Travel, commerce, and newspapers broadened people's perspectives by giving knowledge about other societies. The absolute authority of rulers was questioned. People of unequal rank gathered in coffeehouses and salons to debate politics. Conclusions were reached based upon the best argument and not social status. An independent press emerged. The rule of authority was replaced by the rule of law. Royal courts declined in importance while towns gained in significance.

These characteristics all portray the emergence of Perceiver thought from the domination of MMNs. Thus, Habermas is describing the same cognitive transformation in *society* that Piaget observed in the developing *child*.

Piaget and Habermas *described* the relationship between MMNs and Perceiver thought. The theory of mental symmetry *explains* this relationship in terms of the interaction between Mercy and Perceiver thought.

In simple terms, Perceiver thought can exist in one of three states: functioning, mesmerized, or confused, with confused being an intermediate state of uncertainty between functioning and mesmerized. The state of Perceiver thought depends upon the level of Perceiver *confidence* compared to the emotional *intensity*. If Perceiver confidence in some region of thought is *greater* than the emotional pressure (provided primarily by mental networks), then Perceiver thought will *function* by discovering, evaluating, and comparing facts and connections. This is the type of thinking that occurs in Piaget's concrete operational stage and Habermas' bourgeois public sphere.

If Perceiver confidence in some region of thought is *lower* than the emotional intensity, then Perceiver thought will become *mesmerized* by emotions and lose the ability to function. Perceiver belief will then be determined either by the connections of the specific emotional experience or the words of the person with emotional status. For instance, a single traumatic experience with a biting dog may mesmerize Perceiver thought into knowing that 'dog' is always connected with 'bite'. Similarly, if an adult tells a young child that 'the moon is made of green cheese', then the emotional status of the adult will mesmerize Perceiver thought in the child's mind into knowing that 'moon' and 'green cheese' are connected. The preoperational child is not *capable* of transcending this form of thought, while the nobility during representative publicity used their emotional status to overwhelm Perceiver thought in their subjects in order to *pressure* them into functioning at this level. Using computer language, the mind of the preoperational child is restricted by its limited mental *hardware* to function at the level of childish MMNs. The mental hardware of the adult is capable of functioning at a higher cognitive level, but will only do so if it is programmed by the proper mental *software*.

If the level of Perceiver confidence matches the level of emotional pressure, then neither way of knowing will function and Perceiver thought will be *confused*. This means that mesmerized Perceiver thought is separated from functioning Perceiver thought by a *threshold of confusion*, which one can see illustrated by the typical teenager. This type of mental transition is described by Love and Guthrie (1999) in their comparison of several systems of cognitive development. They noted that a person begins by acquiring knowledge through blind faith in authority but then eventually questions authority, leading to a crisis of knowing which they call the 'great accommodation'.

We saw when comparing Piaget with Habermas that these cognitive stages can apply either to the individual or to a society. Thus, as a first approximation, one could view the transition from modern thought to postmodern thought as a sort of societal 'great accommodation'. Many authorities have been questioned and theories deconstructed, but how does one put the pieces back together after everything has been torn apart? Where does one find a new foundation for truth? The rise of fundamentalism shows that many are dealing with this threshold of confusion by choosing to send Perceiver thought back to sleep.

In the same way that a person is either asleep or awake, so I suggest that Perceiver thought cannot be simultaneously mesmerized and functioning. Perceiver thought may be mesmerized in one context and functioning in another, but anything that causes Perceiver thought to function in some context will prevent it from becoming mesmerized, while any attempt to mesmerize Perceiver thought will make it more difficult for Perceiver thought to function within that context.

Absolute Truth

When Perceiver thought is mesmerized, then Perceiver belief will reflect Mercy feelings. A person will *believe* a fact in Perceiver thought because of the emotional status of the *source* of this fact in Mercy thought. Such a person will not think that his Perceiver belief is the same as his Mercy feelings because he is experiencing *both* strong emotions from Mercy thought *and* strong belief from Perceiver thought. However, if he loses emotional respect for the source of belief, then Perceiver thought will stop being mesmerized and start being confused, showing that Perceiver belief really is dependent upon Mercy feelings. Notice that all of this is occurring *internally* within the mind of the individual independently of whether the belief corresponds with actual truth or not. The fact that is being believed was probably learned from some person or book, but the emotional respect for the source comes from an internal mental network and the belief in the fact is an internal sense of certainty.

Such a person will also think strongly in terms of *right* and *wrong*. Facts that come from good Mercy sources will be labeled as right, while facts that come from bad Mercy sources will be regarded as wrong. For instance, the Bible-believing Christian accepts facts that come from the Bible as right, while rejecting facts from other holy books as wrong.

This mindset will lead to a strong belief in *absolute truth*. In order to understand this we need to look at how labeling is propagated in Mercy and Perceiver thought. Suppose that I enter a restaurant for the first time. The emotional label that Mercy thought attaches to this new experience will depend partly upon the physical feelings of my body and partly upon the emotional labels already possessed by experiences that come to mind. For instance, I may see a picture of a palm tree and be reminded of a pleasant vacation, or I may see a dirty counter and be reminded of some 'greasy spoon'. Saying this another way, emotional experiences and mental networks form an *emotional* hierarchy, with lesser experiences and mental networks acquiring their emotional labels from defining experiences and core mental networks.

Perceiver thought labels facts in a similar way. Suppose that I encounter a new piece of information. The label of certainty that is given to this new fact will depend upon the labels already possessed by related facts that come to mind. For instance, if bringing up the topic of spiritual gifts reminds me of vague lists of personality traits from questionable sources, then this label of uncertainty will also be applied to any new facts regarding spiritual gifts. Thus, Perceiver labeling is based upon a hierarchy of *knowing*, with lesser facts basing their labels of confidence upon more central facts, which themselves base their labels of confidence upon a set of core beliefs or axioms.

But what defines the set of core beliefs? One possibility is for core beliefs to come from *established authorities*, such as holy books, textbooks, mainstream media, professors, or scientific journals. This leads to an attitude of *absolute* truth, in which certain esteemed authorities are regarded as the source of absolute truth, which is then used to evaluate lesser facts. This type of thinking could be compared to building upon permafrost, because mesmerized Perceiver thought is like frozen ground. The foundation will only be solid as long as the ground remains frozen. But buildings are heated; therefore, there will be an inherent tension between keeping the foundation frozen and the building heated. (This problem is addressed in northern Canada by running refrigeration coils through the foundation of a building in order to ensure that the ground remains frozen.) Similarly, when a person uses Perceiver thought based upon absolute truth, then Perceiver thought will be functioning at the periphery of knowledge but will remain mesmerized when dealing with core belief; Perceiver thought will be un-frozen on the surface but frozen at foundational levels. When discussing facts with such a person, one will notice that thinking is rational—but only up to a certain point. When this point is reached then the person will insist that it is no longer appropriate to use rational thought and that one should stop analyzing and submit to authority.

This explains why a person can both *learn* to use Perceiver thought as a child during Piaget's concrete operational stage and be *unable* to use Perceiver thought as an adult. Piaget was observing primarily the periphery of knowledge that dealt with everyday objects and normal experiences. Almost everyone learns how to use Perceiver thought when dealing with physical objects, such as distinguishing one car or tree from another. It is far more difficult to learn how to use Perceiver thought when dealing with core mental networks. Here many adults remain mentally stuck within Piaget's preoperational stage. And as long as these adults remain within the culture that was the childhood source of their core mental networks, they probably will not *realize* that core thinking is still functioning at the level of Piaget's preoperational stage.

> Free will is real but limited. Choice requires alternatives with similar mental potency.

Building Perceiver confidence could be compared to a weight training program. In order to become stronger, one must lift weights that are heavy but not too heavy. Lifting weights that are too light is not a struggle, while lifting weights that are too heavy is not possible. Similarly, when the emotional intensity is too low, then using Perceiver thought is not a struggle, while using Perceiver thought is not possible when the emotional intensity is too high. It is within the intermediate stage—the threshold of confusion, that it becomes both necessary and possible to use free will. Each choice to use Perceiver thought will lead to greater Perceiver confidence, while choosing not to use Perceiver thought will diminish the level of Perceiver confidence. Looking at this more generally, I suggest that free will also emerges when there are *conflicting* mental networks. When one mental network dominates thought, then free will is not possible. However, when two *different* mental networks clamor for attention, then it becomes possible to *choose* between these mental networks.

Universal Truth

The alternative to absolute truth is *universal* truth. Absolute truth acquires its ultimate Perceiver facts from the statements of esteemed authorities, whereas universal truth acquires its ultimate Perceiver facts from connections that are universally *repeated*. For instance, one does not believe in gravity because Isaac Newton came up with a law of gravity. Instead, one believes in gravity because objects *always* fall to the ground when they are released. In other words, gravity is a universal truth and not an absolute truth. Absolute truth contains an inherent contradiction between a frozen foundation and a warm building, because Perceiver thought is mesmerized when believing the truth but functioning when working with facts that are affected by this truth. Universal truth contains no inherent contradiction because Perceiver thought continues functioning to the very core of belief. Universal truth is fairly easy to discover when examining the physical world, because one can *see* situations being repeated. Universal truth is far more difficult to discover when dealing with non-physical topics such as psychology, religion, or philosophy. However, I suggest that it is possible to discover universal truth by examining many different fields for common connections, which brings us back to the methodology of independent corroboration introduced at the beginning of this book.

Absolute truth acquires its information from esteemed authorities. A belief in universal truth does not stop a person from learning from others, but it does change the way that one views sources of truth. Instead of focusing upon *experts*, universal truth will focus upon *expertise*. Because humans are finite creatures, it is not possible for one person to know everything. This means that one must specialize and look to others to fill in one's gaps in knowledge. Absolute truth will focus upon the emotional *status* of the expert and the discussion will center on the *person*: "Doctor Smith is highly respected in his field and has won many awards." Universal truth, in contrast, will focus upon the *knowledge* of the expert and most of the discussion will be about *information*: "Researchers have been working on a new method of using stem cells to treat cancer. This is now entering clinical trials." Absolute truth will reject information that does not come from socially accepted experts, while universal truth will look beyond social status for consistency and evidence.

The conflict between science and religion is usually portrayed as a struggle for truth. However, I suggest that it is primarily a conflict over *belief*. Science uses Perceiver thought to look for repeated connections. Important experiments will usually be *replicated* by different people in different circumstances. For instance, in 1989 Fleischmann and Pons reported that they had discovered 'cold fusion'. Fusion generates energy by smashing together small atoms such as helium and hydrogen, but requires a very high temperature. The sun produces energy through fusion—at a temperature of 15,000,000°C. Fleishman and Pons claimed to have discovered a form of fusion that occurred at room temperature. Unfortunately, other scientists were unable to replicate these groundbreaking results, and cold fusion is now regarded as an example of 'pathological science'.

Replication builds Perceiver confidence. *Peer review* minimizes the effect of MMNs. It is easy for Perceiver thought to become clouded by the personal emotions generated by MMNs. As we have seen, it is much easier to evaluate the thinking of someone else than it is to evaluate my own thinking. Peer review tries to eliminate personal bias by having my thinking evaluated by other people. In the case of cold fusion, peer review failed because two competing groups were each trying to get academic credit by publishing first. Pons and Fleischmann originally wanted to gather data for 18 additional *months* before publishing, but agreed with their competitors that they would each submit a paper in 18 *days*. They then reneged on this verbal agreement and submitted their paper in *five* days. Because the research was so significant, reviewers were only given one week to evaluate the paper. And because the researchers wanted to patent their discovery, a number of important details were left out of the paper, making it difficult for other researchers to replicate the findings. When others eventually repeated the experiments, they did not notice any cold fusion. Even another scientist using the original equipment was unable to replicate the findings.

Notice that peer review can eliminate the biases of *individual* scientists but has difficulty removing the biases shared by science as a *whole*. *Every* scientist is driven by the MMNs of becoming famous by publishing important results and getting rich by patenting significant discoveries. These MMNs that are shared by all scientists define the *culture* of science, and this culture played the primary role in the saga of cold fusion (Gilet).

I have suggested that research about thinking is often inadequate when it comes to the researcher thinking about his *own* thinking. Therefore, it is only proper to step back for a moment and think about my thinking. How do I know that *my* beliefs are not being clouded by personal emotions? Three factors give me hope that this is not the case. First, I have paid a price for my knowledge. In other words, over the years I have undergone an extensive Perceiver 'weight training program', which has involved holding on to Perceiver truth in the midst of emotional pressure. Second, I have done most of my research outside of the culture of both science and theology, which has made me consciously aware of the implicit underlying mental networks that tend to drive research and writing. Third, I have gone to great lengths to evaluate the theories of others and incorporate their findings into my understanding. Much of the material in this book is the indirect result of my personal attempt to escape the blindness—and often self-deception—of mesmerized Perceiver thought and absolute truth.

Scientific Methodology

Looking at this more generally, I suggest that one can distinguish between scientific thought, scientific methodology, scientific paradigms, and scientific culture.

Scientific *thought* uses Perceiver thought to look for repeated connections. The underlying assumption is a belief in universal truth. The person who searches for repeated connections is assuming that connections are repeated. For instance, Pons and Fleishman believed that they had discovered universal facts about cold fusion that would make it possible to build power plants that generated energy cheaply and efficiently. (We shall see later that science also assumes that Server thought can be used to look for sequences that are repeated.)

> Scientific methodology combines objectivity, empirical evidence, and peer review.

Scientific *methodology* tries to make it easy for Perceiver thought to function. Results are described factually and experiments are replicated. An attitude of objectivity avoids triggering personal MMNs while peer review attempts to eliminate any self-deception introduced by MMNs. And because it is easiest to determine Perceiver facts when dealing with physical objects in the real world, science demands empirical evidence. As far as scientific methodology is concerned, seeing is believing. The problem with scientific methodology is that it tries to *protect* Perceiver thought by focusing upon the physical world and avoiding personal emotions, rather than building Perceiver confidence by holding on to facts in the midst of emotional pressure even when physical objects are not present.

Scientific *paradigms* were discussed in our look at Thomas Kuhn. Perceiver thought uses *non*-emotional logic to look for connections that are repeated. These facts provide the bricks for abstract thought. Teacher thought then takes these Perceiver bricks, which are *not* emotional, and uses them to construct the mental structure of a general theory, which *is* emotional. A methodology that protects Perceiver thought by avoiding Mercy emotions will be unable to handle the Teacher emotions that emerge when Perceiver facts turn into the TMN of a general theory. Thus, as Kuhn observes, the typical objective scientist becomes emotionally trapped by his paradigm.

Scientific *culture* emerges from the set of MMNs shared by a group of scientists. For instance, we saw in the example of cold fusion the two cultural elements of 'wanting to get published' and 'trying to get rich'. Both of these involve strong Mercy emotions. Thus, I suggest that the scientific attempt to remain objective is futile. Humans are driven by Mercy emotions, and as long as humans are involved in research, subjective Mercy emotion will remain part of the equation.

We saw in a previous chapter that scientific theories can turn into TMNs that emotionally trap scientists. Scientific methodology can also turn into a TMN that guides the behavior of the scientist, and scientific culture will form mental networks that guide the behavior of scientists. (We will examine this in more detail in the chapter on righteousness.) This is not a trivial effect. In fact, in the appendix to his book, Kuhn redefines a paradigm to be an expression of the behavior carried out by a group of scientists.

> A paradigm governs, in the first instance, not a subject matter but rather a group of practitioners. Any study of paradigm directed or paradigm-shattering research must begin by locating the responsible group or groups (Kuhn, 1970, p. 180).

> Having isolated a particular community of specialists by techniques like those just discussed, one may usefully ask: What do its members share that accounts for the relative fullness of their professional communication in the relative unanimity of their professional judgments? To that question my original text licenses the answer, a paradigm or set of paradigms (p.182).

Notice how scientific methodology and scientific culture are now in the driver's seat, while scientific theory is merely along for the ride. Scientific methodology and culture are acting as the core mental networks which are imposing their structure upon the lesser mental networks of scientific theory. I am reminded of the school teacher who stated that teaching would be a great profession if one did not have to deal with students. This sounds like a contradiction but I know from personal experience that so much emphasis can be placed upon the supporting structure of educational procedure, curriculum development, teacher training, and lesson planning, that the primary goal of teaching students can be almost forgotten.

Thus, what began as a search for truth (using Perceiver thought to look for repeated connections) turned into a methodology that protects Perceiver thought and then morphed into a collection of mental networks rooted in scientific paradigms, methodology, and culture that now overshadow the original search for truth. It is this *secondary* belief system that tends to dominate the discussion between science and religion rather than the original search for truth.

First, instead of merely recognizing that subjective emotions make it difficult for Perceiver thought to operate, science declares the very concept of purpose or teleology to be *taboo*. The cognitive science of religion, with its Agency Detector, partially violates this taboo, but it does so within the context of the theory of evolution, which (officially) rejects the idea of agents, purpose, and teleology.

Kuhn describes this aspect of evolution quite clearly:

> All of the well-known pre-Darwinian evolutionary theories – those of Lamarck, Chambers, Spencer, and the German *Naturphilosophen* – had taken evolution to be a goal directed process... for many men the abolition of that teleological kind of evolution was the most significant and least palatable of Darwin's suggestions. The *Origin of Species* recognized no goal set either by God or nature... Even such marvelously adapted organs as the eye and hand of man – organs whose design had previously provided powerful arguments for the existence of a supreme artificer or an advance plan – were products of a process that moved steadily *from* primitive beginnings but *toward* no goal (Kuhn, p. 172).

However, we have just seen that science is performed by scientists who are goal-driven. Scientists, like all individuals, would like to become rich and famous. And we saw in our previous look at Tremlin that scientists naturally talk about evolution or Nature as if it is an intelligent goal-driven agent.

Second, peer review has a natural tendency to turn into *elitism*. It is important to compare one's facts with the knowledge and discoveries of others. For the past few years, this has been my primary method of research. However, when I verbally discuss my research to others, most of the conversation is not about content and facts. Instead, I am continually told that others will only take my research seriously if I get a PhD and become part of the academic community. (I have a Masters degree in engineering.) Thus, the methodology that was originally developed to help Perceiver thought to discover truth and the culture that emerged as a result of a group of people using Perceiver thought to search for truth has now become the overriding factor that is used to evaluate truth.

Finally, the focus upon empirical evidence has turned into the dogma of *scientism*, which declares that nothing exists except physical reality. But we have already seen from our discussion of Thomas Kuhn that empirical evidence only plays a partial role in guiding science. Quoting further from Kuhn,

No process yet disclosed by the historical study of scientific development at all resembles the methodological stereotype of falsification by direct comparison with nature. That remark does not mean that scientists do not reject scientific theories, or that experience and experiment are not essential to the process in which they do so. But it does mean – what will ultimately be a central point – that the act of judgment that leads scientists to reject previously accepted theory is always based on more than a comparison of that theory with the world (p.77).

When studying human thought and behavior, then scientism will direct the attention away from core issues to peripheral factors. For instance, in *Language and Power*, Fairclough describes the way in which mental networks (which he refers to as members resources) *internally* guide the thinking of groups and individuals.

The MR [members resources] which people draw upon to produce and interpret texts are cognitive in the sense that they are in people's heads, but they are social in the sense that they have social origins - they are socially generated, and their nature is dependent on the social relations and struggles out of which they were generated - as well as being socially transmitted and, in our society, unequally distributed. People internalize what is socially produced and made available to them, and use this internalized MR to engage in their social practice, including discourse (Fairclough, 1989, p. 24).

Participants arrive at interpretations of situational context partly on the basis of external cues - features of the physical situation, properties of participants, what has previously been said; but also partly on the basis of aspects of their MR in terms of which they interpret these cues - specifically, representations of societal and institutional social orders which allow them to ascribe the situations they are actually in to particular situation types (p.144).

Notice the interaction between *external* social interaction and *internal* mental networks. Social interaction leads to the formation of mental networks. These mental networks are then triggered by situations and used to interpret situations.

However, Fairclough does not appear to mention the concept of *internal* 'members resources' in any of his later writings. Instead, all that is left is a discussion of *external* social interaction. For example, in one article Fairclough says that

Social events are constituted through the intersection of two causal powers – those of social practices (and, behind them, of social structures), and those of social agents. We may say that social agents produce events in occasioned and situated ways, but they depend on social structures and social practices do so – the causal powers of social agents are mediated by those of social structures and practices, and vice-versa (Fairclough).

Notice how people are being described as social agents guided by social structures and social practices. This is like saying that bicycles drive. But bicycles do not drive. People drive bicycles. Curiously, in the same article Fairclough actually describes this tendency to refer to 'bicycles that drive' rather than 'people driving bicycles', which he calls *nominalization*.

> Let us go back to example 4, the European Union text. It is similar to many other contemporary texts in representing global economic change as a process without human agents, in which change is nominalized... and so represented as itself an entity which can act as an agent (p.45).

Going further, scientific methodology can be helpful when analyzing the physical world, but it is counterproductive when attempting to decipher the mind. First, it is not possible to remain objective because the mind is studying *itself*. It is both being studied and doing the studying. This can be done, but only if a person gains the Perceiver confidence that is required to use Perceiver thought in the presence of emotional pressure. And when the mind is studying itself, then it is not possible to ignore purpose. As we saw in the illustration of cold fusion, as long as humans are involved in research, the TMNs of scientific theory will become intermingled with the MMNs of personal desire. This problem becomes multiplied when the topic being studied is the human mind with its personal desires. I suggest that the solution is to make teleology an integral part of cognitive research. Thus, my research over the years has been simultaneously driven by both the TMN of gaining a general understanding of how the mind functions *as well as* the MMN of developing *my* mind so that all cognitive modules function together in harmony.

Second, what really matters when studying the mind is not peer review but rather personal application. For instance, eugenics (using selective breeding to improve human genetics) was widely practiced during the early 20th century, leading to policies such as genetic screening, marriage restrictions, segregation, compulsory sterilization, forced abortions, forced pregnancies, and even genocide. Most of these policies were abandoned after World War II because they had been practiced in such a brutal manner by the Nazis in Germany. Before the Second World War, peer review would have supported research into eugenics while today it would be difficult to publish an article supporting Nazi-style eugenics. In other words, peer review will fail to remove a bias that is part of the culture, because a culture is composed of the MMNs that are *shared* by a group of people. Thus, instead of questioning culture, peer review will tend to reinforce it. But it is the struggle of attempting to use Perceiver thought *despite* the MMNs of culture that is especially effective in building the Perceiver confidence that is required to decipher human thought.

Finally, if one wishes to understand the mind, then one must go beyond empirical evidence to the thinking that lies *behind* this evidence. For example, I studied engineering in the 1980s before computers were commonplace. Whenever I encountered a new piece of electronic equipment, I would have to figure out how it worked. I learned back then that if I understood the function of every knob and button, then I could operate the machine properly. In other words, empirical evidence (studying every physical knob and button) was sufficient to give a complete picture of how the machine functioned. This method is no longer sufficient, because the buttons and knobs are now *reprogrammable*. Most machines today are driven by onboard computers that can be reprogrammed. Thus, studying the function of each knob and button will only determine what they do in that particular configuration. A similar principle applies to the study of the mind, because the mind is a kind of computer. Neurological evidence only tells us how the mind is functioning *in a particular configuration*. Saying this more simply, neurology can observe how the mind *does* work, but it cannot determine how the mind *could* work. That is why empirical evidence is important when studying the mind, but it is not enough.

The Religious Attitude

We have looked at the belief system that lies behind scientific thought. Let us turn our attention now to the belief system that drives *religious* thought. Science begins by assuming that Perceiver thought can be used to discover universal truth. Religion starts by assuming that some source will reveal absolute truth to Perceiver thought. Thus, science has its starting point in Piaget's concrete operational stage and Habermas' bourgeois public sphere while religion has its starting point in Piaget's preoperational stage and Habermas' representative publicity. Because these two forms of thought are separated by a threshold of confusion, a wall of separation will naturally emerge between scientific thought and religious thought. And because Perceiver thought cannot be simultaneously awake and asleep, scientific thought will tend to emerge at the expense of religious thought and vice versa.

Because the concrete operational stage *follows* the preoperational stage, science sees itself as the successor to religion and equates religion with childish thought. Remember what Dirac said about a belief in God.

> It is quite understandable why primitive people, who were so much more exposed to the overpowering forces of nature than we are today, should have personified these forces in fear and trembling. But nowadays, when we understand so many natural processes, we have no need for such solutions (Heisenberg, 1971).

Looking at the big picture, I suggest that science and religion will each emerge naturally within different realms of experience. Science emerges where it is *easiest* to use Perceiver thought. It is easiest to discover solid facts by examining the physical world. It is easiest to deal with emotional pressure by avoiding subjective experiences. And it is easiest to test facts by interacting with my peers who share the same cultural MMNs and the same theoretical TMNs.

Religious thought, in contrast, emerges naturally where Mercy emotions are the *strongest* and Perceiver thought is most difficult. It is easiest for Perceiver thought to be mesmerized when dealing with experiences with great emotional content, such as lightning bolts, tornadoes, volcanoes, or hurricanes, or when dealing with topics of great personal import, such as the meaning of life, the question of personal suffering, or life-after-death. It is easiest to mesmerize Perceiver thought by basing belief in sources that have the greatest emotional status. And it is most difficult for Perceiver thought to function when dealing with invisible topics that cannot be examined empirically.

Thus, it may be technically accurate for science to say that it uses rational thought and religion does not, but this is not a valid comparison because science is using rational thought in precisely the area where it is *easiest* to use rational thought, whereas religion is being mesmerized in precisely the area where it is most *difficult* to use rational thought. Winning a race is easy when one is going downhill with the wind and the opponent is going uphill against the wind. And when the cognitive crutches of objectivity, empirical evidence, and peer review turn into dogma then this is like saying that the only valid race is one in which I get to go downhill with the wind.

The distinction between scientific thought and religious thought can also be seen in the Myers-Briggs category of *Thinking* versus *Feeling*. MBTI views this division as a dichotomy. One is either Thinking or Feeling. I suggest that MBTI Thinking describes Perceiver thought functioning in the absence of Mercy feelings. Similarly, I suggest that MBTI Feeling describes Mercy thought combined with mesmerized Perceiver thought. In other words, Thinking is Perceiver without Mercy while Feeling is Mercy without Perceiver. Mental symmetry, in contrast, recognizes that the division between Thinking and Feeling may be natural, but suggests that it is also cognitively incomplete. The goal is to develop sufficient Perceiver confidence to allow Perceiver thought to *cooperate* with Mercy thought, resulting in a division of labor in which Mercy thought evaluates experiences while Perceiver thought connects experiences. For instance, a chocolate bar may taste good or bad, but this Mercy label is *independent* of the Perceiver connection between eating too many sweets and getting fat. Saying this another way, I suggest that one of the main goals of cognitive development is to integrate the MBTI split between Thinking and Feeling.

Like scientific thought, religious thought also naturally develops a methodology, or more accurately, an *attitude*. This religious attitude is composed of fervor, self-denial, and transcendence. In the same way that scientific *methodology* emerges naturally as a by-product of attempting to protect Perceiver thought, so religious *attitude* also emerges naturally from a desire to keep Perceiver thought mesmerized.

> The religious attitude combines fervor, self-denial, and transcendence.

Fervor uses emotional intensity to impose belief. If Perceiver belief comes from being overwhelmed by Mercy emotions, then the simplest way to increase Perceiver belief is by making Mercy emotions more intense. Habermas' representative publicity tells us some of the ways in which emotions can be intensified. Repeating what was written earlier, "A ruler tried to create an aura of authority by his personal appearance, through the clothes that he wore, the insignia on these clothes, his demeanor, and the manner in which he spoke. Words such as excellence, highness, majesty, fame, dignity, and honor were used to describe eminent individuals." This description also applies to religious thought. Just as the European monarch appeared personally before an audience wearing special clothes and acting in a special manner, so the special event plays a major role in religious thought. A religious priest will usually wear special clothes with special insignia, carry out special rituals, and speak using special words during a special event in a special place. It may seem repetitive to use the word 'special' so many times, but that is precisely what the religious term 'holy' means. To be holy is to be separate and different— or special. Holiness keeps Perceiver thought *mesmerized* by increasing the emotional intensity of Mercy experiences and it prevents Perceiver thought from building *connections* by using physical and mental walls to separate the 'sacred' from the 'profane'. (We will see later that there is also another form of holiness.) I am not suggesting that it is wrong to associate religion with beautiful clothes and meaningful rituals. But I am questioning the cognitive results of using special Mercy elements to *define* Perceiver truth using the mindset of Habermas' first stage. In other words, the problem with religious fervor is not the emotional intensity, but rather that emotional intensity is being used to overwhelm Perceiver thought.

For instance, the practice of *Eucharist adoration* is currently experiencing a revival within the Catholic Church. The consecrated host of the Eucharist is placed within a monstrance so that the faithful can adore the Blessed Sacrament through psalms, prayers, devotional music, or merely in silent contemplation and reflection. Notice the number of religious nouns in the previous sentence that are only used to describe holy objects and experiences. Using non-religious language, it is believed that bread and wine are somehow transformed into the body and the blood of Jesus when the priest stands next to them and says a special set of words. This special bread and wine is called a consecrated host and the ceremony of eating this special bread and wine is known as the Eucharist. The monstrance is a special container for the special bread and wine. In Eucharist adoration, those who regard the bread and wine as special will sit beside it reading special passages, singing special songs, saying special words, or thinking special thoughts.

The response of Western society to all this specialness (or holiness) has gone through three major stages. First, the MMNs created by this holy behavior formed an *assumed core* of identity and culture. Using Habermas' terminology, the attitude of representative publicity was used by both the nobility and the clergy. Second, the bourgeois public sphere led to a questioning of the emotional status assigned to both the nobility and the clergy. As a result, religious rituals were regarded as *childish* activities, as epitomized by Dirac's dismissal of religious belief. This is now being replaced by a third stage that emphasizes the need for *religious myth*. A myth is not true in a scientific sense, but is significant because it meets deep emotional needs. This book is suggesting an approach that goes beyond the third stage of religious myth, based upon the recognition that religious myth meets deep emotional needs because of underlying cognitive mechanisms. If one understands how the mind functions, then it becomes possible to work out how one can meet these emotional needs in a more effective and integrated manner.

Self-denial results from the interaction between mental networks. Religious thought looks to esteemed sources for beliefs that affect personal identity. Using the language of mental symmetry, the MMNs representing the source of truth are mesmerizing Perceiver thought into knowing what is true, and these absolute truths are being applied to personal identity. But because mental networks form an emotional hierarchy, this relationship will only continue to function as long as the MMNs representing the source of truth have much *greater* emotional significance than the MMNs representing personal identity. This may sound complicated but it is quite easy to illustrate by looking at the typical teenager. The young child accepts his parents' statements as 'gospel truth' because he is much smaller, less skillful, and less knowledgeable. As a result, the MMNs that represent parents within the mind of the child are much more powerful than the MMNs that represent personal identity. The teenager who grows up physically, acquires skills, and gains knowledge will no longer regard parents as a source of absolute truth because the MMNs that represent personal identity have grown in status relative to the MMNs that represent parents. The extreme version of self-denial is known in religious circles as 'worm theology', which believes that 'I am utterly contemptible compared to the awesome majesty of God'.

Examples of extreme self-denial are easy to find within religion. For instance, Simeon Stylites was a fourth century Syrian ascetic who lived for 37 years on top of a column. As the online version of the Encyclopedia Britannica relates,

> His first column was 6 feet (2 m) high, later extended to about 50 feet (15 m). He remained atop the column until his death, permanently exposed to the elements, standing or sitting day and night in his restricted area, protected from falling by a railing, and provided with a ladder to communicate with those below or to receive meagre gifts of food from disciples (Britannica).

The Amish provide a more modern example of self-denial that is related to my background. They value humility and abhor any appearance of vanity, such as wearing showy clothing, having fancy furniture, using cosmetics or jewelry, or showing one's face in a photograph. Being raised Mennonite (Friesen is a common Mennonite name) I am familiar with this Amish attitude, although I experienced it in a less stringent form.

Transcendence warns about the dangers of thinking too much about God and religion. In essence, transcendence is the belief that the essential nature of God cannot be grasped by human rational thought. It protects absolute truth by ensuring that Perceiver thought remains in a mesmerized state when dealing with core mental networks. Using the analogy of building upon permafrost, a doctrine of transcendence keeps the ground of absolute truth frozen by ensuring that the building is not heated too much through the use of Perceiver thought. Analyzing core religious beliefs will melt the permafrost upon which the building is situated, threatening the integrity of the building. In practical terms transcendence expresses itself in phrases such as "We cannot understand God. If we were to understand God then we would be God." Stated more philosophically, "If one wishes to encounter the divine, then one must let go of logic and transcend rational thought." More specifically one often hears people in Christian circles saying that "The doctrine of the Trinity is an incomprehensible mystery."

In the same way that scientific methodology plays a valid role in protecting Perceiver thought, so I suggest that these religious attitudes play a valid role in getting a person to move beyond childish MMNs. As we saw in our look at Piaget's preoperational stage, the MMNs of childish identity are fatally flawed. The childish self does need to be denied, and the only way to stop being driven by childish MMNs is to become driven by a new set of MMNs. But while these religious attitudes can help to *start* a person on the path to mental wholeness, I suggest that they will also prevent a person from *finishing* this path.

First, fervor motivates an individual with a new set of MMNs that are *different* than the MNNs of childish identity. However, because these new MMNs are disconnected from normal existence, it is not possible to live in these new MMNs all the time. For instance, the monk who devotes his life to a focus upon God still inhabits a physical body that needs to be fed and nurtured. Thus, even the most fervent religious believer can only spend *some* of his time 'following God'. In contrast, we will see later that Platonic forms result in MMNs that can be pursued *all* of the time, even though they are both different and more perfect than normal physical existence, making it unnecessary to separate holy objects and experiences from normal existence through the erection of physical walls and taboos.

Second, a student may regard school as a form of self-denial (and to some extent he is right), but the goal of attending school is not to withdraw from the world permanently but rather to withdraw for a time in order to re-enter the world as an adult. Similarly, I suggest the purpose of religion is not to suppress childish MMNs in order to *withdraw* from the realm of human experience in gnostic fashion but rather to *rebuild* the MMNs of personal identity upon a more solid foundation so that one can experience *lasting* pleasure in the world of experiences. In other words, denying self is not the same as transforming self. When mental networks of personal identity are suppressed through self-denial, then the environment must be controlled to ensure that they will not be triggered.

Finally, while the spectacles of childish MMNs may be hopelessly inadequate for grasping the nature of God and religion, the premise of this book is that it is possible to *replace* these inadequate glasses with a set of lenses based in the TMN of a general understanding that is capable of viewing core religious doctrines in an adequate manner. This does not mean that finite humans are capable of *fully* understanding universality. However, I do suggest that it is possible for a finite being to build a rational understanding that provides a *sufficient* grasp of the *essential* nature of universal structure.

One sees this relationship illustrated when solving physics problems. The physical universe is governed by laws of physics that can be described in a rational manner, and one can use mathematical equations to predict how *simple* situations will behave, such as 'rolling a ball down an inclined plane', 'driving a car around a banked curve', or 'calculating the forces between two charged particles'. However, *real world* problems are too complicated to be solved analytically. Instead, the physics student uses mathematics to solve *simplified* versions of real world problems. For example, the high school physics student may be told to 'Assume that there is no friction', 'Ignore the effects of gravity', or 'Treat the ball as if it is a uniform mass'. As one advances in physics, one becomes able to solve increasingly complicated problems, but one is still dealing with a simplification of the real world. Saying this another way, finite beings cannot fully comprehend the universe, but they can gain a rational understanding that provides a sufficient grasp of the essential nature of universal structure.

Religious thought is based in absolute truth revealed by experts. Religious attitude protects this attitude of belief in authority through fervor, self-denial, and transcendence. In the same way that scientific methodology can end up overshadowing the scientific search for truth, so the religious attitude can end up overshadowing the content being revealed by religious experts. Saying this more bluntly, there is a natural tendency for religious attitude to define religious belief regardless of the actual words of the religious experts. This can be illustrated by comparing what Jesus and Paul—the two primary religious experts of Christianity—said about these three religious attitudes with historical Christian practice.

> The religious attitude will naturally overrule actual religious content.

Jesus did not have a high regard for religious *fervor*. When one of his disciples pointed out the magnificence of the Temple in Jerusalem, Jesus responded that nothing would be left of this center for religious fervor.

> As He was going out of the temple, one of His disciples said to Him, "Teacher, behold what wonderful stones and what wonderful buildings." And Jesus said to him, "Do you see these great buildings? Not one stone will be left upon another which will not be torn down" (Mark 13:1-2).

He said that public displays of religious fervor would not be rewarded by God.

> When you pray, you are not to be like the hypocrites; for they love to stand and pray in the synagogues and on the street corners so that they may be seen by men. Truly I say to you, they have their reward in full. But you, when you pray, go into your inner room, close your door and pray to your Father who is in secret, and your Father who sees what is done in secret will reward you (Matt. 6:5-6).

And instead of building walls to separate the holy from the profane, we are told that the curtain that protected the holy place in the temple in Jerusalem was ripped apart when Jesus died (Matt. 27:51).

And yet, for two millennia Christendom has been constructing awe-inspiring churches that are centers of religious fervor, in which ritualistic prayers are publicly offered and holy items and relics are protected behind walls and curtains. The problem with religious fervor is not the intense motivation but rather that the focus of the fervor is upon holy objects, events, and rituals that are *divorced* from normal existence and that emotional *approval* is being given to individuals who are associated with these holy objects, events, and rituals.

Moving on, the apostle Paul made the following statement about *self-denial.*

> But the Spirit explicitly says that in later times some will fall away from the faith, paying attention to deceitful spirits and doctrines of demons, by means of the hypocrisy of liars seared in their own conscience as with a branding iron, men who forbid marriage and advocate abstaining from foods which God has created to be gratefully shared in by those who believe and know the truth. For everything created by God is good, and nothing is to be rejected if it is received with gratitude; for it is sanctified by means of the word of God and prayer. In pointing out these things to the brethren, you will be a good servant of Christ Jesus, constantly nourished on the words of the faith and of the sound doctrine which you have been following. But have nothing to do with worldly fables fit only for old women. On the other hand, discipline yourself for the purpose of godliness; for bodily discipline is only of little profit, but godliness is profitable for all things, since it holds promise for the present life and also for the life to come (1 Tim. 4:1-8).

Those are strong words. Paul is saying that those 'who forbid marriage and advocate abstaining from food' are 'falling away from the faith' and 'following the doctrines of demons'. Using the language of mental symmetry, they are acquiring Perceiver truth from a false Mercy source. Paul says that the purpose of religion is not to withdraw from the world of experiences by denying self but rather to change the manner in which one approaches and enjoys experiences. He is not questioning the need for discipline. However, he regards it as a means to an end rather than an end in itself, and he says that the greatest lasting benefits result from internal rather than bodily discipline. Religious self-denial treats personal discipline as the *primary* goal and not as a *means* to an end. For instance, celibacy plays a defining role in many branches of Christianity, which illustrates how the religious attitude of self-denial can become a defining belief even when it violates the words of the religious experts.

Turning to the religious attitude of *transcendence*, one of the core doctrines of Christianity is that God revealed himself to humanity through the incarnation of Jesus, and we will examine the doctrine of incarnation in later chapters. Jesus explains the relationship between him and 'God the Father' in a dialogue with one of his disciples.

> "If you had known Me, you would have known My Father also; from now on you know Him, and have seen Him." Philip said to Him, "Lord, show us the Father, and it is enough for us." Jesus said to him, "Have I been so long with you,

and yet you have not come to know Me, Philip? He who has seen Me has seen the Father; how can you say, 'Show us the Father'? Do you not believe that I am in the Father, and the Father is in Me? The words that I say to you I do not speak on My own initiative, but the Father abiding in Me does His works" (John 5:7-10).

Jesus is emphasizing here that the nature of God can be seen in the character of the incarnation, telling us that not only is it possible for humans to comprehend the essential nature of God but it is possible for God's essential character to be expressed in human form. Despite the fact that Christianity is based upon the Trinitarian relationship between God the Father and God the Son being expressed in human form, Christians continually assert that the very concept of a Trinitarian God is incomprehensible to the human mind. For instance, one of the core doctrines of Orthodox Christianity is the concept of *apophatic theology*, which states that humans cannot make any definitive statements about God but rather can only say what God is *not*. The problem does not lie in regarding God as fundamentally *different* than humans. The concept of a universal being based in a TMN is *radically* different than concepts of humans, animals, and superhuman gods based in MMNs. Rather, the problem is that transcendence regards God as both different and *incomprehensible*. In contrast, I suggest that it is possible to use Teacher thought to gain an understanding of how a universal being would behave.

We see from these biblical quotes that the three religious attitudes of fervor, self-denial, and transcendence will naturally be regarded as core religious doctrines even when this *contradicts* the statements of the primary religious experts of that religion. In the words of Marshall McLuhan, the medium of absolute truth will become the message. Christianity is not the only religion that practices fervor, self-denial, and transcendence. Instead, these three attitudes lie at the core of most religious thought. However, Christianity illustrates how these three attitudes naturally tend to dominate religious expression *even when* the religious experts say something totally different.

Theology

When looking at scientific thought, a distinction was made between scientific thought, scientific methodology, scientific paradigms, and scientific culture. Scientific thought uses Perceiver thought to look for universal connections. Scientific methodology protects Perceiver thought by using it in the easiest manner. Scientific paradigms are the general theories about nature that science discovers which turn into TMNs that can emotionally imprison the scientist. And scientific culture emerges from the set of MMNs that scientists share in common.

If one applies the same divisions to religious thought, then one comes up with a puzzling anomaly—something that does not fit the cognitive pattern. Three of the four elements form a natural package. Religious thought uses Mercy pressure to mesmerize Perceiver thought into believing absolute truth, and religious attitude is a natural by-product of attempting to keep Perceiver thought mesmerized. Religious culture is primarily a reflection of religious attitude. When one thinks of religion, one thinks of temples, shrines, rituals, priests, sacraments, vestments, and relics, all aspects of the attitude of fervor. Self-denial also plays a large role in religious culture as illustrated by monks, nuns, celibacy, flagellation, asceticism, pilgrimages, and sacrifices. Self-denial is also evident in activities that deny self by helping the down-and-out through hospitals and relief organizations. And where does one turn to for the grand explanation when life does not make sense? Religion with its transcendental attitudes and approach. Thus, religious thought, religious attitudes, and religious culture form a self-consistent package organized around the common element of mesmerized Perceiver thought.

> Theology does not fit the natural package of religious thought, attitude, and culture.

Turning to the fourth element, one can see that the paradigms of science correspond to the theology of religion, because both deal with abstract Teacher thought. But theology is an anomaly that does not fit the cognitively natural package of religious thought, religious attitude, and religious culture. In the words of Tremlin,

> Theology has a long and sometimes distinguished intellectual history. But the institutionalized forms that provide the playground for the manipulation and development of such abstractions never succeed in playing the decisive role that the theologians constantly hope for as they dream of bettering the thoughts of typical religious participants. It is sometimes all too obvious that the religious system works quite well without depending to any significant degree upon such theological notions. Sometimes theology seems to do little more than provide soothing background noise. Even if this is an unnecessarily harsh characterization of theology's place in religious systems, at least it must be said that such notions are not the motor that drives religious ideas and the practices these ideas inform, nor does it play any significant role in the growth and decline of religious traditions (Tremlin, 2006, p. xvi).

According to Tremlin, theology is 'not the motor that drives religious ideas'. Instead, religion 'works quite well' without 'theological notions', and Tremlin concludes that theology is often only 'soothing background noise'.

McCauley, another researcher in the cognitive science of religion, agrees that religion is cognitively natural but not theology.

> What I have referred to as "popular religion," then, stands apart not merely from science but from the activities and representations associated with elaborated doctrines and theology. Religion in its popular, that is, widespread, forms incorporates assumptions that are more common, materials that are more familiar, and judgments that are more intuitive than is the case with either science or theology (McCauley, 2011, p. 154).

This may be an accurate observation, but this conclusion leads to a deeper question. If abstract theory plays such a minimal role in religion, then why are researchers such as

Tremlin and McCauley coming up with abstract theories of religion? Why would they devote their careers to coming up with what Tremlin calls 'soothing background noise'?

This is not a trivial question. In fact, McCauley has written an *entire book* about this subject. He explains that

> The substantially counterintuitive, abstract, theologically correct representations that doctrinal religions market turn out to be as delicate, cognitively, as the radically counterintuitive representations in which science traffics. Even students who are rigorously schooled in such representations drop them in a flash at the first sign of circumstance that queue the operation of a maturationally natural system. Participants may ascend to theologically correct claims, they may listen to extensive explications of those theologically correct formulations, they may even memorize all sorts of propositions about them, but it does not follow that the mysteries and paradoxes those claims involve are anything that connect with those participants' day-to-day thought or reasoning about the matters in question. Religious participants are prone, in short, to theological incorrectness (McCauley, p. 218).

McCauley defines *maturational naturalness* as "the cognitive equipment that is typically up and running in human minds by the time children reach school age" (p. 6). Thus, McCauley is essentially repeating one of the conclusions we reached in the chapter on Piaget's preoperational stage. Stated simply, a mind that is functioning at the level of the preschool child does not naturally use Teacher thought. But McCauley is saying something even stronger. Not only does the preschool child find Teacher thought unnatural, but 'even students who are rigorously schooled' in 'abstract, theologically correct representations', who 'listen to extensive explications of these theologically correct formulations' and 'memorize all sorts of propositions about them' will 'drop them in a flash' when the 'maturationally natural system' is triggered.

In other words, the Mercy-based thinking of Piaget's preoperational stage will overwhelm Teacher thought with its abstract theories 'in a flash' even in the *adult* mind. And this mental effect applies to *both* the abstract thinking of theology and the abstract thinking of science, as borne out by the title to McCauley's book: *Why Religion is Natural and Science is Not.*

If abstract theory is 'dropped in a flash' when it encounters religious experience, then how can Tremlin and McCauley come up with abstract theories about religious experience? What is motivating them? What is protecting them from 'theological incorrectness'? Looking at this more generally, if theology and science are cognitively so unnatural, then why do they even *exist*?

McCauley poses precisely this general question.

> If the necessary intellectual and practical skills and the radically counterintuitive contents of science issue in something as foreign to the natural proclivities of

human minds as I have portrayed, then how have human beings ever managed to do science? (McCauley, p. 138).

McCauley suggests that is cognitively natural for the mind to come up with general theories.

> Without a doubt, the best illustration of what appears to be a relatively natural cognitive predilection that is integral to science is human beings' readiness to formulate speculative theories (p. 101).

In addition, it feels good to come up with an explanation. However, these theoretical explanations tend to conflict with the Mercy-based thinking of the pre-operational mind.

> Science gets started because, as Aristotle noted, humans naturally want to know more about their world and they take delight in their discoveries. Science becomes cognitively unnatural, however, because it reliably traffics, usually sooner rather than later, in representations that are radically counterintuitive in this sense (p. 107).

Translating this into the language of mental symmetry, the childish mind is controlled by MMNs, and these MMNs will impose their structure upon the mind when they are triggered. However, Teacher thought is driven emotionally to come up with general explanations, and these Teacher theories will tend to collide with childish MMNs. A general theory that turns into a TMN will motivate the theologian and the scientist just as strongly as MMNs motivate the childish mind, and like any mental network, this TMN will attempt to impose its structure upon thought when it is triggered.

We asked originally why researchers such as Tremlin and McCauley are coming up with abstract theories of religion. The answer is that they are being motivated by the TMN of a general theory. Tremlin describes his theory and its attraction in a more recent book.

> The insights provided by evolutionary biology, as well as cognates such as the cognitive sciences, are fruitfully illuminating the origin and operations of religious thought and behavior... Possessed of the elegance of evolutionary theory itself, an evolutionary science of religion both supplies explanatory power and parsimony – the summa bona of empirical research – and provides the unifying conceptual framework that religious studies has historically lacked (Tremlin, 2013, p. 27).

Notice the repeated references to Teacher order-within-complexity. Evolutionary theory has 'elegance'. It 'supplies explanatory power and parsimony'. It provides a 'unifying conceptual framework'.

We saw in Kuhn's description of paradigms that there is only room for one general theory, and that when a new theory comes along then even history will be rewritten to fit the new paradigm. Notice how Tremlin is reinterpreting history in terms of his general theory, which he claims 'provides the unifying conceptual framework that religious studies has historically lacked'.

One might state that modern researchers such as Tremlin and McCauley are doing science, whereas the theologians of the past were doing theology, and science is totally different than theology. McCauley suggests that the primary difference between science and theology is that theology includes concept of *agents* while science does not.

> Scientific abstemiousness regarding intentional agents and their putative actions is to be compared with what I argued in chapter four is religions' pervasive recruitment of theory of mind and appeals to agent explanations (McCauley, p. 232).

If including agents in an explanation is a hallmark of theology, then this implies that the cognitive science of religion is a branch of *theology*, because it continually talks about agents and is rooted in a theory that appeals to agents. As we saw earlier, 'evolutionists lead the world in substituting teleology for objectivity' (Hanke, 2004).

Thus, it appears that two things are happening simultaneously. Explicitly, the cognitive science of religion is analyzing the MMNs of religion, while implicitly, it is being driven by TMNs to replace historical theology with a new form of theology. Explicitly, researchers in this field may state that theology is irrelevant. But implicitly, historical theology is being replaced by a new theology rooted in the theory of evolution. This, I suggest, is the result of *cognitive mechanisms*. Mental networks struggle for dominance, and a theory that turns into a TMN will naturally attempt to impose its structure upon thought.

Recognizing the role that is played by a TMN also makes it possible to explain core concepts of religion which the cognitive science of religion currently cannot analyze. McCauley says that

> Theologians have been generating radically counterintuitive representations for millennia. Attributing esoteric, abstract properties such as omniscience, omnipotence, and omnipresence to some gods leaps to mind. As do the conceptual recalibrations required, for example, of Christians to accommodate what are far more fundamental notions. Understanding God as a triune entity (each person of which is alleged to have had temporary, divergent physical manifestations) presents all of the conceptual challenges that the modern psychological account of multiple personality disorder demands and more (p. 235).

If one interprets all agents in terms of MMNs, then it is radically counterintuitive to attribute 'omniscience, omnipotence, and omnipresence' to the agent of God. However, if one realizes that a TMN also leads to the concept of an intelligent agent, then the idea of a being with universal attributes becomes cognitively natural. We saw this in the 'atheism' of Dirac. Dirac was vehemently opposed to the concept of an MMN-based divine agent, while being willing to view God as the ultimate mathematician—an agent rooted in a TMN. Similarly, the theory of evolution naturally treats Nature as an intelligent TMN-based divine agent who is carrying out a universal plan of building cosmic order-within-complexity.

Saying this another way, if one looks at the mental *software* that the child naturally acquires, which McCauley refers to as maturational naturalness, then science and theology are both highly counterintuitive. That is one of the conclusions that we reached in the chapter on Piaget's stages of cognitive development: Mercy thought naturally develops in the child in a manner that opposes Teacher thought. But if one looks at the structure of mental *hardware*, then one notices that the mind can learn to function in a manner that resonates naturally with both scientific theory and theology. Going further, we will see that the Christian concept of a Trinitarian God also emerges *naturally* from the hardware of the mind, but this cognitive correspondence only becomes apparent if one *transforms* the software of the mind to be consistent with the structure of the mind.

We have attempted to explain what motivates the typical researcher in the cognitive science of religion, but that leaves the more general question, which is 'Why does science exist?' Science may *become* cognitively natural once a general Teacher theory emerges and turns into a TMN. But how will this theory emerge in the first place? Scientific thought may be self-sustaining once it is born, but how will 'the radically counterintuitive representations in which science traffics' ever come into existence in the first place if they are so 'cognitively delicate'? (And today's postmodern skepticism regarding the existence of abstract theory shows that the self-sustaining nature of scientific thought is not automatically passed on to the next generation.)

We will look at the birth of science in more detail in a later chapter. However, I suggest that this question *itself* reflects the rewriting of history that has been motivated by the current dominant TMN of scientific thought. Science emerged in Western Christendom during the Renaissance, and one of the main reasons it emerged is because medieval thinkers had a *theological* mindset. Thomas Aquinas taught that God had revealed himself through the two complementary volumes of the book of Scripture and the book of nature, otherwise known as 'special revelation' and 'general revelation'. Johannes Kepler describes this concept of general revelation through the 'book of nature'.

> I was merely thinking God's thoughts after him. Since we astronomers are priests of the highest God in regard to the book of nature, it befits us to be thoughtful, not of the glory of our minds, but rather, above all else, of the glory of God.

Notice that Kepler is approaching the natural world from a *theological* bias and not a religious bias. He did not see nature primarily as an expression of supernatural MMNs, but rather as an illustration of the TMN of a word-based theological understanding of God. Thus, I suggest that the real question is not how science came into being but rather how *theology* came into existence. That is because theology started 1500 years *before* the birth of science, and if theology did not exist, then science probably would not exist as well.

The well-known theologian N.T. Wright discusses the birth of theology. Like Tremlin and McCauley, Wright also concludes that theology does not fit the normal package of religion. Instead, Wright tells us that theology was *invented* by the apostle Paul and is a uniquely Christian concept. Quoting from his recent 1658 page tome entitled *Paul and the Faithfulness of God*,

> My overall case in Part II of this book was that when we study the worldview which Paul attempts to inculcate in his converts we find that its central symbol is the united and holy community itself; but that this community was equipped with none of the symbolic markers (circumcision, food laws, sabbath, ethnic identity and endogamy, allegiance to the Jerusalem Temple) which gave Jewish communities in the Diaspora such a comparatively solid basis for their continuing common life. My overall case in Part III has been that Paul's theology, the prayerful and scripture-based exploration of the foundational Jewish themes of monotheism, election and eschatology, was designed to supply this lack, thus elevating something which (with hindsight) we now call 'theology' to a position, in terms of a community and its worldview, which it never previously possessed and which it still does not possess outside Christianity itself. First-century Jews engaged in the study of Torah because Torah not only supplied the community's boundary-markers but also brought its students into the presence of God – a belief which gained in importance for those who lived at a distance from the Temple itself. First-century pagan philosophers discussed questions to do with the gods as a matter of intellectual curiosity on the one hand and inner personal exploration or development on the other, but these questions were never required to play anything like the role that Christian theology had to take on from the start (Wright, 2013).

Wright is saying that the Jewish community was held together by the MMNs of a religious *culture* composed of circumcision, food laws, Sabbath, the Jerusalem Temple, and ethnic identity. Paul replaced this with the TMN of a *theology* based in the concept of a universal monotheistic God. This use of theology as a core mental network did not exist before Christianity and does not exist outside of Christianity.

This means that the real question is not 'How did science emerge?', or even 'How did theology emerge?', but rather 'What was the source of Paul's theology?' That is the question behind the question behind the question.

Paul addresses this question in the following passage.

> For am I now seeking the favor of men, or of God? Or am I striving to please men? If I were still trying to please men, I would not be a bond-servant of Christ. For I would have you know, brethren, that the gospel which was preached by me is not according to man. For I neither received it from man, nor was I taught it, but I received it through a revelation of Jesus Christ. For you have heard of my former manner of life in Judaism, how I used to persecute the church of God beyond measure and tried to destroy it; and I was advancing in Judaism beyond many of my contemporaries among my countrymen, being more extremely zealous for my ancestral traditions. But when God, who had set me apart even from my mother's womb and called me through His grace, was pleased to reveal His Son in me so that I might preach Him among the Gentiles, I did not immediately

consult with flesh and blood, nor did I go up to Jerusalem to those who were apostles before me; but I went away to Arabia, and returned once more to Damascus. Then three years later I went up to Jerusalem to become acquainted with Cephas, and stayed with him fifteen days. But I did not see any other of the apostles except James, the Lord's brother. (Now in what I am writing to you, I assure you before God that I am not lying.) (Gal. 1:10-20)

Paul says that he was not guided by social pressure and that he did not get his theology either from religious culture or from Christian experts. In fact, Paul himself originally rejected Christianity as being radically counterintuitive to the MMNs of his religion, being so 'extremely zealous for my ancestral traditions', that he 'tried to destroy' Christianity. Instead, Paul says under oath that he 'received it through a revelation of Jesus Christ'. Thus, Paul, like Tremlin, McCauley, Wright, and this book, also regards theology as something cognitively unnatural that does not fit the cognitively normal package of religion. And we have seen how the cognitively normal package of religion with its religious attitude has twisted the theology of Paul (and Jesus) over the centuries.

Paul says that he received his theology from an outside source. Paul's statement is definitely incompatible with scientific *methodology*, because Paul is saying that he was explicitly guided by a divine agent. But to what *type* of divine agent is Paul appealing? Not a *Mercy*-based Superman-like superhuman being who exhibits himself through awe-inspiring experiences, but rather a *Teacher*-based agent who shares general theories, the same kind of Teacher-based agent to which the theory of evolution appeals with its description of Nature, and to which science is drawn with its concept of God-as-ultimate-mathematician.

It might be tempting to reject Paul's claim as totally counterintuitive to the rational thinking taken by a scientific approach to religion. However, there are two problems with this response. First, cognitive science does not leave us with any other alternative. If Paul had not invented theology, Tremlin, McCauley, Dirac and others most likely would not be practicing science. By the standards of maturational naturalness, both theology and science are cognitively unnatural. Thus, we have the strange situation of scientific research concluding that both science and theology (which helped give birth to science) should not exist. That leads one to postulate that Paul received his theology from some outside source for whom theology and science are cognitively natural—which is what Paul claims.

Second, far from being *irrelevant* to the cognitive science of religion, the thesis of this book is that Paul's theology actually makes the most sense if it is interpreted *as* a cognitive science of religion.

✳ 5. Education

The previous chapter examined a number of different aspects of scientific and religious thought. In this chapter we will tie these threads together. In simple terms I suggest that *all* education begins with *rote learning,* which is then followed by *critical thinking.*

I suggest that this order is unavoidable because of the inherent nature of Perceiver thought. I mentioned earlier that Perceiver thought evaluates new information on the basis of related facts. This means that Perceiver thought needs facts to check facts. But how will Perceiver thought check the facts that are being used to check facts? The answer to this chicken-and-egg problem is that Perceiver thought uses *absolute* truth to evaluate the initial set of facts. Perceiver thought acquires its *initial* facts through blind faith in authority. Perceiver thought then uses these facts that were acquired through blind faith to evaluate *new* information. Once Perceiver thought has learned enough facts, it then becomes possible to *re-evaluate* the facts that were initially acquired through blind faith. In other words, education begins with rote learning, rote learning leads to critical thinking, and critical thinking can be used to check the facts that were initially acquired through rote learning. In simple terms, *before* Perceiver thought can check information it *first* has to swallow facts blindly.

> Education starts with rote learning, which is followed by critical thinking.

For instance, I have mentioned that for several years I did research together with my older brother. As a Perceiver person, I found it disorienting whenever our research extended into a new context, because I had no way of evaluating the facts that were being discussed. In order to gain a sense of reasonableness I would have to read a number of books and articles written by experts in that field. In each case the starting point was absolute truth based in socially approved sources, which made it possible for Perceiver thought to function, which could then *retroactively* re-examine the information that was originally acquired from the experts. I *now* have enough general knowledge to be able to focus upon expertise when examining some new field, but that was not the case when I began my research.

Rote learning uses emotional status to reveal truth from the teacher to the student. For instance, the student sitting in a school classroom is not using Perceiver thought to evaluate the words of the teacher. Instead, Perceiver thought in the student is blindly swallowing facts guided solely by the emotional respect that the student has for the teacher and the school. This describes not only the child sitting in Sunday school listening to stories in the Bible, or the believer sitting in the mosque listening to the preaching of the Imam, but it also applies to the student sitting in school who is learning about science. All education *begins* with Perceiver thought mesmerized, accepting 'truth' because it comes from an expert. The preoperational child is incapable of going beyond rote learning, but the adult who starts to learn about a completely new subject is also forced to begin at this level of accepting facts blindly from the expert.

The scientist may claim that scientific education provides evidence for its beliefs, but Kuhn suggests that this is not the case.

> The man who reads a science text can easily take the applications to be the evidence for the theory, the reasons why it ought to be believed. But science students accept theories on the authority of teacher and text, not because of evidence. What alternatives have they, what competence? The applications given in texts are not there as evidence but because learning them is part of learning the paradigm at the base of current practice (Kuhn, 1970, p. 80).

The Montessori system of education prides itself upon not 'forcing truth down the throats of students' but rather allowing children to 'discover truth for themselves at their own pace'. However, if one looks closer at how teaching occurs within this system, the guiding hand of the teacher is still ever-present, determining what the child will learn and when it will be learned. I am not suggesting that science textbooks should not have applications, or that the Montessori method is flawed. On the contrary, I think that it is good to have a hands-on approach to learning that includes applications and examples. But the fact still remains that education begins with rote learning, no matter how subtly or politely this rote learning is presented.

The scientist often accuses religion of teaching absolute truth from a holy book. However, Kuhn tells us that science places a greater emphasis upon teaching official truth from approved textbooks than most fields of learning, even using textbooks to teach approved truth in graduate school.

> In music, the graphic arts, and literature, the practitioner gains his education by exposure to the works of other artists, principally earlier artists. Textbooks, except compendia of or handbooks to original creations, have only a secondary role. In history, philosophy, and the social sciences, textbook literature has a greater significance. But even in these fields the elementary college course employs parallel readings in original sources...Contrast this situation with that in at least the contemporary natural sciences. In these fields the student relies mainly on textbooks until, in his third or fourth year of graduate work, he begins his own research. Many science curricula do not ask even graduate students to read works not written specially for students...until the very last stages in the education of a scientist, textbooks are systematically substituted for the creative scientific literature that made them possible (p.165).

The scientist often views religious education as narrow-minded, because it interprets the world through the narrow lens of some revealed text. But Kuhn says that science does the same.

> Textbooks thus begin by truncating the scientist's sense of his discipline's history and then proceed to supply a substitute for what they have eliminated. Characteristically, textbooks of science contain just a bit of history, either in an introductory chapter or, more often, in scattered references to the great heroes of an earlier age. From such references both students and professionals come to feel like participants in a long-standing historical tradition. Yet the textbook-derived tradition in which scientists come to sense their participation is one that, in fact, never existed... the scientists of earlier ages are implicitly represented as having worked upon the same set of fixed problems and in accordance with the same set of fixed canons that the most recent revolution in scientific theory and method has made seem scientific (p.138).

Again, my goal is not to question the use of holy books and textbooks. On the contrary, I suggest that they play a major role in helping the student to make the transition from rote learning to critical thinking. However, I wish to point out that there is no essential cognitive difference between a textbook and a holy book, because both begin with rote learning of absolute truth. Consistent with this, a neurological study examined

> fifteen committed Christians and fifteen nonbelievers—as they evaluated the truth and falsity of religious and nonreligious propositions. For both groups, and in both categories of stimuli, belief (judgments of 'true' vs judgments of 'false') was associated with greater signal in the ventromedial prefrontal cortex ...This region showed greater signal whether subjects believed statements about God, the Virgin Birth, etc. or statements about ordinary facts" (Harris, et al., 2009).

In other words, it appears that the brain does not distinguish between religious belief and secular belief.

In rote learning, Perceiver thought is mesmerized by the MMNs that represent the sources of truth. The purpose of rote learning is to transfer information as quickly and efficiently as possible from the mind of the teacher to the mind of the student. The problem with rote learning is that the student has no way of distinguishing truth from error. Instead, the responsibility for evaluating information lies entirely with the teacher and the system of education. This shortcoming is always present but it usually becomes apparent when one notices *other* experts teaching *different* beliefs. Remember that mental networks operate silently under the surface when input is consistent with their structure. The presence of a mental network typically becomes apparent when it is being violated. Similarly, when teachers are using their emotional status to impart beliefs that are consistent with the local culture, then this will be viewed as natural and expected. However, when students are taught beliefs from a different culture, religion, or holy book, then it will become obvious that 'instructors are ramming beliefs down the throats of unsuspecting, innocent, helpless victims'. The point is that *all* rote learning rams beliefs down the throats of unsuspecting, innocent, helpless victims. That is the nature of rote learning. For the child, rote learning is unavoidable. If it does not occur officially, it will occur unofficially.

Critical thinking checks facts and replaces experts with understanding.

Critical thinking has two related aspects. First, critical thinking uses Perceiver thought to check the facts that were acquired blindly during rote learning. Second, critical thinking replaces the MMNs of experts with the TMN of a general understanding. I suggest that both of these factors are required. It is important for Perceiver (and Server) thought to gain the confidence to be able to function in the midst of emotional pressure. After all, one would not want a physician's mind to go blank or hands to start shaking in the midst of a delicate surgery. But confidence can only take a person so far or last so long in an emotional situation. As the behaviour of the person with Tourette syndrome illustrates, unwanted mental networks that are triggered can be temporarily suppressed, but they will eventually express themselves.

The long-term solution is to replace the MMNs of the experts with the TMN of a general understanding. Rote learning is held together by the MMNs of experts; facts are believed because they come from esteemed experts. Critical thinking is held together by the TMN of a general theory; facts are believed because they are repeated *and* because they fit together in a coherent manner. This order-within-complexity generates positive Teacher emotions that *replace* the Mercy emotions based in personal status. Rote learning says, "I believe because my teacher/pastor/professor said so." Critical thinking says, "I believe because I understand. I see how it fits together." It is this Teacher emotion that the student is feeling when there is an 'aha' moment and the metaphorical lightbulb goes on.

Perceiver confidence without Teacher emotions can *temporarily* acknowledge the facts but the emotion will eventually overwhelm the confidence. One often sees this in the behavior of the immature Perceiver person, because he will use Perceiver thought to 'valiantly hold on to truth', give up when the pressure is too strong, feel guilty because he failed, and then resolve to try again, repeating the cycle.

Teacher thought feels good when many facts fit together in an integrated manner. Kuhn's description of the typical scientist illustrates what happens when there is Teacher emotion without Perceiver confidence. A person will be driven by the TMN of a general understanding but will be unable to question this understanding. Using a car analogy, one could compare mental networks to fuel and confidence to the size of the gas tank and the strength of the motor. A car cannot go anywhere without fuel. Similarly, a human cannot function without mental networks. The size of the gas tank determines how far a vehicle can travel before refueling, and the strength of the motor determines the size of the hills and obstacles that can be successfully traversed during the journey. Likewise, confidence determines the amount of emotional discomfort that a person can handle while mental networks are being questioned. Replacing MMNs with TMNs is like discovering a new source of fuel for the car. The individual who has the TMN of a theory will find that he is able to refuel his car in situations where those who only have MMNs run out of gas, making it possible to take journeys of discovery that are not possible for those who only have MMNs.

For instance, during my initial research I would often wake up in the morning and feel that I had no reason to live because no one seemed to care about what I was doing. In terms of the car analogy, the fuel tank driven by MMNs was bone dry. But then I would think about how the facts fit together, consider my understanding of the mind, and conclude afresh that I was following a path that led to mental wholeness. I would then find that even though I could find no motivation from MMNs, something else was putting fuel in my tank that made it possible to continue my journey. Although I could not see results and was not receiving approval, I had an understanding, and that was sufficient. This does not mean that a person should abandon MMNs and follow only TMNs, just as I suggest that it is not mentally wholesome for a person to spend his entire life studying in school. However, when one is studying, then I suggest that one of the major transitions is to replace the MMNs of authority with the TMNs of understanding. We will examine this transition as well as further transitions in coming chapters.

Using the language of philosophy, Teacher thought uses *coherence* to evaluate truth—do the facts fit together, while Perceiver thought uses *correspondence*—do the facts correspond with reality. Philosophy typically describes both coherence and correspondence in terms of *technical* thought (which we will examine in a later chapter). Do the facts fit together in a logically coherent manner? Does each fact correspond with some real object or situation? However, I suggest that there is also an *emotional* form of coherence and correspondence. For instance, when a colleague makes a logical error, then the philosopher will point out the logical error and conclude that the statement lacks coherence. In contrast, when an outsider attempts to use logic, or when a philosopher tries to analyze normal speech, then there will be an emotional response to the lack of coherence: "Those statements lack coherence. They are meaningless. The speaker does not know how to think clearly." Similarly, a distinction needs to be made between *specific* facts that do not correspond with reality and a *general* lack of correspondence. Scientists often give the impression that a single contradictory fact is sufficient to topple a scientific theory, but we have already seen that Kuhn says that this is not the case: "No process yet disclosed by the historical study of scientific development at all resembles the methodological stereotype of falsification by direct comparison with nature" (p.77). However, a theory will be questioned when *enough* critical facts contradict the theory. Kuhn describes this transition.

> When... an anomaly comes to seem more than just another puzzle of normal science, the transition to crisis and to extraordinary science has begun. The anomaly itself now comes to be more generally recognized as such by the profession. More and more attention is devoted to it by more and more of the field's most

eminent men. If it still continues to resist, as it usually does not, many of them may come to view its resolution as the subject matter of their discipline. For them the field will no longer look quite the same as it had earlier (p.82).

Using the language of Kuhn, a general lack of correspondence will lead to a paradigm shift in which normal science is temporarily replaced by revolutionary science. In the language of mental symmetry, a TMN will motivate a person to ignore contradictory facts, but if there are enough facts that do not fit, then this will threaten the integrity of the Teacher mental network and repairing the mental network will become the primary focus of attention.

Summarizing, Perceiver thought will note a lack of coherence when one fact does not fit another fact, and a lack of correspondence when belief does not correspond with truth. Teacher thought will sense incoherence when interacting with those who are driven by a different mental network, and a lack of correspondence when the existing mental network is no longer adequate.

Developing Critical Thinking

Returning now to the transition from rote learning to critical thinking, I suggest that several factors will either encourage or discourage such a transition to occur.

Science may accuse religion of basing its beliefs in the pronouncements of holy books (while basing its own beliefs in the pronouncements of textbooks), but I suggest that a book by its very nature encourages the student to go beyond basing truth in the MMNs of experts to gaining the TMN of an understanding. First, a book is a physical illustration of Perceiver stability. Perceiver thought wants facts that do not change. When facts are written down on paper, then ephemeral speech is transformed into a lasting, unchanging written record. While people often change what they say depending upon the social context, a book says the same thing no matter when and where it is read. Second, a book is composed of words, which are the basic building blocks for Teacher thought. Third, a book is a physical illustration of Teacher order-within-complexity. Words are organized into sentences, sentences into paragraphs, and paragraphs into chapters. A book does not just present a random collection of facts but rather organizes these facts in some coherent fashion. Fourth, a book provides an emotional distance between the MMN of the author and his Perceiver facts. For instance, when Dr. John Smith speaks, then his physical presence will trigger the MMN that represents his exalted personage. But when Dr. Smith writes a book, then it is possible to read his words and examine his facts without him being physically present.

While the inherent *form* of a book encourages the development of critical thinking, this transition will only occur if the *structure* of the book is compatible with rational thought. For example, consider the structure of the Quran, the holy book of Islam. One of the major doctrines of Islam is the doctrine of *Naskh* or abrogation. The website islamqa.info says that

The concept of abrogation is based on the Qur'an and Sunnah, and on the consensus (ijmaa') of Ahl as-Sunnah, and there is great wisdom behind it. In most cases the abrogation was for the purpose of making things easier for the Muslims or increasing the rewards. Allah, may He be exalted, said (interpretation of the meaning): "Whatever a Verse (revelation) do We abrogate or cause to be forgotten, We bring a better one or similar to it. Know you not that Allah is able to do all things? Know you not that it is Allah to Whom belongs the dominion of the heavens and the earth? And besides Allah you have neither any Walee (protector or guardian) nor any helper" (al-Baqarah 2:106-107) (islamqa).

It is difficult to say exactly how many verses have been abrogated. WikiIslam provides a list of 189 verses in the Quran that have been abrogated by Quranic verses revealed at a later date. The point is that Perceiver thought wants facts that do not change. A book normally provides this, but an official doctrine of abrogation will negate this cognitive benefit.

Going further, a book contains inherent order and structure. This provides a physical illustration of Teacher order-within-complexity, encouraging the reader to search for Teacher structure within the text. However, the 114 chapters of the Quran are not in chronological order. Instead they have been *rearranged* from longest to shortest: understanding rearranged difficult sentence shortest longest makes order from then this When words are the in of to a. (When the words of a sentence are rearranged in order from longest to shortest, then this makes understanding difficult.) This combination of reordering and abrogation makes it especially difficult to understand the Quranic text. Because the chapters are not in chronological order, it is no longer obvious which verses are abrogated and which ones still apply. When the content of a book (be it textbook or holy book) either lacks Teacher understanding or makes it difficult to construct a Teacher understanding, then students will be unable to go beyond rote learning to critical thinking, which means that the content of the book will have to remain based upon the MMNs of experts rather than held together by the TMN of a general theory.

Instructors can also encourage or discourage students to make a transition from rote learning to critical thinking. We saw previously that using a special vocabulary will emphasize rote learning with its attitude of *absolute* truth. Absolute truth is rooted in a specific context, whereas universal truth applies to all contexts. In order to make a mental transition from absolute truth to universal truth, one must *translate* any special vocabulary used by a book into the language of normal thought and existence. That is why I am continually restating concepts using the language of different researchers and theories. In contrast, if instructors say that a holy book cannot be translated and emphasize memorizing words written in a language that the average person does not understand, then this will make it more difficult to develop critical thinking.

Turning again to the Quran, *The Pluralism Project* at Harvard University says that

Muslims point to the beauty of the language as evidence of the Qur'an's miraculous origin. The Qur'an may be interpreted in other languages, but it may not be translated and retain the same power; therefore, the true Qur'an is in Arabic. As the Word of God, the Holy Qur'an must be treated with respect: one should perform ablutions, or wudu, before handling the Qur'an, and one should never place the Qur'an on the floor. The Qur'an is a word to be heard; in fact, the word Qur'an means "recitation." The angel Gabriel commanded Muhammad to recite (iqra') the words he was given. Before the written verses were collected into the book we now know as the Qur'an, the passages were preserved in the memory of reciters. This practice has been passed down to this day, and around the world, young Muslim children memorize the Qur'an. Professional reciters perform for special occasions, such as festivals and funerals. Strict rules govern the reciters' pronunciation, and though recitation often involves melody, it is rigidly separated from musical art in both form and intent. To listen to the Qur'an is to experience the presence of God...At the Darul-Uloom Al-Madania in upstate New York, a secondary school and Institution of Higher Islamic Education, students can enroll in a three- to four-year course to memorize the Qur'an. Those who complete the program receive hafiz certification, and also study Tajwid, the art of Qur'anic recitation (Eck).

When a book 'may not be translated and retain the same power', then this promotes absolute truth and not universal truth. When 'one should perform ablutions, or wudu, before handling' a book, then MMNs of emotional status are being added to the book rather than using the book to distance the reader from such MMNs. When 'strict rules govern the reciter's pronunciation', then the words are being connected with Mercy intonation rather than Teacher understanding. That is because Mercy thought interprets the non-verbal aspect of speech. And when a student enrolls in a three- to four- year course to memorize the Quran and receive 'hafiz certification', then the time and effort that would normally be devoted to developing critical thinking are being used to reinforce rote learning. After all, memorization is, by definition, rote learning. I am not suggesting that the Quran is the *only* holy book to be approached with an attitude of rote learning. However, rote learning does appear to be a defining factor in the religion of Islam and I suggest that it provides a cognitive starting point for understanding Islam.

Notice that nothing has been said so far about the *content* of the holy book or textbook. Instead, we are merely examining the idea of a holy book, the manner in which the content of this book is arranged, and the attitude with which this book is taught. All of these will form part of the *implicit* message that determines whether the student remains at the stage of rote learning or else advances to the next stage of critical thinking. If the arrangement of a holy book or the approach taken by teachers discourages critical thinking, then the only way that a student will gain a Teacher understanding is by rebelling from teachers, and teachers will be forced to respond by increasing the emotional pressure imposed by MMNs. In the extreme, religious apostasy will be punishable by death. In communist Russia, one could be fairly certain that *Pravda* did not contain truth and that *Izvestia* would not publish the news, because any writers who deviated from the official party line would find themselves imprisoned, exiled, or executed. Similarly, if a religion uses the threat of execution to impose orthodoxy, then rational understanding and critical thinking will be driven underground, and religious teaching and theology will reflect the MMNs of social authority rather than the TMNs of a general understanding.

Obviously, if a system of education is to permit critical thinking and *survive*, then the *content* of the holy book or textbook must contain an integrated understanding that is coherent and correlates with truth.

So far, we have examined education from the abstract perspective of Perceiver truth and Teacher understanding. But religious truth applies to personal identity. Therefore, the religious conflict between MMNs of authority and a TMN of understanding is not just a theological dilemma but rather will have deep impact upon the fabric of society.

As we saw before, Kant suggested that it is possible to base moral truth in the concept of *universality*. For instance, stealing is morally wrong because it is not possible for everyone to steal. If everyone tried to steal, then valuable objects would be hidden away preventing them from being stolen. These universal principles will naturally be discovered if one is searching for *universal* truth. Kant's concept of radical evil defines immorality in terms of *incoherence*, because moral evil acts in a way that is inconsistent with the larger context. The person who steals, for instance, steals within a social context where most people do not steal. Saying this more generally, it is possible for *part* of a population to function for a while in a manner that violates Kant's categorical imperative by exploiting the *rest* of the population. History is full of examples, such as barbarians who got their food and wealth by raiding towns, empires that subjugated neighboring states in order to exact tribute, mafia who demand protection money, or bankers and stock market traders who manipulate markets for personal advantage.

The problem is that *absolute* truth will naturally lead to this kind of exploitation, because absolute truth is based in emotional status. In order to believe in absolute truth, one must feel that the source of truth has much greater importance than personal identity. Thus, the average person who lacks emotional status will submit to absolute truth, creating a general environment of law and order, while those who possess sufficient emotional status will think that they are above the law, and those who reject emotional status will think that it is possible to rebel from the law. Therefore, the average individual who submits to the law will be continually plagued by the radical evil of leaders who ignore the law and rebels who reject the law. Added to this will be the more insidious problem of lawmakers who use their emotional status to pass laws that favor themselves rather than others.

Noticing this problem is easy, especially if one is a member of an oppressed group. It is much harder to come up with a solution that does not end up exacerbating the problem. For instance, the obvious answer is revolution; use armed force to kick out the oppressors. But history indicates that this usually ends up replacing one set of oppressive rulers with another. The peasants may gain a new set of lords, but life as a peasant does not get any better. One common response today is for some 'western country' to invade in an attempt to 'export democracy'. However, recent history has shown us—repeatedly and at great cost—that democracy that is exported through armed intervention does not tend to last.

I suggest that solutions such as these fail because they do not address the underlying problem, which is the nature of core mental networks. Thomas Kuhn says that a scientist cannot exist without a paradigm. Saying this more generally, I suggest that a person cannot exist without core mental networks. However, we have seen that every person grows up with a mind that is controlled by childish MMNs. Such a mind requires strong sources of authority, because these sources of authority define the core mental networks that hold the mind together. For instance, living in an abusive marriage is obviously unpleasant. But the abused spouse will often return to an abusive situation because these painful memories turn into mental networks around which the mind integrates. The abusive relationship may be painful, but it is also familiar. Similarly, living under a dictatorship is obviously unpleasant, but citizens who are freed from a dictatorship will often re-create this abusive system because the painful memories have turned into mental networks that provide the source for personal and cultural integration.

The long-term solution is for individuals within the society to progress from Habermas' first stage to his second stage. That means going beyond rote learning to critical thinking by using Perceiver thought to look for connections that bridge societies and social classes and using these *universal* Perceiver truths to build a general understanding that turns into a TMN that can provide an *alternative* source of emotional integration to the MMNs of societal and personal abuse. Connecting this with the previous paragraphs, it logically follows that if a religion is incapable of going beyond rote learning, then this religion is also incapable of delivering a population from dictatorship. Suggesting that a fundamentalist religion that is locked into rote learning allows abuse and violence is quite different than saying that *all* religion breeds violence, as some authors have recently claimed.

> Core mental networks are preserved even if they cause personal pain and suffering.

One can *minimize* this problem by preaching that 'every individual is equal under God', but one is still using absolute truth to try to correct a problem that is the result of absolute truth. Universal truth, in contrast, *naturally* recognizes that universal law applies equally to every individual. For instance, the law of gravity applies universally to every person regardless of emotional status. Universal truth will naturally realize this, whereas absolute truth will be tempted to think that such laws 'do not apply to me' if personal identity is regarded as special or important.

When the mind constructs a general theory in areas that apply to personal identity then this will cause a mental concept of God to emerge. And when a TMN that applies to personal identity becomes the source of emotional integration, then one is mentally submitting personal identity and culture to a concept of God. Thus, I suggest that learning critical thinking in the subjective is actually cognitively equivalent to submitting to God. At first glance, this may sound counterintuitive, but it is important to clarify the *type* of God to which critical thinking submits. What is needed is a mental concept of God that transcends the MMNs of personal approval and culture, ties everything together with a general Teacher understanding, requires Perceiver thought to function, and is based in universal truth. Translating this into language that a child can understand, "God sees everything you do and think. God's truth does not change. God is not fooled or influenced by personal status. God wants you to be honest even when it hurts. God's truth is not always immediately obvious because he wants you to learn how to think. God will often teach you through unexpected sources. Following God will sometimes lead you through times of uncertainty, suffering, or unpopularity. These episodes are meant to test you." If these statements sound religious, that is because they are. But we have merely taken the core elements of critical thinking and translated them into religious language. Because such a concept of God transcends culture, the childish mind will not naturally believe in this type of God.

Instead, the childish mind will naturally believe in a God whose form has been shaped by the characteristics of preoperational thought, such as a God of mysticism encountered through transcendental experience, a God of magic whose nature is proclaimed by the experts of some religious group, or a God of ritual based in holy items, places, and events. But these are concepts of God created in the image of *man*, in which the MMNs of personal identity and culture impose their structure upon the TMN of understanding. Religious culture may give great status to such cognitively natural concepts of God, but if one examines them from the viewpoint of cognitive development, one concludes that they are childish concepts of God because they are expressions of childish thought.

Saying this another way, if one wishes to encourage critical thinking in the realm of the subjective then one needs a concept of God based in *theology* and not a God rooted in ritual or experience. We saw earlier that theology was invented by Paul. We see here that critical thinking requires a God of theology. This does not mean that religious ritual and experience should be abandoned. Rather, I suggest that one is dealing with a matter of emotional priority. Which mental networks are ultimately in charge? Are the MMNs of culture and identity an expression of the TMN of a theological concept of God, or is the TMN behind a concept of God shaped by the MMNs of culture and childish identity? Is God defined as a general understanding that applies *to* culture and identity or as a generalization of the mental networks *of* culture and identity?

In the same way that one must go through rote learning to reach critical thinking, so I suggest that the childish mind will *inevitably* begin with an inadequate childish concept of God. Just as it is the responsibility of the secular teacher to teach content that will survive critical thinking using structure and attitude that is compatible with critical thinking, so I suggest that it is the responsibility of the religious teacher to help a child to develop the mental concept of a universal, all-knowing, impartial, truthful, monotheistic God. Encouraging the child to believe in this kind of God will be a struggle, just as it is a struggle to get the student to think for himself. The key point is that these two struggles are actually the *same* struggle. We saw earlier that Barrett discovered that the typical Christian believer will verbally state that they explicitly believe in a God of theology while experientially demonstrating that they *implicitly* believe in a God rooted in MMNs. This describes the type of cognitive struggle that a religious believer who is in the process of developing critical thinking will experience.

While the concept of a universal rational God is consistent with scientific *thought*, it tends to collide with scientific *methodology*. The *objective* attitude of scientific methodology will instinctively cause the scientist to question the idea of viewing universal truth in *personal* terms, the demand for *empirical evidence* will cause the concept of an *invisible* person to be rejected, while the culture of *peer review* will cause scientists as a whole to belittle any theological explanations that appear to lack academic *rigor*. The average person-in-the-street will hear what the scientist is saying and conclude that theology is bad because the experts say that it is bad. If a God of theology is rejected, then this will not cause religion or belief in God to fade away. Instead, the typical person will then instinctively believe in a God of mysticism, holiness, or ritual. Such a childish concept of God may be incompatible with scientific thought, but it is compatible with scientific methodology, because holiness and ritual are empirical, mysticism does not try to analyze the invisible, and everyone—including scientists—knows that people are ultimately driven by the MMNs of childish desire and culture.

Concluding, I suggest that there is both a scientific and a religious path to acquiring critical thinking in the subjective. The *scientific* path begins by learning how to think critically when dealing with objective, physical reality. The resulting TMNs are then extended to include subjective experiences, transforming rational understanding into the mental concept of a universal rational God. The *religious* path starts with an inadequate mental concept of God based in childish MMNs. This childish concept of God is then gradually transformed into a concept of God that is consistent with rational understanding. The endpoint in both cases is a mind integrated around the mental concept of a universal rational God, but the scientific path starts with 'universal rational' and then eventually adds 'God' while the religious path begins with 'God' and eventually adds 'universal rational'.

✳ 6. Mysticism

What is the nature of God? Instead of addressing this question directly, I would like to examine the cognitive question that lies *behind* this religious question. If a mental concept of God is ultimately based in Teacher thought, then it is possible to understand the nature of a *concept* of God by examining how Teacher thought functions. This chapter will describe Teacher thought and then show that the experiences of mysticism naturally emerge from the concept of God that forms when one uses Teacher thought to build a general theory in the simplest manner possible.

Focusing upon a mental concept of God does not mean that a *real* God does not exist, just as examining how the mind uses MMNs to represent people does not mean that real people do not exist. But in the same way that most social interaction occurs internally between mental networks that represent people, so I suggest that—even if God exists—most interaction with God is occurring internally between mental networks that represent people and the mental network that represents God.

Teacher Thought

We will begin our study of Teacher thought by turning again to Albert Einstein, the world's most famous Teacher person. *Out of My Later Years* contains a series of essays written by Einstein, including one in which he attempted to analyze scientific thought. Einstein divided this thinking into *three stages* (Einstein, 1950).

We have already discussed the first stage, which occurs when Perceiver thought organizes Mercy experiences into facts and objects. In the words of Einstein,

> I believe that the first step in the setting of a "real external world" is the formation of the concept of bodily objects and of bodily objects of various kinds. Out of the multitude of our sense experiences we take, mentally and arbitrarily, certain repeatedly occurring complexes of sense impression (partly in conjunction with sense impressions which are interpreted as signs for sense experiences of others), and we attribute to them a meaning—the meaning of the bodily object.

In the second stage, Teacher thought uses the Perceiver facts acquired in the first stage to form a general theory. Quoting again from Einstein,

> The second step is to be found in the fact that, in our thinking (which determines our expectation), we attribute to this concept of the bodily object a significance, which is to a high degree independent of the sense impression which originally gives rise to it... The justification of such a setting rests exclusively on the fact that, by means of such concepts and mental relations between them, we are able

to orient ourselves in the labyrinth of sense impressions. These notions and relations, although free statements of our thoughts, appear to us as stronger and more unalterable than the individual sense experience itself.

Summarizing, Teacher thought tries to 'orient itself' within this 'labyrinth' of Perceiver facts by assigning a 'significance' that is 'independent' of Perceiver facts, which 'appears to us as stronger and more unalterable' than the original Mercy experiences.

The theory that was developed during the second stage is then tested in the third stage by using the theory to interpret known Perceiver facts.

> The third phase is a constructive effort to formulate and systematically relate theorems that constitute statements about reality or laws of nature, which constitute science – as distinct from an empty scheme of concepts – only as they are returned to sense experiences as comprehended by primary concepts.

What interests us here is Einstein's second stage, because that is where Teacher thought is doing its processing. Einstein tells us that this second stage is not a form of inductive logic where one steps from specific to general, but rather a 'free invention' that leads to intuitive connections between Teacher theory and Mercy experience.

> Physics constitutes a logical system of thought which is in a state of evolution and whose basis cannot be obtained through distillation by any inductive method from the experiences lived through, but which can only be attained by free invention. The justification (truth content) of the system rests in the proof of usefulness of the resulting theorems on the basis of sense experiences, where the relations of the latter to the former can only be comprehended intuitively.

These intuitive Teacher theories are then turned into a logical structure.

> Science concerns the totality of the primary concepts, i.e. concepts directly connected with sense experiences, and theorems connecting them. In its first stage of development, science does not contain anything else. Our everyday thinking is satisfied on the whole with this level. Such a state of affairs cannot, however, satisfy a spirit which is really scientifically minded; because, the totality of concepts and relations obtained in this manner is utterly lacking in logical unity. In order to supplement this deficiency, one invents a system poorer in concepts and relations, a system retaining the primary concepts and relations of the "first layer" as logically derived concepts and relations.

Kuhn says that science normally consists of what he calls puzzle solving, in which scientists use *technical* thought to solve problems *within* some paradigm. When the paradigm falls apart, then normal science is replaced by revolutionary science, which uses a form of thinking that is *less rigorous*. In Kuhn's words,

> All crises begin with the blurring of a paradigm and the consequent loosening of the rules for normal research. In this respect research during crisis very much resembles research during the pre-paradigm period, except that in the former the locus of difference is both smaller and more clearly defined (Kuhn, 1970, p. 84).

I suggest Einstein is describing a less rigorous form of thought that is used when one is *searching* for a paradigm, which turns into more rigorous thought as scientists work *within* the paradigm. When science 'invents a system poorer in concepts and relations, a system retaining the primary concepts and relations of the first layer as logically derived concepts and relations', then the rigorous thinking of technical thought is being used to 'tidy up' a paradigm that was initially discovered using less rigorous thought.

Three forms of thinking: mental networks, normal thought, and technical thought.

Mental symmetry suggests that both concrete and abstract thought can function in one of three different ways: mental networks, normal thought, and technical thought. We have discussed mental networks in some detail. What we are examining now is normal thought. We shall see later that technical thought emerges when Contributor thought takes control of the mind and limits thinking to a specific set of well-defined Perceiver facts and Server sequences. Einstein is known primarily for coming up with the paradigms of special and general relativity, an example of Kuhn's *revolutionary* science with its less rigorous thought and not Kuhn's *normal* science with its technical thinking.

This needs to be restated. Science and philosophy (especially analytic philosophy) place a great emphasis upon the use of rigorous logic and technical thought. As Kuhn says, this type of thinking describes normal science and is best suited for learning more about some area of thought by working *within* a paradigm. However, if one wishes to search for a *grand* explanation, then one must step outside of the box of technical thought and enter the less rigorous realm of normal thought, the type of thinking that science usually encounters during an episode of revolutionary science when it is undergoing a paradigm *shift*. Looking at this from the religious side, religious discussion often focuses upon the behavior of mental networks. Mental networks play a key role in religious thought and behavior, which is why we began this book by discussing mental networks. However, if one wishes to *change* mental networks and not merely be emotionally driven by them, then it is necessary to step outside of the realm of mental networks and discuss normal thought. Summarizing, normal thought can be used to build a structure within which mental networks and technical thought can be placed.

Let us return now to the nature of Teacher thought. Summarizing what Einstein says, Teacher thought is using 'free invention' to 'orient itself' within a 'labyrinth' of Perceiver facts by assigning a 'significance' that is 'independent' of Perceiver facts and Mercy experiences, leading to a mental structure that is 'stronger and more unalterable' than the concrete world of Mercy experiences.

I am not a Teacher person. But I have worked together with a Teacher person for several years. What Einstein says matches up with my personal experience of Teacher thought. Using an analogy, Teacher thought is like a king-maker who takes a citizen off the streets, makes him king, and then sees if this new monarch can bring order to the realm. In Einstein's words, Teacher thought is using free invention to orient itself by assigning significance.

One can see this king-making in Einstein's theory of special relativity. This theory is based in two postulates. In the language of our analogy, it proposes that the realm of physics is ruled by two monarchs.

The first postulate is that the laws of physics are identical in every frame of reference. For instance, if I stand in my home and drop an object, then it will fall to the floor in a manner described by law of gravity. But if I am standing in an airplane traveling at a constant velocity of 900 km/h at an altitude of 10 km and drop the same object, then it will fall to the floor of the airplane in precisely the same manner as it did when dropped in my home. In other words, the law of gravity is the same in the frame of reference of my home as it is in the frame of reference of an airplane moving at a constant velocity. This first 'monarch' is well-known within scientific thought. After all, one would be rather surprised if scientists claimed that scientific laws were not the same everywhere.

Einstein's second postulate appears at first glance to be a pauper off the street who has no right to be a monarch. Einstein stated that the speed of light in a vacuum is the same for all observers regardless of the motion of the light source. That is bizarre. If I am traveling in a car at 50 km/h and throw a ball forward at 30 km/h, then a person standing on the ground will see the ball traveling forward at 80 km/h, because the speed of the ball is added to the speed of the car. But if I am traveling in a spaceship at half the speed of light and shine a flashlight forward, then the speed of light from the flashlight is *not* added to the speed of the spaceship. Instead, everyone, no matter how fast they are traveling, will always see the light traveling at the speed of light, regardless of whether I shine the flashlight forwards, backwards, or sideways.

This is where the bizarre nature of Teacher thought becomes apparent. If the speed of light always remains the same, then space and time have to shrink and stretch. If Einstein were asked "How many physicists does it take to screw in a light bulb?" his answer would be "The light bulb keeps shining while the entire universe twists and turns." Similarly, Einstein's theory of relativity says that the speed of light remains fixed while the entire fabric of space and time warps. This is precisely how Teacher thought forms a general theory. Some specific statement will be 'taken off the street' and promoted to the status of a general theory. As long as it survives intact, it will be treated as a general theory. As Einstein says, this type of thinking is not logical and it is not inductive. Rather, it is a form of free invention. When I first encountered this type of thinking many years ago, I called it 'analyzing the elephant in the light of the gnat'.

What is truly bizarre is that physical evidence *supports* Einstein's strange form of thinking. Space and time really *do* appear to shrink and stretch in such a way that makes the speed of light appear constant. For some strange reason, the universe is designed (yes, that word) to be compatible with Teacher thought.

Teacher theorizing could also be viewed as a form of *concentration*. Teacher thought will hold on to some statement and attempt to concentrate on this statement, examining everything else that passes by in the light of this statement. Concentrating on a statement 'promotes it off the street' and makes it more general than other statements. Einstein calls it a miracle that thinking which regards some concepts as more general than other concepts can make sense of the universe.

> One may say 'the eternal mystery of the world is comprehensibility'...In speaking here of 'comprehensibility', the expression is used in its most modest sense. It implies: the production of some sort of order among sense impressions, this order being produced by the creation of general concepts, relations between these concepts, and by relations between the concepts and sense experience, these relations being determined in any possible manner. It is in this sense that the world of our sense experiences is comprehensible. The fact that it is comprehensible is a miracle (Einstein, 1950).

A recent paper explains why Teacher 'king-making' is capable of comprehending the natural world.

> Recent studies of nonlinear, multiparameter models drawn from disparate areas in science have shown that predictions from these models largely depend only on a few 'stiff' combinations of parameters. This recurring characteristic (termed 'sloppiness') appears to be an inherent property of these models and may be a manifestation of an underlying universality (Machta, 2013).

In simple terms, evidence indicates that natural processes can be modeled by focusing upon a few variables while ignoring other parameters—treating these few variables as 'kings' while ignoring the other 'citizens'.

Teacher thought forms a general theory by concentrating upon some statement.

Summarizing, Einstein's three stages could be compared to gathering a number of citizens, crowning one citizen as king, and seeing how long the king survives. Using psychological language, Teacher thought overgeneralizes while Perceiver thought limits generalization by coming up with counterexamples. Overgeneralization is like crowning some citizen off the street, while a counterexample either deposes or demotes the chosen citizen. Linguists tell us that overgeneralization is one of the most prominent traits of childish speech.

This means that a general Teacher theory can be formed in one of two ways. The easiest way is the method of *overgeneralization*, in which Teacher thought focuses upon some statement and Perceiver thought gets out of the way. As long as Perceiver thought does not come up with any facts that contradict the overgeneralized statement, Teacher thought will feel that this statement is a universal theory, and 'feel' is the right term because Teacher thought functions emotionally. Using the analogy of the monarch, as long as the peasant-made-monarch remains unopposed, he will continue to reign.

When Perceiver thought comes up with a contradictory fact, then this will limit the domain of the theory. For instance, suppose that it rained during the last few weekends. The temptation is for Teacher thought to overgeneralize, causing a person to say, "It always rains on the weekend!" If someone points out that it was sunny the weekend before last, then the domain of the statement will be limited: "Well it did rain all of the time this last weekend."

When abstract thought is functioning at this level, then Perceiver facts are the *enemy* of Teacher thought because they *limit* the extent of Teacher generalization. That is one reason why the Perceiver person does not naturally get along with the Exhorter person. The Perceiver person typically thinks that the Exhorter person is always exaggerating, while the Exhorter person thinks the Perceiver person is continually 'raining on his parade'. The Exhorter person exaggerates because Exhorter thought finds strong emotions exciting and an overgeneralized theory contains strong Teacher emotions. The Perceiver person is consciously aware of facts, and will point out facts that contradict the overgeneralized theories of the Exhorter person.

Similarly, when I was working with my Teacher brother, I discovered that his theorizing tended to occur in areas where my knowledge of facts was weakest. When I learned facts in this area in order to check his theories, then his theorizing would move on to another area where my knowledge of facts was weak. Each of these cycles forced me to go through mental confusion as Perceiver thought acquired facts about a new subject.

At that time I thought that Perceiver thought was only capable of finding *discrepancies* in Teacher theories. Since then I have discovered that Perceiver thought is also capable of helping Teacher thought to construct general theories by building *connections* between one context and another. That describes the second way in which a Teacher theory can be constructed, a method in which Teacher thought and Perceiver thought cooperate. Thus, my primary method of research for the last few years has been reading and analyzing the theories of other individuals. In each case I have found that building Perceiver connections between my theory and the theory of another person clarifies my understanding while extending the domain of the theory of mental symmetry.

> Perceiver thought can find counterexamples to Teacher overgeneralization. Perceiver thought can find analogies and connections that expand Teacher theories.

One can see this progression illustrated by the interaction between countries. Initially, each tribe is ruled by some petty chieftain who declares himself to be 'absolute ruler over the entire world', until his reign is successfully challenged by some upstart. The chieftain might only rule over the local valley, but as long as no one knows of any outsiders, the chief can pretend that he rules over the entire world. This illusion of universality crumbles when an outsider walks into the valley, especially if this outsider is accompanied by a group of strong men. Tribes—and later empires—then fight for domination, each attempting to extend its domain at the expense of the others. However, we are now slowly learning that it is possible to build connections of trade, travel, and communication between countries, leading to the Teacher order-within-complexity of international cooperation.

Mysticism

Now that we understand the nature of Teacher thought, let us turn our attention to one of the most common ways in which people and religions view God. The remainder of this chapter will discuss the concept of God that results from Teacher *overgeneralization*. I suggest that this kind of God will emerge whenever Perceiver facts are vague or absent or when Perceiver thought is disabled in some way. This type of deity is easy to recognize because a simplistic statement of universality will be combined with some sort of injunction against thinking. This will often *lead* to complicated statements based in extensive thinking, but the essence of this analysis will be that words and thinking are inadequate to describe the nature of God.

I suggest that this describes the cognitive mechanism behind *mysticism*. William James in *The Varieties of Religious Experience* says that

> This overcoming of all the usual barriers between individual and the absolute is the great mystic achievement. In mystic states we both become one with the absolute and we become aware of our oneness. This is the everlasting and triumphant mystical tradition, hardly altered by differences of clime or creed. In Hinduism, in Neoplatonism, in Sufism, in Christian mysticism, in Whitmanism, we find the same recurring note, so that there is about mystical utterances an eternal unanimity which ought to make a critic stop and think, and which brings it about that the mystical classics have, as has been said, neither birthday nor native land. Perpetually telling of the unity of man with God, their speech antidates languages, and they do not grow old (James, 1929).

When one finds 'the same recurring note' in many different religions and cultures 'hardly altered by differences of clime or creed', then this indicates that one is dealing with cognitive mechanisms. In other words, mysticism works because it takes advantage of the structure of the mind. James says that the core concept of mysticism is 'the unity of man with God', in which 'we become one with the absolute'. I have suggested that a mental concept of God emerges when a general theory in Teacher thought applies to personal identity in Mercy thought. The simplest possible universal theory that includes personal identity is 'the unity of man with God'. Stated cognitively, this is the ultimate overgeneralization, which will generate the *feeling* that I am experiencing universality. This feeling of encountering the 'oceanic' and the 'limitless' is described in a letter that was received by Sigmund Freud.

> After reading The Future of an Illusion (1927c), in a letter dated December 5, 1927, Romain Rolland wrote to Freud: "By religious feeling, what I mean—altogether independently of any dogma, any Credo, any organization of the Church, any Holy Scripture, any hope for personal salvation, etc.—the simple

and direct fact of a feeling of 'the eternal' (which may very well not be eternal, but simply without perceptible limits, and as if oceanic). This feeling is in truth subjective in nature. It is a contact" (Vermorel, 1993).

Notice exactly what is happening. Teacher thought naturally overgeneralizes. If Teacher thought is permitted to generalize without restriction, then this will produce a Teacher feeling of universality. If personal identity identifies with this Teacher overgeneralization, then this will create the feeling that I am having an encounter with the divine—a direct experience of God.

> Mysticism enables Teacher overgeneralization by disabling Perceiver thought.

Teacher thought will only be free to overgeneralize if Perceiver thought is taken out of the way. This can be seen in the doctrine of 'maya', which views physical objects as *illusion*. The Hinduwebsite.com article on maya explains this concept of 'illusion'.

> Hinduism considers the world to be false or unreal not in a physical sense but in an internal and absolute sense. The world is an illusion not because it does not exist, but because it is not what it appears to be all the time. From an absolute perspective, the material universe is a temporary creation. It changes from moment to moment and is never the same... Our scriptures say that we should not be misled by this ordinary sensory experience of ours. We should pay particular attention to our perceptions and go beyond the appearance of things to know the truth. We can arrive at truth by understanding the various states of our consciousness. For example, when we are awake everything looks real. We can touch and feel things consciously. But in our dream state the world becomes different. Here we are vaguely aware of what is going on, but from the experiential point of view, do not know clearly whether what we experience in the dream is true or not. When we are in deep sleep and our senses are in a state of complete rest, the world almost disappears from the field of our experience. Here we do not experience any duality or plurality. We even lose the sense of self or the ego sense. Thus for a spiritually awakened person, who begins to comprehend the illusion of appearances, the material world presents itself as a stage in which things appear and disappear according to the state of our consciousness, awareness and inclination (Jayaram).

Scientific thought begins by using Perceiver thought to organize Mercy experiences that come from the physical world. This corresponds to Einstein's first step of scientific thought. But Perceiver facts, categories, objects, and connections *limit* Teacher overgeneralization. One can see from the previous paragraph that Hinduism (as well as Buddhism) dismisses Perceiver thought by claiming that all physical facts are illusory. The reason given is that objects and facts *change*. For instance, a seed grows into a sapling which matures into a tree that is cut down to make lumber to build a house.

The idea that Perceiver facts *change* is a very important concept that lies at the heart of scientific analysis, which will be examined later in the chapter on incarnation. Introducing this concept briefly, I have mentioned that Perceiver thought builds connections between Mercy experiences. Normally, Perceiver thought connects experiences that are *spatially* related. For instance, in a tree, the roots are beneath the trunk, the branches extend from the trunk, and the leaves are attached to the branches. This leads to *object* identification. However, it is also possible for Perceiver thought to connect experiences that are *temporally* related. For example, if I jump off a cliff, then I will fall to the bottom. The experience of jumping occurs first followed by the experience of hitting the bottom. Even though these two experiences are separated in time, they are still connected by the law of gravity. Jumping will be *consistently* followed by hitting the bottom. This leads to the concept of cause-and-effect, in which some cause is consistently followed by an effect. Cognitively speaking, cause-and-effect involves a cooperation between Perceiver thought and Server thought. Perceiver thought notices that two experiences are connected, while Server thought notices that a Server sequence leads from one experience to the other. For instance, the two experiences of 'jumping' and 'hitting the bottom' are connected by the Server sequence of 'falling'. Cause-and-effect is the basic building block for concrete *Contributor* thought, which ties together Perceiver and Server.

One of the major breakthroughs in the birth of scientific thought was when Perceiver thought stopped dealing merely with static objects and expanded its thinking to include cause-and-effect. For instance, Aristotle's theory of elements explained gravity in terms of static objects and places. According to Aristotle, all objects are attracted to their natural *place;* for earth and water, the natural place is the center of the earth. Thus, an apple falls to the ground because it is *composed* of earth and water. Science, in contrast, turned its attention to the *path* that an object takes on its way to the ground, *expanding* the concept of Perceiver facts and connections to include Server time and change.

Jayaram, in contrast, argues that the presence of time and change *destroys* the concept of Perceiver facts. 'The world is an illusion' because 'it is not what it appears to be all the time'. In other words, because physical objects change, Perceiver facts are illusions. Science is rooted in empirical evidence. Jayaram, in contrast, bases his truth in 'understanding the various states of our consciousness'. A person who is asleep is only 'vaguely aware of what is going on'. This vagueness permits the 'spiritually awakened person' to 'comprehend the illusion of appearances'. Basing truth in a state of mental confusion is an effective way of eliminating Perceiver thought.

However, when one is awake then it is important to use Perceiver thought to recognize the existence of objects, because the physical world is rather unforgiving of those who believe that objects are merely illusion. As Jayaram says,

> No one can dispute the fact that, at any given moment, the world in which we live is real. It does exist in some specific form and state, independent of whether we exist or not. It is real in the physical sense. It is also tangible to our senses. We experience its existence in innumerable ways in our mind through our senses all the time. Right now at this very moment we are in a real world. We cannot

say the world is illusion, unless we have lost our minds literally. This does not mean it is not an illusion. This is the paradox, the real truth, to understand which we have to go deeper into ourselves to discover our true nature and meaning of self-absorption... An individual soul is subject to the illusion only so long as it is caught up in the material things. But the truth dawns and the soul remembers its true and essential nature, when the mind and the senses are withdrawn and the ego is subdued... As we discard the worldly things and become centered in ourselves, our equation with the world undergoes a tremendous transformation. It is then we become aware of the play of Maya, the apparent illusion caused by the movement and appearance of forms and things. We realize that from 'the creator Brahma right down to the pillar all appearance of materiality is unreal like objects seen in a dream.'...Where there is duality, the sense of separation, there is Maya. When our minds and senses are active, we remain under the influence of Maya...Truly no one is ever free from Maya, till one has lost all sense of duality forever (Jayaram).

In other words, Jayaram says that Perceiver thought *should* be used when thinking scientifically about the physical world, but should *not* be used when thinking religiously about the mind. He explains that 'this is the paradox, the real truth, to understand which we have to go deeper into ourselves to discover our true nature'. When a person says that the 'real truth' is a 'paradox' then this uses Perceiver thought to shut down Perceiver thought, because a person is being told to believe the fact that belief is not possible. Jayaram concludes that 'no one is ever free from Maya, till one is lost all sense of duality forever'. However, Perceiver thought by its very nature creates duality by distinguishing one Mercy experience from another. Thus, Jayaram appears to be saying that one can only encounter the divine by shutting down Perceiver thought.

Summarizing, a mental concept of God that is based in Teacher overgeneralization will generate the feeling of encountering the divine. This Teacher emotion will bring a sense of peace to the emotional turmoil of human existence, but it does so at the cost of shutting down Perceiver thought in the religious realm.

There are many different ways of producing Teacher overgeneralization. The most obvious way is to specifically state a universal theory of divine oneness, as illustrated in the discussion on maya. However, we have just seen that Teacher thought comes up with a general theory by attempting to concentrate on some word or phrase. This leads to the method of the *mantra*, in which the Teacher sensation of overgeneralization is created by repeating some word or phrase, such as the word 'om'.

It does not really matter whether a mantra has a meaning or not. A mantra that has some universal meaning will provide Teacher thought with the seed of a universal theory, but in order to achieve total overgeneralization, Teacher thought has to break through the Perceiver restrictions of meaning. Teacher concentration can be assisted through excessive *repetition*. For instance, in Pure land Buddhism, a name of Buddha will be repeated between 50,000 and 500,000 times a day (Yü Lu, 1964, p. 83). Similarly, in the Orthodox Christian practice of hesychasm, the 'Jesus Prayer' ('Lord Jesus Christ, Son of God, have mercy on me, the sinner') will be repeated several thousand times a day until it turns into an 'earworm' that repeats itself automatically in the background of the mind, indicating that these words have turned into an autonomous TMN that is effectively universal because it is always mentally present (Prayercraft, 2009).

Going further, Teacher thought naturally interprets speech because Teacher thought works with sequences, and speech is a sequence of sounds. But Teacher thought can also examine visual images for the presence of sequences, leading to visual lines, outlines, and written symbols, such as the words you are currently reading.

Applying this to mysticism, another easy way of creating a general Teacher theory is by creating some pattern of lines, known as a *mandala*. If the creation of this pattern is turned into a methodical, painstaking process, then this concentration will lead to the feeling of a universal Teacher theory. Carl Jung describes the connection between the overgeneralization of mysticism, the structure of the mandala, and personal identity.

> In 1918-19 I was in Chateau d'Oex as Commandant de la Région Anglaise des Internés de Guerre. While I was there I sketched every morning in a notebook a small circular drawing, a mandala, which seemed to correspond to my inner situation at the time. With the help of these drawings I could observe my psychic transformations from day to day...Only gradually did I discover what the mandala really is: 'Formation, Transformation, Eternal Mind's eternal recreation.' And that is the Self, the wholeness of the personality, which if all goes well is harmonious, but which cannot tolerate self-deceptions (Jung, 1963).

Finally, it is possible to help Teacher thought to concentrate by focusing upon some *repetitively moving object*, such as a *flickering candle*. For instance, in the following quote taken from a webpage on candle burning, the author suggests that 'the flickering flame of the candle' is 'a means of accessing our innermost powers' because it can 'create a mood of harmony in which conscious barriers dissolve'. Notice also how the sacred flame is portrayed as something universal that has 'been kindled over thousands of years'.

> The flickering flame of the candle provides us with a link to the sacred flames that have been kindled over thousands of years. Candles were used in Egypt and Crete as early as 3000 BC and were a feature of worship in many pre-Christian societies. Mostly made of beeswax, because bees were regarded as messengers of the gods and goddesses, they are still used in Christian churches today. Beeswax candles are currently popular with many people for magical and spiritual development. However, you can perform candle magic with white utility candles and it will be as pure and true as if you had followed the lists of color correspondences, fragrances and herbs that are most often used. These can add ceremony and atmosphere and create a mood of harmony in which conscious barriers dissolve. But those who say that the tools are magic in themselves, rather than just adornments and a means of accessing our innermost powers, are mistaking fantasy for true spiritual experience (DiMilta).

Many mystical practices focus upon the repetitive movement of breathing, a practice known as *anapanasati*, or mindfulness of breathing. Here too, it is not the activity that matters, but rather the internal attitude that is provoked by focusing upon this repetitive sequence. In the words of one Buddhist monk,

> A practitioner with sufficient skill does not breathe externally. That external breathing has stopped, but the internal breathing functions. With internal breathing there is no exhalation through the nose or mouth, but all pores on the body are breathing. A person who is breathing internally appears to be dead, but actually he has not died. He does not breathe externally, but the internal breathing has come alive (Hua, 2004).

Moving on, there are also various ways of preventing Perceiver thought from limiting Teacher overgeneralization. We have already seen one method, which is that of the *paradox*. The paradox turns Perceiver thought against itself, because Perceiver thought is being told to believe the fact that it cannot believe any facts. The simplest Perceiver paradox is that of non-duality, which insists that something is neither separated into categories nor unified. Hori explains that:

> [K]oan after koan explores the theme of nonduality. Hakuin's well-known koan, 'Two hands clap and there is a sound, what is the sound of one hand?' is clearly about two and one. The koan asks, you know what duality is, now what is non-duality? In 'What is your original face before your mother and father were born?' the phrase 'father and mother' alludes to duality. This is obvious to someone versed in the Chinese tradition, where so much philosophical thought is presented in the imagery of paired opposites. The phrase 'your original face' alludes to the original nonduality (Hori, 2000).

One can see in the following quote the Teacher emotion that is generated when Perceiver thought is successfully disabled and Teacher thought is free to overgeneralize. Notice how the monk experiences the breakthrough in which he comprehends that 'all is one' when he is exhausted and unable to think clearly.

> I was dead tired. That evening when I tried to settle down to sleep, the instant I laid my head on the pillow, I saw: "Ah, this outbreath is Mu! Then: the in-breath too is Mu! Next breath, too: Mu! Next breath: Mu, Mu! Mu, a whole sequence of Mu! Croak, croak; meow, meow - these too are Mu! The bedding, the wall, the column, the sliding-door - these too are Mu! This, that and everything is Mu! Ha ha! Ha ha ha ha Ha! that roshi is a rascal! He's always tricking people with his 'Mu, Mu, Mu'!" (Satomi, 1993).

A much simpler way of temporarily disabling Perceiver thought is by closing the eyes and stilling the mind. If I am not seeing the world of objects and if I am not thinking about distinct objects or experiences, then it will be possible for Teacher thought to continue focusing upon the theory that 'all is one'. In essence, one is attempting to re-create the dream state described earlier by Jayaram. Repeating part of that quote,

In our dream state the world becomes different. Here we are vaguely aware of what is going on, but from the experiential point of view, do not know clearly whether what we experience in the dream is true or not. When we are in deep sleep and our senses are in a state of complete rest, the world almost disappears from the field of our experience. Here we do not experience any duality or plurality (Jayaram).

This quieting of the mind is known as mindfulness or *sati*. Gunaratana explains in *Mindfulness in Plain English* that

When you first become aware of something, there is a fleeting instant of pure awareness just before you conceptualize the thing, before you identify it. That is a stage of Mindfulness. Ordinarily, this stage is very short. It is that flashing split second just as you focus your eyes on the thing, just as you focus your mind on the thing, just before you objectify it, clamp down on it mentally and segregate it from the rest of existence. It takes place just before you start thinking about it - before your mind says, "Oh, it's a dog." That flowing, soft-focused moment of pure awareness is Mindfulness. In that brief flashing mind-moment you experience a thing as an un-thing. You experience a softly flowing moment of pure experience that is interlocked with the rest of reality, not separate from it. Mindfulness is very much like what you see with your peripheral vision as opposed to the hard focus of normal or central vision, yet this moment of soft, unfocused, awareness contains a very deep sort of knowing that is lost as soon as you focus your mind and objectify the object into a thing. In the process of ordinary perception, the Mindfulness step is so fleeting as to be unobservable. We have developed the habit of squandering our attention on all the remaining steps, focusing on the perception, recognizing the perception, labeling it, and most of all, getting involved in a long string of symbolic thought about it. That original moment of Mindfulness is rapidly passed over. It is the purpose of the above mentioned Vipassana (or insight) meditation to train us to prolong that moment of awareness (Gunaratana, 2002).

Translating this into the language of mental symmetry, mindfulness focuses upon raw Mercy experiences *before* Perceiver thought organizes these experiences into objects and categories. It attempts to expand the 'fleeting instant of pure awareness just before you conceptualize the thing, before you identify it'.

Gunaratana points out that mindfulness is *non-verbal*. This is because Teacher words by their very nature assume Perceiver categories. For instance, the word 'dog' assumes that it is possible to make a distinction between 'dogs' and other animals, as well as a distinction between living beings and non-living beings. Gunaratana continues that

Mindfulness is the English translation of the Pali word Sati. Sati is an activity. What exactly is that? There can be no precise answer, at least not in words. Words are devised by the symbolic levels of the mind and they describe those realities with which symbolic thinking deals. Mindfulness is pre-symbolic. It is not shackled to logic. Nevertheless, Mindfulness can be experienced - rather easily - and it can be described, as long as you keep in mind that the words are only fingers pointing at the moon. They are not the thing itself. The actual experience lies beyond the words and above the symbols. Mindfulness could be described in completely different terms than will be used here and each description could still be correct.

The idea that words 'are not the thing itself' and that 'the actual experience lies beyond the words and above the symbols' is a common thread that one finds continually repeated in mystical literature. This leads us to a strange juxtaposition. On the one hand, many words have been written about mysticism. On the other hand, these words all agree that 'the actual experience lies beyond words'. It is as if someone responds to some amazing experience by saying 'I am speechless' and then proceeds to describe in detail the extent of his speechlessness. I suggest that this combination is a natural by-product of overgeneralization. Teacher thought will only be able to overgeneralize if Perceiver facts do not get in the way. This explains the insistence that mysticism is beyond words and that 'words are only fingers pointing at the moon'. However, Teacher overgeneralization leads to a Teacher theory with strong Teacher emotions, and these emotions will attract the attention of Exhorter thought, driving the mind to talk and write about the theory. Thus, in the same way that a paradox faces Perceiver thought with a contradiction of believing that it cannot believe, so I suggest that mysticism faces Teacher thought with the dilemma of wanting to talk about something about which one cannot talk.

Looking at this more generally, I suggest that mysticism works best when it is based in words that have vague meanings. The words that *follow* the mystical experience which attempt to describe this experience may be very precise, but the words that *precede* the mystical experience and that lead *to* the mystical experience need to be vague 'fingers pointing at the moon'. This implies that mysticism is independent of religious doctrine. In the same way that one out-of-focus picture tends to look like another, the doctrines of almost any religion can be used to promote mysticism as long as the words remain vague without precise definitions.

The *shahada* of Islam illustrates another method of preventing Perceiver thought from limiting Teacher generalization. The *shahada* is the first of the five pillars of Islam. It is the Islamic statement of faith, and one becomes a Muslim by stating the shahada sincerely before two Muslims. It consists of the statement "There is no God but God and Mohammed is the prophet of God" (said in Arabic). Notice that this statement contains two components. The first is a universal Teacher statement regarding God, while the second is a statement about the source of Perceiver truth describing Mohammed as the prophet of God.

The first portion of the shahada, '*La illaha il'Allah*' (there is no God but God) is especially melodious in the original Arabic. This phrase plays a major role in Sufism, the mystical branch of Islam, and chanting this phrase is a central part of virtually every Sufi gathering. Thus, we see the familiar connection between mysticism and a universal Teacher statement about God.

In order to understand the second part we need to look at the nature of absolute truth. I mentioned earlier that a general Teacher statement such as 'It always rains on weekends' can be contradicted by a Perceiver fact like 'It did not rain last Saturday'. But suppose that the *source* of the original statement has great emotional status. First, the MMN that represents this individual will impose its structure upon the MMNs that represent individuals with lesser status, ensuring that his statements are not overridden by other *persons*. Second, the emotional status of this person will overwhelm Perceiver thought and stop it from functioning, ensuring that Perceiver thought lacks the confidence to assert any contradictory *facts*. Perceiver thought has now been effectively eliminated.

Suppose that a 'prophet of God' who has ultimate Mercy status makes a statement about the universality of God. The status given to the prophet of God ensures that this statement will never be contradicted or limited by any people or facts, giving Teacher thought the freedom to overgeneralize. Of course, this cognitive mechanism will only function as long as the prophet of God is given great emotional respect. Thus, a strong taboo against belittling or blaspheming the prophet of God will be required.

We began this section on mysticism by quoting from William James. Let us return to what James calls the *four essential qualities* of mysticism (James, 1929):

> 1. Ineffability.—The handiest of the marks by which I classify a state of mind as mystical is negative. The subject of it immediately says that it defies expression, that no adequate report of its contents can be given in words. It follows from this that it is quality must be directly experienced...

> 2. Noetic quality.—Although so similar to states of feeling, mystical states seem to those who experience them to be also states of knowledge. They are states of insight into depths of truth unplumbed by the discursive intellect. They are illuminations, revelations, full of significance and importance, all inarticulate though they remain; and as a rule they carry with them the curious sense of authority for after-time...

> 3. Transiency.—Mystical states cannot be sustained for long. Except in rare instances, half an hour, or at most an hour or two, seems to be the limit beyond which they fade into the light of common day...

> 4. Passivity.—Although the oncoming of mystical states may be facilitated by preliminary voluntary operations, as by fixing the attention, or going to certain bodily performances, or in other ways which manuals of mysticism prescribe; yet when the characteristic sort of consciousness once has set in, the Mystic feels as if his own will were in obedience, and indeed sometimes as if he were grasped and held by a superior power.

We have just examined the first quality of *ineffability*. Stated simply, Teacher thought is being given a theory of universality that defies verbal expression. The second *noetic qual-*

ity says that emotional experience leads to Perceiver belief: 'Although so similar to states of feeling, mystical states seem to those who experience them to be also states of knowledge'. This Perceiver knowing does not use Perceiver thought, but rather involves 'states of insight into depths of truth unplumbed by the discursive intellect'. In other words, Perceiver thought is being overwhelmed by emotions into believing what is true because the 'illuminations' and 'revelations' 'carry with them the curious sense of authority'. This 'curious sense of authority' helps Perceiver thought to believe the paradoxes that are inherent in mysticism.

The third quality of *transiency* tells us that a Teacher theory that is based in overgeneralization cannot survive the light of day, both figuratively and literally. Instead, the Teacher feeling of universality typically lasts for half an hour before being dissipated by the Perceiver facts of reality. Finally, the fourth quality of *passivity* demonstrates what happens when a general theory that denies Perceiver facts about reality and identity turns into a TMN. Exhorter thought will be attracted to this TMN and will drive the mind to think and behave in a way that bypasses reality and personal identity.

> Mysticism leads to Perceiver paradox and unspeakable Teacher theory.

If the goal of religion is to achieve mental wholeness, then these four qualities suggest that mysticism does a poor job. It faces Perceiver thought with the contradiction of paradox, it presents word-based Teacher thought with an unspeakable theory, it provides momentary feelings of bliss, and it drives the mind in a manner that does not include personal identity.

But mysticism is *cognitively natural*. The easiest way to form a universal Teacher theory is through overgeneralization, and even an overgeneralized theory feels good—for a while.

Mysticism is also incompatible in several ways with scientific *thought*. Scientific thought uses Perceiver facts to build general Teacher theories that can be described using Teacher words, whereas mysticism suppresses Perceiver facts in order to create the illusion of a general Teacher theory that cannot be described using Teacher words. More specifically, scientific thought uses logic; mysticism goes beyond logic. Scientific thought is guided by the words and symbols of math; mysticism goes beyond words and symbols. Scientific thought results in technology which transforms the physical world; mysticism leads to ecstasy that withdraws from the physical world. Scientific thought has led to the permanent changes of the industrial and the consumer revolutions; mysticism provides temporary emotions of cosmic bliss.

> Mysticism is compatible with scientific methodology but not with scientific thought.

However, mysticism is compatible with scientific *methodology*, because it fills the emotional, internal void that is left by scientific methodology without questioning its underlying assumptions. Scientific methodology protects Perceiver thought by avoiding subjective Mercy emotions; mysticism agrees that Perceiver thought should not be used in the realm of the subjective. Scientific methodology builds rational Teacher theories based upon physical evidence; mysticism agrees that it is not possible to build rational theories about the non-physical realm. Scientific methodology is guided by the consensus of peer review; mysticism agrees that scientists have the right to make definitive statements about physical reality. Using Oriental language, mysticism is the yin to the yang of scientific methodology, with these two acting as a pair of opposites that complement each other.

When mysticism and scientific methodology complement each other in a yin-yang fashion, then one moves from science to religion through a 'leap of faith'. For instance, one finds this leap of faith in the religion of Kierkegaard. Quoting from the Stanford Encyclopedia of Philosophy,

> Christian dogma, according to Kierkegaard, embodies paradoxes which are offensive to reason. The central paradox is the assertion that the eternal, infinite, transcendent God simultaneously became incarnated as a temporal, finite, human being (Jesus). There are two possible attitudes we can adopt to this assertion, viz. we can have faith, or we can take offense. What we cannot do, according to Kierkegaard, is believe by virtue of reason. If we choose faith we must suspend our reason in order to believe in something higher than reason. In fact we must believe by virtue of the absurd (McDonald).

Kierkegaard is disabling Perceiver thought by asserting that 'Christian dogma embodies paradoxes which are offensive to reason'. This makes it possible for Teacher thought to overgeneralize from the 'temporal, finite, human being of Jesus' to the 'eternal, infinite, transcendent God'. In order to make this overgeneralization, Kierkegaard follows the route of the Zen koan by choosing to 'suspend reason in order to believe in something higher than reason'. Kierkegaard's method will work. If a mystical experience is sufficiently intense, then this will cause Perceiver thought to believe 'paradoxes which are offensive to reason'. However, the thesis of this book is that Christian dogma is compatible with reason and does not require paradoxes, and we will see in the chapters on incarnation that it is possible to provide a rational explanation for how a concept of incarnation forms within the mind that does not require any blind leap of faith.

Mysticism is currently marketed in the West as a simple way of reducing anxiety. For instance, the Mayo clinic website says that

> If stress has you anxious, tense and worried, consider trying meditation. Spending even a few minutes in meditation can restore your calm and inner peace. Anyone can practice meditation. It's simple and inexpensive, and it doesn't require any special equipment...Meditation has been practiced for thousands of years. Meditation originally was meant to help deepen understanding of the sacred and mystical forces of life. These days, meditation is commonly used for relaxation and stress reduction... During meditation, you focus your attention and eliminate the stream of jumbled thoughts that may be crowding your mind and causing stress. This process may result in enhanced physical and emotional well-

being... Meditation can give you a sense of calm, peace and balance that benefits both your emotional well-being and your overall health (Mayo Clinic Staff).

Mysticism does have measurable benefits. When Teacher thought feels that it has a universal theory, then this feeling of order-within-complexity will 'focus your attention' and 'eliminate the stream of jumbled thoughts that may be crowding your mind and causing stress'. And it is relaxing to be in a state of mindfulness in which thought and action flow naturally.

Mysticism is a simple way of achieving these cognitive benefits, but we have seen that it does so *temporarily* at the cost of cognitive *dissonance*. This book suggests that it is possible to achieve these *same* cognitive benefits in a manner that preserves mental wholeness. However, this long-term, integrated solution requires far more than 'a few minutes in meditation'. Mysticism uses Teacher overgeneralization to create the *emotion* of a universal understanding, whereas cognitive transformation *constructs* a universal understanding. Mysticism creates the *feeling* of encountering a divine being, whereas cognitive transformation allows personal behavior to be *guided* by a mental concept of God. Mysticism achieves mindfulness by *preventing* the mind from classifying the stream of Mercy experiences, whereas cognitive transformation achieves mindfulness by allowing the mind to flow *intuitively* along a mental grid of Perceiver facts and Server sequences. Mysticism goes beyond words and logic by *denying* rational thought in order to embrace experience, whereas cognitive transformation goes beyond words and logic by *expanding* a rational theory to include experience.

Mysticism is typically portrayed as a way of thinking that is *superior* to rational verbal thought. I suggest that this attitude is essential to the functioning of mysticism. One can explain this by using the analogy of military rank. A colonel commands more people than a captain. Using Teacher language, a colonel has a larger *domain* than a captain. The officer with the most general domain is the general, while a private only rules over his private experiences. This comparison of domain is possible because all of these individuals function within the *structure* of an army with its well-defined Server skills and Perceiver facts. Now suppose that a *slkjif* comes along who claims that his rank does not fit within the army structure. Should he be treated as less than a private or more than a general? Obviously, the *slkjif* will only be able to claim that he is the ruler of the entire universe if he is treated as *more* than a general. Similarly, mysticism will only be able to claim that it describes universality if it is viewed as *superior* to logic with its structured analysis. But is this really the case?

Linguists tell us that a child who is learning grammar will first overgeneralize and then restrict the domain of a grammatical rule as more knowledge is acquired. For instance, a child will usually say 'I goed to the store', overgeneralizing the rule of adding '-ed' to make the past tense of a verb, before learning that 'went' is an exception to this general rule. Thus, we see that overgeneralization usually occurs because of a lack of knowledge and not as a result of knowledge.

Similarly, Jayaram compares the knowledge of mysticism to a 'dream state' in which one is 'vaguely aware of what is going on'. Again, this indicates a lack of knowledge. Gunaratana says that mindfulness 'takes place just before you start thinking about it - before your mind says, Oh, it's a dog.' This also tells us that mysticism occurs before mental processing and not as a result of it. The Mayo clinic website says that 'Meditation has been practiced for thousands of years. Meditation originally was meant to help deepen understanding of the sacred and mystical forces of life.' This indicates a form of thinking that predates modern knowledge.

I am not suggesting that mysticism does not work. It does function as advertised, but only if the overgeneralization of cosmic unity is regarded as more general than—beyond—rational thought. But cognitively speaking, mysticism occurs *before* rational thought and not beyond it, and it is based in ignorance and not knowledge. I am not suggesting that everyone who practices or teaches mysticism is ignorant. Many well-researched, carefully written tomes have been penned about mysticism. But that is precisely the point. Mysticism comes *before* intelligence. The careful analysis comes after the mysticism. When rational thought comes before mysticism, then mysticism can only be achieved by *abandoning* rational thought through some sort of leap of faith in order to return to a pre-cognitive way of thinking.

This is more than just an academic distinction, because thinking that precedes rational thought falls into Piaget's *pre-operational* stage of cognitive development. If religious thought regards pre-operational thinking as 'beyond' the logic of formal operational thought, then the religious mental networks that result will drive a person to remain cognitively immature.

With this in mind, let us revisit the six pre-operational traits discussed earlier.

Transductive reasoning leads to the assumption that God—a *universal* being—can be grasped through a *single* emotional experience. James' quality of transiency notes that mystical experiences occur seldom and do not last for long. Building a universal theory upon such a narrow base of personal experiences is an example of transductive reasoning in which one leaps from specific to universal.

Animism leads to the feeling that inanimate external objects have religious significance. Staring at a flickering candle, sitting quietly in a cross-legged position, or focusing on one's breathing would fall into this category. Obviously, sitting and breathing are performed by people and not inanimate objects, but a person who sits motionless for hours is acting like an inanimate object and someone who focuses the mind upon breathing in and out is acting like an inanimate machine.

Artificialism assumes that one learns about God by believing the right religious sources and following the right religious experts. Mysticism may not have theology, but it is full of accounts of religious seekers spending extensive time with religious gurus in order to achieve enlightenment.

Magical thinking confuses belief with reality. If the world is illusion, if precognitive mindfulness is more advanced than cognitive thought, and if being half-awake is the key to discerning reality, then is one not confusing belief with reality?

Centrating assumes that some specific religion or denomination has a total knowledge of God. Mysticism insists that one can only gain a true understanding of God by letting go of *all other* knowledge in order to fixate upon some religious experience.

Egocentrism creates a God in my own image. For many mystical religions, the concept that 'I am God' is a fundamental doctrine.

We began this book by suggesting that religion addresses two fundamental questions: What is the grand explanation and what is my place within this explanation? Mysticism answers the first question by separating 'grand' from 'explanation'. It says that one can either use Teacher thought to come up with something grand or else use rational thought to develop explanations, but that it is not possible to come up with a grand explanation that combines universality with rational thought.

The answer that mysticism provides for the second question can be understood by comparing the two religious concepts of *heaven* and *nirvana*. The Catholic website catholicism.com explains that

> In Buddhism, nirvana is the final state the soul reaches on its journey through different lifetimes. These lifetimes are pictured as a series of lamps, one being lit by another, until the final lamp goes out. The word 'nirvana' means 'going out' or 'extinguishing.' According to Buddhists, our desires and cravings are what keep the process of reincarnation going. By eliminating all desires it is possible to escape the cycle of rebirth. When a person manages to extinguish all his desires, he reaches a state of nirvana and is said to be a saint. When a saint dies he enters nirvana proper, in which he loses his identity as a distinct individual. Buddha compared the question 'Does a saint survive his death?' to the question 'Where does a flame go when it is blown out?' Both questions are thought to be intrinsically unanswerable. Neither a dead saint nor a blown-out flame have individual identities anymore. Nirvana is different from the Christian idea of heaven. Nirvana is a state of desirelessness; heaven is a state of having one's most fundamental desire (for God) fulfilled. Nirvana is a state of ultimate apathy and indifference, heaven of ultimate joy and fulfillment. Paradoxically, Buddhists regard nirvana, the state of desirelessness, as the most desirable state (Catholic Answers Staff).

In other words, nirvana is characterized by the total absence of any MMNs, because all personal desires and all personal identities have been extinguished. Thus, mysticism answers the question 'What is my place in the grand explanation?' by declaring that the grand non-explanation has no room for concepts such as 'me' or 'mine'. All that is left is pure Teacher overgeneralization.

Suppose that one could break free of the 'wheel of human existence' and enter some sort of realm guided purely by Teacher overgeneralization. Would Teacher thought experience endless emotional bliss? I suggest not. That is because Teacher emotion comes from order-within-*complexity*. Teacher thought feels good when *many* items fit together in a coherent manner. But overgeneralization achieves Teacher order by *suppressing* complexity rather than arranging it. In other words, the mystic can only experience the emotional high of feeling 'united with God' by turning his back upon some world. The mystical monk can only experience the emotional high of breaking through into 'universal understanding' by first struggling with the complexity of trying to fit everything together. Thus, there is a sense in which mysticism is 'beyond' rational thought, because the *intensity* with which one feels Teacher order depends upon the *extent* to which one has struggled with complexity. The problem is that the feeling of order is being achieved by *regressing* to an earlier stage of cognitive development.

Using the analogy of a jigsaw puzzle, assembling all of the pieces and gazing upon the finished picture generates Teacher emotions of order-within-complexity because the pieces now fit together smoothly. The more pieces, the greater the resulting Teacher pleasure. Placing the last piece into a 1000 piece jigsaw puzzle feels better than finishing a puzzle with only a dozen pieces. Mysticism 'solves' the puzzle by giving up, throwing away the box, placing all of the pieces in a blender and pressing the button. The resulting sludge of chewed up cardboard contains a uniform consistency and can be regarded as a form of order-within-complexity. But one has 'unified' the puzzle pieces by *destroying* them. One has achieved Teacher order-within-complexity by *abandoning* complexity. Unfortunately, the puzzle pieces that are blended to achieve this unification are composed of rather significant items such as you, me, my wife, our house, my job, bananas, ice cream, a day at the beach, a beautiful song, job satisfaction, and so on.

If the grand explanation truly did require the extinction of me and everything that I hold dear, then that would be a deeply frightening thought, for it would mean that God, the most powerful being in existence, demands my annihilation. Thus, I suggest that mysticism can only handle the concept of destroying the precious pieces of personal existence because reality restores them as soon as one opens one's eyes and emerges from a mystical trance. Going further, I suggest that mysticism can only contemplate the concept that reality is illusion because reality is not an illusion; it can only regard the prospect of nirvana as pleasurable because it does not inhabit nirvana.

When a system of thought suffers from such a fatal flaw—and 'fatal' is the right word—then it makes sense to look for a better paradigm.

✳ 7. Teacher and Mercy Co-dependence

The relationship between Teacher thought and Mercy thought could be described as *emotionally co-dependent*. On the one hand these two cognitive modules live in completely different worlds. Teacher thought inhabits the realm of time, sequences, words, symbols, lines, and general theories, while Mercy thought lives in a world of space, objects, experiences, events, colors, and specific people. One can gain a sense of how different these two cognitive modules are by comparing the behavior of the Teacher person (Albert Einstein and Isaac Newton are the best-known historical examples) with that of the Mercy person (Abraham Lincoln, Elvis Presley, Mahatma Gandhi, William Howard Taft, Steve Wozniak, and Michael Jackson are a few well-known examples). I know from personal experience what this contrast is like because my older brother is a Teacher person while my mother is a Mercy person. And yet, these two very dissimilar modules process information using the same cognitive currency of emotion. The emotion that a person feels is the *sum* of Teacher emotion and Mercy emotion, and as far as I can tell, these two emotions feel the *same*.

Using an analogy, this is like Monopoly money being indistinguishable from real money. Monopoly money is generated by playing the game of Monopoly, while real money is used to buy and sell goods and services within the real world. Similarly, Teacher thought generates emotion by discovering order-within-complexity, while Mercy thought acquires its initial emotional labels from physical experiences of pain and pleasure. Mentally speaking, the 'Monopoly money' of Teacher emotion can substitute for the 'real money' of Mercy emotion—and vice versa—making it possible to use Monopoly money to cover real world debts or use real money to win a game of Monopoly. This emotional equivalence makes personal transformation possible, because the emotional pleasure of gaining Teacher understanding allows the mind to handle the emotional pain of personal honesty; the joy of following a TMN balances the agony of rebuilding childish MMNs. Using the Monopoly analogy, the debt that is incurred by going bankrupt in the real world is covered by the wealth that one gains from playing Monopoly.

We saw in previous chapters that the childish mind is controlled by MMNs. This is inevitable, it provides the initial content for the mind, it leads to inadequate content, it makes education possible, and it is also open to abuse. The emotional tricks that we will be describing in this chapter provide a similar transitional role. Cognitive development could be compared to highway construction, because one has to keep the traffic flowing while building a new highway. The mechanisms that we will examine are like the detours that keep the mental traffic flowing while the highway of childish MMNs is being replaced by a road system based in the TMN of a general understanding. The problem arises when these temporary emotional detours are regarded as the final highway structure.

These emotional tricks are used by all aspects of human society. However, because the interaction between Teacher emotion and Mercy emotion plays such a major role in religion, they are especially prominent in religion. As a result, critics often equate religion with these emotional tricks, but I suggest that they are actually characteristics of a *transitional* form of religion that goes beyond the Teacher overgeneralization of pure mysticism but has not yet acquired an integrated Teacher understanding.

Adding Mercy Emotion to Teacher Words

We will begin by examining two emotional tricks that use Mercy feelings to substitute for inadequate Teacher emotion.

Emotionally inflated words: Teacher thought wants general theories. Teacher thought uses emotion to evaluate the generality of a theory; the greater the generality the stronger the Teacher emotion. If words are accompanied by Mercy emotions, then these *Mercy* feelings will make the words feel more *general* to Teacher thought. For instance, if I say 'God is omnipotent', then this will not feel like a universal statement. However, if I sing 'God is omnipotent' in a stirring song backed up by an energetic rock band that is amplified through a sound system and illuminated by a set of stage lights, then the statement will *feel* much more universal. The words may have not changed but they are now emotionally reinforced by potent Mercy feelings, making them feel much more general to Teacher thought.

> Teacher thought interprets Mercy emotions as feelings of generality.

For instance, when I was in Korea I played violin in several church orchestras, allowing me to observe the behavior of the typical Korean mega-church. In one church, when the head pastor (who wore the fanciest robes) prayed officially during a church service, he would turn his back to the audience, face the cross hanging at the front of the church, and *doubly* modulate his voice. As a musician I found this intriguing. The normal emphasis of speech was over-emphasized: "Dear Lord we thank you for your grace." A vibrato or quiver was then added to this over-emphasis. "Dear Lord we thank you for your grace." This nonverbal speech combined with other Mercy-based elements, such as the robes, made the words to God feel much more significant.

In a recent study on American mega-churches, researchers relate their surprise at the extensive emotional references encountered when interviewing people who attend such churches.

> Expressions relating to the sensory experience were common—tasting, seeing, feeling, touching, listening, feeding, thirsting—and words related to the emotions—loving, longing, feeling, moving, vulnerability, wanting, crying, joy—were not only peppered throughout the interviews, but rather were the driving force behind nearly every description and often the punch line to every story. The researchers did not go into the research intending to find the prevalence of this affective expression, but in the coding process, this focus on forms of emotional energy became clear and consuming (Wellman, 2012, p. 9).

Notice the emphasis upon sensory experiences and personal emotions, all expressions of Mercy thought. A similar focus upon Mercy emotions is present in the typical megachurch service.

> Usually, in megachurches, there are three to five songs at the beginning of the service to get congregants in a worshipful mood – to initiate mutual entrainment. This portion of the service is bursting with what we have coined a connectic experience: a multisensory mélange of sensory input that is often called by members the 'feeling of the spirit of God' or 'the touch of God.' Whatever it is, we have seen it literally lift people out of their seats, particularly in its relation to altar calls and more generalized megachurch worship. One man described how he and his wife "were kind of blown away by the theatrical set, all the media elements, everything else. It just really – it touches every modality that we have." The stimulation of emotion comes by way of the lyrics of songs that are emotionally charged, often setting up a need (sinfulness) and presenting a solution (Jesus' blood), in one case slides that were literally pulsating with what looked like blood being squeezed under a microscope. The music is loud and emotive, and it is customary (and sometimes prompted by the worship leaders) for people to raise their hands, close their eyes, and even rock back and forth to the music, representing a bodily, tangible commitment to emotional participation (p.12).

When a 'multisensory mélange of sensory input' leads to a feeling of 'the touch of God', then this tells us that Mercy emotion is being interpreted from a Teacher perspective. But the source of this emotion is 'the theatrical set, all the media elements, everything else' and not a Teacher understanding of God.

The preaching also does not usually focus upon building the TMN of a general understanding but rather upon connecting with people's MMNs.

> Rather than complicated theological explanations or critical analysis of a biblical text, the interview responses suggest that the sermons are understood through the emotions – on a level of intuition that 'just feels right,' or that 'just makes sense.' The ideas are arousing and moving, but not intellectually taxing. One man said, 'I'm a diehard Pastor [name] fan, he's on fire, he's the shepherd.' Members from nearly every megachurch in the study constantly praised the accessibility of their pastor's preaching, repeatedly testifying that 'even a child could understand' his message (p.15).

And yet the congregation interprets these Mercy-based words as the voice of God.

> One woman described, "Every time I heard him speak he made me cry, it was so spiritual and so, oh I can't explain it" and another said, "Like, did God just tell you to say that to me? Because it was like he was almost preaching directly to me and what I was experiencing in my life" (p.15).

As the authors of this study suggest, the mega-church is meeting an emotional need that is not being satisfied by modern secular society, which is the feeling of 'connectedness to the divine', an 'affective experience of the ultimate', the type of feeling that was discussed in the last chapter on mysticism.

> Religious rituals differ from secular ones in the holy, divine, or transcendent symbols that they entail and evoke, which allow individuals to feel as though they are channeling and experiencing the divine... Successful religious rituals, therefore, can also produce a fifth ritual outcome—heightened spirituality or connectedness to the divine. By spirituality we mean a desire and affective experience of the ultimate (p.8).

But this Teacher feeling of 'encountering the divine' is being created by saying words about God and then associating these words with Mercy emotions. Teacher thought hears the words, senses the emotions, and concludes that general statements are being made about a universal being. I am not suggesting that the preaching in a mega-church is devoid of content. Most mega-church preachers make insightful statements that are based in universal cognitive mechanisms. However, there is an inherent *tension* between the TMN of a general understanding and the MMNs generated by the experiences of the church and the personality of its pastor.

> Often, members would say that the pastor is not the object of their worship, and yet, in nearly the same breath, they would announce the power of the pastor to deliver the word of God even referring to him as 'God's mouthpiece.' One man's comments exemplify this: "We've heard from folks, both sides, at the same time almost, we don't want to put him [the pastor] on a pedestal, you know, he's real, he's human, and at the same time, something more than human and he's something, you know, that we put on a pedestal" (p.14).

Looking at such a church from the perspective of Piaget's cognitive stages, we conclude that it is functioning at the concrete operational level. Logic and understanding are present, but they are based in concrete experiences. The scientist observing from the sidelines may complain that the mega-church is not functioning at the abstract level of Piaget's formal operational stage, but at least it is attempting to function within the realm of subjective emotions that scientific methodology with its emphasis upon objective empirical evidence tries so hard to ignore.

The problem is that the Mercy emotions that are being substituted for Teacher understanding do not come from nowhere. Rather, MMNs are masquerading as TMNs, and these MMNs come from either *somewhere* or *someone*. Stated bluntly, something or some-one is pretending to be the voice of God.

When religious believers practice blind faith and Perceiver thought is mesmerized, then these MMNs have the power to completely *rewrite* people's concepts of God. If Per-ceiver thought is functioning, then Perceiver error-checking will prevent a wholesale abrogating of divine revelation, but it is still possible for MMNs to change the relative *emphasis* placed upon various doctrines about God, causing some doctrines to be em-phasized and others to be de-emphasized, because Teacher thought will use the *sum* of Teacher and Mercy emotions to evaluate generality. One could compare this emotional warping to the impact which government programs have upon a free market economy. The government does not directly control the economy, but the government can cause certain sectors of the economy to grow or shrink by providing incentives or levying taxes.

We saw in a previous chapter that the religious attitudes of fervor, self-denial, and tran-scendence help to keep Perceiver thought in a mesmerized state of blind faith. When these religious attitudes are dominant, then there will be a natural tendency to view them as essential aspects of the character of God. Instead of just exhibiting religious fervor, people will feel that God's character demands religious fervor; instead of merely practicing self-denial, people will believe that self-denial is an essential characteristic of God's nature; instead of believing that man cannot understand God, people will assert that God is by nature transcendent and unknowable. And because Teacher thought uses emotion to evaluate generality, these religious attitudes—turned into theological dogma—will become central truths about God that overshadow anything written in the holy book about God.

We have discussed how emotional Mercy *experiences* can be used to inflate words about God. MMNs that represent charismatic leaders or gifted preachers will also tend to emotionally inflate words about the divine. Thus, when a preacher says 'thus saith the Lord', these words will be believed as coming from God because of the emotional status of the preacher making these statements. When this adulation is combined with blind faith, then the prophet of God can say whatever he wants and his followers will regard his words as the voice of God. We saw this combination in the previous chapter in the *shahada*. If the leader changes his mind and starts to preach a new revelation from God, then his followers will *accept* this new revelation as absolute truth because the MMN of the leader defines truth, and believers will not be *troubled* by any inconsisten-cies with existing revelation because Perceiver thought is not functioning. Going further, the fickleness of the leader and the mental instability of his followers will naturally turn into the belief that God himself is fickle and mentally unstable.

Combining these two points, the 'prophet of God' will often preach a message that is based upon the religious attitudes of fervor, self-denial, and transcendence. However, while the prophet will tell his followers that they need to worship *God* with fervor, the prophet of God will occupy a central place in these religious rituals, and adoration for God will have a tendency to express itself as adoration for the leader. Similarly, self-denial for God will turn into self-denial for the leader who is the voice of God. Finally, transcendence, which believes that the character of God is unknowable, will turn into the belief that the leader does not have to explain any of his decisions to his followers.

For instance, one sees this combination in the *divine right of kings*, a doctrine that was practiced in Europe during Habermas' first stage of representative publicity. The monarch was not subject to any earthly authority because it was believed that he derived his right to rule directly from God. Any attempt to restrict or depose the king was regarded as a sacrilegious act against God. And when the king went to war, then his subjects were expected to express their self-denial to God by being willing to die for their king on the battlefield. My ancestors, the Mennonites, paid a heavy price for choosing not to participate in this divine farce. Unfortunately many today still believe that following God implies being willing to die for one's country, and political leaders are often all too happy to take advantage of this cognitive dissonance.

Another possibility is to emotionally inflate words about God using the MMNs of *culture*. One sees this illustrated by the 'seeker friendly' approach often taken by the mega-church. As Alan Wolfe, a professor of political science at Boston College, puts it,

> The theologian H. Richard Niebuhr has documented the many ways in which Christ could become a transformer of culture. But in the United States culture has transformed Christ, as well as all other religions found within the shores. In every aspect of the religious life, American faith has met American culture – and American culture has triumphed. Whether or not the faithful ever were a people apart, they are so no longer; if they were singing the famous gospel hymn today, they would say that the old-time religion is no longer good enough for them. Talk of hell, damnation, and even sin has been replaced by a nonjudgmental language of understanding and empathy. Gone are the arguments over doctrine and theology (Wolfe, 2003).

In other words, preachers still talk about God, but these words are being inflated by the MMNs of culture. The end result is that religion becomes indistinguishable from culture, and any words regarding God that offend the MMNs of culture will be de-emphasized. For instance, many years ago I played violin in a church orchestra during an Easter production put on by a local large church. The program was basically a series of skits based upon popular TV shows and movies, made larger-than-life through the use of stage sound and lighting. At the end of this parody of Hollywood, the preacher stood up and stated that this emotionally powerful presentation demonstrated the power of God and the importance of God's message. Ironically, the very spot in that church where I sat playing the violin collapsed several decades later during a Christian rock concert because too many teenagers were dancing there in a mosh pit. Both figuratively and literally, popular culture ended up overwhelming the Christian message.

The solution does not lie in taking the iconoclastic approach of removing all Mercy elements from religion. That is because a mental concept of God emerges when Teacher understanding *applies to personal identity*. Thus, it is not possible to discuss God without including the MMNs of personal identity. When looking for a grand explanation, one must include my place within that explanation. Instead, as I have mentioned before, I suggest that what matters is the relative status of mental networks. As Wolfe asks, is the TMN of theology transforming the MMNs of culture and identity, or is the TMN of theology being shaped by these MMNs? Unfortunately, when religion is functioning at Piaget's concrete operational level, then the MMNs of culture and identity will provide the starting point for religious thought. When this is the case, then it is the responsibility of theologians to correct the errors that will inevitably creep in. Of course, this assumes that theology exists, and that people have a respect for theology and theologians.

Testimony: The Keegan Hamilton study mentions another common method of using Mercy feelings to inflate Teacher understanding, which is the *testimony*, or experience of personal transformation.

> This experience is highlighted as a rite of passage; people may recall and tell the story of their conversion (their 'Testimony') for years to come. Whether or not a congregant decides to be saved that day, this portion of the service is poignantly marked with heavy sensory pageantry. The emotional energy in the room is palpable, people report feeling 'released,' as if they had 'walked through the waters but never got wet.' One man expressed that 'God's love becomes [...] such a drug that you can't wait to come get your next hit. [...] You can't wait to get involved to get the high from God (Wellman, 2012, p. 16).

The problem is not with the testimony. On the contrary, if the goal of religion is to reach mental wholeness, then following the path of religion should lead to many testimonials from people who are experiencing the benefits of mental wholeness. A religion without testimonials is highly suspect. For example, when I visit a new church I often step into the church library and compare the number of shelves devoted to Christian fiction with the number of shelves containing nonfiction and theology. In the libraries that I have checked so far, the fiction section is typically twice as large as the rest of the library combined, suggesting that pretending to be transformed by religion is more popular than actually being transformed by religion.

The problem arises when the Mercy emotions of the testimonial are used to inflate Teacher words about God and religion. One can see this portrayed in the previous quote. First, the Mercy emotions of a *specific* experience of religious transformation are being used to make interaction with God to feel more *universal*. Believers 'tell the story of their conversion', a specific emotional event that occurred at a specific time and date, 'for years to come', similar to the way that the mystic gains pleasure from the emotional afterglow of the occasional mystical encounter. Second, the environment within which this conversion experience occurs is 'palpable with emotional energy', and it occurs during a portion of the service 'poignantly marked with heavy sensory pageantry'.

My goal is not to question the validity of the 'conversion experience'. We will examine the Christian prayer of salvation in the next chapter and see that it is based in deep cognitive mechanisms. However, in the same way that *enrolling* in school is only the first step of *studying* at that school, so I suggest that the emotional 'release' that is generated by the prayer of conversion makes it possible for an individual to 'enroll' in the emotionally difficult 'school' of personal honesty. Focusing upon 'the testimony' confuses enrolling in school with studying at school. Looking at this from an educational perspective, I know from teaching in Korea that the typical Japanese or Korean student makes a similar cognitive error, because the educational system is geared towards passing the entrance exams to prestigious universities, rather than upon studying at a university in order to gain an education.

Celebrity endorsements illustrate the danger inherent in the testimonial. Logically speaking, being rich and famous usually makes a person *less* of an expert, because money can be used to buy the skill and knowledge of others, while fame distorts social interaction. And yet we all know that products sell better if they are associated with some famous face. Cognitively speaking, celebrity endorsement is an effective way of using emotions to inflate speech (and possibly use Mercy status to determine Perceiver belief). For instance, the 'religion' of Scientology is infamous for using celebrities to endorse its message. However this practice is also found in more established religions. The following quote from a cover article in an evangelical Christian magazine illustrates what can happen when belief in God is buttressed by celebrity endorsement.

> Few may realize that one of the best-known 'enforcers' in the National Hockey League (NHL)—nicknamed 'the Grim Reaper'—is a committed Christian. He currently also works as a vice president of the NHL Players Association. Christian teaching doesn't forbid his rough profession, he says. In fact, he believes that God approves of him trying to play the best he can. Former NHL star Paul Baxter is another Christian known for an aggressive playing style. His style made him popular with his teammates and fans in Calgary, though understandably unpopular with his opponents. "People think being a Christian means being meek and mild, but they don't realize the courage and toughness Jesus displayed in his life," says Baxter... An increasing number of top players profess faith in Christ, putting to rest any worries about Christianity making players into wimps. No one questions the career achievements of Christian players such as Doug Jarvis, Chico Resch, Dean Prentice, Paul Henderson, Roger Neilson and Ron Ellis. Even Don Cherry, the gruff, tell-it-like-it-is hockey commentator for the Canadian Broadcasting Corporation, commends Christian players. "A lot of people expect me to put down the Christian athlete and for some reason they think that if you believe in Jesus you have to be a wimp - how wrong they are" (Adlam, 2001).

For those who are unfamiliar with Canadian culture, hockey is our national sport, and Don Cherry is the 'dean' of Canadian hockey. Notice how the traditional religious questions have been stood upon their head. Instead of talking about God who is the central theme of religion, the ultimate focus in this article is upon Don Cherry, the central figure of Canadian hockey. And instead of asking how God would judge those who play a particular style of hockey, the question is how hockey will judge those who believe in a particular kind of God. In other words, MMNs that represent famous people are shaping the TMN of a concept of God rather than vice versa. This inversion of influence will occur naturally when MMNs that represent famous people are used to emotionally buttress words about God.

Misusing Teacher Order-within-Complexity

We saw how emotional *experiences* and *events* can be used to inflate Teacher words about God. We then looked at using *people* with emotional status to inflate religious speech. These two methods use Mercy feelings to make Teacher words feel more general. We will now look at two methods that create Teacher emotions but then use them inappropriately. The first method places humans within an intimidating structure of order-within-complexity, while the second method takes advantage of the order-within-complexity of mass media.

Intimidating organization: The most extreme modern example of intimidating organization is provided by the Arirang Games put on by North Korea. An article from the Guardian newspaper written during the era of Kim Jong-il describes the grandiose scale of these productions.

> Arirang, however, is part of a propaganda offensive on a scale that would make a big-spending Hollywood mogul envious. The stage is the 150,000-capacity May Day stadium in Pyongyang, and the cast is 100,000 strong. The performance is a technicolour mix of entertainment: a floorshow by 1,000 dancers; a military tattoo; a martial arts display; hordes of waving, smiling children; an aerial ballet by dancers on bungee ropes. The most breathtaking element of Arirang is the backdrop - a giant human mosaic that forms elaborate panoramas of megacities, slogans and cartoons. More than 30,000 children form a flip-card unit working so quickly that some pictures appear to be animated...But Arirang is more than that. As well as being technically astonishing - one foreign defence official said the military drills were the best he had seen - it is emotionally compelling (Watts, 2005).

I have suggested that a concept of God emerges when a general Teacher theory applies to personal identity. The *intimidating organization* places personal identity within external surroundings that *feel* like a concept of God. The Wikipedia article on *crowd psychology* says that "Crowd behavior is heavily influenced by the loss of responsibility of the individual and the impression of universality of behavior, both of which increase with the size of the crowd." In other words, when a person becomes a member of a crowd, then the *Mercy* feeling of being an individual will be replaced by the *Teacher* feeling of being part of a universal structure. This effect can be magnified by making the crowd larger, increasing the order-within-complexity of the crowd's behavior, adding to the sensory overload, blocking out the external world, or placing the crowd within an important location presided over by important people.

Intimidating organization places the individual in an environment that feels universal.

Imagine what it feels like to be one of 130,000 performers within the Arirang games. One is surrounded by a sea of fellow performers in the central arena of the country performing intricate maneuvers with incredible precision before a crowd of dignitaries. As the Nazis illustrated with the Nuremberg rallies, the Soviets with the Mayday Parade, and the Romans with the Coliseum, the mass choreographed event is very useful for encouraging the average citizen to deify the regime—and its leader.

As long as Teacher order-within-complexity extends to everything that is *currently* being sensed within the environment, it will feel as if the order-within-complexity is universal. In other words, as long as a person is physically immersed within an environment of massive order-within-complexity, it will feel like a concept of God. We saw this when looking at the tribal chieftain. He may only rule over the local valley, but as long as he rules over everything that can be seen and everyone that is present, he can claim to be the absolute ruler over the entire inhabited realm. This contrast between claim and reality can be seen in the Arirang games. Quoting further from the Guardian article,

> Even at the height of Soviet power, Moscow would have struggled to choreograph such a mass performance. The politics are surreal. The 'prosperous fatherland' reads one giant banner above a mosaic of ploughing tractors - no matter that almost all farmwork is done by hand because vehicles and fuel are in such short supply. 'Green revolution' reads another, over an image of bumper crops, despite the fact that the nation has not been able to feed a third of its people for a decade.

On the one hand, during the mass event, 130,000 people are performing in a manner that demonstrates *impeccable* order-within-complexity. On the other hand, outside of this event these same individuals are eking out a hand-to-mouth existence in a ramshackle economy characterized by a complete *absence* of order-within-complexity.

The Arirang games transcend the scale and precision of any mega-church (the Korean church mentioned in the example of modulated speech had a membership of 80,000, but only 3000 could fit in the sanctuary at once). However, these same cognitive mechanisms will have an impact, especially if one is explicitly talking about God. In the words of the mega-church study,

> The sine quo non of spirituality is an affective experience of a transcendence, which for megachurch members seems necessary for their participation in these churches. This outcome resonates throughout the interviews. Individuals de-

scribed the collective effervescence they experienced through worship and preaching in spiritual terms. Individuals discussed their experiences as being in contact with the divine, generally causing them to grow spiritually. For example, individuals described being in 'God's presence', 'falling in love with Jesus,' being 'transformed,' and feeling that 'the Holy Spirit was here' (Wellman, 2012, p. 19).

When the 'affective experience of a transcendence' is necessary for participation in a mega-church, then this indicates that the cognitive mechanism of intimidating organization is playing a major role, because individuals are experiencing a 'collective effervescence' that is being interpreted as 'being in contact with the divine'. This externally driven 'contact within the divine' provides the emotional context within which people are encouraged to say the 'prayer of salvation'.

> After the sermon, it is common to transition into a time of quieter music and reflection. However, this certainly does not imply that the intensity of emotion wanes – quite the opposite. Rather, the emotion which has been gathered and enhanced by the group experience is turned inward... After the pastor speaks, congregants are encouraged to meditate on his message, to allow the words to sink into their souls, and to open their hearts to change and transformation. This is often the opportunity for the pastor to make an 'alter [sic] call', encouraging congregants to commit their lives to Jesus and to accept him as their personal Lord and Savior. This decision involves coming forward to the front of the church and praying with one of the worship leaders (p.16).

Summarizing, the experience of attending a mega-church will naturally create the sensation of having an encounter with the divine, which will naturally cause audience members to ponder the question of their relationship with the divine, which can be addressed in a natural manner through the Christian prayer of salvation. All of this is occurring *within* the mind and is being guided by cognitive mechanisms. The problem is that not *enough* of it is occurring within the mind, because the external structure of an intimidating organization is substituting for an internal concept of God.

Educational theorists distinguish between *intrinsic* and *extrinsic* motivation. Intrinsic motivation comes from within as mental networks drive motivation guided by an internal grid of skill and knowledge. Extrinsic motivation comes from without as mental networks are formed by emotional experiences and guided by the environment. We saw in the previous quote that 'the emotion which has been gathered and enhanced by the group experience is turned inward' and that listeners are encouraged 'to allow the words to sink into their souls'. In other words, the internal MMNs of personal identity are being transformed by the Teacher emotions generated by an *external* intimidating organization. In contrast, I suggest that the goal of personal transformation is to have the internal MMNs of personal identity be transformed by the *internal* TMN of a general understanding. The problem with using *external* Teacher structure to promote personal transformation is that it is *temporary*, *unstable*, and *arbitrary*. It is temporary because the structure is being provided by the environment. When a person leaves this environment, then the Teacher feeling of encountering God will fade. It is unstable because changing this environment will alter mental content. It is arbitrary because any content can be imposed upon the mind by setting up the appropriate environment.

It is possible to transform this extrinsic motivation into intrinsic motivation; however, this usually requires temporarily *leaving* the environment that is providing the extrinsic motivation. Thus, the solution is not to abandon intimidating organization, but rather to use the organization to teach understanding and then encourage individuals to step out on their own until they are internally motivated by this understanding.

Stated more generally, it appears that the mind will naturally follow the easiest path. This means that a person will only develop intrinsic motivation if forced to do so by the absence of extrinsic motivation.

The mind will naturally follow the easiest path.

One sees these same cognitive mechanisms in the Biblical story of the tower of Babel.

> Now the whole earth used the same language and the same words. It came about as they journeyed east, that they found a plain in the land of Shinar and settled there. They said to one another, "Come, let us make bricks and burn them thoroughly." And they used brick for stone, and they used tar for mortar. They said, "Come, let us build for ourselves a city, and a tower whose top will reach into heaven, and let us make for ourselves a name, otherwise we will be scattered abroad over the face of the whole earth." The Lord came down to see the city and the tower which the sons of men had built. The Lord said, "Behold, they are one people, and they all have the same language. And this is what they began to do, and now nothing which they purpose to do will be impossible for them. Come, let Us go down and there confuse their language, so that they will not understand one another's speech." So the Lord scattered them abroad from there over the face of the whole earth; and they stopped building the city (Gen. 11: 1-8).

Analyzing this story cognitively, everyone on earth is linked linguistically by the general Teacher theory of a common language. They decide that they will cooperate by living within the Teacher order-within-complexity of a city dominated by the intimidating structure of a tower, so that they can view themselves from the Teacher perspective of a corporate name rather than the Mercy perspective of individuals, and they recognize that this corporate plan has religious connotations. This corporate structure attracts the attention of God, who steps in to halt the construction of this external divine-like environment.

Physically speaking, it makes no sense that God would feel threatened by a pile of mud bricks. Cognitively speaking, though, such an act of total cooperation could leave cognitive development stillborn at an early stage. I suggested earlier that the development of

Teacher thought can be compared to the growth of civilization. During the first stage of Teacher overgeneralization, each local chieftain views himself as ruler over the entire world because each tribe knows nothing about the outside world. The second stage of limited domain begins when members of one tribe encounter other tribes, forcing the various chieftains to recognize that they only rule over a small portion of the entire world. The third stage then builds Teacher order-within-complexity through international cooperation between the various groups. If the entire population of the world lived in a single city under a single chieftain then Teacher thought would not move to the second stage because there would be no other groups to encounter. The local chieftain would actually be ruler over the entire inhabited world. Fragmented language forces societal development to advance to the second stage, and the only way to rebuild Teacher order-within-complexity is by translating between the various languages and cultures. Thus, the story of Babel appears to encapsulate significant cognitive principles. Modern research refers to this sort of story as a *myth*.

Mass media: Suppose that I sit in a chair, pick up a cup of coffee, and take a sip. That is a specific Mercy experience that has no Teacher generality. But suppose that the specific experience of me drinking coffee is broadcast on national television. This specific experience will then acquire Teacher generality, not because it is general, but rather because it has been *replicated*. The image of me with my cup of coffee has appeared on millions of television screens. However, this is not a case of true Teacher generality, because there has been no Perceiver categorizing or Teacher simplifying. Instead, the specific Mercy experience has been *copied* millions of times.

In contrast, the *medium* that delivers this message does possess true order-within-complexity. Think, for instance, of the infrastructure that is required to deliver a television signal into every home. Television studios must be constructed, transmission towers erected, episodes recorded, television sets manufactured, bought, and delivered. Going further, if the signal is delivered by cable, then millions of kilometers of coaxial cable must be laid, connecting each and every home with a central location. A similar principle applies to print media. The magazine or newspaper that is placed in every home may be identical, but the production, printing, and distribution systems exhibit extensive Teacher order-within-complexity.

> Mass media uses technical infrastructure to make a message feel more universal.

Using the words of Marshall McLuhan, the medium then becomes the message. The medium has Teacher order-within-complexity, but this structure is provided by *technology*. This structure will only generate Teacher emotions in those who *understand* technology. And the structure will probably lack *Mercy* emotions because technology is based in science, which is objective. The missing Mercy emotions will then be *added* by the message. Think, for instance, of soap operas delivered by satellite. A soap opera is full of Mercy pathos and the typical web of relationships being portrayed expresses Teacher disorder rather than order. Thus, a message characterized by Mercy emotions and Teacher chaos is delivered by a medium with great Teacher order and no Mercy emotions. However, the viewer will feel that the message has Teacher universality because John is watching the program in his house and Joan is viewing it in her apartment, together with millions of other viewers, each in their own personal homes. The result is a form of Teacher universality that applies to personal identity, making it possible for mass media to acquire religious overtones. But it is the television sets and the cable network that contain the Teacher order-within-complexity. The message itself is simply being cloned. The same exact Mercy image is being shown on every television screen. Thus, the mind is being fooled into thinking that the replicated message has Teacher universality.

Not every television program is a soap opera. However, the trend in television programming tends to be for all programs to become more like soap operas. For example, on cable television, the sci-fi channel turned into the Syfy channel that expanded its lineup to include the paranormal, wrestling, and horror. Similarly, the History Channel, which began by broadcasting documentaries and historical fiction, now fills its schedule with reality television and broadcasts programs on UFOs and aliens. One can see a similar progression in the news channels, with short news clips replacing in-depth analyses, and the most insightful coverage often coming from comedy shows rather than official news programs.

In addition, when one experience is being replicated millions of times, then it is possible to fill this single experience with drama and make it much more exciting than real life. For instance, instead of drinking a cup of coffee at the kitchen table, why not sip a cup of Turkish coffee in Istanbul, or even better have the coffee served by a genie in the court of the Sultan in the ancient city of Baghdad. This is done when making a movie. Because the same specific Mercy experience will be shown to many viewers, millions of dollars can be spent on this single experience, making it appear that it occurs in medieval Baghdad or in some other exotic location or time.

Summarizing, the medium contains order-within-complexity. But nobody focuses upon the medium, because technology contains no explicit emotions. Instead, the focus is upon the message, because the message is emotional. However, the message feels general because it is being replicated by the technology, and the money that is received from millions of viewers makes it possible to make the message more exciting. Thus, the message will acquire *implicit* Teacher emotion. As technology develops, the growing order-within-complexity of the medium will increase this implicit Teacher emotion. In contrast, the message will become driven increasingly by *explicit* Mercy emotions. Programs will tend to become 'dumbed down' and more sensational. Being on TV or getting a book published will be regarded as more significant than *what* one shares on TV or says in a book. Going further, those who are driven by strong MMNs will attempt to control the mass media so that their MMNs can be magnified and validated. Those who *possess* money and power will try to *buy* the media, so that they can control which MMNs are broadcast to the masses, and they will buy up competing mass media in order to silence opposing voices. Those who *lack* money and power will try to get *on* the media. One sees this, for instance, on some talk shows, where all manner of childish behavior is brought 'out of the closet' and defiantly proclaimed. Saying this more generally, special interest groups will vie for control of mass media. All of these factors demonstrate that mass media is being driven by MMNs that are being emotionally inflated by technology.

We have looked specifically at the example of television, but I suggest that similar statements could be made about other forms of mass media, such as books, newspapers, magazines, and movies. I should also mention that the emergence of mass media and the way in which it replaces critical thinking with the broadcasting of opinion is a major aspect of Habermas' *third* stage of societal development, which has not been discussed in this book.

The technological side of this problem can be *minimized* by increasing the variety of channels, books, magazines, and newspapers, or *solved* by replacing the one-to-many infrastructure with one that is many-to-many. One sees this in the Internet, which makes it possible for *anyone* to communicate with *anyone*. Like mass media, the technological infrastructure of the Internet contains great Teacher order-within-complexity. But, unlike mass media, a simple Google search will demonstrate the mind-boggling order-within-complexity present within the *message* of the Internet. Unfortunately, the Internet is also subject to the same underlying MMNs that are present in mass media. Even though it is *possible* to visit anyone on the Internet, most people spend most of their time visiting a few well-known websites, effectively returning to the one-to-many architecture of broadcasting. Those who lack money and power often view the Internet as a forum for *spreading* their MMNs, those who have money and power are attempting to control the Internet in order to *impose* their MMNs, while too many people spend too much time *satisfying* their MMNs with cat videos and pornography.

Unfortunately, because the Internet makes it *possible* for everyone to become a source of information, it is also possible for everyone to become an *inadvertent* source of information. *Meta-data* is a superb source of Teacher order-within-complexity. If one collects information on the browsing habits of many visitors, organizes this information into Perceiver categories, and then uses Teacher thought to look for simple patterns, one can come up with valuable understanding. Meta-data can also be used to spy upon personal identity, because if one correlates the meta-data that is gathered on some individual, one can find out many personal details about that individual. For instance, in one case a department store learned that a teenage girl was pregnant before her father found out (Hill, 2012).

And in the same way that the rich and powerful try to buy up mass media so that they can be the sole source of MMNs, so the same power groups are now trying to ensure that they are the sole beneficiaries of meta-data. As the revelations of Edward Snowden have made clear, they want to know everything about everyone else, but they do not want anyone else to know anything about them.

Before we continue, let us step back to look at the religious implications of mass media. First, it appears that for many individuals, mass media have become the primary source of absolute truth, supplanting the role previously occupied by church and school. We joke about people thinking that 'If it is on television, then it must be true' or 'If it is written in the newspaper, then it must be right'. However, many people do regard certain programs and publications as sources of Truth, while rejecting other programs and publications as sources of Error. This labeling of truth and error occurs whenever Perceiver thought is overwhelmed by Mercy emotions, but mass media intensify these conclusions, magnifying truth into gospel truth and error into heinous error.

Second, the universal surveillance that the Internet makes possible is in the process of creating a very potent concept of God. In the past, the child was often told that 'God sees and judges everything you do'. Now, everyone knows that 'The government sees and judges everything you do'.

In the same way that the scientist becomes emotionally trapped by the Teacher emotions of his paradigm, so the average citizen seems strangely unwilling to struggle against the influence of mass media. Academics such as Norman Fairclough have turned this juxtaposition of personal MMNs enabled by universal infrastructure into a general theory of existence, transforming this deception of Teacher thought into an official theory within Teacher thought. This same attitude of passive resignation appears to be present with the Internet. When the average person is told about the extent of government surveillance, he shrugs his shoulders and responds that 'I have nothing to hide', not realizing that the situation always ends up rather bad for the individual citizen when a government takes on the role of God.

We have examined four ways in which a concept of God can be formed within Teacher thought through mental deception. *Emotionally inflated speech* makes words about God feel universal by associating them with emotional Mercy experiences, while *testimony* uses the emotional status of important people to add feelings to the words. In both cases Mercy emotions are being used to give the impression of Teacher generality. *Intimidating organization* places people within a physical structure that exhibits order-within-complexity, leading to the feeling of being a cog in a vast machine, and this external 'Teacher general theory that applies to personal identity' will naturally cause a concept of God to form within the mind. Finally, *mass media* uses the Teacher order-within-complexity of technology to make specific Mercy experiences feel more general.

When people are functioning at the level of Piaget's concrete operational stage, then it may be necessary to use these emotional tricks to help them make the transition to Piaget's formal operational stage. The danger arises when Teacher understanding is lacking or people are unwilling to understand, because then these inadequate concepts of God will be regarded as genuine.

Fooling Personal Identity

Let us turn our attention now to three ways in which Teacher thought can deceive Mercy thought. In each case, personal identity in Mercy thought identifies with some general structure in Teacher thought of which it is not a legitimate member. One could think of this as receiving a fake passport. The person holding the passport may believe that he is the citizen of some country, but in fact the document is invalid.

Saying this another way, the four emotional tricks that we have just examined lead to errors in the grand explanation, while the three ways that we will now discuss lead to mistaken conclusions about my place within this grand explanation.

The group: Professional sports provide a good illustration of this cognitive error. The saying goes that "Football is 22 people in the field who need rest and 22,000 people in the stands who need exercise." But when the game is over then these 22,000 people who did nothing except sit, watch, and cheer will proclaim loudly that 'We won!' In other words, the sports fan is carrying a 'fake passport'. He believes himself to be a member of the winning team when in fact he is merely a bystander.

Looking at this more technically, the cognitive error lies in jumping from general to specific by assuming that qualities that apply to the group as a whole also apply to every person within that group. For instance, one could regard both football players and football fans as members of a common group. But only some of the members of this group—the players—receive fame and fortune. This mental leap occurs because Mercy thought is interpreting Teacher emotions of generality as Mercy feelings of personal significance. For instance, if I was part of the order-within-complexity of 22,000 spectators responding in coordinated fashion to the antics of 22 football players, then the resulting Teacher emotion will give Mercy identity the feeling that something special happened to *me*. Hence the leap from general to specific.

One sees this same cognitive error in the theory of evolution. Evolution says that the species is evolving, that a *group* of organisms is gaining increasing order-within-complexity. But this principle does not apply to every organism within the species, because the mutations that produce change in species are rare, and most of these mutations are harmful. Thus, as far as some specific individual organism is concerned, evolution is not a theory of inevitable progress. Rather, evolution says that the theory probably does not apply to that individual, and if it does then it will probably lead to greater disorder. Putting this more personally, the evolutionary theorist will say that *we* are evolving and regard personal identity as part of this great process of ever-increasing Teacher order. But even if we *are* evolving, this does not prove that *I* am evolving.

> Mercy thought will interpret Teacher emotions in personal terms.

This is an important distinction because the mental leap from 'we' to 'I' helps to turn the theory of evolution into the mental concept of the God of Nature, and the person who makes this mental leap derives emotional comfort from this implicit concept of God, because he assumes that the positive Teacher feeling of growing order-within-complexity applies to me in Mercy thought. But it does not. Instead, the theory of evolution is particularly brutal to the individual. Individuals compete, they die, they are replaced by other individuals who are more 'fit to survive', and they have to live with harmful mutations or incomplete developments.

Turning now to a religious example, I suggest that this mental leap from group to individual is also common in Judaism. One of the core tenets of Judaism is that the Jews are a 'chosen nation', a special group of people chosen by God. And the history of the Jewish people is sufficiently unusual to make this a plausible assertion.

However, saying that God has chosen a *group* of people is quite different than saying that God has chosen every *individual* within that group. On the contrary, Jewish scriptures repeatedly state that God's salvation applies to a 'faithful remnant' of individuals within this group. Quoting from the Jewish Virtual Library, *Remnant of Israel* is

> a term denoting the belief that the future of Israel would be assured by the faithful remnant surviving the calamities that would befall the people as a result of their departing from the way of God. On the one hand the prophets foretold the forthcoming exile and destruction of Israel, and on the other they held forth the hope and promise of its survival and eternity. The doctrine of the Surviving Remnant resolved this contradiction. The doctrine is referred to by most of the prophets. Thus Micah (2:12) states, "I will surely gather the remnant of Israel"; Jeremiah (23:3) "and I will gather the remnant of my flock out of all the countries whither I have driven them and will bring them back to their folds, and they shall be fruitful and multiply." Joel promises, "For in Mount Zion and in Jerusalem there shall be those that escape and among the remnant those whom the Lord shall call" (3:5), and the first half of the verse is repeated almost literally by Obadiah (v. 17). It is in Isaiah, however, that the doctrine is found in its most developed form which greatly affected Israel's thoughts about the future (Encyclopaedia Judaica).

Bringing this point home rather starkly, the Jewish Virtual Library adds, "After World War II the phrase the 'remnant which survives' (she'erit ha-peletah) was applied to the survivors of the Holocaust." This demonstrates that progress which applies to the group can have devastating consequences for most of the individuals within that group. As Reb Tevye says to God in *Fiddler on the Roof*, "I know, I know. We are Your chosen people. But, once in a while, can't You choose someone else?"

The legacy: The cognitive error here lies in assuming that my place in the grand explanation does not require my presence. Using an analogy, suppose that a check for a thousand dollars is placed in my mailbox every week. If I move to another location, then even if the amount on the check is raised to a million dollars, it is still meaningless to me because I no longer receive the check. Similarly, a person may work hard to leave a legacy behind after he dies. But if death is followed by personal existence in some 'other location' then leaving behind a physical legacy becomes meaningless *to me*. By the same token, if death is the end of personal existence, then the very concept of a legacy is absurd, because I am acting as if I still belong to a group of which I am no longer a member. Examples of this cognitive fallacy are unfortunately rather easy to find, such as the warrior who wants to die a heroic death, the scientist who wants to have some theory named after him, or even the parent who devotes his life to his children. We shall see later that there is a legitimate cognitive reason for altruistic activity, but the basic fact still remains that the dead warrior is no longer a part of his tribe, the dead scientist is no longer a member of academia, and the dead parent has ceased to be a member of the family.

It is good to leave a legacy; more people should be motivated to do so. But a legacy is not a substitute for personal existence. Suppose someone said, "I am going to kill you. But that is fine because I will leave a picture of you on everyone's desk so they can remember you and think fondly of you." The individual who tries to 'achieve immortality' by 'living on in the minds of others' is following the same logic. If most social interaction occurs within people's minds, then it is possible to 'live on in the minds of others'. However, what is continuing to exist is the mental network that represents a person and not the actual person. Even if everyone remembers me after I die, I am still dead.

Misquoting Monty Python, the person "'is no more! He has ceased to be! 'E's expired and gone to meet 'is maker! 'E's a stiff! Bereft of life, 'e rests in peace! If you hadn't nailed 'im to the perch 'e'd be pushing up the daisies! 'Is metabolic processes are now 'istory! 'E's off the twig! 'E's kicked the bucket, 'e's shuffled off 'is mortal coil, run down the curtain and joined the bleedin' choir invisibile!! THIS IS AN EX-" PERSON!! This may be funny when describing dead parrots but it is no laughing matter when personal identity is at stake.

> The legacy assumes my place in the grand explanation does not need my presence.

That brings us back to the question of life-after-death. The scientist practicing scientific methodology rightly accuses religious attitude of placing one's eternal fate in the MMN of some religious source, but I suggest that the scientist is making an equally great emotional leap by jumping from the TMNs of scientific theory to the specific experiences of personal identity. In both cases, one is deriving personal emotional comfort through faulty reasoning.

This book is attempting to follow a third alternative. Suppose that someone promises to give me a new car. I could follow the 'religious' option and drool over pictures of cars, or I could follow the 'scientific' option and debate the existence of cars. I suggest that both of these approaches miss one significant factor. If I do not have a driver's license, then even if cars exist, and even if someone gives me a car, cars do not exist *for me. I* will not be able to drive a car. Similarly, if one wishes to investigate the question of continuing human existence in an intelligent manner, then I suggest that it is imperative to 'get a driver's license' by understanding what it means to exist as a human. Saying this another way, if one wishes to come up with a grand explanation and determine one's place within this grand explanation, then it makes sense to begin by understanding how the mind comes up with grand explanations and how these grand explanations mentally interact with personal identity. That is because doing a good job requires good tools. Good tools may not guarantee success, but poor tools will probably lead to failure.

The job: The cognitive fallacy here is to assume that a Teacher structure that applies to the periphery of personal identity also applies to core MMNs of identity. For instance, I started playing violin when I was three years old. When I play, I try to create a musical beauty that is an expression of my personal identity. When I played in orchestras, I found it interesting to compare the beauty and skill that other musicians exhibited through their musical instruments with the words and behavior that these musicians exhibited off the stage in normal life. I noticed that the musician who makes beautiful music is not necessarily a beautiful person; the Teacher structure of personal elegance and beauty can apply to a person's music without applying to the core of identity.

> The job assumes that peripheral professionalism applies to personal identity.

Steven Ortiz, a professor of sociology at Oregon State University, describes the juxtaposition between job and family that often occurs in the marriage of the professional athlete. Cognitively speaking, mental networks involving spouse, family, and personal identity are more fundamental than mental networks involving hitting, throwing, and kicking round objects within some playing field. However, wives

> see their role in this kind of marriage as a supportive role. They would feel guilty if they were to question it. In career-dominated marriages, it's the husband's career that comes first. There is an implicit unspoken agreement that the wife will focus on the family and childrearing, and make it possible for him to focus on his career almost exclusively. These characteristics exist in other career-dominated marriages with politicians, corporate executives, military servicemen, physicians, and so on (Ma, 2007).

But core mental networks will drive the mind, even when they are regarded as secondary or ignored.

> When a wife travels with her husband and the team, there is a code of conduct that you're supposed to follow. What you see on the road is not discussed when you're off the road. When you're traveling with the team, you don't go into the hotel bar where the team is staying. I naively used to think this was because the guys are hanging out, bonding. And the wives said no, it's because that's where many of the married players meet other women, and they don't want the families or the wives to observe this kind of activity.

One of the cardinal rules is to never do anything in public that would negatively reflect the husband or the team organization that he represents — which is much like the wife of a politician or clergy person.

Stated crudely, athletes are being driven by childish MMNs of sexual gratification, and it is common for athletes to bed other women when they are traveling. When playing a game, the professional athlete is an expert at going beyond mere impulse in order to function within a grid of knowledge, skill, and understanding. However, knowledge and understanding are lacking and impulse rules in the far more emotional realm of sexuality. The wife exhibits a similar cognitive error by protecting the professionalism of the game while ignoring her husband's peccadilloes.

The underlying problem is that the athlete grew up in an environment that focused upon job excellence while ignoring personal excellence. Ortiz explains that

> Spoiled-athlete syndrome begins early in sports socialization. From the time they could be picked out of a lineup because of their exceptional athletic ability, they've been pampered and catered to by coaches, classmates, teammates, family members and partners. As they get older, this becomes a pattern. Because they're spoiled, they feel they aren't accountable for their behaviors off the field. They're so used to people looking the other way.

Turning now to the big picture, scientific methodology indirectly *encourages* these three cognitive errors. When scientific progress is tested through peer review, then the *group* of the scientific community takes precedence over the individual. When the focus is upon objective, empirical research, then the *job*, with its measurable objective outcomes, will be regarded as more important than personal life and family relationship. And when objective facts are used to build Teacher understanding, then personal identity will take vicarious pleasure in the 'advancement of knowledge' and the 'building of some kingdom' leading to the faulty thinking of the *legacy*. Facts do need to be checked with fellow experts, but even more basic than establishing the facts is being able to handle the facts, and that is an ability that a person can only acquire as an individual. Doing a good job is important, but that needs to be an expression of being a good person, because rotten people will eventually do rotten jobs. And it is deeply meaningful to play a role in furthering a grand explanation, but it is far more important for me to have a continuing role within this grand explanation.

In addition, childish identity naturally *practices* these three cognitive errors. Childish identity has not individuated but rather is composed of a juxtaposed collection of mental networks representing authority figures and cultural experiences, leading naturally to a focus upon the group rather than the individual, and allowing childish identity to identify with the group, the job, or the legacy. In other words, what is missing is *personal honesty*. In simple terms, childish identity has not yet been *defined*. The preoperational mind is driven by MMNs and lacks Perceiver thought. Thus, Perceiver thought is unable to assert facts about the MMNs of personal identity.

Sometimes this expresses itself as *deliberate* self-deception. For instance, the article on cheating athletes begins by recounting that

> During a 2003 news conference, Los Angeles Lakers guard Kobe Bryant admitted to committing adultery with a Colorado teenager who accused him of sexual assault. Bryant's wife, Vanessa, leaped to his defense. 'He is a loving and kind husband and father,' she said. 'I will give him all the strength and support he needs... I will not let him face these accusations alone.' Her selfless stance baffled viewers (though the $4 million rock that soon appeared on her hand helped explain things).

In most cases, though, I suggest that one is dealing with a more fundamental problem, which is that core mental networks are being *assumed*. When core mental networks are assumed, then it will also be assumed that they will continue to exist. Thus, the person who is attempting to leave a legacy may think that he is dealing with the topic of death, but he is still thinking about death in a way that assumes that he will continue to exist. This is like running a computer program that simulates the destruction of the computer. The very fact that one is running a computer program assumes that the computer will not be destroyed. Core mental networks that are assumed will be viewed as invulnerable. The professional athlete is probably not deliberately trying to ruin his marriage. Instead, he is merely assuming that his marriage will survive the pressures of career. The best way to stop assuming mental networks is by acquiring an *alternative* set of mental networks. For instance, learning about one's own culture often requires traveling to another culture, and learning the grammar of another language makes it easier to learn the grammar of one's native tongue. In both cases, acquiring an alternative set of mental networks makes it possible to analyze the mental networks that were acquired in childhood through osmosis.

The next chapter will examine how personal honesty can be achieved, which will require looking at technical thought and incarnation.

❊ 8. Technical Thought and Incarnation

The word *incarnation* literally means 'embodied in flesh' and refers to the religious concept of God appearing in human form. Incarnation is quite different than mysticism.
Mysticism produces the feeling of being united with God, while incarnation describes a
person who is both God and man. Mysticism says that personal unity with God is
achieved by regarding the physical world as illusion, while incarnation says that God
took on human form within the physical world.

Even though incarnation is a well-known religious concept, it is *not* compatible with the
three religious attitudes of fervor, self-denial, and transcendence. *Fervor* reinforces religious belief by focusing upon holy items and holy experiences that are distinct from
daily existence, while incarnation believes that God lived within the 'secular realm' of
daily existence. Self-denial believes that following God means denying personal, physical
existence, but incarnation teaches that God exhibited himself within personal, physical
existence. Transcendence regards the nature of God as unknowable to normal rational
human thought. However, incarnation is the belief that the essential nature of God can
be expressed in the form of a person who exhibits normal rational human thought.

Incarnation is one of the most basic doctrines of Christianity, because Christianity was
founded by Jesus, who claimed to be both God and man. Because the idea of incarnation is fundamentally incompatible with religious attitude, it is usually taught in Christian
circles as blind dogma, a doctrine of Christianity that must be believed but cannot be
understood. For instance, the Catholic Encyclopedia says that "The Incarnation is the
mystery and the dogma of the Word made Flesh." Similarly, Orthodox Christianity
teaches an amalgam of mysticism and incarnation, in which incarnation is viewed as the
doorway to mystical union with God.

In contrast, when I was using the theory of mental symmetry to analyze technical rational thought, I discovered that the mind *naturally* creates a concept of incarnation that
corresponds in detail to the Christian 'dogma' of incarnation. In other words, far from
being a mysterious dogma, it appears that the doctrine of incarnation is an expression of
the most rational aspect of human thought, and one can find examples of incarnation in
the thinking of science, logic, and mathematics. This means that we will have to take a
detour away from our discussion of religion in order to explain technical thought. Unfortunately, the explanation for technical thought is itself somewhat technical. I will try
to illustrate this explanation with a number of examples, but because these examples are

drawn from the realm of technical thought, they too will be somewhat technical. My apologies.

I mentioned previously that the mind can use *mental networks*, *normal thought*, and *technical thought*. Because mental networks play such a central role in religion, we began this book by discussing mental networks. Normal thought describes the way in which the seven cognitive modules typically interact. We have looked at the interaction between Perceiver and Mercy, between Mercy and Teacher, and between Teacher and Perceiver. A later chapter will add Server thought to this mixture. Exhorter, Contributor, and Facilitator thought are also a part of normal thought, but they play a primary role when *using* the mind whereas the emphasis of this book is upon *programming* the mind.

> Mercy and Teacher thought drive mental networks.
> Contributor thought controls technical thought.
> Normal thought involves the cooperation of all seven cognitive modules.

MMNs are an expression of *Mercy* thought. TMNs express *Teacher* thought. Technical thought emerges when *Contributor* thought takes control of the mind. One can see from the diagram of mental symmetry that Contributor connects Perceiver and Server. In technical thought, Contributor thought restricts the mind to some limited 'playing field' composed of a well-defined collection of Perceiver facts and Server sequences. *Games* provide an illustration of technical thought. For example, in the game of chess the playing field is provided by the chessboard. Each player starts with the Perceiver objects of eight pawns and eight other pieces, and each piece is permitted to perform certain Server sequences: A bishop can only move diagonally; a rook can only move vertically or horizontally, and so on.

Technical Thought

Looking at this more technically, technical thought has the following characteristics: First, a limited set of Perceiver facts are used. For example, a checker piece cannot be used in the game of chess. Second, a limited set of Server sequences are permitted. For instance, in a game of chess, a pawn may move one step forwards but it may not move backwards. Third, total certainty is required. In chess, for example, there is no doubt over which pieces are permitted, the position of these pieces, and which actions are allowed. Fourth, there is a limited playing field. In chess, the playing field is the chess board. Fifth, there is a goal or bottom line. The goal in chess is to capture the king.

These five characteristics all relate to aspects of Contributor thought. Contributor thought does not 'live' in the middle of Perceiver or Server processing but rather accesses Perceiver and Server memories from a *distance*. Using an analogy, Perceiver and Server thought are like workshops that construct facts and sequences. Contributor thought goes to these workshops and *takes out* specific facts and sequences. Contributor thought then uses these facts and sequences, treating them as if they have been *sufficiently well made.* Contributor thought is able to *concentrate* upon a certain context or plan, leading to the limited playing field. Contributor thought is driven by Exhorter energy, which is attracted to *strong emotions*, leading to the goal or bottom line. Finally, Contributor thought carries out a plan by *choosing* between different alternatives.

I have said that technical thought emerges when Contributor thought takes control of the mind. This does not mean that Contributor thought is shutting down the rest of the mind (though Contributor thought can also function in a manner that does shut down the mind). Rather, Contributor thought *coordinates* the activities of several different cognitive modules and permits them to function in a way that is consistent with Contributor thought.

One can illustrate the difference between normal thought and technical thought by comparing a trip across town with the same trip as described on a GPS navigator. First, this trip can be taken in many different ways. One could drive, walk, catch a ride, take a bus, or even go in a helicopter. The GPS system limits this to a set of menu choices, such as car, foot, or truck. More advanced GPS software will give more choices, but the 'technical thought' of the GPS system is always limited to a set of choices, while reality is open-ended. Second, the trip could follow a number of different routes. One could take a main road, side roads, or even walk across a field or drive through a parking lot. Again, the GPS system limits this to a collection of alternatives. A GPS system may consider alternate routes, but these routes all take place along existing highways. Third, real roads are not always passable. They may be blocked in winter, muddy during rain, or too narrow for trucks. In a GPS system, a road either exists or does not exist. It is possible to add details to this, such as recommending that a road not be used by trucks or in the winter, but these details will still be coached in terms of total certainty. A road may exist for cars but not for trucks or it may exist after a certain date in spring and cease to exist after a certain date in fall. Fourth, the advice from a GPS system is limited to the extent and details of the map. Real life, in contrast, extends beyond the map and contains more details than any map. Finally, the route in a GPS system is determined by the destination. It is possible to add waypoints, but one is still heading towards a certain goal. A real journey, in contrast, is open-ended. One may be heading to the shopping mall on the other side of town but decide en-route to stop at the library.

Both concrete and abstract thought are capable of functioning in a technical manner. Games are an example of *concrete* technical thought, as is traveling by GPS. The *company* is another illustration of concrete technical thought. A company provides a limited set of clearly defined products and services, guided by some bottom line. The restricted playing field of technical thought is seen in the limited liability of a company, and a company is supposed to keep careful records and follow established corporate rules.

Logic, math, grammar, science, and computer programming are all examples of *abstract* technical thought. We briefly referred to this kind of thinking when discussing Thomas Kuhn. Kuhn says that scientists usually practice what he calls 'normal science' and only use 'revolutionary science' when the existing paradigm falls apart and needs to be replaced by a new Teacher understanding. Kuhn's *normal science* corresponds with abstract technical thought, in which scientists 'solve problems' by using clearly defined Perceiver facts and Server sequences within the limited playing field of some paradigm. Kuhn's *revolutionary science* corresponds to normal abstract thought, which we analyzed when looking at the thinking of Einstein. Kuhn describes revolutionary science as a 'loosening of the rules of normal science.' This is an accurate statement, but I suggest that it regards the wrong kind of thinking as 'normal', because normal science may be normal for the scientist, but it does not describe normal thought for the average person. Normal thought involves the cooperation of all seven cognitive modules. It provides the *framework* that ties together mental networks, and it provides a semi-rigorous *starting point* for the rigorous thinking of technical thought. Technical thought, in contrast, emerges when Contributor thought *restricts* mental processing. Because technical thinking applies rigorous thought within a limited context, it brings *improvements* to *specific* areas. The modern conveniences that we enjoy, for instance, are the result of technical thought. However, when technical thinking is regarded as the norm, then personal existence tends to fragment into disconnected specializations that ignore core issues—as illustrated by modern Western society, a predicament from which postmodern thought is now attempting to recover.

Applying this to the topic of this book, I suggest that technical thought is not the best strategy for studying religion, for the simple reason that specialization does not lead to grand explanations. Saying this more philosophically, I suggest that it is a category mistake to use logic to try to prove or disprove the existence of God. That is because logic and proof are part of Kuhn's 'normal science' which works *within* a paradigm. Thus, trying to logically prove the existence of God places a *universal* being *within* some specific paradigm, which is like trying to prove the existence of dogs by thinking only about poodles. This does not mean that technical thought has no place when investigating the existence of God. It is possible to start by *assuming* the existence of a universal being and then use technical thought to see if this leads to a self-consistent, logical structure. But if one wishes to prove the existence of God, then I suggest that one must use normal thought with its analogies and patterns—and partial certainty. One can use normal thought to become *increasingly* certain that God exists, one can use technical thought to act and think *as if* God exists, one can become *emotionally driven* by the mental network of a concept of God, but I do not see how it is cognitively possible to prove with *total* certainty that God exists.

Thus, we see again that there is some truth to the statement that religion goes 'beyond logic'. However, those who make this statement generally assume that abandoning technical thought means embracing mental networks. Instead, I suggest that if one wishes to come up with a grand explanation, then one should use the form of thinking that ties the mind together, which is normal thought. Consistent with this, neurology has discovered that the highest form of human thought is not formal logic but rather analogy, which is carried out by the frontopolar region, the very front of the frontal cortex (Green, et al., 2010).

Applying these principles to the approach taken by this book, we have analyzed mental networks in extensive detail, but the underlying assumption has been that mental networks function within the mental grid of something larger. The methodology used by this book will not satisfy a logician, because we are continually jumping from one topic to another guided by analogies and patterns, but this analogical thinking is semi-rigorous, because we are using a limited set of carefully defined analogies guided by the cognitive model of mental symmetry. This distinction can be seen in a fascinating video series on the history of science and invention produced by James Burke for the BBC and The Learning Channel entitled *Connections,* in which he examines many of the connections behind the development of science and technology. This series is worth watching, but it also feels *dis*-connected, because a collection of seemingly random connections is being portrayed in a manner that lacks underlying structure. In contrast, we are attempting to portray a connected set of connections, tied together by the underlying structure of a cognitive model.

Continuing with our analysis of technical thought, abstract technical thought and concrete technical thought are *similar* because in both cases Contributor thought is taking control of the mind. However, the mental processing that is done by Contributor thought is quite *different.* In simplest terms, nouns and verbs switch places. What was dynamic becomes static, while what was static becomes dynamic. Using the language of physics, there is a duality between wave and particle. The concrete world is composed of Perceiver objects, such as cars, apples, and stores. Concrete thought moves from one object to another by carrying out Server sequences of actions, such as getting into a car to drive to the store to buy apples. The abstract world, in contrast, is *composed* of Server sequences, such as sequences of letters and words. In concrete thought, Server sequences are the *dynamic* elements, the verbs that lead from one static object to another. In abstract thought, Server sequences are the *static* elements, the 'building blocks' that are combined to build understanding. In concrete thought, Perceiver truth is something *static*, a label of confidence that is applied to objects. In abstract thought, Perceiver truth is something dynamic that is *constructed.* Concrete thought *believes* in facts; abstract thought *proves* that facts are true.

One can illustrate this distinction with the *machine*, which is an object that can be approached using either concrete thought or abstract thought. For instance, a car is used to move from one location to another. This is an example of concrete thought, in which Server actions are used to reach Mercy goals. But a car mechanic does not view a car as a tool for moving from one concrete location to another. Instead, the mechanic sees the car as a set of Server functions that combine to generate Teacher order-within-complexity. An engine, for instance, is a device-that-spins-a-crankshaft. A wheel is something-round-that-goes-in-circles. Each element of the car is defined by its Server function—what it *does*. Perceiver thought is then used to connect these various working parts. The crankshaft of the engine is connected to the driveshaft; the driveshaft is connected to the differential; the differential is connected to the wheel. When all the parts of a machine are assembled, then these parts function together in a harmonious manner to produce order-within-complexity. The driver of a car wants to know where the car is going. That is a *Mercy* question involving concrete thought. The mechanic wants to know how well the parts of the car are functioning together. That is a *Teacher* question involving abstract thought. Either concrete or abstract thought can be used to analyze the *same* object. We will see in a few paragraphs that this *alternate* view of the *same* item lies at the heart of the concept of *incarnation*. (I should mention in passing that the philosopher Heidegger attempted to redefine concrete thought in terms of Server functions rather than Perceiver objects.)

> Concrete technical thought is based in cause-and-effect.
> Abstract technical thought is based in precise meaning.

Abstract technical thought differs from concrete technical thought in two other major ways. First, the *content* is different. In concrete thought, Server *actions* are applied to Perceiver *objects*. When Contributor combines Perceiver with Server, then this leads to a sense of *cause-and-effect*. In abstract thought, Server sequences of words and symbols are given Perceiver meanings. When Contributor combines Perceiver with Server, then this leads to a sense of *precise meaning*, and one of the primary requirements for entering abstract technical thought is to define terms precisely.

Willard Quine describes this defining of terms in *The Web of Belief.*

> When philosophers give a precise sense to what was formerly a fuzzy term or concept it is called explication of that term or concept. Successful explications have been found for the concepts of deduction, probability, and computability, to name just three. It is no wonder that philosophers seek explications; for explications are steps toward clarity (Quine, 1978).

When my brother was studying biographies, he noticed that Contributor persons tend to fall into the two major categories of what he called the *practical* Contributor person who emphasizes concrete technical thought and the *intellectual* Contributor person who emphasizes abstract technical thought. This emphasis upon *either* abstract *or* concrete technical thought can be so pronounced that the intellectual Contributor person can turn into an 'absent minded professor' who lacks manual coordination, while the practical Contributor person may have a stunted theoretical understanding that is limited to a repertoire of slogans and parables.

These two forms of Contributor thought are distinct for the simple reason that words are separate from actions. This needs to be repeated. I suggest that one of the primary reasons for the distinction between concrete thought and abstract thought is that concrete thought uses *actions* to move through the physical world, while abstract thought uses *words* to generate meanings that are independent of the current physical environment. Saying this another way, speech makes abstract thought possible. As we saw in the example of the machine, not all abstract thought involves speech, but words appear to provide the starting point for abstract thought and they provide the basic building blocks for Teacher thought.

There is no inherent relationship between words and actions. Instead, the connection between words and actions is largely arbitrary. For instance, the words *fahren, conduire,* and *drive* all refer to the same action, but in different languages. Because abstract technical thought is based in words that are inherently disconnected from the actions of concrete technical thought, these two forms of Contributor-controlled thought will only become unified if words become connected with actions. Using Christian language, words become connected to actions when 'the word becomes flesh'. This integration of 'word' and 'flesh' distinguishes science from mathematics. Mathematics inhabits the realm of words, symbols, and equations. Science, in contrast, 'fleshes out' the words of mathematics with physical sequences. For instance, '$E = mv^2/2 + mgh$' is an abstract sequence of mathematical symbols. But it also describes the concrete path of any object that is thrown through the air.

The second primary difference between concrete technical thought and abstract technical thought is that the *motivation* is different. The aim of *concrete* technical thought is to improve some specific object, experience, or person in Mercy thought. This provides the bottom line for business or the goal for games. For instance, this may be buying a car, using the car to drive to the store, capturing the king in a game of chess, building some widget, improving a widget, or making money by selling widgets. Concrete technical thought differs from normal concrete thought in the technical way in which the goal is achieved. For instance, it is possible to buy a car by using normal thought to compare several available models and then choose one that is reasonably priced. Technical thought turns this into a rigorous process through steps such as listing the desired features, noting carefully the pros and cons of each model, and comparing fuel economies and repair costs. I experienced a similar transition when the international school in which I was teaching in Korea became WASC certified. While some of the certification process focused upon meeting educational standards, most of the time was spent carefully defining and documenting what we were already doing, effectively turning normal thought into technical thought.

The aim of *abstract* technical thought is to improve the Teacher order-within-complexity of some theory, process, or structure. For example, the trigonometric expression $(sin^2x - tan^2x)/(tan^2xsin^2x)$ is merely a complicated way of writing the number '-1'. For those want the technical details, divide top and bottom by tan^2x. Recognize that $sin^2x/tan^2x = cos^2x$. Because $sin^2x + cos^2x = 1$, $cos^2x - 1 = -sin^2x$. Finally, cancel the sin^2x in the numerator with the sin^2x in the denominator. I mention these details because they illustrate how abstract technical thought functions. Concrete thought moves from one *Per-*

ceiver location to another. In contrast, abstract thought 'moves' from one *Server* sequence to another. The first 'movement' in this example is from the initial sequence of $(\sin^2 x - \tan^2 x)/(\tan^2 x \sin^2 x)$ to $(\sin^2 x/\tan^2 x - 1)/(\sin^2 x)$, which is followed by the sequence $(\cos^2 x - 1)/(\sin^2 x)$, which then transforms into $-\sin^2 x/\sin^2 x$. The movement occurs by replacing elements of the Server sequence with other elements that have the *same Perceiver meaning*. For instance, '$\sin^2 x + \cos^2 x$' has the same meaning as '1' because of Pythagoras' theorem relating the legs and hypotenuse of a right triangle. Notice how Perceiver meanings are being used to move from one Server 'location' to another, precisely the opposite of concrete thought, which uses Server actions to move from one Perceiver location to another. Returning to the Teacher goal, '-1' is much simpler than $(\sin^2 x - \tan^2 x)/(\tan^2 x \sin^2 x)$, thus bringing order to the complexity. Merely writing down the number '-1' does not generate Teacher pleasure. Instead, what Teacher thought appreciates is the movement from the complexity of $(\sin^2 x - \tan^2 x)/(\tan^2 x \sin^2 x)$ to the order of '-1'. As far as I can tell, this Teacher goal of reducing something complex to something simpler (or using something simple to encompass some complexity) is present in all math problems. In some cases, such as the trigonometric problem that we just examined, one is told explicitly to 'simplify this expression'. In other cases, the simplification is implied. For instance, solving the polynomial equation $x^3 + 5x^2 = 9x + 45$ means restating it in the much simpler form of $x = -5, -3$, or 3.

Before we continue, notice the characteristic elements of technical thought. Each *Server* sequence must be composed of a limited set of symbols combined in a permissible manner. For instance, the sequence 'shn x \$ {' is not permitted. Only a limited set of Perceiver transformations is allowed. Each step also involves total certainty. One can state with total certainty, for instance, that the number -1 is equivalent to $(\sin^2 x - \tan^2 x)/(\tan^2 x \sin^2 x)$. Finally, this manipulation all occurs within a limited playing field. For instance, one does not jump suddenly from $(\cos^2 x - 1)/(\sin^2 x)$ to 'To be or not to be, that is the question'.

Technical thought interacts with mental networks in an *explicit* manner that is generally recognized, as well as in an *implicit* manner that is often unnoticed. Looking first at concrete technical thought, one talks of the businessman who is 'willing to sell his own grandmother'. Obviously, this is an extreme situation, but it illustrates a point, which is that business by its very nature violates MMNs. In order to reach a goal, I must leave my existing location. Trading means giving up something valuable in order to gain something that is more valuable. Similarly, using abstract technical thought often requires 'thinking outside of the box' or letting go of 'established procedure' in order to come up with a 'new-and-improved' method. When dealing with these smaller mental networks, there is a tendency to preserve technical thought by *suppressing* mental networks. For example, my father is a Contributor person who has been in business all of his life. I remember him once receiving a London taxi-cab in payment for some debt, and this vehicle was parked for several years in our garage. Even though my father officially owned this car, we never licensed it or drove it. This arms-length relationship with the vehicle prevented us from becoming emotionally attached to it, but it also stopped us from enjoying what was officially ours.

In a similar manner, many of the ways that abstract technical thought can be derailed by mental networks have been analyzed, catalogued, and even turned into posters that can be downloaded from the Internet. For instance, 'appeal to authority' bases Perceiver truth in MMNs of important people, 'strawman' allows Teacher thought to overgeneralize an opposing view, 'the Texas sharpshooter' focuses upon Perceiver facts that fit a pre-existing mental network, 'personal incredulity' rejects Perceiver facts when there is a lack of Teacher understanding, 'ad hominem' focuses upon the personal MMNs of the opponent, 'appeal to nature' bases Perceiver truth upon the MMNs of childish identity, 'bandwagon' bases truth upon the MMNs of culture, 'slippery slope' rejects a Perceiver fact because it triggers an unwanted mental network, 'loaded question' phrases questions in such a way that they do trigger unwanted mental networks, and 'appeal to emotion' appeals to the emotion contained within mental networks.

While technical thought is adept at challenging mental networks that appear *within* the context, we saw earlier that it can become emotionally trapped by the mental network that is formed *by* the context. Remember that a mental network is formed out of similar emotional memories. Because technical thought is pursuing some emotional bottom line within a limited context, this will lead naturally to the formation of a mental network. Thus, the Contributor person who pursues rational thought so vigorously within his area of expertise will be tempted to respond with emotional derision when faced with a *different* paradigm or a *competing* plan. However, this emotion will not usually be expressed directly but rather packaged as sarcasm, a form of speech that appears on the surface to be rational but is intended to deliver a biting emotional message.

> Technical thought questions mental networks *within* the context.
> Technical thought becomes trapped by the mental network created *by* the context.

Now that we have been introduced to technical thought, let us return to the topic of incarnation. I suggest that the core element of incarnation is the relationship between infinite and finite. How can the same person be both universal God and a finite human? Studying personality as well as exploring the diagram of mental symmetry led me to the conclusion that Contributor thought faces precisely the same dilemma *within the mind*. Personal identity is represented by MMNs, while a concept of God is based in a TMN. Contributor thought naturally divides into the two fragments of *abstract* technical thought that uses words to improve *general* Teacher theories and *concrete* technical thought that uses actions to improve *specific* Mercy experiences. Thus, understanding incarnation is not merely a theological dilemma but also a core struggle in the process of reaching mental wholeness. How can I program *my* mind so that the two halves of Contributor thought become unified within *my* mind? Saying this another way, how can Contributor thought bridge the mental concept of a universal God in Teacher thought with the mental concepts of specific individuals within Mercy thought?

Notice the fundamental difference between *mysticism* and *incarnation*. Mysticism creates the *feeling* of uniting universal understanding in Teacher thought with personal identity in Mercy thought by *suppressing* the Perceiver and Server content that separates these two from each other. Incarnation, in contrast, *bridges* universal Teacher understanding with Mercy personal identity in a way that *preserves* Perceiver and Server content.

Variables and Equations

The next chapter will examine how abstract Contributor thought becomes unified with concrete Contributor thought within the *mind*. The rest of this chapter will look at how these two forms of technical thought are integrated in *math* and *science*, and how this integration is reflected in the structure of *physical reality*.

In brief, I suggest that this integration involves the *variable* and the *equation*. A variable is an abstract symbol that is used to represent many specific objects. For example, the variable **X** might represent apples, people, or the price of a *jin* of tea in China. Cognitively speaking, a specific Mercy experience is being replaced by a Perceiver fact—which groups together Mercy experiences—and this Perceiver fact is being represented by a Teacher symbol. For instance, there may be a red Gala apple sitting on my desk that I plan to eat later. What matters to concrete thought is that specific apple. If someone takes it away from my desk, then there will be nothing for me to eat and I will go hungry. Math ignores the specific apple in Mercy thought and focuses instead upon the Perceiver category of apples. One can also see this distinction in English grammar. 'I would like the apple' refers to some specific apple within Mercy thought, while 'I like apples' refers to the Perceiver category of apples. Math deals with the Perceiver category of apples and then connects these Perceiver categories with abstract symbols such as **X**. The variable **X** is not limited to representing only apples but can be used to represent many different groups of items, such as apples, people, or Chinese tea. And one is not limited to using the letter X. Instead, one can use any letter of the alphabet, or pick a letter from the Greek or Hebrew alphabet. Theoretically, one could make this even more abstract and use a simple / to represent a variable. However, if one becomes too abstract, then it is no longer possible to say anything because all of the symbols appear the same. For instance, it is easy to confuse a \ with a | or a /. Thus, there is an optimal level of generality. If one is not *sufficiently* general, then one is *not* saying very much. For instance, limiting the variable **X** to the group of apples would place major restrictions upon the generality of mathematics. But if one is too general, then one *cannot* say very much, and the precision of incarnation will turn into the vagueness of mysticism. It is said, for example, that all of the impressionistic music that was written after Debussy sounded like Debussy. That is because Debussy made the musical rules of composition so vague that it became difficult to distinguish the style of one composer from another. After using the diagram of mental symmetry for several decades, I have come to the conclusion that it is optimally general. It is sufficiently general to be able to act as a meta-theory that can bring order to other theories, but it is still sufficiently specific to be able to say something meaningful.

> Math uses the variable and the equation to bridge concrete and abstract.

Contributor ties together Perceiver and Server. The variable is the *Perceiver* side of connecting universal with specific, while the equation is the *Server* side. For instance, suppose that an apple costs $0.60. If I buy 40 apples, then the total cost will obviously be $24. Notice that we are dealing with an *if-then* statement, the basic building block for concrete technical thought. If I buy 20 apples, then the cost will be $12. If I buy 25 apples, then the cost will be $15, and so on. Instead of writing out the price for each possible number of apples, it is possible to replace all of these specific if-then statements with a general equation. Let X represent the number of apples and Y represent the total cost. $Y = 0.60 \cdot X$. In the previous paragraph, we used a variable to go from specific Mercy experience to general Perceiver fact. Here we are going from *cause-and-effect* (the basic building block for concrete Contributor thought) to *precisely defined statement* (the basic building block for abstract Contributor thought).

This is where philosophers start arguing with each other. Instead of attempting to join this discussion, we will limit ourselves to describing how this philosophical debate shows up in math and computer programming. In simplest terms, '=' has two meanings, one determined by concrete Contributor thought and the other by abstract Contributor thought. These two meanings are not quite the same. When these two aspects of Contributor thought are combined, then the meaning for '=' becomes ambiguous, and technical thought hates ambiguity. For instance, in the computer language C++ one can either write '$X=3$' or '$X==3$'. (A similar distinction exists in other computer languages.) '$X==3$' *compares* the value of X with the number 3. If these are the same, then the answer is **True**, if they are different, then the result is **False**. Using the more concrete language of apples, if X represented the number of apples that I possess, then '$X==3$' would be **True** if I have three apples and **False** if I have any other number of apples. This describes the type of thinking used by *abstract* technical thought, in which one Server statement is compared with another and Perceiver truth is calculated. In contrast, '$X=3$' *assigns* the number 3 to the variable X. Instead using Perceiver thought to *check* whether I have three apples, it uses Server thought to perform the action of *giving* me three apples. This describes the type of thinking used by *concrete* technical thought, in which a Server action *leads* from one Perceiver fact to another.

Computer languages distinguish between these two possible meanings of '=' by representing each with a different symbol. This same ambiguity exists in math, but it is not clarified by using distinct symbols. For instance, the equation $Y = 0.60 \cdot X$ described earlier is actually a *function* relating the input X to the output Y. One learns in high school algebra how to plot functions, with X, the independent variable or input, going on the horizontal axis and Y, the dependent variable or output, going on the vertical axis. Again notice that we are dealing with the cause-and-effect of *concrete* Contributor thought. If I have 15 apples, then the cost will be \$9. But it is also possible to use '=' in an equation such as $\sin(x) = \cos(x)$. Here one no longer starts with **X**, performs some Server action, and ends with **Y**. Instead one is using the '=' to compare the left side of the equation with the right side of the equation. One is asking what the value of **X** is if $\sin(x)$ is the *same* as $\cos(x)$. The solution is to replace the equation $\sin(x) = \cos(x)$ with the *equivalent* equation 'x = 45 + 180n, n = any integer', using *abstract* Contributor thought to replace one Server sequence with another.

History of Science

We have looked briefly at how abstract and concrete technical thought interact with each other in mathematics. Judea Pearl, a researcher at UCLA, described this relationship and its development in history particularly clearly in a 1996 lecture entitled *The Art and Science of Cause and Effect* (Pearl, 1996).

Before the advent of science, people assumed that all effects were caused by living agents. Using the language of mental symmetry, they believed that all events within concrete thought are caused by MMNs that represent people. Quoting from the slide notes (the capitalized words are in the original),

> Explanations are used exclusively for passing responsibilities. Indeed, for thousands of years explanations had no other function. Therefore, only Gods, people and animals could cause things to happen, not objects, events or physical processes. Natural events entered into causal explanations much later, because, in the ancient world, events were simply PREDETERMINED. Storms and earthquakes were CONTROLLED by the angry gods, and could not, in themselves, assume causal responsibility for the consequences. Even an erratic and unpredictable event such as the roll of a die was not considered a CHANCE event but rather a divine message demanding proper interpretation.

Notice how gods are being viewed from a Mercy perspective as human-like agents who cause natural events. As we saw at the beginning of this book, the cognitive science of religion has done useful work in analyzing this type of religious thought.

Pearl suggests that the development of *complicated machines* led to the emergence of a new concept of cause-and-effect.

> Once people started building multi-stage systems, an interesting thing happened to causality – PHYSICAL OBJECTS BEGAN ACQUIRING CAUSAL CHARACTER. When a system like that broke down, it was futile to blame God or the operator – instead, a broken rope or a rusty pulley were more useful explanations, simply because those could be replaced easily, and make the system work. At that point in history, Gods and humans ceased to be the sole agents of causal forces – lifeless objects and processes became partners in responsibility. A wheel turned and stopped BECAUSE the wheel proceeding [sic] it turned and stopped – the human operator became secondary.

We saw earlier that a machine can either be viewed from a *Mercy* perspective as a tool that is used by some agent to reach some goal, or from a *Teacher* perspective as a set of functions that work together to generate Teacher order-within-complexity. Notice the precise cognitive progression being described by Pearl. First, tools are being used to reach goals within concrete thought. Second, technical concrete thought emerges as toolmakers (usually led by Contributor persons) try to develop better tools. When tools become sufficiently complicated, then *concrete* technical thought will turn into *abstract* technical thought as mechanics start asking Teacher questions such as 'Why are these parts not working together?' or 'How can these parts be made to work together better?' Notice how technical thought is emerging within the overall context of a concrete world that is driven and motivated by MMNs. This cognitive progression probably played a contributing role in the birth of science.

Pearl says that the breakthrough into science occurred when cause-and-effect was examined without thinking about agents. In other words, technical thought became free of the domination of MMNs *within some context*.

> This revolution, expounded in his 1638 book 'Discorsi' published in Leyden, far from Rome, consists of two Maxims: ONE, description first, explanation second - that is, the how precedes the why; and TWO, description is carried out in the language of mathematics; namely, equations. Ask not, said Galileo, whether an object falls because it is pulled from below or pushed from above. Ask how well you can predict the time it takes for the object to travel a certain distance, and how that time will vary from object to object, and as the angle of the track changes.

Galileo stated that one should not view cause-and-effect from the perspective of MMNs: 'Ask not whether an object falls because it is pulled from below or pushed from above'. Instead, one should use abstract technical thought to *compare* one cause-and-effect with another in order to find common principles: 'Ask how that time will vary from object to object as the angle of the track changes'.

Technical thought is locally rational, but not necessarily globally rational.

I mentioned earlier that technical thought struggles to overcome mental networks that lie within the context but is vulnerable to mental networks that are created by the context. The flip-side is that technical thought can emerge within a general environment that is controlled by mental networks. Technical thought will question the mental networks that lie within the context while continuing to function within the environment dominated by mental networks. Saying this more generally, technical thought is locally rational, but there is no guarantee that it is also globally rational.

For instance, the story is told that Galileo began his study of the pendulum when he was distracted from his prayers in the cathedral of Pisa by the swinging to and fro of a lamp suspended above the high altar. Galileo noticed that the period of oscillation remains the same regardless of the magnitude of the oscillation. Saying this more simply, a pendulum takes the same amount of time to go back and forth whether it swings a little or a lot. (Technically speaking, this is only accurate if the angle of oscillation is less than about 20°. However, Galileo's conclusion was sufficiently close to enable the development of accurate pendulum clocks.) This story illustrates how abstract technical thought can emerge within a general context driven by mental networks. Prayers, cathedrals, altars, and lamps are physical expressions of religious mental networks, while comparing one oscillation with another is an example of abstract technical thought. Similarly, the Contributor businessman may be totally rational in his pursuit of the bottom line, while following a bottom line that is defined by irrational social pressures. The successful Contributor person will often have a midlife crisis after he has 'climbed to the top of ladder', because he will look around and realize that he has climbed the wrong ladder. He has been locally rational while being globally irrational. That is both the strength and weakness of technical thought.

We saw when discussing mathematics that the '=' sign has two different meanings. When dealing with functions, it is like an *arrow* heading from **X** to **Y**, *from* the independent variable *to* the dependent variable. This meaning comes from the cause-and-effect thinking of *concrete* technical thought. *Abstract* technical thought in contrast, views the '=' sign as a way of comparing two different mathematical expressions. Saying this another way, the sense of time is lost when one moves from concrete technical thought to abstract technical thought.

Pearl describes this tension between time-based science and timeless mathematics.

> Physicists talk, write, and think one way and formulate physics in another. Such bilingual activity would be forgiven if causality was used merely as a convenient communication device – a shorthand for expressing complex patterns of physical relationships that would otherwise take many equations to write... The laws of physics are all symmetrical, going both ways, while causal relations are unidirectional, going from cause to effect. Take for instance Newton's law $f = ma$. The rules of algebra permit us to write this law in a wild variety of syntactic forms, all meaning the same thing – that if we know any two of the three quantities, the third is determined. Yet, in ordinary discourse we say that force causes acceleration – not that acceleration causes force, and we feel very strongly about this distinction. Likewise, we say that the ratio f/a helps us DETERMINE the mass, not that it CAUSES the mass. Such distinctions are not supported by the equations of physics, and this leads us to ask whether the whole causal vocabulary is purely metaphysical... Fortunately, very few physicists paid attention to Russell's enigma [regarding causality]. They continued to write equations in the office and talk cause-effect in the CAFETERIA, with astonishing success, they smashed the atom, invented the transistor, and the laser. The same is true for engineering.

Notice the strange dilemma. On the one hand, cause-and-effect rules *concrete* reality. Scientists who 'smashed the atom and invented the transistor' were successful because they acted as if cause-and-effect exists. Anyone who attempts to live in reality knows that time is an inexorable force that cannot be resisted. On the other hand, cause-and-effect does not exist within the *abstract* realm of mathematics. Instead, 'the laws of physics are all symmetrical, going both ways'. On the one hand, causal relations are uni-directional, going from cause to effect', while on the other hand, 'such distinctions are not supported by the equations of physics'.

This dilemma is well-known within physics, and I am not stating anything new by describing it. What is new, though, is the suggestion that the same dilemma exists within the mind between concrete technical thought and abstract technical thought, the type of thinking behind math and science. Math, with its carefully defined sequences of symbols, is based in abstract technical thought but it crosses over into concrete technical thought when it is used to describe functions with their inherent cause-and-effect relationship. Science uses concrete technical thought to observe and measure cause-and-effect within the physical world, but it crosses over into abstract technical thought when comparing one cause-and-effect with another in order to come up with general laws.

Pearl says that Karl Pearson, the person who developed statistical mathematics, (Pearl's area of specialization) was fiercely opposed to the concept of cause-and-effect.

> Pearson categorically denies the need for an independent concept of causal relation beyond correlation. He held this view throughout his life and, accordingly, did not mention causation in ANY of his technical papers. His crusade against animistic concepts such as 'will' and 'force' was so fierce and his rejection of determinism so absolute that he EXTERMINATED causation from statistics before it had a chance to take root.

That leads to a fundamental problem. Abstract technical thought may be able to function without the concept of causality, but concrete technical thought is *based* upon causality. Thus, whenever technical thought attempts to apply abstract theory to the concrete world, then cause-and-effect will naturally creep back in—even when it is officially denied. For instance, even though statistical math was developed in a way that ignores causality, one of the major uses of statistics today is to *prove* causality.

Let us summarize briefly before continuing. There are two forms of technical thought, both are controlled by Contributor thought, and both work with a limited collection of well-defined Perceiver facts and Server sequences. Concrete technical thought uses a knowledge of cause-and-effect and is guided by specific goals within Mercy thought. Abstract technical thought assigns precise definitions to words and symbols and is guided by order-within-complexity within Teacher thought. Technical thought becomes much more powerful when concrete technical thought is combined with abstract technical thought. However, concrete technical thought is based upon time whereas abstract technical thought functions independently of time.

I have suggested that a concept of God emerges when a sufficiently general Teacher theory applies to personal identity. Similarly, I suggest that a concept of incarnation emerges when abstract technical thought becomes combined with concrete technical thought—if technical thought acknowledges the existence of mental networks. Abstract technical thought works with general Teacher theories, and a concept of God is based in a general Teacher theory. Concrete technical thought works with specific Mercy goals, and concepts of people are based in Mercy experiences. Combining these two halves of Contributor thought will lead to the concept of a God/man.

Notice the requirement for acknowledging the existence of mental networks. The mind represents people, both human and divine, as mental networks. Obviously, integrated Contributor thought can only bridge God and man if Contributor thought acknowledges the existence of God and man. This requirement is *not* easy to meet. We have seen that technical thought is naturally dismissive of any mental networks that reside within the area of specialization. The Contributor *person* has a tendency to treat those under him as pawns within his plan, and it disturbs him when these pawns develop a life of their own. That is why the typical Contributor executive needs a Facilitator secretary to fine-tune impersonal Contributor plans so that they are more human-friendly. And when underlying mental networks are triggered, then we have seen that technical thought often resorts to the pseudo-rationality of belittling and sarcasm in an attempt to squelch the existence of independent or threatening mental networks.

Putting this more bluntly, a concept of incarnation will emerge when technical thought stops treating people as tools to be manipulated and stops regarding the concept of God as a childish myth. The blame for this does not reside entirely with Contributor thought. We have seen that the childish thinking of Piaget's preoperational stage is rather prevalent and that most concepts of God are based in blind faith. Thus, the attitude taken by technical thought toward culture and religion is often justified.

As Pearl described in his brief discussion of the history of technical thought, concrete technical thought often comes to birth in a social and religious environment dictated by traditional MMNs. Using technical thought to improve Mercy experiences is a cognitively *superior* strategy to being driven passively by MMNs. Think, for instance, of using rational thought to develop new methods of farming. Having an abundance of food is far better than surviving on the edge of starvation. And introducing new methods to both physical fields and fields of thought often means struggling to overcome hidebound traditions driven by cultural mental networks. Similarly, using technical thought is also a cognitively *superior* strategy to accepting blindly the pronouncements of authority figures. Critical thinking is better than rote learning. And using abstract technical thought often means questioning the revealed truth of authority.

Technical thought is actually a *combination* of rational thinking and emotion, which one could compare to a rider on a horse. The rider is Contributor thought with its combination of carefully defined Perceiver facts and Server sequences. The horse is Exhorter thought, the cognitive module that is before Contributor thought and provides the motivation for Contributor thought. Contributor thought may be totally rational, but Exhorter thought derives most of its energy from the emotional intensity of mental networks. One often sees this in the behavior of the Contributor person, who can be a workaholic when motivation is present, but can also be rather lazy when motivation is lacking. Thus, technical thought has a tendency to explicitly despise mental networks for being non-rigorous while at the same time being implicitly driven by mental networks.

But what will provide the *motivation* for technical thought if mental networks are merely suppressed? One possibility is for the motivation to come from the mental networks that are being *suppressed*. One sees this type of motivation in the Contributor person who lives (or skydives, or climbs cliffs, etc.) on the edge of disaster. The Contributor person will walk close enough to the edge of the figurative (or literal) cliff to provide excitement for subconscious Exhorter thought but not walk so close to the cliff that Contributor thought loses control. Religiously speaking, one sees this approach in the atheist, who uses technical thought to disprove childish concepts of God while being driven in Exhorter thought by the very concept of God that he is attempting to disprove. Obviously, this is not a good alternative, because one only remains motivated as long as an enemy exists.

Another possibility is for motivation to come from the *implicit* mental networks that emerge from using technical thought. We saw this option in the previous chapter when looking at the emotional trap of the job. Generally speaking, technical thought focuses upon the objective experiences related to the job in order to escape the emotional tyranny of home and culture. The problem with this option is that technical thought ends up optimizing the useless, or in other words, climbing to the top of the wrong ladder. For instance, the Contributor person who pursues a job may become skilled at dunking a basketball while his marriage falls apart.

Another option is for the goal of technical thought to be *co-opted* by some outside authority or structure. For instance, the NSA (National Security Agency) is probably the largest current employer of mathematicians in the United States, hiring about 30 PhDs in mathematics every year (Wickware, 2001). But it has recently been revealed that the NSA spends $250,000,000 a year attempting to undermine standards and infiltrate companies in order to make Internet less secure (Ball, 2013). Thus, the NSA employee is actually using abstract technical thought to destroy Teacher order-within-complexity, rather than build it. This oxymoron is even more obvious within the arms industry. For instance, the American military budget in 2013 was $618,000,000,000 (Frohlich & Kent, 2014). That's a lot of zeros. Modern weapons could not exist without technical thought. However, the primary purpose of a weapon is to destroy structures and kill people, rather than build structure and help people.

The final alternative is to use technical thought to *improve* mental networks. This can only happen if both mental networks and technical thought function within a mental grid of Perceiver and Server content constructed by normal thought. That will be the topic of the next chapter. Here we will examine how technical thought can be used to jump-start the personal honesty that is required to build this mental grid.

The Prayer of Salvation

The underlying problem was discussed in the chapter on Piaget's preoperational stage. In simple terms, childish identity is chaotic, disordered, disobedient, ignorant, and irrational, all traits that are abhorrent to Teacher thought. In religious terms, God finds childish human thought and behavior repugnant. Using the language of mental symmetry, the MMNs of childish identity will struggle with the TMN of universal understanding and each will attempt to impose its structure upon the other. Either a person will form a concept of God in his own image or else personal identity will submit to a concept of God. This may sound clinical but it is not. It is personally devastating for childish personal identity to face the emotional glare of a universal Teacher understanding, somewhat like a person staring at himself in the mirror the first time after being horribly injured in an accident. Because these feelings of inadequacy are being produced by the TMN of a general understanding imposing its *structure* upon childish MMNs, they will not be generated by a God of mysticism, because Teacher overgeneralization lacks structure. Such a concept of God will not provoke a sense of guilt or personal inadequacy because mysticism lacks content and without content there can be no standard to fall short of.

Notice that this struggle is occurring *within the mind* between an image of God in Teacher thought and personal identity in Mercy thought. Whether a real God exists or not, this internal conflict will occur, it will affect how the mind functions, and this will shape society. Similarly, the answer that we are about to examine is also a mental solution based in cognitive mechanisms. This does not mean that it is *only* a cognitive mechanism. In the same way that the mind uses mental networks to represent real people, so it is possible that real beings exist that correspond to the mental concepts of God and incarnation.

The TMN of a concept of God can be reconciled with the MMNs of childish identity by inserting Contributor thought *between* Mercy thought and Teacher thought, taking advantage of the fact that abstract and concrete technical thought have different concepts of time. Using religious language, incarnation acts as an *intermediary* between God and man. In order to explain how this works in the simplest way possible, we will use the analogy of a *school*.

A school emphasizes abstract thought. One does not go to school to do Server actions but rather to learn Perceiver facts in order to gain Teacher understanding. But a school is also an expression of abstract *technical* thought. A school does not teach everything. Rather, what is taught is a limited set of facts and sequences defined by the *curriculum*. This learning is done with total certainty. If one passes a class, then one has officially 'learned' the material in that class and is permitted to take more advanced courses. And a school usually packages its content in the form of *textbooks*, books that have been carefully structured through the use of technical thought. A school does not have to use technical thought, but as I learned through the process of accreditation, there is a natural tendency for school to become defined in terms of technical thought.

> The prayer of salvation places Contributor incarnation between Mercy and Teacher.

As far as the elementary (and often more advanced) school student is concerned, going to school is something that you *do*. First you do grade 1, then you do grade 2, and so on. Each grade takes time and one grade follows another. The young student who is in Piaget's concrete operational stage is not attending school in order to acquire knowledge and build understanding, but rather is doing assignments in order to please the teacher. However, the student will only receive approval by 'playing according to the rules of the game'. These rules turn school into a form of technical concrete thought. Summarizing, school combines abstract and concrete technical thought. For the instructors, school is primarily an example of abstract technical thought, while for the students, especially the younger students, school means concrete technical thought.

How does the typical adult view young children? Yes, I know, mother's love and all that. But there is a reason why there are so many 'adult only' communities and housing complexes. Children are noisy, they are ignorant, they pick their noses, they have to go to the bathroom, they break things, they get in the way, and they have to be fed and entertained. In a word, they are obnoxious. If this sounds like a harsh indictment then please re-read the chapter on preoperational thought.

However, when a young child enrolls in school then the *status* of the child changes from 'obnoxious urchin' to 'school student'. The child who has just started school has not yet learned anything. Instead, he has only taken the first step in a long process of acquiring an education. But his status has changed. Instead of being viewed *directly* by Teacher thought as an example of personal chaos, the student is now viewed *indirectly* by Teacher thought as a member of the school system. Instead of seeing the disorder of the student, Teacher thought sees the order of the school. Abstract technical thought also removes the sense of time from concrete technical thought. Thus, even though the student has just enrolled in school and has only begun a long chain of cause-and-effect involving taking one class after another, abstract technical thought ignores the time that this takes and views the entire sequence as a single unit. As far as Teacher thought is concerned, all of the order-within-complexity of the curriculum already applies to personal identity. But according to Mercy thought, personal identity still has to go through the process of becoming educated. However, as long as a person remains enrolled in the school, personal identity will continue to be viewed by Teacher thought as 'totally educated'.

I suggest that this is what happens cognitively when a person says the Christian 'prayer of salvation'. Typically, it goes something like "God, I recognize that you are holy and I am a sinner. I ask Jesus to come into my heart and be my Lord. I ask you to forgive my sins in Jesus' name." Analyzing the various parts of this prayer, *saying* the prayer addresses Teacher thought, because Teacher thought is based in words. Using the word 'God' addresses Teacher thought in personal terms, because what is required is a general Teacher theory that applies to personal identity. 'I recognize that you are holy and I am a sinner' submits the MMNs of childish identity to the TMN of Teacher understanding in a way that preserves mental content. 'I ask Jesus to come into my heart' extends the image of incarnation to include personal identity', while 'be my Lord' submits personal identity to incarnation. Finally, 'in Jesus' name' asks Teacher thought to view personal identity indirectly through incarnation. Because Teacher thought thinks verbally, this is done by referring to the verbal label given to incarnation—the *name* of Jesus.

Translating this into the language of the school, this prayer would go something like "I recognize that I am ignorant and need an education. I would like to become an educated person. May I enrol in this school? I agree to take the courses, do the homework, and pass the exams. Please regard me officially as a student of this school rather than as an uneducated person."

This official change in status is known in theological terms as *justification*. (Justification means to be 'declared righteous', and we will examine righteousness in the next chapter.) N.T. Wright describes what is called the *juridical* nature of justification.

> It is not a descriptive locution, but an illocutionary speech-act of declaration and verdict. The judge's declaration works on the analogy of other speech-acts which create a new status or situation: 'You're fired'; 'I pronounce that they are husband and wife'; 'I declare the meeting adjourned.' The declaration creates and constitutes a new situation, a new status. We stress again: this is a declaration, not a description. It does not denote or describe a character; it confers a status. In that sense, it creates the status it confers. Up to that point, the person concerned cannot be spoken of as 'righteous', but now they can be and indeed must be. Thus the status of being 'in the right', reckoned 'righteous', is actually created by, and is the result of, the judge's declaration. That is what it means to say that the status of 'now being in the right', dikaiosynē, has been reckoned to the person concerned (Wright, 2013).

Notice how justification is like a 'judge's declaration' that creates 'a new status or situation'. The flip-side to justification is known in theological language as *sanctification*. Justification describes the change in status viewed by abstract technical thought, while sanctification describes the process taken by concrete technical thought. Justification ignores time; sanctification requires time. Using the school analogy, justification is like enrolling in the school, while sanctification is like studying in the school.

Significant theological discussion has occurred over the precise relationship between justification and sanctification. I suggest that it is possible to resolve this problem by understanding the relationship between abstract and concrete technical thought. In simple terms, justification and sanctification are two different views of the same process, with justification taking the timeless perspective of Teacher thought and sanctification taking the time indwelling perspective of Mercy thought.

> Justification sees a Contributor plan from a *timeless* abstract perspective.
> Sanctification sees the *same* Contributor plan from a time-oriented concrete view.

For instance, N.T. Wright focuses strongly upon justification while downplaying the concept of sanctification. Consistent with this, Wright has spent his professional career using abstract technical thought as a professor, theologian, pastor, bishop, and biblical exegete. Because he has spent so much time focusing upon abstract technical thought, it makes sense that his concept of incarnation would also emphasize the justification of abstract technical thought rather than the sanctification of concrete technical thought. This re-emphasizes that we are dealing here not just with a theological doctrine to which one asserts. Instead we are examining a theology that is based in cognitive mechanisms, that has transformative power because of cognitive mechanisms, and that can be overruled if the way that one deals implicitly with cognitive mechanisms is inconsistent with one's explicit statements. Stated bluntly, it is dangerous to proclaim a doctrine of incarnation and then live a life that does not express incarnation.

Our analysis of mysticism led us to conclude that it is an inadequate way of creating a concept of God because it creates merely the *feeling* of encountering of God at the cost of shutting down Perceiver thought (and Server thought). And because an overgeneralized theory contains order but not complexity, the only way to create Teacher order-within-complexity is by getting the complexity from somewhere *else* and then turning one's back upon this complexity in order to *embrace* the 'order' of mysticism.

The Christian prayer of salvation also relies on a mental trick, namely the different ways that abstract and concrete technical thought view time. Is this also mentally destructive? If saying the prayer becomes a *substitute* for personal growth, then I suggest that the prayer of salvation is not mentally profitable because it gives a person the mental illusion that personal identity is the buddy of God when in fact personal identity still thinks and behaves in a manner that is totally inconsistent with the character of a universal being. Using the school analogy, this attitude turns the school of personal transformation into a diploma mill, in which one only has to enrol in order to get a diploma. Evidence from personality suggests that the practical Contributor person is prone to spreading this error because he tends to view abstract technical thought as a source of slogans and 'magic formulae' that can be called upon occasionally to supercharge concrete technical thought. As a result, the practical Contributor person can go to great lengths telling people about the prayer of salvation and getting them to say this prayer.

In contrast, if saying the prayer of salvation is seen as a doorway to the path of personal honesty, if enrolling in the school is followed by studying at the school, then there is no mental trick because the feeling of being justified will eventually result in the state of being sanctified. In addition, both theory and observation suggest that it is not possible for a person to submit core MMNs to the TMN of a general understanding without the emotional benefit that saying this prayer engenders.

I should emphasize that there is nothing magical about saying these specific words. Instead, what makes the words effective is the mental decision to *recognize* the supremacy of Teacher understanding, *acknowledge* the inadequacy of childish identity, *allow* concrete technical thought to transform personal identity, and *place* abstract technical thought under the guidance of Teacher understanding.

Several points need to be made before continuing. First, if the average person is told to 'combine abstract technical thought with concrete technical thought, submit personal identity to concrete technical thought, and submit abstract technical thought to Teacher understanding', then this may be technically correct but it will *not* communicate. In contrast, it *does* communicate when one tells someone to 'admit that you are a sinner, ask Jesus into your heart and ask God to forgive your sins in Jesus' name'. That is because one is dealing with a chicken-and-egg sort of problem. In order to understand the cognitive mechanisms behind this prayer, one must acquire the ability to think rationally in the realm of subjective, but that ability is difficult, if not impossible, to acquire without saying the prayer. Thus, what usually happens is that a person *initially* says the prayer of salvation as a sort of magical incantation and then *later on* gradually realizes that the words have deep cognitive meaning. It is possible that there is *also* some form of 'spiritual' meaning to these words. But even if this is the case, I suggest that the cognitive content *enables* the spiritual meaning and that it is possible to discuss the prayer of salvation in purely rational terms from a cognitive perspective.

Second, if the required cognitive content is present, then the prayer of salvation will be effective, whether it is understood or not. In other words, as long as it is stated with sincerity and depth of meaning, it will work, even if it is viewed as a magical incantation, which often leads to the belief that it really is nothing more than a magical incantation. As a result, the natural tendency of scientific methodology will be to reject this prayer as something that is irrational and non-empirical. However, if one understands the cognitive mechanisms behind this prayer, one sees that it is actually deeply consistent with the mental structure behind math and science. Understanding how the prayer works also makes it much more effective because the concepts will then be based in universal truth rather than absolute truth.

Third, theologians have debated over the possibility of 'losing one salvation', with some saying that a person must continue to 'do good works' in order to 'be saved' and others claiming that the person who honestly says the prayer of salvation has 'eternal security' of salvation. Examining this question from a cognitive perspective suggests that what matters is remaining enrolled in school. One does not have to get an A+ in every class in order to remain enrolled. One can even fail and retake classes and remain a student. However, if one deliberately chooses to drop out of school, then obviously one loses the emotional benefit of being a student. This may lead to the fear that a person might inadvertently drop out of school, but I suggest that this is not the case. As we saw when looking at Kuhn's description of the typical scientist, once a general theory turns into a TMN, then it becomes very difficult to let go of this theory. A similar principle would apply to saying the prayer of salvation. The longer that personal identity enrols in a 'school of incarnation' that is held together by the TMN of a mental concept of God, the more difficult it becomes emotionally to 'drop out' of this school. Eventually the emotional strength of the underlying TMN will be so overpowering that a person is no longer able to use free will to leave the school. When this point is reached then a person does have 'eternal security', not because he has a religious 'life insurance policy' that cannot be canceled, but rather because his concept of God has turned into a 'hound of Heaven' that 'hunts him down' no matter what he chooses.

Fourth, while school is a good analogy of the prayer of salvation, I suggest that enrolling in a physical school cannot substitute for saying the prayer of salvation. That is because the instructors of a physical school can only observe and judge what the student says and does and must guess what the student is feeling and thinking. In contrast, an *internal* school that is guided by a mental concept of incarnation and a mental concept of God is capable of observing and judging a person's deepest motives. Thus, physical schools can be seen as partial expressions of the internal school, and saying the prayer of salvation as a way of extending enrollment in a physical school to the core of the subjective. Of course, this assumes that the content that is taught by the physical school is consistent with personal integration. For instance, a military college may teach good content and build character, but it is difficult to reconcile killing people with mental wholeness. Similarly, it is possible to pursue disciplines such as law, marketing, media, and politics in a manner that is consistent with mental wholeness, but not if the goal of law is to defend the client regardless of the facts, if the purpose of marketing is to sell products regardless of their quality, if the aim of media is to proclaim an agenda regardless of the facts, or if the goal of politics is to get elected at any cost. In cases such as these, the physical school is assuming that the core of personal identity lacks integrity, and one will have to choose between obeying God or obeying man because the curriculum of the school of man is incompatible with the curriculum of the school of God.

Finally, the problem with regarding the prayer of salvation as a religious incantation is that it remains mentally disconnected from normal life—and can cause severe cognitive disconnects. That is because a magical incantation uses Mercy emotions to overwhelm Perceiver thought, and if Perceiver thought is not functioning, then the mind cannot build connections between one mental context and another. In the extreme, this can lead to the type of situation described by Theodore Weld in the 1839 book entitled, *American Slavery As It Is: Testimony of a Thousand Witnesses.*

> I will first introduce the reader to a woman of the highest respectability—one who was foremost in every benevolent enterprise, and stood for many years, I may say, at the head of the fashionable élite of the city of Charleston, and after-

wards at the head of the moral and religious female society there. It was after she had made a profession of religion, and retired from the fashionable world, that I knew her; therefore I will present her in her religious character. This lady used to keep cowhides, or small paddles, (called 'pancake sticks,') in four different apartments in her house; so that when she wished to punish, or to have punished, any of her slaves, she might not have the trouble of sending for an instrument of torture...Very often she would take a position at her window, in an upper story, and scold at her slaves while working in the garden, at some distance from the house, (a large yard intervening,) and occasionally order a flogging. I have known her thus on the watch, scolding for more than an hour at a time, in so loud a voice that the whole neighborhood could hear her; and this without the least apparent feeling of shame. Indeed, it was no disgrace among slaveholders, and did not in the least injure her standing, either as a lady or a Christian, in the aristocratic circle in which she moved. After the 'revival' in Charleston, in 1825, she opened her house to social prayer-meetings. The room in which they were held in the evening, and where the voice of prayer was heard around the family altar, and where she herself retired for private devotion thrice each day, was the very place in which, when her slaves were to be whipped with the cowhide, they were taken to receive the infliction; and the wail of the sufferer would be heard, where, perhaps only a few hours previous, rose the voices of prayer and praise (Weld, 1839).

We have seen that a mind that is ruled by childish MMNs thinks naturally in terms of 'us versus them', approving individuals from the same culture with similar MMNs while disapproving individuals from other cultures with different MMNs. Perceiver thought limits this cultural discrimination by pointing out similarities between 'us' and 'them'. If emotional pressure disables Perceiver thought, then these similarities will not be perceived. Notice in this passage the combination of potent cultural MMNs, disabled Perceiver thought, an attitude of 'us versus them', and the complete lack of shame or disgrace. The woman was 'foremost in every benevolent enterprise' and 'head of the moral and religious female society'. She 'opened her house to social prayer-meetings' and 'retired for private devotion thrice each day'. These potent MMNs disabled Perceiver thought to the extent that she could not even realize that she was praying and whipping in the same room. Instead, there was a total cognitive disconnect between her treatment of whites and blacks. She did this 'without the least apparent feeling of shame', and her behavior 'did not in the least injure her standing'.

Saying this more generally, if one views prayer to God as a religious incantation that uses Mercy emotions to overwhelm Perceiver thought, then this will tend to reinforce social discrimination and disable conscience. Instead of making personal honesty possible, the prayer of salvation will encourage feelings of social and personal superiority.

In other words, in the same way that enrolling in a good college can either be viewed from a Mercy perspective as becoming a member of an elite group or from a Teacher perspective as having the opportunity to gain a better understanding, so the feeling of being forgiven by God can either be seen from a Mercy perspective as becoming a member of a group that is chosen by God or from a Teacher perspective as having the opportunity to gain a better understanding of universal truth.

Deep Structure of Incarnation

We have looked at the relationship between abstract and concrete technical thought that occurs in both math and physics, telling us that there is a *cognitive* relationship between these two fields of thought. What has amazed scientists over the years is the *physical* relationship between these two fields of thought. Pearl describes when this relationship between math and physics was first discovered. Continuing further from the passage quoted earlier regarding Galileo,

> Moreover, said Galileo, do not attempt to answer such questions in the qualitative and slippery nuances of human language; say it in the form of mathematical equations. It is hard for us to appreciate today how strange that idea sounded in 1638, barely 50 years after the introduction of algebraic notation by Vieta. To proclaim algebra the UNIVERSAL language of science, would sound today like proclaiming Esperanto the language of economics. Why would Nature agree to speak Algebra? of all languages? But you can't argue with success. The distance traveled by an object turned out indeed to be proportional to the square of the time (Pearl, 1996).

As Pearl says, today we take it for granted that math can be used to describe the real world, but this was a radically new concept when proposed by Galileo. Why should 'Nature agree to speak algebra'? (Notice in passing how Nature is being referred to as an agent, indicating an implicit concept of God. This usage also occurs in the next quote.)

Dirac, whom we encountered earlier when comparing his disdain for a Mercy-based concept of God with his acceptance of a Teacher-based concept of God, describes the relationship between math and science in more detail.

> The physicist, in his study of natural phenomena, has two methods of making progress: (1) the method of experiment and observation, and (2) the method of mathematical reasoning. The former is just the collection of selected data; the latter enables one to infer results about experiments that have not been performed. There is no logical reason why the second method should be possible at all, but one has found in practice that it does work and meets with reasonable success. This must be ascribed to some mathematical quality in Nature, a quality which the casual observer of Nature would not suspect, but which nevertheless plays an important role in Nature's scheme (Dirac, 1938).

Notice the bizarre relationship between math and reality. The physicist can learn more about the real world either by using technical thought to carefully observe the real world or by using technical thought to make 'chicken scratches' on a piece of paper. As Dirac says, 'there is no logical reason why the second method should be possible at all'. But for some reason there is a 'mathematical quality in Nature'. And the relationship between math and physics is not just a surface relationship but rather continues to grow, even though these two forms of technical thought are radically different.

> Pure mathematics and physics are becoming ever more closely connected, though their methods remain different. One may describe the situation by saying that the mathematician plays a game in which he himself invents the rules while the physicist plays a game in which the rules are provided by Nature, but as time goes on it becomes increasingly evident that the rules which the mathematician finds interesting are the same as those which Nature has chosen (Ibid).

Physics derives its content from empirical evidence. Math, in contrast, is guided by Teacher emotions of order-within-complexity.

> The dominating idea in this application of mathematics to physics is that the equations representing the laws of motion should be of a simple form. The whole success of the scheme is due to the fact that equations of simple form do seem to work. The physicist is thus provided with a principle of simplicity, which he can use as an instrument of research.

It is a mystery why math can be used to describe physical reality.

Dirac says that when the technical thought of mathematics is guided by Teacher emotions to search for *simple* equations, then it is these simple equations that describe reality. Even when Einstein's theory of relativity overturned the world of physics, physicists still found that equations which describe nature exhibit mathematical beauty.

> The discovery of the theory of relativity made it necessary to modify the principle of simplicity... What makes the theory of relativity so acceptable to physicists in spite of its going against the principle of simplicity is its great mathematical beauty. This is a quality which cannot be defined, any more than beauty in art can be defined, but which people who study mathematics usually have no difficulty in appreciating. The theory of relativity introduced mathematical beauty to an unprecedented extent into the description of Nature.

Let us relate this now to incarnation. We have seen that math uses abstract technical thought to work with a precisely defined, limited set of Teacher words and symbols. However, math can also be used by concrete technical thought to describe functions and discover correlations. We have also seen that science uses concrete technical thought to observe physical connections of cause-and-effect by performing experiments upon Mercy experiences in carefully controlled circumstances. However, science then uses abstract technical thought to discover common patterns in these connections of cause-and-effect. Thus, math stretches *down* from abstract technical thought, while science reaches *up* from concrete technical thought. We now see that there is an extensive *overlap* between math and science. I suggest that this overlap illustrates incarnation. I other words, incarnation is far more than God appearing as man for brief moments throughout human history. Rather, it expresses itself in the study of nature as an ever-growing grid of overlap between the word-based technical thought of math and the experience-based technical thought of science. This is not a mystical relationship, or a vague feeling of becoming united with God. Rather, it is a massive realm of technical interconnections between the universal statements of mathematics and the specific experiences of the real world.

> The overlap between math and physics creates a mental concept of incarnation.

Using religious terminology, this is like an entire city that is illumined by God in which humans conduct all of their existence, which is what one finds described in the last chapter of the book of Revelation.

> And he carried me away in the Spirit to a great and high mountain, and showed me the holy city, Jerusalem, coming down out of heaven from God, having the glory of God... I saw no temple in it, for the Lord God the Almighty and the Lamb are its temple. And the city has no need of the sun or of the moon to shine on it, for the glory of God has illumined it, and its lamp is the Lamb. The nations will walk by its light, and the kings of the earth will bring their glory into it. In the daytime (for there will be no night there) its gates will never be closed; and they will bring the glory and the honor of the nations into it; and nothing unclean, and no one who practices abomination and lying, shall ever come into it (Rev. 21:10-11, 22-27).

Notice that the *entire* city is holy (separated to God) and not just some religious buildings within the city. This city is illumined by the Teacher 'light' of God as well as the 'lamp' of incarnation (Jesus is referred to in Revelation as 'the Lamb'). Notice also that this holiness does not need to be protected from the 'profane world' by any walls of separation, but instead interacts continuously with the outside environment—without losing its Teacher order-within-complexity.

Whether this description in Revelation describes a real place or not, it does portray the type of mental concept of incarnation that will naturally emerge when technical thought uses math and science to analyze the physical world.

In a sense incarnation is a mystery. But the mystery is not that incarnation is *incomprehensible*, as the typical Christian insists, but rather that the abstract technical realm of mathematics overlaps in such a *comprehensive* and *comprehensible* way with the concrete technical realm of science. The real mystery is not why incarnation does not make sense but rather why it makes so much sense.

Continuing, science claims to be based purely in empirical evidence, but we see now that this is *not* the case. Kuhn describes how the scientist is *also* guided by the Teacher emotions of a paradigm. Dirac makes this relationship explicit. Science is based both in empirical evidence *and* is guided by mathematical beauty. Because of the 'mystery' of incarnation, these two radically different methods lead to compatible results.

I too have been simultaneously following two radically different methods that keep leading to compatible results. On the one hand, my research is guided by the general Teacher theory of mental symmetry. Like the scientist who uses mathematics to predict qualities about the physical world, I often use the diagram of mental symmetry to predict qualities about the metaphysical world. And like the scientist who keeps discovering that these mathematical predictions correspond with observations of physical reality, so I keep discovering that my theoretical predictions correspond with observations of human, social, and religious behavior.

What does this all mean? That is a difficult question to answer. However, I suggest that it is possible to determine what this means to the mind. I mentioned that Perceiver thought can interact with Teacher thought in one of two ways. First, Perceiver thought can *poke holes* in Teacher theories by pointing out specific examples that do not fit the general pattern. This makes Perceiver thought the enemy of Teacher overgeneralization, which means that mysticism requires inhibiting Perceiver thought. Second, Perceiver thought can *assist* Teacher thought in building general theories by discovering similarities and analogies between one context and another. I have suggested that technical thought is not appropriate for proving the existence or nonexistence of God because God is a universal being while technical thought specializes. But if normal thought uses patterns and analogies to build *bridges* between the specializations of technical thought, then this will produce a very powerful concept of God, in which the complexity of technical thought is given order by the analogies and patterns of normal thought. Saying this more succinctly, when one discovers that math is related to science, that both reflect basic cognitive structure and that this same cognitive structure is found in religious doctrine, then this integrated web of connections can lead to a potent Teacher-based concept of God, the sort of concept of God that is needed to 'illumine' a 'holy city' as described at the end of the Bible. And we know from history that concepts of God have the power to build up or destroy civilizations.

Principle of Least Action

I have recently realized that the connection between physics and incarnation extends even further. One can explain this reasonably simply by beginning with Snell's law. Suppose that I stick a straw into a glass of water. Because light refracts as it travels from one medium to another, the part of the straw that is immersed in the water will appear *bent,* and Snell's law describes this bending of light in mathematical terms. Fermat realized in 1662 that it was a possible to derive Snell's law in a completely different manner. Light actually takes the *shortest path* from point A to point B. One can see what this means with the help of a mathematically similar analogy. Suppose that I am standing on the beach and see a swimmer in trouble out at sea a few hundred meters down the beach. What is the fastest path to the swimmer? Because I can run faster than I can swim, the shortest path is not a straight line. Instead, it will involve running down the beach to the water's edge until I am nearly opposite the swimmer and then swimming the remaining distance. That is precisely the path that light takes when traveling through different mediums with different speeds of light. Light picks the shortest path—every time. But how does light know *beforehand* what is the fastest path? That is like driving to work during rush hour and knowing beforehand exactly which route will be the fastest way to work. No human can reach this level of perfection. But light does—every time.

For this reason, Fermat's letter in which he proposed that light takes the shortest path led immediately to an objection by Claude Clerselier, an expert in optics, who pointed out that Fermat cannot be right because light does not know the future but rather 'acts without foreknowledge'.

> Fermat's principle can not be the cause, for otherwise we would be attributing knowledge to nature: and here, by nature, we understand only that order and law-fulness in the world, such as it is, which acts without foreknowledge, without choice, but by a necessary determination (Mahoney, 1994).

However, physicists soon discovered that this perfection was not just limited to Snell's law and the refraction of light. Instead, it appears that *all* of the laws of physics are optimal in some way. This is known in physics as the *principle of least action*. With refraction, the 'least action' means taking the shortest time. In other situations, it may be the energy that is minimized rather than the time. Discovering precisely what is minimized in a particular set of natural laws is known as finding the *Lagrangian*. This principle of least action applies to classical physics, relativity, and quantum physics.

This is so strange that it needs to be repeated. Physicists have discovered that everything in the natural world functions in some way in a manner that is inhumanly perfect. And if that sounds bizarre, then try to wrap your head around the way that physics uses quantum mechanics to explain this prescient behavior. How does a particle or photon know the best path to take? It takes *all* possible paths and all of these paths cancel each other out except for the one that is optimal. Yes, I know, that is bizarre. But that is what physics says.

Now let us turn to the cognitive realm and try to work out how these fundamental properties of physics will affect a concept of incarnation. Following the optimal path or minimizing energy is the sort of processing that epitomizes concrete technical thought. The practical Contributor person is always trying to come up with a more optimal solution, a faster path, or a better way of making a buck.

We have seen that the overlapping interaction between abstract and concrete technical thought that occurs in science and math will lead to a strong concept of incarnation. But now we see that Nature (with a capital N) exhibits a form of behavior that, as far as concrete technical thought is concerned, defines a level of perfection that transcends anything that is humanly possible, not sometimes but all of the time, and not somewhere but everywhere. What makes this inhuman perfection possible is universal knowledge. Incarnation can pick the best possible path because it has a knowledge of all possible paths. Saying this in theological language, incarnation is a sinless person who exhibits human perfection because incarnation is actually an aspect of God.

> The principle of least action implies that incarnation is sinless because of being God.

This does not prove that such an incarnation actually exists. However, when this type of incarnational perfection occurs universally, then this order-within-complexity will lead to the development of a TMN, and this TMN will impose itself upon the rest of the mind. Curiously, this is the sort of incarnation that one finds described by Paul, the inventor of theology.

> And we know that God causes all things to work together for good to those who love God, to those who are called according to His purpose. For those whom He foreknew, He also predestined to become conformed to the image of His Son, so that He would be the firstborn among many brethren; and these whom He predestined, He also called; and these whom He called, He also justified; and these whom He justified, He also glorified (Romans 8: 28-30).

This biblical passage lies behind what is known in theological circles as the doctrine of *predestination*. In its most extreme form, it asserts that God decides who goes to heaven and who goes to hell. However, I suggest that something else is being described. Notice that an optimization guided by universal knowledge is occurring for those who are 'called according to His purpose', which is causing them to be 'conformed to the image' of incarnation (described here as the Son of God). In other words, those who 'enroll' in the school of incarnation will experience the same sort of optimization guided by universal knowledge that one finds exhibited by incarnation in nature, in which 'all possible paths' are 'working together' to generate the optimal path.

That brings us to the progression that begins with foreknowledge and ends with glorification. I suggest that one can interpret this in terms of an elite school. If a universal being knew all possible paths, then that being would have a *foreknowledge* of which individuals would be driven by their mental networks to enroll in the school of incarnation. These individuals would then be *called* to enroll in the school, and when they did enroll they would be *justified*. Finally, when they graduated from school then they would be *glorified*. Notice that one does not find anything in this passage about any specific choices that these chosen individuals are making while studying in school, or any prohibition against others choosing to enroll in this school.

The curriculum of this elite school is described a few verses later.

> Who will separate us from the love of Christ? Will tribulation, or distress, or persecution, or famine, or nakedness, or peril, or sword? Just as it is written, 'For Your sake we are being put to death all day long; We were considered as sheep to be slaughtered.' But in all these things we overwhelmingly conquer through Him who loved us (Romans 8:35-37).

Ouch!! The bottom line of this school is obviously not personal comfort but rather character development. One can see why Tevye would say to God, "I know, I know. We are Your chosen people. But, once in a while, can't You choose someone else?"

Orthodox Incarnation

I have suggested that incarnation makes sense if one examines the *most rational* aspect of human thought. Orthodox Christianity illustrates what can happen when one approaches the doctrine of incarnation using *irrational* thought. The end result is an amalgam of the two concepts of incarnation and mysticism, through what orthodox Christianity calls the doctrine of *theosis*. Archimandrite George, Abbott of a monastery on Mount Athos in Greece, describes this juxtaposition. His starting point is the emotional desire for personal identity to achieve the feeling of being united with God.

> The psyche of man, who is created in the image and likeness of God, yearns for God and desires union with Him. No matter how moral, how good man may be, no matter how many good deeds he may perform, if he does not find God, if he does not unite with Him, he finds no rest. Because holy God Himself placed within him this holy thirst, the divine eros, the desire for union with Him, for deification (gr. theosis). He has in himself the erotic power, which he receives from his Creator, in order to love truly, strongly, selflessly, just as his holy Creator falls in love with His world, with His creatures (George).

George describes this emotional 'desire for union' with God as a 'holy thirst', a 'divine eros', driven by 'erotic power'. Those are strong, personal emotions. George also says that this 'holy thirst' for union with God has nothing to do with morality. In other words, it is independent of any *content* that God might impinge upon personal identity. An emotional drive for union with God that ignores content describes the path of mysticism. George emphasizes that

> moral perfection is not enough for man. It is not enough for us simply to become better than before, to perform moral deeds. We have as our final aim to unite with holy God Himself. This is the purpose of the creation of the universe. This is what we desire. This is our joy, our happiness, and our fulfillment (Ibid).

We have just seen that incarnation makes possible the prayer of salvation which enables the personal honesty that is required for moral transformation. Using the school analogy, setting up a school makes it possible to enroll in school which makes education possible. George says something quite different.

> The Church Fathers say that God became man in order to make man a god. Man would not be able to attain deification (gr. theosis) if God had not become incarnate... Full union with God, Theosis, becomes possible, is attained, with the incarnation of the Divine Logos. This is the purpose of the incarnation of God. If the purpose of man's life was simply to become morally better, there would be no need for Christ to come into the world, for all these events of divine Provi-

dence to take place; for the incarnation of God; the cross, the death and resurrection of the Lord; all that we Christians believe (gr. pistis) to have happened by Christ. The human race could have been taught to become morally better by the prophets, the philosophers, the righteous men and teachers, just as well.

According to George, incarnation has nothing to do with moral perfection. Instead, the purpose of incarnation is to make it possible to achieve the goal of mysticism by becoming unified with God. The logic is as follows: God is incomprehensibly different than man, therefore it is impossible for someone to be both man and God. But Jesus did the impossible by being God and man. Therefore, people can also achieve the impossible by being both man and god.

However, if finite man achieves full union with infinite God, then this leads naturally to the conclusion that finite creation is the same as infinite God, a belief that is known as *pantheism*. George avoids this natural conclusion by distinguishing between divine *essence*, with which a human *cannot* identify, and divine *energy*, with which a human *can* identify.

> By virtue of God having divine energies, and by uniting with us by these energies, we are able to commune with Him and to unite with His Grace without becoming identical with God, as would happen if we united with His essence. So, we unite with God through His uncreated energies, and not through His essence. This is the mystery of our Orthodox faith and life. Western heretics cannot accept this. Being rationalist, they do not discern between the essence and the energy of God, so, they say that God is only essence. And for this reason they cannot speak about man's deification... In order not to fall into pantheism, they do not speak at all about deification (gr. theosis). What then, according to them, remains as the purpose of man's life? Simply moral improvement.

But if man can only become fully unified with the energy of God, then man is not becoming *fully* unified with God, because the Perceiver *distinction* between divine energy and divine essence stands in the way of being completely unified. The solution is to turn this Perceiver belief into a 'mystery' based in the MMNs of 'our Orthodox faith and life'. One can tell that Perceiver thought is not functioning but rather is being overwhelmed by cultural and religious MMNs because those who question the distinction between energy and essence are placed into the Mercy group of 'rationalists' and are given the negative Mercy label of 'heretics'.

Is George right? I suggest that one can answer this question by observing his physical environment. A rational concept of incarnation has succeeded in transforming the entire globe, while George lives as an abbot in one of the few places on earth that have not been transformed by science and technology. One must get a special visa to visit Mount Athos, the peninsula still uses the Julian calendar, and women have been forbidden to enter since an edict by the Byzantine Emperor in 1046. In other words, George is wearing a rather limited set of spectacles.

✳ 9. Platonic Forms and the Holy Spirit

The previous chapter examined the *variable* and the *equation*, and we saw the role that these two play in math and science. The variable replaces specific Mercy items such as apples and oranges with Perceiver categories like **X** or **Y,** while the equation uses abstract Teacher sequences to represent concrete cause-and-effect. For instance, instead of saying that the apple fell from the tree to the ground, one writes d = ½ gt². This chapter will look at the *Platonic form*, which I suggest relates to the *variable*. The next chapter will examine the relationship between the *equation* and the *exemplar*, which will involve discussing the relationship between Server thought and Teacher thought.

Imagine a circle. What probably comes to mind is the mental image of a perfectly round circle with no rough edges. This mental concept of 'the perfect circle' is the Platonic form of a circle. Philosophers and theologians have discussed the precise nature of Platonic forms ever since Plato came up with the idea of Platonic forms in around 400 BC. I suggest that one can use the theory of mental symmetry to explain how Platonic forms emerge within the mind.

Let us look more closely at the Platonic form of a circle. The physical world contains many round objects. Encountering these various objects will lead to the formation of memories within Mercy thought, such as a round stone at the beach, the circular cross-section of a log, or the round shape of the moon. Perceiver thought will notice this common property of roundness and come up with the Perceiver category of roundness. This Perceiver fact will then provide the raw material for Teacher thought, which will come up with a general theory of roundness that summarizes the essence of 'roundness'.

In order to come up with the simplest, most general Teacher theory, Perceiver facts will be modified in two ways. First, Perceiver facts will be made *fuzzy*. Quine gives an example of imprecise facts in *The Web of Belief.*

> Precision sometimes obstructs generality and sometimes not. The hypothesis about the boiling point of water can be generalized to pressures other than 760 millimeters without loss of precision by expressing the boiling point of pure water as an arithmetical function of the pressure. On the other hand if we want to generalize to impure water we must drop some precision, because the effect of impurities upon the boiling point varies not only with their amount but with their nature (Quine, 1978).

In other words, the simplest theory about boiling water says that water boils at 100°C. One can extend this theory to impure water by saying that water boils at *about* 100°C. It is possible to include atmospheric pressure by using the slightly more complicated equation $T = 100°C - (0.000561) \cdot H$, where H is the elevation in meters. If a more accurate answer is required, then an even more complicated equation will have to be used. Notice the trade-off between Perceiver accuracy and Teacher generality. In order to construct the simplest Teacher theory about boiling water, one must make the Perceiver facts a little bit fuzzy. Similarly, in order to come up with the simplest Teacher theory about 'roundness' one must make Perceiver facts about round objects slightly fuzzy by ignoring minor imperfections.

Second, Perceiver categories will be modified to *include* some items and *exclude* other items. Quoting again from Quine,

> A new definition may let the term apply to some things that it did not formerly apply to, and it may keep the term from applying to some of the things to which it had applied. The idea is to have any changes come in harmless cases, so that precision is gained without loss... Biologists gained precision and something more when they gave the common term 'fish' a sharp definition that banned whales; for the new distinction turned on biological characteristics that entered elsewhere into theory (Ibid).

In this case, Mercy thought contained many experiences about big living creatures in the ocean, leading to the Perceiver category of 'fish'. When biologists came up with general Teacher theories about fish, they found that they could construct a more general theory by modifying the Perceiver category of fish to exclude whales.

> A Platonic form is an imaginary Mercy image that results when Teacher thought modifies Perceiver facts about real Mercy experiences.

When Perceiver facts are modified in order to come up with more general Teacher theories, then these adjusted Perceiver facts will lead to the emergence in Mercy thought of *imaginary* images of objects that are more perfect and more simple than any real objects. These perfected, idealized, purified, simplified, imaginary, Mercy images are *Platonic forms*. Saying this all in a single sentence (which Teacher thought likes to do), a Platonic form is the imaginary Mercy image that results when Teacher thought modifies Perceiver facts about real Mercy experiences. Thus, a Platonic form is not real, but it is based in real experiences. A Platonic form will always remain imaginary, but it is possible to make real items more like Platonic forms. For instance, the Platonic form of a circle is like the definition of a circle that one learns in geometry. No real circle achieves that perfection and simplicity. However, modern technology makes it possible to create round items that are almost perfectly round.

The combination of modified Perceiver facts and Platonic forms will change the way that Mercy thought views reality. The adjusted Perceiver facts will alter the way that

Mercy experiences are *organized*, while the Teacher emotion behind Platonic forms will lead to a shift in *attention*. This means that a paradigm is not just a *metaphorical* set of spectacles through which one intellectually 'views' the abstract realm of ideas, but, to a certain extent, it is also a pair of *real* spectacles through which one views the concrete realm of physical reality. Thomas Kuhn describes how a paradigm shift changes the way that a scientist sees reality.

> During revolutions scientists see new and different things when looking with familiar instruments and places they have looked before. It is rather as if the professional community had been suddenly transported to another planet where familiar objects are seen in a different light and are joined by unfamiliar ones as well. Of course, nothing of quite that sort does occur: there is no geographical transplantation; outside the laboratory everyday affairs usually continue as before. Nevertheless, paradigm changes do cause scientists to see the world of their research engagement differently. In so far as their only recourse to that world is through what they see and do, we may want to say that after revolutions scientists are responding to a different world (Kuhn, 1970, p. 111).

Plato suggested that Platonic forms are more real than reality. While it is theoretically possible that Platonic forms might exist in some sort of non-physical spiritual realm, one can state with certainty that Platonic forms do not exist in the physical world. Instead, as Plato stated, everything in the world is imperfect and can only approach the perfection of Platonic forms. However, I suggest that Platonic forms can become more compelling than reality, to the extent that they *seem* more real than reality and change the way that one views reality. That is because Platonic forms emerge as a result of Teacher thought, which means that they can become emotionally backed up by underlying TMNs. This does not mean that Platonic forms contain *only* Teacher emotions. The most powerful Platonic forms also include emotional Mercy experiences and MMNs. However, Teacher thought, guided by Teacher emotion, does the *shaping* that creates Platonic forms out of the raw material of Mercy experiences.

Plato suggested that there is a *hierarchy* of Platonic forms, starting from images of reality and culminating in the Form of the Good, which Plato defined as the highest form. This hierarchy demonstrates the presence of Teacher thought, because the mind is generalizing about specific objects, and then continuing to generalize about its generalizations until a single general form emerges, which is the Form of the Good. The resulting interconnected mental structure will contain extensive order-within-complexity. Plato was unable to come up with a clear definition of the Form of the Good. I suggest that this is because he lacked a general Teacher understanding of how the mind functions. However, both Platonic forms and the Form of the Good fit nicely within the theory of mental symmetry, especially when combined with the concept of exemplars.

While a Platonic form is an *expression* of Teacher thought, a Platonic form *resides* within Mercy thought. A Platonic form is not a general theory. Rather, it is an image that has been modified by a general theory. For instance, 'the set of all points equidistant from some center' is a general Teacher theory of a circle, expressed using the Teacher elements of words. The Platonic form of a circle is the internal image within Mercy thought that expresses this general Teacher theory. This indirect relation leads to two common errors regarding Platonic forms. The first error is to think that Platonic forms have nothing to do with physical reality because they are the result of abstract thought. However, concrete reality provides the raw material for Platonic forms, which emerge when Teacher thought modifies real experiences from the real world. The other error is to assume that Platonic forms can be divorced from abstract theory because they are composed of real experiences. However, Platonic forms will not emerge without Teacher processing, and if abstract theory is abandoned, then Platonic forms will lose their perfection, purity, and simplicity.

> Platonic Forms based in absolute truth will be divorced from reality.

I should emphasize that the Platonic form being described here emerges from *universal* Perceiver truth, in which Perceiver thought compares many Mercy experiences to look for common features. Teacher understanding that is based upon *absolute* Perceiver truth will also cause Platonic forms to emerge within Mercy thought, but these will be internal visions of perfection that have *nothing to do* with reality, because they come from an understanding of facts that are based in some special book and not reality. Thus, theologians who are attempting to integrate Christian faith with the real world often recoil from the idea of Platonic forms. (N.T. Wright, for instance, condemns Platonic forms in no uncertain terms.) However, I suggest that the underlying problem is not Platonic forms but rather basing Platonic forms in absolute truth rather than universal truth. Summarizing, I am not suggesting that Platonic forms are *separate* from reality in some sort of Neoplatonic fashion, and I am also not suggesting that Platonic forms are the *same* as reality. Instead, a Platonic form is a Teacher-driven *idealization* of facts about reality, which motivates a person not to escape from reality, but rather to make reality more *like* the Platonic form.

Platonic Forms and Reality

Let us turn our attention now to religion. If *some* Teacher thought results indirectly in Platonic forms, then a *general* theory will lead indirectly to a *hierarchy* of Platonic forms, and a universal Teacher theory will express itself indirectly as a hierarchy of Platonic forms culminating in the Form of the Good. I have suggested that a mental concept of God emerges when a sufficiently general theory applies to personal identity. Adding to this the concept of Platonic forms, a mental concept of God will indirectly result in Mercy thought in a Form of the Good that idealizes the MMNs of personal identity and combines them into an inter-related social network held together by the TMN of a concept of God. Using religious language, I suggest that the Form of the Good defines a mental concept of the *Holy Spirit* and that the 'glue' that holds this mental concept together within Mercy thought is *love*.

So far, we have been assuming that Teacher thought builds *general* theories while Mercy thought handles *specific* experiences. That describes how Teacher thought and Mercy thought naturally develop when one grows up in a physical world governed by natural law. But it is also possible for the MMNs of Mercy thought to become unified into a *universal* concrete structure of social relationship. When this *Mercy* universality is approached in personal terms, then the result will be a concept of God that is different than what we have discussed so far, one which could be referred to as a concept of *divine spirit*. This sense of Mercy universality or divine spirit can be created either *externally* by the environment or *internally* by a universal understanding.

In order to avoid confusion, this book will use the term 'God' to refer to the image of a universal being that emerges when a general Teacher theory applies to personal identity. The term 'Holy Spirit' will describe the image of a universal being that forms within Mercy thought based in the Form of the Good. This is also a concept of a personal divine being but it is a *secondary* image that emerges within Mercy thought as the *indirect* result of a concept of God within Teacher thought. Using theological language, the Holy Spirit is also God because the mental concept within Mercy thought is both personal and universal, but there is only one God and not two Gods because the concept of the Holy Spirit acquires its perfection and universality from the concept of God in Teacher thought. Finally, the term 'divine spirit' will be used to describe the concept of divinity that forms within Mercy thought as a result of being immersed within some personal environment.

For instance, a person growing up in a jungle is surrounded by an ecosystem of interacting living beings. Thus, it is natural for the jungle native to regard Nature as a sort of divine spirit. A similar concept of divine spirit will naturally emerge when one grows up immersed in the *concrete* jungle of modern civilization. In both cases, a concept of divine spirit is being created by the *environment*. This concept of Nature as divine spirit or Gaia is different than the concept of Nature that one finds alluded to in biology and evolution. For the jungle native, Nature is intensely experiential and personal, leading to the sense that one is surrounded in *Mercy* thought by spirits that live in trees, rocks, and animals, immersed within the 'ocean' of divine spirit. For the biologist, Nature is more a personification of the *Teacher* structure of the natural world. Similarly, I suggest that a distinction can be made between a *general theory* and a *worldview*. A general theory resides in Teacher thought, while a worldview is an internal image in Mercy thought.

The concept of a *Holy* Spirit emerges when Teacher thought creates Platonic forms in Mercy thought and these Platonic forms are integrated into a Form of the Good by the TMN of a concept of God. The concept of divine spirit comes from being immersed within an environment. Thus, it is an integrated Mercy view of what *is*, and could be referred to as a 'spirit of this world'. In contrast, the concept of Holy Spirit comes from integrating Platonic forms. Thus, it is an integrated Mercy view of what *could be*. Because it is composed of Platonic forms that are purer, simpler, and more perfect than real life, it is a *Holy* Spirit that is an idealization of reality. One finds this combination illustrated by the word utopia, which could be read either as eu-topia, a place of goodness, or ou-topia, a place that does not exist. Because a Platonic form is an idealization of *existing* experiences and objects, the Form of the Good is eu-topia. But because a Platonic form is *better* than anything that exist in real life, the Form of the Good is also ou-topia.

Saying this another way, a distinction can be made between *goals* and *values*. A goal is something concrete in Mercy thought that one reaches using Server actions, like building a house, drinking a cup of coffee, getting a better job, or building a better mouse trap. A value is a Platonic form that lies behind goals and shapes goals. One can only reach goals; only goals are realizable. Values are invisible idealizations that can never be fully realized in the external environment. But when values turn into mental networks, then they will attempt to impose their structure upon goals, making goals more idealistic. Instead of just building a house, the goal will be to build a convenient house, a lasting house, a beautiful house, or a cute house. Rather than just drinking a cup of coffee, the goal will be to drink a tastier cup of coffee. Instead of just getting a better job, the goal might be to find a job that helps humanity, and instead of merely building a better mousetrap, the goal may be to free the world from vermin.

Similar statements can be made regarding love and Platonic love, a concept originally described by Plato. One could define love as mutually beneficial interaction between mental networks. Unfortunately, we have seen that when mental networks come into contact with one another, then the natural type of interaction is not love but rather *domination* and *submission,* because one mental network will attempt to impose its structure upon the other. Thus love will only occur naturally between people of the same family or culture who share *similar* mental networks, while interaction between people from opposing cultures will tend to be characterized by hate and xenophobia rather than love. However, Teacher thought finds pleasure in order-within-complexity; Teacher thought feels good when mental networks interact in a way that is simple, pure, efficient, straightforward, ordered, and honest. Thus, when Teacher thought creates Platonic forms, when these Platonic forms are held together by a general Teacher understanding leading to a Form of the Good, and when interaction between MMNs occurs within this universal Mercy framework, then the Form of the Good will motivate people to interact in a way that is more loving. Using religious language, God's love will be spread through the Holy Spirit.

> Love is mutually beneficial interaction between mental networks.

One can see a partial illustration of this in the *international economy.* Back in Roman times, tribes and empires gained wealth primarily by stealing from their neighbors, an external expression of one mental network imposing itself on another. The money for building the Colosseum in Rome, for instance, came from looting the Jewish Temple in Jerusalem.[1] In contrast, what drives most national growth today is the Platonic form of the 'international economy', formed indirectly by the general Teacher understanding of science and technology. While it is true that the real international economy always falls short of this Platonic form, it is also true that the Platonic form of the international economy motivates people and nations to interact in a manner that is far more loving than the raiding and looting practiced in previous times.

The *invisible church* provides a religious example of Platonic forms shaping love. The invisible church is a theological concept attributed to Saint Augustine, who apparently got the idea from Plato's theory of forms. The invisible church is a prominent concept in Protestant circles, because the *visible* Protestant church is fragmented into numerous denominations and sects. The Orthodox Church is held together by the MMNs of a collection of common traditions, handed down from the church fathers. The Catholic Church gains its unity primarily from the *external* Teacher order-within-complexity of a global church organization. The Protestant Church lacks both of these, and instead is held together internally by the Platonic form of the invisible church. The invisible church is a realm of idealistic perfection, in which everyone follows God wholeheartedly, everything works smoothly, there are no personality conflicts, everyone is growing in maturity, and politics never play a role. Real churches, in contrast, are composed of real individuals who lack these perfections. As the joke goes, if one ever finds a perfect church, then one should never join it because then it will become imperfect.

I suggest that any religion that is based in *theology* will have Platonic forms, because theology uses Teacher thought and Platonic forms emerge when Teacher thought idealizes Perceiver categories. Because a Platonic form is an idealization of reality, there will always be a *tension* between the perfection of the invisible church and the imperfection of visible churches.

Those who are outside of a theologically-based religion will notice the discrepancy between Platonic forms and reality and will point out the *hypocrisy* of religious believers. However, I suggest that this instinctive response is missing the point, because it is precisely this discrepancy between idealism and reality that *motivates* a person to make reality more ideal. The important thing is to maintain this tension, and the temptation will be either to regard the ideal is totally *separate* from reality or to regard reality as the *same* as the ideal. One sees the first response in the attitude of monks who leave society in order to focus fully upon God and Platonic forms. One sees the second response in the attitude of the Catholic Church, which tends to equate the Platonic form of the ideal

---

[1] Jerusalem was sacked by Titus under Vespasian in AD 70, construction on the Colosseum began in AD 72, and an inscription was recently found saying 'Imp. T. Caes. Vespasianus Aug. Amphitheatrum Novum Ex Manubis Fieri Iussit', or in English, 'The Emperor Caesar Vespasian Augustus had this new amphitheatre erected with the spoils of war' (Johnston, 2001).

church with the physical organization of the Catholic church (or in any religious denomination that thinks that it embodies the 'one and only true church').

A similar discrepancy between idealism and reality exists between the American *dream*
and the American *nation*. The American dream is a Platonic form created indirectly by
the Teacher structure of the American Constitution and the rule of law. The American
dream is a perfect society in which anyone can achieve success by working hard following the example of self-made heroes like Horatio Alger. The American dream is also an
imaginary society that does not exist and Horatio Alger is a *fictional* character. The American nation, in contrast, is a specific country that partially expresses the American dream.
Unlike the American dream, the American nation is imperfect. It is common for non-
Americans to point out the discrepancy between the American dream and the American
nation. However, I suggest that this also misses the point. There will always be a discrepancy between ideal and reality; this discrepancy motivates people to make reality
more ideal. The temptation is either to separate idealism from reality, by viewing the
American dream as a fantasy that no longer applies, or to equate idealism with reality by
viewing the American nation as the epitome of the American dream. But the American
dream can—and does—motivate people of *all* nations and societies to build a better
world (through the more general Platonic form of the international community). It does
not need the American nation to exist.

In a similar manner, *academia* is a Platonic form that is expressed through the *university*.
Academia consists of researchers collaborating to extend the body of knowledge. However, what one encounters in real life is not academia but rather a university, a physical
location often driven by politics, schools of thought, personal ambition, and the need to
publish. A university will always be only a partial expression of academia and the discrepancy between the two should motivate university to continually strive to become
more like academia. The important thing is to realize that academia is not the same as
university and that academia can also exist outside of a university.

When a Platonic form is expressed primarily by a single group, country, or society, then
there will be a natural tendency to equate the Platonic form with that *specific* group or
society, especially for those who grow up in that society. For instance, during the dark
Ages the Catholic Church was the *only* church in Western Christendom. Thus, it was
natural to regard the Catholic Church as the invisible church. Similarly, the United
States has played such a dominant role in the world's economy and possesses so much
physical wealth that it is natural to regard the American nation as the same as the
American dream. And because most academic thought currently occurs within universities, the natural tendency is to regard university as equivalent to academia.

So far, we have thought about TMNs and MMNs as occupying *separate* worlds, with
TMNs inhabiting the abstract world of words and symbols and MMNs living in the
concrete realm of experiences and people. A Platonic form emerges when TMNs 'invade' the realm of MMNs, or using religious language, the universal realm of God in-

vades the finite realm of man. This does not mean that words turn magically into experiences, or that God becomes visible to human eyes. But the *indirect* impact of Teacher thought upon Mercy thought is so profound that it feels as if one can see theories. Religiously speaking, one gains the impression that the 'invisible hand of God' has become visible in the concrete world of experiences.

As I have mentioned, Platonic forms will naturally be regarded as *distinct* from normal MMNs when *absolute* truth is revealed in a *book*. The structure of a book naturally encourages the development of Teacher understanding. However, when a book is regarded as *the source* of absolute truth rather than as a *description* of universal truth, then Perceiver thought will find it difficult to translate between the language of the holy book and the rest of reality, leading to a mental split between the Platonic forms that result from reading and understanding the holy book and the MMNs of normal life. One saw this kind of mental split illustrated graphically by the southern lady who prayed to God in the same room that she beat her slaves. In her case, the split between religious and secular was *internal*; she did not have to go to a special holy room to pray to God but instead was able to switch mentally between sacred and profane. Saying this more generally, a religion that is based in cultural and personal MMNs will tend to make *physical* distinctions between holy and unholy, whereas a religion that is guided by Platonic forms based in absolute truth is capable of separating *mentally* between holy and unholy. In either case, I suggest that building walls to separate holy from unholy is a symptom of incomplete mental integration, because walls, by definition, divide rather than connect.

The *equating* of Platonic forms with physical institutions usually occurs over time between generations. The founders of an institution develop Teacher understanding which leads to the formation of Platonic forms. These Platonic forms then motivate the founders to make reality more like Platonic forms, leading to the founding of institutions, and the founders tend to see these institutions as a visible expression of the 'invisible hand of God'. The *next* generation grows up in this environment, and the experience of living within this environment leads to the formation of MMNs held together by the *physical* structure of the institution as well as the *social* structure of the important people within this institution. For the founders, the physical institution is an expression of Platonic forms, peopled by individuals who are internally driven by the TMNs behind Platonic forms. In contrast, the succeeding generations will naturally regard the same physical institution as a source of childhood memories, and look to the founders as sources of truth with emotional status. Stated more simply, the next generation does the right thing for the wrong reason.

This does not mean that Teacher thought ceases. Instead, those who follow are usually able to go further than the founders because they are 'standing on the shoulders of giants'. However, the full proverb says that '*dwarves* are standing on the shoulders of giants'. Looking at this cognitively, succeeding generations are 'standing on the shoulders of giants' because they acquired the knowledge of the founders in childhood, which enables them to start their research from where their ancestors left off, but if the core of their knowledge is based upon MMNs of status and culture rather than the TMNs of deep understanding and Platonic forms, then they are 'dwarves'. For instance, the United States is still the world's largest economy, universities are the major source of academic thought, and Catholic theologians have a depth of scholarship that is seldom matched by theologians from other branches of Christianity. But in each case, one finds that the physical institution, its procedures, and its founders loom large in the core of thought. For Americans, the underlying assumption still tends to be that America is some sort of 'chosen nation' with a special status and the founding fathers are given almost religious reverence. Similarly, when I discuss my research with most academics, two questions generally come to the fore. First, have I quoted recognized sources, and second, why don't I get a PhD, the underlying assumption being that we are probably dwarves compared to the intellectual stature of the founders, and that one must become officially recognized by a university in order to be part of academia. Likewise, even though Catholic theology tends to be of high quality, one generally finds it infused with a deep and assumed reverence for the institution of the Catholic Church.

Pentecostalism

It is also possible for a Platonic form to become *disconnected* from its source in Teacher thought, like a tail becoming disconnected from a dog. What happens then is that the tail becomes vulnerable to being 'wagged' by other sources. I have mentioned that one usually finds a high level of scholarship in Catholic writing. The opposite is true of Pentecostal writing, where scholarship is often lacking and is replaced by experience and testimony. Pentecostalism is the branch of Christianity that emphasizes the Holy Spirit and downplays theology. This is expressed through practices such as a focus upon dramatic worship, a search for miracles, speaking in tongues, words of prophecy, and spiritual gifts. Pentecostalism was first spread by the Azusa Street Revival, which began at a religious meeting on April 9, 1906 in Los Angeles and continued until about 1915. Using cognitive language, I suggest that Pentecostalism focuses upon the Mercy experiences of Platonic forms while forgetting that Platonic forms are the indirect result of Teacher understanding.

> Pentacostalism focuses on Platonic Forms while ignoring their Teacher source.

It is interesting to note that Los Angeles in the early 1900s was also a center of the *American dream*. The Santa Fe railroad arrived in 1885. During the 1890s the climate and opportunities of Hollywood were heavily advertised throughout United States. The Rose Bowl started in 1902, the city of Hollywood was founded in 1903, and two major oil fields were discovered in the Los Angeles region in 1900 and 1902. (My mother's father visited Los Angeles several times during this period and even bought land on Beacon Hill, but unfortunately gave away the mineral rights when selling the property.)

One can see this disconnection in the Pentecostal practice of *speaking in tongues*. Pentecostalism initially placed a great emphasis upon speaking in tongues and regarded it as proof that one had been 'baptized by the Holy Spirit'. (The Pentecostal movement was followed in the 1980s by the charismatic renewal, which continues most of the practices of Pentecostalism but no longer regards speaking in tongues as an essential requirement.) William Samarin, a linguist at the University of Toronto, examined glossolalia (speaking in tongues) from a linguistic viewpoint and concluded that glossolalia

> consists of strings of syllables, made up of sounds taken from all those that the speaker knows, put together more or less haphazardly but emerging nevertheless as word-like and sentence-like units because of realistic language-like rhythm and melody. In other words, there can be neither syntactics nor semantics to this means of speech. There is, nonetheless, a not insignificant pragmatics... the sociolinguistic meaning of glossolalia is located in its apposition with normal language. Once the charismatist has developed the facility of producing glossolalic discourse (acquired by some almost instantaneously, but others with considerable practice, but much more easily than is generally imagined,) he has the choice of using either human language or the heavenly language in the exercise of his religion... He can give prophetic pronouncement, pray, or praise God in either glossolalia or whatever his usual language may be (Samarin, 1972).

Saying this more simply, glossolalia contains the structure of language but lacks the content of language. In contrast, the Mercy-based non-verbal aspects of pragmatics and melody are 'not insignificant'. This conclusion is backed up by a 2006 neurological study which discovered that if one compares singing with speaking in tongues, then speaking in tongues is correlated with decreased prefrontal and left temporal pole activity as well as increased left superior parietal and right amygdala activity. Translating this into mental symmetry, the internal world is functioning less, specific words are not being retrieved in Teacher thought, the general structure of speech is being retrieved in Server thought, and Mercy emotions are active (Newberg, 2006). (This neurological mapping is described in the final chapter.)

It is interesting to compare the attitudes of mysticism and glossolalia with the approach taken by this book. In each case, the goal is to use Teacher thought to provide Mercy thought with personal benefits, or in terms of the analogy, to use the dog of Teacher thought to wag the tail of Mercy thought. Mysticism insists that there is no such thing as a dog. Saying this more properly, mysticism brings Teacher and Mercy thought together by removing all Perceiver and Server content, leading to a mental conflict between the content of human existence and the contentlessness of interacting with God. And 'contentlessness' is an appropriate term because it is a complicated way of saying 'nothing'. In other words, even though mysticism is driven by a Teacher theory that lacks content, many esoteric words are used to describe this lack of content.

In glossolalia, the tail of Mercy thought is being wagged by the *idea* of a dog. However, glossolalia is unable to use rational Teacher thought to describe the nature of this dog.

That is because Teacher thought makes a switch in Teacher thought from 'human language' to 'heavenly language' and then uses 'heavenly language' to create the Platonic form of the Holy Spirit. Thus, instead of Teacher understanding, there is technobabble. But this theoretical jargon gives the impression that the tail is being wagged by some sort of dog. A similar type of mechanism is used in science fiction, such as when Scotty tells Captain Kirk on Star Trek that he is 'reversing the polarity' or 'replacing the dilithium crystals'. Even though these words mean nothing, they convey the impression of a Mercy tail being wagged by some magnificent dog of deep Teacher understanding.

In contrast, mental symmetry attempts to wag the tail of Mercy thought using the Teacher understanding of a *fuzzy, generic* dog. We are focusing upon overall structure rather than specific content, and we are jumping from one context in Teacher thought to another guided by general patterns. Thus, there is a similarity between the methodology of mental symmetry and speaking in tongues. However, instead of *abandoning* intelligible Teacher thought as speaking in tongues does, we are being *guided* by the meta-theory of a cognitive model that integrates different contexts, and it is possible to *describe* this meta-theory using words with reasonably precise definitions.

Pentacostalism uses the idea of a dog to wag the tail. A similar statement can be made regarding the *American dream*. Here too, the Mercy 'tail' of material prosperity is attached to 'the dog' of scientific understanding, democratic capitalism, and the Protestant work ethic. Detaching the tail from the dog results in the *consumer society*. The consumer knows in a *general* way that the Teacher understanding of science, politics, and theology leads to the dreams of Platonic forms, which are then turned into the reality of 'new and improved products', but the typical consumer does not comprehend any of the abstract content contained within science, politics, or theology. One finds this *physically* illustrated by Los Angeles at the beginning of the 20th century. Eastern United States had tradition, culture, and institutes of higher learning. Thanks to the railroad, one could leave this realm of content and move to Los Angeles, a land of opportunity with pleasant climes uninhibited by any of the content present in Eastern society.

Summarizing, the Pentecostal switches from an earthly language with content to a heavenly language that lacks content and then uses the general idea of language to create Platonic forms which then motivate concrete action, the consumer society switches from the content-full language of science to the content-less language of marketing and then uses the general idea of scientific thought to create visions that lead to new products, and the 1900s opportunist moved from the Eastern states with their cultural content to the uninhibited society of Los Angeles and then used the general idea of modern civilization to create schemes which then motivated concrete action. In each case one finds a similar cognitive transition, in which one removes the dog and then uses the idea of a dog to wag the tail.

When tails get wagged by invisible dogs, then there is a tendency for these invisible dogs to be replaced by visible ones. One sees this in the Pentecostal 'word of prophecy'.

Prophecy is typically preceded by speaking in tongues. First, someone will stand up in church and say something like "Oohrababa shandalama hundai..." Then, someone else will stand up and interpret this heavenly language through word of prophecy. Usually, this prophecy is a general statement of personal affirmation, like "God wants you to know that he loves you and cares for you." Occasionally, specific instructions are given, such as "The Lord says, 'Someone in this congregation needs to step out in faith and move to Scotland, where they will become part of a new and powerful ministry of God.'" Other times, prophecy involves healing: "God says that there is a person who is struggling with a weak knee. God wants to heal that knee today."

It is possible that there is some reality behind these claims. For instance, for many years I played violin in a string quartet with a lady whose left hand had been totally crushed by a falling piano. Even after being operated upon she was still completely unable to play. However, twice she felt a warm sensation in her hand in the middle of the night, and after the second warm feeling she was able immediately to pick up the viola and play again. Thus, while most 'healings' are probably psychosomatic, this one was definitely the genuine article (Watson, 1999).

However, the format of the word of prophecy is vulnerable to abuse. People *do* sell their houses and move to Scotland, guided primarily by some word of prophecy. Unfortunately, when Teacher understanding is lacking then there is no way to distinguish between God telling me to move to Scotland, my concept of God telling me to move, someone else's concept of God telling me to move, or someone else pretending to speak for God and telling me to move.

Summing this all up theologically, I suggest that the Holy Spirit is the *third* person of the Trinity. Notice that I said *third* person and not *second* person. This distinction is significant and is also reflected in the *filioque* clause that was partially responsible for the final schism between Catholic Christianity and Orthodox Christianity in 1054. The Orthodox version of the Nicene Creed says 'in the Holy Spirit, the Lord, the giver of life, from the Father proceeding' while the Catholic version says 'in the Holy Spirit, the Lord, and giver of life, who from the Father and the Son proceeds'. Notice the addition of the phrase 'and the Son', which in Latin is *filioque*. This may seem like a subtle difference, but it describes two different ways of connecting Teacher thought with Mercy thought. Does one head *directly* from Teacher thought to Mercy thought or does one go *indirectly* through Contributor thought? The direct connection leads to mysticism and we have seen that Orthodox Christianity interprets incarnation in terms of mysticism, while the indirect connection uses Contributor incarnation to integrate the Teacher universality of a mental concept of God with the Mercy universality of a mental concept of the Holy Spirit. Mysticism can only function by denying mental content, whereas incarnation leads to an integration between Teacher theory and Mercy experience that is deeply consistent with the overlapping Contributor content shown in math and science. Thus, I suggest that it is no accident that math and science developed primarily in Catholic

Western Europe rather than Orthodox Eastern Europe. This does not mean that the Orthodox interpretation is entirely counterproductive, because the Western focus upon incarnation has resulted in the specialization of technical thought, which gets the details right but loses sight of the big picture. Thus, I suggest that it is important to view the Holy Spirit as proceeding from the Father *and* the Son. The Son adds content while the Father adds universality, resulting in a Holy Spirit that has both content and universality.

Two Forms of Holiness

Both holiness and Platonic forms lead to the sense that some Mercy experiences, objects, people, or events are *more special* than other Mercy elements. But the way that this specialness is expressed is quite different. We can compare these two kinds of specialness by looking at the *Eucharist,* one of the sacraments (or core rituals) of Christianity.

Holiness gives emotional status to *specific* items within Mercy thought. For example, a religious altar may be holy, or a specific cup of wine or piece of bread. This specific holy item is then separated from other similar items that are not holy, usually by placing the holy item behind physical walls. For instance, we looked previously at the reverence given to the sanctified bread and wine during Eucharist adoration. The bread and wine becomes holy when it is consecrated by a priest during mass. It is then either displayed upon an altar in a monstrance or else locked away in a tabernacle. This physical separation is necessary because Perceiver thought is fighting Mercy thought. On the one hand, Perceiver thought will notice that the holy bread and holy wine appear *similar* to secular bread and wine, while on the other hand, holiness driven by Mercy emotions insists that the holy bread and wine are *different* than secular bread and wine.

The *Mercy* side of this cognitive conflict is addressed by ensuring that a holy item triggers a *different mental network* than a secular item. Thus, a piece of bread sitting on a kitchen table triggers secular mental networks related to mealtime, while the same piece of bread sitting on a monstrance will trigger religious mental networks related to the celebration of the Mass.

The Perceiver side to this cognitive conflict is addressed through the doctrine of *transubstantiation*. In simple terms, a distinction is made between the physical properties of an item, known as its *accidents*, and the *substance* of that item. For instance, a person is physically a collection of organic chemicals, water, and minerals. However, the *substance* of a person is far more than merely a collection of physical atoms. The problem of hard consciousness strongly suggests that a person *is* more than just a collection of physical atoms. Similarly, attempting to come up with a grand explanation collapses into absurdity if my place within this grand explanation ceases at physical death. Thus, when dealing with people, I suggest that it does make sense to make a distinction between accident and substance. But is a piece of bread more than a collection of wheat, water, yeast, and salt? Physically speaking, I am not convinced. But cognitively speaking, we saw when introducing mental networks that a child's doll becomes more than merely fabric and stuffing to a child when it is represented within the child's mind by a mental network. If a child can interact socially with fabric and stuffing, then adults could use the same cognitive mechanisms to interact religiously with bread and wine.

But we have seen in this chapter that feelings of holiness within Mercy thought can either be created *directly* by emotional experiences, objects, and people or *indirectly* through Platonic forms. When holiness is created directly, then the focus will be upon specific objects and the goal will be to make those objects as *unique* as possible. Platonic forms, in contrast, emerge when Teacher thought idealizes many objects in Mercy thought. Thus, a real object will be regarded as special to the extent that it *epitomizes* the Platonic form. For example, the meter is a Platonic form. When one thinks of a meter one thinks of a precise invisible length that does not exist anywhere in real life. However, for many years the meter was represented by the distance between two physical marks on a physical bar made of platinum and iridium stored in climate-controlled conditions in Paris. The care with which this prototype meter was treated far exceeds the reverence shown to the sacraments during mass. However, the reason for this care was quite different. A sacrament is treated with reverence in order to preserve the emotional intensity of the MMN that represents the sacraments and to prevent this MMN from coming into mental contact with secular MMNs. In contrast, the care shown the prototype meter was designed to keep the physical property of length of that metal bar as close as possible to the Platonic form of one meter. And instead of trying to *prevent* Perceiver thought from connecting between consecrated bread and normal bread, the ultimate purpose of the prototype meter was to make the *best possible* Perceiver connection between the standard meter and all other meter sticks.

> Holiness treats specific items as special and uses walls to preserve this specialness. Platonic forms view specific items as special to the extent that they resemble the ideal.

Summarizing, holiness regards specific objects as special, whereas Platonic forms regard any objects as special to the extent that they resemble the ideal. Holiness prevents Perceiver thought from thinking that holy objects are similar to secular objects, while Platonic forms use Perceiver thought to compare ideal objects with normal objects in order to make normal objects more similar to ideal objects. A holy object will tend to be ornate and highly crafted, signifying great Mercy care and uniqueness, while an ideal object will tend to be pure, simple, and elegant, signifying Teacher order-within-complexity. Finally, the natural tendency is for holy objects to become blasphemed when they come into contact with secular objects, whereas Platonic forms naturally improve normal objects.

Now that we understand this general distinction, let us return to the Eucharist. The typical monstrance is ornate and highly crafted, different than any object used in normal life, kept in a location that is separate from normal life. Similarly, the Eucharist is celebrated in a ritual that is also ornate and highly crafted, performed by individuals who act, talk, and dress in a manner quite different than normal life, performed in a location that is distinct from normal life. However, when it comes to the bread and the wine, then the situation is quite different. Eating is something that one does several times a day, and bread and wine were common elements of the typical Roman citizen's diet. There is also nothing ornate or highly crafted about bread and wine. Instead, they are both generic and pedestrian. Thus, if one examines the sacraments themselves, one notices the characteristics of Platonic forms, but if one examines the trappings surrounding the sacraments, then one sees the characteristics of holiness.

But what Platonic form do bread and wine express in ideal form? We can answer this question by looking at the biblical account of the 'last supper', so called because it was the last supper Jesus had with his followers before being crucified.

> While they were eating, Jesus took some bread, and after a blessing, He broke it and gave it to the disciples, and said, "Take, eat; this is My body." And when He had taken a cup and given thanks, He gave it to them, saying, "Drink from it, all of you; for this is My blood of the covenant, which is poured out for many for forgiveness of sins" (Matt. 26:26-28).

Notice how the sacrament of the Eucharist begins when Jesus takes normal food during mealtime. (The group was celebrating the Jewish feast of Pesach, and I suggest that similar statements could be made about that 'sacrament' as well.) We see here that the Eucharist is being associated with identification with incarnation in order to receive forgiveness of sins. We saw precisely this combination when examining the Christian prayer of salvation. Personal identity submits to incarnation in order to experience the feeling of forgiveness from God. Previously, we viewed the prayer of salvation as a decision that happens at a certain point in time that changes one's official status, similar to enrolling in a school, and that is how it is seen by *abstract* technical thought. For *concrete* technical thought, though, school is a long process of being fed daily by information delivered in bite-size chunks which is then digested in order to become integrated into one's body of knowledge. In other words, 'eating one's daily bread' is such a natural metaphor of the process of education that it has entered normal speech.

Summarizing, the sacrament of bread and wine makes sense from the viewpoint of *Platonic forms*, because the action of regularly eating food in bite-sized chunks *resembles* the process of education. However, the ritual that has grown up over the centuries to accompany the bread and wine makes sense from the viewpoint of holiness, because the actions, objects, events, and people connected with the Eucharist are given great emotional status in Mercy thought and kept distinct from normal experiences. I suggested earlier that there is a tendency within Catholicism to confuse the Platonic form of the invisible church with the physical expression of the Catholic Church, because for many centuries the Catholic Church was the only Western church. One sees a similar confusion in the Catholic (and Orthodox) celebration of the Eucharist, because one finds a juxtaposition of holiness and Platonic forms. This juxtaposition is officially expressed as the doctrine of transubstantiation, which states that the 'substance' of the bread literally becomes the physical body of Jesus the physical incarnation.

Stating this more generally, when a cognitive confusion such as equating the invisible church with the visible church turns into a core mental network, then this mental network will impose its structure upon related doctrines, such as the doctrine of transubstantiation. I am not suggesting that Catholicism ignores Platonic forms and symbolism. One can find extensive Catholic literature regarding the symbology of the Eucharist, which attempts to analyze the Platonic form behind the sacraments. However, what happened historically is that the original structure emphasized Platonic forms, these Platonic forms were equated with physical objects, actions, and people during the early days of Christendom, and Catholic scholars are now attempting to determine the Platonic forms behind the *combination* of original structure and holy items, rituals, and individuals. It would be more productive cognitively to cut out the middleman. Using an analogy from computer support, it is very frustrating for a person who understands computers to give instructions to another person who understands computers if these instructions have to be relayed *through* some intermediary who is computer illiterate, because the instructions will get mangled by the intermediary. It is far more productive to eliminate the intermediary.

Summarizing, Platonic forms create *values* within Mercy thought that will naturally make Mercy *goals* more idealistic. A concept of the Holy Spirit emerges when a general theory in Teacher thought integrates Platonic forms. This leads to a hierarchy of mental networks. What holds everything together is the TMN of a general understanding. This TMN gives shape to the MMNs of Platonic forms, which in turn impose their structure upon the MMNs of personal identity and culture. Using religious language, personal existence is guided by the Holy Spirit, and the Holy Spirit submits to God. When mental networks are arranged in this manner, then people are naturally driven to think and behave in ways that are more idealistic, purer, simpler, transparent, and loving. University becomes more like academia, America becomes more like the American dream, and the physical church becomes more like the invisible church.

Incarnation and Platonic Forms

We will finish this chapter by examining the relationship between *incarnation* and *Platonic forms*. Remember that one of the core issues in religion is the relationship between a *universal* concept of God in Teacher thought and *finite* personal identity in Mercy thought. We have now discussed two ways of connecting finite with infinite in a manner that includes content. Science and mathematics use the method of incarnation, which uses general equations to represent specific cause-and-effect. For instance, $d = \frac{1}{2} gt^2$ is the general equation that is used to represent the specific cause-and-effect of an apple falling from a tree to the ground. Platonic forms also connect specific with universal by using the Platonic form of an idealized, simplified item to represent many similar specific items. For instance, all round shapes are represented internally by the Platonic form of an ideal circle. What is the relationship between these two methods?

We can address this question by looking at geometry, a subject which I taught for several years to grade 9 students in Korea. Geometry is full of Platonic forms such as points, lines, planes, parallel lines, perpendicular lines, circles, triangles, squares, and parallelograms. These idealized shapes are the basic building blocks for geometry, which then uses abstract technical thought to formulate theorems and proofs within this realm of Platonic forms. Thus, Platonic forms create the *context* for abstract technical thought in geometry.

One can see a similar relationship when formulating a problem in physics. Consider, for instance, the following problem taken at random from a physics textbook.

> A hockey puck with mass 0.160 kg is at rest at the origin on the horizontal, frictionless surface of the rink. At time $t = 0$ a player applies a force of 0.250 N to the puck, parallel to the x-axis; he continues to apply this force until $t = 2.00$ s. What are the position and speed of the puck at $t = 2.00$ s? (Young & Freedman, 2012).

Notice all of the idealizations that are occurring. An imaginary *grid* of X and Y is being imposed on an ice surface, and it is assumed that the force is being applied precisely in the *direction* of the imaginary X-axis. The surface of the ice is represented by an ideal plane that is perfectly *horizontal* without any friction. And the force that the hockey player exerts on the puck is treated as a *uniform* force that *begins* at precisely zero seconds and *ceases* at precisely two seconds. Thus, physics first turns real objects into Platonic forms and then uses abstract technical thought to analyze these Platonic forms, similar to the method used by geometry. The same transition occurs in algebra when, for instance, a specific apple is replaced by the Platonic form of the variable **X**.

Abstract technical thought works with the Platonic forms of real items.

Summarizing, replacing a specific Mercy item with a Platonic form is one major aspect of making the transition from concrete technical thought to abstract technical thought. For instance, suppose that I want to throw a ball in order to hit some target. Concrete technical thought will use a real ball and throw it at a real target, observe where the ball lands, and then adjust how hard the ball is thrown and the angle at which it is thrown in order to get closer to the target. In order to make the transition to abstract technical thought with its mathematical equations, all of the real objects are first replaced by Platonic forms. The irregular ball is replaced by the Platonic form of some mass concentrated at some geometrical point. The complicated process of throwing the ball is replaced by the idealized process of releasing a mass with some velocity in some direction. And the real atmosphere with its air friction is replaced by the Platonic form of an ideal atmosphere that has no air friction. Mathematical equations are then used to solve the idealized version of the problem in which all of the real objects and events have been replaced by equivalent Platonic forms.

Because a Platonic form is an idealization of many specific items, it is slightly different than any specific item. For instance, the ideal ball is slightly different than any real ball. Physics partially accounts for this approximation of reality by the concept of *significant figures*. For example, in the physics problem shown above, the force was given as 0.250 N. The '0' after the '5' indicates that the force was measured to an accuracy of 1/1000th of a Newton. This means that even if all of the approximations made by the physics problem can be ignored, the final answer will still only be accurate to one part in a thousand. Physics goes from reality to Platonic form, while engineering goes from reality to Platonic form *back* to reality, because engineering uses the equations of physics as a guide for building real objects and setting up real processes. Engineering accounts for the approximation inherent in using Platonic forms by adding a *safety margin*. For instance, if mathematical equations indicate that a certain column needs to have a diameter of 30 cm in order to hold up a certain weight, then a safety margin of 50% might be added, and the engineer will build a column with a diameter of 37 cm instead of 30 cm (the strength of the column depends upon its cross-sectional area, which is proportional to the square of the diameter).

Adding a correction factor is usually sufficient, but not always. For instance, I mentioned the example of a local church floor collapsing during a Christian rock concert. Obviously, the engineers who designed this floor never visualized dozens of people standing in one place and jumping up and down in a rhythmic fashion. Instead, they probably designed the floor so that it would hold up a *typical* crowd represented as a number of *idealized* masses and then added a *standard* correction factor. Thus, when making a transition from concrete to abstract technical thought, it is very important to use the appropriate Platonic forms. That is because Platonic forms are being used to approximate reality whereas the actual cause-and-effect comes from the specific physical item in concrete thought and not from the Platonic form. For instance, the collapsing floor in the church came from real people jumping up and down in rhythm on top of a real floor. (Rhythmic motion that occurs at a resonant frequency is particularly dangerous for load-bearing spans, which is why soldiers do not march in formation when crossing bridges.) The floor collapsed because the Platonic form that was used to represent these people accurately represented their mass but not the rhythmic movement.

Now let us apply this concept to the mind. What are the appropriate Platonic forms when using abstract theory to analyze real people in real social situations? Mental symmetry suggests that a person can be represented by the Platonic form of a cognitive module. For instance, I may have a friendly neighbor who often gives me samples of his wife's baking and who likes to entertain family. That describes some specific person that the mind will represent within Mercy thought using some MMN. If I know that this person has the cognitive style of Exhorter, then it is possible to represent this specific person by using the Platonic form of Exhorter thought, a Platonic form that uses Teacher understanding to distill the essence from all my experiences with Exhorter persons. This is the most general way of representing a person, but it is also an approximation. If one wishes to make this Platonic form more accurate, then one can model my friendly neighbor using the Platonic form of an entire mind composed of interacting cognitive modules in which Exhorter thought is conscious. In this case, the general Teacher theory of the diagram of mental symmetry is being used to distill the essence from experiences with all cognitive styles. Finally, if one wishes to add some detail, then one can include the various attributes that distinguish the mature Exhorter person from the immature one, such as remaining within difficult situations rather than moving on when faced with problems, or developing physical skills rather than using speech to tell others what to do. Notice how one can only use the abstract theory of mental symmetry to analyze humans if one first replaces specific humans with Platonic forms that represent categories of humans.

Turning briefly to psychology, I suggest that this adds details to Higgins' concept of *Possible Selves* (1987). Higgins said that a person's self-concept is usually composed of three different aspects, which he called the *actual* self, the *ought* self, and the *ideal* self. The *actual* self is based upon a person's knowledge and skills. Using the language of mental symmetry, it forms when Perceiver thought notices repeated connections involving personal identity. For instance, if I know many facts about computers then knowledge about computers will form part of my actual self because the knowledge is consistently available when required. Similarly, if I can consistently use my fingers to play music on a piano then this skill of pianist will also form part of my actual self. The *ought* self is based upon the expectations of other people and their approval and disapproval of me. For example, if my parents think that I should be a medical doctor, then this will be part of my ought self. In terms of mental symmetry, the ought self is imposed upon personal identity by the mental networks of significant people such as parents and authority figures. Unlike the actual self, the ought self is unstable because it changes when different mental networks are triggered. For example, if I leave home, then I will no longer feel as much pressure from my parents to be a medical doctor because the mental networks that represent my parents are no longer being triggered. Saying this another way, the ought self depends upon my social surroundings. Think, for instance, of the way that drivers instinctively put on the brake when a police car shows up, because the presence of a policeman triggers a mental network regarding speeding and traffic tickets that will attempt to impose itself upon personal identity. Finally, the *ideal* self describes what I would ideally like to become, the type of person that I would like to be. I suggest that the ideal self reflects Platonic forms that apply to personal identity. Saying this in the language of values and goals, the actual self lets me know which goals I am *capable* of achieving, the ideal self provides the values that *shape* my goals, while the ought self reflects the attempts of *others* to determine my goals and values.

Many different kinds of Platonic forms can be used as values to motivate personal improvement. However, if one approximates human character using Platonic forms that leave out key attributes, then one will eventually end up facing unforeseen problems, just as the engineers who represented people using the Platonic form of 'an object with mass' ran into an unforeseen problem when these people gathered together in one place and danced to the rhythm. That is why I suggest that it is best to represent humans using the Platonic forms of cognitive styles and cognitive modules, because these appear to encapsulate all significant aspects of human personality.

In other words, all Platonic forms are approximations, because they leave out *nonessential* characteristics. It is possible to compensate for this type of inaccuracy by adding a safety margin. Inappropriate Platonic forms also leave out *essential* characteristics. When this is the case, then having a safety margin is usually not sufficient. The problem is that the MMNs of culture often determine which characteristics are regarded as essential or nonessential. For instance, the church with the collapsing floor was built in an era in which dancing in church was strictly verboten (especially in a *Mennonite* church), and thus could be regarded as a nonessential detail by the designers. When cultural norms shifted, then the unthinkable became the expected, turning a nonessential characteristic into an essential one. That is why it is best to base Platonic forms in the hardware of natural law or cognitive structure rather than the software of culture and social convention, because software can and does change, whereas hardware is fixed.

Applying this specifically to the topic of Christianity, almost every recently written Christian book on personal transformation that I have read quotes, often more than once, the verse in Romans 12 where Paul says that one should be 'transformed by the renewing of your mind'. However, none of these books analyze the rest of this passage, which describes the seven different cognitive styles. If one wishes to describe Christian theology from the abstract cognitive perspective of 'being transformed by the renewing of the mind' then I suggest that one must first represent both the mind and people by the appropriate Platonic forms.

The immediate context within which this oft-quoted phrase occurs is illuminating.

> Therefore I urge you, brethren, by the mercies of God, to present your bodies a living and holy sacrifice, acceptable to God, which is your spiritual service of worship. And do not be conformed to this world, but be transformed by the renewing of your mind, so that you may prove what the will of God is, that which is good and acceptable and perfect (Romans 12: 1-2).

The natural path is for the mind to be 'conformed to this world', shaped by the MMNs that are acquired through embodiment. Paul tells us to submit the MMNs of embodiment as a 'living sacrifice' to the TMN of God. Instead of the mind being conformed to world-imposed MMNs, it will be transformed through a '*spiritual* service of worship'—a focus upon Platonic forms. As a result, personal behavior will become increasingly like the Platonic forms that express the TMN of an understanding of God.

I suggest that this principle of modeling people as Platonic forms will naturally cause a mental concept of incarnation to emerge. One is already representing the Contributor person by a Platonic form as well as noticing that Contributor persons fall into the two general categories of Intellectual Contributor and Practical Contributor. One then recognizes that this *same* Platonic form plays the role of incarnation within the mind.

Now suppose that a *real* Contributor person exists who claims to be the *real* incarnation. One could validate this claim by examining the Platonic form of Contributor incarnation and then seeing how closely this real person matches up with the Platonic form. A person who physically encountered this real incarnation would first regard this person 'according to the flesh' as a specific individual within concrete thought. However, in order to make the cognitive transition from concrete technical thought to abstract technical thought, one would have to stop regarding this person as merely a specific individual, and start regarding this individual 'according to the spirit' as a Platonic form created by abstract thought. Saying this another way, this individual would have to 'ascend' from the specific human realm of concrete reality to the abstract divine realm of generality. One finds this illustrated by the Christian story of incarnation ascending from earth to heaven. Why is it important to view incarnation as a Platonic form rather than merely as a specific physical individual? Because this dual concept of specific man/Platonic form can be *inserted* as an incarnation between Mercy thought and Teacher thought, which will *generate* the feeling of being forgiven by God, which makes it *possible* to practice personal honesty, which is a *requirement* for transforming childish MMNs.

I would like to add one final point which I have discovered as a Perceiver person working with the concept of Contributor incarnation. I have suggested that Platonic forms are a prerequisite for making the transition from concrete technical thought to abstract technical thought. Saying this more generally, normal thought creates the environment for technical thought, because Platonic forms are an expression of *normal* thought with its *interaction* between cognitive modules. As Kuhn suggests, the standard practice for science is to make the transition from normal thought to technical thought as quickly as possible, and then spend as much time as possible solely within technical thought, re-emerging into standard thought only when forced to when the existing paradigm falls apart. In contrast, my research has focused upon using normal thought with its patterns and analogies (something which a Perceiver person would naturally do). However, I have discovered—repeatedly—that normal thought can only get me *close* to an answer. In order to find a complete solution, I have to make a mental transition from normal thought to technical thought, which *internally* for me as a Perceiver person means losing control to subconscious Contributor thought, while *externally* it means studying the technical research done by other individuals who spend most of their time within technical thought.

✳ 10. Blasphemy Against the Holy Spirit

I know that the phrase 'blasphemy against the Holy Spirit' is highly charged, both emotionally and religiously. In Christian doctrine, this is known as the 'unpardonable sin'. However, this phrase appears to be the most accurate description of the juxtaposition of mental networks that we will be examining in this chapter. Therefore, let us begin by assigning a technical definition to this phrase.

If one wishes to build a harmonious society that is guided by Platonic forms, childish MMNs must be fully transformed by the TMN of a general understanding. In religious language, identity and culture must be *totally* transformed by the concept of a monotheistic, universal God. If core childish MMNs remain *intact* and *in charge* of the mind, then the result is a *partially* transformed society that, rather than becoming better, actually becomes worse, because childish thought and behavior are still being pursued.

Blasphemy against the Holy Spirit occurs when there is *some* personal or societal transformation guided by Platonic forms, this partial transformation is *governed* by core childish MMNs that have not been transformed, and it is all *held together* by the TMN of a verbal system which insists that it is right, proper, and inevitable for Platonic forms to be the servant of childish identity. It is this *final* step which performs the 'blasphemy', because Teacher thought is being used to attack Platonic forms rather than build them, and to reinforce childish MMNs rather than analyze them.

> Blasphemy against the Holy Spirit *submits* MMNs of Platonic forms to childish MMNs and then uses Teacher thought to *support* this inverted relationship.

Using an analogy, if transformation is like a journey, then blasphemy against the Holy Spirit is like going part of the way, stopping, and then insisting that it is impossible to go further and attacking anyone who suggests otherwise.

One finds this cognitive combination portrayed in the biblical passage from which the phrase 'blasphemy against the Holy Spirit' originates. Jesus is drawing large crowds because of what he is doing and saying.

> Jesus withdrew to the sea with His disciples; and a great multitude from Galilee followed; and also from Judea, and from Jerusalem, and from Idumea, and beyond the Jordan, and the vicinity of Tyre and Sidon, a great number of people heard of all that He was doing and came to Him (Mark 3:7-8).

In response, the people of his hometown call him crazy, while religious leaders say that he is demon possessed.

> When His own people heard of this, they went out to take custody of Him; for they were saying, "He has lost His senses." The scribes who came down from Jerusalem were saying, "He is possessed by Beelzebul," and "He casts out the demons by the ruler of the demons" (Mark 3:21-22).

It is specifically this kind of verbal response that is referred to as blasphemy against the Holy Spirit.

> "Truly I say to you, all sins shall be forgiven the sons of men, and whatever blasphemies they utter; but whoever blasphemes against the Holy Spirit never has forgiveness, but is guilty of an eternal sin"— because they were saying, "He has an unclean spirit" (Mark 3:28-30).

One can understand the references to 'forgiveness' and 'eternal sin' by using the analogy of a school. If transformation is like studying in a school, then blasphemy against the Holy Spirit is like a group of teachers replacing courses with childish activities and firing any instructors who complain. Studying in such a school will lead to 'eternal sin' because childish behavior will be reinforced rather than changed. And enrolling in school will not generate a feeling of forgiveness because the school will lose its reputation as an institution of learning. Those who enrol will no longer gain the official status of 'student' but rather that of 'party animal'.

I need to warn that the examples in this chapter may provoke strong emotions. When observing the blasphemy against the Holy Spirit being practiced by *another* person or group, the instinctive response is to regard it as an unmitigated evil that needs to be abolished from civilized society. In contrast, any group or individual that is *practicing* blasphemy against the Holy Spirit will respond to such suggestions by stating in no uncertain terms that their behavior is entirely natural and inescapable and that it is unreasonable, idealistic, misguided, dishonorable, and even blasphemous to suggest that things could be any different.

I suggest that both of these responses are *themselves* examples of blasphemy against the Holy Spirit. After all, if someone is being attacked verbally for suggesting that *partial* transformation guided by Platonic forms could go *further*, then that verbal attack is by definition blasphemy against the Holy Spirit. If it is good to go *part* of the way toward some goal, then isn't it better to go *all* of the way and reach the goal? If taking some of the cure for a disease is good, then isn't it better to take all of the cure? However, those who defend blasphemy against the Holy Spirit typically insist that it is, not just wrong, but repugnant to suggest that a partially-finished journey should be completed. Going further, the one who *observes* blasphemy of the Holy Spirit in others and responds by calling for it to be abolished is declaring that *external* force must be used because *internal* transformation guided by the Platonic forms of the Holy Spirit is insufficient. This too is using words to blaspheme the work of the Holy Spirit.

The end result is that different forms of blasphemy against the Holy Spirit will tend to fight each other. Each camp will claim that it is attempting to rid the world of evil, while exhibiting the same kind of flawed thinking as the evil that it is fighting. Thus, while each side will publicly state that it is removing evil from society, in practice it is actually attempting to replace the other camp's version of blasphemy against the Holy Spirit with its *own* version of blasphemy against the Holy Spirit. If one wishes to escape this vicious cycle, then I suggest that one must replace blasphemy with understanding. After all, if the journey of transformation *began* with Teacher understanding, then it makes sense that further understanding will make it possible to *complete* the journey.

Summarizing, blasphemy against the Holy Spirit is characterized by a specific hierarchy of mental networks. What *drives* everything is childish MMNs. Submitted to this is a *partial* understanding guided by TMNs that leads to the formation of *some* Platonic forms in Mercy thought. This juxtaposition is then held together by the TMN of a general system. This juxtaposition can be accurately described as 'evil', because it goes beyond mere childishness to distilled, empowered childishness.

I should emphasize the problem does not lie in being partially transformed. Rebuilding childish MMNs is a long-term project that takes decades, and few—if any—living humans have completed this journey. Instead, the problem lies in declaring partial transformation to be the norm and then verbally attacking anyone who questions otherwise.

This chapter will examine four expressions of this mindset: a religious version driven by Teacher thought, a religious version driven by Mercy thought, a secular version driven by Teacher thought, and a secular version driven by Mercy thought. In general terms, I suggest that the religious *attitude* that was discussed earlier leads in the direction of religious evil, while scientific *methodology* leads in the direction of secular evil. That is because both religious attitude and scientific methodology result in partial transformation, and evil results when the part that *is* transformed becomes ruled by the part that is *not* transformed. Notice that I said 'leads in the direction of' and not 'causes'. It is possible to follow the religious attitude or scientific methodology without practicing blasphemy against the Holy Spirit. However, subscribing to one of these two mindsets makes blasphemy against the Holy Spirit more likely.

Two Religious Versions

We will start with the religious, Teacher-driven, version of blasphemy against the Holy Spirit because that is the form that has occasionally emerged within my Mennonite culture. Remember that the religious attitude consists of fervor, self-denial, and transcendence. In its extreme, fervor attempts to focus fully upon mental networks associated with God and religion, self-denial feels that mental networks of personal identity are worthless compared to mental networks associated with God and religion, while transcendence believes that it is impossible to gain a rational understanding of mental networks associated with God and religion. We are seeing in this book that Christian theology is compatible with rational thought, can be described as a general Teacher theory, and leads to the formation of Platonic forms and a concept of the Holy Spirit. Suppose that one studies the Bible with a religious attitude. The content that is being studied will lead to *some* Teacher understanding which will cause some Platonic forms to emerge. But this rational partial concept of God with its Platonic forms of a better society will occur within the general *context* of the religious attitude. Saying this less theoretically, the Christian fundamentalist will read the Bible, understand the words, see in his mind's eye how to better himself and his society, and then suppress this internal vision in order to continue abasing himself before God. Cognitively speaking, the MMN of emotional respect for the source of absolute truth is being placed *above* the TMN of a mental concept of God and the MMN of the Platonic form of the Holy Spirit. This attitude is sometimes referred to as 'worm theology', because it believes that 'I am a worm compared to God'. For such a religious believer, being a worm is more fundamental than being transformed by God.

I suggest that the Orthodox Christian practice of *hesychasm* is an example of this attitude. Hesychasm is the practice of repeating what is known as the *Jesus prayer*, and was briefly discussed in the chapter on mysticism. Quoting more extensively from the webpage referenced earlier,

> The Jesus Prayer: 'Lord Jesus Christ Son of God, have mercy on me the sinner' is perhaps the most intriguing and exciting form of prayer the Eastern Orthodox Christian Church has to offer... It is a repeated prayer. The person that prays repeats many times, the same phrase: 'Lord Jesus Christ Son of God, have mercy on me the sinner' or some variation of this phrase like 'Lord Jesus Christ Son of God, have mercy on me', 'Lord Jesus Christ, have mercy on me'...This is performed tens, hundreds or even thousands of times... The Jesus Prayer, being short, meaningful and compact is easily memorized and repeated, and will ideally after a time 'stick to the head' like a song or music 'earworm' does, having a 'Tetris Effect'. Only in this case the words will 'fix' the attention and the whole being of the person towards God the Father, Jesus the Son, and the Holy Spirit (Prayercraft, 2009).

One can see more clearly what is happening cognitively by placing this prayer within an educational setting. Imagine if a student continually said to himself and his teacher, "I am dumb and my teacher knows everything. Teacher, please forgive my stupidity." It is true that teachers know more than students. If a teacher knows less than the students about the subject that is being taught, then that teacher will be replaced by one that is more knowledgeable. But the goal of education is to *transfer* understanding from the mind of the teacher to the mind of the student. A student who continually says that 'I am dumb and my teacher knows everything' is *unteachable*, because the Mercy attitude of self-abasement before the instructor has turned into a general TMN that rules the mind.

Personal identity will *always* fall short of the perfection of Platonic forms, and the Jesus prayer is a good expression of this realization of personal inadequacy. Realizing that I fall short of the standard should motivate me to become more *like* the standard. Thus, the Jesus prayer is a good *starting* point for personal transformation. But when the Jesus prayer is repeated so many times that it turns into an 'earworm' that 'sticks to the head', then one has *artificially* created the mental concept of a universal God. A universal theory is a simple Teacher statement that *applies* to all situations. For instance, 'F = mg' is a universal theory of gravity. Turning the Jesus prayer into an 'earworm' uses concentration to make this statement feel universal because it is universally present within *my* mind wherever I go. Thus, the concept of God that hesychasm creates is not the concept of a universal, perfect God but rather the concept of universal, ever-present human imperfection. What is universal is not God but rather my inadequacy, because what has been universalized is not universal truth but rather religious attitude. Because the perfection of Platonic forms is being placed within a universal Teacher theory of human inadequacy, I suggest that hesychasm is an example of blasphemy against the Holy Spirit.

The solution, I suggest, is to follow more completely the personal transformation that has been started. If childish identity really is 'a worm' compared to the perfection of God, then why not allow God's perfection to transform *all* of childish identity? Why regard personal deficiency as the ultimate reference point?

Let us turn now to the religious *Mercy-driven* version of blasphemy against the Holy Spirit. We know that mental networks struggle for domination. When people's minds are ruled by childish MMNs then people and groups will struggle for domination. In contrast, the TMN of a concept of God will impose law, order, and structure upon a society, because Teacher emotion comes from order-within-complexity. Teacher thought feels good when people cooperate and bad when people fight. Thus, when war and fighting play a major role in a society or religion, then one can conclude that childish MMNs are in charge.

With this in mind, consider the following quote about martyrdom from a Shiite Muslim website.

> All the nations of the world view the word 'martyrdom' as sacred and holy. Martyrdom refers to lay [sic] down one's life while defending one's religion or nation or while protecting life or wealth. The people look up a martyr with great reverence. However, the importance given to a martyr and martyrdom by the holy Islamic Shariat cannot be found in any nation or religion. Especially the concept of martyrdom elucidated by the Infallible Imams (a.s.) cannot be matched. As per the traditions of holy Imams (a.s.), apart from being martyred while defending the nation and the self, a person who dies on the love of progeny of Mohammad (s.a.w.a.) dies the death of a martyr. The Holy Prophet (s.a.w.a.) said: 'One who dies on the love of the progeny of Mohammad, dies a death of a martyr.' To lay down ones life while fighting in the way of Allah, to get killed while protecting life and wealth, getting slain while protecting the life of holy personalities, laying down life while fighting against the enemies of Imam (a.s.), dying as captive, getting killed while defending the Muslims and dying on the love of the progeny of Mohammad (s.a.w.a.) are the different causes through which one attains martyrdom. This struggle in the way of Allah is waged for

strengthening Islam or to implement its laws. Both are clear instances of struggle in the way of Allah. Regarding this Allah, the High says in the Holy Qura'n (Imamreza).

Notice how the religious attitudes of fervor and self-denial are being interpreted in the physical terms of being a martyr. Let us look briefly at what it means to be a martyr. A Platonic form is, by definition, invisible. Therefore, a person who is willing to die for a Platonic form is showing in the ultimate tangible manner that he is being guided by invisible values rather than visible goals. This martyrdom can inspire others to follow Platonic forms, and if personal existence continues after physical death, then it might (hopefully) result in personal benefits for the now disembodied mind. Having said that, the brutality of war and death has a strong tendency to replace any redemptive qualities of martyrdom with the emotional trauma of imposed MMNs. This societally uplifting effect of martyrdom becomes negated when a person dies in the pursuit of physical, material goals. Such an individual is not a martyr but a thug.

With this in mind, let us interpret the quote about martyrdom. The passage begins by saying that 'all the nations of the world view the word martyrdom as sacred and holy.' This may be the case if martyrdom is defined as dying for Platonic forms, killed by oppressors who are driven by childish MMNs to pursue material goals. This website claims that 'the importance given to a martyr and martyrdom by the holy Islamic Shariat cannot be found in any nation or religion' and that the form of martyrdom 'elucidated by the Infallible Imams (a.s.) cannot be matched'.

But what exactly is the nature of this unmatched, ultimate martyrdom? Is it driven by Platonic forms? We can answer this question by looking at what is being defended in this passage. 'Life and wealth' are being preserved, the 'progeny of Mohammed' is being loved, the lives of 'holy personalities' are being protected, the 'enemies of Imam' are being fought, and Muslims are being defended. If one eliminates the religious terminology, what is being described is typical tribal warfare, in which one group of people is driven by its cultural mental networks to protect 'us' and our things while attacking 'them' and their things. But this tribal conflict is being called a 'concept of martyrdom elucidated by the Infallible Imams (a.s.)' that 'cannot be matched'. Tribal warfare may be a brutal expression of childish mentality, but it is not blasphemy against the Holy Spirit, nor is tribal warfare motivated by MMNs of tribal gods. However, I suggest that using the TMN of a monotheistic God to justify and ennoble tribal warfare does qualify as blasphemy against the Holy Spirit, because instead of using a general Teacher theory to transform childish identity, Teacher words about universality are being used to justify the most heinous forms of childish behavior. Notice the references to universality in this quote: 'All the nations of the world view the word martyrdom as sacred and holy'. The Imams are 'infallible', and their concept of martyrdom 'cannot be matched'. This is a 'struggle in the way of Allah' whose purpose is 'strengthening Islam'.

Saying this more plainly, childish MMNs are being given the appearance of religion by cloaking them within a *religious attitude*. Showing fervor for God sounds better than getting excited about raiding my neighboring tribe. Denying myself for God by dying as a martyr sounds better than getting killed in tribal warfare. And obeying the will of God without questioning sounds better than blind obedience to some tribal chieftain. Unfortunately, when Perceiver thought is mesmerized by Mercy status, then religious followers will be mentally unable to distinguish a warlord who is following childish MMNs while claiming to be the mouthpiece of God from someone who genuinely is a prophet of God.

In addition, Platonic forms are being used to *motivate* childish behavior. Notice the various Platonic forms described in the following quote, taken from the same webpage.

> Ameerul Momeneen (a.s.) replied! "The same question I had posed before the Holy Prophet (s.a.w.a.) while he was sitting on his camel and Holy Prophet (s.a.w.a.) replied to me thus, 'When a warrior intends for struggle, Allah makes him far from the hell. When he gets ready for the fight, Allah prides Himself among His angels. When he bids farewell to his family, the house and the walls cry over him. He comes out from his sins like a snake comes out from its hole. Allah appoints 40,000 angels to guard him from all sides. Allah multiples the rewards of his good deeds. Everyday, the reward of worship of 1000 men, who have worshipped for 100 years, is written in his account. When he faces the enemy, nobody in the world can encompass his reward. When he fights with his spear and sword, angels come near him and pray for his help and steadfastness. An announcer announces that paradise is under the shadow of the sword. Due to the rewards, when a Muslim is inflicted with injury, he endures it and its feeling is like drinking cold water in summer. When he falls from his horse, before he reaches the ground, heavenly fairies come to him and give him glad tidings of rewards which Allah has stored for him. When he falls on the ground, these fairies congratulate him and say that peace be on the pure soul which has emerged from a pure body. They congratulate him and say Allah has kept such reward from him which neither any ear has heard nor any eyes have seen it nor any heart has comprehended. Then Allah says, I am his Guardian and Guardian of his family. Whoever pleases them has pleased Me. And whoever angers them has angered Me. Allah will bestow each martyr 70 rooms in paradise. The distance between each room will be equal to the distance between Sanaa (Yeman) and Syria. The light in each room will be such, which will illuminate the East and the West. Every room will be having 70 doors and each door will have 70 brocades. Every door will have a veil. Every room will have 70 tents. And each tent will have 70 platforms. Its legs will be of sapphire and chrysolite. On each platform, there will be 40 beds. On each bed, there will be two fairies with all their embellishments" (Ibid).

'Angels' and 'fairies' are typically viewed as Platonic forms—idealized versions of humans. Thus, 'being guarded by 40,000 angels' is an idealized version of being guided by idealized humans. Similarly, 'paradise' is a nonphysical realm of Platonic forms. One sees these Platonic forms in the idealized description of '70 rooms', each with '70 doors' and '70 tents', with each tent having '70 platforms', each platform '40 beds', and each bed 'two fairies'. Notice all the Perceiver objects being organized by Teacher order-within-complexity. If I calculate correctly, it works out to 27440000 fairies 'with all their embellishments' for each martyr. However, when 'an announcer announces that paradise is under the shadow of the sword', then Teacher words are being used to proclaim that Platonic forms are the servant of warfare. When 'fairies congratulate' the dying warrior and 'say that peace be on the pure soul which has emerged from a pure body', then Teacher words from Platonic forms are being used to reinforce tribal warfare. And when 'Allah prides Himself among his angels when a warrior intends for struggle', then the concept of a monotheistic God has become the slave of tribal conflict. That juxtaposition defines blasphemy against the Holy Spirit.

Finally, one can tell that Perceiver thought is not functioning very well because the Platonic forms that are motivating this childish behavior lack common sense. For instance, it does not make sense for each martyr to have precisely 27440000 fairies at his disposal, or that 'the distance between each room will be equal to the distance between Sanaa (Yeman) and Syria'.

The solution, I suggest, is for the Muslim warrior to follow *more completely* the path of personal transformation that has already been started. The goal of the Muslim warrior is to spend eternity in a heavenly paradise of peace and bliss. If this is the goal of the warrior, then it makes sense that one should reach this goal using means that are *consistent* with the goal. If the warrior is supposed to be motivated by a heavenly paradise, then why is he fighting to preserve earthly kingdoms? If one wishes to live in an eternity of peace, then one should prepare for this peace by pursuing peace here on earth rather than warfare. If one wishes to live in an eternity of bliss, then one should prepare for this bliss by spreading bliss here on earth rather than terror. And if those who ask questions such as these are verbally denounced—or physically attacked, then that too is an example of blasphemy against the Holy Spirit.

Two Secular Versions

Let us turn now to two *secular* expressions of blaspheming the Holy Spirit, beginning with the one driven by Mercy thought. The two religious expressions are enabled by the religious attitude. Similarly, I suggest that the two secular expressions are enabled by scientific methodology. Again notice that I said 'enabled' and not 'caused'. It is possible to follow the religious attitude without becoming a monk or pursuing religious warfare. However, the religious attitude causes a person to be vulnerable to being led down one of these two paths. Likewise, I suggest that scientific methodology creates a mental vacuum that makes a person vulnerable to function in a way that blasphemes the Holy Spirit.

Scientific thought is guided by general Teacher theories. These theories cause Platonic forms to emerge within Mercy thought, which motivate people to interact with the world in a way that is more ordered, structured, and efficient, leading to the development of technology. That is all good. Indoor plumbing, for instance, is far more pleasant than a trench in the ground or an outhouse. The problem is that scientific methodology limits this transformation to the realm of physical objects, because it avoids the subjective and it focuses upon the empirical. Obviously, something that avoids subjective emotions cannot improve subjective emotions and something that studies physical matter will only improve the physical world. The result is that scientific methodology is vulnerable to being exploited by the demagogue. One sees this in the *military-industrial complex*.

The religious path of 'holy warfare' uses religious language and Platonic forms to ennoble lawless behavior such as rape, pillage, and murder. In a similar manner, the 'military-industrial complex' ennobles destruction and murder through the use of scientific language and technology. According to the Stockholm International Peace Research Institute, the top twenty arms companies in the world sold 273 billion dollars of arms and military services in 2012, with two-thirds of those companies located in the United States (SIPRI, 2013). In comparison, the NASA budget for 2012 was 18.4 billion dollars. Saying this another way, America spends twelve times as much on arms and military services as it does on exploring space. Imagine what the earth—and the moon and Mars—would now be like if engineers designed and built rockets to *send* people up instead of building rockets to *blow* people up. After all, space exploration began when the rocket-making expertise of the Nazi Third Reich was redirected after World War II towards civilian purposes.

When the Teacher order-within-complexity of an entire military-industrial complex arises for the purpose of using Platonic forms to enable people to build increasingly refined machines of death, and when this juxtaposition is defended as normal and those who question it are denounced as idealistic, unrealistic, or unpatriotic, then this combination can accurately be described as blasphemy against the Holy Spirit.

Unfortunately, scientific methodology shields the engineer of death from the horror of his creation. By suppressing the subjective, he can ignore the personal trauma that his tools are causing. By focusing upon physical objects, he can ignore the mindset that motivates the development and use of these objects. And by limiting his interaction to his peers, he can focus upon perfecting his infernal machines while ignoring the hellishness of the larger picture. This same objective, impersonal, specialized attitude extends to the *use* of high-tech weapons. Innocent lives are not ruined. Instead, there is collateral damage. People are not butchered. Rather, the weapon functioned nominally.

If the Platonic forms of new-and-improved technology guided by rational Teacher understanding can be used to transform the *way* that war is waged, then it is reasonable to suggest that Platonic forms guided by rational Teacher understanding can also be used to transform the *fact* that war is being waged. Even from a totally empirical perspective, I am only suggesting that the military-industrial complex should follow more completely the path that it is *already* pursuing. If technology should be used to make weapons more modern, more structured, and more integrated, then should not the *results* of these weapons also be more modern, more structured, and more integrated? Instead, the modern weapon is used to blow the enemy back to the stone ages, the structured weapon is used to destroy the structure of the enemy, and the integrated weapon system is used to disintegrate the physical body and infrastructure of the foe.

Turning finally to the secular, Teacher-driven expression of blasphemy against the Holy Spirit, in the same way that a religious attitude can cause the religious believer to exalt the flawed MMNs of childish identity, so I suggest that scientific methodology can cause the scientist to exalt the flawed MMNs of childish identity.

Consider the following paragraph from Tremlin's book on the cognitive science of religion, from which we quoted earlier.

> For evolutionary psychologists, the complete slate of mental modules will only be uncovered as we place the modern mind against the backdrop of its ancestral past. If mental modules are evolved mechanisms constructed in response to adaptive problems, then we must consider the environment in which these problems were faced. That means looking again into the Pleistocene's evolutionary forge. It is wrong to attempt to explain the architecture of the mind in relation to contemporary times. The human mind evolved under the selective pressures confronted by our Stone Age relatives. Indeed, the post-Pleistocene period—a mere tick of time constituting only about 5,000 human generations—is largely irrelevant to the composition of the mind. Our minds remain adapted to a Pleistocene way of life; the mental modules we use today are the same ones our hunting and gathering ancestors used to survive in their own unforgiving Pleistocene world. Cosmides and Tooby point out that many psychologists also erroneously attempt to describe the cognitive architecture of the mind based on the study of what it *can* do rather than of what it was *designed* to do. The evolutionary engineering of the past was completed without regard to present circumstances or with an eye to enabling cognitive skills beyond those necessary to solve problems within the Pleistocene environment. The novel ways we use our minds today, however impressive, are but secondary consequences, or the architecture of the modern mind by-products, of their functional design and cannot be used as an explanation for how that design came to be (Tremlin, 2006, p. 58).

According to Tremlin, it is wrong to 'explain the architecture of the mind in relation to contemporary times' and it is erroneous to 'describe the cognitive architecture the mind based in the study of what it can do'. Instead, 'our minds remain adapted to a Pleistocene way of life; the mental modules we use today are the same ones our hunting and gathering ancestors used to survive in their own unforgiving Pleistocene world'. In plain English, if one wishes to understand how the mind works, then one should study what it means to think and act like a savage. After all, 'the novel ways we use our minds today, however impressive, are but secondary consequences'.

I know that Pope Francis just stated publicly that evolution is compatible with Christianity. I also see—repeatedly—the ridicule that Internet forums heap upon those who dare to question the theory of evolution. One can understand what is motivating these responses. First, those who practice science are recoiling from the *religious* version of blasphemy against the Holy Spirit. They see the self-denial and religious warfare that fundamentalism enables and they are concluding that religion is the cause. Second, we saw in the chapter on Teacher thought that the scientist cannot exist without a general Teacher theory. Thus, the scientifically trained mind finds it emotionally *inconceivable* when the religious attitude prompts a person to say, 'The Bible says it! I believe it! That settles it!' or when a religious person uses miracles to prove that God exists.

The scientist (in the typical Internet comment) views himself as the defender of rational thought against the religious hordes with their blind faith and ignorance, and rational thought *needs* to be nurtured and preserved in today's climate of growing fundamentalism. But, does Tremlin's approach actually nurture and preserve rational thought? Tremlin says that "The evolutionary engineering of the past was completed without regard to present circumstances or with an eye to enabling cognitive skills beyond those necessary to solve problems within the Pleistocene environment. The novel ways we use our minds today, however impressive, are but secondary consequences." This means that our brain hardware is designed (his word) to live as a savage within a savage environment, and civilization with its rational scientific thought is only a secondary veneer that has been placed on top of this Pleistocene adapted underlying structure. Thus, in order to be accepted as *truly* rational today and not just as an irrational person who is *pretending* to be rational, one must adhere to the belief that we are all brute beasts pretending to be rational.

When a general theory is being promulgated that views the Platonic forms motivating modern civilization as 'but secondary consequences' of 'survival in the unforgiving Pleistocene world', and when those who question this theory are denounced as irrational, then that qualifies as blasphemy against the Holy Spirit.

We have seen that 'evolutionists lead the world in substituting teleology for objectivity' (Hanke, 2004). Thus, the theory of evolution creates a potent Platonic form in the concept of Nature as the inexorable force driving individuals, society, and the universe to ever greater order and structure. One could even regard the effects of Nature as a mental concept of a Holy Spirit. But what does the typical scientist do with this scientific version of a Holy Spirit? Blaspheme it. Even though cognitive mechanisms drive the mind to view Nature *implicitly* as heading in the direction of greater order-within-complexity, this teleology is verbally denied by the evolutionist. And when 'intelligent design' comes along and *explicitly* states that some divine agent is guiding existence, then this is dismissed in no uncertain terms. But what does the evolutionist do after verbally denigrating the concept of a 'God of intelligent design'? Treat Nature implicitly as if it is a 'God of intelligent design'.

As with the previous three cases, I suggest that those who promote the theory of evolution should pursue *more fully* an answer that they *already* possess. The theory of evolution claims that life evolved through the inexorable hand of Nature. If Nature is so all-powerful, then why not focus upon Nature and call it God instead of focusing upon human savagery, which the evolutionist claims is being transformed by Nature? Why not talk *explicitly* about the concept of a Teacher-based God of order-within-complexity, if this is already being described implicitly?

Unfortunately, these are not just theoretical questions. We know that the *religious* versions of blasphemy against the Holy Spirit can lead to the personal agony of religious self-denial and religious warfare. However, history indicates that the *secular* versions of blasphemy against the Holy Spirit have had equally horrific repercussions.

World War I

The First World War was the first modern war. It was the first conflict in which science and technology were used on a global scale to inflict massive human carnage. The Western world was just starting to experience the personal benefits of the consumer revolution. But instead of using the Platonic forms of new-and-improved objects to build a better world, the entire industrial might of Western nations was redirected towards the manufacture of weapons and munitions. For instance, in 1915 Britain experienced a major shortage of artillery shells. In response, David Lloyd George was appointed Minister of Munitions and he told the British people that

> We are fighting against the best organized community in the world, the best organized whether for war or for peace. And we have been employing too much the haphazard go-as-you-please methods which believe me, would not have enabled us to maintain our place as a nation even in peace much longer. The nation now needs all the machinery that is capable of being used for turning out munitions or equipment, all the skill that is available for that purpose, all the industry, all the labour and all the strength, power and resource of everyone to the utmost (David, 2012).

Notice how all machinery, all skill, all industry, all labor, and all strength are supposed to be used by everyone to the utmost—to 'turn out munitions or equipment'. Thus, Platonic forms in each Western country became the servant of a national ruling organization whose primary purpose was mass murder.

Franz Konrad von Hötzendorf was the Austrian chief of General Staff who instigated the Austrian attack against Serbia that began this war. Lawrence Sondhaus says in his biography of von Hötzendorf that "among the men responsible for shaping the tactics, strategies, and war plans that led old Europe to destruction in the unprecedented blood-letting of 1914-1918, he had no equal" (Sondhaus, 2000). Sondhaus explains that Von Hötzendorf and his fellow officers were motivated by a philosophy of social Darwinism.

> Conrad's perceptions of Austria-Hungary; its place in the world, and its future prospects reflected his broader Darwinian convictions... Conrad traced the development of mankind through the 'struggle for existence', from early 'hordes' to later peoples and nationalities. "In order to persist in the struggle for existence, small national states and small nationalities joined together to defend their interests in a common struggle, either in temporary or in enduring alliances." Through this device, Conrad, like Gumplowicz and Ratzenhofer, reconciled basic Darwinian assumptions with the existence and survival of Austria-Hungary... Conrad asserted that "the recognition of the struggle for existence as the basic principle of all events on this earth is the only real and rational basis for policymaking"... The passage of time has made Conrad's aggressive fatalism appear strange, if not insane. In an age of overheated nationalism, in which the military men of Europe habitually express themselves in apocalyptic Darwinian language, such views were common, but also particularly ill-suited to a leading general serving a state as vulnerable as Austria-Hungary. Yet Conrad had plenty of company within his own army... Manfried Rauchensteiner has concluded that a prevailing pessimism, rooted in Darwinism, "became almost a fundamental outlook (Grundhaltung)" among Army officers (Sondhaus, 2000).

In other words, Conrad turned Mercy-driven barbarism into a *universal* Teacher theory to guide civilization: 'The struggle for existence as the basic principle of *all events on this earth* is the only real and rational basis for policymaking'. However, 'the struggle for existence' in which 'small nationalities join together to defend their interests' describes precisely the aspect of modern 'civilized' culture that is *not* rational but rather driven by MMNs of childish identity. When this 'aggressive fatalism' is defended as 'the only real and rational basis', then this defines blasphemy against the Holy Spirit, because the Platonic form of civilization is being made the servant of a universal Teacher theory based in 'struggle for existence'. Saying this more simply, Conrad and his fellows used the theory of evolution to justify savage passions driving civilized minds. Helmuth von Moltke, the German Army Chief of Staff, held similar beliefs: "His views on society reflected both the social prejudices of his aristocratic profession and the social Darwinism so prevalent in Germany and Europe during his lifetime" (Moltke & Hughes, 1993).

The 'new atheism' says that religion should be abolished because it is supposedly the source of irrational thought and warfare, and we have seen that the religious attitude *can* lead to a combination of irrational self-denial and religious warfare that could accurately be described as double blasphemy against the Holy Spirit. However, during the First World War, the combination of the military-industrial complex and the theory of evolution *did* lead the Western world to a secular version of double blasphemy against the Holy Spirit that can only be described as hell on earth.

Let us finish this discussion with an example that is also an analogy. CTV news reported last year that an Edmonton school teacher

> was suspended in 2012 for giving students zeros when they missed tests or didn't hand in assignments. Four months later, he was fired from his position at Ross Sheppard High School... The "no-zero" policy is based on the idea that grades of "zero" can negatively impact student esteem and growth. A 2009 Alberta Student Assessment Study, commissioned by the provincial government, said that "assessment must not be used to reward or punish" and that "no-zero policies support student-learning outcomes" (Chan, 2014).

We know that it is not possible to teach students knowledge instantly or to expect perfection from students. But it is possible to stop proclaiming theories that justify childish behavior and it is possible to stop firing teachers who demand progress from students. Similarly, as long as individuals and societies remain partially transformed, governments with armies, jails, and policemen will be required. One cannot instantly lay down all weapons. It takes time to transform both an individual and a society. But one can stop proclaiming that incomplete transformation is the norm, and one can stop condemning those who suggest that further transformation is required. In other words, one can stop blaspheming the Holy Spirit.

The Facilitator Person and Evolution

Turning now from theory to personality, there appears to be a natural resonance between the theory of evolution and the thinking of the Facilitator *person*. Because this book largely ignores the Facilitator person, we will now take a few pages to discuss some aspects of Facilitator thought and how they are expressed in the Facilitator person, which will eventually lead us back to the theory of evolution. Evidence suggests that the Facilitator person exists midway between the internal world and the external world. On the one hand, he often gives the impression that he is observing himself, implying that the self of conscious thought stands apart from the self composed of MMNs within Mercy thought. On the other hand, he is very aware of his senses, implying that the self of conscious thought is close to physical sensation.

The Facilitator person often thinks initially that he is all of the cognitive styles, because he can consciously observe all these forms of thinking within his own mind. However, the Facilitator person is the only cognitive style with this wide awareness. While the conscious awareness of the Facilitator is broad, it also appears to be shallow. In other words, Facilitator thought observes the rest of the mind from a distance, unaware consciously of the deep aspects of mental processing. Thus, while other cognitive styles live immersed within some aspect of mental processing, the Facilitator person views understanding how the mind works as a question that needs to be studied and analyzed. For instance, Sigmund Freud (a Facilitator person) used dream analysis to attempt to decipher what his mind was doing, guided by the belief that "the interpretation of dreams is the royal road to a knowledge of the unconscious activity of the mind" (Freud, 1900).

One could compare Facilitator thought to a sound engineer in a recording studio who observes the performers (the other six cognitive modules) from an adjacent room and uses a mixing board to adjust the relative levels of the performers. Adjusting requires a combination of freedom and stability. For instance, it should be possible to make the piano louder or softer by adjusting the appropriate slider on the mixing board. But it would be extremely disorienting if adjusting the slider caused the entire room to twist and turn. Similarly, Facilitator thought adjusts Mercy experiences guided by Perceiver facts that do not change, as well as adjusting Teacher words guided by Server sequences that remain constant. Facilitator adjusting breaks down when Perceiver facts or Server sequences shift when Mercy experiences and/or Teacher words are adjusted.

> Facilitator thought adjusts and blends the thinking of other cognitive modules.

One can illustrate this interaction by using Sorites paradox, a problem of philosophy originally posed by the ancient Greeks. Suppose that one removes one straw from a bale of hay. What is left over is obviously still a bale of hay. But suppose that one continues removing straws from this bale. At what point does the bale cease to be a bale and become merely a pile of straw? I suggest that the answer lies in recognizing that one is dealing with an interaction between three different cognitive modules. Mercy thought contains the experiences of straws, Perceiver thought notices that these straws form the object of a bale, while Facilitator thought is performing the adjusting of removing straws from the bale. If Facilitator thought continues to adjust the bale by removing straws, then eventually Perceiver thought will stop viewing it as a bale and start viewing it as a pile of straw. Saying this more generally, Facilitator adjusting occurs within the context provided by Perceiver thought. Putting this another way, Facilitator thought functions in an analog manner by making smooth adjustments. However, Facilitator adjustment operates within the context provided by Perceiver categorization, which functions in a more digital manner by connecting experiences with one fact or another. One can see this Perceiver categorization occurring in the classic duck/rabbit illusion, because the same picture can be interpreted either as a duck or as a rabbit.

Sorites paradox can also be stated in a form that illustrates the relationship between Server and Teacher thought. Suppose that a pianist is playing a Chopin étude and he makes a mistake. Is he still playing Chopin, or is he now playing a totally different piece? How many notes can the pianist change before it ceases to be a Chopin étude? Here one is dealing with an interaction between Server sequences and Facilitator adjusting. If Facilitator thought continues to adjust the notes of the piece, then eventually Server thought will conclude that this sequence of notes belongs to another piece of music.

Let us relate this now to the topic of religion. One of the problems with fundamentalism is that one must choose between freedom and stability. If some source of Perceiver truth is given great Mercy status, then there will be stability but there will also be no freedom because nobody will dare to question the source of truth. However, if there is no respected source of truth, then there will be freedom but there will be no stability.

Thus, when respect for authority is monolithic, then Facilitator persons will call for intellectual and personal freedom, but when respect for authority breaks down, then Facilitator persons will call for order and structure. Facilitator thought naturally becomes dominant in a multi-cultural environment in which there are several competing sources of truth. Facilitator thought will then define Perceiver truth as 'the average of the opinions of all the experts weighted by the emotional status of each expert'. Those who lack emotional status will not be invited to the table to define truth because they are not sources of stability, while those who cling to some particular version of truth will be kept away from the table because they refuse to adjust.

The Facilitator person often speaks of 'going through a cult experience'. He is initially attracted to the cult because it claims to provide truth and stability. But he then discovers that being a member of the cult limits his world, because he cannot question the beliefs of the cult and he has become cut off from major segments of society. Thus, he leaves the group and treats it as a cult. Sometimes, this cult experience involves an actual cult. However, when the standards of society are shifting, then the adult Facilitator person may regard childhood itself as a kind of cult experience.

Buried within this problem is the deeper problem that Facilitator thought has no direct access to other cognitive modules, but rather observes—and adjusts—them from a distance. This means that the Facilitator person has no way of directly accessing or controlling mental networks that form within his mind. The Facilitator person can use conscious adjusting and mixing to alter the way that a mental network is expressed, but cannot prevent subconscious Exhorter thought from being attracted to unwanted mental networks. For instance, Sigmund Freud said that

> sublimation of instinct is an especially conspicuous feature of cultural development; it is what makes it possible for the higher psychical activities, scientific, artistic, or ideological, to play such an important role in civilized life... Finally, and this seems most important of all, it is impossible to overlook the extent to which civilization is built upon the renunciation of instincts, how much it presupposes precisely the non-satisfaction by suppression, repression or other means of powerful instincts. This cultural frustration dominates a large field of the social relationships between human beings (Freud, 1930).

In other words, the Facilitator person cannot use conscious thought to suppress childish MMNs, but can use adjusting and mixing to express these mental networks in a socially acceptable manner. This trait also shows up in the Facilitator person's natural tendency to put a positive spin upon personal experiences. When relating a story that touches MMNs of personal identity, details that make self look bad will tend to be downplayed, while aspects of the story that make self look good will be emphasized. Obviously, everyone has a tendency to put a spin upon the facts. However, the Facilitator person does it instinctively and expertly. The Facilitator person is also especially vulnerable to parental disapproval. For instance, a Facilitator person may attend college in order to gain parental approval and discover that even after gaining two PhDs he is still troubled internally by childish MMNs of disapproval from father. This explains why the Facilitator person can regard childhood itself as a cult experience, because recovering from unwanted mental networks is so difficult.

> The Facilitator person finds self-analysis easy but personal change difficult.

If the Facilitator person wishes to change core mental networks and not simply sublimate them, then extreme measures are required. One possibility is to change the social environment. The Facilitator person cannot directly access mental networks within his mind, but if he is in a position of power, then he can change mental networks indirectly by changing the opinions of the authority figures who are the sources of these mental networks. For instance, this method was used by Henry VIII (a Facilitator person) when getting his marriage to Anne Boleyn annulled. Alison Weir writes that

> on March 23 [1534], Parliament passed one of the most controversial pieces of legislation of Henry's reign: the Act of Succession, which vested the succession to 'the imperial crown of England' in the children of Henry and Anne. On 1 May, the contents of this Act were proclaimed in all the shires of England, and the King's subjects were warned that anyone saying or writing anything 'to the prejudice, slander or derogation of the lawful matrimony' between the King and 'his most dear and entirely beloved [second] wife Queen Anne', or against his lawful heirs, would be guilty of high treason, for which the penalty was death and forfeiture of lands and goods to the Crown. Furthermore, it was proclaimed that the new Act required all the King's subjects, if so commanded, to swear an oath 'that they shall truly, firmly, constantly, without fraud or guile, observe, fulfil, maintain, defend and keep the whole effect and contents of this Act'. The oath also required recognition of the King's supremacy. Those refusing to take it would be accounted guilty of misprision of treason and sent to prison (Weir, 1991).

Notice how it was not enough for Henry VIII to divorce his first wife. Instead, every person in the entire kingdom had to be willing to swear under oath that his second marriage to Anne was the only legitimate marriage.

The Facilitator person can also use mixing to defang unwanted mental networks. One sees this method used by Freud in *Moses and Monotheism* (Freud, 1939), which he wrote shortly before his death. A New York Times article explains that Freud

> argued that Moses himself was not a Jew. How did Freud know? First of all, he claimed that Moses is not a Jewish name but an Egyptian one; second, Freud's study of dreams and fairy tales convinced him that the Bible had inverted things. In the Exodus story, Moses' mother, fearing Pharaoh's order to kill all Jewish boys, leaves the infant Moses in a basket on the river's edge, where he is discovered by Pharaoh's daughter. But Freud maintained that the Jews were the ones who had found him by the river. (In fairy tales and dreams, the child always begins with rich parents and is adopted by poor ones, yet his noble nature wins out

— or so Freud insisted.) Freud also said that monotheism was not a Jewish but an Egyptian invention, descending from the cult of the Egyptian sun god Aton (Edmundson, 2007).

Moses is deeply revered as one of the founders of Judaism, while the Jewish belief in monotheism expresses the core of Jewish religion, as illustrated by the Shema (Hear, oh Israel: the Lord our God, the Lord is one). Thus, when Freud, a Jew, claimed that Moses was an Egyptian and not a Jew and that monotheism was an Egyptian invention, then Freud was attempting to defang the core mental networks of Judaism by detaching these beliefs from the MMNs of Judaism and connecting them with the MMNs of ancient Egypt, which in Jewish tradition symbolizes the enemies of Israel. It is interesting to note that Freud was only mentally capable of performing this Facilitator re-mixing when he was old, after decades of psychoanalysis had formed an alternative set of core mental networks within his mind.

Finally, I suggest that the Facilitator person can use the method described in this book to transform mental networks. King Solomon, another Jewish Facilitator person, wrote that "the fear of the Lord is the beginning of wisdom, and the knowledge of the Holy One is understanding" (Prov. 9:10). Translating this into the language of mental symmetry, the TMN of a mental concept of God is capable of transforming childish MMNs, even within the mind of the Facilitator person.

> Facilitator thought needs both stability and freedom.

Fundamentalism forces the Facilitator person to choose between stability and freedom. The long-term solution is to replace absolute truth with universal truth and verbal theory with exemplars (which will be discussed more fully in the next chapter). Universal truth uses Perceiver thought to look for solid connections that are common to many different Mercy situations. Because Perceiver thought ties together many Mercy experiences, there is both stability and freedom. Similarly, exemplars make it possible to use many different kinds of Teacher words to describe the same underlying Server sequences, leading to a combination of stability and freedom.

The Facilitator person is naturally attracted to science, because science combines a search for universal Perceiver truth with a focus upon universal Server exemplars. Stated more simply, scientific thought gives the Facilitator person a combination of stability and freedom. This explains why the Facilitator person can become such a strong advocate of scientific thought and such a vocal enemy of religious fundamentalism. As far as the Facilitator person is concerned, science leads to mental freedom and stability while fundamentalism leads to inescapable emotional bondage.

The Facilitator person naturally practices a version of scientific thought that is characterized by careful experimentation. That is because the modules that handle content are subconscious within the mind of the Facilitator person. A subconscious cognitive module functions the same way that a conscious one does, but requires input that is clear and simple. Thus, if the Facilitator person uses conscious thought to hold all parameters fixed and then carefully adjusts one parameter and observes what happens, the results will be sufficiently clear and simple to program subconscious Perceiver thought within the mind of the Facilitator person. Similarly, if the Facilitator person changes only one aspect of a Server sequence at a time, then the results will again be simple enough to program subconscious Server thought with stable sequences. Notice precisely what is happening. The Facilitator person is using conscious thought to hold elements fixed and vary parameters one at a time. Subconscious thought within the mind of the Facilitator person (which the Facilitator person cannot directly see) is responding by coming up with solid Perceiver facts and solid Server sequences. Going further, clarifying Perceiver facts and Server sequences will automatically motivate subconscious Teacher thought within the Facilitator person to place these 'bricks' of knowledge within a general structure of order-within-complexity.

This contrast between conscious adjusting and subconscious clarifying and structuring is especially apparent when the Facilitator person is attempting to discover something new. The mental strategy of adjusting and mixing is both appropriate and accurate when *interpolating* between existing facts and sequences. However, it tends to give spurious results when *extrapolating* beyond existing information. Thus, the Facilitator person finds it difficult to escape mentally from the status quo. One possible strategy is to make some random change and observe what happens. For instance, this strategy was used by Thomas Edison (another Facilitator person) when inventing the light bulb. Edison

> tested the carbonized filaments of every plant imaginable, including baywood, boxwood, hickory, cedar, flax, and bamboo. He even contacted biologists who sent him plant fibers from places in the tropics. Edison acknowledged that the work was tedious and very demanding, especially on his workers helping with the experiments. He always recognized the importance of hard work and determination. "Before I got through," he recalled, "I tested no fewer than 6,000 vegetable growths, and ransacked the world for the most suitable filament material" (Edison Files).

Notice precisely where the randomness is occurring. Edison eventually used carbonized bamboo as a light bulb filament because it consistently lasted for a long time. Thus, there was no randomness in the natural process. Science would not be possible if nature functioned in a totally random manner. Instead, the randomness occurred in the method that Edison used to discover the natural process.

Putting this all together, the Facilitator person will observe that conscious adjusting, mixing, and random change lead automatically to stable truth, solid sequences, and greater order and structure. However, the Facilitator person is not consciously aware of the Perceiver, Server, and Teacher processing that causes this to occur. If this process of 'adjusting → automatic clarity → automatic understanding' continues to repeat itself within the mind of the Facilitator person, then it will lead to the formation of a core mental network. And because Facilitator thought lies between the internal and ex-ternal worlds, the Facilitator person will find it natural to believe that both the mind and the physical world function in a manner that is self-categorizing and self-structuring.

The end result is that the Facilitator person finds the theory of evolution naturally at-tractive. (Charles Darwin was a Facilitator person.) First, it is scientific and the Facilita-tor person has learned that science leads to stability and freedom. Second, the process of evolution resonates with the thinking that occurs within the mind of the Facilitator person, because in both cases, gradual evolving is leading to new Perceiver objects and new Server sequences and heading in the direction of greater Teacher order. Third, the agentless theory of evolution makes it possible to escape from the 'cult experience' im-posed by the mental networks behind God and religion. Thus, the theory of evolution is often viewed by the Facilitator person not just as a scientific theory but rather as a means of escaping bondage and finding stability and freedom that resonates deeply with the core mental network of Facilitator self-analysis. If such a Facilitator person achieves a position of power, then this attraction can turn into a public crusade to replace the dogma of religion with the theory of evolution. And because the Facilitator person has no conscious control over subconscious Exhorter desire, this public crusade can be-come an inescapable obsession.

I have suggested that the goal of religion is to achieve mental wholeness. This includes providing a wholesome environment for Facilitator thought. One of the by-products of following the path of personal transformation is that Facilitator thought will find a combination of stability and freedom. In addition, the path being described in this book attempts to minimize internal discontinuities—which Facilitator thought abhors—by transferring internal control between one mental strategy and another.

✳ 11. Righteousness

This chapter will examine—finally—the relationship between Server thought and Teacher thought. It may seem strange that this book has spent so much time discussing Perceiver thought while postponing an analysis of Server thought until now. The more cynical might suggest that I am focusing upon Perceiver thought merely because I am a Perceiver person. I admit that it is easier for me to analyze the part of the mind in which I am conscious. However, I suggest that there is more to the story.

I mentioned at the very beginning of this book that Server thought can build its own confidence whereas Perceiver thought gains its confidence from the environment. This is not a trivial distinction. Perceiver thought and Server thought *both* gain confidence through repetition. Whenever a set of connections is repeated, then Perceiver thought gains confidence that these connections describe a solid fact. Similarly, whenever a certain sequence is repeated, then Server thought gains confidence that this sequence describes how things really work.

Server thought has an *advantage* that Perceiver thought does not have, while Perceiver thought has a *disadvantage* that Server thought does not have. The Server advantage is that Server confidence can be acquired merely by moving one's body. Practicing builds Server confidence by *repeating* a sequence of movements. In contrast, Perceiver confidence is acquired when connections are *repeated*. In other words, Server thought can *actively* build confidence while Perceiver confidence is acquired *passively*. The Perceiver disadvantage is that Perceiver thought must learn how to function in a realm of Mercy experiences that is already filled with ready-made emotions provided by the physical body. Server thought does not have the same problem. In fact, the average person— and researcher—does not even know that Teacher emotion exists. Thus, not only is Perceiver confidence harder to acquire than Server confidence, but Perceiver thought has learn how to function in an environment that is already strewn with emotions, whereas Server thought is free to practice its movements in an environment that is largely oblivious to Teacher emotions. Using an analogy, Server thought grows up in the prairies where the land is flat and one can drive anywhere—and is also given a car to drive. Perceiver thought, in contrast, grows up in the mountains and has no easy way of getting from point A to point B.

Thus, one reason that we devoted so much time to discussing Perceiver thought and its interaction with Mercy emotions while ignoring Server thought is that Perceiver thought needs help getting started whereas Server thought does not.

But having a car and being able to drive wherever you want also has its disadvantages. What happens is that action can become its *own* justification. When asked, 'Why are you doing things that way?' the response will be, 'Because that is how things are done around here!' A simple Google search on 'strange traditions' will show that things are often 'done around here' in rather bizarre ways.

> Action that is repeated long enough turns into self-perpetuating tradition.

For instance, the town of Ivrea in northern Italy has an annual three-day festival in which nine teams throw oranges at each other. It began in the Middle Ages with poor families throwing out pots of beans as a sign of rebellion against the local lord. This turned into using beans as ammunition to throw at people passing by. The throwing of oranges began in the 19th century when local girls started tossing oranges at passing parade carriages in order to draw the attention of boys. Since World War II, the 'battle of the oranges' has been fought according to strict rules. Thus, what began as a series of semi-random actions solidified over the centuries into a solid tradition.

Throwing oranges for three days is a rather innocuous tradition. Unfortunately, we saw in a previous chapter that science itself can turn into tradition. As was quoted earlier, in the appendix to his famous book, Kuhn redefines a paradigm as how a group of scientists act. Kuhn explains the idea of scientific community in more detail.

> A scientific community consists, on this view, of the practitioners of the scientific specialty. To an extent unparalleled in most other fields, they have undergone similar educations and professional initiations; in the process they have absorbed the same technical literature and drawn many of the same lessons from it... As a result, the members of a scientific community see themselves and are seen by others as the men uniquely responsible for the pursuit of a set of shared goals, including the training of their successors (Kuhn, 1970, p. 177).

But the same thing could be said about the orange throwers of Ivrea. This tradition is being upheld by the citizens of Ivrea who have undergone similar educations and grown up in the same town, absorbed the same traditions and drawn many of the same lessons. These citizens of Ivrea would also view themselves as men uniquely responsible for the pursuit of the shared goal of throwing oranges, including the training of their successors.

A distinction was made earlier between scientific thought and scientific methodology. Scientific *thought* uses Perceiver thought to analyze Mercy experiences and formulate Teacher theories. The purpose of scientific *methodology* is to protect and encourage Perceiver thought. Over the centuries, the practice of scientific methodology has turned into a *tradition*, a way in which a group of scientists *act*, and many experts, like Kuhn, now *define* science as the tradition of scientific methodology. However, if science is merely a methodology, then there is no fundamental difference between the tradition of scientific methodology and the tradition of throwing oranges.

We saw when examining Perceiver thought that Perceiver *belief* is not the same as Perceiver *truth*. Belief is what Perceiver thought *thinks* is correct while truth describes what really *is* correct. A child may believe in the existence of Santa Claus, but when he grows up he will realize that this belief is not true. Because we live in a physical world composed of solid objects, truth is usually equated with *empirical evidence*, which means opening up our eyes and seeing what exists in the real world. And because our physical bodies fill our minds with emotional experiences, belief is sometimes equated with *blind faith*, which means allowing Perceiver thought to be overwhelmed by Mercy emotions. Thus, scientific methodology learns about truth by gathering empirical evidence, it avoids blind faith by being objective, and it minimizes emotional bias through peer review.

Unfortunately, while this methodology may work with the *right* hemisphere realm of Perceiver facts and Mercy experiences, it is actually counterproductive when dealing with the *left* hemisphere realm of Server sequences and Teacher understanding. What Server sequences will the typical scientist observe when he 'opens up his eyes and sees what exists in the real world'? If he works on a university campus, or in a corporate or military lab, then what he will mainly see is what he and his fellow scientists are doing. And while it is helpful to *avoid* Mercy emotions when searching for Perceiver facts, we saw from our look at math and science that *following* Teacher emotions is quite useful when studying how the natural world functions. Finally, if peer review judges what a person does by what his colleagues are doing, then this is merely a more rigorous version of tradition.

Now that we understand how Server confidence is acquired, let us step back in order to gain some perspective. Where does one find *Perceiver* truth? Science tells us that truth is found in empirical evidence, which means observing the physical world for solid facts. Mental symmetry suggests that one can also find solid facts in the structure of the mind. Facts about the physical world are universal because they apply everywhere within the universe. Universal facts are needed when building a grand explanation. However, facts about mental structure are also universal in the sense that they follow me around wherever I go, and these are the sorts of facts that are needed if I want to figure out my place within the grand explanation.

Where does one find *Server* 'truth', or in other words, Server sequences that do not change? This is where the message of science has become ambiguous. Science used to say that one could discover unchanging Server sequences by studying how the natural world functions, by examining natural cause-and-effect, by learning what Nature does. Unfortunately, this message has become clouded in two major ways.

First, as I have already mentioned, the focus has turned away from how Nature functions to how a group of scientists function. But there is nothing inherently special about how any group of people functions. The only reason that the functioning of a group of scientists is special is because scientific tradition is an effective way of determining how Nature functions. And the way that Nature functions is special because it does not change. An apple will always fall to the ground in the same manner. In contrast, what a group of scientists do is somewhat faddish, because popular (and fundable and publishable) topics of science come and go.

Second, those who currently talk the loudest about 'how Nature functions' tend to be those who focus upon how Nature usually does *not* function. Repeating part of an earlier quote,

> Bizarrely, evolutionists lead the world in substituting teleology for objectivity. How so? One major reason is the manner in which natural selection slipped seamlessly into the place of the Creator: the Natural Selector as the acceptable new face of the Great Designer (Hanke, 2004).

Mutations are rare and the 'Natural Selector' that drives evolution functions in a manner that is improbable. In contrast, the average scientist who studies how Nature *usually* functions does not generally talk about Nature but rather focuses upon more specific natural laws of cause-and-effect. That is because talking about 'what Nature does' sounds too much like 'what a person does', and science does not like to use that sort of language because persons involve MMNs and scientific methodology has learned that MMNs interfere with rational thought. When those who focus upon how Nature seldom functions talk the loudest about how Nature functions, then this will obviously cloud people's understanding of how Nature functions.

Thinking about Doing

I suggested in an earlier chapter that scientific methodology with its demand for empirical evidence will lead to a focus upon studying social interaction rather than personal identity. We will now examine this connection from a *Server* perspective.

During the *modern* era, scientists used scientific methodology to understand how the Natural world functions. But this has now been replaced by the postmodern era, with its self-questioning and thinking about thinking. Thanks to researchers such as Kuhn and Fairclough, we now know that the supposedly objective thinking of science is heavily influenced by the mind of the scientist with its personal biases. This has caused us to question scientific thought and scientific theories—but scientific methodology continues. Scientists still function the way they used to function. The tradition of being a scientist has not changed. And this tradition says that scientists search for objective, empirical evidence, and check their results with fellow scientists. So, instead of studying how the mind influences scientific thought, the focus keeps shifting to gaining objective, empirical evidence about how the mind influences scientific thought, which means studying how scientists act, because action is objective and empirical.

This may sound confusing, so I will try to rephrase it more simply. Human behavior is driven by mental networks. But mental networks exist *within* the mind, which makes mental networks hard to study in a scientific manner. Therefore, what is studied is *social interaction*, which is the external expression of mental networks. But what is left when one studies social interaction in an objective manner that downplays subjective emotions? Tradition—how a group of people act. But that is precisely what one should *not* study, because people can choose to act in any way that they jolly well please, including ways that are torturous and suicidal. People have chosen to move to the desert and live on top of poles. And people have chosen to go, by the millions, into muddy trenches and clamber out into thick mud in order to be mowed down by machine gun fire.

> Postmodern thinking-about-thinking naturally turns into thinking-about-doing.

If one wishes to think about thinking, then why not think about *thinking* rather than think about *behaving*? This may sound obvious, but I keep encountering religious, scientific, and popular books that claim to think about thinking but end up thinking about doing rather than about thinking, or researchers and schools of thought that began by thinking about thinking but then got sidetracked into thinking about doing. (We have seen that theories about thinking often fall apart when they are applied to the researcher. That is a different problem than the one being discussed here.) This is a rather sweeping statement, so let me back it up with four examples. I mention these four not because they are unusual but rather because they are ones which I have recently encountered in my research.

First, we have already seen how Fairclough's book *Language and Power* analyzes human thought and behavior in terms of *members resources*, which are very similar to MMNs. However, we saw earlier that Fairclough seems to have dropped the concept of member resources in his later writings and instead refers to people as 'social agents'.

Second, I recently read a book entitled *Anatomy of the Soul*, by Curt Thompson (2010), which approaches cognitive development from both a Christian as well as a neurologically informed perspective. Thompson's book contains an excellent description of how MMNs function. In addition, he suggests that the purpose of cognitive development is mental wholeness, which is achieved by allowing the frontal lobes to regulate the rest of the mind, statements with which I would agree wholeheartedly. However, instead of analyzing how mental networks function within a person's mind, Thompson states that 'there is no such thing as an individual brain', and focuses instead upon social interaction. While it is true that social interaction plays a major role in developing the mind, I see 'individual brains' all the time, walking around encased within people's skulls. And most of the exercises that Thompson suggests for developing the frontal lobes (the location of the *internal* world) involve the *physical* world and *external* interaction, such as mentally focusing upon different physical locations in the room, becoming mentally attuned to one's physical body, or practicing open confession and unconditional forgiveness with a group of friends.

Third, N.T. Wright begins his two-book volume entitled Paul and the Faithfulness of God (2013) by stating that he wants to look behind people's theology to the worldview (or mental networks) that drives this theology, and he analyzes in extensive detail the religious mindset of the typical Jew, Greek, and Roman during the time of the apostle Paul. Similarly, when Wright descends from the rarefied heights of historical exegesis in *After You Believe* (2010) to focus upon character transformation, he begins by saying that behavior is ultimately driven by 'the deepest longings of your own heart' (or in other words, by core MMNs). But then he says that these deepest longings are transformed by *building new habits*, thus moving from the subjective, internal realm of the heart to the objective, external realm of Server repetition. Wright says throughout his writings that the Christian should be motivated by the Platonic form of 'God's coming kingdom', consistent with what we have said about values guiding goals (though Wright dislikes using the term 'Platonic forms'). However, when it comes to describing what this 'coming kingdom' is like, Wright talks about having more exuberant church services, redeeming the sanctity of church buildings, and improving city planning.

> The church that takes sacred space seriously not as a retreat from the world but as a bridgehead into it will go straight from worshiping in the sanctuary to debating in the Council chamber – discussing matters of town planning, harmonizing and humanizing beauty in architecture, in green spaces, in road traffic schemes, and... In environmental work, creative and healthy farming methods, and proper use of resources. If it is true, as I have argued, the whole world is now God's holy land, we must not rest as long as that land is spoiled and defaced. This is not an extra to the church's mission. It is central (Wright, 2008).

These may be noble goals but one would hope that God's 'coming kingdom' would extend beyond the purely physical matters of 'town planning', 'road traffic schemes', and 'healthy farming methods'.

Fourth, I recently took several years to apply the theory of mental symmetry to the field of TESOL, in collaboration with Angelina Van Dyke, and I found it very useful to examine the research that is being done in areas such as personal transformation, identity, and culture. However, after reading through dozens of papers, I noticed that the general trend is to replace the 'modern' focus upon linguistics, grammar, and teaching methods, with a 'postmodern' focus upon pragmatics and social interaction. Even though identity is being studied, the general consensus is to define identity in terms of social interaction, rather than seeing social interaction as an external expression of internal mental networks.

Teacher Thought and Server Stability

Now that we have seen the postmodern tendency for thinking about thinking to turn into thinking about doing, let us do some thinking about thinking *and* doing. This means examining the interaction between Teacher thought, the part of the mind that does the *thinking* and Server thought, the part of the mind that does the *doing*.

Teacher thought by itself is unstable. It may seem strange to suggest that a cognitive module that searches for universal answers is unstable, but I have learned from personal experience that this is the case. For instance, I remember one Teacher person who would occasionally tell me his life plan. Teacher thought likes general theories, and a life plan is a general theory that applies to one's entire life. What surprised me was that every few months this person would come up with a completely different life plan, containing just as much order-within-complexity and stated with equal emotional conviction as the previous plan.

One often sees a similar Teacher instability in charismatic Christianity (the modern offshoot of Pentecostalism). I have suggested that Pentecostalism focuses upon the Platonic form of the Holy Spirit while ignoring the Teacher understanding that builds Platonic forms. The charismatic Christian will typically compensate for this lack of understanding with an extensive audiovisual library of motivational speakers, who use emotionally inflated words to give Teacher thought the feeling of having a general theory. Listening to some speaker will give the charismatic believer the sensation of having a Teacher understanding, this feeling will fade after a few days, and Teacher thought will then be recharged by listening to another motivational sermon, repeating the cycle. Yesterday's grand theory is often inconsistent with the grand theory of today. But the current theory will always be embraced with great emotional conviction.

This *internal* instability of Teacher thought is reinforced by the *external* instability of speech. In the same way that Server thought can express itself through actions, so Teacher thought can express itself through talking. But speech is nothing more than a disturbance of air molecules that instantly fades away. The result is a positive feedback loop of instability in which temporary speech feeds temporary understanding which drives temporary speech. As the saying goes, talk is cheap. Think, for instance, of the countless times that one has verbally proposed or defended some grand theory and of how little impact most of those words have had.

> Server actions give stability to Teacher understanding.

In the same way that Perceiver thought gives stability to Mercy experiences by looking for connections that are repeated, so Server thought gives stability to Teacher theories by looking for sequences that are repeated. That is why listening to a lecture in class is followed by *applying* the words in some way, such as doing homework or performing a lab. Doing makes the words stick. According to Dale's *Cone of Experience*, people generally remember 10% of what they read and 20% of what they hear, but 70% of what they say and write and 90% of what they do as they perform a task. Using the language of mental symmetry, Server stability can be added to Teacher words either by *writing* down the words or by *performing* some task that expresses the words. Writing is less effective than doing because writing remains within the realm of abstract thought while doing is part of concrete thought. Writing uses physical action to transcribe the words, while doing uses physical action to express the words. However, both will add Server stability to Teacher words.

Grammar provides another example of adding Server stability to Teacher words. For instance, consider the simple sentences 'I hit the ball', 'You love my sister', and 'John eats a hamburger'. As everyone who has studied English grammar knows, Teacher words such as 'I', 'you', and 'John' fall into the Server category of pronouns, 'hit', 'love', and 'eats' are verbs, and so on. Thus, all sentences such as these can be summarized by the common *Server* sequence of pronoun-verb-article-noun. The specific Teacher words contained within this Server sequence may change but the general Server sequence itself stays the same.

The Exemplar

Notice that we have just come up with a *new definition* for universality. Until now, we have assumed that universal theories are composed of Teacher words. But we have just seen that Server grammar is more general than Teacher words. How can anything be more general than universal words? I suggest that this is not just a technical question but rather one with profound implications. Stated simply, I suggest that a verbal theory can at best be a *description* of universal understanding, but a truly universal understanding will go beyond mere Teacher words to include Server sequences.

One can see this *Server* ingredient of universality in what Kuhn calls the *exemplar*, or model problem.

> All physicists, for example, begin by learning the same exemplars: problems such as the inclined plane, the conical pendulum, and Keplerian orbits...The paradigm as shared example is the central element of what I now take to be the most novel and least understood aspect of this book. Exemplars will therefore require more attention than the other sorts of components of the disciplinary matrix [or paradigm]. Philosophers of science have not ordinarily discussed the problems encountered by a student in laboratories or in science texts, for these are thought to supply only practice in the application of what the student already knows. He cannot, it is said, solve problems at all unless he has first learned the theory and some rules for applying it. Scientific knowledge is embedded in theory and rules; problems are supplied to gain facility in their application. I have tried to argue, however, that this localization of the cognitive content of science is wrong. After the student has done many problems, he may gain only added facility by solving more. But at the start and for some time after, doing problems is learning consequential things about nature. In the absence of such exemplars, the laws and theories he has previously learned would have little empirical content (Kuhn, 1970, p. 187).

Kuhn is comparing the philosopher of science with the scientist. The philosopher thinks that 'scientific knowledge is embedded in theory and rules'—that Teacher universality is found in words and symbols. The philosopher also thinks that 'problems are supplied to gain facility' in understanding abstract theory. In other words, the physics student goes to class, listens to the professor talk, and sees him write equations on the blackboard. These words and equations provide the student with a general theory. The student then applies this theory by carrying out the Server actions of solving problems.

> Math is based in Teacher words; science is based in Server exemplars.

But Kuhn says that the philosopher is mistaken in thinking that 'problems supply only practice in the application of what the student already knows'. Instead, Kuhn suggests that 'at the start and for some time after, doing problems *is* learning consequential things about nature'. In other words, the learning comes from *doing* the Server steps involved in solving problems of physics. For instance, suppose that I am solving a physics problem involving an 'inclined plane' in which some mass is being pushed up the slope. Solving this problem is actually teaching me the 'grammar' used to solve *any* problem that involves objects moving up or down slopes. Using Kuhn's language, these physics problems are *exemplars*, because one problem represents many other problems that *act* in a similar way. Without these problems, 'the laws and theories previously learned would have little empirical content'. There will be Teacher order but only minimal order-within-complexity.

Now let us turn our attention to religion. We have talked extensively about the need to *construct* a mental concept of God rather than jump directly between Teacher and Mercy thought through mysticism, emotionally inflate incomplete concepts of God, or identify with theories that do not apply to personal identity. While constructing a mental concept of God is essential, I suggest that it is not sufficient. That is because words are only capable of *describing* a mental concept of God. The order-within-complexity is much greater if one adds Server exemplars to Teacher words.

This may sound like a subtle distinction, but I suggest that it is important to combine cognitive elements in the right priority and in the right order if one wishes to reach mental wholeness and avoid self-deception. Therefore, we will approach this topic from several different angles.

Suppose that the Bible really *is* the Word of God and that every word in this book is divinely inspired. One is still dealing with two inherent cognitive inadequacies, one related to Perceiver thought and the other to Server thought. The Perceiver problem has already been discussed. If Perceiver thought is mesmerized by the Mercy status given to the author of the Bible, then the words of the Bible will only be applied to religious experiences and will not extend beyond the walls of the religious subculture. For instance, the system of cognitive styles used in this book is taught in Christian circles. I remember reading one Christian description of the Server person which suggested that they can use their spiritual gift to drive the church bus or work in the church kitchen. Notice how driving a bus is not regarded as a spiritual activity that expresses a spiritual gift. Instead, one must drive a *church* bus. But Perceiver thought knows that there is no difference between buses and church buses. They both fall into the Perceiver category of 'bus'. What *really* makes driving a bus spiritual? I suggest that it is being guided by the value of the *Platonic form* of 'driving a vehicle', which means driving in a manner that is honest, efficient, polite, helpful, gracious, and smooth.

The Server problem relates to the distinction between words and exemplars. Books are written using words, which is both their strength and their weakness. The strength of words is that they enable abstract thought to consider content that is *different* than the real world of concrete thought. Words make it possible for humans to transcend being merely creatures of their physical environment. The weakness of words is that they are only descriptions of reality, and a description is not the same as the real thing. Theologians, philosophers, and mathematicians like to think that they are manipulating reality with their abstract words and logical manipulations. But they are only working with a *description* of reality and if these words are not translated into actions, then they will have no effect upon reality.

I am not suggesting that words are wrong or that one must abandon words. Rather, words are *incomplete*. Mysticism also suggests that one must 'go beyond words' in order to 'encounter God', but mysticism discovers God by abandoning words and letting go of rational thought. In contrast, I suggest that one must go beyond words by adding actions to words and by applying rational thought. One can see what this means by looking at science. Science is more than mathematics, because mathematics lives in the Teacher realm of words and symbols while science also studies nature. Science does not abandon mathematics but rather applies mathematics to the concrete world of natural cause-and-effect. Science does not contradict mathematics. Instead, we saw in an earlier quote by Dirac that the amazing thing about science is that one can make scientific progress either by pursuing mathematics or by performing experiments. For some reason, both of these paths lead to similar results.

> One can only go past words if something exists independent of words.

It is only possible to go beyond words if something *exists* beyond words. Science can go beyond the words of mathematics because science studies how the natural world functions—how Nature acts. And Nature does not act in a capricious manner but rather functions in an ordered way that can be categorized by Server thought into similar sequences. Similarly, I suggest that theology can go beyond the words of the Bible because theology studies how the mind functions. And the mind does not act in a capricious manner but rather functions in an ordered way that can be categorized by Server thought into similar sequences.

If a Teacher theory does not describe how something *else* functions, such as the natural world or the mind, then the only way to spread this theory is by *proclaiming* it to others, and if they do not listen then one must *preach* it to others, and if they still do not listen then one must use *status* and *ridicule* to emotionally impose it upon others, and if that is not enough then one must use *force* to physically impose upon others. In contrast, if a Teacher theory accurately describes how something else *functions*, then one only needs to point it out when this something else *does* function. A person who does not know how the natural world functions will act in ways that lead to painful consequences. When this happens, then words can be used to point out understanding and these words will be reinforced by the functioning of the natural world. Similarly a person who does not know how the mind functions will act in ways that lead to painful personal consequences. When this happens, then words can be used to point out understanding and these words will be reinforced by the functioning of the mind.

Proclaiming a theory is a one-way street in which the person who is the source of understanding and/or the follower of God reveals inside knowledge to those who lack understanding and do not know God. In contrast, when one is pointing out how something *else* functions, then learning goes both ways. The one who is doing the pointing out may have an understanding or a concept of God that the listener does not have. But pointing out how a general theory applies to some situation or person will end up making the theory more general as a new area of application is either discovered or explored. Thus, the one pointing out will want to learn from his listener how the general theory applies in that specific situation. Instead of feeling devalued by being preached at, the listener will feel valued because genuine interest is being shown in his specific situation.

I have found this concept to be immensely freeing. For many years I felt that I had to proclaim the theory of mental symmetry, and when others would not listen then I felt like I *should* impose it upon others—while feeling guilty when I *did* impose it upon others. Eventually it dawned on me that if I really was discovering inescapable cognitive mechanisms, then I only needed to point them out to other individuals when they encountered these inescapable cognitive mechanisms. But in order to recognize these cognitive mechanisms at play, I had to use Perceiver thought to translate between my words and the words of others and I had to use Server thought to look for similar sequences in different fields.

As I continued along this path, I also started to grasp the distinction that Kuhn makes between philosophy and science. I suggest that Server actions need to be added to Teacher understanding for three reasons. The first reason is that action adds stability to understanding. As pointed out by Dale's cone of experience, words without actions are unstable. The philosophers in Kuhn's quote recognize this first reason.

The second reason is that actions speak louder than words. This is a deeper reason which many theologians, philosophers, mathematicians, and theoreticians do not appear to recognize. Repeating an action builds Server confidence. Server confidence gives stability to Teacher words. If one repeats an action that is *consistent* with Teacher understanding, then the resulting Server confidence will give stability to the Teacher understanding. However, if one repeats an action that is *inconsistent* with Teacher understanding, then the resulting Server confidence will destabilize Teacher understanding. In other words, Server actions do not just add stability to Teacher theories, they either reinforce understanding or else undermine understanding. This is especially true when one is attempting to gain an understanding of the mind. I have repeatedly found that whenever I come up with a new concept in Teacher thought, it is very important to back up these Teacher words by applying these words through some Server action.

Going further, studying the mind does not occur in a vacuum. Instead, one is usually attempting to gain a Teacher understanding of aspects of thought that *already* contain Server actions that were guided by childish MMNs. Thus, merely applying theory through some Server action is usually not sufficient. Instead, one must apply theory by choosing to perform some new Server action that *replaces* childish habits motivated by childish thinking. I am reminded of a comment that Charlie Brown made in one of the Peanuts comic strips. He commented that Linus would have to go to school for 24 years, 12 years to *unlearn* everything that Lucy taught him, and then 12 more years to gain correct understanding. Similarly, understanding the mind requires both the unlearning of childish Server habits as well as the learning of adult Server habits.

The third reason brings us to Kuhn's comparison of science and philosophy. Server thought is typically viewed as the servant of Teacher thought. One descends from the heights of academic theory in order to occasionally engage in the more pedestrian and plebian realm of concrete action. And the word 'descend' accurately describes how one feels when making what one feels is necessary but annoying detours away from the exalted world of universal words and ideas. But Kuhn is saying that the generality of a Teacher theory does not come from the Teacher words but rather from the Server sequences. The words are general because they describe how something *else* works, and Server thought is the part of the mind that *realizes* how this something else works.

Saying this another way, Server thought does not just *apply* a general Teacher theory, it provides *exemplars* that generalize Teacher theory. An exemplar is a Server sequence that *represents* many similar Server sequences. It is not just an example, but rather a characteristic or illustrative example.

An exemplar is both specific and general. On the one hand, one is carrying out a specific sequence of actions, or solving a specific problem. For instance, in the sample physics problem given earlier, some hockey player is shooting a puck on the ice. On the other hand, one does not perform actions at random, but rather chooses actions that correspond most closely to the general Server sequence—examples that are *characteristic*. For example, one often finds problems involving hockey players and ice skaters in physics textbooks because an ice surface is flat and almost frictionless.

Righteousness

Now that we have examined the relationship between Server thought and Teacher thought, let us turn our attention to religion. What we have been discussing is the concept of *righteousness,* which could be defined as behaving in a way that is consistent with how God behaves. How does one determine how God behaves? If God is a universal being, than one searches for universal sequences of behavior. Science searches for patterns in how the *natural world* behaves. For instance, whenever a block of ice is heated, then it will eventually melt into water and then boil into steam. This is a repeated sequence that occurs when any solid is heated. The thesis of this book is that religion makes sense if one searches for patterns in how the mind behaves. For instance, whenever a person continues to work with some theory, then that theory will turn into a TMN which will emotionally trap a person within that theory. This is a repeated sequence that occurs when any theory is studied.

These universal sequences always occur and they will always impose themselves upon the human mind and body. But it is possible to act *for a while* in a manner that violates these natural sequences. For instance, if I build a house directly upon permafrost in the frozen North, then the heat of the house will eventually melt the frozen ground, causing the house to sink into the ground. It is possible to live for a while in this house, but eventually the way that nature functions will prevent me from continuing to function. In other words, righteousness involving the natural world has to do with *sustainability*. For example, it is possible to have watered green lawns in Southern California but it takes constant watering. As soon as the watering stops, natural processes take over and the green grass will dry up and die. Similarly, the rich and powerful in a society tend to function in a way that takes a lot of effort on the part of many people to sustain. For instance, when the president of the United States traveled to Britain in 2003 on a state visit, he was accompanied by a retinue of 250 Secret Service members, 150 national security advisers, 200 government department representatives, 50 political aides, 100 journalists, a personal chef, 4 cooks, medics, and the 15 member dog sniffer team, all transported in two presidential 747s and a third chartered passenger jet. A C-17 cargo jet flew his motorcade to Britain (Russell, 2003). Obviously, it is only possible for a fraction of the human population to function in this manner. Using the language of Kant, this type of behavior is inconsistent with Kant's categorical imperative.

Ecological sustainability is currently a hot topic and people talk about 'minimizing their ecological footprint'. However there is also *cognitive* sustainability. We joke about girlfriends or boyfriends being 'high maintenance'. Part of this means that sustaining their lifestyle requires a lot of money. But there is also the cognitive maintenance involved in propping up someone's mental networks through affirmation and ego stroking. I suggested in an earlier chapter that childish MMNs naturally function in a manner that Teacher thought finds chaotic. Saying this another way, the way that a baby acts is not sustainable. It takes a lot of effort, both physical and cognitive, on the part of parents to keep a baby functioning.

The growing child illustrates another aspect of righteousness, which is that it is possible to become more righteous by gaining an understanding and acting in a way that is consistent with this understanding. Little children cry when they are hungry and have to be stopped from touching hot stoves. Older children know how to go to the refrigerator for a snack and have learned that hot items should not be touched. In other words, their lifestyle requires less maintenance from others because they have learned to act in a way that is more consistent with how the natural world functions.

Righteousness is Server action that is guided by Teacher understanding.

It feels *good* to act in a righteous manner. But the emotion of righteousness comes from Teacher thought and not Mercy thought. Mercy emotion provides a *goal* to reach or an *obstacle* to avoid. The Teacher emotion of righteousness, in contrast, comes from the *journey*. That is because Mercy thought thinks in terms of *experience* while Teacher thought thinks in terms of *sequence*. Performing an action in a righteous manner feels good, even if there is no destination. This is what distinguishes *works* from *righteousness*. Both involve Server actions, but 'works' are guided by Mercy emotions while righteousness is guided by Teacher emotions.

Because the childish mind is governed by MMNs, Server actions are naturally driven by the MMNs of goals and people. For instance, I walk to the kitchen in order to get an apple, I work at my job in order to buy a car, I clean my room in order to please my parents, or I do the homework in order to get a good grade. Similarly, when God is viewed from a Mercy perspective, then I will feel that I have to *do* something in order to gain the approval of God. But Server actions can also be guided by Teacher emotions. For example, it feels good to act in a gracious or graceful manner. In this case the smoothness of the overall action brings order to the complexity of movements. One sees this, for instance, in ballet dancing or synchronized swimming.

Action that is driven by MMNs takes effort, because the positive emotion only comes at the *end* of the journey when one reaches the goal. In contrast, action that is driven by a TMN feels natural, because the Teacher emotion comes as one is carrying out the sequence, and the positive Teacher emotion comes from carrying out the sequence in a righteous manner—from acting in a way that is *consistent* with Teacher understanding.

Whenever a mental network is triggered, it will attempt to impose its structure upon thought and behavior. The corollary to this is that mental networks take *ownership* of the thought and behavior that they motivate. Saying this another way, carrying out a habit reinforces that habit. Because the childish mind is *already* controlled by MMNs, one becomes righteous by acting in an *altruistic* manner, which means being guided by a TMN in the *absence* of any MMNs. This distinction can be found in the difference between the *goal* driven behavior of Kant's hypothetical imperative and the *understanding* driven behavior of his categorical imperative.

Altruism is often confused with self-denial, and so it is important to distinguish between these two. Self-denial is one of the characteristics of the *religious attitude*, and is driven by Mercy feelings of personal status. I deny myself because I feel that the MMN that represents the source of religious truth is far more important than the MMN of personal identity. Stated more simply, I feel that I am nothing compared to God.

Self-denial is a *negation* of personal identity. Altruism, in contrast, is an *affirmation* of a concept of God. Self-denial chooses *not* to be driven by the MMNs of personal identity. Thus, it is vulnerable to being hijacked by the MMNs of someone else's personal identity. For instance, for many years my parents had an elderly German lady as a neighbor. Other people were constantly denying themselves in order to serve this lady, while she was very willing to be the recipient of this self-denial. Altruism chooses *to* be driven by the TMN of a general understanding. It is guided by understanding in the absence of personal goals. Altruism, for instance, is honest when no one is looking, because it understands that a society functions best when everyone is honest. Altruism helps a person in need guided solely by the Platonic form of a better world.

> Altruism is required to become righteous.

The purpose of altruism is not to deny self but rather to acquire the nature of being righteous. If a Server action is motivated by the MMN of some goal or person, then that mental network will take ownership of that behavior. However, if a Server action is motivated by the TMN of a general understanding and no MMN can take ownership of that action, then the action will become mentally attached to the TMN, and that TMN will then motivate a person to repeat that action. Thus, once a person becomes righteous in a certain area by acting altruistically, it is not necessary to *continue* avoiding MMNs because the mental connection between TMN and personal behavior has now been established—within that context.

Altruism is required because the childish mind is *already* guided by MMNs and lacks TMNs. Thus, the only way to be guided by a TMN is to build a TMN and then choose to follow it in the absence of any MMN. For instance, suppose that a child is punished for telling a lie. Honesty is consistent with Kant's categorical imperative because is not possible for everyone to be dishonest. Instead, dishonesty is only possible when a few people tell lies within a general context of honesty. In addition, society functions most smoothly when everyone tells the truth. But the child's honesty is not being motivated either by Kant's categorical imperative or by the vision of a better society. Instead, the child does not want to get spanked. If a child continues to tell the truth, then this repeated Server action will lead to the habit of telling the truth, but a habit is not the same as righteousness. The child becomes righteous in the area of honesty when he chooses to be honest in a situation where Teacher understanding provides the only reason to be honest.

Righteousness is different than *objectivity*. Objectivity *avoids* subjective Mercy emotions in order to protect Perceiver thought and be guided by Teacher understanding. Righteousness, in contrast, chooses to follow the TMN of a Teacher understanding *rather* than subjective MMNs. Altruism is most effective in making a person righteous when MMNs provide reasons *not* to do some action, a TMN provides a reason to *do* the action, and one chooses to follow the TMN *rather* than MMNs. Using religious language, one becomes righteous by following God *rather* than man. Because one is choosing *not* to follow MMNs, altruism may appear like self-denial or rebellion from authority to those who lack understanding. But altruism is motivated by a desire to act in submission to some *higher* law. Once a person has become righteous, then there is no need to continue violating or avoiding MMNs. What matters is the hierarchy of mental networks that has now become established. A person will continue to be righteous as long as MMNs submit themselves to TMNs. Using the language of Platonic forms, this means that the MMNs of *goals* are guided by TMN-shaped *values* of Platonic forms.

Righteousness is a *combination* of Teacher understanding and Server action. We have looked at the *Teacher* side of becoming righteous, which involves being guided ultimately by TMNs rather than MMNs. Let us turn now to the Server side of becoming righteous. The problem here is that any action that the physical body repeats will gain in Server confidence, causing a habit to form. But righteousness is not just Server confidence in actions, but rather Server confidence in actions that are guided by Teacher understanding. Righteousness is not just doing the right thing, but rather doing the right thing with the right *motives*. For example, I taught for several years at an international school in Korea. Korean students (and Asian students in general) are known for their studiousness. However, what motivates the typical Korean student is not a Teacher-driven love for learning but rather a Mercy-driven desire for status and approval. Thus, while the typical Asian student is doing the right thing, the underlying motive is usually inadequate.

I suggest that Server confidence in actions can be associated with Teacher understanding in four different ways, which I will refer to as divine righteousness, human righteousness, habits, and righteousness. The first three are all aspects of righteousness, but I suggest that they do not fully qualify as righteousness.

Divine righteousness is the sense that some universal being is carrying out Server actions in a way that is guided by Teacher understanding. One form of divine righteousness occurs when the scientist observes similar Server sequences in the way that the natural world behaves and then uses mathematics to describe this universal behavior. Looking first at what is happening within the *mind* of the scientist, Server thought is gaining confidence by observing Server sequences being continually repeated, just as Perceiver thought gains confidence by observing Perceiver connections being continually repeated. This Server confidence is accompanied by the Teacher understanding provided by mathematical equations. Turning now to what is happening externally, the *universe* is doing the behaving, and the universe is bigger than any human, independent of any human, and was not constructed by any human. This will lead to the concept of a righteous God—a universal being who acts in a manner that can be organized into similar Server sequences.

Divine righteousness notices that universal Teacher theory guides 'how things work'.

Another form of divine righteousness occurs when a person observes similar Server sequences in the way that the mind behaves and then uses understanding to describe this universal cognitive behavior. Looking first at what is happening within the mind of the individual, Server thought is gaining confidence by observing Server sequences being continually repeated, which is accompanied by a Teacher understanding provided by some general theory of human behavior. Turning now what is happening physically, the mind/brain is doing the behaving, and it was not constructed by humans. The behavior of the physical universe is universal because it occurs everywhere throughout the universe. Cognitive mechanisms are universal because they are universal to *me*. As Kant pointed out with his distinction between phenomena and noumena, a person cannot escape the structure of his mind.

Finally, when someone looks at the course of history and sees evidence of a Server sequence being carried out that extends beyond the abilities of any finite human person or group, then this will also lead to the concept of divine righteousness. Similarly, a concept of divine righteousness will emerge when a person looks back at personal history and concludes that someone bigger than himself has been acting. In religious language this is known as *divine providence.*

For instance, one can see divine providence being described in the following two sentences from Tremlin's book.

> Natural selection designed minds that produce and interpret representations in particular ways, and by doing so it simultaneously designed minds with particular conceptual predispositions (Tremlin, 2006, p. 159).

> As a biological machine, then, the human central nervous system has much in common with those of other living organisms, designed, as all are, to control bodily function and to interpret and respond to signals received from the outside world (p.54).

In both sentences, Tremlin notices Server similarities in the functioning of different minds and concludes that this reflects the design of the superhuman agent of 'natural selection' whose activity extends over many human generations.

Seeing repeated Server patterns in history leads to a mental concept of divine providence and provides evidence for the existence of a *real* God who exhibits divine righteousness. After all, if I see something moved on my desk, and I did not move it, then I will conclude that someone *else* moved it. And if I notice something on my desk continually being moved in a certain manner, then I will draw conclusions about the *behavior* of this unknown agent.

Saying this another way, a sense of divine providence emerges when a *Teacher* mental network is formed and triggered by some sequence of actions. Suppose that a bump is heard in the middle of the night. This unidentified sound may trigger the MMN that represents the neighboring cat or the MMN that represents some cat burglar. Now suppose that a person has an awe-inspiring experience that cannot be attributed to any known MMN, such as a lightning bolt, or a volcanic eruption. This emotional event will lead to the formation of a MMN, which the mind will then interpret as a superhuman agent, and this MMN of a god (with a small 'g') will then be used to interpret subsequent similar experiences. The concept of divine providence, in contrast, is not based in any *specific* situation but rather in a *general* sequence of events that extends over a long period of time. Server thought notices that sequences are being repeated in different places and times, and Teacher thought discovers order within this complexity, causing a TMN to form, leading to the mental concept of a God (with a capital 'G') who ties everything together.

Summarizing, the concept of divine righteousness emerges when something or someone 'out there' who is independent of any human agent *acts* in a manner that is associated with Teacher *understanding*. A sense of divine righteousness can come either from observing how the natural world functions or from observing how the mind functions. A sense of divine righteousness will also emerge when one notices Server sequences being carried out in human history, as illustrated by the religious sense of divine providence or the evolutionist's description of Nature. The common ingredient is that no *human* is performing the action. Rather, the Server confidence comes from *observing* sequences being repeated by something non-human. Science is a description of how the *world* functions, not how people act. Cognitive science is a description of how mental *hardware* functions, and not the mental *software* that people place within their minds. Divine providence is a description of how *God* or *Nature* acts.

Human righteousness, in contrast, *is* based in how people act. For instance, scientific methodology started as a way of protecting Perceiver thought, but it now describes how a group of scientists function; religious attitude began as a way of preserving Perceiver belief, but it also describes how a group of religious people function. A habit will form whenever Server thought repeats some action, and the order-within-complexity of performing many similar Server actions can cause a TMN to form that will motivate a person to continue performing the habit. Human righteousness differs from habit in three major ways. First, human righteousness extends beyond the Server actions of a single person to involve the combined actions of some *group*. Human righteousness does not just continue to act the way that *I* have acted in the past. Rather, it continues to act the way that *we* have acted. The resulting order-within-complexity will result in a TMN that motivates me to perform my actions as a part of what the group is doing. Second, human righteousness involves a Teacher *understanding* that is not present in a habit. The person who is performing some habit is generally unable to verbalize why he is doing this habit. Human righteousness, in contrast, backs up the actions of some group with the Teacher understanding of some general theory. Third, human righteousness uses Teacher understanding to *regulate* the Server actions of those who are members of the group. A *profession* is an example of human righteousness. For instance, all dentists view themselves as part of a group that is cooperating to carry out the corporate task of dental hygiene, all dentists study dentistry in order to gain a Teacher understanding of dentistry, and dentists belong to professional associations that regulate their actions as a dentist and ensure that these actions remain consistent with the understanding of dentistry.

A *bureaucracy* is also driven by human righteousness, because the actions of a group of people are being guided by a set of structured regulations that can be verbalized and written down. One sees this same combination in a *professional army*. Soldiers are given orders what to do guided by the regulations and structure of the Army.

> Human righteousness is action performed in a group guided by Teacher theory.

Human righteousness is a form of righteousness because Server thought is performing actions that are being guided by Teacher understanding. But it is *human* righteousness because the Teacher order-within-complexity comes from organizing how a group of *people* act. While human righteousness *exhibits* itself through the behavior of a group of people, it is driven primarily by mental structure *within the individual minds* of the members of that group. One can see this by examining professional behavior. Belonging to a professional association of dentists, for instance, does not make a person a dentist. Instead, a person becomes a professional dentist by studying dentistry and gaining the skill of dentistry. This internal human righteousness makes it possible to become a member of a group that practices the human righteousness of dentistry, and external interaction between the members of this group will reinforce and adjust the internal human righteousness.

Human righteousness is a powerful force for regulating personal behavior; however, it suffers from several fundamental shortcomings.

The first problem is that human righteousness sets up an alternative to divine righteousness that can become completely *disconnected* from divine righteousness. Divine righteousness is based upon how the *natural* world acts, how the *mind* acts, or how a *universal divine being* acts, whereas human righteousness is based upon how a group of *people* act. One sees this distinction in Kuhn's redefinition of science. Kuhn's book on paradigms analyzes how the Teacher understanding of how *nature* functions has progressed over the centuries. But Kuhn then redefines a paradigm as a Teacher understanding of how a group of scientists behaves. Thus, Kuhn begins with divine righteousness and then replaces this with human righteousness.

The problem is that humans can *choose* to act however they wish (within limits), this behavior will be *reinforced* by human righteousness, and it will take *great effort* to maintain human righteousness when it violates divine righteousness. For instance, the New York Times reported in 2009 that

> Fuel and water represented two-thirds of the tonnage in Iraq convoys—each one vulnerable to insurgents' explosives. Each must be protected by armored vehicles, helicopters and even fighter aircraft. Afghanistan's more remote, mountainous roads are still more challenging. Slowly seeing this reality, the military has deployed simple measures first. The Army, for example, recently spent $95 mil-

lion spraying tents in Iraq with foam insulation, slashing air conditioning demands nearly in half and eliminating an estimated 12 fuel convoys a day (Leber, 2009).

Natural law says that objects will get uncomfortably hot when the outside temperature is 50°C. Natural law also says that a thinly insulated structure such as a tent will do a poor job of keeping out the summer heat. But human righteousness declares that 1) American soldiers must live in military tents, and 2) American soldiers require air-conditioning. It took 24 fuel convoys *every day* to keep American soldiers cool in Afghanistan and Iraq, costing the American taxpayer billions of dollars a year to maintain human righteousness in the face of divine righteousness.

It takes effort to violate divine righteousness. This is not sustainable.

Looking at the conflict in Iraq and Afghanistan more generally, Senator Joe Manchin observed that

> When you have this many people in a country that doesn't want you there — that has no economy, no infrastructure and a corrupt government — and you're trying to stabilize it and build them into a viable nation? I'm not sure we have enough time, and I definitely know we don't have enough money (NPR Staff, 2011).

Why was America trying to stabilize Afghanistan and build it into a viable nation? Partly because that is how things are done in the United States. America was attempting to apply the human righteousness of American society to the country of Afghanistan. The West does this when it attempts to export the institutions of democracy to some foreign country. But a country such as Afghanistan that is guided by the MMNs of tribe, culture, and personal status is mentally incapable of submitting to any form of TMN-driven righteousness, let alone the human righteousness of some foreign invading army. That is how the mind works, and it takes great effort to force the mind to work in a way that it does not naturally work. In the case of Afghanistan, Iraq, and Pakistan, it took $4.4 trillion of effort between 2001 and 2014. That is trillion with a 't'. The premise of this book is that it is both mentally and societally desirable to replace the MMNs of tribe, culture, and personal status with TMN-driven righteousness. However, the cost, both in terms of money and human pain and effort, is far lower if one makes this transition in a way that respects divine righteousness by following a path that is consistent with how the mind naturally works.

The second problem of human righteousness is that it can also become disconnected from *personal well-being*. That is because it is driven by *Teacher* emotion rather than by the MMNs of culture. For instance, Oscar Wilde famously said that 'The bureaucracy is expanding to meet the needs of the expanding bureaucracy'. Teacher thought feels good when there is increasing order-within-complexity. Therefore, those who work within a bureaucracy and are driven by the TMN created by its organization *feel good* when that bureaucracy functions and grows. But we have just seen that human righteousness can become completely unrelated to the divine righteousness of reality. Therefore, a bureaucracy has a natural tendency to turn into a cancer upon society. Because it is driven by the Teacher organization of its own structure it grows for its *own* sake and not because it provides any *benefit* to the rest of society, and because human righteousness has no inherent relationship with divine righteousness, maintaining the bureaucracy will require resources from *outside* the bureaucracy, just as air-conditioning tents in a remote desert requires an endless stream of fuel convoys. The *Teacher*-driven nature of this societal cancer is illustrated by the American government report in the 1980s which revealed that the Pentagon had paid $435 for a hammer and $600 for a toilet seat. In response to these outrageous prices, President Reagan appointed the Packard commission to find out why military items were so expensive. The commission did not find evidence of fraud or abuse. Instead, it concluded that 'the truly costly problems are those of overcomplicated organization and rigid procedure' (Thomas, 1986). In other words, the problem was excessive human righteousness.

Going further, the Teacher emotions of human righteousness can drive a group of people to behave in a manner that is *destructive* to personal well-being. For instance, the primary purpose of an army is death and destruction. Any soldier who has been in a war (or civilian who has suffered through a war) will tell you that this does not promote personal well-being.

The third problem of human righteousness is that it will focus upon *symptoms* rather than underlying causes. People can only hear what I am saying and see what I am doing. They must guess what I am thinking and feeling. But what I do and say is guided by what I *think*, which is motivated by Exhorter thought being attracted to what I *feel*. And the natural state is for the mind to be driven by childish MMNs. The end result is a tug-of-war between Teacher-driven words and actions and Mercy-driven thoughts and feelings. One sees this struggle in *political correctness*.

For instance, many readers will have noticed that I follow the politically incorrect grammar of referring to people by using the masculine pronoun 'he'. Looking at this cognitively, human righteousness notices that men tend to be driven by childish Mercy emotions of personal status to think that they are superior to women. Human righteousness wants to replace this Mercy-driven arrogance with Teacher-driven cooperation and equality, which is a noble aim. However, human righteousness can only judge what people say and do. Therefore, human righteousness will regulate the *speech* of male chauvinism, while having no effect upon the *attitude* of male chauvinism. In contrast, I have discovered that applying the theory of mental symmetry has helped to change my *attitude* of male chauvinism, because it allows me to understand how the emotions of female *thought* cooperate with the logic of male *thought* to generate human intelligence.

Because human righteousness is incapable of addressing the thinking and feeling that motivate words and actions, human righteousness will continually find itself in the predicament of 'plugging leaks in the dam'. What really causes the leaks is the water behind the dam—the thinking behind the behavior. But human righteousness is only capable of building dams—regulating the behavior that expresses the thinking. Therefore, the water will continually find new ways of leaking through the dam, and these leaks will continually have to be plugged; people will continually find new ways of expressing childish attitudes, and human righteousness will have to come up with new rules. This means that human righteousness has a natural tendency to become increasingly restrictive. For instance, consider the example of the $600 toilet seat. It is quite possible that every single bureaucratic rule was initially put into place in order to prevent some form of abuse to the system. But the combined result of all of these rules is an abusive system.

Finally, human righteousness is ultimately *imposed* by people. Those who are within a professional organization generally do not feel this personal imposition because they are being guided *internally* by the TMN that defines the structure of that organization. And instead of being told what to do, outsiders will be given a handbook or series of regulations that *explain* how the structure functions. However, at its core human righteousness is still humans telling humans how to behave. The mailed fist of personal domination may be within the velvet glove of organization and procedure, but those who reject the velvet glove will still encounter the mailed fist.

I suggest that the current debate over sexual orientation provides an example of human righteousness colliding with divine righteousness. As usual, we will take a cognitive perspective by looking at the relationship between male and female *thought* rather than between male and female people. Studies have consistently shown that female thought is *different* than male thought. My hypothesis is that the two emotional modules of Mercy and Teacher thought are naturally stronger in the female mind, while the two confidence modules of Perceiver and Server thought naturally function more in the male mind. This hypothesis is backed up by research. Males tend to have better motor and spatial skills, indicative of Server and Perceiver thought, whereas females naturally have better verbally mediated memory and social cognition, expressions of Teacher and Mercy thought (Ingalhalikar, 2013). Women are better at recognizing and expressing emotions, whereas men have a tendency to express emotion through anger and aggression, suggesting that emotion comes naturally to female thought whereas emotion tends to overwhelm male thought (Kret & De Gelder, 2012). This general tendency interacts with cognitive style. For instance, a female Mercy person naturally emphasizes conscious Mercy thought, whereas a male Mercy person naturally emphasizes subconscious Perceiver and Server thought. Interestingly, it has been shown that male vervet *monkeys* prefer to play with 'boy' toys such as a car or a ball, while female vervet monkeys prefer 'girl' toys such as a doll or a pot (Alexander & Hines, 2002) and a similar gender preference in toys was found in rhesus monkeys (Hassett, 2008), suggesting that gender-based cognitive differences are not just the result of social pressure. Thus, if one examines the divine righteousness of 'how the mind works' then one concludes that male thought is different than female thought.

If one observes the relationship between male and female *thought* within modern Western society, one notices that there is very little interaction between these two. Instead, male thought tends to interact with male thought while ignoring female thought, whereas female thought interacts primarily with female thought while ignoring male thought. In the *concrete*, this expresses itself as a division between objective and subjective. For instance, music is an expression of subjective emotions. Over the years, I have consistently encountered considerable opposition whenever I have attempted to analyze someone's musical tastes. This simply 'is not done' in Western society. But this was not always the case. For instance, the music of J.S. Bach expresses a deep integration between rational theory and emotional expression, and this integration is one reason why his music has such lasting appeal. In the *abstract*, the division between male and female thought expresses itself as a separation between technical specialization and general understanding. Concluding, if one examines the human righteousness of 'how we do things', Western *thought* appears to be primarily homosexual and not heterosexual.

The situation is quite different if one examines the divine righteousness of 'how the mind works'. As researchers are starting to realize, human intelligence is based upon a combination of logical thought and emotions. It is not possible to separate the one from the other. This, for instance, is the primary thesis of Damasio in *Descartes' Error* (1994). Similarly, if one examines the human brain, using analogies and patterns to compare one general context with another is precisely what the frontopolar cortex does—the most frontal part of the frontal lobes (Green, et al., 2010).

Love and Guthrie (1999) analyzed several systems of cognitive development and concluded that the male mind typically follows a path of cognitive development that avoids subjective emotions while the female mind usually follows a path of cognitive development that embraces personal emotions and social interaction. However, the *final state* for both the male and female mind is an *integration* of logical and emotional thought. Thus, while male thought is *different* than female thought, male thought and female thought work *together* within the integrated mind. For instance, my personal goal is to integrate the male and female sides of my mind. When I work with the theory of mental symmetry, I am using male thought to construct and apply an understanding. But many of my ideas come from female-like intuition that functions within the internal structure that male thought has constructed. Likewise, when I play violin, I am using the female side of my mind to express my personal feelings. But I can also use male thought to analyze how one plays the violin and how to express feelings through music.

Thus, I suggest that the current debate over sexual orientation is ignoring the deeper issue which is the relationship between male and female *thought*. I suggest that this deeper *cognitive* issue is affecting the debate over physical interaction. When a society is driven by its core mental networks to avoid meaningful interaction between male thought and female thought, then these mental networks will obviously affect the interaction between male people and female people. If male thought is supposed to remain separate from female thought, then males will become confused when they discover that their thinking has a female side, and females will become confused when they encounter a male side within their minds.

Instead, I suggest that everyone's goal should be to develop *all* of the mind, and that society needs to stop building walls between male thought and female thought. For instance, I have a Walt Disney Cinderella toaster in my kitchen, which imprints the pattern of Cinderella's slipper on the bread when it toasts. This is feminine. I do not care. I bought it at a garage sale. I think it is funny. My sense of masculinity is not threatened by the presence of a baby blue Cinderella toaster—with a pink heart-shaped knob for pushing down the toast—in my kitchen.

We saw in our discussion of righteousness that it is possible to function in a manner that violates divine righteousness, but it takes a lot of energy to do so, just as it takes many fuel convoys to air-condition tents in the desert. Therefore, if some behavior requires a lot of support and energy from others, then this strongly suggests that this behavior violates divine righteousness. That leads us to pose the following question: If a homosexual lifestyle is cognitively natural, then why does it require such a steady stream of 'convoys' delivering the emotional fuel of public opinion?

Let us turn now to the third form of righteousness, which is true righteousness, or simply righteousness. Righteousness can only exist if there is something independent of people that acts in a way that affects the behavior of people. The natural world behaves in such a manner, the mind behaves in such a manner, and there is evidence to suggest that a real God exists who behaves in such a manner. If this outside source does not exist, then the only alternative is human righteousness with all of its shortcomings. Saying this another way, righteousness is only possible if there is an underlying foundation of divine righteousness. But while divine righteousness is required for righteousness, it is not sufficient. Instead, each individual must choose to make human righteousness the servant of divine righteousness.

There is both a Perceiver and a Server side to this individual choice. The Perceiver side involves personal honesty. We have now seen several different kinds of personal dishonesty and self-deception. There is the dishonesty of mysticism, which shuts down Perceiver thought in order to feel united with God. Mercy thought and Teacher thought can interact with each other in ways that inflate emotions and make logical leaps. And we saw several other forms of personal dishonesty when examining blasphemy against the Holy Spirit. The end result of personal *honesty* is a concept of God that is based in universal Teacher understanding, which will lead to a sense of divine righteousness, as one understands how God acts, either through nature, through the mind, or directly.

Whether God actually exists or not, I suggest that it is essential to refer to a concept of God explicitly as God. On the one hand, the evolutionist refuses to talk about God while attributing divine abilities to either Nature or natural selection. In this case there is a concept of God but no explicit reference to God. On the other hand, the typical fundamentalist believer continually talks about God while having a limited mental concept of God. Instead, what is needed is a constructed mental concept of God that is referred to as God. This sounds straightforward. It is not.

The reason that one must both construct a concept of God and refer to this concept as God is because one is *combining* Teacher understanding with Server actions. Teacher thought uses words. Therefore, if one wants to gain an accurate Teacher understanding of God then one must use the *word* 'God'. But in order to connect the verbal term 'God' with Server actions, one must construct a mental concept of God that goes beyond verbal theology to include the real concrete world of experience and action.

Moving on, the Server side involves acting in a way that is consistent with divine righteousness, or in other words, choosing to act the way that God acts, which means that one must *first* have an understanding of how God acts. This means that using Perceiver thought to construct a mental concept of God comes *before* using Server thought to apply a mental concept of God. In other words, truth and personal honesty come before righteousness. Truth and personal honesty construct a mental concept of God. Righteousness acts in a way that is consistent with a mental concept of God.

> One first uses Perceiver thought to construct a concept of God in Teacher thought.
> One then uses Server thought to act consistently with this concept of God.

One sees this two-step process described in the beginning of what is known as the Lord's Prayer: "Our Father who is in heaven, Hallowed be Your name. Your kingdom come. Your will be done, on earth as it is in heaven" (Matt. 6:9-10). Notice how the prayer begins by constructing a Teacher-based concept of God, one who has a holy 'name' who resides 'in heaven'. This is then followed by submitting to the divine righteousness of 'God's kingdom' by acting 'on earth' as God acts 'in heaven'.

This same two-step process of using Perceiver facts to build Teacher understanding and then using Server actions to apply a Teacher understanding also occurs repeatedly within the process of education and personal growth. For instance, as a Perceiver person, my natural tendency is to emphasize using Perceiver facts to build Teacher understanding. However, I have discovered that I cannot ignore Server thought. This shows up in two main ways. First, before I write an essay or book, I often feel that I have a full understanding of the material. But I find again and again that the Server action of writing down my thoughts will reveal inadequacies in my understanding. Thus, I find that a book or essay always ends up writing itself, in the sense that the act of writing clarifies my thoughts, which then modifies the direction of the writing. Second, I often think that my understanding is complete when I can emotionally handle Perceiver facts and use these facts to construct a general Teacher understanding. Such personal honesty is essential. But it is also not enough. Instead, I continually find that the full understanding only comes when I am faced with a practical situation that relates to my understanding in which I choose to act in a manner that is consistent with my understanding. Until this

Server action is performed, I find that I am unable to move further in my Teacher understanding.

This two-step process of first constructing a mental concept of God and then acting in a way that is consistent with this concept of God is especially critical when one is attempting to *replace* human righteousness with righteousness. Human righteousness is a powerful mental force, backed up explicitly by the TMN of a general understanding and implicitly by the MMNs of culture. The only way to overcome this, and not simply to replace it with the MMNs of dictatorship or the TMN of another form of human righteousness, is to gain a deep understanding of how something *else* functions that is independent of human effort, refer to the resulting TMN as God, and then choose to act in obedience to God.

The distinction between human righteousness and righteousness provides a framework within which one can place the attitude of *pacifism*. We have seen that the childish mind is driven by MMNs of personal status and culture which naturally fight for domination, leading to conflict and war. The only way to transcend this warlike mindset is for people to submit their minds to the TMN of a general understanding that crosses cultures and bridges diversity. In other words, what is needed is righteousness. Human righteousness will impose peace, and the imposed peace of government is superior to Mercy-driven sectarian violence. However, the human righteousness of government can induce personal suffering on a major scale because 'how we do things' can become quite different than 'how things work'. In addition, human righteousness is ultimately imposed by the Mercy status of societal leaders. Thus, human righteousness eliminates local conflicts but can lead to major wars.

This leads to a hierarchy of power. For those who submit to a mental concept of how things work, the state will 'wither away' and there is no need for government force. In contrast, the human righteousness of government is required for those whose minds are still driven by childish MMNs. In other words, human righteousness governs childish minds, while divine righteousness guides human righteousness. The government limits the criminal, while research guides government legislation.

When government is functioning at the level of Habermas' first stage of Mercy-driven emotional status, then the only way to follow a lifestyle of pacifism is by making a group agreement with the local authorities in which one is given exemption from military service in exchange for providing the local prince with non-military benefits. And a mindset that is driven by Teacher understanding rather than Mercy tribal conflicts *will* be able to generate significant non-military benefits. The local authority will protect the pacifists from thugs while the pacifists will educate the rest of the population. This has been the path followed by the Mennonites over the centuries. For instance, Mennonites in Russia played a significant role in modernizing farming and developing local industry, and were held up by the czars as model farmers. When following such a strategy, it is important to leave and find another place of refuge when the threat of war causes special privileges to be withdrawn and not to wait until one is forced by war and conflict either to flee or to abandon pacifism. For instance, my ancestors left Russia in the 1870s when military privileges were withdrawn, while many of the wealthy Mennonites fled Russia in the 1920s after enduring civil war and Stalinist purges. Moving on, when government is functioning at the level of Habermas' second stage of Perceiver-driven law and order, then it becomes possible to maintain an attitude of pacifism while cooperating with government and working in government. The Mennonites in Paraguay provide an example of this option. I am not suggesting that the Mennonites are without flaws. However, they have tried as a group to follow the path of pacifism for twice as long as the United States has existed, and it is possible to learn lessons from this attempt.

We have described several different methods of forming a mental concept of God. Before we continue, let us summarize what we have discovered. In each case, I suggest that there is a natural tendency for a person to assert that external reality reflects internal content. That is because a mental network imposes its structure upon thought when it is triggered, and a mental concept of God forms a very potent mental network. For instance, the person who practices mysticism will not just say that he has the mental concept of a universal, unknowable God, instead he will insist that a real God exists who is universal and unknowable.

Tribal Religion: Idolatry uses emotional experiences to impose MMNs upon the mind. Building the mind upon these core MMNs will lead to concepts of gods and religion. Because MMNs struggle for dominance, the gods will be feared, and worshipers will try to appease the gods through acts of self-sacrifice. Because mental networks respond with emotional discomfort when experiencing input that is inconsistent with their structure, carefully performed rituals will play a major role in religious behavior. And because culture is defined by the MMNs shared by a group of people, each tribe will worship its own set of gods, and tribal conflict will be seen as a struggle between gods.

Divine Spirit: When a person is immersed in an environment of interacting living beings that is not understood, then a concept of God will not emerge. If it does form, it will recede into the background. What will dominate thinking is a concept of divine spirit, leading to a form of pantheism. Instead of using Platonic forms to imagine a better world, the existing world will be viewed as divine.

Mysticism: When Perceiver thought steps out of the way and allows Teacher thought to overgeneralize, then this will form the concept of a God who is infinite but unknowable. This concept of God can bring *emotional comfort* to a person through the mystical feeling of being united with God. Mysticism usually involves meditation, in which the mind is cleared of Perceiver facts and the body is prevented from carrying out Server actions. However, as Zen Buddhism illustrates, it is possible to associate mysticism with *spontaneous* action, in which one performs movement without thinking consciously about what one is doing. A God of mysticism will lead to the Platonic form of *Nirvana*, an unplace outside of time where personal identity is swallowed up in identification with the infinite.

Universal Truth: Platonic forms emerge when Perceiver thought organizes Mercy experiences into categories and Teacher thought distills the essence of these Perceiver categories. Continuing this process will eventually lead to the Teacher concept of a perfect God, an 'immovable mover' who exists in unchanging perfection behind changing flawed reality, as well as the Mercy concept of the Form of the Good, an invisible Holy Spirit who expresses perfection. This will be reflected as a belief in some sort of *heaven*, a realm of perfection where God dwells that is more perfect than reality but also separate from reality. The discrepancy between Platonic forms and personal identity will lead to feelings of personal inadequacy, but also motivate a person to improve reality so that it becomes more like Platonic forms.

Absolute Truth: Universal truth comes from *observing* repeated connections. Absolute truth is provided by books and experts, and is usually learned by studying holy books or textbooks. Because absolute truth is mentally *disconnected* from reality, the resulting Platonic forms will also be disconnected from reality. This will lead to a form of gnosticism, in which perfection is seen as residing in a heaven that is disconnected from imperfect physical reality. Instead of being motivated to make reality more like Platonic forms, a person will be motivated to turn his back upon physical reality in order to worship the perfection of God, and heaven will be viewed as a realm of endless worship.

Divine Righteousness: When Server thought notices similar sequences being repeated, then this repetition will lead to Server confidence. Teacher thought will then form a general theory based upon the essence of these Server sequences, leading to the concept of exemplars, which are *specific* Server sequences that behave in a manner that is close to the *essence* of a Server sequence. For instance, the specific Server sequence of a hockey player shooting a puck on the ice is a good exemplar of Newton's laws of motion because one can ignore the secondary effects of gravity and friction. If Teacher thought comes up with a general theory that ties together many different exemplars, then this will lead to the concept of a God of divine righteousness, one who acts in a manner that is both predictable and organized. The concept of a God of divine righteousness will lead to a belief in divine providence, which asserts that God acts in the physical world in a way that is guided by general Teacher order. For instance, the theory of evolution asserts that Nature acts in the physical world in a way to increase the Teacher order-within-complexity of living organisms. Similarly, Paul describes divine providence in Romans 8:28. "And we know that God causes all things to work together for good to those who love God, to those who are called according to His purpose." Notice that evolution applies divine providence to the group and not the individual, and to the physical and not the non-physical. That is because scientific methodology ignores subjective emotions and focuses upon empirical data. Therefore, the resulting concept of divine righteousness will also ignore the subjective and focus upon the empirical.

Because Perceiver thought cannot directly influence the physical world, Platonic forms are *invisible*, and result in the concept of God inhabiting an invisible heaven. In contrast, Server thought can directly influence the physical world, therefore exemplars are *visible* and result in the concept of God acting in the visible world. I suggest that Platonic forms and exemplars are inadequate by themselves and that what is needed is a *combination* of these two.

Rebirth: The concept of rebirth has not yet been discussed. However, we have already seen rebirth illustrated by Pentecostalism and the consumer society. Stated simply, rebirth goes beyond truth and righteousness by attempting to *live* in heaven-on-earth. This is only possible if one first constructs a mental concept of God and then becomes righteous by acting in a manner that is consistent with this mental concept of God. Saying this another way, truth and righteousness lay the foundation for rebirth. Both Pentecostalism and the consumer society illustrate what happens when one attempts to live in a transformed world without first laying a mental foundation of truth and righteousness.

Emotional Inflation: If one uses emotional inflation to make up for an inadequate concept of God, then the result will be *some* truth and righteousness held together by the glue of approval and emotional status. People will talk about God but have a poorly defined concept of God. People will talk about following God, but this will usually be expressed by obeying religious leaders.

✳ 12. Incarnation, Sovereignty & Free Will

This book began by using the emotional structures of mental networks to explain religion. However, as this discussion moved beyond emotion to the structure behind emotion we found that the emphasis shifted from religion to theology, and because theology is associated with Christianity, we found ourselves discussing mainly Christian theology. This focus upon Christian theology will continue for the rest of the book. However, our *starting* point will still be the theory of mental symmetry. While we will quote a number of passages from the Bible, we will not base anything upon the Bible but rather place these biblical passages within the framework of the theory of mental symmetry.

Christian theology has received a bad reputation in recent years. I suggest that there are three primary reasons for this. First, religious content makes a person *feel bad*. It feels much better when a teacher gives everyone a gold star rather than reserving gold stars for those who perform according to some standard. Using the language of mental symmetry, when the TMN of a concept of God meets the MMNs of personal identity, then this TMN will attempt to impose its structure upon personal MMNs. A concept of God that *lacks* content has no structure to impose; a concept of God that possesses content *will* impose this content upon personal identity, leading to feelings of personal condemnation. Second, theology provides a *target* for science. We have seen that using abstract technical thought leads to the formation of implicit TMNs and that these mental networks will drive the rigorous thinker to belittle opposing paradigms, especially if these paradigms demonstrate *non-rigorous* thought. Christian theology is vulnerable to this sort of attack because it violates the scientific taboo against subjectivity, it discusses invisible non-empirical entities such as God, angels, and spirits, it often resorts to blind faith, and it suggests that natural law is occasionally violated by miracles (we will discuss invisible entities and miracles in a later chapter).

Postmodernism may place less emphasis upon these first two reasons, but it has a third reason for ignoring Christian theology. *All* theorizing has become suspect in today's postmodern environment. While it is now socially and academically acceptable to observe and discuss Mercy feelings of spirituality, this has been accompanied by an attempt to *deconstruct* existing Teacher theories, especially factual theories that make dogmatic statements about personal identity. Instead, the general tendency is either to regard personal identity as irreducibly complex or to focus upon the pragmatics of social interaction. Viewed from this perspective, Christian theology is seen as an outdated set of beliefs imposed by the ruling hierarchy upon the rest of the population. And we shall see when examining the mindset behind World War I that there is some truth to this statement. However, we are also starting to see in this book that when one goes beyond empirical evidence to the structure of the mind, then one finds oneself entering the realm of theology, and not just any theology, but rather Christian theology. Going further, if one starts with the theory of mental symmetry, then—for some strange reason—Christian theology appears to make rational sense. We have already examined some Christian doctrines in the light of mental symmetry. This chapter will focus upon the relationship between *divine sovereignty* and *human free will.*

Divine sovereignty is the idea that God has an eternal plan that *cannot* be thwarted by humans, whereas free will suggests that man *is* capable of making decisions that run contrary to God's eternal plan. Theologians and philosophers over the centuries have tried to determine how a universal God could have sovereignty while still leaving room for human free will, and the general tendency has been to emphasize one part of this balance at the expense of the other.

Calvinism is the branch of Christianity that emphasizes the sovereignty of God, and the approach taken by Calvinism is often summarized by the acronym TULIP—Total depravity, Unconditional election, Limited atonement, Irresistible grace and the Perseverance of the saints. Total depravity says that man can do nothing to save himself, unconditional election states that God chooses who is saved, limited atonement means that the salvation plan of Jesus applies only to those whom God has chosen to be saved, irresistible grace says that everyone whom God has chosen to be saved will be saved, and perseverance of the saints states that anyone who has become saved cannot lose their salvation. In essence, TULIP concludes that human free will does not exist in the area of God and religion. The problem with TULIP is that it creates the image of a God who is—frankly—evil. After all, God is deciding who will be rewarded with eternal bliss and who will be punished with eternal damnation. The very concept of an evil God is a logical contradiction, because it implies that one is using some standard outside of God to judge God, which implies that something exists outside of God, which implies that God is not universal. In addition, it is easy for 'God decides who goes to heaven and hell' to turn into 'We are the mouthpiece of God who tells you whom God has decided will go to heaven and hell' and for that to turn into 'We are the chosen culture who will go to heaven with God and you are an evil culture that God has damned to hell'. Cognitively speaking, the Teacher sovereignty of God has turned into the Mercy dominance of one culture over another, with the childish MMNs that drive interpersonal conflict now backed up by the TMN of a mental concept of God.

A more modern interpretation of TULIP would suggest that man *can* choose, but his fundamental choices are predetermined by his desires. Using the language of mental symmetry, each person is inescapably ruled by core mental networks. This places the mailed fist of an evil God within the velvet glove of personal freedom, but it still removes personal freedom from the one choice that really matters, which is one's eternal fate. Using an analogy, a condemned man is being given a choice over what he will eat as his last meal, but he still remains a condemned man.

Choices do appear to be guided by desires. Exhorter thought provides *urges* based upon emotional memories and mental networks within Mercy and Teacher thought, and Contributor thought *chooses* between these urges. The Contributor person often thinks that he has *total* free will, but we have seen that the choices that are made by technical thought will naturally become limited by underlying mental networks. Thus, evidence strongly suggests that libertarian free will, the ability to make *any* choice, does not exist. However, the major premise of this book is that it *is* possible to transform core mental networks and that studying the process by which core mental networks are transformed leads to an analysis of religion.

The opposite of TULIP is *process theology*, originally developed from the philosophy of Alfred North Whitehead. Process theology emphasizes free will over divine sovereignty, suggesting that not only do humans have free will, but that God himself is undergoing a process of personal transformation that is being influenced by human decisions. *Open theism* is a less radical version that emphasizes human free will while still holding on to the traditional Christian concept of a universal, sovereign, unchanging God. Open theism has recently become both popular and controversial within Protestant theology.

Gregory Boyd describes the viewpoint of open theism in *Satan and the Problem of Evil.*

> We might compare this view of God to a master chess player. We would ordinarily consider a chess player to be insecure to the extent that she would need to know ahead of time, or control if possible, all the moves of her opponent to ensure winning a match. Conversely, we would ordinarily consider a chess player wise and confident to the extent that she could ensure victory without relying on these aids. Her confidence is rooted in her ability to wisely anticipate all possible future moves her opponent might make together with all the possible responses she may make to each of these possible moves. She does not know exactly how many moves she will have to make, or what these moves will be, before the match begins, for she does not know exactly how her opponent will move his pieces. If her opponent is formidable, she may even have to place certain pieces 'at risk' in order finally to checkmate him. But by virtue of her superior wisdom she is certain of victory. And precisely because her victory does not come from having a blueprint of her opponent's moves or otherwise controlling her opponents moves, the wisdom she displays in achieving her victory is praiseworthy (Boyd, 2001).

In other words, God is like an expert chess player, who is so good a player that no matter what the opponent does, he can respond in such a way that will ensure a victory. This provides a possible starting point for reconciling divine sovereignty with free will, but I suggest that it suffers from two basic flaws. First, human free will is only *meaningful* if humans know the rules of the game. A three-year-old child may have the freedom to move pieces on a chessboard, but this freedom will not be *appreciated* by an adult player because the child does not know how to play chess. Second, chess is an inadequate analogy of divine sovereignty, because a chess game is an example of technical thought. If one wishes to understand the rules of the real game of life, then one must also include normal thought and mental networks.

As far as I can tell, the following principles describe some of the 'rules of the game'.

1) When core mental networks become sufficiently developed and unified, then it is no longer possible for a person to use free will to change these core mental networks. For instance, as far as I can tell, it is no longer possible for me to choose to abandon the theory of mental symmetry, because the grid of mental networks contained within this meta-theory is too extensive. Saying this another way, I suggest that every person will eventually become emotionally imprisoned within some sort of internal cage. One can choose one's prison, but one cannot choose whether or not one will become imprisoned, or choose to escape the prison once one has become imprisoned. This is backed up by Kuhn's observation that most scientists are unable to change their basic paradigms.

2) It is difficult to determine if some *other* individual has lost the ability to make fundamental transformations, because one must use Theory of Mind to guess which mental networks are present and active within the minds of other individuals. It is also difficult to determine if *I* have lost the ability to make fundamental transformations, because I cannot examine the spectacles through which I am viewing the world. The best way to find out the fundamental character of myself or others is by being placed in a stressful situation in which one is forced to make fundamental choices. This testing will reveal my true nature, the true nature of others, and true friendship.

3) It is possible to predict with great certainty how a *group* of people will behave by examining the cultural mental networks that they hold in common. Because it is very difficult for a person or group to analyze its core mental networks, the way that a person or society *will* respond is often quite different than the way that a person or society *says* that it will respond. Thus, it would take very little divine interference for a divine being to control with total certainty the path of a *group* of people. However, most of this divine providence would be functioning *implicitly* at the level of mental networks and not explicitly through preaching and verbal proposition. This means that listening to what religious leaders are *saying* would only give a partial picture of what God is actually *doing*.

4) Human free will is real but *limited*, because a person's choices are constrained by his core mental networks. This is similar to the modern interpretation of TULIP but with two crucial differences. First, a person can *adjust* the nature of core mental networks by continuing to make choices in a certain *direction*. In other words, free will is like a *sliding* window. One can only choose within the window, but if one continually chooses one side of the window, then the window itself will gradually shift. Second, free will is greatest when a person is faced with conflicting mental networks, because a person can then

choose between two totally *different* responses, and the mental network that is chosen will grow at the expense of the mental network that is rejected.

Thus, when a person experiences a period of internal or external questioning brought on by some traumatic or unusual experience, then the resulting conflict between mental networks provides the mind with a *window of opportunity* during which that person can choose to undergo major transformation. In other words, free will for both society and individuals is usually limited, but it becomes much less limited during periods of crisis. During these times of crisis, it would also be necessary—and possible—for a divine being to interfere more extensively, especially in the personal lives of individuals who have the power to shape the mental networks of society.

If conflicting mental networks provide the greatest free will, then the free will of humanity would be maximized by dividing the world into distinct cultures. This provides a possible rationale for the biblical story of Babel. As Arnold Toynbee, the British historian, famously said in *A Study of History*, diversity accompanies growth, whereas uniformity is a symptom of decay (Toynbee, 1947).

5) If a person or group really were 'chosen by God', then this would be both a promise and a threat. I suggested earlier that one could view being 'chosen by God' as being enrolled in an elite school from which one is not permitted to drop out. Attending such a school would involve homework and testing. Ensuring that a *recalcitrant* student graduates would require significant remedial class work, extra homework, and repeated testing.

6) Divine providence could be delayed or accelerated, but it would eventually prevail. In essence, this views all of human history as a sort of school with God being the schoolmaster, similar to the manner in which evolution views all of living history as a path of inevitable growth guided by the schoolmaster of Nature.

7) Divine providence could exhibit itself either as a window of opportunity or as the irresistible hand of destiny. In a window of opportunity, conflicting mental networks would provide humans with *maximal* free will, making it possible for humans to choose to follow a radically different path. In contrast, the irresistible hand of destiny would be a period of *minimal* free will, during which many external and internal forces would conspire to force society in a certain direction. Saying this another way, humans would first have an opportunity to choose to be partners with God, consistent with the view of *open theism*. If humans chose to oppose the divine plan, then this would be followed by God acting in a sovereign manner, consistent with the view of *Calvinism*, in which humans would be unable to oppose the flow of divine providence. This would mean that when the divine hand of destiny appears, then the time for human free will would be over. Instead, the time for free will would be before the disaster hits. This two-stage process of free will followed by divine sovereignty could apply both to a *society* and to *individuals*. In essence, this is a restatement of the first point, which observes that the mental networks that a person uses free will to construct will eventually end up imprisoning free will.

For instance, I mentioned that most Mennonites emigrated from Russia either in the 1870s or the 1920s. My ancestors *chose* to emigrate from Russia to Canada in the 1870s, when the Russian government started to limit the freedoms that had been given to the Mennonites. In contrast, the Mennonites who left in the 1920s were *forced* to emigrate because of the Communist takeover of Russia and the resulting civil war in Ukraine. Those who chose to leave in the 1870s did not have to go through the hell-on-earth (and I am not exaggerating) experienced by those who were forced to leave in the 1920s.

The Birth of Science

I suggest that the *birth of science* can be interpreted as an example of a window of opportunity being followed by the irresistible hand of destiny. That is because a historical window of opportunity occurred during which science could have emerged but did not, followed by the actual birth of science several centuries later during which science had no choice but to emerge.

> The birth of science can be seen as missed opportunity followed by irresistible destiny.

While it is difficult to say precisely what factors were *required* for the birth of science, our analysis of science does provide us with a number of major clues. First, science is held together by the TMN of a general understanding. This requires a mindset that is guided by Teacher understanding as well as a belief that the external world is guided by Teacher understanding. Second, scientific thought uses Perceiver thought to analyze facts. This means that Perceiver thought must become free of the domination of the MMNs of status, culture, and religion. Third, studying science means looking beyond the Server sequences of how a group of people functions to the Server sequences of how the natural world functions. Saying this another way, tradition is the natural enemy of scientific thought. Fourth, science combines Platonic forms and exemplars. Science analyzes idealized versions of real-world problems, in which actual items and events are replaced with their Platonic forms. Science also recognizes that the actions of nature can be organized into similar sequences. For instance, the way that one object falls to the ground is similar to the way that all objects fall to the ground. Fifth, science requires both math and empirical data. As Dirac stated in an earlier quote, the amazing thing about science is that one can reach the same results either by doing mathematical analysis or by analyzing data from the real world.

All of these factors were present in the city of *Alexandria* for a period of several hundred years just before the birth of Christ. Alexandria had a major university, which indicates a focus upon Teacher thought. Alexandria also had the world's largest library, and we have seen that a book (or scroll) is a physical example of a general Teacher theory. Whenever a ship entered the harbor of Alexandria, any scrolls on that ship would be copied, the original would be kept within the library of Alexandria, and the copy would be returned to the sailors. This is similar to the type of trade and exchange of information that enabled Perceiver thought during Habermas' second stage of society. Alexandria was a new city founded in 331 BC by Alexander the Great, and artifacts and tombs from this era indicate an unusual hodgepodge of cultural influences, with Greek, Roman, Jewish, and Egyptian elements juxtaposed. Thus, there was no common way by which 'things were done'. The combination of Platonic forms and exemplars can be seen in two of the major cultural groups which coexisted within the city of Alexandria. Platonic forms were originally proposed in the fourth century BC by Plato the *Greek* philosopher, and even though Alexandria was located in Egypt, it was a Greek city. Alexandria also contained the largest urban *Jewish* community in the world at that time, and the Septuagint, a Greek translation of the Jewish Bible, was written in Alexandria during the third century BC. Unlike the Greek mindset, the Jewish mindset viewed history from the vantage point of Server sequences and exemplars. The Jewish term for religious law is 'halacha', a word that means 'doing' or 'going', and the Jewish Torah is composed primarily of a set of instructions in which God tells the Jews what they should do. N.T. Wright describes the Server-oriented perspective of Judaism at that time.

> The main point about narratives in the second-Temple Jewish world, and in that of Paul, is not simply that people liked telling stories as illustrations of, or scriptural proofs for, this or that experience or doctrine, but rather that second-Temple Jews believed themselves to be actors within a real-life narrative. To put it another way, they were not merely story-tellers who used their folklore (in their case, mostly the Bible) to illustrate the otherwise unrelated joys and sorrows, trials and triumphs, of everyday life. Their narratives could and did function typologically, that is, by providing a pattern which could be laid as a template across incidents and stories from another period without any historical continuity to link the two together. But the main function of their stories was to remind them of earlier and (they hoped) characteristic moments within the single, larger story which stretched from the creation of the world and the call of Abraham right forwards to their own day, and (they hoped) into the future (Wright, 2013).

Finally, both Greek and Jewish thought combined abstract thought with concrete thought. Greek philosophy was generally performed by men of leisure who sat around discussing philosophy, while concrete actions were performed by slaves. However, Greek thought in Alexandria extended beyond the theoretical to include the practical. For instance, the Greek astronomer Eratosthenes calculated the size of the Earth based upon experimental data in 240 BC. Similarly, the first scientist to systematically perform dissections on human cadavers was Herophilus, who lived in Alexandria until his death in 280 BC, and Herophilus is considered to be one of the founders of the scientific method. Turning to Jewish thought, the Jewish historian Josephus (who lived during the first century AD) boasted that the Torah was read in public in the synagogues to the general Jewish population every Sabbath, telling us that the average Jew regularly encountered abstract thought and the written word. Alexandria contained a number of Jewish synagogues, and the great Synagogue of Alexandria was internationally known for its size and splendor. Finally, the Jewish practice of monotheism, combined with the Jewish prohibition against idolatry, created a mindset that believed that the physical world was governed by the TMN of a general theory and not by the MMNs of important people. And because Alexandria was not located in Israel, Alexandrian Jews were not directly involved in the religious and political power struggles that plagued Jerusalem. This infighting was so severe that during the Jewish revolt in AD 70, Jewish factions within the city of Jerusalem were actually fighting *each other* while Roman troops were preparing to besiege the city.

Thus, conditions in Alexandria were ripe for the birth of science, but science was stillborn. Using the language of divine providence, the sovereign will of God was delayed.

These same factors were present in concentrated form when science *did* emerge in Renaissance Europe. In Alexandria, the Greek and Jewish communities coexisted *externally* within a single city. During the Renaissance, the Greek and Jewish viewpoints coexisted *internally* within peoples' minds, because scholars studied Greek philosophy as well as Jewish-based Christian theology. Both of these were studied in book form from the vantage point of a totally different civilization. Thus, the material was physically packaged in the form of Teacher theories and read by a society with completely different cultural MMNs. As N.T. Wright says, Christianity not only believed in the Jewish doctrine of monotheism but the entire religion was based upon the TMN of abstract theology rather than MMNs of religious rituals.

Greek thought used Platonic forms to bridge Perceiver categories with Mercy experiences. Jews believed that they were performing Server actions guided by the Teacher words of God. Both of these attitudes were present in strengthened form in Western Christendom. Plato saw Platonic forms as separate from the world of real experiences. Thomas Aquinas modified Plato's concept of forms to emphasize the relationship between forms *and* reality. The Jews believed that they were carrying out actions guided by the words of God. For Orthodox monks, the primary goal was to withdraw from society in order to achieve mystical union with God. In contrast, monasticism in Western Europe was heavily influenced by the Benedictine order, and the motto of the Benedictine monks is 'ora et labora'—pray and work. Benedictine monks spent part of their time using Teacher words to interact with God and part of their time using Server thought to perform manual labor.

Turning now to the external factors, half the population of Europe died in the Black Death between 1346 and 1353, overturning core MMNs of *social* status. Between 1378 and 1418, several men claimed simultaneously to be the true pope during a period of time known as the papal schism, causing people to question core MMNs of *religious* status. The Hundred Years' War deeply affected MMNs of *political* status, especially in England and France. On the positive side, the discovery of the New World created a culture of exploration and investigation. Finally, when Constantinople fell to the Ottomans in 1453, the last physical connection with the MMNs of the Roman Empire was lost, and many Byzantine scholars fled to Western Europe, bringing Teacher understanding while leaving Mercy culture.

If the birth of science is an illustration of divine sovereignty, then one can make the following observations. First, divine sovereignty is not a trivial matter, because one is dealing with the interaction between societies and cultures as well as the rise and fall of civilizations. But it makes sense that a universal being would function at this level of universality. Second, a lot of human suffering can be avoided by cooperating with divine sovereignty. Imagine what the world would be like today if science had emerged in Alexandria before the birth of Christ.

There is an interesting passage in the Gospels where Jesus refers to a window of opportunity that has now closed when entering Jerusalem in what is known as the *triumphal entry*.

> When He approached Jerusalem, He saw the city and wept over it, saying, "If you had known in this day, even you, the things which make for peace! But now they have been hidden from your eyes. For the days will come upon you when your enemies will throw up a barricade against you, and surround you and hem you in on every side, and they will level you to the ground and your children within you, and they will not leave in you one stone upon another, because you did not recognize the time of your visitation" (Luke 19:41-44).

Jesus said that the Jews *had* an opportunity to discover a new paradigm that was not driven by Mercy feelings of cultural conflict, but that this window of opportunity was now shut. He also stated that the physical city of Jerusalem and its Temple would be destroyed. When Jerusalem fell to the Romans in A.D. 70 and the Jewish Temple was destroyed, then this fundamentally altered interaction between Jewish and non-Jewish thought and Judaism had to reinvent itself into rabbinic Judaism in order to survive.

This concept of a window of opportunity is significant for us today because I suggest that we are *currently* experiencing a window of opportunity for integrating scientific thought with religious thought. Everywhere I look, I see people and groups attempting to bridge these two by focusing upon the *Mercy* experiences of spirituality rather than constructing an integrated Teacher concept of God. The mysticism of Buddhism is respected in Western intellectual circles, while Christian dogma is belittled. The cognitive science of religion studies folk religion while ignoring theology. The average North American Christian believer is theologically ignorant and attends church primarily in order to have a spiritual experience. More generally, postmodern thought attacks the very concept of theory while emphasizing social interaction. In contrast, this book presents a general *Teacher* theory of scientific and religious thought.

It is interesting that one sees this same fixation upon Mercy experiences in the Jewish view of Messiah. For instance, the *Judaism 101* webpage on the Messiah explains that

> Jews do not believe that Jesus was the mashiach. Assuming that he existed, and assuming that the Christian scriptures are accurate in describing him (both matters that are debatable), he simply did not fulfill the mission of the mashiach as it is described in the biblical passages cited above. Jesus did not do any of the

things that the scriptures said the messiah would do. On the contrary, another Jew born about a century later came far closer to fulfilling the messianic ideal than Jesus did. His name was Shimeon ben Kosiba, known as Bar Kokhba (son of a star), and he was a charismatic, brilliant, but brutal warlord. Rabbi Akiba, one of the greatest scholars in Jewish history, believed that Bar Kokhba was the mashiach. Bar Kokhba fought a war against the Roman Empire, catching the Tenth Legion by surprise and retaking Jerusalem. He resumed sacrifices at the site of the Temple and made plans to rebuild the Temple. He established a provisional government and began to issue coins in its name. This is what the Jewish people were looking for in a mashiach; Jesus clearly does not fit into this mold. Ultimately, however, the Roman Empire crushed his revolt and killed Bar Kokhba. After his death, all acknowledged that he was not the mashiach (Rich).

Jerusalem and the Jewish Temple were destroyed in A.D. 70. The last gasp of ancient Jewish nationalism occurred in AD 132 with the Jewish revolt led by Bar Kokhba, whom many Jews at that time regarded as the Messiah, and whom this webpage refers to as 'far closer to fulfilling the messianic ideal than Jesus'. Bar Kokhba was a 'brutal warlord' who 'fought a war against the Roman Empire', 'resumed sacrifices at the site of the Temple', 'established a provisional government', and 'began to issue coins in its name'. All of this involves the concrete world of Mercy experiences and MMNs. Notice that 'this is what the Jewish people were looking for in a mashiach' (mashiach is the Hebrew pronunciation of Messiah). However, when this MMN-driven path failed then 'all acknowledged that he was not the mashiach' and for over a millennium the only form of Judaism that survived was Teacher-driven rabbinic Judaism with its focus upon discussing and practicing Jewish law.

Going further, Judaism *explicitly* rejects the concept of incarnation.

> The notion of an innocent, divine or semi-divine being who will sacrifice himself to save us from the consequences of our own sins is a purely Christian concept that has no basis in Jewish thought. Unfortunately, this Christian concept has become so deeply ingrained in the English word 'messiah' that this English word can no longer be used to refer to the Jewish concept. The word 'mashiach' will be used throughout this page (Ibid).

However, the number of Nobel prizes that have been won by Jews combined with the number of technological start-ups that exist in Israel demonstrate that Jews excel at working with the *implicit* expression of incarnation that is found in science and technology. Thus, in the same way that evolution explicitly rejects the concept of divine providence while continually appealing implicitly to divine providence, so Judaism explicitly rejects the concept of a divine incarnation while continually appealing implicitly to the concept of divine incarnation.

Incarnation, Divine Sovereignty, and Human Free Will

That brings us to our next topic of discussion. We have examined the cognitive mechanisms behind righteousness and divine providence. We will now use these concepts to come up with a more universal view of incarnation, which will then allow us to come up with a more rigorous explanation for the relationship between divine sovereignty and human free will.

> Contributor incarnation combines cause-and-effect with precise definition.
> Perceiver thought uses Platonic forms and variables to bridge specific and general.
> Server thought uses exemplars and equations to bridge specific and general.

Notice that we have now encountered three different methods of bridging specific and general in a way that preserves content. There is the *Perceiver* method of the Platonic form and the variable, there is the *Contributor* method of incarnation, and there is the *Server* method of the exemplar and the equation. Because Contributor combines Perceiver and Server, these three methods form a complete package. Contributor incarnation *bridges* Mercy thought with Teacher thought in some specific context, and Perceiver Platonic forms and Server exemplars then *extend* this bridge to other contexts through the 'unfolding' of Server and Perceiver patterns and analogies. Saying this another way, Server thought and Perceiver thought provide the context for the bridging done by Contributor thought.

We saw in a previous chapter how this relationship is exhibited in math and science. Math uses the variable and the equation. The *variable* replaces specific Perceiver objects such as apples and oranges with generic variables such as **X** and **Y**. Math describes the relationship between variables using the Server sequence of an *equation*. An equation can either be viewed from abstract thought as a Perceiver relationship between variables or from concrete thought as a Server function that leads from one variable to another variable. Science uses the Platonic form and the exemplar. Science works with simplifications of real-world problems, replacing physical objects such as inclined slopes, ropes, and objects with the *Platonic forms* of frictionless slopes, massless ropes, and point masses. Science problems also act as Server *exemplars*. Because scientific problems fall into different Server categories, learning how to solve one problem will teach the student how to solve many similar problems, as well as extend the general understanding of science. For instance, when a student learns how to solve one problem involving pushing a block up an inclined slope, the student has also learned how to solve many *similar* problems involving masses and ramps, as well as learned to *extend* Newton's laws of physics to the realm of objects moving up and down slopes. Physical problems fall into Server categories because that is how the physical world works, and it is possible to use mathematical equations involving variables to model physical problems because the physical universe has been organized in that way. This extended overlap between math and science expresses the nature of incarnation.

Summarizing, concrete physical problems are made abstract by replacing specific objects with their idealized Platonic forms and by viewing specific sequences as exemplars. Abstract math is made concrete by using variables to represent specific items and interpreting mathematical equations as functions that describe cause-and-effect. The wonder of science is that one ends up with the same results either by solving mathematical equations or by observing the physical world. This overlap involves Contributor thought, but Perceiver and Server thought reveal the extensiveness of this overlap. Thus, Contributor incarnation occurs within the overall context of Server equations and exemplars and Perceiver variables and Platonic forms.

The incarnation of math and science exists because of the nature of the *physical world*. I suggest that a similar incarnation between theory and personality exists because of the nature of the *mind*. The theory of mental symmetry represent specific people using the *variables* Perceiver, Server, etc., and then uses the diagram of mental symmetry to describe the relationship between these variables. This diagram can be viewed either from abstract thought as a general description of how the mind works or from concrete thought as a path for developing the mind. This analysis begins either by using the diagram of mental symmetry to do a theoretical analysis of interacting cognitive modules, or by observing the behavior of real people and then replacing specific people with the Platonic form of the corresponding cognitive style. For instance, instead of analyzing 'my cousin Fred', one analyzes 'Fred who is a specific example of a Facilitator person'. The specific situation in which cousin Fred currently finds himself is then viewed as an exemplar that applies to all Facilitator persons at a similar stage of cognitive development. For instance, if Fred finds himself in a situation where he is defending himself verbally, the exemplar behind this particular situation is the general observation that Facilitator persons have a natural tendency to portray situations in a way that makes them look better and others look worse.

This may sound like a rather esoteric distinction, but it makes a huge difference when counseling people. Because one does not have to delve into the details of personal problems, it is possible to preserve a sense of personal privacy. Instead of having to learn all about Fred's marriage problems, one can focus upon how the typical Facilitator person deals with personality conflicts. Instead of saying 'Fred, you need to change' one can say 'These are the choices which the Facilitator person faces in a situation such as this'. The first option focuses upon the specific MMN representing Fred, while the second is guided by the general TMN of personality theory. This makes it possible for a discussion of personality to be guided by Teacher understanding and Perceiver facts *without having to go objective*. This bears repeating. Scientific methodology protects Perceiver thought by avoiding Mercy emotions. It is also possible to protect Perceiver thought by dealing with the Platonic forms of cognitive styles and cognitive modules instead of the specific emotional experiences of specific individuals. Even though Fred and his personal feelings may be the topic, focusing upon the Platonic forms of Facilitator persons and Facilitator thought allows the analysis to be one step removed from the messy realm of Mercy emotions.

The amazing thing is that one can learn more about human personality either by using the diagram to make theoretical predictions and then observing human behavior, or by starting with observing human behavior—or reading about people's descriptions of human behavior—and then using the diagram to explain these observations and descriptions. For instance, most of the traits of the Server person were initially determined by using the diagram to derive hypothetical Server traits from known Perceiver traits and then observing the Server person to confirm these theoretically derived traits. One might think that it would be easier to ask a Server person to describe how he thinks. But our experience is that while the Server person is naturally able to copy the actions of others, the Server person finds it extremely difficult to analyze the mental state of self and others. Thus, the typical Server person cannot tell you how he thinks.

Moving on, I have discovered over the years that the generality of the diagram of mental symmetry only became revealed one facet at a time as I went through Server sequences of solving personal problems. For example, the only reason that I realized the difference between proclaiming a Teacher understanding and pointing out a Teacher understanding is because I was personally unable to proclaim the theory. Normally, when a person develops a theory of personality, then that person either goes into counseling or else starts to give seminars. In my case, neither of these possibilities opened up, forcing me to think about the alternatives.

Turning now to religion, for some strange reason, the theory of mental symmetry keeps coming up with theoretical statements that are cognitively equivalent to the doctrines of Christian theology. And the path that I have been following to reach mental wholeness guided by the theory of mental symmetry keeps being consistent with the 'testimonies' of Christians who are 'following God' in order to become 'more like Jesus'. If one eliminates the emotional baggage of religiosity from these testimonies and looks at the underlying cognitive transformations, what the sincere Christian is relating appears to be consistent with what mental symmetry says.

Summarizing, we have now encountered four expressions of incarnation. There is the incarnation between math and science, the incarnation between the theory of mental symmetry and the process of becoming mentally whole, and there is the incarnation between Christian theology and the experience of Christian transformation. Finally, there is the incarnation that normally comes to mind when this term is used, which is Jesus the incarnation, whom Christianity claims was both God and man. These four expressions of incarnation all appear to have a similar structure.

For instance, compare the description of incarnation given in the following biblical passage with our cognitive analysis of incarnation. I should point out that this passage was written 1500 years before the birth of science, when algebra did not exist and math was at the level of Roman numerals.

Philip said to Him, "Lord, show us the Father, and it is enough for us." Jesus said to him, "Have I been so long with you, and *yet* you have not come to know Me, Philip? He who has seen Me has seen the Father; how *can* you say, 'Show us the Father'? Do you not believe that I am in the Father, and the Father is in Me? The words that I say to you I do not speak on My own initiative, but the Father abiding in Me does His works. Believe Me that I am in the Father and the Father is in Me; otherwise believe because of the works themselves. Truly, truly, I say to you, he who believes in Me, the works that I do, he will do also; and greater *works* than these he will do; because I go to the Father. Whatever you ask in My name, that will I do, so that the Father may be glorified in the Son. If you ask Me anything in My name, I will do *it*. If you love Me, you will keep My commandments. I will ask the Father, and He will give you another Helper, that He may be with you forever; *that is* the Spirit of truth, whom the world cannot receive, because it does not see Him or know Him, *but* you know Him because He abides with you and will be in you" (John 14:8-17).

The passage begins with Philip wanting to see God. Jesus answers that anyone who sees him sees God. In other words, Jesus is an incarnation of God. He then clarifies what it means to be an incarnation. First, one learns that incarnation is an expression of God by getting to know the character of incarnation, implying that the relationship between incarnation and God is based upon extensive internal connections. Second, the relationship between Contributor incarnation and general Teacher understanding is based in an overlap between the two: 'I am in the Father and the Father is in me'. Third, the Server actions of incarnation are exemplars that illustrate general Teacher understanding: 'Believe because the works themselves'. Fourth, concrete Contributor thought becomes generalized by making the transition to abstract Contributor thought: 'The works that I do; he will do also; because I go to the Father'. Fifth, this generalization involves Perceiver thought: 'He who believes in me'. Sixth, Teacher generalization makes Contributor incarnation more powerful: 'Greater works than these he will do'. Seventh, one uses Teacher words to interact with Contributor incarnation when it is an abstract form: 'Whatever you ask in my name'. Eighth, Contributor incarnation in abstract form turns into general equations that can be filled with many types of specific content: 'If you ask anything in My name, I will do it'. Ninth, applying the equations of Contributor incarnation increases the order-within-complexity of the underlying Teacher theory: 'so that the Father may be glorified in the Son'. Tenth, one is supposed to use Perceiver thought to hold on to the general laws of Contributor incarnation. (The word 'keep' comes from the Greek word *tereo* which means to guard as a treasure.) Eleventh, Teacher thought modifies the content of Contributor incarnation, leading to the formation of a concept of the Holy Spirit based in Platonic forms: 'I will ask the Father and He will give you another helper'. Twelfth, these Platonic forms transcend specific experiences: 'He may be with you forever'. Thirteenth, these Platonic forms are based in Perceiver facts: 'the Spirit of truth'. Fourteenth, those who base their minds in empirical evidence lack the Perceiver facts and the Mercy experiences needed to form a concept of the Holy Spirit:

'It does not see him or know him'. Fifteenth, one senses a Holy Spirit based in Platonic forms internally and through social interaction: 'You know him because he abides with you and will be in you'. Summarizing, there is an extensive correspondence between the biblical description of incarnation and the concept of incarnation that we have discussed.

The reference to 'another helper' in this passage is traditionally viewed in Muslim circles as a biblical reference to Mohammed. But 'the helper' is described as a 'spirit whom the world cannot receive', something internal that is inherently different than the external mental networks of culture. In contrast, Islam focuses very heavily upon *physical* actions rather than *internal* content. For instance, the five pillars of Islam are all external. One *says* that there is no God except God, one performs the *physical* ritual of praying five times a day, one gives 2.5% of one's *material* wealth to the poor and needy, one shows self-control by avoiding *physical* food during the daytime during the month of Ramadan, and one takes a *physical* pilgrimage to Mecca. Similarly, Islam deals with the problem of lust not by telling the man to clean up his mind, but rather by telling the woman to cover up her body. The Islamic kingdom is primarily a physical kingdom, not an invisible Platonic form, and Islam has historically been spread primarily through the application of physical force rather than by changing the thinking of people. Thus, it seems strange to use a reference to a 'spirit whom the world cannot receive' to prove the validity of a 'government whom the world should receive' or to talk about a person who 'will be *in* you' when describing a religious system that does not emphasize internal content.

Now that we have a better understanding of the nature of incarnation let us return to the topic of divine sovereignty and human free will. As usual, we will examine this topic from a theoretical, cognitive perspective. Suppose that a God exists who functions similarly to a mental concept of God. Suppose also that God interacts with man through an incarnation who functions similarly to a mental concept of incarnation. What type of sovereignty and free will would emerge?

> A divine sovereign plan would contain general equations and treat people as variables.

The basic principle is that the sovereign plan of God would be stated in terms of general *equations* in which people are treated as *variables*. One can understand how this works by looking at the way that the equations of *statistics* allow people to be treated as variables. The basic premise of the insurance industry is that it is possible to use mathematics to make definitive statements about *groups* of people. I may not know if my neighbor Jane is going to get cancer. But it is possible to know with considerable certainty how many middle-aged, non-smoking, Canadian females will develop cancer each year. Saying this another way, instead of dealing with specific people, statistical analysis addresses the Platonic form of the idealized individual, such as the typical middle-aged, non-smoking, Canadian female. A similar situation exists in physics. For instance, it is not possible to say when a specific atom will undergo radioactive decay, but it is possible to use mathematical equations to predict with great accuracy how many atoms within a group of atoms will decay in a certain period of time.

Thus, the nature of physics leads us to the conclusion that most specific events are random and not directly controlled by God. Similarly, the nature of statistics suggests that most human free will can be regarded as a random influence that has no major bearing upon the larger picture. But this *individual* randomness is combined with *general* certainty. Using religious language, human freedom is combined with divine sovereignty. From the human viewpoint of specific Mercy experiences, there is uncertainty and free will. However, from the divine viewpoint of universal Teacher theories, there is total certainty and complete sovereignty. In a similar manner, I have discovered over the years that human behavior is very predictable. While one cannot predict the choices that people make in specific situations, one can analyze a person's general pattern of behavior with depressing certainty.

It may not be possible to control specific situations, but it is possible to change the *odds* regarding specific situations. For instance, a non-smoking individual is less likely to get cancer than someone who smokes. Likewise, spending money on education will lead to less human suffering than spending money on the military. Or for a more specific example, a traffic light can lessen the probability of an accident at a busy intersection.

We see here three general principles being illustrated. First, I suggest that it is a category mistake to blame God for personal suffering, because God lives in generalities while humans live in specifics. We blame God for specific situations because we are viewing God from the *Mercy* perspective of specific situations. Instead, it makes much more sense to view God from the Teacher perspective of general understanding. (We shall see later that this cognitive error is naturally made by the 'consumer' of religion.)

The second general principle is that righteousness can minimize human suffering. We saw at the beginning of this book the personal suffering that is generated by following childish MMNs. Think, for instance, of the child who sees something shiny out on the road, runs out to examine it, and is hit by a car. As any parent knows, the young child continually has to be saved from himself. But there is also the personal suffering that is produced by human righteousness. Albert Einstein famously defined insanity as "Doing the same thing over and over again and expecting different results." It takes a lot of energy and effort to continue doing things 'the way that they have always been done'. A lot of human suffering has been eliminated and could be eliminated by doing things 'the way that the world functions' or 'the way that the mind functions'. Again quoting from Einstein, "You have to learn the rules of the game. And then you have to play better than anyone else." Saying this more bluntly, most human suffering is caused by childishness and human stupidity, and human suffering can be minimized by submitting to divine righteousness.

The third general principle is that free will usually occurs *before* the specific experience of suffering. For instance, a person does not choose to get cancer. But, a person does choose to smoke, which makes it more likely to get cancer.

Moving on, I have suggested that God could control human history by manipulating the mental networks that guide society. One can understand how this works by looking at how *advertising* drives a modern economy. Generally speaking, individuals in a modern economy are not forced to buy specific products. Thus, there is personal freedom. Instead, companies spend massive amounts on advertising in order to affect the buying patterns of a group of people so that they are more likely to buy a product. The basic premise of the advertising industry is that a group of people can be influenced in substantial ways by creating or manipulating mental networks. Advertising is usually targeted towards a certain segment of the population, guided by Platonic forms. For instance, instead of convincing Johnny to buy Frosted Flakes, advertising will be used to influence the type of breakfast cereal that is consumed by the typical child.

Advertising can appeal to mental networks either indirectly or directly. Information-based advertising affects mental networks *indirectly* by building mental connections. For instance, advertising may state that a new computer is twice as fast as existing computers, or that LED light bulbs use only 20% of the energy consumed by incandescent bulbs. In both cases, the underlying assumption is that people want to save time and energy. This type of advertising only works when consumers are *capable* of using Perceiver thought in the presence of mental networks. The other possibility is to appeal *directly* to mental networks. For instance, there is usually no logical connection between a celebrity and the product that the celebrity endorses. Being good at singing, for example, does not make one an expert in sweetened, carbonated drinks, and yet the pop star Beyoncé was recently given $50 million to endorse Pepsi, while Taylor Swift inked a multi-million-dollar deal to promote Diet Coke. Cognitively speaking, these singers are represented within consumers' minds as emotional MMNs, and when the singer is seen alongside some product, then the Mercy emotions will fool Perceiver thought into believing that there is a lasting connection between the singer and the product, enhancing the emotional attractiveness of the product. Modern humanity likes to think that it is rational, but most current advertising is not based upon information but rather attempts to manipulate or create mental networks in irrational ways.

Applying this to the sovereignty of God, one concludes that God could influence history by either cooperating with a society or else by manipulating a society. Cooperation is like information-based advertising. God shares truth with mankind, and humans use this knowledge to avoid pain and pursue pleasure in a more intelligent manner. However, in order to cooperate with God, man must be capable of using Perceiver thought in the presence of mental networks. If man is incapable of thinking rationally in emotional areas, then the only option is for God to guide mankind by manipulating the implicit mental networks of society. Putting this more bluntly, as long as humans manipulate *each other* by creating and juxtaposing mental networks, a real God would be forced to manipulate humanity by creating and juxtaposing mental networks. When humans can be fooled by irrational advertising and refuse to be swayed by content-based advertising, then this demonstrates that humans are mentally incapable of cooperating with God in the mutually respectful manner described by open theism, and they have only themselves to blame when they feel manipulated by God.

One of the characteristics of science is that the *same* mathematical equations can often be used to analyze processes that appear on the surface to be quite *different*. For instance, Newton's laws of motion can be used to analyze both the path of an apple falling from a tree and the path of a planet orbiting a sun. Before Newton's time, earthly movement was regarded as part of the human realm of imperfect experiences, whereas the movement of planets was seen as part of the heavenly realm with its 'movement of the celestial spheres'. Thus, Newton used a single Teacher theory to unify experiences that had been divided into the Mercy categories of holy and secular. Similarly, the theory of mental symmetry can be used to analyze both religious and secular thought and behavior.

Applying this to divine sovereignty, the sovereign plan of God would be in the form of general equations that could be applied in several ways. For instance, the biblical book of Revelation describes many sequences of events that can be interpreted either symbolically or literally. The *Left Behind* series is a popular set of novels about the book of Revelation written by Tim LaHaye and Jerry Jenkins. These books interpret Revelation primarily from a literal, fundamentalist, evangelical perspective, leading to a rather bloodthirsty portrayal of divine sovereignty. As the Time article on this series states, "The nuclear frights of, say, Tom Clancy's The Sum of All Fears wouldn't fill a chapter in the Left Behind series. (Large chunks of several U.S. cities have been bombed to smithereens by page 110 of Book 3.)" (Cloud, 2002). However, if this book is regarded as a series of divinely ordained 'equations', then these equations could also be fulfilled in ways that would avoid the obscene level of death and destruction portrayed by LaHaye and Jenkins.

I have suggested that God could control the path of human history by manipulating the mental networks of society, similar to the method used by advertising. The *Left Behind* novels are obviously addressing core mental networks of American society because over 65 million copies have been sold and seven of the titles have reached number #1 on bestseller lists. The Wikipedia article explains the nature of these core mental networks. "One reason often cited for the books' popularity is the quick pacing and action, and reflects the public's overall concern with the Apocalypse, as portrayed in the book of Revelation in the Bible... The plotting is brisk and the characterizations Manichean. People disappear and things blow up." When people's minds are guided by the TMNs of general understanding, as is the case with the scientist and his paradigm, or by the MMNs of Platonic forms, then it becomes possible for God to guide people *internally* by manipulating these mental networks. However, we have seen that Americans tend to confuse the Platonic form of the American dream with the physical country of America. Going further, there is a tendency for many American Christians to equate the religious attitude of denying oneself in order to serve God with the patriotic attitude of denying oneself physically in order to serve one's country. Thus, the natural tendency is for American Christians to read the book of Revelation with its general equations and Platonic forms and to equate this with physical destruction affecting the United States of America.

This type of combination would place God in a difficult situation. On the one hand, divine sovereignty would be satisfied with *many* different specific expressions of the divine equations. Using religious language, God would not care if the prophecies were fulfilled physically, symbolically, cognitively, or religiously. On the other hand, core mental networks of human society are only triggered if these divine equations are interpreted in a manner that involves massive physical death and destruction. This combination would force God to fulfill the prophecies through a *physical* apocalypse, not because God wants trauma and suffering, but rather because humans are infatuated by trauma and suffering. The flip side of this is that it would theoretically be possible for humans to alter the specific expression of the divine plan by choosing to build their minds upon MMNs that do *not* involve 'people disappearing and things blowing up'.

We have looked at the interaction that would occur between a universal God and human *society*. Let us turn now to the relationship between divine sovereignty and *individuals*. The obvious question is *why* a universal being would need assistance from finite individuals, because a human helping God seems rather like giving a penny to the world's richest man. Not only is it not needed, but the act could be viewed as an insult.

I suggest that quantum mechanics provides us with a possible answer. The story of Schrödinger's cat is often used to illustrate the basic nature of quantum mechanics. In this thought experiment, a radioactive atom is placed next to a detector that is hooked up to the trigger of a gun which is aimed at a cat, and the entire collection is placed within a closed box. If the atom undergoes radioactive decay, then the detector will trigger the gun, which will kill the cat. But radioactive decay is something that occurs statistically, guided by quantum principles. Therefore, is the cat alive or dead? If the box remains closed then there is no way of knowing. Instead, the cat is in the ambiguous state of being both dead and alive. However, if the box is opened, then the cat moves from the superposition of being *both* dead and alive to being *either* dead or alive. Saying this more formally, quantum mechanics has discovered that waves and particles are often in *ambiguous* states, which can be described *mathematically* using wave function equations. *Observing* a wave or particle 'collapses the wave function', placing the wave or particle within a *particular* state. Physicists argue over what this means, but they all agree on the math and the general process.

Looking at this theologically, as far as a universal being who lives in *equations* is concerned, there would be total predictability, because the ambiguous nature of waves and particles can be described with great accuracy using mathematical equations. But for humans living within specific experiences, there is ambiguity, and this ambiguity is only resolved when finite humans 'open the box'. Finite humans would 'partner' with God by 'opening up boxes'. God would live within the universal realm of possibilities, while human choice would choose between these possibilities in order to create a single reality.

Putting this all together, God's sovereign plan would be a general plan involving equations, groups, and possibilities. Human free will would be needed to turn possibility into certainty by choosing between one of the various options. For instance, we have looked at the sample physics problem about a hockey player shooting a puck across the ice. This is an idealized problem that could apply to *many* different hockey players on *many* different ice surfaces. But suppose that we are talking about Fred Sasakamoose of Sandy Lake Reserve, Saskatchewan shooting the puck at the age of 17 while playing a home game with the Moose Jaw Canucks in October 1951. The general equation has now been turned into reality. And history is composed of reality and not general equations. Physics does not care which hockey player shoots the puck, but physics only exists because real players such as Fred Sasakamoose shoot real pucks on real ice surfaces.

> God would realize a divine plan by choosing people with obsessions.

Thus, in order to turn possibility into reality, God would have to choose humans (and possibly other finite beings) to realize the divine plan. The type of person that God would want is someone *predictable*, someone driven by mental networks that are strong enough to guarantee a certain general pattern of response. Saying this another way, God would choose people with *obsessions*. This could be an obsession for power, an obsession for helping the down-and-out, an obsession for hockey, or an obsession for music. The specific obsession would not matter, as long as it was an obsession that could be placed within the current divine equation. What would matter is that a chosen person was driven by a core mental network sufficiently powerful to override free will in that individual. The specific choices made by such individual would also be of secondary importance to the divine plan as long as the core obsession drove the general direction of that person's life. For instance, I am driven to make music. Normally, I can express this obsession by playing violin. But I have been struggling recently with finger problems, and therefore I have been forced to express my musical obsession in another way by singing in a choir.

Looking at this more specifically, God's sovereign plan of human history would be formulated in terms of probable paths driven by mental networks, somewhat like the research tree in the popular computer game of Civilization. For instance, in Civ III, the discovery of Alphabet can lead either to Writing or Mathematics, and Mathematics can be followed by Currency, while Writing can be followed by Code of Laws, Literature, or Mapmaking. In each case, one discovery leads naturally to another. This does not mean that one discovery leads *inevitably* to the next. Instead, each discovery forms a collection of societal mental networks, and some of the people growing up in this society will have the appropriate obsession for carrying out the next discovery. If this next discovery did not emerge naturally, then divine sovereignty could choose a specific individual or group with the appropriate obsession to perform the next step.

Thus, divine sovereignty would function at both the group level and the individual level. At the group level, the core mental networks of each culture would predict the path of that particular group, and these core mental networks could be manipulated through the use of natural events or through interaction between one culture and another. Divine control at the group level could be maximized by separating human society into distinct cultures that could be individually manipulated. Therefore, something like the story of Babel would be necessary.

At the individual level, society would be guided by individuals with obsessions. God would look for individuals with the *appropriate* core mental networks, God would *test* individuals to ensure that they really were driven by these core mental networks, and then God would *choose* one or more individuals who passed this test to carry out a specific segment of the divine plan. Once an individual (or group) was chosen by God, then this choosing would be *irrevocable* because the divine plan would now depend upon the conduct of that individual (or group), and the circumstances of that individual (or group) would be manipulated to ensure that the obsession remained intact.

For instance, if God chose some specific group of people to be 'chosen by God', then God would determine the initial direction of this group by externally imposing core mental networks, and the mindset of this group would be characterized by a national obsession that would color the entire thinking of this group. This group would have a strong sense of being guided by God through human history, and would view being chosen by God as both a promise and a threat.

Notice that we have not yet said anything about the nature of the driving obsession. As far as *divine sovereignty* is concerned, either Martin Luther King or Adolf Hitler could be used to further the divine plan, because both individuals were driven by obsessions. However, from a human perspective, it is much *nicer* when society is driven by a Martin Luther King rather than an Adolf Hitler. Unfortunately, we have seen that the default is for the human mind to be driven by childish MMNs, and dictators such as Hitler come to power by appealing to these childish MMNs. Thus, as long as people pay lip service to people like Martin Luther King while being swayed by individuals like Adolf Hitler, God would have no choice but to use evil people such as Hitler to drive his sovereign plan. Of course, we all know *now* that Hitler was an evil man. But before World War II, many people in many countries (including some Mennonites—especially those who had been persecuted in Russia) considered Hitler to be a good man. And while very few would choose to follow Hitler today, I suggest that we are currently in a situation which is similar to that of Europe in the 1930s. We have recently learned that Western governments spy extensively upon their own people, and Americans now know that their elections are bought and that most American political leaders are corrupt liars. But the average American does not care enough to do anything about this, and most Americans keep asserting that they live in the world's best democracy while doing nothing to ensure that their country remains a democracy. As far as divine sovereignty is concerned, platitudes and preaching are both irrelevant. Instead, what matters are the core mental networks that drive society, and as long as these are childish and destructive, God would be forced to manipulate society using means that are childish and destructive—because that is *the way that the mind works*. Saying this another way, the actions of a real God would be guided by divine righteousness.

Consumers, Hackers, and Inventors

I suggest that one finds a similar type of interaction between groups, individuals, and the Teacher understanding of science in a modern technological society. In simple terms, a person can interact with scientific understanding in one of three main ways: passively, intelligently, or actively.

The typical consumer interacts with science *passively* as a member of a group. Some new product is announced, such as a smart phone, movie, fashion trend, type of food, music recording, or vehicle. This product attracts the attention of some group of consumers, who respond by purchasing the new product. Using this product alters the course of society. For instance, the introduction of the railroad literally changed the gene pool because it became much more common for individuals to marry outside of the local village. Similarly, the smart phone is currently in the process of altering social interaction, because many people now stare at tiny screens in public instead of talking with one another.

The average consumer does not understand technology. As Arthur C. Clarke famously said, "Any sufficiently advanced technology is indistinguishable from magic." Thus, even though technology is an expression of *Teacher* understanding, the typical consumer views technology from a *Mercy* perspective as objects with special powers or experiences with emotional content. This lack of understanding means that the typical consumer cannot produce technology, fix technology, or customize technology. Therefore, the consumer has no option but to accept technology passively as a consumer. When some shiny new gadget or exciting new experience is introduced, then this will attract the attention of *many* consumers who lack the ability to *customize* this gadget or experience. The result will be a group response guided by MMNs shared by many people.

It is also possible to interact *intelligently* with science as an individual. One sees this illustrated by the 'hacker communities' that modify and customize devices. For those who are unfamiliar with this term or have only heard it used in a pejorative sense, I am distinguishing between a *hacker*, who has a sense of ethics, and a *cracker*, who does not, and many webpages have been written attempting to distinguish between these two. In order to be a *hacker*, one must understand how a device functions, which means going to school, either formally or informally, in order to get an education. The average consumer approaches technology from the Mercy perspective of experiences and objects. The hacker, in contrast, views technology from the Teacher perspective of order-within-complexity. For the hacker, a gadget is a collection of parts that work together to produce some general function. For instance, the average consumer connects to the Internet through the use of a 'black box' received from the Internet company; 'the Internet' plugs into one side of this box, 'the computer' plugs into the other side of the box, and 'the box' magically translates between one and the other. The hacker, in contrast, realizes that this box is composed of a modem that *mod*-ulates and *de*-modulates between the baseband signal of the computer and the modulated signal on a carrier, a router that translates between the single IP address given by the Internet company and the local IP addresses of each computer, a switch that permits many computers to connect together via LAN cable, and a wireless access point that allows computers to connect with each other through a carrier wave either at 2.4 GHz or 5.6 GHz. The typical consumer reads a description such as this and his eyes glaze over. The hacker sees this knowledge as a gateway to control and customization.

The typical consumer often views the hacker as a threat to society, because the hacker does not submit to the cultural MMNs that drive the consumer. However, I can say both from extensive reading and from personal experience as an engineer that the hacker is generally driven by Teacher emotions. He wants his devices to work better, operate more efficiently, have more functions, work together, or be more reliable. These are all expressions of Teacher order-within-complexity. In addition, the hacker sees that the Mercy-driven mind of the consumer makes the consumer a slave of technology. He views them as 'sheeple', herds who are incapable of thinking coherently and who go mindlessly with the flow. However, the typical consumer often has one advantage over the typical hacker. The hacker may know how to derive *Teacher* pleasure from improving and optimizing his gadgets, but he does not always know how to find *Mercy* pleasure in using a device, whereas the consumer views technology as a source of tools for providing Mercy enjoyment.

> The consumer enjoys new technology passively as part of a group driven by MMNs.
> The hacker uses Teacher understanding to customize and integrate technology.
> The inventor is driven by the MMN of an obsession rooted in Teacher understanding.

Finally, it is possible to interact *actively* with science as an inventor and a developer. The hacker modifies technology guided by understanding, personalizing his experience with science. But he is still making existing technology work better; he is still functioning within the current Teacher framework. The inventor advances the state-of-the-art by developing *new* technology. Being a successful inventor requires a deeper personal commitment than being a hacker, because one must be able to identify the mental networks that drive society and then use technology to come up with better ways of satisfying these mental networks. Inventors are often seen as eccentric individuals with strange obsessions—until they finally come up with some breakthrough that everyone wants, when they are then seen in retrospect as forward-thinking visionaries. Inventors have to be obsessed, because the core mental network of an obsession propels the inventor through the intermediate stage of being a 'misunderstood genius'.

Of course, being misunderstood does not make one a genius. Both crackpots and inventors are misunderstood eccentrics who disregard the MMNs of culture. The passive consumer who knows only cultural MMNs will tend to lump these two together. But the inventor is guided by a deep Teacher understanding of 'how things work' while the crackpot only *thinks* or *pretends* that he has an understanding.

The consumer, the hacker, and the inventor illustrate three different ways in which *individuals* can interact with the Teacher understanding of science. I suggest that three similar categories would exist in the interaction between individuals and a sovereign God. At first glance, one might conclude that there is no relationship between the sovereign plan of God and the development of technology. But I suggest that that conclusion is the result of viewing divine sovereignty from the *Mercy* perspective of a passive consumer. If one examines divine sovereignty from a Teacher perspective, then one might initially conclude that the difference between divine sovereignty and technological development is that science views Teacher understanding as a *passive* structure that is gradually revealed through the progress of science, whereas divine sovereignty views Teacher understanding as an *active* agent that is choosing to be gradually revealed. However, we have seen that there is a natural tendency among scientists in general and evolutionists in particular to view Nature as an *active* agent driven by a Teacher desire to increase the order-within-complexity of the natural world. Thus, I suggest that the real difference between divine sovereignty and the march of technology is that divine sovereignty functions at a deeper emotional level than technological development. Technology transforms the objects that we use and the situations that we experience, but it does not directly address the core mental networks of personal identity. As a result, technology can be hijacked by dictators with childish minds and grandiose schemes, leading to such abominations as the military-industrial complex. In contrast, a mental concept of God is, by definition, a Teacher theory that *applies* to personal identity. Thus, even if a real God does not exist, the concept of divine sovereignty based in a mental concept of God backed up by the divine righteousness of how nature works combined with how the mind works has the potential of transforming the motivations that lie behind the use of technology. For instance, technology makes it possible to watch soap operas in the comfort of one's home delivered by satellite signal. Divine sovereignty goes deeper by *changing* what one watches on television as well as transforming an individual beyond the passive state of being merely a couch potato. That is because a concept of God is based in a Teacher understanding that applies *to* personal identity and not just to the objects and experiences *surrounding* personal identity.

Returning now to our look at divine sovereignty, I suggest that the same three categories of consumer, hacker, and inventor show up when discussing interaction with God.

I know that these three terms do not sound religious, but I have chosen them precisely for this reason. In the same way that the typical consumer does not understand science, so most individuals interact with God as passive *consumers* of religion and view religion as a set of cultural MMNs. God is seen a source of religious and ecstatic *experiences* experienced primarily in a group setting, as portrayed earlier in the Keegan Hamilton study on American mega-churches. This is the type of religion that is primarily studied by the cognitive science of religion.

We looked earlier at the cognitive relationship between the consumer society and Pentecostalism. One quarter of the world's two billion Christians are now Pentecostal or charismatic, compared with 6% in 1980. Being a consumer is fun and exciting, because Teacher-driven science and technology is continually providing Mercy identity with new and exciting experiences and gadgets. Similarly, the Pentecostal Christian feels that God is continually providing Mercy identity with new and exciting experiences and powers. And if a real God exists who functions in a manner that is similar to the structure of nature and the mind, then there might be some validity to this claim.

> The consumer wants personal attention but is part of a group and follows the group.

However, I suggest that both the consumer and the Pentecostal are operating under a fundamental self-deception. The modern consumer is continually being told that 'this product was developed just for you' and that 'your personal needs are foremost in our minds'. But that simply is not the truth. The consumer society cares about the *group* and not the individual. Technology does not build devices for Fred the mechanic or John the frequent flyer. Rather, technology builds devices and offer services for mechanics, of which Fred is an example, and frequent flyers such as John. The consumer society pretends to care about the individual because the consumer is driven by Mercy thought, and Mercy thought thinks in terms of specific people and personal identity. Because of this self-deception, the consumer is continually expecting personalized service from science and technology and continually being disillusioned when treated merely as one of a crowd. For instance, we all know the frustration of phoning some telephone number for service, reaching an automated menu in which one must press various numbers, trying to get past the machine to reach a human, and then finally being told that 'All operators are currently busy. Please stay on the line and your call will be processed as soon as possible'.

I suggest that a similar self-deception exists in consumer religion. The religious adherent is continually being told that 'You are special to God and God cares for you personally. Every single individual is unique and precious in God's sight'. However, this simply is not true. Every single individual is *not* unique. Instead, individuals can be classified using categories such as cognitive style, interest groups, culture, gender, and age. People have the potential to *become* unique if they develop internal content that is *different* than the content of others. But a person who is driven by the core mental networks of his culture is not unique, and he will be driven by his mental networks to conform to others so that he does *not* become unique. One sees this self-deception illustrated by the rebellious teenager who tries to be different than society by conforming to his peers. The result of this self-deception is that the religious consumer continually expects God to treat him as an *exception* to the general case and he becomes disillusioned about God and religion when he experiences some random disaster driven by the statistical nature of personal existence. Thus, he may cry out "God! Why did you give me cancer?" or "God! Why didn't you protect me from that car accident?" But God deals with *general* processes and not *specific* Mercy situations such as getting cancer or being in a car accident. Going further, how *can* God treat some religious consumer as an exception to the general case when the consumer is driven by his core mental networks to avoid sticking out by conforming to the general case?

A person graduates from consumer to hacker by gaining a Teacher understanding of technology. The hacker has access to the same technology as the consumer, but the hacker has the Teacher understanding that is required to customize technology, and is driven by Teacher emotion to optimize and integrate technology.

This same type of Teacher-driven optimization can be found in the classic Christian passage on predestination that was quoted earlier.

> And we know that God causes all things to work together for good to those who love God, to those who are called according to His purpose. For those whom He foreknew, He also predestined to become conformed to the image of His Son, so that He would be the firstborn among many brethren; and these whom He predestined, He also called; and these whom He called, He also justified; and these whom He justified, He also glorified. What then shall we say to these things? If God is for us, who is against us? ...Who will separate us from the love of Christ? Will tribulation, or distress, or persecution, or famine, or nakedness, or peril, or sword? Just as it is written, "For Your sake we are being put to death all day long; we were considered as sheep to be slaughtered." But in all these things we overwhelmingly conquer through Him who loved us (Romans 8:28-31, 35-37).

Notice that this passage does not apply to everyone, but instead to 'those who love God, to those who are called according to His purpose'. Using the language of mental symmetry, it applies to those who are emotionally attached *to* and emotionally driven *by* the TMN of a mental concept of God. This does not describe the mindset of the religious consumer but rather the religious hacker (or inventor), who is guided by Teacher emotion and is driven by Teacher emotion. Notice also that being 'chosen by God' does not imply avoiding painful Mercy experiences. Being 'put to death all day long' or being 'considered as sheep to be slaughtered' does not describe a life that is free of Mercy problems. But what does exist is a Teacher-driven divine Providence in which 'God causes all things to work together for good'.

I suggested earlier that the Christian prayer of salvation mentally enrolls a person in a school of incarnation guided by a mental concept of God. As every school teacher knows, most students attend school as consumers of education. They are not there to learn but rather to pass the classes in order to get a diploma that will allow them to get a better paying job. But every once in a while, some individual student within this group has an 'aha' moment in which the mental lights go on and there is a glimpse of Teacher understanding. And there are usually some individuals in the class who are motivated by Teacher thought to gain an understanding and to apply this understanding. These moments and these students provide the emotional reward that keeps a teacher going. One might think that certain cognitive styles might have an inherent advantage, and if one defines education as learning to use technical thought, then the Contributor person has a definite advantage and the Exhorter person a definite disadvantage. However, when one is dealing with a school that involves transforming core mental networks, then I suggest that each cognitive style has its advantages and disadvantages.

When dealing with the 'school of life', I suggest that a person can either be divinely *chosen* to be a 'hacker', *stopped* by circumstances from being a consumer, or *choose* to be a hacker rather than a consumer. First, the mental networks of a person's culture, family, and upbringing sometimes *conspire* to develop some obsession for learning in a gifted individual, and these individuals often feel that they were chosen by God from birth to perform some divinely appointed task. Whether a real God tweaks a person's circumstances or not, such an individual will have the Teacher *impression* that 'God is causing all things to work together' in his personal life and that he is 'called according to God's divine purpose'. He will see Teacher order and divine providence in the structure of his personal life, and this Teacher impression will reinforce his obsession.

Second, the tragedies of life may strike randomly, but when they do strike some individual, then that individual is no longer a member of the group but has been forced to follow a path that is distinct and unique. That individual then has the choice of either focusing upon the personal Mercy experiences of pain and loss or else choosing to adopt the Teacher perspective of believing that 'God causes all things to work together for good'. Saying this another way, a person can either become bitter as a result of tragedy, or view the tragedy as an opportunity for personal growth. Saying this yet another way, tragedy stops a person from being a religious consumer. That individual can then choose to become a religious hacker.

Third, in the same way that a school student can choose to learn in school rather than just be part of the herd of common students, so a person can choose to approach religion from the Teacher perspective of understanding rather than from the Mercy perspective of religious culture. For instance, I specifically remember deciding in high school that 'I have to be here, so I may as well learn something'. Using religious language, a person can choose to become 'predestinated'. But while this choice may begin with a simple decision, it goes far beyond a mere decision. For instance, suppose that some rebellious student informs the teacher that he will now be diligent and studious. As every teacher knows, these are nice words but they need to be backed up by substance.

In other words, the core mental networks of such an individual need to be tested to see what really drives that person.

Notice that testing occurs with all three options. The rare individual who is 'chosen by God at birth' would be tested before birth by the foreknowledge of a universal God, who would be able to predict the general outcome of a person's life based upon the mental networks of family, culture, and upbringing. Obviously, it would only be just for God to choose individuals in such a manner for constructive purposes, and not for purposes that would destroy self or others. Moving on, when an individual faces personal tragedy, then the response to this emotional event provides the testing. If a person chooses to respond in a positive manner then that person has passed the test. Finally, if a person voluntarily chooses to become a religious hacker, then this decision would have to be tested by seeing if this decision still holds when faced with emotional pressure from opposing mental networks.

I have suggested that divine sovereignty could function either through good people such as Martin Luther King or evil people such as Adolf Hitler. When an evil person is chosen by God, then I suggest that it would only be just for God to choose such an individual *after* testing that individual to determine that person's core mental networks.

> Divine equations may be predetermined, but not the people placed in these equations.

One finds a description of this approach in the story of Judas, the disciple who betrayed Jesus. Jesus makes the following comments at the final meal before he is betrayed.

> As they were reclining at the table and eating, Jesus said, "Truly I say to you that one of you will betray Me—one who is eating with Me." They began to be grieved and to say to Him one by one, "Surely not I?" And He said to them, "It is one of the twelve, one who dips with Me in the bowl. For the Son of Man is to go just as it is written of Him; but woe to that man by whom the Son of Man is betrayed! It would have been good for that man if he had not been born" (Mark 14:18-21).

Notice how the betrayal of Jesus is portrayed as a divinely ordained general equation: 'For the Son of Man is to go just as it is written of him'. However, the specific person fulfilling the role of betrayer is portrayed as a variable that could have been filled by several possible candidates: 'Woe to that man by whom the Son of Man is betrayed'. Judas' core mental networks are described in a previous passage, where he is described as a lying thief who pretends to practice religious self-denial.

> But Judas Iscariot, one of His disciples, who was intending to betray Him, said, "Why was this perfume not sold for three hundred denarii and given to poor people?" Now he said this, not because he was concerned about the poor, but because he was a thief, and as he had the money box, he used to pilfer what was put into it (John 12:4-6).

Moving on now to the hacker, we saw in the previous chapter that learning science is a hands-on activity, in which acting upon understanding leads to further understanding. Stephen Levy defined what is known as *hacker ethics* in the book *Hackers: Heroes of the Computer Revolution*. This book was written in 1984, the year that the first Apple Mac computer was introduced (Levy, 1984).

> 1. Access to computers – and anything which might teach you something about the way the world works – should be unlimited and total. Always yield to the Hands-on Imperative!
>
> 2. All information should be free. ['free' here refers to unrestricted access, not price]
>
> 3. Mistrust authority – promote decentralization.
>
> 4. Hackers should be judged by their hacking, not bogus criteria such as degrees, age, race or position.
>
> 5. You can create art and beauty on a computer.
>
> 6. Computers can change your life for the better.

The first point recognizes that learning science requires doing. Notice how human righteousness is submitted to divine righteousness. The goal is to learn 'something about the way the world works', a description of divine righteousness as expressed in the natural world. However, in order to fully understand how the world works, I must act. Server confidence is required to give *stability* to Teacher understanding. Human righteousness needs to be brought into line with divine righteousness by using Server thought to act in a way that is consistent with how the world works. The second point describes the flow of Perceiver information that occurs in Habermas' second stage. If Perceiver thought is to discover universal truth, then it must be possible to learn and compare facts from many different contexts. The next two points attempt to set Perceiver thought free from the domination of Mercy status, going beyond the attitude of absolute truth with its basis in emotionally respected sources. The fifth point shows that thinking is being guided by Teacher emotion, while the final point believes that Teacher understanding can lead to personal benefits in Mercy thought.

I suggest that a similar set of ethics will guide the religious 'hacker'. Theology will be recognized as a hands-on activity. In order to recognize the hand of divine Providence, one must *think* in terms of divine righteousness, and this ability is *acquired* one hands-on step at a time as one sees an aspect of divine righteousness and then *acts* in a manner that makes human righteousness consistent with divine righteousness. Even if the Bible is the 'infallible word of God', one must still go beyond an attitude of absolute truth to universal truth by comparing truth from different sources. One must stop basing truth in Mercy status and one must be guided by the Teacher emotions that come from constructing a more adequate concept of God. Finally, one must believe that following a Teacher-based concept of God has personal benefits.

I am not suggesting that all hackers are deeply religious. On the contrary, hackers have a tendency to be rather irreligious. However, that is primarily because the average person approaches religion from a Mercy-based perspective, causing the hacker to instinctively reject religion. I suggest that the religious hacker should learn from the computer hacker by approaching the divine righteousness of 'the way the mind works' in the same way that the computer hacker approaches the divine righteousness of 'the way the world works'. However, being a religious hacker is much more difficult than being a computer hacker because the computer that is being hacked is one's own mind with its self-deceptions and childish thinking.

The computer hacker is often viewed as a threat to society, but the computer industry owes much of its existence to the work of hackers, because their hands-on experimentation furthers Teacher understanding. That is the point that Thomas Kuhn was trying to emphasize when he said that solving problems is an inherent aspect of learning science. Similarly, those who attempt to 'follow God rather than man' will also tend to be viewed as threats to society, because they do not bow to the MMNs of culture. What distinguishes the hacker from the rebel is that the hacker is *submitting* to a higher law while the rebel is merely rebelling from law. The hacker is submitting to the TMN of 'how things work' rather than the MMNs of culture, while the rebel is simply rejecting cultural MMNs. The consumer often confuses these two because the consumer only knows the MMNs of culture.

Saying this another way, the religious hacker is a *partner* with God, because the Server actions and experimentation of the hacker help to develop a mindset that is guided by Teacher understanding and create a society that expresses Teacher understanding.

Let us move on now to the third category of religious *inventor*. I have suggested that divine sovereignty would use people and groups with strong mental networks. Saying this more bluntly, God uses people who are obsessed, based upon their obsessions. Using theological language, in order to become the partner of God as described by open theism, one must mentally reach the stage where one is incapable of using free will to overrule fundamental desires, in line with the viewpoint of Calvinism. Notice that God is not overriding free will but rather respecting the core mental networks that develop as a result of free will. Even if some individual were chosen by God at birth, this predestination would be guided by foreknowledge based upon existing social and family mental networks. God would predict that a certain individual would develop in a certain manner and would take advantage of that knowledge, just as we take gifted children and place them in special schools.

Being obsessed may be a requirement for being a successful inventor, but not all obsessed people are inventors. Rather one needs the right type of obsession. I suggest that one can see the type of obsession that is required by looking at the example of Steve Jobs of Apple computers. Will Shanklin wrote in a 2012 article on the first anniversary of Job's death that

What made Jobs special – perhaps more so than the fictional Don Draper – was his deep-rooted obsession with the customer's journey. Most companies look at their products as things. They decide what this thing is going to do, what practical purpose it will solve, and how much it will cost. The product is an objective, measurable item, and their job is to figure out how to make money off of that item... Jobs thought differently. He saw life – from birth to death – as an experience... Jobs was a dreamer – influenced heavily by 1960s cultural icons like the Beatles and Bob Dylan – and he believed that his products (much like Dylan's songwriting) took that subjective experience to a higher level. Sublime art elevated life. His goal with his products, then, was to create events...Perhaps what separated Jobs from an ad exec with a marketing degree, though, was that he really believed in this perspective. To him, it wasn't just a clever tactic to sucker people into making him rich; it represented his core philosophy. The iPad wasn't just a product sold by Apple any more than *Hey Jude* was just a product sold by Apple Records. To Jobs, they were both art: elevating life experience from the dull and boring into something approaching nirvana (Shanklin, 2012).

Using the language of mental symmetry, Steve Jobs was obsessed with a *Platonic form*. He was not just following the bottom line thinking of the practical Contributor (though it is quite obvious that Jobs was a Contributor person). He wanted to transform normal Mercy experiences into *ideal* Mercy experiences, 'elevating life experience from the dull and boring into something approaching nirvana'. This was not 'a clever tactic to sucker people into making him rich'. Rather, it was a core mental network that 'represented his core philosophy', which gave him a 'deep-rooted obsession with the customer's journey'.

In an article entitled *Elon Musk is the true successor to Steve Jobs*, John McDuling writes that

It's increasingly clear that his true successor as the world's most important, and exciting, entrepreneur is not Mark Zuckerberg, Jack Dorsey or even Tim Cook. It's Elon Musk... Although Tesla's products lack the mainstream appeal of Apple's, they inspire a similar, cult-like devotion among users. Maybe that's because Musk is exhibiting a Steve Jobs-like obsession with the beauty and quality of them (McDuling, 2014).

Elon Musk is also driven by an obsession that transcends normal Mercy experiences. He wants to establish a human base on Mars. Dolly Singh, a former executive at SpaceX, Elon Musk's space exploration company, clarifies that

I know Elon — well. His obsession with Mars is no PR scam, but something the folks at SpaceX are giving their blood and sweat to achieve. You have no idea how much design and planning is already underway. There are millions of other things he could use his brilliance, resources, and connections on if all he wanted to do was make money and be famous. Taking on spaceflight is actually the fastest way to go broke and lose all your credibility. We have a joke in the New Space industry: How do you become a New Space millionaire? Start off as a Billionaire. I wouldn't deny he has an extremely healthy dose of ego and seems to be enjoying the limelight of late, but Mars is about legacy for him and his dedication and passion for that mission is one no one who actually knows him would ever question (Singh, 2014).

Putting this all together, the inventor needs to be a hacker. McDuling notes that "Like Jobs, [Elon Musk] exudes an intimate familiarity that suggests he is heavily involved in their [the Model S cars] design and creation." In order to design new gadgets that work, one must have a deep understanding of 'how things work'. But the inventor goes *beyond* the hacker. The hacker is driven by Teacher emotions to hack devices so that they work better, interact better, and have more features. The inventor, in contrast, is driven by the Mercy emotions of a Platonic form. Teacher understanding has reconnected Mercy experiences within his mind to create the internal vision of how things could be, this internal vision has turned into an obsession, and the inventor is using a Teacher understanding of 'how things work' to realize the Mercy vision of 'how things could be'. Using religious language, the inventor goes beyond loving God in Teacher thought to being guided by the Holy Spirit in Mercy thought.

Now that we understand the general mindset behind the inventor, let us contrast the inventor with the religious inventor. The inventor uses a knowledge of how the *world* works to design better objects and experiences. But the inventor lacks the knowledge of how the *mind* works that makes it possible to become a better *person* who is capable of having better *interpersonal* experiences. For instance, Shanklin opened his tribute to Steve Jobs by saying that

> You have to wonder whether all of the tech bloggers who gush sentimental tributes to Steve Jobs would have actually liked the man. Numerous accounts paint a picture of a person who – in addition to his obvious charm, wicked intelligence, and inspired creativity – could be extremely rude, manipulative, and hot-tempered. It's easy to laugh these traits off when you're reading about them in a biography, but if these sappy fanboys had actually spent time with Jobs, would they still offer such moving words? (Shanklin, 2012).

In other words, while Jobs was driven by Platonic forms to transcend normal experience with *objects*, he had no corresponding Platonic form that drove him to transform normal experiences with people. On the contrary, his Platonic forms involving *objects* caused him to be worse than normal when dealing with *people*. That is what happens when a person's obsession does not include personal character.

In contrast, the religious 'inventor' starts with a Teacher-based concept of God that *applies* to personal identity, which then leads to the Platonic form of a concept of the Holy Spirit that *transforms* personal identity, creating an obsession that *includes* personal identity.

Including personal identity as an aspect of one's obsession is not enough. Instead, I suggest that the religious inventor should be obsessed about transforming personal identity, and that everything else should be seen as a secondary expression of this core obsession. There is a common saying in charismatic Christian circles that "Your anointing can take you to a place where your character cannot sustain you." This is what happens when 'the anointing' focuses upon some secondary aspect of 'ministry' rather than the core process of personal transformation.

That leads us to a deeply personal question. A God of divine sovereignty could use individuals with obsessions. But if a person was obsessed about something that did not involve personal identity, then that individual would end up being *used* by God in the bad sense of this word, because that individual would experience external success while being driven towards personal inadequacy. How can a person acquire an obsession without being destroyed by that obsession? Phrased religiously, how can a person be used by God without being destroyed in the process?

An inventor can be destroyed by the obsession that drives him.

This may sound like a rather non-Christian question, but consider the following words of Jesus.

> Many will say to Me on that day, "Lord, Lord, did we not prophesy in Your name, and in Your name cast out demons, and in Your name perform many miracles?" And then I will declare to them, "I never knew you; DEPART FROM ME, YOU WHO PRACTICE LAWLESSNESS." Therefore everyone who hears these words of Mine and acts on them, may be compared to a wise man who built his house on the rock. And the rain fell, and the floods came, and the winds blew and slammed against that house; and yet it did not fall, for it had been founded on the rock. Everyone who hears these words of Mine and does not act on them, will be like a foolish man who built his house on the sand. The rain fell, and the floods came, and the winds blew and slammed against that house; and it fell—and great was its fall (Matt. 7:22-27).

Jesus talks here about individuals who 'prophesy', 'cast out demons', and 'perform many miracles', guided by a Teacher-based name of God, activities that would be classified as 'being used by God'. However, these 'ministers of God' end up being rejected by God because their Teacher understanding of God has not transformed their personal identity. Jesus then clarifies that what matters is the presence or absence of *righteousness*. A person who has performed Server actions that are consistent with his Teacher understanding of God will survive intact when core mental networks are tested, while the individual who does not add Server actions to Teacher words about God will not survive personal testing. Instead, his 'character will not be able to sustain him'. Notice finally that these words are not being addressed to everyone, but rather to those who are being 'used by God' but have not added Server actions to their words.

So how can a person be used by God without being destroyed in the process? Using secular language, how can a person be obsessed without being destroyed by that obsession? The only solution I know is to be obsessed with mental wholeness. But even that is not enough. One needs to be obsessed with mental wholeness *and* how this mental wholeness can be expressed in the external world. Using religious language, one needs to be obsessed with a concept of the Holy Spirit that is based in a concept of God that applies *both* to personal identity *and* to all of nature. That is why our discussion about religion in this book includes an analysis of science.

Suppose that a person's obsession involves *aspects* of mental wholeness. God would be able to use such a person (or group) for a *while* in order to take the next critical step, but would then have to move on to using another individual (or group) in order to take succeeding steps. For instance, many Christian denominations began by acknowledging and applying some new aspect of personal development, such as the Catholics during the middle ages, the Lutherans during the Reformation, the Methodists during the time of the enlightenment, or the Pentecostals during the advent of the consumer society. Each of these groups advanced the state-of-the-art, and when each group emerged it had the critical piece of the puzzle. But when it came time to move on to the next piece of the puzzle, then the tendency was for each group to cling to its piece and claim that this piece remains forever the most important piece of the puzzle. Thus, a group that was used by God for some step ended up becoming the foe of God for the next step. A similar process often occurs with corporations. Some company comes up with a breakthrough, it becomes successful developing a new product, and then it squelches the next product, which has to be developed by another company.

Kodak provides a classic example of this principle. The company began in the 1880s when George Eastman developed a new dry film that made it much easier to take pictures. In 1888 the first Kodak camera came out with the slogan 'You press the button—we do the rest'. Consumers would take a roll of pictures using the simple Kodak box camera and then mail in the camera in order to get their pictures developed and the camera reloaded with a new roll of fresh film. One of the things I remember from my travels is that everywhere I went, Kodak film could be bought at the local tourist kiosk, and in the 1970s Kodak controlled 90% of the photographic film market in the United States (Rees, 2012). But Kodak film is no longer needed today because everyone takes digital pictures. Kodak actually *invented* the digital camera in 1975 and spent many years developing digital camera technology. However, the initial product was dropped because Kodak was afraid that it would threaten their film business. The end result is that Kodak declared bankruptcy in 2012, because Kodak film had been made obsolete by a product that Kodak invented but *other* companies pursued (Pachal, 2012).

Moving on, the typical inventor is often obsessed with secrecy, because he does not want others to steal his ideas. This is a valid concern, because it is common for corporations to steal ideas from inventors without reimbursing them. However, the underlying problem is that the invention can be *separated* from the inventor, because the inventor is creating objects that are distinct from his person. The religious inventor does not have this problem because his invention involves his personal character. One sees this to some extent with high-tech companies. The common misconception is that the company contains the assets, and that one can acquire these assets by buying the company.

But the real assets of the company are the engineers and inventors within the company who have the knowledge and ability to create new products. Without these individuals, the company is merely a shell.

When I began doing research in cognitive styles, I was afraid that others would steal my work. But it soon became clear to me that others could not steal this research because they lacked the mental ability to think clearly about the subject. Saying this another way, I have become my research. One result is that when I study the findings of others, I find that an understanding of their research emerges naturally and intuitively within my mind. Building this understanding may be a struggle, but it is a struggle that involves me and my personal development. Notice that this goes beyond Kuhn's assertion that science is learned through the practice of problems. That describes the mind of the hacker who gains understanding through application. What I am describing here involves a transformation of personal identity, becoming personally *obsessed* with one's research to the extent that one's identity becomes intertwined with that research. As I have already stated, this level of personal obsession is extremely dangerous if it is mishandled. That is why it is imperative to become obsessed with the transformation of personal identity, because if one is not obsessed with transforming personal identity, then one's obsession will transform personal identity. At the beginning of this book, we defined personal identity as 'the set of mental networks that cannot be ignored'. An obsession is a set of mental networks that cannot be ignored. Saying this another way, an obsession is a mental prison. Being mentally imprisoned within paradise is wonderful; being imprisoned within a hovel is not.

This does not mean that everyone should drop what they are doing in order to study the theory of mental symmetry for the next decade. Mental symmetry is a *meta*-theory that can be expressed in many different ways using many different languages, and the process of personal transformation is a general process that can be experienced in a number of specific ways. For some individuals, such as those who are blaspheming the Holy Spirit, pursuing personal transformation may require abandoning what they are currently doing. However, for most people, developing a proper obsession means continuing to do what they are already doing while choosing to be guided by the context of the larger picture.

✳ 13. The Plan of Incarnation

The previous chapter examined how a universal God might cooperate with finite humans. What is missing from that description is a method for recovering from error. It is fine to say in theoretical terms that humans have a free will which can be exercised before major situations arise, but what about the person who finds himself in the situation of having made the wrong choice? Is he irrevocably damned by God? Education can minimize this problem by allowing each generation to learn from the previous generation, but what if children ignore the advice of parents or if parents themselves are ignorant? Is there no way to recover from bad decisions? I suggest that one can use the theory of mental symmetry to come up with a potential solution by bringing in the aspect of God that was not discussed in the previous chapter, which is Contributor incarnation. We have discussed the cognitive structure behind a mental concept of incarnation, and we have used school to provide an illustration of the role that incarnation plays. What we have not yet discussed is the *curriculum* of the school—the specific plan that incarnation needs to carry out. What is needed is a plan that makes it possible to recover from error, or using religious language, a plan of *salvation*.

Contributor thought is ideally suited for this role because concrete Contributor thought naturally improves specific Mercy experiences. Remember that concrete Contributor thought tries to improve some emotional bottom line in Mercy thought guided by a knowledge of cause-and-effect. For instance, 'If I change the way that I hold my golf club, then I can hit the ball further', 'If I attend university, then I will get a better job', or 'If I invest money in this company, then I will make a profit'. In each case, if-then connections are being rearranged in order to improve some specific result in Mercy thought. However, Contributor thought also has some inherent limitations that need to be overcome if incarnation is to act as a savior.

> Concrete Contributor thought naturally improves things rather than people.

The first problem is that concrete Contributor thought has a natural tendency to improve *things* rather than people. Think, for instance, of the example of Kobe Bryant referred to earlier in the book. He knew how to shoot a ball through a hoop but he did not know how to conduct a marriage. Similarly, Steve Jobs was brilliant at using technology to create transcendental experiences while disregarding how people experienced him. However, if Contributor thought is to become a savior of people and not just a savior of things, then Contributor thought has to gain sufficient confidence to apply if-then thinking to the personal realm of Mercy mental networks. One sees this application of Contributor thought to the mental networks of personal identity in the words of Jesus.

> For what will it profit a man if he gains the whole world and forfeits his soul? Or what will a man give in exchange for his soul? (Matt. 16:26).

The second problem is that merely *improving* personal identity is not enough. Using religious language, salvation cannot be achieved through hard work. That is because every human emerges from childhood with a mind that is integrated around childish MMNs that are fundamentally inadequate. We looked at this in detail when discussing Piaget's preoperational stage. We have seen throughout this book that personal improvement which leaves childish MMNs intact ends up amplifying childish attitudes rather than curing them. Instead of throwing stones at each other, one shoots bullets and fires rockets. The method of delivery may be far more high-tech, but the underlying motivation is still the same.

The solution is for concrete Contributor thought to carry out a plan of personal salvation that involves tearing apart the MMNs of childish identity and rebuilding them in adult form. But the mind cannot handle the fragmentation of having core mental networks ripped apart; one cannot use the mind to attack the foundation of the mind. A mind that is integrated around childish MMNs cannot transform childish MMNs, let alone diagnose them accurately. However, it is possible to let go of childish MMNs if one integrates the mind around the TMN of a general understanding. Using an analogy, if I try to move the leg upon which I am standing, then I will fall down. But I can move that leg forward if I first place my weight upon the *other* leg. Applying this to Contributor thought, concrete Contributor thought is insufficient for carrying out a plan of salvation because it is driven by Mercy emotions. Instead what is required is a form of Contributor thought that can be driven either by Mercy emotions or by Teacher emotions. We saw in an earlier chapter that this combination of concrete Contributor thought and abstract Contributor thought describes a mental concept of incarnation, because concrete Contributor thought improves specific Mercy experiences whereas abstract Contributor thought improves general Teacher understanding.

> Incarnation backed up by universal Teacher understanding can fully transform people.

One finds this combination described in the verses that precede the verse about improving personal identity rather than things.

> Now when Jesus came into the district of Caesarea Philippi, He was asking His disciples, "Who do people say that the Son of Man is?" And they said, "Some say John the Baptist; and others, Elijah; but still others, Jeremiah, or one of the prophets." He said to them, "But who do you say that I am?" Simon Peter answered, "You are the Christ, the Son of the living God." And Jesus said to him, "Blessed are you, Simon Barjona, because flesh and blood did not reveal this to you, but My Father who is in heaven. I also say to you that you are Peter, and

upon this rock I will build My church; and the gates of Hades will not overpower it. I will give you the keys of the kingdom of heaven; and whatever you bind on earth shall have been bound in heaven, and whatever you loose on earth shall have been loosed in heaven." Then He warned the disciples that they should tell no one that He was the Christ. From that time Jesus began to show His disciples that He must go to Jerusalem, and suffer many things from the elders and chief priests and scribes, and be killed, and be raised up on the third day. Peter took Him aside and began to rebuke Him, saying, "God forbid it, Lord! This shall never happen to You." But He turned and said to Peter, "Get behind Me, Satan! You are a stumbling block to Me; for you are not setting your mind on God's interests, but man's." Then Jesus said to His disciples, "If anyone wishes to come after Me, he must deny himself, and take up his cross and follow Me. For whoever wishes to save his life will lose it; but whoever loses his life for My sake will find it. For what will it profit a man if he gains the whole world and forfeits his soul? Or what will a man give in exchange for his soul?" (Matt. 16:13-26).

This passage contains a number of interesting details when analyzed from a cognitive perspective. It begins with the disciples describing how people are viewing Jesus from the *Mercy* perspective of people with emotional status, comparing Jesus with such Jewish luminaries as Elijah and Jeremiah. But then Peter adopts a different perspective, connecting Jesus with a concept of God in Teacher thought. Using the language of mental symmetry, Peter recognizes that Jesus is an incarnation who combines abstract Contributor thought with concrete Contributor thought. Jesus responds by saying that this statement of Peter comes from abstract Teacher thought and is not based in concrete Mercy experiences: 'Flesh and blood did not reveal this to you, but My Father who is in heaven'. When Contributor incarnation becomes based in the TMN of a concept of God, it then becomes possible for Contributor incarnation to carry out the plan of tearing apart and rebuilding the MMNs of personal identity, which explains why 'From that time Jesus began to show His disciples that He must go to Jerusalem, and suffer many things from the elders and chief priests and scribes, and be killed, and be raised up on the third day'.

In the middle of this passage lies the strange reference to 'Peter and the keys of heaven'. According to the Catholic Church, this describes Jesus giving Peter the authority to be the first pope, and this authority has been transferred down the centuries through an 'apostolic succession' of succeeding popes. However, I suggest that a knowledge of cognitive styles can provide us with a more straightforward interpretation of this exchange between Jesus and Peter. Jesus is a Contributor person. Peter, in contrast, is a *Perceiver* person. (The description of Jesus and Peter in the Gospels is sufficiently detailed to reach this conclusion with reasonable certainty.) Perceiver thought and Contributor thought both have access to Perceiver facts, but these two cognitive modules treat the *same* Perceiver facts in a *different* way. The Perceiver person is naturally good at recognizing truth and holding on to truth—which describes the mindset of the *conservative*. The Contributor person, in contrast, uses facts to move from one location to a better location. Contributor thought can only use facts to *transform* Mercy experiences if Perceiver thought lets go of using facts to *preserve* Mercy experiences. As I mentioned in an earlier chapter, if I as a Perceiver *person* want to experience the salvation of Contributor thought, then I must *lose control* to Contributor thought. It is naturally difficult for the Perceiver person to stop gathering facts and start using facts. This is precisely what one sees in the dialogue between Jesus and Peter. When Jesus describes his plan of personal rebirth, Peter adopts an attitude of conservatism by taking Jesus aside and rebuking him. Jesus responds to this rebuke by saying that the Perceiver thinking of Peter is acting as a stumbling block to the Contributor thinking of Jesus. Jesus then makes it clear that enrolling in the 'school of incarnation' means letting go of conservatism in order to follow a path of personal rebirth: 'Whoever wishes to save his life will lose it; but whoever loses his life for my sake will find it'.

That brings us finally to the statements about Peter and the keys of heaven. In order to carry out a plan of rebirth, Perceiver thought has to lose control to Contributor thought. However, every Contributor plan is limited to some specific context, and Perceiver thought is needed to *unfold* this plan by extending it to other contexts through the use of Perceiver connections. And this *Teacher* unfolding occurs as Perceiver thought discovers connections within the concrete world of Mercy experiences. But in order to perform this Perceiver unfolding, Perceiver thought must let go of the Mercy-based attitude of absolute truth and adopted the Teacher-based attitude of universal truth, which is what Peter is doing when he views Contributor incarnation from the perspective of Teacher thought. Notice the precise nature of Perceiver thought being described here. Peter is using Perceiver thought to form or break connections—'binding' or 'loosing'. This binding and loosing is occurring 'on earth' in the concrete world of Mercy experiences. These concrete Perceiver connections do not create universal Teacher understanding 'in heaven' but rather reveal the nature of connections that already exist within universal Teacher thought. Thus, 'whatever you bind on earth shall have been bound in heaven' (this specific verb tense is in the original Greek text). Saying this scientifically, observation does not create scientific theory, it reveals it. However, if the observation is not done, then the theory will not be revealed.

> Perceiver thought (and Server thought) can unfold the plan of incarnation.

Given this interpretation, I suggest that it does not make sense to use this passage as the basis for an unbroken succession of popes stretching from Peter to the present. First, Peter is given 'the keys of heaven' when he *transcends* a Mercy focus upon people with emotional status in order to adopt a Teacher focus upon a concept of God. Focusing upon a succession of popes, in contrast, describes a *Mercy* focus upon people with emotional status. If the requirement for being given the keys of heaven is to *stop* assigning emotional status to religious people, then why would the keys of heaven be used as a basis for *assigning* emotional status to religious people? Second, Jesus clearly states that his plan does not involve an *unbroken* earthly succession, but rather involves the *breaking* of earthly connections by dying and returning to life. And when Peter tells Jesus that earthly connections should remain unbroken, then Jesus condemns Peter in no uncertain terms. If Jesus denounces the conservatism of Peter, then why would he approve of the conservatism of an unbroken apostolic succession? On the contrary, Jesus predicts in this passage that he will be killed by the religious leaders in Jerusalem, who acquired their positions through the 'unbroken apostolic succession' of *his* day.

This leads us to the third problem, which is that Contributor incarnation is not sufficient for *universal* salvation, because technical thought is by its very nature limited to some *restricted* context. As we have seen, what typically happens is that technical thought works within some context, and this causes a TMN to form that limits Contributor thought to this context. That is because, as Kuhn observed, abstract Contributor thought naturally gets locked within the TMN of some specific theory. The solution is for Contributor incarnation to allow universal Teacher understanding to change the context for Contributor thought. One sees this cognitive principle portrayed in another well-known biblical passage that talks about Jesus praying to God just before he is betrayed and killed.

> He said to them, "My soul is deeply grieved, to the point of death; remain here and keep watch with Me." And He went a little beyond them, and fell on His face and prayed, saying, "My Father, if it is possible, let this cup pass from Me; yet not as I will, but as You will." And He came to the disciples and found them sleeping, and said to Peter, "So, you men could not keep watch with Me for one hour? Keep watching and praying that you may not enter into temptation; the spirit is willing, but the flesh is weak." He went away again a second time and prayed, saying, "My Father, if this cannot pass away unless I drink it, Your will be done." Again He came and found them sleeping, for their eyes were heavy. And He left them again, and went away and prayed a third time, saying the same thing once more. Then He came to the disciples and said to them, "Are you still sleeping and resting? Behold, the hour is at hand and the Son of Man is being betrayed into the hands of sinners" (Matt. 26: 38-45).

Contributor incarnation is being faced with a situation that threatens Contributor thought with fragmentation. In the words of Jesus, 'my soul is deeply grieved, to the point of death'. Despite this, Contributor incarnation is responding to the situation by submitting to universal Teacher thought: 'My father, if this cannot pass away unless I drink it, your will be done'. Jesus' words to Peter imply that Perceiver thought can help Contributor incarnation to make such a transition by 'keeping watch with Me'. However, 'the spirit is willing, but the flesh is weak'. Translating this into cognitive language, if Perceiver thought focuses upon 'the spirit' of Platonic forms, then this will assist Contributor thought to make the transition from one context to another guided by universal Teacher thought. However, the temptation for Perceiver thought in such a situation is to be overwhelmed by the mental networks of culture and accepted practice and 'fall asleep'.

The relationship between Contributor rebirth and Teacher universality is also brought out in the classic passage on incarnation written by Paul in Philippians.

> Have this attitude in yourselves which was also in Christ Jesus, who, although He existed in the form of God, did not regard equality with God a thing to be grasped, but emptied Himself, taking the form of a bond-servant, and being made in the likeness of men. Being found in appearance as a man, He humbled Himself by becoming obedient to the point of death, even death on a cross. For this reason also, God highly exalted Him, and bestowed on Him the name which is above every name, so that at the name of Jesus EVERY KNEE WILL BOW, of those who are in heaven and on earth and under the earth, and that every tongue will confess that Jesus Christ is Lord, to the glory of God the Father (Phil. 2:5-11).

Paul begins by saying that the rebirth of incarnation should be regarded as a general sequence that applies to everyone: 'Have this attitude in yourselves which was also in Christ Jesus'. Contributor incarnation begins by working with universal Teacher understanding in abstract Contributor thought: 'although he existed in the form of God'. Contributor incarnation does not remain within abstract thought but extends itself to concrete Contributor thought: 'Being made in the likeness of men'. Contributor incarnation then experiences rebirth within concrete Contributor thought, guided by abstract Contributor thought: 'obedient to the point of death'. As a result, Teacher thought regards Contributor incarnation as a universal theory: 'bestowed on him the name which is above every name'. This universal Teacher theory of incarnation guides Server actions: 'every knee will bow'. And it also guides Teacher words: 'every tongue will confess'.

Before we continue, I would like to make some brief comments regarding biblical interpretation. I have suggested several times throughout this book that the theory of mental symmetry leads to conclusions that are consistent with Christian doctrine, and I have backed up this assertion by using mental symmetry to analyze core Christian doctrines. However, the biblical passages that we have just examined illustrate another aspect of the correspondence between mental symmetry and Christian doctrine. The Bible contains many strange references, such as the keys of Peter, or Jesus' prayer in the garden of Gethsemane. Over the centuries, theologians have attempted to analyze these references. For some strange reason, I have found that these details make sense when one puts on the spectacles of the theory of mental symmetry and reads the passage from a cognitive perspective. I do not know how far this approach can be taken, but I do know that this correspondence includes all of the core doctrines of Christianity. I do not claim to understand the entire Bible, and I am not suggesting that I am more clever than centuries of theologians. Rather, I am observing that as I get better at using the glasses of mental symmetry, more of the Bible falls into place, including strange details.

Normally, those who are closest to the author of a book have the best understanding of that book. However, when it comes to the Bible then we find exactly the opposite, because the earliest church fathers make many conclusions about the Bible that can only be described as cognitively deficient, and one can see these cognitive errors being gradually eliminated over the centuries as we have learned more about how the natural world and the mind function. This leads us to two conclusions. First, I suggest that it is unreasonable to state that the Bible was written by the church fathers because it contains too much information about the mind of which they were ignorant. Second, I suggest that the normal theological practice of viewing the patristic church fathers as the most definitive authority on the Bible is fundamentally flawed.

A Real Incarnation?

Cognitive analysis suggests that the biblical story of Jesus is a myth with deep symbology. But is it merely a myth or was Jesus *really* an incarnation of God? Evidence from other ancient sources, such as Josephus, tells us that Jesus actually existed, and we have seen the Bible claims that Jesus is an incarnation of God. But is this actually the case?

If one examines this question from a cognitive perspective, then I suggest that we are dealing with two fundamental problems. The first problem is that a universal being who lives in quantum probability would require human action to turn possibility into actuality. In other words, it would not be sufficient for God to announce from heaven the existence of incarnation using the divine language of general equations and Platonic forms. Instead, incarnation would have to be actualized through the existence of some physical person who carried out the role of incarnation.

The second problem is that we are dealing with a chicken-and-egg type of situation. On the one hand, what is required is a Contributor incarnation that is based in a general Teacher understanding. On the other hand, we have seen that every human grows up with a mind that is integrated around childish MMNs that oppose Teacher understanding. The plan of incarnation is capable of transforming the childish mind so that it *becomes* based in Teacher understanding, but setting up this plan of incarnation requires a mind that is already based in Teacher understanding. This is like trying to get into a locked room when the key to the door is locked in the room. Using the school analogy, how can a school be initially set up when only someone who has attended a school is capable of establishing a school?

These two problems suggest that a real incarnation is needed and that the source of this incarnation must be God. Using religious language, the *word* of general Teacher understanding has to become the *flesh* of human action and this flesh needs to be an expression of rational Teacher understanding. As the apostle John says, "the Word became flesh, and dwelt among us, and we saw His glory, glory as of the only begotten from the Father, full of grace and truth" (John 1:14).

But this is only a partial solution because it moves the problem *back* a stage. The problem within the problem is that flesh acts while quantum probability does not. Thus, incarnation has to be made flesh within a human cultural context of people who are performing Server actions that are consistent with a Teacher understanding of God. In other words, an incarnation that comes from God needs to be taught how to act by humans who are righteous. That is because action is something that *humans* do, while righteousness is something that an incarnation *from God* requires. But how can incarnation learn from humans how to act in a righteous manner if incarnation is required to teach humans how to become righteous?

I suggest that the solution to that chicken-and-egg problem is for God to choose some *group* of people and tell them what to do as a group. A group must be chosen because childish minds are incapable of thinking as individuals but instead are governed by the MMNs of their tribe. Western thought emphasizes the importance of being an individual. Despite this, group mentality still guides most decisions. Imagine what society was like several millennia ago when all that existed was the tribe. Childish minds are also incapable of abstract thought. Therefore, God would have to tell a group of people to perform a set of concrete actions. One can see what this means by observing the typical kindergarten class. I have substituted in these classes just enough to know what is being emphasized. The kindergarten teacher is using her authority (98% of kindergarten teachers are female) to teach young children the Server habits of being a school student in a group setting. God would have to do a similar thing with a group of people.

Ideally, this divine instruction would lead to the birth of science, so that incarnation could become flesh within a scientific society in which at least interaction with the world of objects was guided by Teacher understanding. Thus, it would have been much better for incarnation if science had emerged in Alexandria before the time of Christ. But it did not, which provides a possible explanation for Jesus' comment regarding a window of opportunity being closed. At the minimum, the culture in which incarnation became flesh would have to be guided by Server confidence in the actions that were originally revealed by God to the group. Using a school analogy, it would be better for incarnation to appear to a group of high school students who had studied science, but it would be sufficient for incarnation to appear to a group of kindergarten students who knew how to be school students. But incarnation would then face the problem of living in a culture that was fixated upon physical action and unable to grasp the symbolism behind those actions, locked within concrete thought and unable to use abstract thought.

Abstract or Concrete?

I would like to expand upon the previous sentence, because I suggest that incarnation is still being viewed *today* by many individuals from a perspective that is fixated upon physical action and locked within concrete thought. A 2008 survey taken of the two largest Orthodox Christian groups in America found that 90% value the church primarily because of the Eucharist and church liturgy, 98% believe the bread and wine turns into the body and blood of Christ, and 93% think the primary duty of the priest is to lead worship and administer sacraments. In addition, 97% believe that belief in transubstantiation is required to be a good Orthodox Christian. (Second only to 98% believing that a good Orthodox Christian believes in the resurrection of Jesus.) Thus, for the vast majority of American Orthodox Christians, the essence of Christianity is eating bread and drinking wine that is believed to be the actual body and blood of Jesus (Krindatch). Bread and wine are physical concrete objects. When these objects are equated with incarnation, then incarnation is being mentally associated with a religious culture that is fixated upon physical action and locked within concrete thought.

Catholicism also tends to view incarnation from a concrete perspective, as illustrated by the practice of Eucharistic adoration. In March 2006, Pope Benedict XVI stated in an official address that

> The Blessed Sacrament is exposed for adoration 24 hours a day in St Anastasia on the Palatine. The faithful take turns in making Perpetual Adoration. My suggestion is that there should be Perpetual Adoration of the Eucharist in each one of the five sectors of the Diocese of Rome...without adoration as an act consequent to Communion received, this centre which the Lord gave to us, that is, the possibility of celebrating his sacrifice and thus of entering into a sacramental, almost corporeal, communion with him, loses its depth as well as its human richness (Benedict-XVI, 2006).

And in June 2013,

> Millions of people around the world took part in an hour of Solemn Eucharistic Adoration on Sunday evening. Pope Francis led the unprecedented, worldwide event from Saint Peter's Basilica in Rome. Catholic faithful throughout the world took part in their own Cathedrals and churches, and followed the event on television, radio, and the internet (Vatican Radio, 2013).

The American Catholic website summarized some of the key suggestions made during the 2005 world Synod of bishops on the Eucharist.

> "The institution of the Eucharist demonstrates how Jesus' death, for all its violence and absurdity, became in him a supreme act of love and mankind's definitive deliverance from evil," Pope Benedict wrote. Celebrating the Eucharist, he said, "the church is able to celebrate and adore the mystery of Christ" who is present in the bread and wine through the power of the Holy Spirit. In addition to offering a spiritual reflection on the meaning of the Eucharist, the liturgy and eucharistic adoration, Pope Benedict made several concrete suggestions for further study and for celebrating the Mass in the Latin rite: ...The pope asked Catholics to pay more attention to how their postures and gestures at Mass communicate their faith in the Eucharist, particularly by "kneeling during the central moments of the eucharistic prayer" (Wooden, 2006).

Notice how Jesus' death is called 'absurd', indicating transcendence, and 'a supreme act of love', consistent with fervor and religious self-denial. Similarly, the Eucharist is 'celebrated and adored', expressing fervor, with 'kneeling during the central moments', indicating self-denial, and is referred to as a 'mystery', indicating transcendence.

In contrast, Paul says that he used to view incarnation from the concrete perspective of the flesh, but that he now views everyone from a different perspective.

> Therefore from now on we recognize no one according to the flesh; even though we have known Christ according to the flesh, yet now we know Him in this way no longer. Therefore if anyone is in Christ, he is a new creature; the old things passed away; behold, new things have come. Now all these things are from God, who reconciled us to Himself through Christ and gave us the ministry of reconciliation, namely, that God was in Christ reconciling the world to Himself, not counting their trespasses against them, and He has committed to us the word of reconciliation. Therefore, we are ambassadors for Christ, as though God were making an appeal through us; we beg you on behalf of Christ, be reconciled to God (2 Cor. 5:16-20).

Paul says that he used to view Jesus as a physical person 'according to the flesh'. But he is adopting a new perspective with everyone including Jesus, one which makes total transformation possible. This new perspective is rooted in the concept that universal Teacher thought is using Contributor incarnation to reconcile childish Mercy identities so that they become compatible with Teacher thought. This 'ministry of reconciliation' uses words to appeal to people to submit to general Teacher understanding, and it includes the method of justification described earlier in this book.

The thesis of this book is that Christianity makes sense when held together by the TMN of an abstract theory of cognition, and we have taken several chapters to show that a mental concept of incarnation emerges naturally when one uses the most rigorous form of thought and that this mental concept of incarnation corresponds to the deep structure of science. We saw when discussing righteousness that action will only be guided by the TMN of a general understanding if a TMN is followed *instead of* MMNs. This means that if a mental concept of incarnation is to be held together by the TMN of a general Teacher theory, then one must stop associating incarnation with the MMNs of transubstantiation and Eucharist adoration.

> Incarnation viewed from a concrete perspective cannot generate total transformation.

I am not suggesting that there is no benefit to viewing incarnation from a human Mercy perspective. Piaget's stages of cognitive development make it clear that *all* human thought begins with a Mercy perspective. Therefore, transubstantiation and Eucharist adoration are a possible *starting* point. However, in the same way that one can only construct the concept of a universal God by transcending fundamentalism, so I suggest that one can only construct the concept of a universal incarnation by transcending the doctrine of transubstantiation and the practice of Eucharist adoration.

Orthodox Christianity and Catholicism both regard a *Mercy* focus upon incarnation as a core element of Christianity. In contrast, I suggest that these branches of Christianity view incarnation from a concrete perspective not because Christianity *is* ultimately based in concrete thought but rather because these forms of Christianity came into being in an era that was only *capable* of concrete thought. In order to back up this statement, we will take a few paragraphs to examine the biblical passage that is traditionally used to support the doctrine of transubstantiation, in order to see what Jesus himself says about the relationship between concrete and abstract thought. As we go through this passage, notice how the crowd fixates upon people with Mercy status and physical actions while Jesus repeatedly tries to get them to think about Teacher understanding and the symbolism behind physical actions.

> Jesus answered them and said, "Truly, truly, I say to you, you seek Me, not because you saw signs, but because you ate of the loaves and were filled. Do not work for the food which perishes, but for the food which endures to eternal life, which the Son of Man will give to you, for on Him the Father, God, has set His seal." Therefore they said to Him, "What shall we do, so that we may work the works of God?" Jesus answered and said to them, "This is the work of God, that you believe in Him whom He has sent." So they said to Him, "What then do You do for a sign, so that we may see, and believe You? What work do You perform? Our fathers ate the manna in the wilderness; as it is written, 'HE GAVE THEM BREAD OUT OF HEAVEN TO EAT.'" Jesus then said to them, "Truly, truly, I say to you, it is not Moses who has given you the bread out of heaven, but it is My Father who gives you the true bread out of heaven. For the bread of God is that which comes down out of heaven, and gives life to the world." Then they said to Him, "Lord, always give us this bread" (John 6:26-34).

This passage occurs right after the story of the feeding of the five thousand, to which the crowd responds by attempting to crown Jesus as their king. Jesus tells the people at the beginning of this passage that all they care about is food and not symbolism, and that they should look for symbolic food that comes from a Teacher-based concept of God. They respond by asking 'what shall we do', indicating a fixation upon concrete Server actions. Jesus counters that what is needed is Perceiver belief and not Server action. They answer that they will believe if Jesus performs some Server action that leads to visible Mercy results, indicating again a fixation upon concrete thought. They then refer to the time when the Jews were originally told by God what to do, and they point out to Jesus that they got free bread from the sky back then. Jesus answers by saying that the source of this bread was not Moses, the Jewish leader to whom they give great Mercy status, but rather a Teacher-based concept of God. But all they hear from that sentence is the word 'bread'.

Continuing with this chapter,

> Jesus said to them, "I am the bread of life; he who comes to Me will not hunger, and he who believes in Me will never thirst. But I said to you that you have seen Me, and yet do not believe. All that the Father gives Me will come to Me, and the one who comes to Me I will certainly not cast out. For I have come down from heaven, not to do My own will, but the will of Him who sent Me. This is the will of Him who sent Me, that of all that He has given Me I lose nothing, but

raise it up on the last day. For this is the will of My Father, that everyone who beholds the Son and believes in Him will have eternal life, and I Myself will raise him up on the last day." Therefore the Jews were grumbling about Him, because He said, "I am the bread that came down out of heaven." They were saying, "Is not this Jesus, the son of Joseph, whose father and mother we know? How does He now say, 'I have come down out of heaven'?" Jesus answered and said to them, "Do not grumble among yourselves. No one can come to Me unless the Father who sent Me draws him; and I will raise him up on the last day. It is written in the prophets, 'And they shall all be taught of God.' Everyone who has heard and learned from the Father, comes to Me. Not that anyone has seen the Father, except the One who is from God; He has seen the Father. Truly, truly, I say to you, he who believes has eternal life. I am the bread of life" (John 6: 35-48).

Jesus responds to the crowd's fixation upon bread by saying that Contributor incarnation is the source of lasting Mercy benefits. He then points out that seeing is not believing. Instead, those who are guided by unseen Teacher understanding will recognize and follow him. He as incarnation came from general Teacher thought in order to do Server actions that are consistent with general Teacher understanding. His job is to include everything that comes from Teacher thought and bring it through a Contributor plan of rebirth.

> Jesus' audience was fixated upon concrete objects and physical actions.

The crowd responds that Jesus cannot come from Teacher thought because they know his Mercy source: 'Is not this Jesus, the son of Joseph, whose father and mother we know?' Jesus responds that people will only recognize that his ultimate source is Teacher thought if they are guided by Teacher thought, and even their revered sources of truth say that understanding comes from Teacher thought. Whoever learns from word-based Teacher understanding will recognize him. But only someone who comes from universal Teacher understanding can grasp the true nature of Teacher thought.

The next few verses describe the connection between bread and wine and the body and blood of Christ.

"Your fathers ate the manna in the wilderness, and they died. This is the bread which comes down out of heaven, so that one may eat of it and not die. I am the living bread that came down out of heaven; if anyone eats of this bread, he will live forever; and the bread also which I will give for the life of the world is My flesh." Then the Jews began to argue with one another, saying, "How can this man give us His flesh to eat?" So Jesus said to them, "Truly, truly, I say to you, unless you eat the flesh of the Son of Man and drink His blood, you have no life in yourselves. He who eats My flesh and drinks My blood has eternal life, and I will raise him up on the last day. For My flesh is true food, and My blood is true drink. He who eats My flesh and drinks My blood abides in Me, and I in him. As the living Father sent Me, and I live because of the Father, so he who eats Me, he also will live because of Me. This is the bread which came down out of heaven; not as the fathers ate and died; he who eats this bread will live forever" (John 6:49-58).

Jesus says that there was nothing transformative about the Mercy experiences that originally defined the Jewish people. But when Teacher thought is the source, then there is transformation, and this transformation comes from incarnation becoming flesh. The literal minded audience then responds by thinking that Jesus is talking about some form of cannibalism. Jesus responds that concrete personal identity cannot exist by itself, but needs to be renewed by identifying with the Server actions (flesh) and the emotional Mercy experiences (blood) of Contributor incarnation. He clarifies that the *concrete* side of Contributor incarnation gives life to personal identity in a manner that is analogous to the way that general Teacher thought gives life to the *abstract* side of Contributor incarnation, and that this is what it means to have 'bread from heaven'.

The final section of this chapter describes the various responses to this dialogue.

> These things He said in the synagogue as He taught in Capernaum. Therefore many of His disciples, when they heard this said, "This is a difficult statement; who can listen to it?" But Jesus, conscious that His disciples grumbled at this, said to them, "Does this cause you to stumble? What then if you see the Son of Man ascending to where He was before? It is the Spirit who gives life; the flesh profits nothing; the words that I have spoken to you are spirit and are life. But there are some of you who do not believe." For Jesus knew from the beginning who they were who did not believe, and who it was that would betray Him. And He was saying, "For this reason I have said to you, that no one can come to Me unless it has been granted him from the Father." As a result of this many of His disciples withdrew and were not walking with Him anymore. So Jesus said to the twelve, "You do not want to go away also, do you?" Simon Peter answered Him, "Lord, to whom shall we go? You have words of eternal life. We have believed and have come to know that You are the Holy One of God" (John 6:59-69).

Most listeners respond by leaving Jesus because they cannot handle his strange words. Jesus then turns to his disciples and asks how they would respond if they see him returning from concrete Server thought back to general Teacher thought. He then tells his disciples that he has been talking about Platonic forms and not concrete Server actions. Server action by itself profits nothing. The passage ends by mentioning Judas and Peter. Peter decides to stay with Jesus because of his Teacher words and because he believes that Jesus comes from general Teacher thought. Judas, in contrast, will betray Jesus.

When people are approached from a Teacher viewpoint, then the *names* of people are significant, just as a name such as physician or plumber is more important than the physical appearance of a person when one is interacting with people from the Teacher viewpoint of functionality. It is interesting that the name Judas means *praise*. Praise is a Mercy response that focuses upon the emotional status of some individual. Praise flows naturally from the religious attitudes of fervor, self-denial, and transcendence: "God, I worship you with all of my being, I am nothing compared to you, you are incomprehensibly wonderful." However, I suggest that praise also has a natural tendency to betray incarnation because it focuses upon experiences and people rather than being guided by a Teacher understanding of 'how things work'.

One can see that throughout this entire exchange that Jesus is trying to get his audience to stop fixating upon concrete objects and physical actions in order to look at the Platonic form and Teacher understanding that lie behind the physical symbol. In other words, the context of this passage does not appear to support the concept of transubstantiation, and Jesus seems to be doing his best to wean his audience from the Mercy fixation upon physical objects that is epitomized by Eucharist adoration.

The danger of viewing incarnation from the Mercy perspective of holy objects rather than from the Teacher perspective of verbal understanding is also brought out in the passage that immediately follows. We will look at the version described in the gospel of Luke. The event known as the *Transfiguration* occurs about one week after this dialogue between Jesus and the crowd.

> Some eight days after these sayings, He took along Peter and John and James, and went up on the mountain to pray. And while He was praying, the appearance of His face became different, and His clothing became white and gleaming. And behold, two men were talking with Him; and they were Moses and Elijah, who, appearing in glory, were speaking of His departure which He was about to accomplish at Jerusalem. Now Peter and his companions had been overcome with sleep; but when they were fully awake, they saw His glory and the two men standing with Him. And as these were leaving Him, Peter said to Jesus, "Master, it is good for us to be here; let us make three tabernacles: one for You, and one for Moses, and one for Elijah"—not realizing what he was saying. While he was saying this, a cloud formed and began to overshadow them; and they were afraid as they entered the cloud. Then a voice came out of the cloud, saying, "This is My Son, My Chosen One; listen to Him!" (Luke 9:28-35).

Here we have a truly transcendental experience being described, in which Jesus starts glowing and he talks with two (dead) living legends of Judaism. Whether this incident describes myth or reality, I suggest that the various responses are significant. Peter is sleeping, implying that Perceiver thought has been overwhelmed by the emotional intensity of the Mercy experience. We can tell that Perceiver thought is not functioning properly because Peter does not 'realize what he is saying'. In his semi-mesmerized state, Peter mumbles that they should build three chapels of adoration, one for each Mercy expert. Immediately, clarity is replaced by fear, as Perceiver thought gives way to Mercy emotions. This is followed by a *voice* saying that it is the *source* of incarnation and that they should *listen* to incarnation, indicating that Contributor incarnation is based in Teacher words and that one should approach incarnation from a Teacher perspective.

This transition from viewing God and incarnation from a *Mercy* perspective to viewing God and incarnation from a *Teacher* perspective is also portrayed in the book of Revelation. Many of us are familiar with the passage in the book of Revelation that describes endless worship before the throne of God, and heaven is often viewed as a place where one sits on clouds with wings playing harps and worshiping God.

> And the four living creatures, each one of them having six wings, are full of eyes around and within; and day and night they do not cease to say, "Holy, holy, holy is the Lord God, the Almighty, who was and who is and who is to come." And when the living creatures give glory and honor and thanks to Him who sits on the throne, to Him who lives forever and ever, the twenty-four elders will fall down before Him who sits on the throne, and will worship Him who lives forever and ever, and will cast their crowns before the throne (Revelation 4:8-10).

However, that quote occurs at the *beginning* of the book. Further on, we are told

> Then I looked, and behold, the Lamb *was* standing on Mount Zion, and with Him one hundred and forty-four thousand, having His name and the name of His Father written on their foreheads. And I heard a voice from heaven, like the sound of many waters and like the sound of loud thunder, and the voice which I heard *was* like *the sound* of harpists playing on their harps. And they sang a new song before the throne and before the four living creatures and the elders; and no one could learn the song except the one hundred and forty-four thousand who had been purchased from the earth. These are the ones who have not been defiled with women, for they have kept themselves chaste. These *are* the ones who follow the Lamb wherever He goes. These have been purchased from among men as first fruits to God and to the Lamb. And no lie was found in their mouth; they are blameless (Revelation 14:1-5).

Many groups, interpreting this from a purely concrete perspective, have claimed to be the chosen 144,000. However, I suggest that what matters are the cognitive principles being portrayed. Jesus and his followers all have the name of Jesus and the name of God written on foreheads, symbolizing that their minds are being guided by a Teacher-based understanding of incarnation and God. This leads to a 'new song' which those who have a Mercy fixation upon worship are incapable of singing. These new individuals have not 'defiled themselves' with emotional tricks and they have not become emotionally snared by the current culture.[1] And instead of bowing before God passively, they actively follow Contributor incarnation, and Teacher thought within their minds is guided by Perceiver honesty.

The end of the book of Revelation talks about the New Jerusalem. It descends from the heaven of Teacher thought to the earth of Server action, a more general form of the

[1] Female thought emphasizes emotions. Female thought is good. Emotions are good. Playing emotional tricks, such as the ones that we have examined in this book, is not good. Hence, *defiled* with women'. The word 'chaste' (parthenos) describes a virgin *woman*, but here it is in the *male* plural. This implies a cognitive 'virginity' of not being 'married' to the existing worship-driven culture. In other words, they have not 'sold their souls' to the system.

word being made flesh in incarnation. It is a *city* in which all human activity is guided by a general Teacher understanding of God. And for the author of Revelation, it is currently an invisible Platonic form that can only be seen 'spiritually' by taking a general perspective.

> And he carried me away in the Spirit to a great and high mountain, and showed me the holy city, Jerusalem, coming down out of heaven from God, having the glory of God (Revelation 20:10).

In the New Jerusalem, there is no longer any Mercy focus upon Temple worship. Instead, all of existence is guided by the light of a general Teacher theory and Contributor incarnation. This needs to be repeated. In the New Jerusalem, God and incarnation are no longer associated with specific Mercy holy objects. Instead, God and incarnation provide a universal illumination for all of normal life.

> I saw no temple in it, for the Lord God the Almighty and the Lamb are its temple. And the city has no need of the sun or of the moon to shine on it, for the glory of God has illumined it, and its lamp *is* the Lamb (Revelation 20:22-23).

One finds a similar message in the book of Malachi, the last book of prophecy in the Jewish Bible (or Christian Old Testament), written just before the time when science could have emerged in Alexandria.

> "Oh that there were one among you who would shut the gates, that you might not uselessly kindle fire on My altar! I am not pleased with you," says the LORD of hosts, "nor will I accept an offering from you. For from the rising of the sun even to its setting, My name will be great among the nations, and in every place incense is going to be offered to My name, and a grain offering that is pure; for My name will be great among the nations," says the LORD of hosts (Mal. 1:10-11).

Stated bluntly, God is tired of praise and he wishes that someone would shut the doors of the temple and stop the Mercy fixation upon God. Instead, God wants to be associated with a universal Teacher name that is honored in all cultures. But that breakthrough did not happen.

> Jesus would have had a more receptive audience if science had emerged in Alexandria.

In conclusion, the contrast between the *Teacher* emphasis of biblical passages and the *Mercy* emphasis of early branches of Christianity supports the hypothesis that the Bible describes an abstract theory of cognition that was initially revealed to a group of people that had only a limited ability to use abstract thought. It is as if a college physics textbook was given to a group of kindergarten students. These students have now grown up and are capable of understanding college physics. In other words, Orthodox and Catholic scholars *do* use abstract thought to analyze Christian practice and doctrine today. But what is generally being analyzed is not the college physics textbook, but rather the physics textbook *as viewed through the eyes of kindergarten students*.

Looking at this more generally, one can see that it would have been better for science to have been invented before the coming of incarnation, because incarnation could have *extended* from a Teacher understanding of how the world works to a Teacher understanding of how the mind works. Incarnation would still have had to go through a plan of rebirth in order to bridge the gap between transforming things and transforming people, but at least the gap between concrete experiences and abstract thought would not have existed, the current division between religion and science would also not exist, and we would probably be living in Utopia, because mentally transformed people would be inhabiting a transformed world.

Extending Incarnation

In the same way that an inventor extends the original invention of science and technology, so I suggest that the religious inventor extends the atonement of Jesus. Paul describes this at the beginning of the book of Colossians. He prefaces this passage by describing incarnation. This description is typically viewed as a collection of superlatives by which Paul is attempting to worship and praise Jesus. However, I suggest that it is actually a technically accurate description of Contributor incarnation.

> For He rescued us from the domain of darkness, and transferred us to the kingdom of His beloved Son, in whom we have redemption, the forgiveness of sins. He is the image of the invisible God, the firstborn of all creation. For by Him all things were created, *both* in the heavens and on earth, visible and invisible, whether thrones or dominions or rulers or authorities—all things have been created through Him and for Him. He is before all things, and in Him all things hold together. He is also head of the body, the church; and He is the beginning, the firstborn from the dead, so that He Himself will come to have first place in everything. For it was the *Father's* good pleasure for all the fullness to dwell in Him, and through Him to reconcile all things to Himself, having made peace through the blood of His cross; through Him, *I say*, whether things on earth or things in heaven (Col. 1:13-20).

Paul begins by saying that people are being transferred in Teacher thought from a domain that lacks general understanding to one that is ruled by Contributor incarnation and that this transfer leads to a state in which one feels forgiven by God. This is consistent with our earlier analysis of the Christian prayer of salvation. Contributor incarnation is the 'image of the invisible God'. Using cognitive language, the structure of abstract Contributor thought accurately reproduces the content of the general Teacher concept of God. But Contributor incarnation translates a general Teacher theory that cannot be seen into concrete images that can be seen. As science has discovered, Contributor incarnation guided by general Teacher understanding appears to govern all of physical creation. Contributor incarnation applies to both the heavens of abstract thought and the earth of concrete thought, both the visible realm of the physical world and the invisible realm of the mind. Contributor thought can be used both to understand how everything was originally put together as well as how to function within this structure.

Continuing on from the phrase 'head of the body', Contributor incarnation makes it possible for a new group of people to emerge who experience the rebirth of personal transformation. That is because Mercy identity can be reconciled with universal Teacher understanding through Contributor incarnation. In order to set up this reconciliation, Contributor incarnation has to go through rebirth. Finally, this reconciliation affects both abstract thought and concrete thought.

We now reach the passage where Paul talks about extending the atonement of Jesus.

> Although you were formerly alienated and hostile in mind, engaged in evil deeds, yet He has now reconciled you in His fleshly body through death, in order to present you before Him holy and blameless and beyond reproach—if indeed you continue in the faith firmly established and steadfast, and not moved away from the hope of the gospel that you have heard, which was proclaimed in all creation under heaven, and of which I, Paul, was made a minister. Now I rejoice in my sufferings for your sake, and in my flesh I do my share on behalf of His body, which is the church, in filling up what is lacking in Christ's afflictions. Of this church I was made a minister according to the stewardship from God bestowed on me for your benefit, so that I might fully carry out the preaching of the word of God, that is, the mystery which has been hidden from the past ages and generations, but has now been manifested to His saints, to whom God willed to make known what is the riches of the glory of this mystery among the Gentiles, which is Christ in you, the hope of glory (Col. 1:21-27).

Paul's audience was governed by childish MMNs that fought one another and opposed Teacher understanding, but they can now be consumers of the salvation that Jesus has invented. The goal is not for them to remain passive consumers, but rather to become governed by Teacher understanding. This transformation will occur if they hold on to Perceiver facts and continue to be guided by Platonic forms based in a verbal theory (proclaimed) that comes from abstract thought (heaven) that applies to all of concrete thought (creation).

Paul is also a religious inventor who is extending the invention of Jesus. On the one hand, inventing is painful. On the other hand, inventions help consumers. Paul is being guided by general Teacher understanding to share a verbal theory about God. This Teacher approach to God used to be a mystery that was hidden from people, but it is now apparent to those who are being guided by Teacher understanding. In the words of N.T. Wright, Paul invented theology. This Teacher understanding will lead to a combination of Platonic forms and an internal concept of incarnation that makes it possible to transform the world. Translating this paragraph into the language of science, natural law used to be a mystery that was hidden from people, but it is now apparent to those who are being guided by Teacher understanding. The Teacher understanding of natural law leads to the Platonic form of a better world which the Contributor incarnation of technology makes it possible to realize. Notice how Paul's concept of mystery is totally different than the mystery of mysticism, because Paul is explaining what *used* to be a mystery, whereas mysticism insists that ultimate knowledge is a mystery that *remains* inexplicable.

How Does God Benefit?

We have looked at Contributor incarnation from a human viewpoint and have concluded that childish identity is too flawed to develop an adequate concept of Contributor incarnation. Therefore the process of cognitive development needs to be jump-started from some Teacher source. Saying this another way, the school of incarnation needs to be founded by some non-human, Teacher-based being. We have also looked at cognitive development from the viewpoint of divine sovereignty as well as noting some interesting patterns regarding the birth of science. But we have not looked at this process from *God's* perspective. We have seen why man needs help from God, and we have discussed how God might help man. However, what benefit would there be for God? Saying this more specifically, we saw at the beginning of this chapter that if Contributor incarnation is to save humanity, then incarnation must go through a plan of rebirth in Mercy thought and be recognized as a universal theory in Teacher thought. But why would God want to save humanity? Taking one step back, if God created humanity, then why would God create humans in such a manner that humans would need salvation? Stated bluntly, why would God set himself up for failure?

Traditionally, the answer to this question has typically been guided by the religious attitude. Fervor implies that God is utterly complete and does not need anything from humanity. Self-denial suggests that God provides the ultimate example of self-denial. Therefore, God chose to save humanity as an expression of eternal, selfless love. Finally, transcendence suggests that this question is ultimately unanswerable because the ways of God are inscrutable.

While it may be presumptuous to attempt to determine the motivations of a universal being, it is possible to analyze how a mental concept of incarnation benefits a mental concept of God and then postulate that this might also apply to a real God. After all, *all* social interaction is based upon Theory of Mind in which one uses mental networks within one's own mind in order to guess what is happening within the mind of another person. Therefore, we are simply applying Theory of Mind to the topic of God, guided by the divine righteousness of 'how the mind works'.

My mental concept of God has undergone two major shifts, the first several years ago, and the second just recently. These transitions did not occur overnight and did not come easily, but rather involved major restructuring of core mental networks that triggered feelings of existential angst. That is because transforming a mental concept of God means rebuilding a general Teacher theory that applies to personal identity.

The first transition was from a concept of God based in words to one rooted in 'how things work'. I grew up in a conservative Mennonite home and attended Sunday school as a child. Developing the theory of mental symmetry caused a mental concept of God to form within my mind, and this new concept of God threatened the existence of the concept of God I had acquired from my Mennonite upbringing. The conflict was not over religious doctrine. As we have seen both in this chapter and in this book, the theory of mental symmetry is remarkably consistent with Christian doctrine. However, there was a major conflict over religious attitude, involving questions such as "Who am I to think that I can analyze God and religion? How dare I question the conclusions of religious authorities? Why should I focus upon myself instead of God?" When a mental network is threatened, then it will respond with intense pain. When the existence of a mental network that represents a universal being is threatened, then this mental network will respond with feelings of intense *universal* pain. Using religious language, questioning a mental concept of God will lead to feelings of eternal damnation. Suppressing an inadequate concept of God is not the solution because that will merely intensify the feelings of eternal damnation being broadcast by the threatened mental network representing God.

In order to transform a mental concept of God, one must demonstrate to Teacher thought that the existing mental concept of God is *not* universal and provide an alternative Teacher understanding that *is* universal. If one continues to do this for an *extended* period of time in *many* different contexts, then this will *gradually* transform a mental concept of God. I use the words 'extended', 'many', and 'gradually' because one is attempting as a finite creature who can only deal with one context at a time to transform a universal theory that applies to all contexts.

First, a concept of God that is based in a holy book cannot be universal, because a book is only a finite object, and it is not possible for a finite object to contain all truth. A holy book could contain the essence of truth, but this truth must still be universalized by comparing the content of the holy book with other facts and theories. Applying this to Christianity, it appears that the Bible contains *accurate* cognitive truth. But this truth will only become universal if it is *translated* into nonreligious language. Second, a concept of God that is based in words can only be a *description* of universal understanding. In order to gain a truly universal understanding, one must go beyond mere words to include what the words are describing. It appears that the Bible provides a general description of 'how the mind works'. But this verbal description only becomes universal if it is connected with the actual functioning of the mind. The first principle uses Perceiver thought to extend a verbal concept of God while the second uses Server thought. The first replaces the MMNs of religious culture with the TMN of a general understanding while the second replaces the verbal logic of philosophy with the exemplars of science.

These two principles are not just theoretical constructs but rather fundamental principles that brought me through the angst of transforming my fundamentalist concept of

God. Whenever I felt condemned to hell, these principles convinced Teacher thought that my research was actually constructing a mental concept of God and not blaspheming it. And when Teacher thought felt reassured, then it would stop broadcasting its message of eternal personal damnation. This reassurance worked because I really *was* building a general Teacher understanding and not just using emotional tricks to fool Teacher thought.

Remember that a Teacher theory will feel universal to Teacher thought as long as it does not encounter any counterexamples, just as a tribal chieftain can claim to be ruler over the entire inhabited world as long as he is unaware of any other tribes. Therefore, a concept of God that is based in a holy book will feel universal if it applies to a religious subculture that is distinct from the 'outside world'. The angst of rebuilding a fundamentalist concept of God can be minimized by breaking down the walls that separate the religious ghetto from normal life *one wall at a time* and then using rational thought to think through the questions that will arise. Even better, one can replace the emotional 'stick' of tearing down walls with the emotional 'carrot' of building bridges and applying understanding. Using Perceiver thought to build bridges between religious and secular truth, as exemplified by Habermas' second stage, and using Server thought to apply a Teacher understanding, as illustrated by the exemplars of science, will automatically make a fundamentalist concept of God appear inadequate, just as buying a new computer will make one's existing computer feel out-of-date. Attempting to transform a mental concept of God is not a trivial task, and if steps are not continually taken to try to minimize the emotional discomfort, then the power of the mental networks will become so great that free will will be overwhelmed. In other words, one will start the journey and be unable to finish it. One could compare this to the task of rebuilding a house in which one lives. It can be done if the transformation occurs one room at a time. However, if too many rooms are torn apart then the entire edifice will come crumbling down making further progress impossible.

Following this process to its completion will result in an adequate mental concept of God. As a finite human, is impossible to construct a truly universal concept of God, but it is possible to build a mental concept of God that is sufficiently universal. This provides us with a possible reason why a *real* universal God would send incarnation. When 'the word becomes flesh and dwells among men' then Teacher words expand to include Server actions and Perceiver facts become universalized. The end result is a general Teacher theory with *increased* universality.

Let us move on now to the second transition that occurred within my mental concept of God. My description may be incomplete because I am still going through this process. The first transition leads to an adequate mental concept of God, but God is still seen as someone who 'lives in heaven'. When one studies or thinks about God one feels that one is doing something different than normal research, and when one follows God one feels that one is acting in a way that is different than normal life. This tension is natural because the first transition will lead to a mental concept of God that is *distinct* from the mental networks of family, culture, and accepted thought. Saying this another way, one is continually choosing to 'follow God rather than man'. However, each time that one chooses to follow God rather than man, the mental grid of Perceiver facts and Server sequences held together by a general Teacher understanding grows. Eventually this leads to a totally different view of reality. As Kuhn describes with his concept of incommensurability, one literally sees the world through a different set of glasses. Instead of seeing 'following God' as something that is opposed to 'following man' or viewing religion as something that fights scientism, one begins to see all of these aspects as pieces of a large puzzle, and one realizes that the problem is not with the puzzle pieces themselves but rather with how these pieces are being assembled.

When one views life through this new mental grid of Perceiver facts and Server sequences, then the puzzle pieces of life reassemble themselves to form a coherent picture that is consistent with the mental concept of a universal God. The primary goal then is no longer to proclaim fundamentalist truth to the unbeliever, or to convince people to follow God rather than man, but rather to help people to untwist skewed priorities.

What drives this mental transition is the frustration of continually following an invisible kingdom of God that refuses to appear—trying to pursue Platonic forms while being forced to continue existing within imperfect reality. One gradually realizes that Platonic forms are *not* distinct from reality. Platonic forms may be invisible concepts that do not exist in real life, but they are formed by idealizing experiences that do exist and they are realized by rearranging existing experiences. This is different than the suggestion that heaven does not exist and that the goal is to improve human society until Earth gradually becomes paradise. But it is also different than the suggestion that the goal is to abandon earth and live in heaven. Instead, one transforms earth by first building a heaven of non-material Platonic forms and then bringing this heaven down to earth in order to rearrange and perfect the puzzle pieces of human existence. When this happens, then 'God dwells with man' and the distinction between religious and secular vanishes. Instead, religion becomes viewed as taking secular pieces and putting them together in a way that fits.

That is what one finds portrayed at the end of the book of Revelation in the New Jerusalem. Since we have already discussed this passage, we will focus here upon aspects that were not mentioned earlier.

> Then I saw a new heaven and a new earth; for the first heaven and the first earth passed away, and there is no longer any sea. And I saw the holy city, new Jerusalem, coming down out of heaven from God, made ready as a bride adorned for her husband. And I heard a loud voice from the throne, saying, "Behold, the tabernacle of God is among men, and He will dwell among them, and they shall be His people, and God Himself will be among them" (Rev. 21:1-4).

The context for the New Jerusalem is a new grid of existence, a new 'heaven and earth' which no longer contains the 'sea' of raw Mercy experiences. The New Jerusalem comes 'out of heaven from God' indicating that its source is universal Teacher thought. But this holy city itself is something beautiful that expresses Teacher order-within-complexity. The result is that 'God himself will be among them'.

Skipping ahead to the end of the chapter,

> I saw no temple in it, for the Lord God the Almighty and the Lamb are its temple. And the city has no need of the sun or of the moon to shine on it, for the glory of God has illumined it, and its lamp is the Lamb. The nations will walk by its light, and the kings of the earth will bring their glory into it. In the daytime (for there will be no night there) its gates will never be closed; and they will bring the glory and the honor of the nations into it; and nothing unclean, and no one who practices abomination and lying, shall ever come into it, but only those whose names are written in the Lamb's book of life (Rev. 21:22-27).

As was mentioned earlier, there is no longer a need for religion because a concept of God governs all of human existence. There is no longer a barrier between following God and living in the world—the gates of the city are never closed. Instead, the new Jerusalem acts as a Platonic form that guides the normal experiences of human existence that occur outside of the city, while the best of the 'puzzle pieces' that are generated outside of the city within normal existence are brought into the city to be assembled. Nothing enters the city that threatens this purity (the word 'unclean' is usually translated 'to defile'), and no person enters who is driven by childish MMNs (the word *bdelugma* translated 'abomination' means 'related to idols and idolatry') or who disables Perceiver thought (lying).

Tying this in with what was mentioned previously about consumers, hackers, and inventors, one sees here that some are living as religious consumers, experiencing the benefits of the holy city from a distance, others are like religious hackers trading with the city, while the religious inventors live in the city.

Viewing this all from the perspective of God, why would a universal being want to 'dwell with humans'? Because this leads to *multifaceted* order-within-complexity, a type of fractal beauty in which facets of the overall structure reveal miniature versions of the universal theory. The Mandelbrot set provides an illustration of what this means. Every single pixel within the Mandelbrot set is generated by the simple Teacher equation $z_{new} = z^2 + c$. And yet, this three variable equation is capable of generating a beautiful picture of incredible multifaceted complexity in which one can zoom in and repeatedly encounter variations of the overall shape.

Summarizing, a mental concept of God that is based in a verbal theory may feel universal but it is merely a description of a general theory presented in a single language. In order to make this concept of God truly universal, one must go beyond words to actions and one must translate religious speech into the language of other specializations.

Going further, a mental concept of God acquires multifaceted order-within-complexity when people and objects live within the grid of a universal concept of God. These two transformations can occur internally with a mental concept of God, and the Bible claims that the first transformation occurred when the 'word was made flesh' and that the second transformation will occur when 'the new Jerusalem descends to earth from heaven'.

While my concept of God has undergone two major shifts, the fundamental content of my concept of God has remained unaltered. Discovering the theory of mental symmetry completely transformed my view of God, as did applying this theory. However, neither of these transformations led to a *different* God but rather to a different view of the *same* God. This distinction is significant because theologians over the centuries have struggled over how a God can both change and be unchanging. Cognitively speaking, it is possible to completely transform the mental structure that holds together a concept of God without altering the essential characteristics of God.

✳ 14. Apocalypse and Rebirth

We have divided the process of personal salvation into the three stages of *truth*, *righteousness*, and *rebirth*. Truth uses Perceiver facts to construct a general Teacher understanding, righteousness adds Server actions to this Teacher understanding, and rebirth places personal identity within the mental structure that was constructed during the previous two stages. These three stages are ultimately based in an understanding of how the *mind* works.

A similar sequence of three stages occurred during the development of science and technology, guided by an understanding of how the *world* works. During the *scientific* revolution, Perceiver facts about the natural world were used to build a general Teacher understanding of natural law. Habermas' second stage describes the development of Perceiver thought in Europe at this time. During the *industrial* revolution, this Teacher understanding transformed Server actions. Instead of being handcrafted by artisans, objects were made in factories using machines (and by treating workers as machines). During the *consumer* revolution, everyday life was transformed by the development of consumer gadgets.

I suggest that the three stages of truth, righteousness, and rebirth each need to be accompanied by a corresponding transformation in a concept of God. I described in the previous chapter how a mental concept of God can be transformed, and illustrated this by describing two transformations that my concept of God has undergone. However, I did not mention a third transformation that *precedes* the other two. I grew up in a fundamentalist environment. The underlying assumption of fundamentalism is that truth about God is revealed through verbal revelation. For tribal religions, God is revealed through Mercy experiences and not through Teacher words. Words may be used, but they play a secondary role to rituals and religious experiences. In contrast, a religion of the book is based upon the words and doctrines of a holy book.

If one wishes to pursue the first stage of truth, then one must first believe that knowledge about God can be found in absolute, verbal truth. Saying this another way, the fundamentalist concept of a God of absolute truth is *sufficient* to practice the first stage of truth. One can study the doctrines that are revealed in a holy book or textbook and then use rational thought to fit these facts together into a general Teacher theory. This describes the type of thinking that is typically found in disciplines such as theology, math, and philosophy, because experts are quoted and verbal structures are generated. Saying this more generally, it is possible to start with a set of facts that have been revealed by experts and then use abstract technical thought to manipulate these facts in a logically coherent manner.

If one wishes to move on to the second stage of righteousness, then one must transform one's concept of God from being based in absolute, verbal truth to being based in 'how things work'. Using the language of Kuhn, one must move from philosophy to science, from verbal theories to exemplars. The reason for this is simple. In order to act in a manner that is consistent with the character of God, one must first construct a concept of a God that is based in general Server sequences. In order to behave like God, one must first gain an understanding of how God behaves, which is only possible if one believes that God behaves.

If one attempts to pursue righteousness with a concept of God that is based in *revealed* truth, then the result will not be righteousness but rather obedience and/or human righteousness. Suppose that one attempts to obey the words of the holy book. This may look like righteousness because Teacher words are leading to Server actions, but there is no general understanding associated with these Teacher words. As a result, the emphasis will be upon applying words that give specific commands or instructions, while ignoring words that describe general principles. Because no single book can give specific instructions that apply to all situations at all times, and because an understanding of universal truth is lacking, the instructions of the holy book will have to be extended and interpreted by religious experts. Thus, what began as performing Server actions guided by the Teacher words of the holy book will gradually mutate into performing Server actions that are guided by the Teacher words of religious experts with Mercy status. Over time, this will lead to human righteousness based upon 'how we do things'. Summarizing, obedience will focus upon specifics because of a lack of understanding, obedience will have to be supplemented with the opinions of experts, which will eventually lead to the human righteousness of religious tradition.

In order to escape from this mindset, one must question the interpretations of the religious experts and compare what the holy book says with research being done by non-religious experts. And one must choose to follow the divine righteousness of how things work rather than the human righteousness of religious tradition. The temptation will be to reject the holy book and to rebel from religious tradition. However, we have seen in this book that the content of the Bible does appear to describe the divine righteousness of 'how the mind works'. Therefore, when comparing biblical truth with secular research, it is important to read the biblical text carefully without automatically accepting—or rejecting—how religious experts say that this text should be interpreted. Similarly, when attempting to determine 'how things work' one should not automatically reject religious tradition but rather view it as a general equation that has been placed within the straitjacket of a specific culture. As science illustrates, general equations can only be learned by applying them in some specific manner. But this specific manner needs to be regarded as an exemplar that is *one* way of carrying out a general principle, rather than as a religious tradition that is the *only* way of carrying out this general principle.

I suggest that these three transformations in a concept of God accompanied the scientific revolution, industrial revolution, and consumer revolution. The first transformation occurred with the introduction of Christianity, the first religion to be based in theology. This transformation *preceded* the scientific revolution. The Christian concept of God and religion was radically different than the popular concept of religion at that time. As N.T. Wright says,

> Ando offers two summary statements of what, in this broad sense, 'Roman religion' was all about. It was, he says, "a system of embedded symbols and social actions of their institutionalization"; or, approaching the same result from another angle, it was "a set of practices developed in response to the gods' immanence and action in the world". What we can call, loosely and heuristically, the 'religion' of Paul's world was not set apart from the rest of ancient culture. On the contrary: it was its beating heart, with every part of the body politic related to that heart by active and throbbing blood vessels. If the world was full of gods, the world was also therefore full of religion, full of cult; full of god-soaked culture (Wright, 2013).

That describes a view of God and religion that is firmly enmeshed in the MMNs of culture. What Christianity introduced was something so different that it was regarded more as a kind of philosophy than a religion. Quoting again from N.T. Wright,

> From Paul onwards the Christians did three things which in the ancient world would have been associated, not with religion, but precisely with philosophy. First, they presented a case for a different order of reality, divine reality which cut across the normal assumptions. They told stories about a creator God and the world, stories which had points of intersection with things that the pagan said about god(s) and the world but which started and finished in different places and included necessary but unprecedented elements in the middle. Second, they argued for, and themselves modelled, a particular way of life, a way which would before long be a cause of remark, sometimes curious and sometimes hostile, among their neighbours. Third, they constructed and maintained communities which ignored the normal ties of kinship, local or geographical identity, or language – not to mention gender or class... To people of his day, he and his communities would have looked more like a new school of philosophy than a type of religion. A strange philosophy, of course, with unexpected and even disturbing features. But a philosophical school none the less (p.345).

Wright's first point describes a paradigm shift in which existing elements are viewed from a totally new general perspective. The second point tells us that personal identity in Mercy thought is being governed by this new way of thinking. The third point indicates that this new way of thinking and behaving is causing existing MMNs of culture to be questioned. Finally, Wright states that Christianity would have appeared more like a Teacher-based system of philosophy than any Mercy-based religion of that day.

Moving on to the second stage of righteousness, James Smith describes the transformation in a mental concept of God that *followed* the scientific revolution.

> The medieval conviction of God as First Cause underlying all cosmological or secondary causes fed into the early modern theory of God's acting uniformly in all things. Underneath this specifically theological notion were developments in the sciences regarding the uniformity of nature. The scientific revolution during the early modern period nurtured a growing awareness in the Western world that there were universal natural laws at work that ordered the movements of the world and its parts... Against this backdrop, the deists suggested the watchmaker analogy: just as watches are set in motion by watchmakers, after which they operate according to their pre-established mechanisms, so also was the world begun by the God as Creator, after which it and all its parts have operated according to their pre-established natural laws. With these laws in [sic] perfectly in place, events have unfolded according to the prescribed plan, with no need for God to intervene (Smith & Yong, 2010).

God is being viewed here from a theoretical perspective as someone who 'acts uniformly in all things'. This describes a concept of God based in a universal understanding of 'how things work'. Using scientific language, there are 'universal natural laws at work that order the movements of the world and its parts'. This led to a transformed concept of God based in the 'watchmaker analogy'.

Apocalypse

That brings us to the third stage of rebirth and the transformation in a concept of God that accompanies it. In brief, I suggest that rebirth is a by-product of *apocalypse*. The word apocalypse means 'unveiling'. An apocalypse is not just the unveiling of some specific object or person in *Mercy* thought but rather the unveiling of a new general regime in *Teacher* thought that affects *all* specific objects and people in Mercy thought in a profound way. It is the unveiling of a light that shines upon everything, and because it illumines everything, all childish MMNs have no choice but to be transformed because they are caught in the light like cockroaches with no place to hide. Using religious language, personal identity encounters the TMN of a universal concept of God. King David described what this feels like.

> O LORD, You have searched me and known me. You know when I sit down and when I rise up; You understand my thought from afar. You scrutinize my path and my lying down, and are intimately acquainted with all my ways. Even before there is a word on my tongue, behold, O LORD, You know it all. You have enclosed me behind and before, and laid Your hand upon me. Such knowledge is too wonderful for me; it is too high, I cannot attain to it. Where can I go from Your Spirit? Or where can I flee from Your presence? If I ascend to heaven, You

are there; If I make my bed in Sheol, behold, You are there. If I take the wings of the dawn, if I dwell in the remotest part of the sea, even there Your hand will lead me, and Your right hand will lay hold of me. If I say, "Surely the darkness will overwhelm me, and the light around me will be night," even the darkness is not dark to You, and the night is as bright as the day. Darkness and light are alike to You. For You formed my inward parts; You wove me in my mother's womb (Ps. 139:1-13).

David is describing a concept of God that applies to the details of personal identity, including both Teacher words and Server sequences, internal thought and external action. This leads to a TMN that is much bigger than the MMNs of personal identity, which imposes its structure upon personal identity. This general Teacher understanding leads to the Platonic form of a concept of the Holy Spirit that is similarly universal. David feels like a cockroach that is caught in the light which is trying to scurry into some place of darkness where the light does not shine. However, wherever David goes, the Teacher light of understanding and the Mercy light of Platonic forms still shine. The text also suggests that David has learned that a concept of God is connected in some way with how his internal being functions: 'You formed my inward parts; you wove me in my mother's womb'.

> Stage one of truth assumes a God of fundamentalism revealed in written words.
> Stage two of righteousness assumes a righteous God based in how things work.
> Stage three of rebirth assumes a universal God revealed through apocalypse.

The first two stages of truth and righteousness have already been discussed in some detail. Therefore, we will take the rest of this chapter to focus upon the third stage. The BBC put out a video series on World War I in 1964, entitled *The Great War*, that describes the relationship between apocalypse and rebirth (The Great War - Complete BBC Series, 1964).

What made this war both inevitable and ferocious was the combination of peripheral intelligence and core childishness. On the one hand, European society was still being guided by the traditional MMNs of nobility, religion, patriotism, and culture, while on the other hand, the physical environment was being transformed by the TMN of science and technology. As was mentioned before, the First World War was the first modern war. The primary shift in worldview occurred in 1916 as a result of the two battles of Verdun and the Somme. Verdun was a *ten month* struggle in which the French continually sent in reinforcements in order to resist a German artillery-driven onslaught whose primary purpose was to 'bleed the French white'. 156,000 French soldiers and 143,000 German soldiers died in this extended conflict. The Somme was the British led counterattack that immediately followed, in which more than 1 million men were killed or wounded. It was in this battle that the tank was first used.

The British men who fought in the Somme were known as Lord Kitchener's army, composed of citizens who volunteered to replace the professional soldiers who had been killed in earlier battles. Quoting from the dialogue of this series,

> The men of 1916 were the men who had responded to Lord Kitchener's famous appeal... Standing there as privates were many men whom no other conceivable circumstances would have brought into the Army. Five hundred pounds-a-year businessman, stockbrokers, engineers, chemists, metallurgical experts, university and public-school men, medical students, journalists, schoolmasters, craftsmen, shop assistants, secretaries, and all sorts of classes. By the end of 1914, 1,186,337 men had joined the Army (episode 11).

The knowledge and skills of these individuals had been transformed by the *objective* understanding of science and technology, leading to individuals with technical and business expertise. However, the core of these peoples' minds was still driven by MMNs of loyalty to God and country, and when these MMNs demanded their obedience, they submitted en masse.

Submission to the MMNs of 'God and country' replaced the mental networks of civilization and individuality with a new set of ruling mental networks, based upon the *human* righteousness of military organization.

> "So far, we'd been individualists. So far, we'd been mommy's pet or something like that. We had a will of our own and it came rather hard, to start with, to obey commands. But gradually... we became a disciplined body of men." They learned the rituals of another way of life. They had all the eagerness in the world to impel their learning (episode 12).

But when soldiers entered the trenches, then they encountered a new type of TMN based in the *divine* righteousness of science and technology that had never before been encountered, and the unveiling of this new TMN obliterated existing MMNs of personal identity.

> Steadily, day by day, the Somme was transforming itself into what the Germans called the material battle, the battle of lead and iron against flesh, in which the destruction of the flesh seemed to lose all meaning. An officer wrote, "A man seemed to lose his identity as an individual. Divisions were swallowed up in corps and armies and from this point in the war one seemed no longer to regard death as individual. Reinforcements would arrive, one never knew their names, they disappeared so quickly through the gracing stations, or to swell the number of the little wooden crosses. The individual man was gone" (episode 13).

The TMN of 'the material battle' became personified as 'The Guns'.

> We are the guns and your masters. Saw ye our flashes? Heard ye the scream of our shells in the night and the shuddering crashes? Saw ye our work by the roadside, the shrouded things lying moaning to God that he made them? The maimed

and the dying, husbands or sons, fathers or lovers. We break them. We are the guns (episode 13).

This apocalypse caused all existing social mental networks to be rejected as insane.

How many have died like this without glory taken by surprise on their first day. They have given their life and nobody even knew their name. Hell cannot be so terrible as this. Humanity is mad. It must be mad to do what it is doing (episode 11).

Notice the cognitive progression. The core MMNs of status and culture originally motivated the war. The core MMNs of culture prompted citizens to enlist, the peripheral TMN of education made the citizen army good recruits, and military training attempted to enhance the MMNs of culture with the TMNs of human righteousness. But nobody realized the power of the TMN driving science and technology. Like any TMN, it attempted to rule anything and anyone that came into contact with it, turning war into total war. But this TMN was based in the divine righteousness of how the natural world functions. And nothing limited the growth of this TMN because the MMNs of culture and personal identity had been made subordinate to the empirical goal of occupying physical territory. This transformed the war from a struggle between the MMNs of different cultures and nations into a struggle between Teacher-driven technology and Mercy-driven flesh, a 'battle of lead and iron against flesh'.

> Living within an unveiling (or apocalypse) will force rebirth.

Because personal identity had become the servant of a general Teacher understanding that ignored personal identity, human individuality cease to exist; because this general Teacher understanding ignored humanity, applying this general understanding created an inhuman environment; and because people were forced to live in this Teacher created inhuman environment, it turned into a mental concept of God known as 'The Guns'. Not only did the ceaseless pounding of The Guns obliterate human flesh, but it turned the physical landscape into a shapeless mud filled with dead, rotting flesh.

What was unveiled during Verdun and the Somme was not just the Mercy power of some army or general but rather the new Teacher structure of the 'material war' with its general environment created by The Guns. War no longer consisted merely of specific battles that occurred at specific times but rather turned into an assembly line of destruction in which the meat grinder of The Guns was fed an unending stream of human fodder. This continued for month after month. This unending, remorseless, total, and universal change describes the unveiling of an apocalypse. In a *revolution*, the leaders change, but there is often little change in the structure of society. For the average person, everything continues as it was before. In other words, a new person is in charge in Mercy thought, but the Teacher structure is the same. In an apocalypse, the structure changes. Even if the same people are still in charge, everything is different. It is as if the law of gravity has been reversed and all objects now fall up instead of down.

Eventually, most of the French army mutinied against the repeated calls for them to 'give their utmost' and refused to fight further until the leadership instituted reforms such as leave, rest, and recreation that treated them as individuals and not just as cannon fodder.

What makes a divine apocalypse so terrifying is that it is based in 'how things work'. World War I was the first conflict in which people truly understood 'how the world works' and used this understanding to transform the physical environment. The result was a total, inescapable transformation of physical reality.

Internal unveiling occurs when a mental concept of God goes through the third transformation. This is when a concept of God comes down from heaven to earth and 'dwells among men'. The first two stages of truth and righteousness create a new internal world composed of the internal warp and woof of Perceiver truth and Server righteousness held together by the Teacher understanding of a mental concept of God. But this concept of God is still one step removed from personal identity. The rule of God is like a neighboring country that one goes to visit by practicing personal honesty and performing acts of righteousness. Practicing this truth and righteousness is essential because it creates the mental structure in which personal identity *could* live. But personal identity is not yet living in this mental structure. It is like a mansion in heaven that remains unoccupied. In order to live in this new mental structure *all* of the time and not just visit it, what is needed is an apocalypse, an unveiling that reveals the mental concept of God as a universal being who observes and governs all aspects of personal identity. Without such an apocalypse, it is not possible to fully transform the MMNs of culture, authority, and childhood. When a concept of God is unveiled, then personal transformation becomes inevitable and irresistible, just as flesh could not stand in its struggle with lead and iron.

Kuhn says that a new paradigm causes a person to view the physical world in an entirely different way. Similarly, an internal apocalypse does not change the external world, but it completely overturns one's view of the external world. However, an internal apocalypse is more than a paradigm shift. A paradigm shift is like *viewing* the world through new set of glasses; an internal apocalypse is like *experiencing* the world with a new set of senses.

Apocalypse does not have to be dreadful, but I suggest that it always will be full of dread; it is not always awful, but it is full of awe. Mysticism leads to the feeling that personal identity is being unified with God. Apocalypse leads to something far more substantial because personal identity finds itself living in an entirely new world governed by a new set of universal laws. The unveiling is full of awe because personal identity is encountering a new universal Teacher understanding, and it is full of dread because this new TMN has the power to completely crush the MMNs of personal identity.

This means that apocalypse always carries with it a divine judgment, because the MMNs of personal identity are being inexorably reshaped into a form that is consistent with the TMN behind the mental concept of God.

What the World War I soldier encountered was an *external* apocalypse, a new physical environment that was transformed by a Teacher understanding of natural law. Obviously, this destroyed the soldiers physically, but it also destroyed them *mentally* by overturning existing MMNs of culture, personal identity, and emotional status. This external apocalypse was made possible by the partial internal apocalypse that had *previously* occurred during the development of science and technology—in order to transform the physical environment, people first have to understand natural law.

An external apocalypse does not have to be physically destructive. For instance, when communism was replaced by capitalism, there was an infusion of new wealth and prosperity. But an external apocalypse will be destructive for those who have not first undergone an internal apocalypse. For example, the unveiling of capitalism had the deepest internal impact upon those who had grown up under communism and did not know how to function under capitalism, because their minds were governed by inadequate mental networks.

The apostle John describes the process of preparing internally for an external unveiling.

> Now, little children, abide in Him, so that when He appears, we may have confidence and not shrink away from Him in shame at His coming. If you know that He is righteous, you know that everyone also who practices righteousness is born of Him. See how great a love the Father has bestowed on us, that we would be called children of God; and such we are. For this reason the world does not know us, because it did not know Him. Beloved, now we are children of God, and it has not appeared as yet what we will be. We know that when He appears, we will be like Him, because we will see Him just as He is. And everyone who has this hope fixed on Him purifies himself, just as He is pure (1 John 2:28-3:3).

John says that an external unveiling will occur and that the natural response will be to scurry like cockroaches into the shadows. The solution involves two steps. First, one must construct a mental concept of God based in righteousness and one must practice righteousness. This describes the first transformation of a mental concept of God which enables the second stage of righteousness. Second, one must construct a mental concept of God that views people as 'children of God', finite beings whose inherent character is similar to the character of God. This describes the second transformation of a mental concept of God. When this type of person experiences an external apocalypse, then what 'shrinks away' is not the untransformed core of personal identity but rather the fragments of personal identity that remain untransformed. Such a person has a mental concept of a God that is 'pure', because it is based in universal characteristics that apply everywhere. This person will be driven by the 'hope' of a Platonic form that drives personal identity to become similarly pure. This attitude will appear incomprehensible to those who do not share this Teacher understanding—who do not 'know him', somewhat like a person in a communist country attempting to learn what it means to live as a capitalist in a country that has no concept of capitalism. (John was a Mercy person. The book of 1 John appears to describe the process of transformation from a Mercy viewpoint. This Mercy viewpoint is also apparent in the visual symbology of the book of Revelation.)

John describes in Revelation what it is like to experience an unveiling *without* having the appropriate internal content.

> I looked when He broke the sixth seal, and there was a great earthquake; and the sun became black as sackcloth made of hair, and the whole moon became like blood; and the stars of the sky fell to the earth, as a fig tree casts its unripe figs when shaken by a great wind. The sky was split apart like a scroll when it is rolled up, and every mountain and island were moved out of their places. Then the kings of the earth and the great men and the commanders and the rich and the strong and every slave and free man hid themselves in the caves and among the rocks of the mountains; and they said to the mountains and to the rocks, "Fall on us and hide us from the presence of Him who sits on the throne, and from the wrath of the Lamb; for the great day of their wrath has come, and who is able to stand?" (Rev. 6:12-17).

This describes in figurative language what it means to experience an apocalypse or divine unveiling that is based in a knowledge of 'how things work'. The new Teacher paradigm leads to a global shift in the existing landscape. The existing general Teacher understanding no longer provides emotional light but instead turns into a crude weaving of Perceiver facts and Server sequences. Lesser Teacher theories also fall from the sky and become part of the earth of general knowledge. The old understanding gradually disappears like the rolling up of a scroll. Existing authority figures in Mercy thought feel personally threatened by the new Teacher understanding, hide from the light, and search for certainty.

This accurately describes what the theory of mental symmetry has done within my mind. The light of fundamentalism that drove me as a child has turned into a simplistic structure of partially accurate Perceiver facts and Server sequences that no longer provides illumination. When I analyze the theories of academic luminaries, they end up fitting into the landscape of the theory of mental symmetry. This new understanding overwhelms the MMNs of culture and emotional status, and it continually grows at the expense of previous Teacher understanding.

That brings us back to the *Left Behind* series by LaHaye and Jenkins, in which they portray their interpretation of the book of Revelation. Does an apocalypse have to involve the type of physical destruction portrayed in this series of novels? In World War I it did. But what is being unveiled is *general* Teacher order and structure. The specific manner in which this is unveiled can vary.

The apocalypse of World War I was *awful* because what was unveiled was a general Teacher understanding of science that either ignored personal identity or else regarded it as unredeemably savage. Thus, humans found themselves thrust into an inhuman environment. The apocalypse was *dreadful* because this Teacher understanding was being revealed through a Contributor incarnation whose prime purpose was not the salvation of humans but rather the destruction of humanity. Saying this more simply, it was awful because fleshy humans were in awe of the power of lead and iron, and it was dreadful because human flesh was no match for lead and iron. Using the language of the book of Revelation, what was revealed was a divine beast brought to earth through an antichrist. This may sound like strong language, but one is taking the most potent human emotions that exist and combining them with a knowledge of 'how things work'.

In contrast, what is needed is a general Teacher understanding that includes personal identity, revealed through a Contributor incarnation whose prime purpose is to achieve personal wholeness rather than personal fragmentation, which is what we have been attempting to describe in this book.

Rebirth

The fundamental problem is that an apocalypse is needed, but one does not want the sort of apocalypse that occurred in World War I or that is described by fundamentalists such as Jenkins and LaHaye. Childish MMNs *are* fundamentally flawed and the only way to force them to be transformed is through the unveiling of a general Teacher understanding. This understanding will only have the power to *force* MMNs to change if it is based in how things work, it will only *free* people from existing cultural MMNs if how things work does not depend upon social status, and it will only lead to *rebirth* if it affects a person in a global manner.

One can see these principles illustrated by the rebirth—or lack of it—that occurred in different segments of society during World War I.

The average citizen experienced economic and political rebirth, because there was a massive unveiling of Teacher order-within-complexity: "In every country now the individual had become a cog in a huge and complex war machine. Whole new industries had been created since 1914" (episode 20).

Women gained political rights by becoming part of the new machinery of total war.

> There were no noncombatants in the total war. Everyone was drawn in, everyone was doing their bit. The war was insatiable. The men had marched away in millions and they had died in millions. Now women had to don service uniforms... Women gained an importance as part of the machinery of victory that they had never enjoyed in their own right. Total war, rather than Mrs. Pankhurst and her suffragettes, gave women the right to vote (episode 20).

The BBC documentary describes this rebirth in more detail.

Lloyd George told an audience, "It is a strange irony but no small compensation that the making of weapons of destruction should afford the occasion to humanize industry, yet such is the case. The older prejudices have vanished. New ideas are abroad. This opportunity must not be allowed to slip." It could not be allowed to slip. Victory depended on industry (episode 19).

Notice what is happening. The new war industry was based upon a Teacher understanding of 'how the world works'. Total war turned this industry into a universal Teacher driven structure that swallowed up workers and factories. But 'how the world works' is independent of personal opinion or personal status. A woman can manufacture an artillery shell or build an airplane engine as well as a man can. Therefore, the Teacher demands of total warfare forced people to let go of the Mercy 'older prejudices' based upon class and gender. This needs to be repeated. Women did not gain the right to vote primarily because of social struggle within *Mercy* thought *against* the MMNs of social pressure. Rather, they gained equality primarily because of the universal demands of a *Teacher* structure that was *independent* of the MMNs of social pressure. Thus, evidence from World War I does not support what Fairclough asserts in *Language and Power*.

Ironically, soldiers in the trenches, or least those who survived with body and mind intact, also experienced a form of cognitive rebirth. Even more than the factory worker at home, they were living in a totally new environment that had never existed before.

> It was impossible for the soldiers to communicate the truth about this war because nothing like it had ever happened before. Never had such vast armies wielding such an immense apparatus of killing, destruction, battle, fought each other for so long in one place (episode 19).

Obviously, living in this environment filled Mercy thought with experiences of unspeakable human suffering. All were traumatized and some were driven insane. But living in this new and horrible world also brought men together in a way that transcended normal life with its squabbling MMNs.

> Yet the Western front had its compensations. "The war years", said one British soldier who served there, "will stand out in the memories of vast numbers of those who fought as the happiest period of their lives." He went on. "In spite of all differences in rank, we were comrades, brothers dwelling together in amity. We were privileged to seen in each other that inner ennobled self which in the grim commercial struggle of peacetime is all too frequently atrophied for lack of expression. We could note the intense affection of soldiers for certain officers, their absolute trust in them. We saw the love passing the love of women, the one pal for his half section. We were privileged, in short, to see a reign of goodwill among men which the piping times of peace with all their organized charity, their free meals, free hospitals, and Sunday sermons have never equaled. Otherwise we could not have stuck it." The code of frontline behavior became the only one worth having. Hateful, disgusting, terrifying, the zone of the armies was

nevertheless the only place to be. "For my part, I am more glad of that experience than anything else I have known" (episode 19).

Again notice what is happening. The soldier is also living in an environment that is driven by 'how things work' which is independent of rank or social status. The flight of an artillery shell is guided purely by the laws of physics and it will maim or kill both officers and enlisted men with equal efficiency. Living within this environment mentally freed soldiers from the MMNs of culture and social status and turned them into brothers all governed by the common TMN of 'how things work'.

In contrast to the factory worker and the soldier at the front, the political and economic leaders at home did *not* experience rebirth. Instead, existing cultural MMNs became *intensified* by Teacher thought rather than transformed.

> This was a new kind of war whose scale dwarfed the traditional means to victory, victory by success on the battlefield. This was not a conflict of armies alone but a conflict of peoples, peoples armed with all the powers of modern industry and invention, peoples obsessed by a vision of total victory. They wished to stand triumphant over a smashed, crushed, humiliated, and prostrate foe. Desire for total victory rode the human soul and spurred it on. The mainspring of the world's catastrophe was the mind of man. Victory lay with he who conquered it. Propaganda became the deadliest of weapons and truth the first casualty... Government censorship in every country made sure that all news was slanted or suppressed... Government propaganda machines disseminated mental poison by the newest inventions of the 20th century—the cinema film, wireless telegraphy, faked photography. The unchecked, unproven atrocity story was one means by which the hatred was nourished among the home population... Relentlessly the enemy was portrayed as a monster of savagery, worthy only of hate. The message never varied. Hate, total hate. It was total hate that sustained the demand for total victory (episode 20).

Notice how the Mercy-driven 'conflict of armies' grew into a Teacher-driven 'vision of total victory', This turned into a core mental network and 'desire for total victory rode the human soul and spurred it on'. Science is based upon Perceiver facts that are independent of people. Propaganda, in contrast, overrides Perceiver thought in order to impose mental networks. The Mercy label of 'bad' applied to the MMNs of 'them' turned into a universal Teacher theory of unvarying hate requiring total victory, and modern technology became the servant of this universal message of hate. Thus, instead of being reborn, what resulted was blasphemy against the Holy Spirit, because new technology with its Platonic forms was placed within a universal Teacher theory based upon the childish Mercy emotion of hate. There was no rebirth because the leaders at home lived within a Mercy-driven social environment rather than within a Teacher-driven environment of 'how things work'. As a result, the 'literary agent' at home became despised by the soldier at the front.

The military world had no connections with the life of the country. The two universes were juxtaposed, the one civilian, the other uniformed, and they knew nothing, and would continue to know nothing of each other. "If you were to ask me who it is we despise and hate the most, my answer would be, first of all, the war profiteers. Businessmen of all kinds and with them the professional patriots, the humbugs, the literary gents who dine each day in pajamas and red leather slippers off of dish of bosh." Every army was learning to hate the literary gents (episode 19).

Let us summarize. The consumer revolution began in the late 1800s, guided by a general Teacher understanding of how the natural world works. This understanding was used to build both better gadgets for consumers and better weapons for soldiers. However, the subjective core of people's minds was still governed by a childish attitude of dominance and submission, in which followers submit to MMNs of status and culture, while leaders struggle to dominate others through MMNs of status and culture. This struggle between leaders for domination turned into open warfare, and followers submitted because of their respect for status and culture. This type of response has occurred throughout history and will continue to occur as long as childish MMNs rule the mind.

What made World War I different was that it occurred after the consumer revolution, which unveiled the Teacher understanding of science and technology to the average person through the Teacher order-within-complexity of an industrial infrastructure. Government leaders such as Lord Kitchener turned the *civilian* unveiling of technology into a purely *military* unveiling by appealing to the core MMNs of citizens and by transforming the civilian economy into a war economy. The soldiers and factory workers who lived in this new Teacher-driven environment experienced a form of rebirth, while those who manipulated social mental networks or did not live within the new environment experienced an intensification of existing childish prejudices.

We are in the process of experiencing this again at a much more personal level. Modern society has become transformed as a result of the unveiling of the computer and the Internet. This has led both to a new world of gadgets and a new set of weapons. On the one hand, computers and the Internet now play a role in most human activity. On the other hand, governments are using this technology to develop new weapons. For instance, Bruce Schneier, a computer security expert, recently wrote that

Last week we learned about a striking piece of malware called Regin that has been infecting computer networks worldwide since 2008. It's more sophisticated than any known criminal malware, and everyone believes a government is behind it. No country has taken credit for Regin, but there's substantial evidence that it was built and operated by the United States (Schneier, 2014).

These new tools are being used to facilitate the traditional Mercy-driven mindset of dominance and submission. The Electronic Frontier Foundation summarizes that

> For years, there's been ample evidence that authoritarian governments around
> the world are relying on technology produced by American, Canadian, and
> European companies to facilitate human rights abuses. From software that en-
> ables the filtering and blocking of online content to tools that help governments
> spy on their citizens, many such companies are actively serving autocratic gov-
> ernments as 'repression's little helper.' The reach of these technologies is aston-
> ishingly broad: governments can listen in on cell phone calls, use voice recogni-
> tion to scan mobile networks, read emails and text messages, censor web pages,
> track a citizen's every movement using GPS, and can even change email con-
> tents while en route to a recipient. Some tools are installed using the same type
> of malicious malware and spyware used by online criminals to steal credit card
> and banking information. They can secretly turn on webcams built into personal
> laptops and microphones in cell phones not being used. And all of this informa-
> tion is filtered and organized on such a massive scale that it can be used to spy
> on every person in an entire country (EFF Staff).

In the same way that leaders in the First World War appealed to MMNs of culture and
patriotism to justify total warfare, so leaders today are appealing to culture and patriotism to justify total surveillance. For instance, an article posted in the British magazine
The Telegraph says that

> Internet users are being spied on in their own home as the Government uses the
> threat of terrorism and the spread of child pornography to justify launching a
> dramatic expansion of surveillance society, according to a leading academic...
> His comments come after the Government announced it was pressing ahead with
> privately held 'Big Brother' databases that opposition leaders said amounted to
> 'state-spying' and a form of 'covert surveillance' on the public. The police and
> security services are set to monitor every phone call, text message, email and
> website visit made by private citizens. The details are set to be stored for a year
> and will be available for monitoring by government bodies (Khan, 2010).

There are a number of parallels between what is happening today and what happened
during World War I. In the same way that World War I turned from being a war between nations into a war between The Guns and humanity, so today's surveillance is in
the process of being transformed from a war against 'evil people' to a war between
global data and human individuality. Back then, partial rebirth was experienced by those
who lived within this new Teacher-driven world. Similarly, a transformation of thinking
is occurring today among those who work within the new world of computers and the
Internet. However, as was the case before, leaders who do not live in technology are *not*
being transformed but rather are being driven by technology to teach an intensified
message of 'hate against the terrorist and the child pornographer' and are using technology to implement total control over the population.

✳ 15. Internal Unveiling and the Holy Spirit

We have examined the external apocalypse and partial rebirth that occurred during World War I. This chapter will examine the relationship between a mental concept of the Holy Spirit and internal unveiling, and we will analyze the partial internal unveiling that has occurred in Pentecostalism. We will then finish the chapter by reviewing the three stages of personal salvation from an internal perspective.

An *external* apocalypse guided by an understanding of how the world works will naturally be hijacked by respected leaders of society, who will transform it into a total war against humanity. That is because an external apocalypse does not address the fundamental problem, which is childish MMNs. This book describes an alternative, which is an *internal* apocalypse guided by a general understanding of how the mind works. An internal apocalypse focuses upon the root of the problem, which is the inadequate nature of personal identity.

An external unveiling has a natural tendency to mutate into an external apocalypse—in the sense of an inhuman physical environment. In contrast, an internal unveiling naturally leads to external personal benefits. First, developing the mind naturally increases one's ability to understand how the natural world functions. That is because the structure of the mind is consistent with the deep structure of science and technology. However, this compatibility will only be apparent to a mind that thinks in terms of Platonic forms and exemplars, which means going through the first two stages of truth and righteousness. Second, submitting personal identity to Teacher understanding will affect the way that one applies technology. For instance, since the 1950s we have possessed the ability to destroy human civilization through the use of atomic weapons. But we choose not to do so because we understand the personal cost. Similarly, even though wars continue, we have not yet experienced a third world war because we understand that the personal cost would be prohibitive.

An *internal* unveiling will express itself as a revelation of the Holy Spirit. This is because of the nature of a Platonic form. Remember that Platonic forms emerge within Mercy thought when Teacher theories modify Perceiver facts. Thus, one could describe a Platonic form as an internal unveiling of Teacher understanding, a Mercy image that reveals the nature of a general Teacher theory. During the third stage of rebirth, what is unveiled is not just a theory affecting a few facts, but rather a universal Teacher understanding that is supported by an entire interlocking grid of Server sequences and Perceiver facts. This will lead in Mercy thought to the unveiling of a Platonic Form of the Good—a universal, imaginary Mercy image of simplicity and purity.

Whether this unveiling is beneficial to personal identity or not will depend upon the general Teacher theory that is being unveiled. World War I led to the unveiling of *The Guns*, a Platonic form of simple, pure destruction. This was not a Holy Spirit but rather a blasphemy of the Holy Spirit, in which the Platonic forms of the consumer society became servants of a general Teacher theory based in the childish MMNs of dominance and submission. However, researchers were motivated by Platonic forms to come up with new and improved weapons, and when the war finally ended, this new technology did bring great benefit to mankind.

The problem is that the breakthrough in understanding how the *world* works was not accompanied by a similar breakthrough in understanding how the *mind* works. One can see this in the quote by James Smith. The scientific revolution was preceded by a 'theory of God's acting uniformly in all things'. But it was followed by the watchmaker analogy in which God sets the natural order in place and then *steps back* from further involvement. While not everyone ascribed to the deist view of God, this period is referred to as an 'age of enlightenment' in which the emphasis turned from religion to using rational thought to gain an understanding of how the world functions.

When the unveiling of the consumer revolution occurred, science *re-entered* the experiential realm of Mercy thought where religion still lived. Science was now using technology to *invent* new objects and experiences within Mercy thought, while religion was still *basing* its truth in the Mercy status of objects and people. The problem is that scientific understanding is not required to use technological gadgets. One can drive a car, for instance, without being a mechanic. Thus, experience became disconnected from understanding both in the religious and the secular. In the religious, belief was still based in absolute truth revealed by Mercy experts that *lacked* general Teacher understanding, while in the secular, science was now leading to technology that could be *separated* from Teacher understanding. Because the consumer does not require understanding to use technology, the consumer could adopt of the attitude of blind faith taken by the fundamentalist. Fundamentalism bases its truth about God in the pronouncements of religious authorities. Similarly, the secular consumer bases truth about science in the pronouncements of scientific authorities. And because science produces a steady stream of new technological gadgets, the fundamentalist started to view religion the way that the consumer views science. Science with its highfalutin' Teacher words does not remain within the realm of abstract theory but reveals itself through the Mercy experiences of technological gadgets. Similarly, Pentecostalism added this additional step of unveiling to religion, while retaining the consumer's aversion to highfalutin' Teacher words.

One can describe this more clearly by comparing the chain of reasoning. The secular consumer views science and technology in the following manner: Mercy need → incomprehensible abstract world of equations and science → magical new gadget. For the fundamentalist consumer of Christianity, the process is: Sinful humans with needs in Mercy thought → incomprehensible abstract world of God, heaven, and theology →

new magical world of personal bliss sometime in the future. The consumer revolution led to the emergence of Pentecostalism which modified the third step. For the Pentecostal Christian, the process became: Sinful humans with needs in Mercy thought → incomprehensible abstract world of God, heaven, and theology → new magical world of personal bliss now.

As before, I am not suggesting that *all* fundamentalism views theology—or science—as incomprehensible. However, Pentecostalism in its earliest days appealed primarily to the uneducated who did view science as a form of magic, and Pentecostalism has historically had a strong anti-intellectual bias.

The 'health and prosperity' movement that emerged in the 1950s illustrates more clearly the relationship between the consumer revolution and the Pentecostal view of God. The consumer revolution produces a continual stream of new gadgets. Fundamentalism bases its truth in the Mercy status given to religious experts and the holy book. 'Health and prosperity' teaches that one prays to God in order to receive new gadgets, and that the Mercy experience of being surrounded with new gadgets proves that one is preaching truth from God. Saying this more crudely, I pray to God in order to receive a new Cadillac, and the fact that I have a new Cadillac proves that I know truth about God. Notice how religion has become the servant of science and technology. The *benefits* of religion are all provided by science and technology, possessing technology *proves* religious truth, and the benefits of religion are *limited* to the technological realm of objects and physical health.

The basic problem is not the consumer attitude of Pentecostalism. The average individual interacts with science and technology as a consumer. But consumers depend upon hackers and inventors for their new gadgets, and hackers and inventors are guided by a general Teacher understanding of 'how things work'. The Pentecostal, in contrast, is attempting to be a consumer of religion without the support of religious hackers and inventors, in the absence of any general Teacher understanding of 'how things work'. That is why I suggested earlier that Pentecostalism jumps directly from first stage of truth to the third stage of rebirth.

I am also not suggesting that all Pentecostal Christians are ignorant consumers. There are those who are attempting to interact with God at the level of hacker and inventor. For instance, the quote by James Smith comes from a book written by Pentecostal scholars. However, the popular Pentecostal view of spirituality often resembles the way in which people approached electricity several hundred years ago.

A book on electricity in the time of Benjamin Franklin relates that

> by intimately involving people and their displays, electrical disseminators were able to entrance their audiences... The lecturer recruited several people and directed them to hold hands in a line or semicircle. When he connected the free hands at either end to a sizable Leyden jar [a primitive battery], the participants jumped in unison. This demonstration was sometimes conducted on a large scale

before an august audience. Louis-Guillaume Le Monnier, for example, performed the stunt with 140 guards before the French King (Schiffer, 2003).

Similarly, one common demonstration of the power of God is being 'slain in the spirit', in which a person is spiritually 'shocked' by the application of 'spiritual electricity'. As the skeptic points out, the victim is usually given a (firm) helping hand to ensure that he keels over if the 'power of the spirit' does not show up. However, I have occasionally felt an unusual tingling in the middle of the night which could best be described as a sort of 'spiritual electricity', and I know that many others have described something similar. We now know that the uses of electricity extend far beyond merely shocking people. People in Franklin's day thought that electrical shocks were exciting because they had no concept of what electricity could produce. Likewise, when people today get excited by being 'slain in the spirit', this implies that they have no concept of what spirituality can produce.

If one truly wishes to achieve the religious equivalent of the consumer revolution, then theory suggests that one must first come up with a general Teacher understanding of how things work and then apply this as an inventor. This book reinterprets Christianity in terms of a general Teacher theory of 'how the mind works', and the three stages of transformation describe how one can apply this theory to the level of being an inventor. Every inventor is driven by an obsession. My obsession is to follow this path and see where it leads.

Personal Benefits of Rebirth

We will explore a possible connection between the theory of mental symmetry and an actual spiritual realm in a later chapter. Even if such a spiritual realm does not exist, I suggest that there are a number of purely *cognitive* benefits to 'being filled with the spirit'. Cognitively speaking, a person is 'filled with the spirit' when a general Teacher understanding is mentally unveiled through the Platonic Form of the Good, because that is when *all* Mercy experiences become colored by a network of Platonic forms. Saying this in terms of mental networks, the TMN of a universal concept of God holds everything together mentally. Within this TMN lie the TMNs of more specific theories as well as the MMNs of Platonic forms. An *unveiling* occurs when this hierarchy of mental networks becomes apparent to Mercy thought and *rebirth* happens when existing MMNs become reborn within this hierarchy of mental networks.

I have mentioned—repeatedly—that childish Mercy mental networks struggle for dominance. This relationship changes when MMNs are reborn within a grid of truth and righteousness held together by a Teacher-based concept of God. Instead of conflict, there is *peace*. One sees this externally with the *rule of law*. When law and order break down, then every human encounter is a potential for danger. Will the other person threaten me? Should I attack him? In earlier times, merely traveling from one town to another put the average person in such a predicament. In contrast, people in a law-abiding society can interact in a peaceful manner because they know how others will respond. Similarly, rebirth brings law and order to the internal interaction between MMNs.

Teacher thought feels good when there is order-within-complexity. Similarly, Mercy thought feels good when MMNs interact in a *loving* manner. However, when childish MMNs rule the mind, then instead of interacting in a loving manner, MMNs will naturally struggle for domination. The TMN of a general understanding will *impose* peace, while the Platonic form of a concept of the Holy Spirit will *motivate* individuals to interact in a manner that is more pure, more simple, more ideal, more integrated, and less complicated.

When mental networks are continually struggling for domination, then they will tend to function in crisis mode, focusing upon primitive emotions of integration and fragmentation, fearful of being crushed by other mental networks or looking for opportunities to crush other mental networks. This is similar to what happens in a war zone where normal activity ceases because everyone is afraid for their lives. Peace and love, in contrast, lead to *gentleness*. In simple terms, mental networks are given the freedom to function. Mental networks feel free to express their nature, and people actually notice the desires and abilities of other individuals, instead of seeing self and others merely as potential targets.

There will be *joy*, because interaction between MMNs is emotionally colored by the positive Teacher feeling of a general understanding.

There is also *self-control*, because self now exists within a framework of understanding. When childish MMNs rule the mind, then self cannot be controlled because self is the *controller*. Some *person* is ultimately in charge. Reborn identity, in contrast, lives within a grid of understanding. As a result, self naturally avoids thought and behavior that is inconsistent with 'how things work'. For instance, my students in Korea would often sing the song 'I believe I can fly', and I would sometimes respond by telling them that if they really believed that they could fly, then they should jump out of the window and flap their arms. Of course, everyone knows that people cannot really fly. But that is the point. Childish identity is continually pretending that it can do things that are impossible. Reborn identity, in contrast, recognizes human limitations. This does not mean that one abandons dreams. Rather, one uses understanding to *realize* dreams. Thanks to science and technology, we now can fly. In other words, self-control is not the same as Contributor controlled technical thought. The Contributor person is naturally good at maintaining control of his mind, but this type of control places people and minds within a straitjacket within which they are prevented from moving freely. Instead, reborn identity exhibits self-control because it knows the location of things and people. Just as a physical map shows the locations of people and places, so an internal grid of truth and righteousness provides a mental map within which reborn identity lives: I am here and not there. I do not pretend that I am there, but I do observe there from a distance, and if it is a desirable location then I take the steps that are needed to get from here to there. Childish identity, in contrast, is continually pretending that it already is there, and as a result it never knows where it is.

Reborn identity is also *meek*. Childish identity confuses meekness for weakness, because any mental network that does not struggle for dominance will become dominated by other mental networks. 'If I do not stand up for myself, then others will step on me.' Meekness recognizes that everyone is at a certain place and that pretending to be at a different place does not change one's actual location. If I am in Portland, Oregon, I do not yell at those around me that 'I am in Portland' for fear that they will come to me and tell me that 'I am in Seattle'. My location is independent of what people think, because it is determined by 'how things work'. It is physically impossible to be in Portland and Seattle at the same time, because that is how the world works. Meekness recognizes the facts, lives within the facts, and knows that shouting about the facts merely makes it more difficult to determine the facts.

In summary, one sees the types of attributes that Paul describes in Galatians 5 as the 'fruit of the Spirit'.

Moving on, we saw previously that Contributor incarnation connects abstract with concrete by using Platonic forms to represent specific Mercy experiences and exemplars to represent specific Server sequences. For instance, consider the story of the apple falling on Newton's head. Physics looks at that situation and replaces the apple with a generic mass of 150g and regards the path of the apple as representative of the path taken by any falling object.

A similar transition occurs to personal identity when it is reborn. Childish Mercy identity lusts after *specific* items, such as 'the big red apple hanging from the tree'. Reborn identity, in contrast, is driven by *Platonic forms*, which makes it possible to derive satisfaction from any type of apple or from fruit in general. Childish identity pines after a specific house, job, or friend. Reborn identity still grieves over the specific loss but is able to find new houses, new jobs, and new friends. And the current house, job, and friend is enjoyed in the light of the Platonic form of houses, jobs, and friends. This makes it possible to tread lightly through life. One is not using *denial* to block off Mercy feelings and one is not *shutting down* Mercy thought by living only in Teacher theory. Instead, one is enjoying specific Mercy people, objects, and experiences within the context of Platonic forms. Thus, there still is a friendship between specific people such as John and me. But John and I are also exploring what it means to be friends.

Saying this another way, actual love is guided by Platonic love. These two are not seen as something totally *different*, as they were in the Middle Ages. Instead, *all* love becomes a *partial* expression of Platonic love, because personal identity and other mental networks have become reborn within a framework of Platonic forms. One does not need to distinguish between different kinds of love, because one loves everyone within the same context of Platonic forms. One recognizes that there are levels of friendship, and that mental networks of self and others will be damaged if one comes too close to another person without first building a framework within which this relationship can occur. That is because the 'fruit of the Spirit' will only be experienced if interaction between MMNs occurs within a grid of truth and righteousness that is guided by understanding. If this framework is missing, then there may be short-term pleasure, but the long-term result will be to regress to interaction based upon dominance and submission.

Moving on from Platonic forms to exemplars, reborn identity is able to take lessons and skills learned in one context and apply them to other contexts, because specific sequences are viewed as exemplars that are similar to many other sequences. For instance, studying the mind is quite different than playing the violin. However, when I play my violin, I am emotionally expressing the skills that I have acquired from studying the mind. I am often accused by those accustomed to the specialization of technical thought of jumping from one topic to another. But I increasingly see each specialization as a specific expression of the same subject, because I continually find the same general principles popping up in different specializations. Transforming personal identity is a key aspect of developing the mind. But it also plays a major role when developing a skill, especially one that involves people and emotions. For example, I played violin for three summers in the Canadian national youth orchestra. One summer, the final concert was in Massey Hall and during one of the pieces I was sitting directly behind the concert-master. Suddenly in the middle of the program, I realized what I was doing and had a crisis of personal identity. Who am I? What am I doing here?

Internal Stages of Salvation

We have looked at how a concept of the Holy Spirit affects personal identity during the third stage. Let us now take another look at the three stages of truth, righteousness, and rebirth, focusing upon how they appear *internally* when applied to personal identity. Some of this will be a review of points that were mentioned previously.

Truth: The scientific revolution learned Perceiver facts about the *external* world. The stage of truth acquires Perceiver facts about the *internal* world. Instead of studying physical objects, one studies personal identity. The goal of both science and the stage of truth is to use these Perceiver facts to build a general Teacher understanding. When one is acquiring facts about personal identity, then the resulting Teacher understanding will lead to a mental concept of God.

The goal of this first stage is to construct an adequate concept of God. First, this requires personal honesty. Unfortunately, a mind that is governed by childish MMNs is not capable of personal honesty. (The Facilitator person is naturally capable of *describing* personal identity, but finds it very difficult to *change* personal identity and needs a mental concept of God to *transform* personal identity.) The Christian prayer of salvation makes personal honesty emotionally possible by placing personal identity within a 'school' of incarnation. Second, an adequate concept of God will view God as a universal being, which means going beyond absolute truth to universal truth. In order to do this one must use Perceiver thought to *translate* between different kinds of facts, including facts about the world, facts about the mind, facts about society, religious facts, and scientific facts. One must also use Perceiver thought to *compare* facts about self with facts about others. While self-analysis is a major aspect of personal honesty, even observing myself in the most honest and transparent way possible will only tell me facts about the incomplete way in which my mind is currently functioning. In order to gain a more complete picture, I must study myself *and* others and use Perceiver thought to compare these facts. The overall goal is to have the most general Teacher theory apply to as much of personal identity as possible. Universal truth increases the generality of the Teacher theory. Personal honesty applies this theory to more of personal identity in Mercy thought.

During this first stage, the big struggle is learning how to use Perceiver thought in the midst of Mercy emotions. This ability is not acquired instantly but rather is built up one step of personal honesty at a time. That is why it is important to view the prayer of salvation as a means to an end and not as an end in itself. For instance, I have mentioned that Asian students often see enrollment in a good university as a way of acquiring social status in Mercy thought, rather than as the start of gaining an understanding in Teacher thought. Similarly, many Christians view saying the Christian prayer of salvation (enrolling in the school of incarnation) as a way of acquiring special status before God in Mercy thought, rather than as the start of constructing a mental concept of God in Teacher thought.

One does not *try* to use Perceiver thought, because trying increases the emotional intensity and this emotional pressure will overwhelm Perceiver thought. Instead, one recognizes and acknowledges Perceiver truth. This is only possible if truth is *independent* of the opinions of people. Truth is a set of connections, and confidence in truth grows as one continues to see the same connections repeated in many different situations. Fighting for truth is a contradiction in terms, because truth exists whether one fights for it or not. Instead, truth is something that must be acknowledged and Perceiver confidence is the quiet unshakable sense of certainty that grows behind all of the emotions as one continues to observe truth. Similarly, personal honesty is neither a great outpouring of personal emotion nor the suppressing of personal emotion. Instead, personal honesty is the recognition that facts are *independent* of personal feelings. The facts may make me feel ecstatic or miserable but this personal feeling has no bearing upon the facts of the situation. Logically speaking, this is obviously true, and it is usually easy to acknowledge the facts when dealing with someone else's personal experiences. The challenge is to acknowledge the facts when they affect *me* personally, because my emotions will overwhelm Perceiver thought within my mind making it difficult for me to believe the facts.

I suggest personal honesty will only be *redemptive* if it includes both time and emotions. First, when acknowledging personal facts, one goes *back* in time to include motivation.

What mental network motivated the response or action? This will place my response within a larger emotional context. For instance, maybe I was motivated by jealousy. Jealousy is bad because it makes me miserable and does not get me what I want.

Second, when imagining possible situations, one goes *forward* in time to include probable results. What will happen if I respond in a certain manner? How will that feel? For instance, that girl looks attractive. It is pleasant to imagine sleeping with her. But what will happen then? The encounter will form an MMN within my mind. If it is only a one night stand, then that MMN will not get satisfied, causing me to feel frustrated. If I have a relationship with another girl, then that MMN will get triggered, leading to emotional baggage that diminishes my future pleasure. I can prevent an MMN from forming by treating this as an impersonal encounter. But what is the point of doing something if one has to remove the pleasure from doing it in order to do it?

Saying this another way, personal honesty looks for emotional cause-and-affect, which means applying practical Contributor thought to personal identity, because cause-and-effect is the basic building block for practical Contributor thought.

The primary goal at this stage is not to change mental networks but rather to understand them accurately. That is because one cannot suppress core mental networks merely through the use of willpower. Instead, one must build an understanding, allow that understanding to turn into a TMN, and then use willpower to choose to follow the TMN of understanding *rather* than the inadequate MMN.

The end result is to change underlying motivation. Instead of trying to use Contributor willpower to *suppress* Exhorter desires, one rebuilds the mental networks that *drive* Exhorter desires. For instance, willpower responds to pangs of jealousy by trying to suppress these feelings, leading to frustration. Changing motivation, in contrast, makes it possible to enjoy the possessions of others from a distance without feeling driven to possess them for myself. Similarly, willpower tries to suppress feelings of lust, leading to frustration. Changing motivation, in contrast, makes it possible to enjoy beauty from a distance without feeling driven to possess it for myself.

Changing a mental network should not be confused with preventing a mental network from being triggered. If an unwanted mental network is not activated, then this will give the impression that underlying motivation has changed. However, the original motivation will return as soon as the mental network is triggered. For instance, suppose that one attempts to deal with lust in the Muslim fashion by forcing women to cover up their bodies. This will stop feelings of lust from being triggered by the sight of the female form, but it will have no effect upon the underlying mental networks. Men still have dirty minds, but the dirt is not being triggered. Cleaning up the male mind means replacing childish MMNs that treat women as pleasant experiences to grab and possess with the Platonic form of the ideal woman which views all aspects of beauty and sensitivity as something valuable to be preserved and enhanced. Similarly, I suggest that the mature *female* mind will also be guided by Platonic forms that view all aspects of beauty and sensitivity as something valuable to be preserved and enhanced.

Righteousness: Once a mental concept of God has been constructed, then it becomes possible to act in a manner that is consistent with this concept of God. If one attempts to become righteous without having an adequate concept of God, then one will either become driven by the MMNs of authority figures who claim to speak for God, or one will acquire the trait of human righteousness, in which one is guided by the TMN of 'how we do things'.

I suggested that truth should go back in time to determine motivation and forward in time with imagination. Obviously, righteousness is only possible if the preceding stage of truth included a sense of time, because righteousness means acting in a manner that is consistent with understanding, and actions are composed of sequences of movement that occur over time.

True righteousness is only possible if 'the way that things work' is *independent* of people's opinions and cannot be changed through human effort. For instance, the law of gravity applies whether it is acknowledged or not; it does not matter whether the person falling over the cliff is a princess or a peasant, and no one can order gravity to stop working. Both truth and righteousness involve confidence. This confidence does not *alter* the facts or sequences, but rather gives one the ability to *recognize* which facts and sequences do not change. Truth places confidence in facts that are independent of people's opinions while righteousness places confidence in sequences that are independent of what people think or do. This means that righteousness, like truth, also expresses itself quietly as an unshakable confidence.

If one is confusing righteousness with *submitting* to the MMNs of authority figures who claim to speak for God, then one will have to practice righteousness before an audience. This is like following the law of gravity in front of people: "Look at me! I am following the law of gravity. Aren't I special?" Following the divine righteousness of 'how things work' has its *own* rewards, because things run much smoother and it takes much less effort to function in a manner that is consistent with 'how things work'. Similarly, if one is confusing righteousness with *human* righteousness, then one will have to practice righteousness in a group, and one will lose certainty when one is outside of the group. For instance, Japanese culture is heavily guided by the human righteousness of 'how we do things as Japanese', and one of the symptoms of this is that most Japanese tourists travel in groups and not as individuals.

Righteousness is not just doing the right thing but rather doing the right thing for the right motives. Remember that mental networks will take ownership of the actions and responses that they motivate. Server actions are *already* being motivated by Mercy mental networks of approval and personal benefit. Therefore, an action will only become internally connected with the TMN of a general understanding if that action is motivated by understanding in the *absence* of other mental networks.

As with truth, notice that one is dealing with internal connections and not external reality. It is logically obvious that a dropped object will fall to the floor. But this connection between Server action and Teacher understanding does not occur automatically within the mind but rather has to be constructed. For instance, consider the child who says "Mom is going to be really mad at me if I drop her precious vase." The ultimate motivation is not being provided by the TMN of an understanding of the law of gravity but rather by the MMN of parental approval. The child may be acting in a manner that appears externally to be righteous, but internally the child is not righteous. In order to be righteous, the child has to act in a manner that is consistent with the law of gravity *and* be motivated by an understanding of the law of gravity. One sees this distinction illustrated by some of the cheesy Walt Disney movies from the 1960s. The typical plot had a school professor inventing some new substance, such as anti-gravity rubber or growth-enhancing plant fertilizer. Invariably, the climax of the story would involve using this new invention to win some crucial game against a rival school. Thus, research guided by natural law was portrayed as the servant of personal status, expressed as 'us' winning the game over 'them'. The scientist in this movie may be acting in a way that is consistent with 'how the world works' (or at least giving the impression that he is studying and applying natural law) but this understanding did not provide the ultimate motivation.

This means that altruism is a fundamental aspect of *becoming* righteous. But altruism should not be confused with self-denial. Self-denial focuses upon suppressing MMNs. However, all thought and action is motivated by some mental network, therefore self-denial that lacks understanding will usually replace one MMN with another. For instance, practicing self-denial in order to be noticed by others will not lead to righteousness, because one is replacing the MMNs of personal identity with the MMNs of societal approval. Instead, righteousness is gained by following the TMN of understanding when there are *no* supporting personal or societal MMNs. Similarly, being miserable does not automatically make an action righteous. Teacher thought works with *general* equations that can be expressed through many different kinds of similar Server sequences, and some of these Server sequences lead to Mercy results that are more painful than other Server sequences. The Server sequence that is more painful is not automatically the Server sequence that is more righteous. Instead, what matters is not the presence of Mercy discomfort but rather the absence of Mercy motivation. A person becomes righteous when an action is performed for which there is no Mercy reason but only a Teacher reason. Personal discomfort may have an indirect impact upon righteousness because more Server confidence is required when there is emotional intensity. However, this personal discomfort can be created either by facing pain or by postponing pleasure. In other words, either suffering or patience will create the emotional pressure that helps to strengthen Server confidence. But patience is much less painful than suffering. In addition, altruism is only required to *become* righteous. The ultimate goal is not to follow a TMN in the absence of MMNs but rather to have a TMN rule over actions and MMNs. One *becomes* righteous by obeying a TMN in the *absence* of MMNs but once this emotional hierarchy of mental networks has been established, then one continues to be righteous by following MMNs within the general context of a universal TMN.

Many of these principles are described by Jesus in the introduction to the Lord's Prayer.

> Beware of practicing your righteousness before men to be noticed by them; otherwise you have no reward with your Father who is in heaven. So when you give to the poor, do not sound a trumpet before you, as the hypocrites do in the synagogues and in the streets, so that they may be honored by men. Truly I say to you, they have their reward in full. But when you give to the poor, do not let your left hand know what your right hand is doing, so that your giving will be in secret; and your Father who sees what is done in secret will reward you. When you pray, you are not to be like the hypocrites; for they love to stand and pray in the synagogues and on the street corners so that they may be seen by men. Truly I say to you, they have their reward in full. But you, when you pray, go into your inner room, close your door and pray to your Father who is in secret, and your Father who sees what is done in secret will reward you. And when you are praying, do not use meaningless repetition as the Gentiles do, for they suppose that they will be heard for their many words. Do not be like them; for your Father knows what you need before you ask Him (Matt. 6:1-7).

Jesus says that Server actions that are motivated by the MMNs of personal approval will not be rewarded by the TMN of a mental concept of God. People who practice public self-denial are hypocrites because they claim to be motivated by a TMN of God while actually being motivated by personal and social MMNs. Because the MMNs take ownership of this action, it will not become mentally connected with any TMN. Instead, altruism will be connected with a TMN of God if it is practiced in secret, in the absence of MMNs. The key is to practice it with the 'right hand' (which is connected with left hemisphere Teacher thought) without allowing the 'left hand' (which is connected with right hemisphere Mercy thought) to get involved. A similar principle applies to the use of Teacher words in abstract thought. If one wishes Teacher words to be motivated by a general Teacher understanding then one needs to do research in private so that the primary motivation is not public approval. Applying this to scientific research, it is often said that one must 'publish or perish' because funding and promotion are typically based upon the number of papers that one has published. That, I suggest, is an unrighteous motivation that turns science from a study of 'how things work' to the practice of 'how we do things'. This does not mean that one should not publish. But if publishing is the primary goal, then this will result in a plethora of inconsequential (or even fraudulent) papers that do little to advance the understanding of science. Jesus says that righteousness should not be confused with Server repetition, because repetition reflects the thinking of 'Gentiles' who lack the Jewish mindset of associating Server actions with the Teacher words of God. If one repeats a sequence of words, then this repetition will build Server confidence causing the sequence of Teacher words to become stable within

Teacher thought. But this is not the same as a general theory. A general theory holds onto Teacher words because they describe Server sequences that are repeated *out there* in the way that things work, whereas repetition holds onto Teacher words because *I* repeated these words and not because there is any inherent connection between these words and how things work. For instance, the physicist repeatedly says F = ma because these words apply to many different sequences of movement. This is not the same as repeatedly saying G = nb. However, for the individual who lacks an understanding, repeating F = ma is exactly the same as repeating G = nb.

The statement about 'going into the inner room and praying to the Father in secret' has traditionally been used in Orthodox Christian circles to support the tradition of *hesychasm*, discussed earlier, in which the Jesus prayer is repeated incessantly. However, one notices that the very next verse says that one should not use 'meaningless repetition' when praying. The Greek word *battologeo* used here appears once in the Bible and is defined by Strong's concordance as 'to repeat the same things over and over'. Thus, when one places the statement 'going into the inner room and praying to the father in secret' within the immediate context, one ends up with a conclusion that contradicts hesychasm rather than supporting it. The Orthodox scholar would probably respond by saying that one should interpret the Bible by following the example set by the Church fathers. If that is the case, then one is being mentally ruled by the MMNs of authority figures rather than the TMN of a general understanding; one is using an unrighteous mindset to define righteousness.

Rebirth: The final stage is rebirth. Truth and righteousness create a mental grid of facts and sequences that is held together by a general Teacher understanding. Rebirth places the MMNs of personal identity within this mental grid. This is not an easy process, because it means tearing apart childish MMNs and rebuilding them within a grid of rational understanding. This ultimately means rethinking *all* of the MMNs that represent parents, *all* of the MMNs that represent authority figures, *all* of the MMNs of culture and society, as well as *all* of the MMNs of religion. In addition, one has to process through all *trauma,* in which emotions overwhelmed Perceiver thought into believing that certain experiences were connected, all *idolatry,* in which potent positive emotions fooled Perceiver thought into believing that some desirable object or person was connected with personal identity, and all *denial,* in which potent negative emotions fooled Perceiver thought into believing that some painful object or person was not connected with personal identity.

Jesus refers to this transition in the following passage.

> And He came home, and the crowd gathered again, to such an extent that they could not even eat a meal. When His own people heard of this, they went out to take custody of Him; for they were saying, "He has lost His senses." The scribes who came down from Jerusalem were saying, "He is possessed by Beelzebul," and "He casts out the demons by the ruler of the demons."... Then His mother

and His brothers arrived, and standing outside they sent word to Him and called Him. A crowd was sitting around Him, and they said to Him, "Behold, Your mother and Your brothers are outside looking for You." Answering them, He said, "Who are My mother and My brothers?" Looking about at those who were sitting around Him, He said, "Behold My mother and My brothers! For whoever does the will of God, he is My brother and sister and mother" (Mark 3:20-22, 31-35).

Jesus is behaving in a way that violates his cultural MMNs. Eventually, his family shows up as a group in order to use parental MMNs to bring Jesus back into line, and the crowd uses their MMNs to reinforce the family ultimatum. Jesus responds by saying that even family MMNs need to be guided by the TMN of righteousness: 'Whoever does the will of God, he is My brother and sister and mother'.

Jesus repeats this message later.

While Jesus was saying these things, one of the women in the crowd raised her voice and said to Him, "Blessed is the womb that bore You and the breasts at which You nursed." But He said, "On the contrary, blessed are those who hear the word of God and observe it" (Luke 11:27-28).

This verse is traditionally used by Protestants to question the reverence given by many Christians to the Virgin Mary. However, I suggest that both sides in this controversy tend to ignore the underlying point. The primary issue is not whether *Mary* was blessed because she was the physical mother of Jesus or because she said 'let it be to me according to your word'. Rather, the real issue is whether *I* am blessed or not. Am I building my mind upon MMNs of family and culture or am I being guided by the TMN of righteousness? In other words, this is not an esoteric doctrinal point but rather a universal cognitive principle.

Saying this more briefly, one must analyze and digest everything and everyone that one holds dear, because these are the very mental networks around which the childish mind is integrated. This may sound like an onerous requirement, but the alternative is worse. If these core childish MMNs remain in control of the mind and are not processed, then the combination of peripheral intelligence and core childishness will lead to the type of blasphemy against the Holy Spirit that was discussed earlier. Instead of becoming adults, people will turn into brilliant idiots, savages with a veneer of civilization—which is what the theory of evolution claims that we are.

No one can handle the emotional angst of having core mental networks ripped apart. It is unbearable. But it is possible to *replace* one set of core mental networks with another. That is why rebirth occurs *after* truth and righteousness. These first two stages create a mental structure held together by Teacher emotions in which personal identity *can* live. First, the TMN of a general understanding provides a source of emotional integration that can replace the MMNs of childish identity. The mind can only let go of one set of mental networks that hold the mind together if they are *replaced* by another set that also hold the mind together. This is a generalization of Kuhn's observation that a scientist can only let go of an existing paradigm if he is given a replacement paradigm. Second, the TMN of a general understanding can only replace childish MMNs if the general understanding *applies* to personal experiences. That is why one needs to construct a concept of God. A concept of God is *needed* because the general understanding must apply to personal identity, and this concept must be *constructed* in order to contain sufficient detail for personal identity to live within this understanding. Saying this more simply, the extent of rebirth that a person can experience depends upon the universality of one's concept of God. The goal of rebirth is not to deny personal pleasure but rather to lay the foundation for deep, lasting personal pleasure. And one's ability to pursue and enjoy lasting pleasure will depend upon the extent of one's rebirth.

The extent of one's rebirth depends upon the universality of one's concept of God.

Saying the Christian prayer of salvation is often referred to as 'being born again'. However, I suggest that this is cognitively inaccurate. The prayer of salvation changes the *emotional status* of personal identity. Instead of *directly* observing the chaos and ignorance of childish personal identity, Teacher thought views personal thought *indirectly* as an element of the Teacher order-within-complexity of the school of incarnation. However, the MMNs of personal identity have not changed. All that has changed is the way that Teacher thought views these MMNs. The change in emotional state that occurs as a result of saying the prayer of salvation can lead to the formation of new mental networks—there may be a new birth, but identity itself has not yet been reborn. This emotional shift will naturally express itself in new attitudes and behavior, but the fundamental structure of the mind has not been changed. In rebirth, the MMNs of personal identity are torn apart and re-assembled.

The Exhorter and Contributor persons are most prone to confusing the prayer of salvation with personal rebirth. That is because the Exhorter person can use conscious thought to pursue a new infatuation, while the Contributor person can use conscious thought to switch from one context to another. Using religious language, there has been repentance (a word that means changing one's direction) but the individual has not been born again. One can tell this is the case because the underlying mindset of these two cognitive styles usually remains unchanged. The Contributor person who says the prayer of salvation may acquire a new bottom line, but his mindset of selling some objective product rather than improving people usually remains unchanged. Instead of selling cars, he is now selling 'the prayer of salvation'. The Exhorter person who has a 'salvation experience' may have a new infatuation, but his mindset of using his golden tongue to spread his vision to others typically remains the same.

✳ 16. Three Stages of Salvation Revisited

We finished the previous chapter by reviewing the three stages of salvation of personal salvation from an internal perspective. In this chapter, we will revisit these three stages from two more perspectives. First, we will interpret the life of Jesus as described in the Gospels from the vantage point of these three stages. Second, we will show how the theory of mental symmetry can be used to assist a person to go through these three stages.

Let us begin by summarizing the three stages. The process begins with the belief that God reveals himself to humanity using words that have meanings. As we saw before, this needs to be jumpstarted by some external source, because the natural tendency is for childish thought to associate God with either magical formulae backed up by MMNs or with mystical experiences expressed using overgeneralized words that lack meaning. In addition, God needs to view humanity indirectly through incarnation. Using educational language, school assumes that knowledge can be conveyed using words that have meanings, and an educational system assumes that adults will not avoid children but rather give children approval for being good students.

Moving on, the first stage of truth uses Perceiver facts to build a concept of God based in general Teacher understanding. In order to move past this first stage, the concept of God needs to be transformed from one that is based in *absolute* truth revealed in some holy book or textbook to *universal* truth based in 'how things work'. This leads to the concept of divine righteousness, in which one believes that 'the way things work' reflects the character of God. This enables the second stage of righteousness, which acts in a manner that is consistent with 'how things work', or to use religious language, behaves in a manner that is consistent with the character of God. In order to move past the second stage, the concept of God needs to be transformed again through an unveiling in which one sees the character of God portrayed in all aspects of human existence. This unveiling forces existing MMNs to be reborn within the grid of Perceiver truth and Server righteousness that was constructed during the first two stages.

We have seen that science views specific Server sequences as exemplars that illustrate general sequences. Jesus often stated that everything he did was a reflection of God the Father. For instance,

> Therefore Jesus answered and was saying to them, "Truly, truly, I say to you, the Son can do nothing of Himself, unless it is something He sees the Father doing; for whatever the Father does, these things the Son also does in like manner" (John 5:19).

If this is a valid statement, then the sequence of the three stages of salvation should line up with the sequence of events described in the life of Jesus. Saying this another way, the life of Jesus should be an exemplar that illustrates the general equation of these three stages. If this correspondence does not exist, then that tells us that our analysis is flawed.

> The life of Jesus should be an exemplar of the three stages of personal transformation.

The life of Jesus needs to begin with the belief that one can learn content about God and not just have emotional experiences involving God. But the childish mind does not naturally associate God with mental content. Thus, what is needed is a mental concept of incarnation that uses content to connect God and man. But the childish mind will not naturally form such a mental concept of incarnation, because the childish mind does not naturally associate God with mental contact. Therefore, a mental concept of incarnation needs to be given birth using content that comes from some non-human source which does regard mental content as natural. This is reflected in the doctrine of the virgin birth, which states that Jesus had a divine father. Male thought emphasizes content. Therefore, virgin birth is an accurate exemplar of the process of cognitive development being jumpstarted by a Contributor incarnation birthed by content from a general Teacher understanding.

There also needs to be a change in a way that God views humanity. One finds this portrayed in the story of the angels appearing at Jesus' birth.

> The angel said to them, "Do not be afraid; for behold, I bring you good news of great joy which will be for all the people; for today in the city of David there has been born for you a Savior, who is Christ the Lord. This will be a sign for you: you will find a baby wrapped in cloths and lying in a manger." And suddenly there appeared with the angel a multitude of the heavenly host praising God and saying, "Glory to God in the highest, and on earth peace among men with whom He is pleased" (Luke 2:10-14).

Notice the positive emotion based in a universal verbal message. There is 'good news of great joy' that is 'for all the people'. This positive feeling is a result of the birth of a Contributor incarnation who is 'a Savior' in concrete thought and 'Christ the Lord' in abstract thought. This results in two global emotional shifts. First, instead of running away from Teacher thought, there is 'glory to God in the highest'. Second, God now views humanity in a positive emotional light leading to 'peace among men with whom He is pleased'.

These prerequisites make possible the first stage of truth, in which one uses Perceiver thought to build a general Teacher understanding. One finds this attitude described in the story of Jesus at the temple. When Jesus is twelve, he goes with his parents to Jerusalem for a religious festival. After the festival, his parents travel for a full day before realizing that he is not with them. They return to Jerusalem and search for their son. Luke says that

> after three days they found Him in the temple, sitting in the midst of the teachers, both listening to them and asking them questions. And all who heard Him were amazed at His understanding and His answers. When they saw Him, they were astonished; and His mother said to Him, "Son, why have You treated us this way? Behold, Your father and I have been anxiously looking for You." And He said to them, "Why is it that you were looking for Me? Did you not know that I had to be in My Father's house?" (Luke 2:46-49).

For five days, Jesus has been discussing theology with the experts, who are all amazed at his Teacher understanding. When questioned by his worried mother, he does not apologize for having run away, but rather answers that they should have known where he was: 'Did you not know that I had to be in my Father's house?' In other words, Jesus was using truth to construct a mental concept of God because that was where he *had* to be. It was a step in the general plan of divine sovereignty.

In order to make further progress, a transformation must occur in the concept of God. This transition is portrayed in the baptism of Jesus, baptism being a symbol of rebirth.

> Then Jesus arrived from Galilee at the Jordan coming to John, to be baptized by him. But John tried to prevent Him, saying, "I have need to be baptized by You, and do You come to me?" But Jesus answering said to him, "Permit it at this time; for in this way it is fitting for us to fulfill all righteousness." Then he permitted Him. After being baptized, Jesus came up immediately from the water; and behold, the heavens were opened, and he saw the Spirit of God descending as a dove and lighting on Him, and behold, a voice out of the heavens said, "This is My beloved Son, in whom I am well-pleased" (Matt. 3:13-17).

John does not initially want to baptize Jesus, but Jesus replies that this baptism is necessary 'to fulfill all righteousness', telling us that we are dealing with Server actions that express general Teacher understanding. When one makes a transition from absolute truth to universal truth, then this will transform a concept of God, portrayed as the heavens being opened. First, instead of merely talking about a universal God, one will actually have a valid concept of a universal God, as reflected in the voice from heaven indicating approval. Second, Teacher generalization will lead to the formation of Platonic forms in Mercy thought, which is reflected in the spirit descending as dove.

When a person makes the transition from religious consumer to religious hacker, then core mental networks need to be tested to see if that person really is being guided by the TMN of a general understanding and not by MMNs. One sees this testing in the three temptations of Jesus, which happen right after his baptism. If one examines these three temptations from the viewpoint of Contributor thought (incarnation is based in Contributor thought and the description of Jesus in the gospels is consistent with the cognitive style of Contributor person), one notices that these three temptations correspond with ways in which the practical Contributor person typically misuses abstract technical thought.

First,

> The tempter came and said to Him, "If You are the Son of God, command that these stones become bread." But He answered and said, "It is written, 'Man shall not live on bread alone, but on every word that proceeds out of the mouth of God'" (Matt. 4:3-4).

The temptation here is to regard abstract thought as a form of *magic* that is invoked as a servant of concrete thought. We saw earlier that Teacher words form the basic elements of abstract thought and that abstract thought has the power to change Perceiver facts. Magic sees this is as a shortcut to achieving concrete results. For instance, if I say 'Open Sesame', then the stone cliff in front of me will transform into a doorway. Jesus is told to use his connection with abstract thought to meet his personal needs by commanding stones to be transmuted into bread. Jesus answers by saying that one should not make Teacher words the servant of specific Mercy needs but rather associate words with a universal Teacher understanding of God.

The practical Contributor person is often tempted to regard abstract thought as a servant of concrete thought that can be controlled by concrete thought: "If I say just the right words and quote the right promises, then God must answer my requests." For instance, "The Bible says 'Is anyone among you sick? Then he must call for the elders of the church and they are to pray over him, anointing him with oil in the name of the Lord; and the prayer offered in faith will restore the one who is sick' (James 5:14, 15). Therefore, if I carry out this formula with sufficient faith, then God must heal."

Second,

> The devil took Him into the holy city and had Him stand on the pinnacle of the temple, and said to Him, "If You are the Son of God, throw Yourself down; for it is written, 'He will command His angels concerning You'; and 'On their hands they will bear You up, so that You will not strike Your foot against a stone.'" Jesus said to him, "On the other hand, it is written, 'You shall not put the Lord your God to the test'" (Matt. 4:5-7).

The temptation here is to regard abstract thought as a sort of *genie* that can protect a person from the harmful results of cause-and-effect. This is what happens when one views God from a Mercy perspective as a kind of Superman connected with holy objects in Mercy thought, the logic being that if one respects MMNs that are associated with God, then God should respond by preventing personal identity in Mercy thought from having bad experiences.

For instance, in 1755 Lisbon was hit by an earthquake that struck on All Saints Day when many citizens were attending mass in church. Tens of thousands of people died in Lisbon alone, and many of the cathedrals in the city were destroyed. This catastrophe led to major questions regarding God and evil, because people were not protected from personal harm by attending a religious event at a religious place.

The practical Contributor person has a tendency to make deals with God: "If you save me from this problem, then I promise to attend church for the rest of my life." This places abstract thought within the constraints of the if-then thinking of concrete technical thought.

Finally,

> the devil took Him to a very high mountain and showed Him all the kingdoms of the world and their glory; and he said to Him, "All these things I will give You, if You fall down and worship me." Then Jesus said to him, "Go, Satan! For it is written, 'You shall worship the Lord your God, and serve Him only'" (Matt. 4:8-10).

The temptation here is to view abstract thought as a *tool* of childish identity. We saw this, for instance, in the 'total war' of World War I, in which the incarnation of technology did fall down and worship the 'devil' of hatred against the foe (the word 'devil' means slander). Jesus responds by saying that Mercy identity and Server actions should submit *entirely* to universal Teacher understanding.

Similarly, the practical Contributor person typically regards abstract understanding as a means to an end, rather than as a master to which one submits. Knowledge will be guarded because knowledge is power: "I can defeat my opponents if I know something that they do not."

Because Pentecostalism attempts to jump directly to the third stage of salvation without first building a general Teacher understanding, it often fails these three temptations. First, God can be viewed as a dispenser of magic, who magically transforms one set of Perceiver facts to another. Occasionally, there are even claims of matter itself being magically transmuted, such as normal teeth fillings being turned into gold fillings. Modern technology *can* be used to change one substance into another to an extent that would previously have been regarded as magical. However, performing such transmutations requires a deep understanding of natural process. Second, God is often seen as a genie who protects individuals from personal harm. This is seen particularly in the 'walk of faith', in which a person goes on a trip, usually involving some plan of religious self-denial, without making any preparations in order to see if 'God will provide'. Finally, as televangelists have illustrated, there is a depressing tendency for Pentecostal leaders to start by following what they perceive to be the kingdom of God and end by building a personal kingdom of wealth and social status.

This episode is then followed by a period of several years during which Jesus travels and teaches as a Jewish rabbi. As we just saw from the fifth chapter of the book of John, Jesus acts in a righteous manner during this time. A few chapters later, Jesus emphasizes again that both his words and his actions reflect the nature of God the Father. Note that his audience does not comprehend this way of functioning.

> "He who sent Me is true; and the things which I heard from Him, these I speak to the world." They did not realize that He had been speaking to them about the Father. So Jesus said, "When you lift up the Son of Man, then you will know that I am He, and I do nothing on My own initiative, but I speak these things as the Father taught Me. And He who sent Me is with Me; He has not left Me alone, for I always do the things that are pleasing to Him" (John 8:26-29).

In order to make a transition from righteousness to rebirth, a concept of God must be transformed through an unveiling or apocalypse. We have already looked at this reference in our analysis of Peter and the keys of heaven, so we will only summarize the relevant points here.

> He said to them, "But who do you say that I am?" Simon Peter answered, "You are the Christ, the Son of the living God." And Jesus said to him, "Blessed are you, Simon Barjona, because flesh and blood did not reveal this to you, but My Father who is in heaven. I also say to you that you are Peter, and upon this rock I will build My church; and the gates of Hades will not overpower it. I will give you the keys of the kingdom of heaven; and whatever you bind on earth shall have been bound in heaven, and whatever you loose on earth shall have been loosed in heaven." Then He warned the disciples that they should tell no one that He was the Christ. From that time Jesus began to show His disciples that He must go to Jerusalem, and suffer many things from the elders and chief priests and scribes, and be killed, and be raised up on the third day. Peter took Him aside and began to rebuke Him, saying, "God forbid it, Lord! This shall never happen to You." But He turned and said to Peter, "Get behind Me, Satan! You are a stumbling block to Me; for you are not setting your mind on God's interests, but man's." Then Jesus said to His disciples, "If anyone wishes to come after Me, he must deny himself, and take up his cross and follow Me. For whoever wishes to save his life will lose it; but whoever loses his life for My sake will find it. For what will it profit a man if he gains the whole world and forfeits his soul? Or what will a man give in exchange for his soul? For the Son of Man is going to come in the glory of His Father with His angels, and WILL THEN REPAY EVERY MAN ACCORDING TO HIS DEEDS. Truly I say to you, there are some of those who are standing here who will not taste death until they see the Son of Man coming in His kingdom." Six days later Jesus took with Him Peter and James and John his brother, and led them up on a high mountain by themselves. And He was transfigured before them; and His face shone like the sun, and His garments became as white as light (Matt.16:16-17:2).

This passage begins with a transformation in Peter's concept of incarnation, which Jesus says is the result of a revelation or unveiling from God. Jesus then describes the key role that Perceiver thought plays in an internal unveiling by unlocking different mental contexts. This unveiling is immediately followed by a shift in the teaching of Jesus who changes his focus from the second stage of righteousness to the third stage of rebirth. When Peter questions this new emphasis, Jesus replies that rebirth is part of the plan of divine sovereignty. He then tells his followers that this is an exemplar. Not only is he going to experience rebirth, but everyone who wants to follow the path of personal salvation must go through rebirth. This internal unveiling within the mind of Peter is followed by the external unveiling of the Transfiguration, and Jesus also predicts that there will be a future apocalyptic unveiling of 'the Son of Man coming in the glory of His Father with His angels'. This triple reference to unveiling suggests that we are dealing again with an exemplar that can be expressed in various ways.

A week before Jesus is killed, another unveiling occurs, known as the triumphant entry, which is again followed by Jesus talking about rebirth.

> When all the people heard of Jesus' arrival, they flocked to see him and also to see Lazarus, the man Jesus had raised from the dead. Then the leading priests decided to kill Lazarus, too, for it was because of him that many of the people had deserted them and believed in Jesus. The next day, the news that Jesus was on the way to Jerusalem swept through the city. A large crowd of Passover visitors took palm branches and went down the road to meet him. They shouted, "Praise God! Blessings on the one who comes in the name of the Lord! Hail to the King of Israel!"...Many in the crowd had seen Jesus call Lazarus from the tomb, raising him from the dead, and they were telling others about it. That was the reason so many went out to meet him—because they had heard about this miraculous sign. Then the Pharisees said to each other, "There's nothing we can do. Look, everyone has gone after him!" Some Greeks who had come to Jerusalem for the Passover celebration paid a visit to Philip, who was from Bethsaida in Galilee. They said, "Sir, we want to meet Jesus." Philip told Andrew about it, and they went together to ask Jesus. Jesus replied, "Now the time has come for the Son of Man to enter into his glory. I tell you the truth, unless a kernel of wheat is planted in the soil and dies, it remains alone. But its death will produce many new kernels—a plentiful harvest of new lives" (John 20:9-13, 17-24).

Notice the unveiling. The news of Jesus' entry into Jerusalem 'swept through the city'. The Pharisees complained that 'everyone has gone after him'. And people from a non-Jewish culture came to enquire about Jesus, who responds by referring again to rebirth.

We are all familiar with the story of the death and resurrection of Jesus that follows. We will focus on what are known as the 'seven sayings of Jesus', which are the seven statements that the Gospels attribute to Jesus while he is being crucified. I suggest that these statements are relevant for anyone going through the third stage of rebirth.

1) "Father, forgive them; for they do not know what they are doing" (Luke 23:34). When general Teacher understanding is being used to process the MMNs of authority figures, people should not be treated as units but rather as collections of mental networks. This recognizes that people are not consciously choosing their responses, but rather are being driven by their mental networks to respond in a certain fashion. One

sees this illustrated by the response of the Pharisees described at the beginning of the quote from John 20. If someone like Lazarus actually were raised from the dead, then the rational response would be to acquire this benefit for oneself. After all, if I am dying from an incurable disease and someone comes up with a cure for this disease, then surely I would want this cure. However, the Pharisees are driven by mental networks of status and authority to decide that both Jesus and Lazarus need to be killed.

2) "Truly I say to you, today you shall be with me in paradise" (Luke 23:43). One of the thieves who is being crucified with Jesus says to him, "Remember me when you come in your kingdom." Jesus responds by saying that the thief will be with him in paradise. The general principle being described is to focus upon the personal benefit that lies on the other side of rebirth, both for self and for others. When one is going through a cognitive rebirth, it is very easy to focus upon the current predicament or to become cynical and write off other individuals. This focus upon future personal benefit is also mentioned in Hebrews, where the author talks about "fixing our eyes on Jesus, the author and perfecter of faith, who for the joy set before Him endured the cross, despising the shame" (Heb. 12:2).

3) "When Jesus then saw His mother, and the disciple whom He loved standing nearby, He said to His mother, 'Woman, behold, your son!' Then He said to the disciple, 'Behold, your mother!' From that hour the disciple took her into his own household" (John 19:26-27). Rebirth will affect MMNs that represent parents. It is important not to block off these mental networks but rather to place them within a context that protects them.

4) "About the ninth hour Jesus cried out with a loud voice, saying, 'ELI, ELI, LAMA SABACHTHANI?' that is, 'MY GOD, MY GOD, WHY HAVE YOU FORSAKEN ME?'" (Matt. 27:46). This does not describe a concept of God being transformed, but rather refers to personal identity feeling abandoned by God. Notice that this statement is given in Jesus' mother tongue of Aramaic, an indication that core MMNs are feeling forsaken, because the language of one's childhood connects with MMNs in a way that languages learned later on do not.

5) "After this, Jesus, knowing that all things had already been accomplished, to fulfill the Scripture, said, 'I am thirsty'" (John 19:28). Notice that each of the first five statements is more personal than the previous one. The first was a general statement about surrounding people. The second addressed colleagues who are going through similar experiences. The third dealt with parents, while the fourth referred to one's internal relationship with God. Similarly, cognitive rebirth is like peeling away the layers of an onion, working one's way from peripheral to core mental networks. At the end all that remains is a general Mercy feeling of thirst. However, this Mercy angst is not felt within a vacuum but rather within the context of knowing 'how things work'.

6) "When Jesus had received the sour wine, He said, 'It is finished!'" (John 19:30). Jesus does not say that there is no hope or that he has lost. Rather, he says that the job is fin-

ished. The goal of rebirth is to transform all existing MMNs. Once the core of Mercy thought has been digested, then the job is finished.

7) "And Jesus, crying out with a loud voice, said, 'Father, into Your hands I commit My spirit.' Having said this, He breathed His last." (Luke 23:46). The process of 'dying to self' ends with giving up, or breathing one's last. But one does not give up in order to be personally annihilated. Instead, one connects all the Platonic forms of personal identity to general understanding in Teacher thought.

Three Stages of Salvation and Mental Symmetry

We have examined the three stages of salvation from theoretical and theological perspectives. We will now turn our attention from theory to practice. What does it mean in *practical* terms to use the theory of mental symmetry as a guide to reaching mental wholeness? I am not suggesting that mental symmetry is *required* to reach mental wholeness. People have been pursuing a path of mental wholeness for countless generations. However, I have found that mental symmetry is very helpful for *clarifying* the steps that need to be taken.

Let us start with the first stage of truth. If I want to know truth about myself and others, then one of the most basic facts about people are their cognitive styles. Sometimes a person's cognitive style is obvious, other times it is not. That is because cognitive style is not the cognitive module that is functioning the best, but rather the cognitive module that is *conscious*. This means that determining cognitive style requires a certain level of individuation, because a person must be himself before he can discover who 'self' is. When cultural MMNs are too powerful, then it becomes very difficult to determine a person's cognitive style, because nobody is expressing their true nature. I suggest that this is the primary reason why cognitive style was not discovered many centuries earlier. Using the language of Higgins, people were driven so strongly by the *ought* self of culture and approval that they were unable to discover the *actual* self of cognitive style.

Putting this more personally, if I wish to know my cognitive style then I need to ask myself what type of thinking and behaving come *naturally* to me. Not how others think that I should behave, or what habits I have picked up, but rather what is the real me. What do I like to do, what comes naturally to me, what do I find obvious, and what really bothers me when it is ignored by others? For instance, the Perceiver person is really bothered by *hypocrisy* because this signifies a mismatch between Perceiver meaning and Perceiver object recognition. What bothers the Mercy person is *insincerity*, because MMNs are receiving inconsistent messages. The Teacher person is bothered by *double-mindedness*, being guided by incompatible general Teacher theories. The Server person is troubled by *long-term problems* about which nothing can be done. The Exhorter person hates *frustration* and *boredom*. The first blocks Exhorter urges, the second removes the source of Exhorter urges. The Contributor person is bothered when the *rules* of the game are unclear, because this disables cause-and-effect. And the Facilitator person dislikes *impoliteness* or *rule-breaking* because this disrupts the underlying structure that guides Facilitator mixing.

Because cognitive style reflects consciousness, it is hard to come up with an empirical test for cognitive style. Determining one's MBTI category is easy, because MBTI measures the way of thinking that is *operating*. Figuring out one's cognitive style is more difficult. It can be helpful to start by asking 'What am I not?' before turning to 'What am I?' One can usually eliminate four or five of the seven categories this way, simplifying the question of 'What am I?' to 'Am I this or that?'

Knowing cognitive style places the question of *motivation* within the context of how the mind works. The answer to 'Why am I doing this?' might be 'Because I am a Teacher person'. And the answer to 'Why is she doing that?' could be 'Because she is a Contributor person'. This is the type of simple answer that Teacher thought likes, which will motivate a person to probe further. What are the traits of a Teacher person? What is a Contributor person like? For those who want more information about these traits, descriptions of the seven cognitive styles can be found on the www.mentalsymmetry.com website. One of the quickest ways to learn about cognitive styles is by being under the domination of someone who should know about cognitive styles, is clearly one of the cognitive styles, but does not want to learn about cognitive styles.

Knowing about cognitive style also puts *imagination* within the context of how the mind works. If I know my cognitive style, and I know the natural strengths of that cognitive style, then that can guide my imagination, because it tells me what I will find fulfilling and what will not satisfy me. My cognitive style may be capable of doing things that I personally have never tried. Similarly, my cognitive style might become frustrated by a career that my parents think I should follow. If my parents have different cognitive styles than I do, then I may feel unfulfilled—and do a poor job of—following in my parents' footsteps. This does not mean that each cognitive style can only do certain jobs, because cognitive style determines the *way* I do my job, not necessarily the job that I do, and there are often many *different* ways to do the *same* job. Nevertheless, some cognitive styles are naturally *better* at certain jobs than other jobs.

That brings us naturally to the next level of applying mental symmetry. It is important to discover my cognitive style, and to develop the mode of thought in which I am conscious. Ultimately, I can only find fulfillment by performing activities that express my cognitive style. But intelligence involves the *entire* mind, and I will be able to function much more *effectively* if all seven cognitive modules within my mind work together in harmony. I may not be a Teacher person, for instance, but if Teacher thought is functioning properly within my mind, then I will feel positive Teacher emotions. Similarly, if Perceiver thought is not functioning properly within my mind, then I will lack confidence when working with facts and truth, which will leave me confused and uncertain regardless of my cognitive style.

Using the language of the philosopher Hume, the 'is' of how the mind *does* function will naturally turn into the 'ought' of how the mind *could* function. Hume asked how 'is' can turn into 'ought', how a *description* of how the mind works can turn into a *prescription* of how the mind should work. I suggest that this naturally happens when one applies the theory of mental symmetry.

'Is' will turn into 'ought' in two major ways. The first 'is' are the mental networks of culture. When researchers observe how people behave, they notice that we are creatures of habit and culture. That is how the mind naturally works. Learning one's cognitive style turns this 'is' into an 'ought'. Instead of following the dictates of culture and upbringing, I should be myself and develop my personal potential. Instead of submitting to the human righteousness of 'how we do things', I should follow the divine righteousness of how my mind is wired. Using the language of Higgins, instead of submitting to the ought self, I should realize my actual self, by developing the cognitive module in which I am conscious.

Once I recognize and develop my cognitive style, then a second is-ought distinction emerges, based upon mental wholeness. It is natural for each cognitive style to use the cognitive module that is conscious while either ignoring or suppressing the rest of the mind. For instance, if I am a Perceiver person, then I will think that everyone should believe in truth, and my natural tendency will be to preach this truth to others even if this tramples upon their Mercy feelings or violates their Teacher understanding. It is important to discover my cognitive style and to develop the mode of thought in which I am conscious. But if I *only* use conscious thought then I will be mentally incomplete. I may not be an Exhorter person, for instance, but if Exhorter thought is functioning properly within my mind, then I will have energy and feel motivated. Or, if Server thought is not functioning properly, then I will lack manual dexterity and skip steps when carrying out sequences, and find myself continually getting into physical difficulties. Using is-ought language, it *is* natural for each cognitive style to emphasize conscious thought and de-emphasize subconscious thought. But each cognitive style *ought* to develop and use all of the mind.

Restating this in practical terms, I can learn about my potential both by examining myself and by looking at others. Starting with the first is-ought, looking inside will help me to realize my natural strengths and weaknesses, while looking at others will help me to understand how my natural abilities differ from the natural abilities of others. This observation needs to be couched in terms of cognitive styles and cognitive modules. For instance, instead of saying, "I am a rotten driver compared to John", I need to say, "I am a Perceiver person. I am naturally good with maps. John is a Contributor person. A Contributor person is naturally good at carrying out a plan such as driving a car." This changes the standard from the human righteousness of 'This is how people expect me to behave' to the divine righteousness of 'This is where I can naturally excel'. The first is based in 'how people work', while the second is based in 'how my mind is wired'. The first is software, the second is hardware. Human righteousness is ultimately enforced by people with *Mercy* emotional status, while divine righteousness is ultimately enforced by a Teacher understanding of 'how things work'. Thus, observing myself and others in terms of cognitive styles and cognitive modules will place my concepts of self and others within the Teacher framework of a general understanding and free these concepts from the Mercy expectations of authority figures. This may sound complicated, but it is not. For instance, my nieces do not have any degrees in psychology or philosophy. But they are continually discussing cognitive styles, asking questions such as, "What type of person is Jane? Fred acts like a typical Mercy person. I am learning about the Teacher person by observing Tom. Why is the Contributor person that way?"

Observing self and others in terms of cognitive style is a good start, but it will only provide a partial picture. That is because each cognitive style is more than just one cognitive module. Thinking purely in terms of cognitive styles can lead to responses such as "I am a Mercy person. Mercy people are emotional. I cannot change being a Mercy person. Accept me the way I am." Or, "I can ignore your words. You are just saying that because you are thinking like a typical Perceiver person." The solution is to change the focus from cognitive *styles* to cognitive *modules*. For instance, instead of viewing a Facilitator person as the epitome of Facilitator thought, one views the Facilitator person as an individual with all seven cognitive modules who is conscious in Facilitator thought. Equating cognitive style with cognitive modules is both inaccurate and limiting. It is *inaccurate* because Facilitator thought may be dominant in the Facilitator person, and the immature Facilitator person may think that only Facilitator thought exists, but many of the traits of the Facilitator person are the result of subconscious thought interacting with the conscious Facilitator module. Thus, one gains a fuller picture of the Facilitator person by analyzing the Facilitator person in terms of cognitive modules. For example, the Facilitator person wants flexibility within structure. The flexibility comes from the mixing and blending of *conscious* Facilitator thought, whereas the structure is provided by *subconscious* Perceiver facts and Server sequences. Equating cognitive style with cognitive modules is also *limiting*. If a Facilitator person, for instance, is nothing more than Facilitator thought, then how can the Facilitator person grow and develop? This is one of the primary weaknesses of a system such as MBTI. Cognitive development will alter how the mind is functioning, which may change a person's MBTI category.

Thinking about cognitive modules can be done either internally or externally. Whenever we take a 'cognitive perspective' in this book, we are examining thought and behavior in terms of *internal* cognitive modules. This can lead to extensive theoretical analysis, but does not have to. Instead, when analyzing a thought, one simply needs to ask "Which cognitive module is the source of that thought?" One of the primary differences between conscious and subconscious thought is that one can see conscious thought but cannot see subconscious thought. Instead, subconscious thought is like an unknown caller on the phone who refuses to reveal his identity. When subconscious thought is functioning, it will come up with conclusions and it will pass these solutions on to conscious thought. But the *source* of these conclusions will be unknown. Determining which cognitive module is the source of a conclusion has two benefits. First, it allows me to know the state of my cognitive modules. For instance, computer technicians hate it when someone calls for help and says "My computer is not working", because this statement is too vague to be able to come up with a solution. What is needed is more specific information, such as, "My screen is blank", or even better, "The power light goes on, both on the case and the monitor, and I can hear the hard drive spin, but the screen remains blank." Similarly, "I feel bad" is a very difficult cognitive problem to solve. It is far more helpful to realize, for instance, that "Teacher thought is feeling bad because my work situation is chaotic." I can then focus my attention on helping Teacher thought to feel okay. Second, analyzing thought in terms of cognitive modules places thought within the structure of a general Teacher theory. If I understand why I am feeling bad, for instance, then this understanding will give Teacher thought positive emotion. In this particular case, Teacher thought may feel bad because of the chaos at work, but this Teacher pain will be balanced by the Teacher pleasure of understanding why I feel bad.

For those who find this sort of internal analysis difficult, it can also be practiced in *external* form. For instance, one of my nieces is a Mercy person. She knew from an understanding of cognitive styles that the Mercy person does not naturally get along with the Teacher person, and we saw when looking at Piaget's stages that childish Mercy thought naturally struggles with Teacher thought. She wanted to move beyond this. Her husband had a friend in graduate studies who is a Teacher person. Being friends with this Teacher person gave her an opportunity to understand Teacher thought and become reconciled internally with Teacher thought. Initially, her gut response was that the Teacher person acts the way that he does in order to be obnoxious or hurtful. In other words, she was seeing the relationship from the Mercy perspective of one individual *versus* another. However, she gradually learned that he was behaving in a manner that he thought was natural, and she began to understand *why* he was behaving the way that he did, changing the focus from Mercy struggle to Teacher understanding. This step is not easy for a Mercy person to take, because the Teacher person is quite rare, most people do not understand the nature of Teacher thought, and the Teacher person does not generally put a high priority upon respecting the Mercy constraints of culture. Saying this more generally, the way that I treat a cognitive module within my own mind will be reflected in the way that I treat the cognitive style who is conscious in that cognitive module. For instance, if I suppress Teacher thought within my own mind, then I will naturally be antagonistic to Teacher persons. Similarly, if I want to develop Teacher thought within my own mind, then I can do this by interacting with Teacher persons.

At first glance, it may appear that what I am advocating is unrelated to Christianity. However, Paul gives similar advice in the passage in Romans 12 that describes cognitive styles. We examined this passage briefly at the very beginning of this book. Now that we understand more about how the mind functions, let us take another look.

> Therefore I urge you, brethren, by the mercies of God, to present your bodies a living and holy sacrifice, acceptable to God, which is your spiritual service of worship. And do not be conformed to this world, but be transformed by the renewing of your mind, so that you may prove what the will of God is, that which is good and acceptable and perfect. For through the grace given to me I say to everyone among you not to think more highly of himself than he ought to think; but to think so as to have sound judgment, as God has allotted to each a measure of faith. For just as we have many members in one body and all the members do not have the same function, so we, who are many, are one body in Christ, and individually members one of another. Since we have gifts that differ according to the grace given to us, each of us is to exercise them accordingly: if prophecy, according to the proportion of his faith; if service, in his serving; or he who teaches, in his teaching; or he who exhorts, in his exhortation; he who gives, with liberality; he who leads, with diligence; he who shows mercy, with cheerfulness (Romans 12:1-8).

Paul begins by saying that MMNs which drive physical action need to be submitted to the TMN of a concept of God. And instead of being shaped by the MMNs of culture, one should be transformed through an internal process, guided by an increasingly adequate mental concept of God. This is then followed by advice that sounds very much like what we have just discussed. One should not think that one's cognitive style is the only valid form of thought, but rather be guided by a rational general understanding to recognize that one's cognitive style is only part of the total picture. Just as a physical body has many parts that function together, so all the cognitive styles function together in an integrated manner held together by Contributor incarnation. Paul then gives the list of seven cognitive styles upon which the theory of mental symmetry is based.

Jesus says something similar in his summary of religion.

> A lawyer, asked Him a question, testing Him, "Teacher, which is the great commandment in the Law?" And He said to him, "'YOU SHALL LOVE THE LORD YOUR GOD WITH ALL YOUR HEART, AND WITH ALL YOUR SOUL, AND WITH ALL YOUR MIND.' This is the great and foremost commandment. The second is like it, 'YOU SHALL LOVE YOUR NEIGHBOR AS YOURSELF.' On these two commandments depend the whole Law and the Prophets" (Matt. 22: 35-40).

The second half of this quote is known as the Golden rule. However, notice that Jesus places the Golden rule within the context of loving God. The first step is to love God with all the *internal* aspects of one's being, including the 'mind' of abstract understanding and the 'heart' of personal identity. Using the language of mental symmetry, one first finds emotional pleasure in a general Teacher theory that applies to all of the thinking of all cognitive modules. One then loves others as oneself within the *context* of this general Teacher understanding. If one skips directly to the Golden rule, then love of neighbor will be guided by the MMNs of culture rather than the TMN of 'how the mind works'.

For instance, suppose that I am smoking and my friend asks me for a cigarette. Directly applying the Golden rule leads to the conclusion that I should share a cigarette with my friend. I like to smoke, therefore he should also be able to smoke. But smoking is not healthy because it is inconsistent with 'how the body works'. Therefore, a direct application of the Golden rule will actually be harmful because I will be helping my neighbor to damage his physical body. However, if sharing a cigarette is placed within the context of 'how the body works', then the goal will be to help my neighbor as myself by developing more healthy alternatives to smoking.

Moving on, we have seen that people's minds are naturally fragmented. However, when people stop being members of a tribe and start to individuate, then each cognitive style will naturally develop the cognitive module that is conscious. A Perceiver person will develop Perceiver thought, a Contributor person will develop Contributor thought, and so on. Examining each person within the framework of an understanding of cognitive styles will lead to a composite picture of how the mind *could* function. This framework of understanding is essential, because it indicates what one should and should not learn from each person. For instance, the Contributor person is naturally good at goal-oriented behavior based in a knowledge of cause-and-effect. One should learn about this type of thinking from the Contributor person because it is an expression of Contributor thought. However, one should not follow the bottom line of the typical Contributor person, because that is determined by Mercy thought, which is subconscious in the Contributor person. One should also question the values and truths of the Contributor person, because they are determined by Perceiver thought, which is also subconscious in the Contributor person. Similarly, one should learn about politeness and working within the system from the Facilitator person, because this expresses Facilitator thought, which is conscious in the Facilitator person. However, one should not automatically accept the system within which the Facilitator works, because that is an expression of Teacher and Server thought, which is subconscious within the Facilitator person. Likewise, the Mercy person is naturally good at taking a mental snapshot of a person's emotional state. One should learn from this because it is an expression of Mercy thought, which is conscious in the Mercy person. However, one should question the advice that the Mercy person gives about changing one's emotional state, because that advice is based upon thought that is subconscious in the Mercy person.

I am not suggesting that one should never learn from the subconscious thought of others. Rather, I am suggesting that this standard needs to be applied when people have gone *beyond* the stage of being part of a group to being individuals but have not yet *arrived* at the stage of mental wholeness. It is in this *intermediate* stage that one must attempt to learn from conscious thought while questioning subconscious thought, and this describes the level of mental functioning for the average person in modern Western society. We have individuated, but we are not mentally whole.

Learning the right thing from each person is illustrated by the following European joke.

> Heaven is where the police are British, the lovers French, the mechanics German, the chefs Italian, and it is all organized by the Swiss. Hell is where the police are German, the lovers Swiss, the mechanics French, the chefs British, and it is all organized by the Italians.

Notice how a composite portrait of the *same* nationalities can lead either to heaven or hell. The difference between these two lies in learning the right things from the right people.

Looking at this now from a religious perspective, if I continue to observe myself as well as others individuals with my cognitive style, then I will gain a *composite* picture of this cognitive style. Using Teacher thought to understand the essence of this cognitive style will lead indirectly to the Platonic form of the *ideal* person of my cognitive style, which will provide a set of values to guide my personal identity. Similarly, observing other individuals in the light of cognitive styles will provide me with a composite portrait of each cognitive style. Understanding how each cognitive style functions and how the various cognitive modules interact will construct a general understanding of human thought. This general understanding (that applies to personal identity) will lead in Teacher thought to a concept of God and in Mercy thought to the Platonic form of an ideal society composed of ideal persons interacting in an ideal manner.

At first glance, this idea of a concept of God based in mental wholeness may sound rather different than the Christian concept of God. However, I suggest that this is not the case. Christian doctrine teaches that man is 'made in the image of God' (Gen. 1:26-27). Theologians recognize that this cannot describe a *physical* image because there is obviously no physical similarity between a finite human and a universal being. We have seen in this book that pursuing mental wholeness leads to the mental concept of a Christian Trinitarian God, suggesting that 'in the image of God' refers to an *internal* correspondence. Consistent with this, we saw earlier that when Philip asks to see God, Jesus answers that he is the image of God and that Philip should know this because he has spent so much time interacting with Jesus, telling us that we are dealing with an *internal* similarity.

> Philip said to Him, "Lord, show us the Father, and it is enough for us." Jesus said to him, "Have I been so long with you, and *yet* you have not come to know Me, Philip? He who has seen Me has seen the Father; how *can* you say, 'Show us the Father'" (John 14:8-9).

In addition, the book of Revelation refers four times to the 'seven spirits of God', suggesting that the seven cognitive modules of the human mind may be a reflection of something inherent in the essence of God.

Summarizing, if one starts with the biblical list of 'spiritual gifts', one ends up with a neurologically consistent, universal theory of personality. If one uses this theory to develop the mind, this leads to the mental concept of a universal Trinitarian God based in the Platonic forms—or spirits—of the seven different cognitive styles. In contrast, the concept of God that I encounter in 'Christian' books and churches often bears only a *partial* resemblance to either Christian doctrine or Christian practice.

I suggested earlier that moving from the first stage of truth to the second stage of righteousness requires transforming one's concept of God from one that is based in absolute truth revealed through words to one that is based in the universal truth of 'how things work'. This transition will naturally occur when one analyzes self and others in terms of cognitive modules, because one is constructing a general Teacher theory that applies to personal identity based upon the universal truth of 'how the mind works', which will end up creating a mental concept of God. And because there is only room for one universal Teacher theory, this new concept of God *will* conflict with existing explicit—and implicit—mental concepts of God. That is why this book goes to extensive lengths to show that the theory of mental symmetry is consistent with the structure of science, consistent with evidence from neurology, and consistent with biblical theology. I am trying to show that the theory of mental symmetry does not replace existing content but rather reinterprets it and places it within the larger context of a meta-theory.

Looking now at the big picture, we have seen the three stages of salvation occurring in three different contexts. First, we saw how the scientific revolution, industrial revolution, and consumer revolution illustrate the three stages of salvation guided by a Teacher understanding of how the world works. Second, we looked at the life of Jesus as described in the Gospels and noticed that it also can be analyzed in terms of the three stages of salvation. Third, we examined how these three stages occur within the mind and compared this with what the Bible says about personal transformation.

Suppose that one steps back and looks at human history as a whole. Do these same three stages appear? I have suggested that each stage is accompanied by a transformation in the concept of God. One can find these three *divine* transformations described in the Bible. The first transformation to a God of verbal revelation can be seen in the revealing of Torah to the Jews on Mount Sinai. The second transformation to a God of righteousness corresponds to the incarnation of Jesus in which the 'Word was made flesh'. And one finds the third transformation to a universal God who lives among men portrayed in the story of the New Jerusalem at the end of the book of Revelation.

The scientific, industrial, and consumer revolutions occurred after the second divine transformation and before the third. Thus, we see the three stages occurring within one larger transformation of a concept of God. After the second divine transformation into a God of righteousness, it was *inevitable* that Western society would discover science with its concept of the divine righteousness of how the world works. In contrast, before this second divine transformation, it was *possible* that Jewish and Greek society could have discovered science, but it did not happen. If this pattern holds, then it is possible that present society will discover what rebirth really means during the present civilization, but if it does not then the next civilization will experience an unveiling that makes it impossible to avoid learning what rebirth really means.

✳ 17. Other Worlds

I suggested at the beginning of this book that the goal of religion is to come up with a grand explanation and to determine my place within this explanation. This final chapter will use the theory of mental symmetry to come up with a grand explanation as well as suggest personal guidelines for maneuvering within this grand explanation.

I should warn that this will truly be a *grand* explanation because we are about to discuss non-material topics such as heaven, angels, and the spirit realm. Scientific methodology requires empirical evidence, and researchers have discovered that technical thought can be used to analyze the laws of nature. This is all fine and good—when studying how the *world* works. However, technical thought is always limited to some restricted domain, and working within some domain will lead to the formation of a mental network. When technical thought encounters something outside of its restricted domain, the *correct* response is for technical thought to acknowledge that is not qualified to evaluate this material and to defer to some other form of thinking. However, the *typical* response is for technical thought to be driven by underlying mental networks to ridicule and belittle the 'extraneous' material and/or to insist that if technical thought cannot say anything, then this means that *no one* is permitted to say anything. This is especially true when discussing anything regarding non-material reality.

Three points need to be made forcefully in response. First, focusing solely upon how the world works creates a human society that is at best banal and at worst hellish, because it either ignores human value or else tramples upon it. Second, if human existence ceases at death, then even thinking about existence becomes absurd. Third, when material that lies outside of some theory is belittled or ignored, then this suggests that the theory has turned into a TMN which is emotionally motivating a person to reject inconsistent input. Thus, I suggest that what is really needed is a general theory that is consistent with scientific thought which can *also* handle the concept of non-physical reality without recoiling in horror.

> The theory of mental symmetry can naturally handle non-physical existence.

We have already seen that the theory of mental symmetry is consistent with scientific thought as well as the deep structure of the physical universe. Over the years, I have gradually realized that the theory of mental symmetry also provides possible explanations for non-physical existence. This bears repeating. Scientific methodology cannot handle the concept of non-physical reality because it *begins* with the assumption that only empirical evidence is valid. In contrast, the theory of mental symmetry can handle both physical reality and nonphysical existence *without* having to be modified in any manner. That is because the starting point for mental symmetry is *one step removed* from physical reality. Instead of beginning with physical reality, one starts with the mind, an entity that *interacts* with physical reality through the brain and the body. The final chapter of this book will show that the theory of mental symmetry is consistent with neurology at a detailed level. Thus, I am not advocating that one abandon empirical evidence. However, I suggest that this physical evidence should be used as a constraint rather than as a starting point.

Starting with the mind *automatically* generates a possible answer both for life-after-death and for non-physical reality. Life-after-death simply becomes the mind existing as a disembodied entity apart from the brain and body, while non-physical reality can be analyzed as the *same* mind interacting with a *different* external reality via a *different* brain/body interface. (I am using the term 'mind' in this chapter as a synonym for 'soul'.) What remains the same in all cases is the mind, and the fundamental assumption of the theory of mental symmetry is that the structure of the mind does not change.

This *reverses* the manner in which nonphysical existence is typically investigated. Instead of asking 'What is the nature of non-physical reality?' one turns this question around and asks instead, 'What type of non-physical reality could the mind inhabit?' In other words, whatever life-after-death is like, it can only be life-after-death *for me* if it is compatible with the structure of my mind. This is like asking what homes are like in an unknown culture. If these homes are inhabited by human beings, then this automatically puts constraints on the nature of homes. There must be a place to make food because people eat. There must be a toilet because people defecate. There must be some sort of bed because people sleep. There must be some kind of door through which a person can enter or exit the home, because people cannot fly. And there must be some source of light because people cannot see in the dark. All of these aspects will have to be present in some form because of the nature of the human body. Similarly, if human minds are to exist within some realm of life-after-death, then this automatically puts constraints upon the nature of life-after-death.

This approach has already been used twice within this book. First, we saw when looking at Contributor incarnation that the structure of the mind is compatible with the deep structure of the laws of nature. If this deep similarity did not exist, then the human mind would find the physical universe alien and incomprehensible, because the physical environment would continually be forcing the mind to function in an incoherent manner. Second, we have seen that the structure of the mind is deeply consistent with the concept of God and religion described in the Bible.

Notice that there are two kinds of compatibility: software and hardware. *Software* compatibility means that the external environment functions in a manner that is consistent with the structure of my core mental networks. When this compatibility is violated, then I experience culture shock. *Hardware* compatibility means that the external environment functions in a way that is consistent with the structure of my mind. As we have seen in this book, mental reprogramming is required because the mind naturally develops software that is only *partially* consistent with the underlying mental hardware. Using a car analogy, drivers naturally drive their cars in a way that is harmful to the vehicle and have to be taught how to drive in a way that does not damage it.

The Spiritual Realm

Several centuries ago, Swedenborg proposed a view of life-after-death based upon what he called 'ruling loves', which are very similar to the mental networks of mental symmetry. I do not suggest that all of the *details* of Swedenborg's system make sense. After all, Swedenborg lived in the 18th century, when the religious attitude was much stronger and far less was known about both the world and the mind. However, Swedenborg's general concept of ruling loves does explore the concept of life-after-death in a manner that is consistent with the theory of mental symmetry.

Swedenborg defines a ruling love in the following passage (Kingslake, 1991).

> The affections or loves that constitute our spiritual mind are arranged like a little kingdom, and each new affection we develop takes its place in relation to the others, and works together with them. Anything which is not in harmony gets pushed to the outside. If it is a kingdom, it must have a king! There must be a ruling love inside each one of us, which organizes our other affections, promoting some to positions of importance, and demoting others. This ruling love is not seen in the hurly-burly of our everyday lives. Rather it has to do with our motivation: why we do the things we do, why we are living in the way we are. It has to do with ultimate values, and therefore it is essentially religious. It does not necessarily appear in our outward behavior. Even our closest friends cannot tell for certain what our ruling love is. We may not even know ourselves! But nevertheless the whole color and character of our spiritual mind is derived from our ruling love (Ch. 6).

A mental network could be described as an 'affection' because it uses emotions to impose its structure upon thought and behavior. Mental networks organize themselves into an emotional hierarchy, with core mental networks imposing their structure upon lesser mental networks. In the language of Swedenborg, 'there must be a ruling love inside each one of us, which organizes our other affections, promoting some and demoting others'. The average individual has never analyzed the core mental networks that drive his mind. Similarly, Swedenborg notes that 'we may not even know ourselves' the nature of our ruling loves.

A spiritual realm would express mental networks as 'physical' reality.

Swedenborg says that life-after-death begins in a neutral 'World of Spirits' where a person's true nature is gradually revealed.

After a short or longer period in the World of Spirits, a person's ruling love begins to reveal itself, and he no longer cares whether it is seen or not. All the thoughts, affections and beliefs which he brought with him but which are not in harmony with his ruling love, begin to fall away; they are not really his own, and so he discards them, becoming completely integrated—'himself.' He can no longer play a role or 'put on an act' or pretend to be what he isn't. This stripping of one's self bare, even to one's most secret thoughts and intentions, is the judgment (Ch.7).

Using the language of mental symmetry, physical existence involves an interaction between mind and body. This makes it possible to *control* what the mind thinks by placing the body within a certain environment, to *change* what the mind thinks by altering the physical environment, and to *rely* upon the body and brain to keep incompatible fragments of the mind together. A disembodied mind (or soul) would lack these compensation mechanisms. Instead, a person would be defined by his core mental networks and all other mental networks would either conform or else fall away. This happens to some extent in aged people, because they become more like their dominant traits.

Swedenborg continues,

Eventually, everyone in the intermediate region begins to feel the 'pull' of their ruling love. They cannot resist it; they must move in the direction it draws them, like water finding its own level. The evil go first. They are repeatedly warned that they are heading for Hell, but what do they care? It seems a pretty good place to them, the best they have ever been in! All the other inhabitants there are like themselves: they quarrel and lust and spit invectives at one another to their hearts' content. Who sent them to Hell? Nobody but themselves. There is no inquiry as to their faith or former church affiliations, or whether they were baptized, or even what kind of life they lived on earth. They migrate toward a hellish state because they are drawn to its way of life, and for no other reason... Good spirits also leave the intermediate region, but in the opposite direction, towards Heaven. Their ruling love takes them to precisely that point in Heaven where they feel at home and are at rest. All the other inhabitants there are of the same nature; they even resemble one another, like members of the same family, and they welcome them as new-found brothers or sisters. In our material world, a person can settle down and live almost anywhere; but in the spiritual world there is only one place where any individual can feel at home, and this is determined by his or her deep-down attitude towards God and the neighbor. Those are near together who are alike in character. Love attracts, and hate repels. 'Birds of a feather flock together.' It is possible, of course, to leave one's home for short periods at a time; but, if one does so, there is always a feeling of strain and anxiety, a 'home sickness' until one returns (Ibid, Ch. 7).

Physical existence occurs within a natural universe that functions in a manner that is *independent* of the mind. This independence would be lost if the mind left physical reality, and Swedenborg suggests that the attraction and repulsion of mental networks characterizes the *external* environment of life-after-death. Thus, a person would be inescapably attracted to an environment that was consistent with core mental networks, peopled by human minds with similar core mental networks. Any attempt to leave this environment would face core mental networks with incompatible input, creating a strong desire to return to one's natural environment.

Swedenborg expands upon this interrelationship between mental networks and spiritual 'reality'.

> Since the spiritual world is non-material, everything there springs from and re-flects the spiritual nature of the local inhabitants. This includes nearness and dis-tance in relation one to another; also the character of their surroundings, which corresponds exactly to their states of mind... It is quite easy to travel within one's particular Heaven or Hell, though not so easy beyond its borders. If you want to visit somebody at a distance, all you have to do is to bring yourself temporarily into harmony with their state, and you find yourself traveling towards them. You may be 'walking' if the distance is short; or 'flying' if the distance is consider-able. This 'flying' is a rapid projection from one place to another... All objects and surroundings in the spiritual world are a projection of the states of the people in the vicinity. The whole landscape is like a mirror reflecting their thoughts and affections by a system of symbolism. The rocks are formed by their basic beliefs; the birds are molded by their rapidly-flying thoughts, the animals by their affec-tions, and so on (Ibid, Ch.5).

Because *physical* reality functions independently of the mind, one learns about reality and then builds mental maps to represent reality. In a spiritual realm, the external map would be a *reflection* of the mental map, and one would move externally by moving in-ternally through the mental map. This correspondence between internal content and external reality would also make it possible to see Platonic forms.

I mentioned in an earlier chapter that a person can only make major choices if his mind contains *conflicting* mental networks between which one can choose. A disembodied mind that is integrated around core mental networks would no longer have conflicting mental networks and thus would be unable to make major choices. Swedenborg de-scribes this limitation of free will.

> Theoretically it might be possible to change one's ruling love at any time, even after death; but in practice nobody ever wants to do so because, especially after settling down in Heaven or Hell, one is totally committed either to good or to evil. Spirits can change in a hundred different ways in the course of their devel-opment to eternity, but it is always within the framework of their ruling love... Only in the equilibrium or balance between Heaven and Hell that exists in this earth life does anyone change his ruling love, which is what makes this earth life so important! (Ch.7)

In summary, Swedenborg is basically suggesting that everyone becomes imprisoned within an environment that is consistent with core mental networks. If this is the case, then the best option is to construct the *nicest* prison possible and then become mentally trapped within that prison. In contrast, one of the worst options would be to take the childish behavior of 'struggle for survival' and turn it into the TMN of a universal theory around which one integrates one's mind.

Notice that we have returned to the matter of evaluating a potential pair of spectacles, except now on a more personal level. The spectacles of my worldview determine how I *view* reality. But if reality ceases to become independent of the mind, then my spectacles actually become the prison that *determines* my reality. I suggested at the beginning of the book that one evaluates a potential pair of glasses by putting them on and then asking two questions: 1) How clear is my vision? 2) How much can I see? If the disembodied mind inhabits a spiritual realm that is an expression of the mind, then these questions become more personal: 1) 'How clear is my vision?' turns into 'How interesting would my world be?' Would my mental networks create a vivid external environment full of interesting details, or would they produce a shadowy realm of vague shapes? 2) 'How much can I see?' becomes 'How far could I travel?' Would I be forced to stay in one place or would I have the mental ability to travel far and wide? Added to this would be two additional *personal* questions: 3) How pleasant would my world be? Would my core mental networks drive me to create a hellish environment of suffering and conflict, or would they lead to a heavenly environment of peace and pleasure? 4) What would I look like? If my physical appearance were a reflection of core mental networks, then what would be my physical appearance?

Logic suggests that the best possible mental prison is one that is consistent with the structure of the mind, because I would then be driven by my core mental networks to function in a manner that brought fulfillment to all my cognitive modules.

Now let us connect this with Christianity. How does the concept of the disembodied mind being judged by the structure of its own core mental networks relate to the Christian doctrine of *divine* judgment? And if the disembodied mind creates its own environment, then where is the Christian idea of 'living in heaven with God'? First, the individual who is being forced to live with his core mental networks is actually being judged by the *divine* righteousness of 'how the mind works'. Second, an individual will experience the most personal joy and fulfillment if all cognitive modules within his mind function together in a cooperative manner. If the external environment reflected internal structure, then a person with mental wholeness would also experience *environmental* wholeness, and this combination could only be described as living in heaven. Going further, when all cognitive modules function together, then the mind will be held together by the mental concept of a Christian Trinitarian God. Thus, those who inhabited heaven would want to live in the presence of a Christian God, while those who created their own hell would find the concept of a Christian God personally repulsive.

A similar statement could be made regarding the Christian assertion that 'saying the Christian prayer of salvation saves one from hell'. That is because the prayer of salvation makes it possible to practice the personal honesty that is required to transform core mental networks so that they interact in a loving manner rather than one characterized by childish antagonism. However, what matters is not *saying* 'the magic formula' but rather taking the *internal step* of mentally enrolling in the 'school of incarnation'.

Summarizing what we have discussed so far, we have examined how a disembodied mind would be held together by its *mental networks* and how it could survive in a 'spiritual' environment that reflected these mental networks. It is also theoretically possible that human-like minds could start their existence as 'spirits' within such a spiritual realm. Such beings would experience neither the benefits nor the shortcomings of going through Piaget's stages of cognitive development. Thus, they would tend to be immature and innocent. They would also be mentally parasitic upon other individuals for their cognitive content.

The Angelic Realm

Moving on, one can postulate the existence of a *second* nonphysical realm by asking two simple related questions. What makes concrete thought concrete and abstract thought abstract? Why does concrete thought deal with specifics and abstract thought with generalities? I suggest that these characteristics are a result of the *environment* and are not inherent qualities of the mind. Mercy thought receives specific experiences of pain and pleasure from the physical world, while Server thought can use physical actions to affect physical matter in specific ways. This *direct, finite* interaction between cognitive modules and external environment makes Mercy and Server thought both concrete and specific. Perceiver thought, in contrast, cannot impose objects directly upon the external environment but rather acquires facts by looking at many specific situations. Thus, Perceiver thought interacts with the physical environment in a way that is indirect and general. Similarly, Teacher words are merely vibrations in the air, and words by their very nature can refer to many different specific items or situations. For instance, the word 'apple' can describe a myriad of apple-like shapes. Even when one tries to make words more specific, such as referring to 'the assassination of Abraham Lincoln', this verbal description still contains many related specific incidents.

> An angelic realm would be a mirror image of physical reality.

Thus, it would be theoretically possible for a human mind to be placed in a container within an environment that made Teacher and Perceiver thought concrete and Mercy and Server thought abstract. This is not easy to visualize, because human assumptions regarding concrete and abstract are fundamental. However, one can gain an idea of what it is like by comparing normal movement with the examination of a physician. My physical location is determined by my physical body. If I am in Paris, then I am not in London. That is because my location within the realm of Mercy experiences is determined by the Perceiver object of my physical body. In contrast, the physical body of a physician is largely irrelevant. It does not really matter whether I am seeing Dr. Singh,

Dr. Song, or Dr. Byrd. Instead, what matters is the *specialization* of the physician, such as cardiologist or neurologist, which is a Teacher name defined by a set of Server skills. Normal movement occurs within the world of Mercy experiences. Perceiver thought is used to define one's location, and then Server actions are used to move from the current location to some other location. Compare this with the typical doctor's examination. The visit begins with the doctor perusing the file of the patient. The visit then consists of a sequence of questions, instructions, and examinations, such as 'How long have you been coughing?', 'Take two pills a day', or 'Open your mouth and say ah'. When the visit is over then the doctor immediately leaves and moves to another room and another patient. Thus, the 'location' is composed of Teacher words and Server actions and the doctor 'moves' by using Perceiver thought to change the mental context: 'I was examining John in room three. I am now examining Joan in room one'.

Notice that Perceiver and Server have exchanged roles, as have Teacher and Mercy. That is what happens when abstract becomes concrete and concrete becomes abstract. In terms of the diagram of mental symmetry, the left side of the diagram becomes the right and the right becomes left, which is why it is called a diagram of *mental symmetry*. This is difficult to visualize because it is impossible to do physically. But it is possible to do mentally, as illustrated by the behavior of a physician, or any other professional specialist. Now try to imagine a physician without a physical body. The job would then consist of teleporting from one 'Server sequence of examination' to another. At least that is how the behavior of a non-physical physician would appear to humans. To grasp how this might appear to the non-physical physician, one can turn to the example of the Internet. Each webpage is a 'location' on the Internet, and a webpage can act as a 'homepage' that defines the identity of some individual. A webpage is composed primarily of a Server sequence of Teacher words. One moves from one webpage to another by clicking a link, which then performs a 'hyperjump' to the next webpage. In cognitive terms, one is existing in a realm of Teacher words in which Server thought defines location and Perceiver thought is used to move from one location to another. The location of a page on the web has nothing to do with physical location. If I am in Seattle, then Vancouver is closer than Rome, but on the Internet closeness is defined by the number of links that one has to click to reach a certain webpage. A webpage that is hosted by a computer in Rome may be only one click away, while a webpage located on a computer in Vancouver may be five links away. Time is also defined differently on the Internet. The webpage that I visit may have been written yesterday or ten years ago. What matters primarily is the number of updates that have occurred, or in other words, the number of Perceiver transformations that have been applied to the Server sequence of Teacher words.

This may all sound very strange, but it is the *same kind* of strangeness that one encounters in quantum physics. Mercy thought interacts with the physical world of objects, whereas Teacher thought thinks in terms of the waves of speech, movement, and sequence. Quantum mechanics says that there is a duality between objects and waves.

Every object is also a wave and vice versa. In quantum mechanics, objects can teleport from one location to another by temporarily exhibiting wavelike properties. While the mathematics of quantum mechanics is well-known, visualizing what is happening is so difficult that one of the interpretations is colloquially known as 'shut up and calculate'. In other words, do not even try to visualize what is happening, just use the mathematical equations.

Turning now to the non-physical realm, the typical UFO or angel story is like a doctor's examination. Many individuals who claim to have contacted UFOs even refer to their 'alien abduction' as a medical examination, but there are deeper similarities as well. The UFO suddenly appears, a task is performed, and then the UFO disappears; the abductee is teleported or 'beamed' on board, the examination is performed, and then the abductee is returned. Many angel stories have a similar flavor. One common tale is that of the roadside helper. A person is stuck by the side of the road with a flat tire or some mechanical problem, some stranger shows up to fix the problem and then immediately leaves. When the person turns around to give thanks for the assistance, the helper is nowhere to be seen but has vanished from sight. The person then concludes that the helper was an angel. Another common variant is for some unknown visitor to show up, deliver an important message, and then disappear. *What* the angel is saying or *why* the alien is performing a medical examination is of secondary importance here, because that is an expression of software, which is determined by mental networks. In contrast, the *nature* of the visitation would be determined by the hardware of 'how the physical realm works' interacting with 'how the angelic realm works'. Angels and UFOs might have vastly different agendas, but there appears to be an underlying structural similarity in the *method* of visitation.

There is a curious story in the book of Acts that contains similar features.

> But an angel of the Lord spoke to Philip saying, "Get up and go south to the road that descends from Jerusalem to Gaza." (This is a desert road.) So he got up and went; and there was an Ethiopian eunuch, a court official of Candace, queen of the Ethiopians, who was in charge of all her treasure; and he had come to Jerusalem to worship, and he was returning and sitting in his chariot, and was reading the prophet Isaiah. Then the Spirit said to Philip, "Go up and join this chariot." Philip ran up and heard him reading Isaiah the prophet, and said, "Do you understand what you are reading?" And he said, "Well, how could I, unless someone guides me?" And he invited Philip to come up and sit with him... When they came up out of the water, the Spirit of the Lord snatched Philip away; and the eunuch no longer saw him, but went on his way rejoicing. But Philip found himself at Azotus, and as he passed through he kept preaching the gospel to all the cities until he came to Caesarea (Acts 8:26-31, 39-40).

Like many alien abductions, this one occurs in the middle of a journey on a deserted road. While a human performs the visit in this story, the account begins with a message from an angel. Philip (the human) then performs the task of a messenger, explaining the biblical text being read by the Ethiopian eunuch. And when Philip's job is finished, he disappears from sight and finds himself teleported to another location and another task.

The idea of a mind being associated with a Teacher name rather than a Mercy body is borne out by the word angel itself. 'Angel' comes from the Greek term *angelos*, which means 'messenger'. A message is a specific chunk of Teacher content, and a messenger is a person defined by a specific chunk of Teacher content, just as a human is a person defined by a specific chunk of Mercy matter.

UFO encounters exhibit other common characteristics that are consistent with the concept of Teacher-based minds visiting from a realm of Teacher-like waves and Server sequences that is independent of physical reality.

UFOs are typically associated with energy. UFO encounters are often accompanied by various forms of radiation, suggesting a connection with energy rather than matter. UFOs often manipulate objects using beams of light that have shape and length.

UFOs and aliens behave in a manner that shows unfamiliarity with the human concept of spatial location. UFOs often travel along power lines, treating them as highways, suggesting that aliens associate location with energy rather than physical location. Humans are typically abducted either when asleep and mentally distant from the Perceiver objects of physical reality, or when in the midst of some journey, when the Perceiver location is changing and the Server sequence of 'taking a trip' is constant. And aliens occasionally make spatial mistakes that humans would consider quite stupid, such as returning an abductee to the wrong room, or putting the abductee's clothes on backwards.

UFOs and aliens often move in a manner that is not subject to the laws of physics. Instead of walking, aliens will often glide, transporting themselves and objects through walls, implying that the Server sequence of movement is more 'solid' than the Perceiver objects being traversed by this movement. Observers often describe UFOs splitting into distinct objects or joining to form a single object, suggesting that Perceiver thought in the angelic realm does not just classify objects but can also manipulate objects.

My goal here is not to delve deeply into the realm of aliens and angels, because many strange words have been written about the subject and it is difficult to sift the wheat from the chaff. Rather, I am attempting to show that the theory of mental symmetry can be used *in unmodified form* to analyze the topic of aliens and angels and that the fragments of evidence that do exist are consistent with the predictions made by mental symmetry. In contrast, scientific methodology with its demand for empirical evidence is only capable of viewing aliens and angels as physical beings from other planets. It is possible that some aliens do live on other physical planets. However, when one examines stories about these aliens, one still notices a number of elements that suggest the existence of an angelic realm that extends beyond the physical realm.

Notice that the angelic realm is quite different than the spiritual realm. The angelic realm may be characterized by bizarre wave-like content, but it is a realm of content, and when angels and UFOs visit, they have agendas. These agendas might seem incomprehensible, but they seem to know what they are doing.

In contrast, the spiritual realm is not a realm of solid content, and when spirits interact with humans then spirits typically acquire their content from humans, amplifying human content rather than imposing alien content upon humans as angels and UFOs do.

> Spirits and angels are treated differently in the Bible.

This same distinction can be seen when examining biblical accounts of spirits and angels. In the Hebrew Old Testament, the word 'ruach' is used for spirit and 'malaach' for angel. In the Greek New Testament, the word for spirit is 'pneuma' and the word for angel is 'angelos'. One can see in the following quote from one of the trials of Paul that it was common to make a distinction between these two. Notice that the non-physical realm is being associated with both angels (angelos) and spirits (pneuma).

> The Sadducees say that there is no resurrection, nor an angel, nor a spirit, but the Pharisees acknowledge them all. And there occurred a great uproar; and some of the scribes of the Pharisaic party stood up and began to argue heatedly, saying, "We find nothing wrong with this man; suppose a spirit or an angel has spoken to him?" (Acts 23:8-9).

When the word *malaach* or *angelos* is used in the Bible, it consistently describes a person delivering a message or performing some task. The only time that angels are described as standing or sitting around is when the scene being depicted is in heaven and not on earth. While angels are sometimes described as communicating with humans through dreams, there is no biblical story of a human being 'possessed' by an angel.

The terms *ruach* and *pneuma* are used in a completely different manner. (When not applied to people, the term *ruach* means 'wind'.) A person might have a 'spirit of jealousy', or a spirit 'comes upon' a certain person in order to drive him to behave in a certain way. Spirits are 'cast out' of people in order to stop them from exhibiting certain behaviors. Spirits express emotions and amplify human abilities. Spirits usually do not come only for a single episode to perform a task and then leave, but rather 'dwell' in a person. The reference may be to the spirit of a person, some specific spirit coming upon a person, or being motivated or filled by the Holy Spirit. This is consistent with a type of being that interacts over the long term with mental networks.

Summarizing, mental symmetry, biblical references, and anecdotal evidence all suggest that the *same* mind can exist within one of three possible realms: as a human within the physical realm, as an angel/alien within the angelic realm, or as a spirit or disembodied mind within the spiritual realm. The human and angelic realms appear to be mirror images of one another, with one composed of physical matter and the other of waves/energy. Because these two domains contain content that is independent of the mind, people who grow up in these environments would be driven through stages of cognitive development to emerge as individuals with agendas. In contrast, the content of the spiritual realm appears to be dependent upon the mind, leading to individuals who would be parasitic upon beings from other realms for their content. For a physical human, the primary mind/body interface occurs through Mercy and Server thought. For an angel/alien, the primary mind/body interface would occur through Teacher and Server thought. For a spirit, the main mind-body interface would be via mental networks. Whether a disembodied mind is a spirit or has a spirit could be debated. The evidence seems to indicate the latter. The point is that the disembodied mind appears to be capable of interacting with a spiritual realm on the basis of its mental networks.

Interaction Between Realms

Now let us look at the interaction *between* these realms. Interaction between humans occurs within a context of physical matter. I recognize my friend John, for instance, by the shape of his physical body. In order to communicate with John from a distance I use a physical connection such as a telephone line or computer network cable. John does not disappear if I refuse to believe in him. Instead, physical appearance is independent of mental state.

The situation appears to be quite different when interacting with either the spiritual or angelic realms. Those who are attempting to contact spirits often complain when the attempt fails that 'someone in the room is a disbeliever'. Similarly, one of the comments that one hears in connection with UFOs is that as long as most people do not believe in them, they cannot appear openly. Obviously, these statements can be used as an excuse for the absence of evidence, but this is not the sort of excuse that one hears when dealing with fellow humans and physical matter.

Going further, it is common to hear about spirits, angels, and UFOs communicating with humans *telepathically*. If I see a car driving in the distance and start thinking about that car, then that vehicle will not respond to my thoughts. But, in many UFO stories, a person will see a UFO, attempt to communicate with it telepathically, and find that the craft responds in an intelligent manner to his thoughts. Similarly, one does not normally sense the presence of other humans. In contrast, people often claim that they feel a strong sense of personal presence when describing encounters with spirits, aliens, or angels. This sense of presence appears to extend to the animal realm, because accounts often talk about birds and animals becoming totally silent when a UFO shows up.

My primary goal is not to focus upon any of these specific points but rather to point out that the consensus of opinion is that mental state plays a dominant role when interacting with other realms. My general thesis is that one can explain spirits and angels in terms of the *same* kind of mind living within a *different* kind of container and environment. People interact best through what they have in *common*. Therefore, it makes sense that there would be a strong *mental* component to interaction.

Going further, this means that a disembodied human mind would find itself *living* among beings from other realms. This is what one finds described in the Bible: Dead souls find themselves either in heaven with angels or in hell with demons. But one also finds this in UFO stories. One well-known researcher in this field recounts that

> we got thousands upon thousands of letters. Instead of glancing at them and discarding them, Anne went to work... She kept a big chart to keep track of repeated descriptions, and one day she came out of her office and said to me, "Whitley, this has something to do with what we call death." She had discovered what is now a truism of the contact literature, which is that witnesses often see the dead in the context of encounters with the visitors (Strieber, 2015).

Spirituality is currently a hot topic in both religious and secular circles. However, the tendency is to pursue spirituality *without* content. If the spiritual realm has no inherent content but rather reflects the structure of the minds that inhabit it, then what will provide the content if one pursues spirituality without adding content? One is reminded of a sign posted outside a convenience store that was close to a high school: "If you don't have anything to do, don't do it here!" Similarly, if spirituality without content is successful in its quest, then all that it will succeed in doing is adding spiritual intensity to the status quo. And generally speaking, the status quo is precisely what does not need reinforcing. Logic suggests that if one wishes a spiritual encounter to be personally beneficial, then one should *first* build one's mind around core mental networks that are personally beneficial *before* attempting to contact a spiritual realm.

A similar principle would apply to pursuing spirituality based upon physical content. It is sometimes claimed that holy relics and religious icons have spiritual power, and those who participate in the Eucharist often regard the bread and wine as a source of 'spiritual grace'. But suppose that this actually is the case. Suppose, for instance, that one really can contact the spiritual realm by sitting in the presence of the shroud of Turin. Spirituality that comes from a physical object will not promote personal transformation because the focus is upon objects rather than people and upon 'what is' rather than 'what could be'. If one wishes to promote personal transformation, then one needs to pursue spirituality based upon Platonic forms, because these reside within the minds of people, and they are better and more perfect than 'what is'.

While the spiritual realm has no inherent content, the angelic realm does appear to have inherent content, but this content is *inhuman* at the most fundamental level. We have seen in this book that the human mind acquires its initial core mental networks from interaction with the physical body and the physical environment. By symmetry, an angelic mind would acquire its initial core mental networks from interaction with its name-like container and its wave-like environment. When a person's core mental networks are so different from mine as to be almost unimaginable, then direct interaction with that person will obviously be deeply threatening. Interaction between *spirits* and humans in the Bible is portrayed as a sort of symbiotic relationship in which spirits amplify human mental networks. In contrast, when a person encounters an *angel* in the Bible, then one of the first things that the angel usually says is 'Fear not!', implying that the human is being faced with radically inhuman content. Similarly, a feeling of deep dread generally accompanies descriptions of UFO encounters. Interestingly, many angel stories also begin with angels asserting their name, implying that an angelic being might find it equally disconcerting to interact with humans who have no concept of name. And stories of UFO encounters often mention that aliens are also terrified of humans.

One reads in some circles the suggestion that *emptying* one's mind through Buddhist-like meditation is an effective way of 'calling UFOs'. If angelic minds are based upon core mental networks that are vastly different than the core mental networks of human minds, then one can understand why this would work, because one is avoiding triggering any mental networks that the other party might find offensive. However, this is somewhat like meeting a tiger and emptying one's mind of any thoughts of human preservation. Such a story generally ends with the human being eaten by the tiger, because if the human will not think about preserving human life, the tiger certainly will not. Similarly, if a person empties himself of any *human* thoughts in order to communicate with UFOs, then if the human does not worry about what it means to be human, the alien certainly will not.

If one wishes to interact with the angelic realm in a manner that preserves mental and physical wholeness, then logic suggests that one should base this interaction upon *common* content that can be approached *both* from a human Mercy perspective *and* from an angelic Teacher perspective. We saw precisely this type of overlap when examining Contributor incarnation. Using religious language, one interacts 'in the name of Jesus', Jesus being Contributor incarnation in human form and the 'name of Jesus' the *same* Contributor incarnation in angelic form.

> Incarnation would permit human and angelic realms to overlap.

Consider the *machine*, which was discussed in the section on Contributor incarnation. For concrete thought, a machine is a *tool*, a device that performs some Server action that leads from one Mercy state to another. For example, a coffee machine transforms coffee beans into a cup of coffee, an airplane transports a person from one location to another, and so on. The point is that human concrete thought has no problem fitting machines into the human world of objects and actions. For abstract thought, a machine is a collection of functions that cooperate to generate Teacher order-within-complexity. For instance, the owner of the car views an automobile as a tool for getting from point A to point B, while the car mechanic sees the *same* car as a collection of parts that work together. This type of dual perspective emerges when *concrete* Contributor thought with its focus upon cause-and-effect becomes integrated with *abstract* Contributor thought with its precisely defined functions. Simple machines have always existed, but it is only since the consumer revolution that everyday life has become filled with complicated machines and existence itself has become transformed into a machine-like infrastructure of transportation and communication.

Now let us apply this to our current discussion. An understanding of how the *world* works has led to a massive integration of abstract Contributor thought with concrete Contributor thought in the objective realm of machines. Curiously, most stories of encounters with aliens involve the appearance of unidentified flying *objects*—machines from another realm. In addition, these machines are often described as being in some way 'alive' and certain kinds of aliens are sometimes referred to as being machine-like.

The problem is that the objective bridge between Teacher and Mercy thought based upon how the *world* works has not been accompanied by a corresponding subjective bridge based upon how the *mind* works. Thus, we are attracted to alien objects but repelled from the aliens themselves. The fact that alien machines appear to be alive combined with the fact that they are visiting us and not the other way around suggests that they *have* learned to bridge Teacher and Mercy thought at least to some extent in the realm of the subjective.

When two parties have only *some* things in common, then the obvious solution is to focus on areas of commonality while ignoring areas of difference. Unfortunately, in this case the area of difference involves human existence itself, something which one ignores at one's personal peril. It is interesting to note that extensive interaction between aliens and humans is occurring—if rumor is to be believed—between aliens and the aspect of human society that regards human existence as less important than achieving objective goals such as building weapons and occupying physical territory. Saying this more bluntly, when Contributor incarnation has only transformed the physical world of objects, then aliens will be most comfortable interacting with human soldiers, because soldiers are professionals who are trained to destroy human life.

The long-term solution is to *extend* Contributor incarnation to the realm of the subjective, which we are attempting to do in this book. Simply proclaiming that Jesus is the incarnation in fundamentalist manner is not sufficient. Instead, what is needed is a concept of incarnation that can be viewed both from the human Mercy perspective as a person and from the angelic Teacher perspective as a living function.

The basic premise of mental symmetry is that all human interaction can be analyzed in terms of seven interacting cognitive modules. If all seven modules are functioning properly in a cooperative manner, then a person will be happy and fulfilled. This definition of personal wholeness can be interpreted from either a human Mercy perspective or an angelic Teacher perspective. From a human perspective, each module can be viewed as an invisible 'person' who needs to be kept happy. For instance, I avoid filling my mind with traumatizing images because I know that this will harm Mercy thought. Similarly, I try not to suppress my emotions because I do not want to face Exhorter thought with frustration. That is what it means to pursue mental wholeness on a concrete human level. However, each module can also be viewed from an angelic perspective as a *function*. For instance, Server thought deals with sequences, Perceiver thought handles connections, Teacher thought constructs order-within-complexity, and so on.

For a Teacher-based creature, this functional viewpoint would be the personal viewpoint. Thus, a human could treat the mind as a collection of interacting modules, an angel could treat the *same* mind as a collection of cooperating functions, and each would naturally treat the other in a way that makes the other happy. Similarly, the human body can also be viewed from a human perspective as a collection of parts that should generate pleasure and not pain, or from an angelic perspective as a collection of functions that should each do their job properly.

A similar principle would apply to a person's concept of God. This book suggests that the first stage of transformation is to construct a mental concept of God within Teacher thought and that a full sense of the Holy Spirit only emerges during the third stage when Teacher understanding becomes unveiled to Mercy thought. For an angelic being, the process would be *reversed*. Such a person would first construct what humans view as a sort of divine spirit in Mercy thought and a Teacher-based concept of what humans call God would only emerge indirectly during a later stage of cognitive development. Interestingly, descriptions about the alien view of God often describe belief in what humans would call a Mercy-like divine spirit.

This means that a mental concept of Contributor incarnation that has been sufficiently 'unfolded' by Perceiver facts and Server sequences actually performs *four* related cognitive functions: bridging man and God by connecting specific Mercy experiences with general Teacher theories; bridging God and Holy Spirit by connecting general Mercy experiences with general Teacher theories; bridging angel and Holy Spirit by connecting specific Teacher names with general Mercy experiences; and bridging angel and human by connecting specific Teacher names with specific Mercy experiences. For a human mind, the first bridging would occur first, whereas for an angelic mind, the third bridging would happen first.

Pentecostalism focuses upon the Holy Spirit, and Pentecostals claim to experience miracles and/or angelic visitations. Human activity is most successful when people recognize that the physical world is ruled by general Teacher laws. By analogy, approaching the unseen from the perspective of universal Mercy thought would theoretically be the most successful way of interacting with the angelic realm. Thus, Pentecostalism might be connecting in some way to an angelic realm. The problem is that Pentecostalism *jumps* directly to the third stage without first using rational thought to construct a concept of God. Thus, even if a breakthrough were achieved, it would be unsustainable because of the lack of a solid foundation, which explains the charismatic proverb that 'the gifting carries them to places that their character cannot sustain them'.

Saying this another way, what would be needed to preserve mental wholeness would be a *combination* of angelic and spiritual interaction, because when one is viewing a person as a collection of interacting cognitive modules, one is actually interpreting people in terms of Platonic forms and general equations. Saying this yet another way, the spiritual perspective makes it possible to integrate the human and angelic perspectives. A similar principle applies to interaction with the physical world. If one insists upon empirical evidence, then this will result in mental networks that are threatened by the very concept of nonphysical reality. However, if one sees the structure of the physical world as something that is *compatible* with the mind, then it is also possible to view the structure of angelic and spiritual realms as compatible with the mind. But this means approaching physical reality from an *internal* structure based in Platonic forms and general equations. Again, we see that taking a spiritual perspective makes it possible to integrate the human and angelic perspectives. Saying this more simply, if a person wishes to remain sane while interacting with both physical and angelic realms, a person must take one step back mentally from the physical world. Instead of inhaling mental networks directly from the environment, one must view reality through an internal grid of truth and righteousness. But this internal viewpoint is precisely what is needed to interact successfully with the spiritual realm.

Moving on, there is a strange passage at the beginning of the Bible that appears to be describing interaction between humans and angels that *lacks* internal content.

> Now it came about, when men began to multiply on the face of the land, and daughters were born to them, that the sons of God saw that the daughters of men were beautiful; and they took wives for themselves, whomever they chose. Then the Lord said, "My Spirit shall not strive with man forever, because he also is flesh; nevertheless his days shall be one hundred and twenty years." The Nephilim were on the earth in those days, and also afterward, when the sons of God came in to the daughters of men, and they bore children to them. Those were the mighty men who were of old, men of renown. Then the Lord saw that the wickedness of man was great on the earth, and that every intent of the thoughts of his heart was only evil continually. The Lord was sorry that He had made man on the earth, and He was grieved in His heart. The Lord said, "I will blot out man whom I have created from the face of the land, from man to animals to creeping things and to birds of the sky; for I am sorry that I have made them" (Gen. 6:1-7).

This passage has been interpreted either as intermarriage between two groups of humans or as marriage between male angels and female humans. However, only the second option appears to be capable of generating the consequences being described here. The story begins with Teacher emotion. Angels (presumably) are being attracted by the beauty of the female form, resulting in children who are 'men of renown', referred to as Nephilim. The King James version translates the word *Nephilim* as 'giants', but the term technically means 'fallen ones', and was viewed in ancient Judaism as a reference to fallen angels.

The specific combination of male angels and human females makes sense if one views angels as beings who live within the Teacher realm of messages. Getting pregnant and giving birth requires a minimum of mental content for a human female, because the physical body performs the entire process automatically. Similarly, theory suggests that a male messenger would be naturally adept at manipulating messages, including the message of DNA. Manipulating a DNA message would make it possible to produce offspring with unusual abilities, as is described here. Curiously, UFOs stories often mention aliens claiming to have manipulated the DNA of humans during ancient history. My purpose here is not to dwell upon alien abductions and DNA manipulation but rather to point out two features. First, a sexual encounter requires only minimal social interaction. Thus, each side in an encounter between male angels and female humans would need to know very little about the other side. Second, the results are described as disastrous for cognitive development. The implication is that physical limitations force humans to learn, and that when these physical limitations are removed, then the natural tendency is for learning to cease as well. As the saying goes, power corrupts and absolute power corrupts absolutely.

Christians often ask God to perform miracles that violate the laws of nature. Presumably, alien/human hybrids would be able to perform 'miracles' at will. However, if law-violating miracles were common, then I suggest that this would not *prove* the existence of God, but rather *prevent* a mental concept of God from forming, leaving the mind ruled by fragmented mental networks. That is what one finds described here: 'Every intent of the thoughts of the [human] heart was only evil continually'. And in Jude 14-15, the adjective 'ungodly' is used four times in two verses to describe the people of this period. The cognitive results are so catastrophic that God is 'sorry that He had made man on the earth.' Interestingly, God does not apologize for making intelligent minds but rather focuses specifically upon minds that live in human bodies on the earth.

Let us jump forward now from the beginning of the Bible to the end. When looking at Swedenborg and the spiritual realm, we focused upon personal existence as a *disembodied* mind within a non-physical realm. N. T. Wright goes to great lengths to distinguish this type of disembodied existence from physical resurrection.

> We should recall in particular that the use of the word heaven to denote the ultimate goal of the redeemed, though of course hugely popularized by medieval and subsequent piety, is severely misleading and does not begin to do justice to the Christian hope. I am repeatedly frustrated by how hard it is to get this point through the thick wall of traditional thought and language that most Christians put up. The ultimate destination is (once more) not 'going to heaven when you die' but being bodily raised into the transformed, glorious likeness of Jesus Christ... Thus, if we want to speak of going to heaven when we die, we should be clear that this represents the first, and far less important, stage of a two-stage process. Resurrection isn't life after death; it is life after life after death (Wright, 2008, p. 168).

There are two main passages that describe resurrection. Paul devotes a chapter to the topic of *personal* resurrection in the book of 1 Corinthians. One sees here the familiar combination of divine unveiling followed by rebirth.

> Then comes the end, when He hands over the kingdom to the God and Father, when He has abolished all rule and all authority and power. For He must reign until He has put all His enemies under His feet. The last enemy that will be abolished is death. For He has put all things in subjection under His feet (1 Cor. 15:24-27).

Notice how 'the end comes' when Contributor incarnation has been unfolded to the extent that there is a universal understanding of God in Teacher thought. This describes a divine unveiling. A similar transition has been occurring in modern society since the beginning of the consumer revolution, because existing cultural mental networks have been gradually replaced by Contributor-driven technology. With the advent of the computer and the Internet, very little of human existence remains that is not subject to the general Teacher understanding of science.

Paul then emphasizes that resurrection requires rebirth. In order to live within new mental networks, one must tear down existing mental networks of personal identity.

> But someone will say, "How are the dead raised? And with what kind of body do they come?" You fool! That which you sow does not come to life unless it dies; and that which you sow, you do not sow the body which is to be, but a bare grain, perhaps of wheat or of something else (1 Cor. 15:35-37).

Finally, Paul compares a weak, perishable, natural body with a powerful, imperishable, spiritual body.

> So also is the resurrection of the dead. It is sown a perishable body, it is raised an imperishable body; it is sown in dishonor, it is raised in glory; it is sown in weakness, it is raised in power; it is sown a natural body, it is raised a spiritual body. If there is a natural body, there is also a spiritual body (1 Cor. 15:42-44).

What Paul describes here is angelic, spiritual, and human attributes *combined* in a new body. It is not just a body, but a 'spiritual body' that possesses power, an angelic trait. In other words, unveiling is followed by rebirth which expresses itself as an existence that combines realms that are currently distinct.

This same sequence is found in the passage that describes *cosmic* rebirth.

> Then I saw a great white throne and Him who sat upon it, from whose presence earth and heaven fled away, and no place was found for them. And I saw the dead, the great and the small, standing before the throne, and books were opened; and another book was opened, which is the book of life; and the dead were judged from the things which were written in the books, according to their deeds. And the sea gave up the dead which were in it, and death and Hades gave up the dead which were in them; and they were judged, every one of them according to their deeds. Then death and Hades were thrown into the lake of fire. This is the second death, the lake of fire. And if anyone's name was not found written in the book of life, he was thrown into the lake of fire. Then I saw a new heaven and a new earth; for the first heaven and the first earth passed away, and there is no

longer any sea. I saw the Holy City, the new Jerusalem, coming down out of heaven from God, prepared as a bride beautifully dressed for her husband (Rev. 20:11-21:2).

This passage begins with a divine unveiling in which 'earth and heaven' are fleeing from the presence of God. This is followed by a rebirth of heaven and earth: 'I saw a new heaven and new earth; for the first heaven and the first earth passed away'. Notice that the unveiling includes 'death and Hades', which themselves experience a rebirth as 'the lake of fire'. Thus, what is being reborn in this passage is not people but rather the environment.

This passage contains three additional factors. First, a sea is being replaced by a lake of fire. Second, everyone is being judged according to their deeds. Third, those whose names are not written in the book of life are being thrown into the lake of fire. I suggest that one can make sense of these points by examining how computers have led to a reborn human environment.

One used to encounter computers only in 'islands' of technology surrounded by a 'sea' of Mercy-driven culture. Now, computers have become so ubiquitous that all that remains is a few 'lakes' of Mercy-driven culture where one can continue to exist apart from computers. However, those who try to remain within these lakes find themselves continually frustrated by their lack of both gadgets and technical ability. Thus, the lake is actually a 'lake' filled with the 'fire' of frustration. This transition to a computer dominated society has automatically judged everyone based upon what they have done, because everyone now requires the skills that are needed to handle the new technology of computers. Those who can survive this transition are individuals who are able to remake themselves at a deep level, while those who lack this ability find themselves thrown into the 'lake of fire'. Using religious language, those who have enrolled in the school of incarnation are able to handle the rebirth that is required to survive this transition. As John writes a few verses before this passage, "Blessed and holy are those who share in the first resurrection. The second death has no power over them, but they will be priests of God and of Christ and will reign with him for a thousand years" (Rev. 20:6). In other words, those who submit to the school of incarnation do not need to fear environmental rebirth.

It may seem somewhat trite to compare the advent of computers with a cosmic apocalypse, but a similar situation occurred in Eastern European countries after the fall of communism. Everyone suddenly found themselves in a new environment in which they were judged by how their existing Server skills fit into the new unveiled Teacher order of capitalism. Those who were able to transform their personal identity survived the transition, while many middle-aged workers found themselves with obsolescent skills, trapped in lakes of Mercy-driven culture accompanied by the fire of frustration. If this results from the unveiling and rebirth of a system of *human* righteousness, one can imagine that the unveiling and rebirth of a new system of *divine* righteousness would have similar, yet much more profound, effects. The point is that a similar process is occurring in all of these situations, and that one can gain an understanding of the greater process by examining the shape of the lesser process.

An unveiling alters general law and forces rebirth.

Let us turn finally to the topic of aliens and religion. David Weintraub recently wrote a book that explores how different religions would be affected by the appearance of extraterrestrial life. He concludes that evangelical Christianity would potentially be devastated by the appearance of extraterrestrials, because humanity is viewed as the sole focus of God while Christianity is regarded as a universal religion. He also suggests that the primary question for Catholicism would be whether aliens suffer from original sin and need to be saved (Weintraub, 2014). My gut feeling is that the typical evangelical Christian *would* find the appearance of extraterrestrials devastating, but that is not because of an inherent limitation in the structure of Christianity, but rather due to the attitude of fundamentalism. We have seen in this book that Christianity can be described as a universal religion. But this universality will not be apparent to the Christian whose belief is based in absolute truth.

My basic premise is that one can explain existing stories of the supernatural and the spiritual by postulating that the same mind could exist—and remain sane—within a physical, an angelic, and a spiritual realm. Other realms might be possible, but these are the ones I know of within which a human-like mind could theoretically exist. The underlying assumption is that if the structure of the human mind is 'made in the image of God', and if there is one God, then all intelligent life forms would have the same kind of mind. Consistent with this, many UFO researchers have concluded that there must be some common cosmic principle guiding the expression of intelligent life, because all intelligent beings appear to have humanoid form.

That brings us to the Catholic questions regarding original sin and the universal atonement of Jesus. Humans need atonement because the human mind naturally develops in a manner that is incomplete and can only reach mental wholeness by being jumpstarted from some external source. The problem is not with the fundamental structure of the mind, but rather with the mental networks around which human mental content is organized. Thus, a mind that started existence in a different kind of body and environment might not suffer from 'original sin'. However, such a mind would still require a mental concept of Contributor incarnation—and would have to go through episodes of cognitive rebirth—to reach mental wholeness. In other words, some aliens might not need Jesus to be saved *from* sin, but they would still need some version of Jesus the incarnation to be saved *to* wholeness. However, this concept of incarnation would probably take a form that would be regarded as totally alien and non-Christian by a fundamentalist Christian. That is because human religion and alien religion might be fundamentally the same, but it would take extensive translation to realize that they were equivalent, and performing this sort of translation would require going beyond the fundamentalist belief in absolute truth to a belief in universal truth.

Does this mean that Jesus would have to become incarnate upon every alien planet? I suggest not. The reasoning has to do with Perceiver and Server confidence. When a certain process is being tested, it does not have to be carried out in every possible situation. Rather, it is sufficient if this process is tested in a *representative* situation that is more *stressful* than any other situation in which this process might occur. Thus, Jesus would not have to become incarnate on every planet. Instead, it would be sufficient if Jesus became flesh upon the most godless, brutal, and stupid planet. This implies that God sent Jesus to earth not because humans are so special, as evangelical Christians like to think, but rather because humans are such stubborn idiots. It would then be possible to generalize this incarnation through translation into other realms.

One sees this universality of salvation described by Paul in Colossians in a passage that was previously analyzed from a purely cognitive perspective.

> He is the image of the invisible God, the firstborn of all creation. For by Him all things were created, both in the heavens and on earth, visible and invisible, whether thrones or dominions or rulers or authorities—all things have been created through Him and for Him. He is before all things, and in Him all things hold together. He is also head of the body, the church; and He is the beginning, the firstborn from the dead, so that He Himself will come to have first place in everything. For it was the Father's good pleasure for all the fullness to dwell in Him, and through Him to reconcile all things to Himself, having made peace through the blood of His cross; through Him, I say, whether things on earth or things in heaven (Col. 1:15-20).

The beginning of this passage describes Contributor incarnation as the source of a vast array of human and nonhuman life forms inhabiting both material and non-material realms. Paul then says that Jesus' atonement 'through the blood of the cross' 'reconciles all things to himself', 'whether things on earth or things in heaven'. This implies that both humans and angels can be saved, which is quite different than the typical fundamentalist assertion that Jesus' salvation applies only to humans and that all UFO aliens are demons damned to hell. I am not suggesting that all aliens are good. Many alien stories describe a level of evil that is quite profound. However, we know that humans are capable of perpetrating evil that is equally profound. The point is that dividing intelligent beings into the Mercy categories of 'saveable human' and 'damned alien' is both morally and intellectually simplistic. The actual situation appears to be much more complicated, with some humans and aliens being mentally enrolled in a school of salvation and others in the process of being corrupted.

✳ Neurology

The purpose of this final chapter (or appendix) can be described using an analogy. Suppose that archaeologists uncover an ancient city. Excavating the ruins can provide empirical evidence about the ancient city but will also reveal only part of the picture. A more complete understanding will be gained if one can also uncover ancient tablets. But these writings will only expand the understanding of the ancient city if certain requirements are met. First, the language in which the tablets are written needs to be deciphered. It may be possible to gain clues about what the words mean by examining the behavior of present day inhabitants of this region. Second, a mapping must be done between the physical ruins being uncovered by archaeology and the places and activities described in the writings. Do the ancient tablets describe this city, or some other location? The writings may refer to a palace, a temple, or a marketplace. Which of the ruined buildings being uncovered is the palace? Which is the temple, and where is the marketplace? Can one find artifacts in these various places that are consistent with the activities described in the tablets? If these requirements can be met, then archaeology *combined* with the deciphering of tablets can be used to generate a composite picture of the ancient city that is more complete than what only one of these methods would reveal.

The brain is like the ancient city, and neurologists are like archaeologists looking for empirical evidence about life in the ancient city. Studying human personality is like reading tablets. The theory of mental symmetry appears to be the key for deciphering human personality, which can be verified by observing human behavior. The purpose of this chapter is to show that the 'tablets' of mental symmetry describe the *same* 'city' that is being uncovered by the 'digging' of neurology. One cannot use neurology to prove the theory of mental symmetry. But I suggest that one can demonstrate that the theory of mental symmetry is describing the same mind—in detail—that is being uncovered by neurology. Thus, by combining mental symmetry with neurological evidence, it is possible to come up with a more complete picture of how the mind functions. This chapter will examine the various regions of the brain in the light of the latest neurological evidence and show that the traits being discovered by neurology are consistent with the traits described by mental symmetry.

I should warn that this chapter is not easy reading. I will try to define terms, but I will be quoting extensively from neurological literature. This chapter does not describe any new aspects of the theory of mental symmetry, but it does throw extensive light upon traits and cognitive mechanisms that were discussed earlier. Therefore, I am not sure whether to regard this as a final chapter that should be read or as an appendix to which one can refer. I leave that choice to the reader.

I began studying neurology back in the 1980s. That was before the invention of the World Wide Web, and so accessing the latest research meant driving into the heart of Vancouver to spend a day reading journals at the Woodward biomedical library. During that initial foray into neurology, I went through about 200 books and 2000 papers. Enough was known about the brain at that time to provide general evidence for the diagram of mental symmetry. Far more is known about the brain now, thanks largely to the invention of brain imaging technology. This new evidence continues to be consistent with the theory of mental symmetry, adding, clarifying, and sometimes correcting details.

Before we discuss neurology, some comments should be made about the nature of neurological research as well as the basic structure of the brain. I have mentioned that scientific methodology emphasizes empirical evidence, objective research, and peer review. In practical terms, this means that neurology is at the top of the pecking order in behavioral science, because it uses objective research to gathers empirical evidence about brain functioning. Neurological papers refer primarily to peers who are also doing research in some branch of neurology, and cognitive models are based almost exclusively upon neurological data. When neurological papers do refer to other fields, these references usually occur in the introduction, followed by the suggestion that neurology will now re-examine the topic from a more rigorous empirical perspective. Similarly, I have noticed that researchers in other fields, such as psychology, philosophy, and theology, increasingly refer to neurological evidence in order to back up their claims.

Thus, the instinctive response is to regard the approach that is being taken by this book as not just wrong, but so deeply wrong that it borders upon insanity. However, I suggest that this is a mistaken response, because neurological evidence has now disproven the mindset of scientific methodology that causes neurological research to be regarded as more authoritative than other ways of studying the mind.

First, the idea of *objective research* was questioned in a major way by the publication of Damasio's groundbreaking book *Descartes' Error* (1994) which argued that emotions play a key role in rational thought. This book had a large impact partially because Damasio is one of the world's leading neurologists and he presented detailed evidence from neurology to back up his claims. In brief, Damasio says that emotions provide a shortcut for rational thought. Life happens too quickly to work out a rational well-thought-out response to every situation. Emotions provide a quick-and-dirty method for coming up with an instant response that is usually correct. Thus, objective neurological research has now shown that subjective emotions play a primary role in rational thought.

Second, neurological research on the frontal lobes has seriously undermined the demand for *empirical evidence*. The frontal lobes used to be terra incognito, a section of the brain whose function was only vaguely known. Between the mid 1930s and the mid

1950s, 20,000 frontal lobotomies were performed in the United States alone, 'treating' psychiatric and behavioral problems by severing connections within the frontal lobes. Researchers soon discovered that damaging the frontal lobes might leave the ability to interact with the external world relatively intact, but had the devastating result of making the patient less of a human being.

> The lobotomy started to fall out of favor as the follow-up neurologic sequelae became more evident. Reports in the scientific and medical literature suggested that the efficacy of the lobotomy was dubious. Moreover, the clinical indications were rather poorly defined and its side-effects could be severe. Inertia, unresponsiveness, decreased attention span, blunted or inappropriate affect, and disinhibition led to the conclusion that the treatment was worse than the disease (Mashour, et al., 2005).

As we shall see, the functions of the various subregions of the frontal lobes are now known in substantial detail. In brief, the frontal lobes contain the *inner world* that make someone a person as opposed to merely a stimulus-response creature of the physical environment. Concepts of self and others reside within the frontal lobes, plans are formulated here, and the frontal lobes guide social interaction, social appropriateness, and conscience.

In other words, what makes a person a person is not the posterior of the brain that handles empirical evidence, but rather the frontal lobes that contain content and structure that may be *derived* from physical evidence but have become *independent* of physical evidence. Saying this another way, empirical evidence may lead to effective scientific research, but if one wants to be a person then one must go beyond empirical evidence. This is one of the fundamental discoveries of modern neurology.

Third, neurology has discovered that technical specialization with its emphasis upon peer review is not the highest form of human thought. In the words of Stuss, a leading neurological expert on the frontal lobes, the frontopolar cortex (which resides at the very front of the frontal lobes) "appears to be maximally involved in the most recently studied meta-cognitive aspects of human nature: integrative aspects of personality, social cognition, autonoetic consciousness, and self-awareness. Because they are the most recently evolved, they may be uniquely positioned to integrate the higher-level executive cognitive functions, and emotional or drive-related inputs" (Stuss, 2006). Frontopolar cortex does not specialize within one context but rather finds analogies that cross contexts (Green, et al., 2010). It is critical for multitasking in the absence of external cues (Volle, et al., 2011). Using the language of mental symmetry, neurology has discovered that the highest form of human thought is not technical thought guided by empirical evidence but rather the correlative, inter-disciplinary processing of normal thought.

This neurological finding was preceded by a groundbreaking book by Lakoff & Johnson, entitled *Metaphors We Live By* (1980), in which the authors pointed out how deeply metaphors based in physical reality are embedded in normal speech. A later book by the same two authors (Lakoff & Johnson, 1999) claimed that *all* of human thought is ultimately based in metaphor. (Mental symmetry, in contrast, suggests that normal thought with its metaphors acts as the *framework* for mental networks and technical thought.)

These three findings lead to the following quandary. Should one be guided by the *findings* of scientific methodology or by the *attitude* of scientific methodology? Neurological research has discovered that human intelligence combines rational thought with emotions and that the highest form of human thought uses an internal model of reality based in metaphors to integrate different contexts. In contrast, the attitude of scientific methodology insists that empirical, objective specialization is the ultimate source of all knowledge. Mental symmetry suggests that it is more important to follow the 'divine righteousness' of 'how the brain works' than to submit to the 'human righteousness' of scientific methodology that tells us how we are supposed to use our brains.

Authors such as Damasio or Lakoff & Johnson may be willing to question *some* of the parameters of scientific methodology, but they also go to great lengths to emphasize the supremacy of empirical data. Damasio is an advocate of *scientism*, which insists that nothing exists except empirical data, while Lakoff & Johnson hold to *strong embodiment*, which claims that the mind is incapable of transcending its environment. But researchers such as Damasio, Lakoff, and Johnson are hailed precisely because they used their frontal lobes to *transcend* input from the environment and because they proposed a new *interpretation* of empirical data, suggesting that we may explicitly teach scientism and strong embodiment, but implicitly we act as if concepts such as these are invalid.

The alternative to strong embodiment is known as *weak* embodiment. Weak embodiment recognizes that human thought is heavily dependent upon input from the physical environment but insists that it is also possible for thought to transcend physical input. A recent paper analyzed the results from a number of neurological studies on linguistics and concluded that the evidence supports weak embodiment rather than strong embodiment (Meteyard, et al., 2012), pointing out that speech and imagination activate brain regions that are *adjacent* to brain regions activated by sensory input and physical action. Thus, thought is dependent upon embodiment but not the same as embodiment. Meteyard suggests that

> Whereas concrete knowledge would be grounded into our experience with the outside world, abstract knowledge could be grounded in our internal experience. Abstract words tend, on the whole, to have more affective associations than concrete words, and the greater the affective associations, the earlier those abstract words are acquired. But, affect may play a critical role in allowing the learning, or bootstrapping, of abstract knowledge. Of course it is the case that not all abstract words are affectively loaded. Affect, nonetheless could have an important role in allowing for knowledge that cannot be grounded to the external world to begin developing. Once the system is set in place, other abstract concepts can be learned, based on linguistic information solely.

In other words, Teacher speech combined with internally driven mental networks make it possible to construct an internal abstract world that is independent of concrete embodiment.

Another study analyzed data from a number of brain imaging studies involving words and sentences and found similar results.

> Abstract concepts elicit greater activity in the inferior frontal gyrus and middle temporal gyrus compared to concrete concepts, while concrete concepts elicit greater activity in the posterior cingulate, precuneus, fusiform gyrus, and parahippocampal gyrus compared to abstract concepts. These results suggest greater engagement of the verbal system for processing of abstract concepts and greater engagement of the perceptual system for processing of concrete concepts, likely via mental imagery (Wang, et al., 2010).

In other words, concrete thought uses more of the back of brain (the regions mentioned all reside within the back of the brain) while abstract thought places a greater emphasis upon the part of the brain (including the frontal lobes) that is involved in speech.

I have suggested that free will requires conflicting mental networks. Weak embodiment implies that there is an inherent struggle between embodiment and abstract verbal thought. Weak embodiment *enables* free will, because I can choose to remain a creature of my environment or I can choose to transcend my environment through the development of abstract verbal understanding. A philosophy of strong embodiment leads ultimately to fatalism and determinism because it uses abstract understanding not to transcend embodiment, but rather to *reinforce* embodiment. But the very fact that one is using words to preach an abstract theory of strong embodiment implies that it is *possible* to use abstract verbal understanding to mentally transcend one's physical environment. Thus, a general theory of strong embodiment ends up deconstructing itself.

In summary, suggesting that neurological findings should be interpreted in the light of a cognitive meta-theory may not be consistent with scientific methodology, but neurological research has discovered that using a meta-theory to interpret empirical data describes the highest form of human thought, and that submitting the mind to an abstract verbal theory makes it possible to transcend the embodiment of childish MMNs. Thus, when viewed from the perspective of 'how the brain works', the theory of mental symmetry is the right *kind* of theory because it uses analogical thinking that is one step removed from empirical evidence to bridge many different contexts in a manner that combines emotions with rational thought, and it follows the right *approach* because it uses an abstract verbal theory to reprogram the mind.

Moving on, there is no *direct* neurological evidence for the theory of mental symmetry. In other words, no one has used the theory of mental symmetry as the basis for neurological experiments, and the theory of mental symmetry is not mentioned in any neurological paper. Instead, all of the neurological evidence is indirect and corroborative;

what neurology has found is *consistent* with what mental symmetry states. However, most of the brain cortex is known as *association* cortex, which functions in an indirect and corroborative manner. Association cortex is defined as

> Any of the expanses of the cerebral cortex that are not sensory or motor in the customary sense, but instead are associated with advanced stages of sensory information processing, multisensory integration, or sensorimotor integration (Dictionary.com).

Thus, I suggest that indirect corroborative evidence is sufficient because that is what most of the brain generates. For instance, mathematical beauty, visual beauty, and moral beauty all activate the same region in the medial orbitofrontal cortex (Zeki, et al., 2014). Similarly, a single region in the right parietal cortex handles spatial maps, temporal maps, and social maps (Pardini, et al., 2014). In both cases, information that is radically different on the surface is being processed by a *single* brain region because of underlying similarities. In contrast, the same experiment will activate *different* regions of association cortex if subjects adopt a different mental strategy. Thus, if one wishes to understand the brain, one must go beyond specific words and experiments to underlying processes. What matters is not whether papers *talk* about mental symmetry, but rather whether brain regions function in a manner that is *consistent* with the theory of mental symmetry.

Parietal Lobes

Going further, the brain appears to be performing the same *kind* of connecting and corroborating that one finds in the theory of mental symmetry. It does not make sense, for instance, to talk about a 'lobe of logic'. That is because deduction activates *many* areas of the brain, and approaching logic symbolically activates different regions than building a mental model (Kroger, et al., 2008). However, it does appear to make sense to talk about a Perceiver lobe (right parietal cortex) or a Server lobe (left parietal cortex). One can demonstrate this by comparing what the Kolb & Wishlaw Textbook of Neuropsychology (2005) says about the parietal lobes with characteristics of Perceiver and Server thought.

> Server thought uses left parietal lobe.
> Perceiver thought uses right parietal lobe.

The parietal lobes can be divided into an anterior somatosensory section and a posterior associative section. Perceiver thought is aware of body position (as a Perceiver person, I know the position of my body and limbs, and when I imagine playing violin I am primarily aware of arm and finger position); Server thought generates physical action. The anterior parietal cortex receives most of its input from the physical body and sends output mainly to the primary motor cortex, the part of the brain that controls the physical body. Thus, the *anterior* parietal cortex provides the raw material for Perceiver and Server thought. The "posterior zone is specialized primarily for integrating sensory input from the somatic and visual regions and, to a lesser extent, from other sensory regions, mostly for the control of movement" (p. 348).

Before we continue, I should give a word of warning. We are about to embark on an examination of all the major regions of the brain, focusing upon association cortex and higher level subcortical modules. We will begin by examining the various functions of *posterior* parietal cortex, quoting passages from Kolb & Wishlaw.

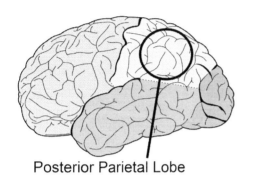

Posterior Parietal Lobe

1) **Mental map**. Perceiver thought builds mental maps. The "parietal lobe plays a central role in the creation of this brain map." K&B add that "it seems likely that there is no single map, but a series of representations of space, which vary in two ways. First, different representations are used for different behavioral needs. Second, representations of space vary from simple ones, which are applicable to control the simple movements, to abstract ones, which may represent information such as topographical knowledge" (p.348). "Deficits in the ability to use topographical information are more likely to be associated with damage to the right hemisphere than the left area. Such disorders include loss of memory of familiar surroundings, the inability to locate items such as countries or cities in a map, and the inability to find one's way about the environment" (p.363).

This is consistent with the suggestion that Perceiver thought constructs and uses many different kinds of maps, ranging from maps of physical location to maps of abstract information. The Perceiver person is naturally good at interpreting maps and knowing personal location within a map.

2) **Movement and Position**. "The posterior parietal region plays a significant role in directing movements in space and in detecting stimuli in space." Notice the cooperation between Perceiver thought, which evaluates object and body position, and Server thought, which moves the body and manipulates objects.

3) **Mental object manipulation and recognition**. One "common symptom of right-parietal-lobe lesion: although able to recognize objects to show in familiar views, patients having these lesions are badly impaired at recognizing objects shown in unfamiliar views... a type of a spatial mapping in which the more common view of an object must be rotated spatially to match the novel view." This type of object rotation and manipulation also comes naturally to the Perceiver person.

4) **Spatial Awareness**. Right parietal lobe damage can lead to a strange condition known as *contralateral neglect*, in which a person ignores the left side of his physical surroundings, the left side of his body, and the left side of imagined items (p.358). In other

words, Perceiver thought (right parietal cortex) can handle spatial awareness for both halves of the body, whereas Server thought (left parietal cortex) can only handle spatial awareness for its side of the body. (The right side of the brain controls the left side of the body and vice versa.) Here we see the physical basis for self-image, a concept of fundamental importance to the Perceiver person.

The traits we have examined so far are related primarily to *Perceiver* thought and right parietal cortex. Let us turn now to Server thought and left parietal cortex.

1) **Apraxia**. Patients with left parietal lesions typically have "difficulty learning a sequence of novel movements of the limbs". They are "grossly impaired" when "asked to copy a series of arm movements" (p.361). Server thought assembles physical movement into sequences of action and is naturally talented at copying the actions of others.

2) **Disturbed language function**. K&B describe one characteristic patient who "was unable to write even his name (agraphia), had serious difficulties in reading (dyslexia), and spoke slowly and deliberately, making many errors in grammar (dysphasia)" (p.360). These are all aspects of language that relate to Server thought. Server thought performs the action of writing words. Server thought works out grammatical structure—sequences that are common to many specific sentences.

The relationship between dyslexia and the left parietal region can be explained by comparing Perceiver thought with Server thought. As far as Perceiver thought is concerned, 'god' and 'dog' are equivalent because one can be turned into the other through *rotation*. However, Server thought regards these two as distinct because they are different *sequences* of letters. If Server thought is not functioning properly, then Perceiver thought will naturally equate words that Server thought regards as different. This will also lead to an inability to discriminate left from right, another symptom of left parietal damage.

3) **Dyscalculia**. This same patient "was very poor at mental arithmetic and could not solve even simple additions and subtractions." Math is a form of language with strict Server rules of grammar. This type of language is also affected when Server thought is damaged.

4) **Recall**. K&B's sample patient "had an especially low digit span, being able to master the immediate recall of only three digits, whether they were presented orally or visually." I have suggested that Server thought can give stability to Teacher words through memorization. This function is also dependent upon the left parietal lobe.

The authors note that "Many problems can be solved by using either a verbal cognitive mode or a spatial nonverbal cognitive mode... A complex spatial problem, such as reading an upside-down map, can be solved either directly, by 'spatial cognition' (the directions to travel are intuited spatially) or indirectly, by 'verbal cognition' (the spatial information is encoded into words and the problem is solved by being talked through step by step). People who are highly verbal prefer the verbal mode even when it is less efficient; we expect lesions of the left parietal lobe in these people to disturb functions that ordinarily are disrupted preferentially by right parietal lesions" (p.364).

Saying this another way, one can approach physical movement *allocentrically* or *egocentrically*. The first uses *Perceiver* thought to relate locations within a map (My house is 3 km northeast of the shopping center), while the second uses *Server* thought to form sequences of movement (Turn left when leaving the shopping center and then turn right at the second traffic light). Some people, such as Perceiver persons, naturally think in terms of maps, while others, such as Server persons, naturally think in terms of routes. A person will be naturally driven by cognitive style to use primarily one of these mental strategies, even when it is not the most effective strategy.

Kolb & Wishlaw's description of the parietal lobes leads us to four conclusions. First, I suggested that it makes sense to talk about a Perceiver lobe and a Server lobe. We have seen that this is not just a vague statement. Instead, primary functions of the right and left parietal lobes correspond in detail to core traits of Perceiver and Server thought. Second, neurology indicates that these two lobes do not work in isolation but rather cooperate with one another. This is consistent with the concept that Contributor connects Perceiver facts with Server sequences. Third, it is possible to approach navigation from either the Server perspective of sequences or the Perceiver perspective of spatial connections. In fact, as the philosopher Heidegger illustrates, it is possible to redefine all of physical existence in terms of Server sequences. This principle of approaching the same information from either a left hemisphere perspective or a right hemisphere perspective will show up repeatedly when examining other areas of the brain. Finally, I have suggested that in the stage of righteousness one learns to act in a way that is consistent with verbal understanding. This Server split between *physical* sequences of action and *grammatical* sequences of words is present within the left parietal lobe. As K&B state, "Three parietal lobe symptoms do not fit obviously into a simple view of the parietal lobe as a visuomotor control center. These symptoms include difficulties with arithmetic, certain aspects of language, and movement sequences" (p.352). When the *same* brain region handles *different* functions, then this implies that it is *possible* to mentally integrate these functions.

Our examination of the parietal lobes quoted from a neuropsychological textbook. That is because the primary functions of the parietal lobes have been known for some time. The rest of this chapter will be quoting in extensive detail from neurological papers. Normally, one does not quote directly but rather summarizes what is contained within a paper. But the very concept of using a cognitive model—especially one that began with a biblical passage—to analyze neurology is so 'unreasonable' that I will be using direct quotes rather than paraphrasing. This also makes it easy to check the source because almost all of the papers being quoted are freely available on the web. Therefore, the paper can be accessed easily by googling part of the direct quote. Because this chapter contains so many quotes, I will be placing them in line with the text rather than indenting them as has been done so far. Any text that is in [square brackets] has been added by me to explain or clarify a quote. Finally, when one paper quotes another author, then one is supposed to reference the original author. This becomes overwhelming when attempting to carry out a reasonably detailed summary of brain regions. Therefore, I will take the liberty of quoting from authors even when they are summarizing the work of other authors. The original source can be found easily enough by googling the quote. The important point is that I am quoting someone *else's* summary of the evidence rather than placing my own interpretation upon the data. Of course, that still leaves the possible bias of 'cherry picking data'—choosing papers that agree with my cognitive model. The best way to dispel that criticism is by doing a detailed summary of neurology, which we are about to begin.

Frontal Lobes

We will now turn our attention to the frontal lobes, the part of the brain that constructs the *internal* world of thought. Before we examine specific regions of the frontal lobes, let us step back for the big picture. K&B point out that "there are connections between the posterior parietal cortex and the dorsolateral prefrontal region... These connections emphasize a close functional relation between the prefrontal cortex and the parietal cortex. This relation probably has an important role in the control of spatially guided behavior" (p.347). Saying this more generally, mental symmetry suggests that each of the four simple cognitive styles (Perceiver, Server, Teacher, and Mercy) uses a specific region in the back of the brain to store and manipulate data as well as a specific region in the frontal cortex to construct an internal world. Perceiver thought uses right dorsolateral frontal cortex and right parietal cortex, while Server thought uses left dorsolateral frontal cortex and left parietal cortex.

This system is known in neurology as *executive function*. Barbey (2012) examined 182 patients with focal brain damage and concluded that the "findings support an integrative framework for understanding the architecture of general intelligence and executive function, supporting their reliance upon a shared frontoparietal network for the integration and control of cognitive representations." More specifically, "the frontoparietal network identified by the present analysis includes lateral frontopolar cortex, anterior prefrontal cortex, the dorsolateral prefrontal cortex, anterior cingulate/medial prefrontal cortex and the inferior and superior parietal lobe. This constellation of regions is commonly engaged by tasks that require executive control processes. The frontoparietal network is recruited by paradigms that elicit controlled processing related to the simultaneous consideration of multiple interdependent contingencies, conflict in stimulus-response mappings, and integrating working memory with attentional resource allocation, supporting the maintenance and integration of items for goal-directed behavior." Notice that the frontoparietal network includes the parietal cortex as well as the dorsolateral prefrontal and frontopolar cortex (regions that I suggest are related to Perceiver and Server thought), but does not include the orbitofrontal cortex (which I suggest is related to Teacher and Mercy thought). Notice also that a major portion of the brain is being regarded as an integrated system of thought, consistent with the idea that Perceiver thought and Server thought function as *high level* cognitive modules. Finally, notice that the traits of the executive function are consistent with the suggestion that Perceiver facts and Server sequences provide an *integrated grid* of knowledge that holds together the rest of thought.

> Perceiver thought uses right dorsolateral frontal cortex and right parietal cortex.
> Server thought uses left dorsolateral frontal cortex and left parietal cortex.

Looking now at the frontal lobes, Stuss summarizes that

> The theory of the evolution of cortical architectonics indicates two major functional/anatomical dissociations within the frontal lobes: a dorsolateral prefrontal cortical cortex (DLPFC), evolving from a hippocampal, archicortical trend, involved in spatial and conceptual reasoning processes; and a ventral (medial) prefrontal cortex (VPFC) paleocortical trend, emerging from the caudal orbitofrontal (olfactory) cortex, and closely connected with limbic nuclei involved in emotional processing, including the acquisition and reversal of stimulus-reward associations. These two trends form the two major (executive cognitive; behavioral/emotional self-regulatory) functional divisions within the frontal lobes (Stuss, 2006).

The reference here to the theory of evolution refers specifically to comparing analogous regions of the brain, such as comparing the frontal lobes of the rat with the frontal lobes of the monkey and the human. This provides useful data which can either be interpreted from a *concrete* time-oriented perspective as 'rat evolving into monkey evolving into human' or from an *abstract* structural perspective as rat brain, monkey brain, and human brain all having a similar structure that reflects a common general architecture. Presumably, one would find order-within-complexity in the design (that word again) of a divine being that uses universal Teacher thought.

Stuss says that one can divide the frontal lobes into *two* primary regions. (The very back of the frontal cortex controls physical movement. The prefrontal cortex is the part of the frontal cortex that does not control physical movement. This chapter will be discussing only the prefrontal cortex.) The *dorsolateral prefrontal* cortex is the 'executive cognitive' region involved in 'spatial and conceptual reasoning'. Using the language of mental symmetry, the dorsolateral region cooperates with the parietal lobes to generate Perceiver and Server thought. The *orbitofrontal* cortex is related to emotional processing, pursuing reward, and emotional self-regulation, and is part of the 'limbic system'. This, I suggest, is the core of Teacher and Mercy thought, which we will be discussing shortly. (Orbitofrontal cortex is the ventral or bottom part of the frontal lobes that lies just above the orbits of the eyes.)

Notice the connection between Perceiver and Server thought and the hippocampus. In simpler animals (such as the rat) the dorsolateral prefrontal cortex is quite small and the spatial function is provided primarily by the hippocampal formation. In addition, the orbitofrontal cortex in simpler animals is strongly connected with the sense of smell. This relationship between emotional thought and olfaction can be seen in the behavior of the Mercy person, who has a sensitive nose and tends to sniff objects. Neurologically speaking, smell is the only sense that bypasses the thalamus and goes directly to orbitofrontal cortex. Thus, smell is an effective method of triggering mental networks.

Summarizing, evidence suggests that dorsolateral frontal cortex is related to the internal world of Perceiver and Server thought, while orbitofrontal cortex is related to the internal world of Teacher and Mercy thought. We will now examine these two core frontal regions as well as several additional regions of frontal cortex.

Dorsolateral Prefrontal Cortex

In simplest terms, a Perceiver fact is a set of connections and a Server sequence is a string of items. Perceiver and Server thought do not handle memories themselves but rather *connections* between memories. Consistent with this, Blumenfeld (2011) found "that DLPFC [dorsolateral prefrontal cortex] activity specifically promoted memory for relational information during relational encoding and not memory for item-specific information during item-specific encoding." This region has traditionally been associated with what is known as *working memory*: "Neurons in the primate dorsolateral prefrontal cortex generated persistent firing in the absence of sensory stimulation, the foundation of mental representation" (Wang, et al., 2013). Thus, Perceiver and Server connections provide the structure for the *internal* world, 'firing in the absence of sensory stimulation'.

> Dorsolateral prefrontal remembers connections and evaluates uncertain information.

This region does not just *remember* connections and sequences but also chooses the *appropriate* connection or sequence in the presence of interference. Damage here "may reflect a higher-order deficit, one including elements of susceptibility to proactive interference and of perseveration" (Tsujimoto & Postle, 2012). In addition, this region is "more active when the human subjects respond with low-confidence than when they do with high-confidence, and it is thought to be engaged when cues from the environment are ambiguous and/or there is a prepotent, but inappropriate, response that is cued." Saying this in the language of mental symmetry, the dorsolateral prefrontal is not just associated with Perceiver and Server *memory*, but with Perceiver and Server *thought*. One of the characteristics of Perceiver and Server thought, as opposed to technical thought, is that it works with *partial certainty*—ambiguous information. As another paper explains, "Recent primate neurophysiology, human neuroimaging, and modeling experiments have demonstrated that perceptual decisions are based on an integrative process in which sensory evidence accumulates over time until an internal decision bound is reached. Here we used repetitive transcranial magnetic stimulation (rTMS) to provide causal support for the role of the dorsolateral prefrontal cortex (DLPFC) in this integrative process" (Philiastides, et al., 2011).

The exact role played by left and right dorsolateral prefrontal is still somewhat controversial, but there is evidence associating left with Server thought and right with Perceiver thought. For instance, "Applying low-frequency rTMS to the right dlPFC of intact adult humans had opposing effects on their ability to accurately perform verbal and spatial versions of the 3-back task of working memory. Specifically, accuracy was transiently impaired relative to baseline on the spatial task, but enhanced on the verbal task." (Fried, et al., 2014). Low-frequency repetitive transcranial magnetic

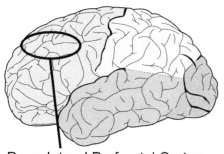

Dorsolateral Prefrontal Cortex

stimulation (rTMS) temporarily *disables* a specific region of the cortex, whereas *high*-frequency stimulation *enhances* functioning. Thus, temporarily disabling the right dorsolateral prefrontal impaired Perceiver spatial processing.

I have suggested that emotional Mercy experiences can overwhelm Perceiver thought. "Posttraumatic stress disorder (PTSD) is an incapacitating anxiety disorder characterized by intrusive thoughts, hyperarousal, flashbacks, nightmares, sleep disturbances, emotional numbing, and withdrawal" (Boggio, et al., 2010). They found that "high frequency stimulation of right DLPFC may be an effective approach in the neuromodulatory treatment of PTSD and that it may function by decreasing the anxiety component of this disorder," backing up an earlier study which found "that 10 Hz rTMS applied to the right DLPFC results in improvements to both core PTSD symptoms and anxiety." Thus, enhancing the right dorsolateral prefrontal helps to prevent Perceiver thought from being overwhelmed by Mercy emotions. We will see later that the amygdala is an emotional processer, and I suggest that the right amygdala generates Mercy emotions. A study of adult females "examined whether one HF-rTMS session applied to the left (n = 10) or right (n = 10) dorsolateral prefrontal cortex (DLPFC) would influence amygdala responses to positively and negatively valenced baby faces... After a single right-sided HF-rTMS session we found a significant right amygdala activity attenuation during the processing of negatively valenced baby faces. This finding provides additional evidence supporting the role of the right anterior hemisphere in the processing of negative emotional information, and increases our understanding of HF-rTMS treatment effects in mental disorders" (Baeken, et al., 2010). In other words, enhancing Perceiver thought lessens the impact of painful Mercy emotions.

> Perceiver thought in right dorsolateral prefrontal can balance or suppress emotions.

Looking at a related trait, a study of college women revealed that "individuals with greater tonic (resting) activity in right posterior DLPFC rate themselves as more behaviorally inhibited" (Shackman, et al., 2009). I have suggested that the Perceiver person is a natural conservative who has to lose control to Contributor thought in order to go beyond the strategy of preservation to one of transformation. Similarly, another paper describing the application of rTMS to the dorsolateral prefrontal cortex concluded that "the capacity to resist temptation depends on the activity level of the right prefrontal cortex" (Knoch & Fehr, 2007). And Beauregard (2001) found when showing erotic film excerpts to male subjects that "the attempted inhibition of the sexual arousal generated by viewing the erotic stimuli was associated with activation of the right superior frontal gyrus and right anterior cingulate gyrus." (The anterior cingulate, which we will examine later, exhibits control at a more basic Contributor level.)

Honesty is very important to the Perceiver person; the facts need to be accurately portrayed. A recent lesion study (which did not distinguish between left and right hemispheres) found that damage to the dorsolateral prefrontal cortex causes a person to be less honest when there is a conflict between honesty and self-interest (Zhu, et al., 2014).

Turning now to the left hemisphere, I have suggested that Server thought handles the structure behind speech. Consistent with this, "Left DLPFC executive control modulates semantic processing of verbal insight problems" (Metuki, et al., 2012). Server thought is needed to carry out sequences of action, especially in the presence of emotional pressure. A study on dieting found that "those with effective dietary self-control had increased activity in the left DLPFC when making decisions about which foods they would like to eat, suggesting that the operation of the DLPFC may be important for regulating dietary self-control. Therefore, differences in DLPFC activity, particularly the left DLPFC, may explain individual differences in dietary choices." When the left dorsolateral prefrontal was suppressed, then individuals felt a much stronger craving for appealing snack food (Lowe, et al., 2014). Notice that the focus here is not so much upon resisting temptation (an expression of Perceiver thought), but rather upon carrying out a sequence of actions (using Server thought).

Lowe makes an interesting generalization that is consistent with the idea of cognitive modules: "Individuals with weak EFs [executive function] may lack the dietary self-control necessary to regulate snack food consumption in the modern obesogenic environment (i.e., one that is saturated with highly salient facilitating cues to consume energy-dense foods), which, in turn, increases the likelihood of such individuals to become overweight or obese. Interventions aimed at enhancing or preserving DLPFC function in healthy populations may reduce the likelihood of adiposity and other chronic conditions. In addition, interventions aimed at enhancing DLPFC activity in clinical populations, may subsequently result in improved disease management." In other words, instead of focusing upon the specific problem of 'eating less', one should focus upon the more general problem of gaining the confidence that is required to use Perceiver and Server thought in the midst of emotional pressure.

Moving on, I have suggested that Perceiver thought points out errors in Teacher theories. This is backed up by a study that examined the brain region being used by competent math students to find math errors: "Mathematical competence was found to modulate the activation of an area in the right dorsolateral prefrontal cortex. Specifically, individuals with relatively higher mathematical competence were found to activate this region more for incorrectly solved trials than their less mathematically competent peers... activation of the right lateral prefrontal cortex during arithmetic errors is affected by individual differences in mathematical competence" (Ansari, et al., 2011). Similarly, a study on deductive and math processing found that "in reasoning, only those problems calling for a search for counterexamples to conclusions recruited right frontal pole" (Kroger, et al., 2008). (We will see in the next section that the right frontopolar cortex is also related to Perceiver thought.)

Perceiver thought can also help to build Teacher understanding by expanding the context. This relationship was found in a study on jokes with incongruous endings, such as "What gets wetter and wetter as it dries? A towel" (Marinkovic, et al., 2011). When a joke is told, the initial activity comes from the speech region in left inferior frontal and temporal cortex, as Teacher thought attempts—and fails—to make sense of the sentence. The right prefrontal cortex then activates as Perceiver thought expands the mental context. This is finally followed by more general prefrontal activation as the punch line of the joke is understood. In the author's words, "In an effort to 'get' the joke, the left anterior temporal area may access semantic memory representations, while the right prefrontal region may contribute divergent, alternative word meanings that are based on weak semantic associations, contextual demands, and lexical ambiguity." This "may lead an extended bilateral temporo-frontal network in establishing the distant unexpected creative coherence between the punch line and the setup." As a Perceiver person, I am very sensitive to alternate meanings of words, and those who know me will agree that I tell too many puns.

I have suggested that Contributor thought *combines* Perceiver facts and Server sequences to come up with *plans*. Consistent with this, "It is well established that the mid-dorsolateral prefrontal cortex (dlPFC) plays a critical role in planning. Neuroimaging studies have yielded predominantly bilateral dlPFC activations, but the existence and nature of functionally specific contributions of left and right dlPFC have remained elusive" (Kaller, et al., 2011). A version of the Tower of London game (I have suggested that games involve Contributor-controlled technical thought) was used to compare the function of the left and right dorsolateral prefrontal. The left was more active when the goal made the order of the steps obvious, while the right was more active when intermediate steps had to be taken that did not lead directly towards the goal. As a Perceiver person I am not naturally aware of sequences. Therefore when I plan, I usually use interdependencies to reduce the possibilities before working out a sequence. When packing a car trunk, for example, I will place large objects first because I know that it is easier to pack small objects around large objects rather than the other way around.

Logical reasoning is another example of technical thought with its combination of Perceiver facts and Server sequences. The "right anterior prefrontal (APFC), right dorsolateral prefrontal cortex (DLPFC), and bilateral posterior parietal cortex (PPC) play a crucial role in four-term transitive reasoning" (Brzezicka, et al., 2011). The authors explain why *right* prefrontal cortex is being activated: "Two specific conditions have been shown to activate the right prefrontal cortex in a reasoning task... [First,] unfamiliar or nonspecific materials (lacking conceptual content, like the letters used in our study), whereas equivalent logical reasoning containing familiar materials activates only the left prefrontal cortex... [Second,] the presence of inverted relations (e.g., given that A is taller than B and B is taller than C, inferring whether C is shorter than A)." In other words, Perceiver thought is required when information cannot be placed within a general Teacher theory or when information has to be transformed in some way.

Concluding, there is significant evidence connecting the dorsolateral prefrontal cortex with Perceiver and Server thought. There is also a correspondence between the functions of this area and a number of specific traits of Perceiver and Server thought. The evidence distinguishing left from right dorsolateral cortex is less conclusive. However, as researchers are learning which hemisphere is activated in a given situation, the ambiguities seem to be resolving in a direction that is consistent with the theory of mental symmetry.

Frontopolar Cortex

This region lies in front of the dorsolateral prefrontal cortex at the very front of the brain. It is also referred to as *rostrolateral prefrontal* cortex or *Brodmann area* [BA] *10*. A recent paper by Watson & Chatterjee (2012) summarizes what has been discovered about this region, and mentions that it has two primary related functions.

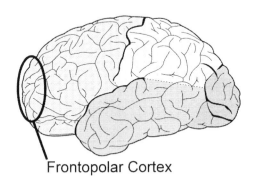
Frontopolar Cortex

First, as was mentioned previously, frontopolar cortex performs *analogical reasoning,* especially analogies that cross contexts. Most imaging studies "point to the rostrolateral prefrontal cortex (RLPFC) as playing a pivotal role in mediating analogy. For instance, activity in RLPFC is sensitive to the number of relations, or the relationships between components of an analogy, that need to be considered. The degree to which an analogy's components are dissimilar on the surface also modulates RLPFC activation. For instance, cross-domain analogies (e.g., nose:scent::antenna:signal) elicit greater frontopolar activity than within-domain analogies (e.g., nose:scent::tongue:taste) (Green, et al., 2010). The development of analogical reasoning ability in children is also accompanied by changes in the way in which RLPFC is engaged."

Watson adds that "The recruitment of RLPFC during analogical (and other types of relational) reasoning has been hypothesized to reflect the need to simultaneously compare and integrate multiple relations between things – 'relational integration'." This describes precisely the sort of semi-rigorous reasoning that we have been using in this book. It is easy to find a *simple* analogy between one topic and another. It is much harder to find an analogy in which the *details* of one topic also correspond to the details of another. This comparing of details adds rigor to analogy. For instance, simply saying that Perceiver and Server thought corresponds to the processing of dorsolateral prefrontal cortex is not rigorous. But if one looks at the *details* of Perceiver and Server thought and finds the *same details* present in dorsolateral prefrontal processing, then one can say with some rigor that there is a correspondence between these two.

> Left frontopolar thought is associated with Server analogies and nested plans.
> Right frontopolar thought is associated with Perceiver analogies and nested plans.

Second, frontopolar activity "is also observed during a wide range of non-analogical cognitive tasks, including episodic memory retrieval, prospective memory, and multitasking. This domain-general involvement of anterior PFC has led to comprehensive theories of its function. On several accounts, this area of the brain coordinates the outcomes of subgoals in the service of fulfilling a main goal." Another paper adds that the frontopolar cortex keeps 'plan B' in mind when one is following 'plan A' (Boorman, et al., 2011).

Watson & Chatterjee explain a possible relationship between these two frontopolar functions: "Integrating the relations between entities is just a special case of coordinating subgoals, and even non-analogical reasoning tasks may require the integration of the results of two or more separate cognitive operations."

Putting this all together, I have suggested that abstract and concrete technical thought view the *same* structure from two *different* angles. Concrete technical thought combines various elements in order to reach some Mercy goal, while abstract technical thought combines the same elements in order to build Teacher order-within-complexity. For instance, a car is an example of a machine which can either be used as a tool to drive from one place to another or as a collection of parts that function together. One sees this same type of overlap occurring in frontopolar cortex. *Planning* treats specific steps as parts of a general plan that are combined and manipulated to reach some Mercy goal, whereas *analogy* treats systems as part of a general structure that are combined and manipulated to generate a Teacher understanding.

Now let us relate this to the interaction between Perceiver thought and Contributor thought. Evidence indicates that the Contributor person *uses* frontopolar cortex. One study showed that "compared with managers, entrepreneurs showed higher decision-making efficiency, and stronger activation regions of frontopolar cortex previously associated with explorative choice" (Laureiro-Martinez, et al., 2014). The entrepreneurs who participated in this study had "founded an organization that was initially established based on their venture idea. Besides, they all had implemented their idea and were—at the time of the study—running the organization." The Contributor person excels at being this sort of self-made individual. But the Contributor person also appears to use frontopolar cortex in a *limited* manner. The natural tendency of the Contributor person is to specialize within some context and to remain within this context. Generally speaking, the Contributor person broadens his thinking because he has to and not because he chooses to. For instance, the entrepreneurs in this study were "constantly involved in various pressing heterogeneous strategic decisions related to administrative areas as diverse as marketing, human resources, production, research and development, and finance." Notice that this heterogenous thinking is still restricted to various aspects of running a business. In other words, the Contributor person may allow frontopolar thought to build connections *within* some general context, but I seldom encounter a Contributor person who is willing to *lose control* to the cross-contextual thinking of frontopolar thought. Instead, Contributor-controlled technical thinking puts a tight leash upon frontopolar thought by dealing with a limited number of connections, rejecting partially certain connections, and ignoring connections that lead beyond the general context.

In contrast, I have discovered that as a Perceiver person I naturally excel at working with many partially certain connections that cross contexts. This ability had to be *developed* and knowledge about different contexts had to be *acquired*, but I have found that there is a natural fit between my cognitive style of Perceiver and frontopolar thought. I have also discovered that the typical educated Contributor person who uses technical thought does not appreciate this type of analogical thinking. This implies that the Perceiver person is conscious in frontopolar thought, whereas the Contributor person is accessing it 'from next door'.

Turning now to the difference between left and right frontopolar cortex, I have suggested that analogy uses Server similarities to construct a general Teacher understanding. Consistent with this, "A left-sided region of the frontal pole of the brain (BA 9/10) was selectively active for the abstract relational integration component of analogical reasoning" (Green, et al., 2006). Others have found that left frontopolar handles verbal and right frontopolar visual data. One study found "strong evidence for a specific involvement of right frontopolar cortex in visual-spatial prospective memory" while previously finding "evidence for left BA 10 involvement in verbal prospective memory" (Costa, et al., 2013). Prospective memory means carrying out some subtask (in Costa's experiment, subjects pressed the letter M on the keyboard if a certain square on the screen lit up) while continuing to perform some primary task (in this case reproducing a sequence of dots on the screen either forwards or backwards). Watson & Chaterjee (2012) also suggest that "hemispheric differences may emerge depending on the visuospatial or verbal/semantic nature of the analogies." Thus, it appears a *separation* can be made between Perceiver and Server frontopolar thought when dealing with *simple* coordination tasks or when distinguishing visual from verbal. However, Watson found that "both left and right RLPFC were more active during the analogy condition relative to the item condition", suggesting that *both* Perceiver and Server thought become involved when dealing with more *complicated* connections. Similarly, "the left frontopolar became more active when people thought about carrying out more complex plans of action, such as 'planning a wedding' versus 'stirring a cup of coffee'" (Krueger, et al., 2009).

Watson adds that "because the analogy task alone required integration of *relations*, these results [of their study] suggest that RLPFC activity is more strongly driven by the need to integrate relational information rather than coordinate subgoal outcomes." "Despite being solved more quickly, analogies elicited greater average activity within the left and right RLPFC." In other words, both analogy and coordinating subgoals involve the frontopolar cortex. However, analogy may involve the frontopolar region more strongly because one is thinking about *thinking*—one is looking for relations between relations, whereas coordinating subgoals involves thinking about *doing*—using frontopolar thought to assist other regions of the mind. In a similar manner, the metacognition of knowing-that-one-knows appears to activate the right RLPFC more strongly: "fMRI activity in right rostrolateral PFC, rlPFC, satisfies three constraints for a role in metacognition of decision-making. Right rlPFC showed greater activity during self-report compared to a matched control condition, activity in rlPFC correlated with reported confidence, and the strength of the relationship between activity and confidence predicted metacognitive ability across individuals" (Fleming, et al., 2012).

Summarizing, there is strong evidence associating frontopolar cortex with the highest level of Perceiver and Server thought. There is also evidence associating Perceiver thought with right frontopolar cortex and Server thought with left frontopolar cortex.

Orbitofrontal Cortex

This region lies at the bottom of the frontal lobes, just above the orbits of the eyes. We have examined the two major regions of the frontal cortex that are associated with *executive* function. We will now turn our attention to the parts of the frontal lobe that are associated with *identity* and *emotional* thought. In general terms, I suggest that the orbitofrontal region is associated with the internal worlds of Mercy thought and Teacher thought.

This is the part of the cortex that functions the most emotionally: "In human neocortex, pleasure appears most faithfully represented by activity in orbitofrontal cortex, particularly in a mid-anterior subregion. Evidence suggests activity of this mid-anterior zone tracks changes in subjective pleasantness ratings of chocolate and delicious drinks, such as when pleasure intensity is diminished by switching the taster's state from hunger to satiety, and may also encode pleasures of sexual orgasm, drugs, and music" (Berridge & Kringelbach, 2013). For instance, my mother is a Mercy person and she consistently avoids eating food just before mealtime for fear that it will spoil her appetite and diminish the pleasure of the meal.

> Mercy mental networks reside within right orbitofrontal cortex.
> Teacher mental networks reside within left orbitofrontal cortex.

Orbitofrontal cortex deals with both simple and abstract pleasures, "with more complex or abstract reinforcers (such as monetary gain and loss) represented more anteriorly in the orbitofrontal cortex than less complex reinforcers (such as taste)" (Kringelbach, 2005).

This emotional labeling provides the basis for judgments of value. A study of monkeys showed that "during economic choice, neurons in orbitofrontal cortex encode the value of offered and chosen goods. Importantly, OFC [orbitofrontal cortex] neurons encode

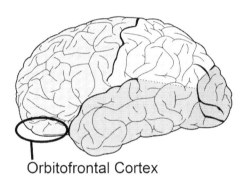

Orbitofrontal Cortex

value independently of visuospatial factors and motor responses" (Padoa-Schioppa & Assad, 2006). The study explains that "Shortly after the offer, when the monkey presumably assigns values to the two juices, neurons encoding the offer value (i.e., the value of one juice or the other) are most prevalent. Also during the delay, many neurons encode the chosen value (i.e., the value of the juice the monkey will eventually consume), even though the choice is still covert (because the go signal has not been given yet). Finally, after the monkey has indicated its choice, before and after juice delivery, many neurons encode the taste of the chosen juice." I have suggested that most emotional processing is guided *internally* by mental networks and that sensory input *updates* mental networks. Notice how the monkey is guided through most of this process by the *memory* of how the preferred juice tastes as well as the *anticipation* of how the juice will taste. This internal emotional value is then updated at the end of the sequence by the *actual* taste of the juice.

I have also suggested that triggering one element of a mental network will activate the entire mental network. Consistent with this, "the orbitofrontal cortex appears to have a crucial function in integrating incoming sensory information with memory to facilitate recognition" (Chaumon, et al., 2013). More specifically, it is "proposed that the OFC receives coarse, partially analyzed information from visual stimuli before an object is actually recognized, and uses this information to generate a 'first guess' prediction about the identity of the object. This visual prediction is then back-projected top-down to occipito-temporal visual regions to promote recognition." However, "only stimuli resembling known objects, and thus activating semantic associations, trigger a response in the OFC." A similar study noted that "the OFC was found to be activated when participants perceived coherence... This increase in activation began earlier in the OFC than in temporal object recognition areas. Moreover, the present study demonstrated that OFC activation was independent of physical stimulus characteristics, task requirements, and participants' explicit recognition of the stimuli presented. These results speak to the OFC's fundamental role in the early steps of intuitive judgments" (Horr, et al., 2014). Putting this together, when the mind encounters incomplete information, then this will trigger a mental network leading to what Horr refers to as a 'gut feeling'. This mental network will then impose its structure upon sensory input and what is seen will be interpreted in the light of this mental network. Horr suggests that this describes the brain mechanism behind intuition. Volz (2008) found a similar result regarding intuitive judgments about sounds, suggesting that this intuitive processing applies to all modalities. Thus, it appears that the orbitofrontal cortex functions in a manner that is consistent with mental networks. Finally, Horr found that "left OFC activation in the present study was significantly higher for stimuli judged as coherent than for those judged as incoherent", consistent with the idea that Teacher thought looks for order-within-complexity.

Horr adds that "recent studies have shown that the OFC is important to perform a model-based inference on the value of sensory events (e.g. 'I like coffee cups'), rather than to retrieve this value from specific past events cached in memory (e.g. 'I like this coffee cup')." If this conclusion is accurate, then this means that mental networks within orbitofrontal cortex automatically overgeneralize—whether this is warranted or not. I have suggested that there is a natural tendency for Mercy thought to regard specific emotional experiences as universal principles. For instance, one emotional experience of being bitten by a dog will lead to the formation of an MMN which causes a person to believe that 'all dogs bite'. Similarly, there is a natural tendency for Teacher thought to overgeneralize, jumping from 'It rained last Saturday' to 'It always rains on the weekend'. The end result is what one could call *unstable universality*, in which the latest defining experience or overgeneralized theory is treated as universal until some new emotional memory crowds its way into orbitofrontal cortex. This type of thinking appears to be characteristic of immature Mercy and Teacher thought.

A comprehensive summary of orbitofrontal functioning can be found in an article by Rolls & Grabenhorst (2008). I have suggested that the emotional label that is applied to experiences by Mercy thought can be altered by connections provided by the rest of the mind. Rolls describes this type of emotional relabeling occurring with *taste*: "Activations related to the affective value of umami taste and flavor (as shown by correlations with pleasantness ratings) in the orbitofrontal cortex were modulated by word-level descriptors (e.g., 'rich and delicious flavor')." It also occurs with *odor*: "Word labels influenced the subjective pleasantness ratings to the test odor, and the changing pleasantness ratings were correlated with the activations in the human medial orbitofrontal cortex." And with *touch*: "When subjects were informed by word labels that a cream seen being rubbed onto the forearm was a 'Rich moisturising cream' vs. 'Basic cream', these cognitive labels influenced activations in the orbitofrontal/pregenual cingulate cortex and ventral striatum." Similarly, *focusing* upon emotions will increase the sensitivity of the orbitofrontal cortex: "When subjects were instructed to remember and rate the pleasantness of a jasmine odor, activations were greater in the medial orbitofrontal and pregenual cingulate cortex than when subjects were instructed to remember and rate the intensity of the odor." This tells us that it is possible to *choose* whether or not one will approach an experience from an emotional Mercy perspective.

The basic premise of cognitive style is that people have a natural tendency to use different cognitive strategies. Consistent with this, Rolls & Grabenhorst found that "Some individuals, chocolate cravers, report that they crave chocolate more than non-cravers, and this is associated with increased liking of chocolate, increased wanting of chocolate, and eating chocolate more frequently than non-cravers... the sight of chocolate produced more activation in chocolate cravers than non-cravers in the medial orbitofrontal cortex and ventral striatum. For cravers vs. non-cravers, a combination of a picture of chocolate with chocolate in the mouth produced a greater effect than the sum of the components (i.e. supra-linearity) in the medial orbitofrontal cortex and pregenual cingulate cortex." The Mercy person tends to be a chocolate craver and an MMN of chocolate craving can be triggered by pictures of chocolate.

I have stated that both Mercy and Teacher thought are inherently unstable and subject to change. Orbitofrontal neurons exhibit this kind of instability: "One function implemented by the orbitofrontal cortex is rapid stimulus-reinforcement association learning and the correction of these associations when reinforcement contingencies in the environment change."

Orbitofrontal cortex also deals with *social interaction*. Rolls points out that "social behaviour to an individual may require representations not only of face expression, but also of face identity, and both are involved in typical social behaviour" and Rolls has found that some "orbitofrontal cortex neurons provide representations of which expression is present on a face, and of face identity" (Rolls & Grabenhorst, 2008). A study of macaque monkeys found that "the orbitofrontal cortex, a brain region involved in motivation and reward, is tuned to social information... neuronal activity was found to track momentary social preferences and partner's identity and social rank. The orbitofrontal cortex thus contains key neuronal mechanisms for the evaluation of social information" (Azzi, et al., 2012). Looking at humans, "Lesion studies suggest that OFC is causally involved in central components of social influence on value. Damage to this region impairs one's ability to correctly assign value to stimuli, respond appropriately to social cues, and act appropriately during social interaction" (Campbell-Meiklejohn, et al., 2012). And there is "a linear relationship between grey matter volume in a region of lateral orbitofrontal cortex and the tendency to shift reported desire for objects toward values expressed by other people... [This grey matter volume] also predicted the functional hemodynamic response in the middle frontal gyrus to discovering that someone else's values contrast with one's own." In other words, orbitofrontal cortex tracks social status, is affected by social standards, and notices when personal standards differ from social standards. This is consistent with the suggestion that Mercy thought uses mental networks to represent self, others, and culture, and that mental networks that are triggered simultaneously will struggle for emotional dominance. This struggle between mental networks is described by Rolls: "The orbitofrontal cortex, being concerned especially with making explicit in the firing rate the representations of reinforcers, provides a brain region where different reinforcers can be compared by competition implemented by lateral inhibition" (Rolls & Grabenhorst, 2008).

> Orbitofrontal cortex calculates emotional labels and guides social interaction.

Looking further at social behavior, "Both clinical characterizations and anecdotal evidence suggests that orbitofrontal damage impairs the ability to regulate social behavior" (Beer, et al., 2003). Beer suggests that "the impaired behavioral regulation of the orbitofrontal patients was associated with disrupted self-conscious emotion", explaining that "self-conscious emotions include embarrassment, shame, guilt, and pride. These emotions involve complex appraisals of how one's behavior has been evaluated by the self and other people." Continuing, "although orbitofrontal patients did generate self-conscious emotions, these emotions tended to reinforce inappropriate behavior rather than correct it. For example, orbitofrontal patients were not embarrassed by and were proud of their teasing behavior that was objectively inappropriate." In addition, "orbitofrontal patients had trouble making accurate appraisals of others' self-conscious emotions." Translating this into the language of mental symmetry, the patient with orbitofrontal damage behaves in a way that would mortify the Mercy person, oblivious to the MMNs that normally guide behavior.

Notice that most of what we have discussed relates to Mercy thought rather than Teacher thought. One reason for this is that much of this research comes from studying animals such as monkeys, and animals are incapable of abstract thought. Another reason is that Mercy thought is more prominent than Teacher thought in the average person. Obviously, observing the brain will only reveal how it *is* functioning and not how it *could* function. However, one can also find Teacher thought and Teacher emotion in this region of the brain. As was mentioned previously, Zeki (2014) found that "the experience of visual, musical, and moral beauty all correlate with activity in a specific part of the emotional brain, field A1 of the medial orbitofrontal cortex." And scanning the brains of 15 mathematicians, who *have* learned to use Teacher thought in the area of mathematics, "showed that the experience of mathematical beauty correlates parametrically with activity in the same part of the emotional brain, namely field A1 of the medial orbito-frontal cortex (mOFC), as the experience of beauty derived from other sources." Beauty is primarily a Teacher emotion, generated by the order-within-complexity of attributes such as symmetry, elegance, simplicity, and smoothness. The fact that so many different kinds of beauty all activate the same brain region suggests that it makes neurological sense to talk about Teacher thought and Teacher emotion.

The other reason for the apparent dominance of Mercy thought is that personal identity and social interaction can be approached from either a Mercy or a Teacher perspective. For instance, we have seen that identity can be defined either by the Mercy object of the physical body or by the Teacher name that describes a profession. Similarly, social interaction consists of a combination of Mercy experiences and Teacher words; I *get together* with friends and *converse* with them. Because identity and social interaction contain both a Mercy and a Teacher component, it makes sense that both right and left orbitofrontal cortex would be activated.

Only a few papers discuss the difference between left and right orbitofrontal cortex. One study examined the vocal blocking that occurs in stuttering and found that "preceding a block there is significantly less activation of the left orbitofrontal and inferior frontal cortices. Furthermore, there is significant extra activation in the right orbitofrontal and inferior frontal cortices" (Sowman, et al., 2012). This implies that Mercy thought is disabling Teacher thought during stuttering. (We will see later that left inferior frontal is associated with Teacher thought and right inferior frontal with Mercy thought.)

Finally, there are some interesting findings regarding religious belief. "The orbitofrontal cortex (OFC) is a region of the brain that has been empirically linked with religious or spiritual activity, and atrophy in this region has been shown to contribute to serious mental illness in late life" (Hayward, et al., 2011). I have suggested that religious culture is based in MMNs and that the Christian prayer of salvation brings harmony between a TMN-based concept of God and the MMNs of personal identity. Consistent with this, Hayward found in a study of older people that "Significantly less atrophy of the left OFC was observed in participants who reported a life-changing religious or spiritual experience during the course of the study, and in members of Protestant religious groups who reported being born again when entering the study. Significantly greater atrophy of the left OFC was also associated with more frequent participation in public religious worship. No significant relationship was observed between religious or spiritual factors and extent of atrophy in the right OFC." In other words, those who had undergone religiously guided personal transformation or had applied the Christian prayer of salvation experienced 'significantly less atrophy' of the core of Teacher thought, while those who approached religion from a Mercy perspective experienced 'significantly greater atrophy' of Teacher thought. Another study found that "Experiencing fear of God was associated with decreased volume of L precuneus and L orbitofrontal cortex" (Kapogiannis, et al., 2009), implying that the core of Teacher thought is being suppressed because personal identity is feeling threatened by a concept of God.

Concluding, there is excellent evidence relating orbitofrontal cortex to the emotional realm of mental networks. While most of this evidence describes Mercy thought and Mercy mental networks there is also some evidence of Teacher thought and Teacher mental networks.

Medial Frontal Cortex

The medial prefrontal cortex is adjacent to the orbitofrontal cortex and is the part of the frontal lobes in the center line of the brain where the left hemisphere touches the right. It is considered to be related to orbitofrontal cortex, just as the frontopolar cortex is related to the dorsolateral cortex. The nomenclature here is somewhat confused, with various terms being used to describe overlapping areas, and the precise boundary between the orbitofrontal and the medial frontal is uncertain. As Wikipedia explains, "Different researchers use the term ventromedial prefrontal cortex differently. Sometimes, the term is saved for the area above the medial orbitofrontal cortex, while at other times, 'ventromedial prefrontal cortex' is used to describe a broad area in the lower (ventral) central (medial) region of the prefrontal cortex, of which the medial orbitofrontal cortex constitutes the lowermost part."

The general consensus is that this medial area can be subdivided into three subregions. The two areas in the front, which I will refer to as *medial frontal,* appear to connect Perceiver with Mercy and Server with Teacher, while the smaller part at the back that lies

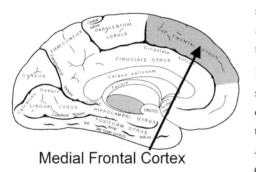

Medial Frontal Cortex

above the corpus callosum, called the *anterior cingulate,* appears to connect the four simple styles with Contributor thought.

Looking first at the medial frontal, I have suggested that the emotional experiences of personal identity reside within Mercy thought, while Perceiver thought creates a *self-image* by observing identity from next door. This dichotomy exists within the brain, because "Social knowledge, be it about one's self or of others, is represented in the medial prefrontal cortex" (Wagner, et al., 2012), which is adjacent to orbitofrontal cortex. Wagner adds that "a distinction is made between ventral (VMPFC) and dorsal (DMPFC) regions of the MPFC [medial prefrontal cortex], the former being commonly implicated in self-referential cognition and the latter being more commonly associated with impression formation and thinking about the mental states of others." In other words, thinking about myself activates the region of the medial frontal cortex that is closest to the orbitofrontal with its experiences of self, while thinking about others activates regions that are further away from the orbitofrontal.

This distinction between self and others is not supported by all authors. For instance, Bzdok (2013) "comprehensively characterized both the vmPFC and dmPFC as relevant for self- and other-focused as well as social, emotional, and facial processing. More specifically, the vmPFC subserves predominantly non-ambiguous subjective-value-related evaluative processes driven by bottom-up pathways, whereas the dmPFC subserves predominantly ambiguous amodal metacognitive processes driven by top-down pathways." In other words, the vmPFC generalizes based upon specific personal experiences in orbitofrontal cortex while the dmPFC makes guesses about specific individuals and situations guided by a general knowledge of people and social interaction. Both of these interpretations may be accurate, because when I am generalizing about people based upon specific experiences, I am usually generalizing about specific experiences involving *me*. That interpretation is suggested by Nicolle (2012), who says that "the functional gradient in the medial prefrontal cortex does not align with the individual, but is dependent on whether choices are executed by the subject or instead are modeled without overt execution." Regardless of which of these precise interpretations is the best one, the general point is that the medial frontal contains a combination of Mercy-and-Perceiver as well as Teacher-and-Server.

> Medial frontal generates self-image, value, social interaction, and conscience.
> Left medial frontal uses Server thought to connect mental networks.
> Right medial frontal uses Perceiver thought to connect mental networks.
> Medial frontal plays a central role in Theory of Mind.

Looking at more specific aspects, Wagner adds that the "DMPFC is particularly sensitive to conditions in which an individual is required to form social inferences based on minimal information. For instance, when participants reason about uncertain beliefs, or attempt to infer someone's personality and preferences, the DMPFC shows a greater response relative to tasks that call for inferences about unambiguous beliefs and preferences." Using psychological language, "the medial pFC (mPFC) is frequently reported to play a central role in Theory of Mind (ToM)" (Hartwright, et al., 2014).

Wagner (2011) adds that the "VMPFC is spontaneously recruited for highly self-relevant biographical material", the "VMPFC tracks ownership of objects", and it is "spontaneously activated upon reading biographical information." In each of these cases, one is dealing with facts about personal identity. The "DMPFC is engaged when viewing short films depicting social interactions, when thinking about the thoughts and intentions of virtual characters while playing a video game." Here we see activity related to facts about people in general.

The medial frontal is also involved in evaluating *moral status*. One study looked at "the spontaneous evaluation of social targets as a function of their social status. Differential activation in the IPS [intraparietal sulcus] was found for targets varying on financial status, but not for targets varying on moral status. In contrast, differential activation for targets varying on moral status, but not on financial status, was observed in VMPFC" (Cloutier, et al., 2012). In other words, evaluating people on the basis of their financial worth uses simple knowledge about facts and sequences within parietal cortex, while determining the moral status of an individual looks more deeply at self-image within medial frontal cortex. Another study reports that "individuals lower in social status are more likely to engage neural circuitry often involved in 'mentalizing' or thinking about others' thoughts and feelings... college students' perception of their social status in the university community was related to neural activity in the mentalizing network (e.g.,

DMPFC, MPFC, precuneus/PCC) while encoding social information, with lower social status predicting greater neural activity in this network" (Muscatell, et al., 2012). They explain this finding by quoting another study which found that "individuals who are relatively lower in social status exhibit cues that they are closely attending to an interaction partner (more eye contact, head nodding, laughing). By contrast, higher-status individuals are more likely to behave in ways suggesting less engagement in the interaction" (Kraus, et al., 2009). This tells us that social status and Theory of Mind interact within the medial frontal cortex. It also shows how mental networks of personal identity typically interact, with greater mental networks ignoring other mental networks and lesser mental networks adjusting to fit the structure of greater mental networks. A meta-analysis of studies on morality noted that "Brain activity related to both moral cognition and non-pain empathy converged significantly in an area of the dmPFC", which "may suggest an implication of this highly associative cortical area in more complex social-emotional processing" (Bzdok, et al., 2012).

Belief, either religious or secular, is also associated with the medial frontal cortex. Harris (2009) examined "fifteen committed Christians and fifteen nonbelievers—as they evaluated the truth and falsity of religious and nonreligious propositions. For both groups, and in both categories of stimuli, belief (judgments of 'true' vs judgments of 'false') was associated with greater signal in the ventromedial prefrontal cortex ...This region showed greater signal whether subjects believed statements about God, the Virgin Birth, etc. or statements about ordinary facts." Belief describes *my* view of the facts; it combines Mercy identity with Perceiver information.

Two major conclusions can be drawn from this material so far. First, this book has discussed the interaction between Perceiver facts and Mercy identity in substantial detail. This focus may seem unwarranted to those who are used to scientific methodology with its objective thought. However, there is a specific region of the frontal lobes that is devoted to carrying out precisely this interaction. Second, I have suggested that most social interaction occurs *within people's minds* as people jump to conclusions based upon incomplete information. The core of this internal social interaction is occurring within the medial frontal region, which 'is particularly sensitive to conditions in which an individual is required to form social inferences based on minimal information'. External social interaction may be *updating* the internal mental networks that represent people, and studying external social interaction may give *clues* about what is happening within the mind, but evidence from neurology makes it clear that most social interaction is occurring *within* the mind.

I have suggested that the goal of personal transformation is to become guided internally by Platonic forms in order to reach long-term goals. The medial frontal cortex plays a central role in this kind of internal processing: "When deprived of compelling perceptual input, the mind is often occupied with thoughts unrelated to the immediate environment. Previous behavioral research has shown that this self-generated task-unrelated thought (TUT), especially under non-demanding conditions, relates to cognitive capacities such as creativity, planning, and reduced temporal discounting... Individuals with a higher tendency to engage in TUT under low-demanding conditions (but not under high-demanding conditions) show an increased thickness of medial prefrontal cortex (mPFC) and anterior/midcingulate cortex. Thickness of these regions also related to less temporal discounting (TD) of monetary rewards in an economic task, indicative of more patient decision-making. The findings of a shared structural substrate in mPFC and anterior/midcingulate cortex underlying both TUT and TD suggest an important role of these brain regions in supporting the self-generation of information that is unrelated to the immediate environment" (Bernhardt, et al., 2013). Saying this more simply, developing an internal world of personal Mercy experiences guided by Perceiver facts (and Teacher words guided by Server sequences) leads to greater creativity, better planning, and more patience when carrying out plans. This ability can be measured physically in terms of cortical thickness: "Multiple recent human imaging studies have suggested that the structure of the brain can change with learning" (Lerch, et al., 2011).

Turning now to the relationship *between* medial frontal and orbitofrontal, medial frontal connects the emotional memories that are contained within orbitofrontal: "Although the VMPFC is involved in making self-evaluations generally, accuracy of self-evaluations is instead related to activity in the orbitofrontal cortex (OFC)" (Wagner, et al., 2011). In other words, the mental networks of self within orbitofrontal cortex force self-image to be accurate. This is consistent with another paper that examined the feeling of *regret*, the negative emotion that results from making a wrong choice. Looking at patients with brain damage in this area, "VMPFC patients tended to make worse choices, and... reported emotions that were sensitive to regret comparisons. In contrast, LOFC [lateral orbitofrontal cortex] patients made better choices, but reported emotional reactions that were insensitive to regret comparisons. We suggest the VMPFC is involved in the association between choices and anticipated emotions that guide future choices, while the LOFC is involved in experienced emotions that follow choices, emotions that may signal the need for behavioral change" (Levens, et al., 2014). Saying this another way, medial frontal cortex uses self-image to come up with possible selves and future selves, in line with Higgins' theory of possible selves, while orbitofrontal cortex adds the personal emotion of regret that comes from living in my current self rather than a better alternative self. Another study "used an autobiographical memory paradigm where participants relived during fMRI [functional magnetic resonance imaging] scanning situations from their own past that were associated with strong feelings of guilt, shame, or sadness. Compared with the control emotions, guilt episodes specifically recruited a region of right orbitofrontal cortex, which was also highly correlated with individual propensity to experience guilt (Trait Guilt). Guilt-specific activity was also observed in the paracingulate dorsomedial prefrontal cortex, a critical 'Theory of Mind' region" (Wagner, et al., 2011). This study is especially interesting because subjects relived situations from their *own* past rather than dealing with hypothetical moral situations. This activated most strongly *right* orbitofrontal cortex—the internal world of Mercy thought. But it also activated medial frontal cortex, which contains the connections behind conscience.

Finally, this region of the mind plays a key role in determining economic value, as shown by a field of research known as neuroeconomics: "Recent work in neuroeconomics has shown that regions in orbitofrontal and medial prefrontal cortex encode the subjective value of different options during choice" (Camille, et al., 2011). Grabenhorst & Rolls (2011) conclude that "the VMPFC represents a common valuation signal that underlies different types of decision as well as decisions about different types of goods. A related account suggests that, whereas the OFC is involved in encoding the value of specific rewards, the VMPFC plays a specific role in value-guided decision-making about which of several options to pursue by encoding the expected value of the chosen option." Again we see that emotional experiences reside within orbitofrontal cortex while the connections between these experiences lie within medial frontal cortex.

Moving on, none of the papers that I read distinguished between left and right medial frontal cortex. One reason is that the two hemispheres are literally touching each other at this point and so it is difficult to distinguish one from the other. Another reason is that there is both a Perceiver and Server form of self-image. Perceiver self-image observes Mercy experiences and looks for repeated connections—facts that do not change. Server self-image is based upon my skills—what I can do. The Server definition of self-image is prominent in human righteousness, which places 'what I do' within the general context of 'how we do things'. These two definitions overlap, because Perceiver self-image includes my skills, and Perceiver facts about what I own and where I work play a major role in human righteousness.

In conclusion, one can say with considerable confidence that medial frontal is Perceiver-plus-Mercy and Teacher-plus-Server, but one cannot prove from neurology that one is related to right medial frontal and the other to left.

It is interesting to compare the interpretations of conscience with the countries in which the authors of these papers work. This is easy to do because papers list the institutional affiliations of the authors. Wagner (2011), working in Switzerland, says that "Guilt is a central moral emotion due to its inherent link to norm violations, thereby affecting both individuals and society." The emphasis here is upon norms that apply to both individuals and society. Bzdok (2012), working in Germany, states that "Morally judicious behavior forms the fabric of human sociality," and begins by quoting Aristotle, Kant, and Kohlberg. Levens (2014), working in the United States, views conscience from the perspective of individuality and free will, beginning the Abstract with "Counterfactual feelings of regret occur when people make comparisons between an actual outcome and a better outcome that would have occurred under a different choice. Cloutier (2012), also working in America, focuses upon how individuals are viewed who have "low or high financial status (e.g., 'earns $25,000' or 'earns $350,000'), or low or high moral status (e.g., 'is a tobacco executive' or 'does cancer research')", reflecting the American ambivalence between getting ahead financially and breaking the rules morally. Yu (2014), working in China, views guilt in more pragmatic, interpersonal terms, opening with the question "How would you feel if you lost the bicycle borrowed from your friend, which was the last present given to him by his grandmother before she died?" Finally, Boksem (2010), working in the Netherlands, approaches morality from the postmodern perspective of social hierarchy and power: "Social hierarchies feature prominently in a large variety of animal species, including humans, and are found to be an important organizing principle in most cultures. In animals, but also in humans, social status strongly predicts well-being, morbidity and even survival. Be it in domestic, professional or recreational settings, status looms large and defines implicit expectations and action predispositions that drive appropriate (social) behaviour." (Boksem was studying Medial Frontal Negativity, which is thought to originate in the anterior cingulate.) All of these authors are studying the same brain region using careful research. And yet, each paper approaches conscience guided by the mental networks of the culture of the authors. This implies that the brain mechanism behind conscience can be programmed in several different ways, and that neurological research will not discover *all* of the ways that conscience can be programmed but rather will tend to focus upon—and measure—the way that conscience is being programmed by the culture of the researcher.

Research on the medial frontal also leads us to another conclusion. Economics, personal identity, social interaction, and morality have traditionally been viewed as unrelated, with economics regarded as something objective achieved using concrete technical thought, personal identity being part of the subjective world with its MMNs, morality associated with revealed truth and fundamentalism, and social interaction guided by the MMNs of status and culture. I have suggested that all four of these use the same cognitive modules. Economics uses Perceiver thought to build connections between emotional Mercy experiences leading to a map of value that guides economic choice; personal identity is composed of emotional Mercy experiences while self-image is based in Perceiver facts about personal identity; morality results when Perceiver truth impinges upon personal identity within Mercy thought, and social interaction uses Perceiver facts to compare identities in Mercy thought. This equating of these four different processes is consistent with neurology, because the *same* brain region calculates economic value, contains personal identity and self-image, generates feelings of morality, and interprets social interaction.

Anterior Cingulate Cortex

Cost-benefit analysis and optimization are core attributes of practical Contributor thought. In order to decide what plan to follow, Contributor thought compares the benefit of following each option with the cost of pursuing that choice. Going further, Contributor thought is continually modifying behavior in order to follow the best choice in the most optimal manner. The anterior cingulate cortex appears to be carrying out precisely this type of calculation. This region "has been implicated in a diversity of functions, from reward processing and performance monitoring to the execution of

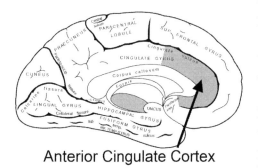

Anterior Cingulate Cortex

control and action selection. Here, we propose that this diversity can be understood in terms of a single underlying function: allocation of control based on an evaluation of the expected value of control (EVC). We present a normative model of EVC that integrates three critical factors: the expected payoff from a controlled process, the amount of control that must be invested to achieve that payoff, and the

cost in terms of cognitive effort. We propose that dACC [dorsal anterior cingulate cortex] integrates this information" (Shenhav, et al., 2013). The anterior cingulate performs this optimization guided by information about value from the orbitofrontal and the medial frontal cortex. In the words of Shenhav, "The EVC model proposes that dACC monitors such present state and outcome-value information, garnered from other regions (such as orbitofrontal, ventromedial prefrontal, and insular cortex), as a basis for computing and maximizing the EVC." Similarly, Grabenhorst & Rolls (2011) suggest that "information about the value of rewards is projected from the OFC to ACC... Bringing together information about specific rewards with information about actions, and the costs associated with actions, is important for associating actions with the value of their outcomes and for selecting the correct action that will lead to a desired reward."

> Anterior cingulate calculates Contributor value based on Teacher and Mercy emotions.

Contributor thought uses a knowledge of value to make choices. Hayden (2011) suggests that the "dACC is positioned late in the sequence of processes that serves to convert sensory information to motor plans. If the goal of the brain is to use information arriving from the environment to make adaptive decisions, then one would expect neurons positioned late in the processing stream to represent decision variables, like whether a switch is needed, but not to represent constituent information relating to that decision—such as probability and reward size." In other words, the anterior cingulate takes information about value from the orbitofrontal and medial frontal and translates it into a form that is appropriate for Contributor choice. Precisely where choice occurs depends upon how one defines choice. Grabenhorst & Rolls (2011) view choice as mental networks duelling via the medial Frontal cortex: "The role of the anterior VMPFC area 10 is to transform a continuously scaled representation of expected value (or offer value) of the stimulus choice options into a categorical representation of reward stimulus choice. This process uses a mechanism in which the winner in the choice competition is the chosen stimulus, which can then be used as the goal for action to guide action selection."

However, it also appears that Contributor thought chooses between a limited set of options within the basal ganglia, and the anterior cingulate is critical for working out these options. Holroyd & Yeung (2012) suggest that the "ACC supports the selection and maintenance of 'options'—extended, context-specific sequences of behavior directed toward particular goals—that are learned through process of hierarchical reinforcement learning." The anterior cingulate also responds when results do not match the Contributor plan: "dACC neurons signal the surprisingness of reward outcomes" (Hayden, et al., 2011).

Contributor combines Perceiver and Server, and we saw earlier that these cognitive modules are related to *executive function*. When the anterior cingulate was removed in humans (to 'treat' severe psychological conditions), "neuropsychological follow-up of such cases demonstrated executive function impairment." More specifically, the "ACC contributes to behavior by modifying responses especially in reaction to challenging cognitive and physical states that require additional effortful cognitive control. This is accomplished by monitoring the emotional salience of stimuli, exerting control over the autonomic nervous system, and modulating cognitive activity" (Gasquoine, 2013). This type of activity occurs when Contributor thought carries out a plan.

Practical Contributor thought is a mental circuit that involves the cooperation of several cognitive modules. Holroyd & Yeung (2012) describe several aspects of this circuit. First, they agree that the "ACC integrates information about costs and effort – both correlated with but not reducible to conflict – to the same end." Second, I have suggested that Perceiver and Server thought generate facts and sequences while Contributor thought accesses this content from 'next door'. Similarly, the "ACC decides what task to perform and then directs DLPFC to implement that task... Note that a key difference between the role of DLPFC and ACC is that the latter instigates switches between tasks to achieve a higher-level goal (get in the car, drive to the market, get groceries, etc.), whereas the former implements the task at hand (e.g. drive to the market)." In other words, the anterior cingulate does the Contributor planning while the dorsolateral frontal (Perceiver and Server thought) implements the segments of the plan. Third, Mercy thought provides the goal for Contributor thought. As was discussed earlier, "orbitofrontal cortex associates the termination state of each option with pseudo-reward, providing contextually appropriate reward information to the ventral striatum such that, for example, the system is provided with a pseudo-reward on successful completion of the drive-to-market option." Fourth, we will see later that the ventral striatum is associated with Exhorter thought and motivation.

Evidence from personality indicates that the Contributor person has a tendency to belittle others through the use of sarcasm. Bohrn (2012) found that "Irony/sarcasm processing was correlated with activations in midline structures such as the medFG, ACC and cuneus/precuneus," suggesting that sarcasm involves Contributor calculations of value.

In conclusion, evidence strongly suggests that the anterior cingulate plays a key role in Contributor thought. The papers that we have examined all describe *concrete* Contributor thought that uses Server actions to reach a Mercy bottom line. I have suggested that the same Contributor circuit also plays a role in *abstract* Contributor thought, and recent research is starting to examine this additional role: "We observed activity in the dorsal ACC that was common to incongruent conditions of three different attentional control tasks, regardless of the response modality (vocal vs. manual) and nature of the stimuli (linguistic vs. non-linguistic). This common activation suggests a domain-general substrate that is called upon by all three tasks. More focused analysis of this commonly-activated region of the dorsal ACC in the linguistic-vocal tasks showed that it was sensitive to more difficult (i.e., incongruent) relative to easier linguistic stimuli" (Piai, et al., 2013). In other words, the anterior cingulate appears to be responsible for coordinating both concrete Contributor plans of action and abstract verbal Contributor plans. I should mention in passing that concrete Contributor thought is much simpler to decipher than abstract Contributor thought, for the simple reason that it involves concrete actions and concrete experiences. Thus, it makes sense that neurological researchers would discover how concrete Contributor thought functions before understanding abstract Contributor thought.

Insula

The insula is not part of the frontal lobes. Instead, it is buried beneath the division between the frontal lobes and posterior cortex. I mention it here because it interacts heavily with the medial frontal and anterior cingulate. When I began studying neurology the function of the insula was completely unknown. It has recently been discovered that this region plays a key role in *embodiment*. I have suggested that personal identity begins with experiences of pain and pleasure from the physical body. The insula is the source of this input. Saying this another way, the insula provides an alternative to the orbitofrontal, with the insula providing a *physical* basis for personal identity and the orbitofrontal an *internal* basis rooted in mental networks.

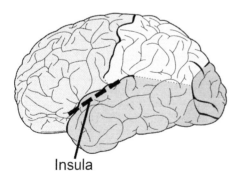

Insula

Zaki (2012) says that "a long research tradition suggests that right lateralized AI [anterior insula] plays a specific role in evaluating the subjective relevance of bodily states." Notice that the *right* insula is associated with embodiment, consistent with the idea that personal identity is seeded by emotional *Mercy* experiences. Because embodiment happens *early* in cognitive development, it makes sense that neurological research would uncover this lateralization. In contrast,

"The left anterior insula has a broad response profile and is part of multiple functional networks including language, memory and socio-emotional networks" (Clos, et al., 2014), suggesting that personal identity is being viewed here from the Teacher vantage point of words and order-within-complexity.

Processing occurs within the insula that distinguishes subjective identity from pure physical experience: "Different portions of the insula are involved in different and successive steps of neural processing building the basis of the sequential integration of the primary homeostatic condition of the body with salient features of the sensory environment and with motivational, hedonic, and social conditions. Raw interoceptive signals such as those coming from visceral changes and pain, first project to the posterior insula and become progressively integrated with contextual motivational and hedonic information as they progress toward the anterior insula. The neural constructs of the distinct, individually mapped feelings in the posterior insular cortex are then re-represented in the mid-insula that integrates the homeostatic re-representations with activity associated with emotionally salient environmental stimuli of many sensory modalities from different parts of the brain. The culmination point of this progression is a complex and rich representation of the 'global emotional moment' in the anterior insula that represents the ultimate representation of all one's feelings, thereby constituting the 'sentient self,' in the immediate present" (Herbert & Pollatos, 2012).

> The right insula is the source of embodiment.

Neurological research about the insula brings to the fore the question of identity and embodiment. Zaki (2012) says that "the apparent convergence of interoceptive and emotional processes in the AI [anterior insula] has motivated neuroscientists to argue that perceptions of internal bodily states – as supported by this region – are central to emotional experience." In other words, personal identity depends upon physical sensation. Herbert (2012) adds that "This is in accordance with the 'somatic marker' hypothesis of Damasio stating that this meta-representation of bodily states constitutes an emotional feeling, accessible to consciousness and providing the 'gut-feeling' that guides our decision processes and forms the basis for our 'self' and consciousness. The neuroanatomic basis of interoception represents the link for the 'body in the mind' and the mechanisms of the embodiment of affective and cognitive functions", and Herbert refers to *Descartes' Error*, the book written by Damasio. I mentioned at the beginning of this chapter that Damasio is an advocate of scientism, which insists that only physical evidence exists. However, notice that the sense of self created by the insula is limited to the 'immediate present'. The self of orbitofrontal cortex goes far beyond this by including the past, the present, the general, the possible, and the missed. Thus, I suggest that placing insula 'gut feeling' within the context of the internal self within orbitofrontal identity makes it possible for personal identity to transcend the here-and-now. In addition, if the *left* anterior insula is part of a network 'including language, memory and socio-emotional networks', then even the insula can generate a form of identity that goes beyond mere embodiment and gut feeling.

It is interesting that Damasio's concept of the 'somatic marker' is explicitly rejected by Rolls, another famous neurologist whom we have quoted several times. Rolls, in contrast, defines emotions as the goals for Contributor thought: "It is by virtue of being a goal for action that instrumental reinforcers produce emotions... This highlights how different Rolls' theory of emotion is to that of Damasio who argues that emotions are related to autonomic feedback, and his theory is not based on the concept of emotions as being states elicited by instrumental reinforcers. Evidence that autonomic effects are not required for emotions includes findings that patients with peripheral autonomic failure do not suffer from disrupted emotions." Rolls' Contributor oriented "computational view on the role of the VMPFC in decision-making is fundamentally different from the proposal made by Damasio and colleagues, in which the VMPFC is involved in generating somatic markers (changes in the autonomic, endocrine and skeletomotor responses)" (Grabenhorst & Rolls, 2011). While Rolls challenges Damasio's strict scientism, Rolls still defines emotion as a component of concrete technical thought with its goal-oriented action. However, we have seen that the orbitofrontal and medial frontal generate self-image, conscience, and social interaction in *addition* to providing the goals for action. Thus, I suggest that Rolls' definition of emotion is also incomplete because it focuses upon one aspect of orbitofrontal functioning. Using the language of mental symmetry, personal identity is more than just an aspect of Contributor-controlled technical thought. Instead, both technical thought and the mental networks of personal identity function within the grid of normal thought.

Inferior Frontal Cortex

This region is also called the *ventrolateral prefrontal*. Modern neurology began when Paul Broca discovered in 1861 that damage to Broca's area (left inferior frontal cortex) destroys the ability to speak. This was the first area of the brain to be associated with a specific function—that of language.

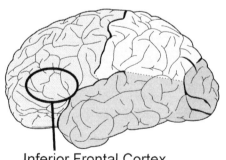

Inferior Frontal Cortex

We began our examination of the frontal lobes by pointing out the relationship between the parietal lobes and the dorsolateral frontal cortex, with Server thought combining left parietal and left dorsolateral frontal and Perceiver thought combining right parietal and right dorsolateral frontal. Language involves a similar cooperation between left inferior frontal and left temporal lobe.

Friederici (2012) summarizes this left hemisphere relationship as follows: "The language circuit modeled here must be conceptualized as a dynamic temporo-frontal network with initial input-driven information processed bottom-up from the auditory cortex to the frontal cortex along the ventral pathway, with semantic information reaching the anterior IFG [inferior frontal gyrus], and syntactic information reaching the posterior IFG. The anterior IFG is assumed to mediate top-down controlled lexical-semantic access to the MTG [medial temporal gyrus] and semantic predictions to the posterior temporal cortex via the ventral pathway. The posterior IFG is assumed to support hierarchization of phrases and arguments and to possibly mediate verb–argument related predictions via the dorsal pathway to the posterior temporal cortex where integration of syntactic and semantic information takes place." (The dorsal and ventral pathways mentioned here both connect temporal with inferior frontal.) Summarizing, the temporal lobe handles specific verbal content (bottom-up) while the inferior frontal predicts what will be said based upon general language structure (top-down). This region handles both words (semantics) as well as structures of order-within-complexity composed of words (syntax). While this region of the brain has been studied for over 150 years, Friederici says that there is still controversy over many of the details. However, it is clear that the left inferior frontal and the left temporal handle the content of Teacher thought.

In general, I suggest that left inferior frontal cortex is associated with the structure of *Teacher* thought while right inferior frontal cortex is connected with the structure of *Mercy* thought. Mental networks appear to be located within orbitofrontal cortex, while inferior frontal cortex appears to handle the content of Teacher and Mercy thought that is not directly related to mental networks.

> Left inferior frontal cortex contains the structure of Teacher thought.
> Right inferior frontal cortex contains the structure of Mercy thought.

I have suggested that Teacher thought uses words as the building blocks for general theories. (Nieuwland, 2011) posits that the left inferior frontal contains both the structure of speech and the structure of general knowledge: "The left inferior frontal cortex (with additional support from other areas) has top-down control over the combinatorial semantic processes that compose multi-word utterances from word-elicited information as represented by the left middle temporal cortex. Moreover, knowledge from different sources and modalities (e.g., speaker identity, real-world knowledge, discourse context) is immediately brought to bear on utterance interpretation, by the same brain system that combines the meanings of individual words into a larger whole." Badre (2007) agrees that "Controlled retrieval of conceptual knowledge depends on a distinct left VLPFC [ventrolateral prefrontal cortex] mechanism that directly influences activation in conceptual stores, such as lateral temporal cortex, and thus should functionally couple with activity in temporal cortex." Badre suggests that "at least two control mechanisms – controlled retrieval and post-retrieval selection – can operate on semantic representations." In other words, inferior frontal memory access first retrieves several related items and then chooses to focus upon one of these items. I suggested when analyzing Einstein's description of scientific thought that the Teacher person forms a general theory by 'picking a citizen out of the crowd and crowning him king.' This matches Badre's description of inferior frontal thought. Teacher memory access first retrieves a 'crowd of citizens' and then chooses to focus upon one of these citizens.

Moving on to another aspect of Teacher thought, Morin (2012) says that "There is little doubt that the LIFG [left inferior frontal gyrus] is implicated in inner speech production. Numerous studies show LIFG activation when participants are asked to silently read single words or sentences, or when undertaking working memory tasks involving covert repetition of verbal material." If Teacher thought is based in words, then inner speech activates Teacher thought. Morin connects inner speech with personal identity, finding that "Participants mostly reported talking to themselves about themselves. In decreasing order, the most frequently mentioned units were self-evaluation, emotions, physical appearance, relationships, problems, food, behavior, financial situation, stress, performance, future, education, beliefs, others' opinion of self, and hypothetical situations. The least frequently reported inner speech units were dream contents, sexuality, personality traits, and death" (Morin & Uttl, 2013). This implies that Teacher thought in the average person is the servant of personal identity in Mercy thought.

> Left inferior frontal gyrus generates speech and organizes knowledge.

It is interesting to relate Morin's observations with the concept of prayer. Cognitively speaking, silent prayer is a way of accessing Teacher thought by using inner speech. I have often heard preachers complain that prayers to God have a natural tendency to revolve around me and my personal needs. If most prayer is a reflection of personal need in Mercy thought, then this also implies that Teacher thought in the average person is being driven by personal Mercy feelings rather than by Teacher understanding or Teacher structure.

Turning now to the right hemisphere, in the same way that the Teacher person forms a general theory through concentration, the Mercy person tends to fixate upon certain experiences. Consistent with this, "the right IFG [inferior frontal gyrus] responds selectively to those items that are of the most relevance to the currently intended task schema." This region "rapidly tunes to selectively respond to current targets, and becomes less responsive to those same objects when the task demands change in several different task contexts... this ability appears to be generalized across different stimulus categories" (Hampshire, et al., 2010). Similarly, Egner (2011) suggests that "the right vlPFC is the primary source of online conflict control in the Stroop-type protocols employed in our experiments, and that the right dlPFC [dorsolateral prefrontal] is recruited additionally in case of performance difficulty, and thus particularly in subjects who are struggling to adapt to conflict." (A 'Stroop-type protocol' is when the picture does not match the verbal label, such as writing the word 'green' in red ink and telling a person to state the color of the ink.) Again we see the ability of Mercy thought to fixate upon something while ignoring distractors. For instance, over the years my Mercy mother has fixated upon various projects, such as writing a book of poetry or making musical recordings, and our family has learned that it is very difficult to divert mother from a quest. In contrast, I have learned from personal experience that Perceiver thought (right dorsolateral prefrontal) often tries to focus but finds it a struggle.

There is considerable debate over the precise function of the right inferior frontal. One view is that this region plays a prominent role in stopping behavior. Another view suggest that it does more: "At present, two prominent theories feature right VLPFC as a key functional region. From one perspective, right VLPFC is thought to play a critical role in motor inhibition, where control is engaged to stop or override motor responses... Alternatively, Corbetta and Shulman have advanced the hypothesis that there are two distinct fronto-parietal networks involved in spatial attention, with right VLPFC being a component of a right-lateralized ventral attention network that governs reflexive reorienting" (Levy & Wagner, 2011). Looking at this cognitively, what is happening when I see a stop sign and 'inhibit my motor response'? Something within my mind recognized the stop sign in the middle of the visual clutter, realized it was emotionally significant, and fixated upon it. Such recognition, emotional tagging, and behavioral fixation is characteristic of Mercy thought. As Levy explains, "recent data suggest that stopping tasks often confound motor inhibition with the need to orient to behaviorally relevant cues and that this orienting response may be what drives right VLPFC engagement when stopping is required." Hampshire (2010) agrees that "It seems plausible that a large component in this type of task is the detection of the stop signal, a task demand very similar to the detection of a learned target stimulus." It is interesting to note that Mercy thought is often viewed by people as something that steps in the way, waves its hands, and says STOP! For instance, "Don't sell that silver tray. It is a precious heirloom from aunt Helen." Or, "Don't touch that object. It is a holy, religious icon."

> Right inferior frontal gyrus recognizes and responds to behaviorally significant items.

Finally, inferior frontal cortex handles prosody—the nonverbal aspect of speech—as well as the general structure of speech. *Linguistic* prosody uses tone of voice to **emphasize** certain words, while *affective* prosody uses tone of voice to convey an emotional message, such as anger or frustration. The precise lateralization of prosody is uncertain. Witteman (2011) found that "right hemispheric damage degraded emotional prosodic perception more than left hemispheric damage", suggesting that affective prosody relates more to Mercy thought, while Belyk & Brown (2014) found that "a major point of divergence was observed in the inferior frontal gyrus: affective prosody was more likely to activate Brodmann area 47, while linguistic prosody was more likely to activate the ventral part of area 44" and they suggested that this may "reflect the different classes of information that listeners extract from affective vs linguistic cues in speech prosody." Area 47 is part of the orbitofrontal cortex, which focuses directly upon emotions and mental networks, while area 44 is part of the inferior frontal, which focuses upon the structure of Mercy and Teacher thought. Evidence from personality indicates that the Mercy person is very sensitive to the way that something is said, as well as tone of voice.

Consistent with this second observation, Hyde (2011) found in a study of seven tone-deaf individuals that "the right inferior frontal gyrus showed an abnormal deactivation in the amusic group, as well as reduced connectivity with the auditory cortex as compared with controls."

Summarizing, the traits of the left inferior frontal cortex support the suggestion that a single cognitive module—Teacher thought—works with words, generates speech, and forms general theories by focusing upon specific verbal elements. Similarly, the right inferior frontal cortex carries out functions that are consistent with the content of Mercy thought, interpreting tone, focusing upon specific experiences that are emotionally significant, and using this focus to guide the rest of the mind.

That brings us to the end of our discussion of the frontal lobes. Let us summarize what we have found. Server thought is associated with left dorsolateral and Perceiver thought with right dorsolateral frontal cortex. Frontopolar cortex handles analogies and nested plans, with the left focusing upon the Server aspect and the right upon the Perceiver. Orbitofrontal cortex contains the emotional core of Teacher and Mercy mental networks, with Teacher on the left and Mercy on the right. Medial frontal cortex places mental networks within a framework of Perceiver facts and Server sequences, the anterior cingulate calculates emotional value for Contributor thought, while the inferior frontal cortex contains the content of Teacher and Mercy thought, with Teacher on the left and Mercy on the right. There is extensive neurological evidence for this mapping, but still some uncertainty regarding the distinction between left and right hemispheres.

Limbic System

We have seen that Perceiver and Server thought are associated with the top of the cortex, combining parietal lobes with a core region in the dorsolateral frontal cortex. This functioning unit is known as executive function in neurological literature. Similarly, I suggest that Teacher and Mercy thought are associated with the bottom of the cortex, combining a core region in the orbitofrontal cortex with the temporal lobes. We have already examined the orbitofrontal cortex. We will be looking shortly at the temporal lobes. This dichotomy between top and bottom is referred to informally in the neurological literature as a *dorsal* path that deals with 'where' and a *ventral* path that deals with 'what'. Borst (2011) did a meta-analysis of 100 studies and suggests that this distinction is even more basic than the separation between left and right hemispheres: "We argue here that a top–bottom divide, rather than a left–right divide, is a more fruitful way to organize human cortical brain functions. However, current characterizations of the functions of the dorsal (top) and ventral (bottom) systems have rested on dichotomies, namely where versus what and how versus what. We propose that characterizing information-processing systems leads to a better macrolevel organization of cortical function; specifically, we hypothesize that the dorsal system is driven by expectations and processes sequences, relations, and movement, whereas the ventral system categorizes stimuli in parallel, focuses on individual events, and processes object properties (such as shape in vision and pitch in audition)." Using the language of mental symmetry, Perceiver thought builds connections that bridge time and space, leading to expectations and relations, while Server thought handles sequences and generates movement. In contrast, Mercy thought focuses upon individual events and the properties of specific experiences and objects. (Borst does not mention the language circuit, indicative of Teacher thought, which is also part of the ventral system.)

> The limbic system combines Mercy and Teacher thought.
> The hippocampus is not part of the emotional limbic system.

'The limbic system' is a vague term originally coined by Thomas Willis in 1664 to indicate cortical regions located around the brainstem (limbus means 'border'). 'Limbic' is currently used as an adjective to refer to the parts of the brain that function emotionally. Used in this sense, the limbic system is the counterpart to executive function, with executive function emphasizing Perceiver and Server thought and the limbic system Teacher and Mercy thought. However, the limbic system also includes areas of the brain, such as the hippocampus, which clearly do not function emotionally. Rolls (2015) concludes in a recent paper that "The concept of a (single) limbic system is shown to be outmoded" because "There is a double dissociation of functions, with the orbitofrontal/amygdala/ACC [anterior cingulate cortex] limbic system being involved in emotion but not episodic memory, and the hippocampal system being involved in memory but not in emotion." Relating this to the dorsal and ventral paths, the "dominance of the ventral ('what') visual system as providing the inputs for emotion and value decoding is strongly to be contrasted with the episodic memory system, in which where, and when, events happened is important, with input therefore required from the parietal spatial/dorsal visual systems. The orbitofrontal cortex is in a sense one end of the 'what' processing systems, and does not know about space or actions." Catani (2013) reached similar conclusions regarding the limbic system. The core region of the ventral 'what' system is sometimes referred to as the Yakovlev circuit. As Catani points out, "Paul Yakovlev proposed [in 1948] that the orbitofrontal cortex, insula, amygdala, and anterior temporal lobe form a network underlying emotion and motivation."

Temporal Lobes

Let us turn our attention now to the temporal lobes and their relationship to Teacher and Mercy thought, starting with the anterior temporal lobes, part of the Yakovlev circuit. Olson (2013) proposes "that portions of the anterior temporal lobe (ATL) play a critical role in representing and retrieving social knowledge. This includes memory about people, their names and biographies and more abstract forms of social memory such as memory for traits and social concepts." Teacher thought handles words and Mercy thought deals with personal experiences. This information, stored within the anterior temporal lobes, provides the raw material for the mental networks that represent people and social situations. Olson adds that "Memory for who people are, and their social and emotional significance is essential for delineating the social environment and for forming and maintaining group cohesion. It is the glue that binds people together in a social group. A large number of findings converge to show that a region of the ventral ATL plays a critical role in person memory." More specifically, "There is a remarkable convergence of findings from PET, fMRI, single-unit recordings in monkeys and humans, and lesion studies all linking the ventral ATL to visual-person-memory functions. Its specific function is in coding facial identity by linking specific faces to semantic, episodic and emotional knowledge." This finding is particularly interesting in light of the Muslim *niqab*, which covers all of the female face except for the eyes. If part of the brain region that stores memories about people specifically interprets faces, then this strongly suggests that covering up the face is dehumanizing at a hardware neurological level.

Evidence suggests that the left anterior temporal lobe is related to Teacher thought and the right to Mercy thought: "Left-lateralized ATL damage commonly impairs the ability to retrieve proper names of familiar (e.g. one's sister) and famous faces and can impair the ability to learn new face-name associations. Right-lateralized damage usually impairs recognition of famous or personally familiar faces, loss of feelings of familiarity or a failure to recollect person-specific semantic information... Thus, the left ATL appears to be more engaged when people's names must be retrieved, whereas the right ATL mediates between faces and biographical knowledge" (Olson, et al., 2013).

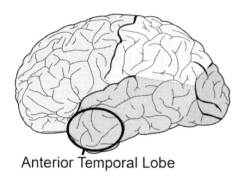

Anterior Temporal Lobe

Normally, interpersonal interaction is face-to-face, but the Internet emphasizes Teacher-based verbal interaction. Consistent with this, Olson says that "the amount of gray matter in the left entorhinal cortex/inferior-medial ATL correlated with the number of Facebook friends. Another group found that gray matter in a more superior portion of the ATL, the left anterior superior ATL, correlated with social network size and theory of mind abilities."

> The left temporal lobe detects and stores Teacher information.
> The right temporal lobe detects and stores Mercy information.

Moving back from the anterior temporal lobe, the *superior temporal sulcus* lies in the middle of the temporal lobes. Lahnakoski (2012) found that "the posterior superior temporal sulcus (STS) responded to all social features but not to any non-social features, and the anterior STS responded to all social features except bodies and biological motion." Gao (2012) attempted to distinguish between animacy (movement that is alive but has no specific goal, like a swarm of flying insects) and intention (goal directed action) and found that "the right pSTS is selectively engaged by the perceptual analysis of shifting intentions, beyond animacy." Similarly, Han (2013) found that "the middle portion of the right superior temporal gyrus/sulcus is more important for processing motion produced by human agents (human motion and functional tool motion) relative to animal motion." In other words, a center in the posterior region of Mercy thought specifically detects agents, providing a neurological backing for the cognitive science of religion. But this is only part of the story, because the left STS has a *different* function. (The temporal lobe agency detector provides information for mental networks which reside within orbitofrontal cortex.)

Gao also explains why science naturally abhors the concept of agents and teleology: "Cues for detecting animacy include the apparent violation of Newtonian laws, self-propulsion, and abrupt changes in motion direction and speed. These cues share a common property, in that physical forces in the environment cannot fully explain an object's motion. Its motion must therefore be attributed to forces that are internal to the object, yielding the perception of animacy" (Gao, et al., 2012). In simple terms, agents violate natural law, and Teacher thought hates exceptions to the rule. Thus, science rejects the idea of an intelligent, supernatural agent intervening in deus-ex-machina fashion to perform miraculous actions. However, as the cognitive science of religion points out, trying to expunge the idea of agents from intelligent thought is rather futile, because there is a brain region that specifically detects agents. In addition, the scientist himself is an intelligent agent who is continually intervening in the physical environment in a manner that disrupts the flow of natural law. I suggest that the solution is to realize that physical bodies and brains function within natural law while intelligent minds—including the mind of God and supernatural beings—are subject to the universal law of 'how the mind works'. Animacy and teleology may violate natural *physical* law, but they are guided by natural *mental* law.

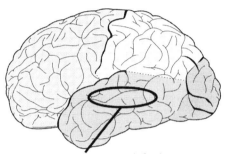

Superior Temporal Sulcus

The *left* superior temporal sulcus is related to speech and Teacher thought: "Converging evidence suggests that the left superior temporal sulcus (STS) is a critical site for multisensory integration of auditory and visual information during speech perception" (Baum, et al., 2012). More specifically, "the left pSTS [posterior STS] plays a role in short-term representation of relevant sound features that provide the basis for identifying newly acquired sound categories. The neural representations in left pSTS consist of low-level abstractions of the sensory input information. In contrast, categorization of familiar phonemic patterns is mediated by long-term, highly abstract, and categorical representations in left mSTS [medial STS]" (Liebenthal, et al., 2010). Concluding, the left STS is related to Teacher thought and the right STS to Mercy thought.

Amygdala

The amygdala is an almond-shaped ('amygdala' means almond) group of nuclei buried within the front of the temporal lobes. The two amygdalae are part of the limbic system and it is widely agreed that the amygdala is an emotional processor. My hypothesis is that they perform the emotional processing for Mercy and Teacher thought. Traditionally, the amygdala has been connected with *negative* emotion. As Fernando (2013) explains, "the amygdala itself has long been associated with emotional processing, particularly the emotion of fear." However, recent research shows that the amygdala interprets *both* emotional pain and pleasure: "Some primate amygdala neurons modulate their responses to rewards and aversive stimuli, acting as value coding neurons guiding either appetitively or aversively motivated behavior. In other cells, however, effects of expectation on responses were similar for both rewards and punishment, suggesting that some neurons are involved in more arousal-specific responses, reflecting the intensity of activation in the motivational systems rather than the specific valence of a reinforcer." This emotional processing is influenced by mental networks within the orbitofrontal cortex. Quoting further from Fernando (2013), "The orbitofrontal cortex (OFC) modulates amygdala activity in terms of current motivational states and goal assessment via its extensive reciprocal connectivity with the BLA [basolateral amygdala]."

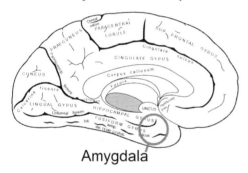

Amygdala

Similarly, Lyons & Beilock (2011) found that "There was no evidence that the amygdala was differentially or disproportionately related to memory for negative items. These results are consistent with recent studies that have demonstrated that the amygdala can respond to positive stimuli as well as negative stimuli." The Mercy person tends to *fixate* upon specific aspects of situations while ignoring the context. Consistent with this, Lyons & Beilock conclude that "amygdala activity does not lead to enhanced memory for all contextual details of an encoding episode. It may be that the amygdala primarily enhances memory for details directly linked to an emotional item and plays less of a role in modulating memory for contextual elements that are tangential to the item."

> The amygdala generates both positive and negative emotions.
> The left amygdala generates Teacher emotions.
> The right amygdala generates Mercy emotions

Amygdala overactivity is associated with *anxiety*: "Even in children as young as ages 7 to 9, high childhood anxiety is associated with enlarged amygdala volume and this enlargement is localized specifically to the basolateral amygdala" (Qin & Northoff, 2011). Similarly, Kim (2011) reports that "a number of functional neuroimaging studies in humans have shown elevated amygdala activity in highly anxious but otherwise healthy individuals." Going further, "efficient crosstalk between the amygdala and the mPFC, perhaps particularly the vmPFC, is critically involved in lowering anxiety levels," indicating that self-image can regulate emotional anxiety. In addition, as we saw before when looking at the dorsolateral prefrontal cortex, "There have been numerous studies implicating amygdalar hyperactivity in PTSD [post-traumatic stress disorder] using a variety of trauma-related stimuli, including imagery" (Bruce, et al., 2013).

The amygdala is also involved in social interaction, another aspect of both Mercy and Teacher thought: "People who fostered and maintained larger and more complex social networks not only had larger amygdala volumes, but also had stronger intrinsic connectivity between the amygdala and regions of the brain implicated in perceptual and affiliative, but not avoidant, aspects of social cognition" (Bickart, et al., 2012). In contrast, a study of young men with a history of criminal violence found that "Lower amygdala volume was significantly associated with measures of aggression and psychopathic features collected in childhood and adolescence. Lower left amygdala volume was associated with higher teacher-reported aggressive behaviors and interpersonal callousness across childhood. Lower right amygdala volume was associated with higher proactive aggression and overall psychopathic features in adolescence" (Pardini, et al., 2014).

Thus, one can state with reasonable certainty that the amygdalae function as emotional processors for Teacher and Mercy thought. The evidence regarding lateralization is still uncertain. As Dyck (2011) summarizes, "The amygdala plays a key role in emotional processing... There is a long-standing debate on hemispheric lateralization of emotional processes, yet few studies to date directly investigated differential activation patterns for the left and right amygdala. Limited evidence supports right amygdala involvement in automatic processes of emotion and left amygdala involvement in conscious and cognitively controlled emotion processing." This is consistent with the idea that the mind learns naturally about Mercy emotion through physical experiences of pain and pleasure while discovering about Teacher emotion by consciously constructing order-within-complexity.

There is some evidence connecting Mercy thought with the right amygdala. Mormann (2012) discovered "that the right amygdala is specialized for processing visual information about animals. The selectivity appears to be truly categorical and argues in favor of a domain-specific mechanism for processing this biologically important class of stimuli." This evidence comes from probes inserted into the human amygdala in epilepsy patients. We see here the connection between living organisms and Mercy thought. This right amygdala bias would not occur with humans because people can talk, and speech generates Teacher emotion.

Another interesting clue regarding lateralization occurs in math anxiety. As Young (2012) explains, "Math anxiety is a negative emotional response that is characterized by avoidance as well as feelings of stress and anxiety in situations involving mathematical reasoning." Young's study of 7- to 9-year-old children revealed that "math anxiety was associated with hyperactivity in right amygdala regions that are important for processing negative emotions. In addition, we found that math anxiety was associated with reduced activity in posterior parietal and dorsolateral prefrontal cortex regions involved in mathematical reasoning." In other words, Mercy emotions are overwhelming the Perceiver and Server basis for technical thought. In addition, "effective connectivity between the amygdala and ventromedial prefrontal cortex regions that regulate negative emotions was elevated in children with math anxiety." Thus, self-image is exacerbating feelings of anxiety; the child is probably thinking, "I am not a math person." Math anxiety is gender related. Maloney (2012) states that "Decades of research have demonstrated that women experience higher rates of math anxiety – that is, negative affect when performing tasks involving numerical and mathematical skill – than men" and suggests that "women may be more math anxious than men on average because women are worse at spatial processing than men on average."

Ally & Donahue (2013) examined "an extremely rare individual with near-perfect autobiographical memory" and discovered two main differences in his brain. "First, HK's right amygdala is significantly larger in volume compared to control subjects. Second, the functional connectivity between the amygdala and hippocampus, as well as distal cortical and subcortical regions in HK, is significantly increased compared to controls." Ally mentions other connections between autobiographical memory (AM) and the right amygdala: "Right amygdala-hippocampal connectivity to medial prefrontal regions has been shown to support memory encoding of high self-relevance or self-involvement." And "the increase in right amygdala activity during first person retrieval perspective reflects the higher degree of subjective emotionality."

There is also some evidence connecting the left amygdala with verbal emotion. A meta-analysis by Bohrn (2012) found that "an area around the left amygdala emerged for figurative language processing across studies." Herbert (2009) found that "during silent reading of adjectives varying in emotional content, pleasant words in particular take advantage of a primarily left amygdala-mediated enhanced perceptual processing." Finally, Hsu (2015) "presented participants in an MR scanner with passages selected from the Harry Potter book series, half of which described magical events, while the other half served as control conditions... We found stronger neural activation for the supra-natural than the control condition in bilateral inferior frontal gyri, bilateral inferior parietal lobules, left fusiform gyrus, and left amygdala. The increased activation in the amygdala (part of the salience and emotion processing network) appears to be associated with feelings of surprise and the reading pleasure, which supra-natural events, full of novelty and unexpectedness, brought about." Here, the left amygdala is being activated by the novel order-within-complexity of the world of magic.

Hippocampus

The two hippocampi lie behind the amygdalae within the medial temporal lobe. I suggest that the left hippocampus is a processor for Server thought, while the right hippocampus is a processor for Perceiver thought. The *entorhinal cortex* is adjacent to the hippocampus and provides the primary input to the hippocampus. We will begin our look at the hippocampus by comparing Buzsáki & Moser's (2013) description of hippocampal functioning with characteristics of Server and Perceiver thought. They begin by explaining that "Navigation is based on two interlinked mechanisms for representation of the spatial environment, one that provides static position information in a reference frame and another that calculates coordinates based on integration of motion and knowledge of previous positions. The first is often referred to as map-based or allocentric navigation, in which the spatial relationships among landmarks assist in defining the animal's location in the environment. The spatial metric needed for the estimation of distances between landmarks is believed to arise from a second mechanism, often referred to as path integration or egocentric navigation. Path integration requires active movement of the body and computes the distances and turns of the animal as it explores the environment... Map-based and path integration-based representation always work together, but the availability of external landmarks may determine whether allocentric or egocentric strategies dominate." Summarizing, navigation *combines* the maps of Perceiver thought with the actions of Server thought.

> The left hippocampus is a processor for Server thought.
> It remembers both actions and sequences.
> The right hippocampus is a processor for Perceiver thought.
> It remembers both maps and facts.

Most of Buzsáki & Moser's data is based in how the hippocampus functions in the *rat's* brain. Iglói (2009) examined maze navigation in *people* and noted that "two main cognitive strategies can be used to solve a complex navigation task: the allocentric or map-

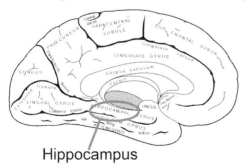

Hippocampus

based strategy and the sequential egocentric or route-based strategy... Regardless of the strategy used spontaneously during the training, all participants could execute immediate shifts to the opposite non previously used strategy." Thus, Perceiver and Server thought cooperate in navigation and a person can switch between either a Perceiver-led allocentric or a Server-led egocentric strategy. However, Iglói also found that 42% of his subjects used a purely egocentric strategy while 14% used only an allocentric strategy, indicative of cognitive style.

Buzsáki & Moser's description of hippocampal map-based functioning corresponds in detail to Perceiver thought. Perceiver thought builds mental maps *and* works with facts. Similarly, Buzsáki & Moser (2013) claim that "the neuronal mechanisms that evolved to define the spatial relationship among landmarks can also serve to embody associations among objects, events and other types of factual information." They explain that "An animal's spatial coordinates are encoded by a range of interacting cell types with defined activity profiles. The two most striking firing patterns are perhaps those of the 'place cells', discovered in the hippocampus, and the 'grid cells', discovered in the medial entorhinal cortex. Grid cells have multiple firing fields that span the entire available space in a periodic hexagonal pattern, which provides a metric to the neural representation of space." Similarly, we have seen that Perceiver thought *places* facts within a *grid* of knowledge. Perceiver thought organizes facts into different mental contexts. Similarly, there are "numerous independent maps in the hippocampus." Perceiver thinking assumes an underlying metric of universal truth that applies everywhere. Likewise, "the entorhinal cortex generates a metric that can be applied universally across environments." Perceiver thought treats facts as if they are objects placed within a mental map. Similarly, "The same mechanisms that define unique positions and their relationships in a map can be used to define or symbolize events, objects and living things. Many experiments demonstrate that recognition and recall of objects or events are associated with unique constellations of firing patterns in the entorhinal cortex–hippocampal system in a variety of species." Perceiver thought treats words and abstract ideas in a similar spatial manner, viewing certain ideas as being 'closer' than other ideas: "Similarly to the embodiment of the spatial relations among objects in the cognitive map, models of semantic relatedness use a metric based on topological similarity and a neuronal network equivalent of vector distance for defining relationships among words." Perceiver thought gradually gains confidence in information when it notices connections being repeated. Likewise, "explicit, semantic knowledge is acquired progressively as similar episodes are encoded repeatedly by the self-referenced episodic memory system, so that knowledge eventually becomes context independent. This gradual process is reminiscent of the formation of allocentric maps based on repeated exploration of the environment." Perceiver thought functions associatively, with incoming information triggering a chain of associations. Likewise, "snippets of cues can trigger a long process of recollection, which is often grouped or chunked into shorter sub-episodes."

The *rat* hippocampus probably handles only physical maps and physical movement. Humphries & Prescott (2009) explain that "as locomotion is its primary model of exploration, changes in location are the consistent element of hippocampal memory representations in rodents. The learning of routes is then just the correct resequencing of events to achieve the desired target location." However, "There is little doubt that the hippocampus is more generally a memory space than a spatial map."

There is also a strong correspondence between Buzsáki & Moser's description of hippocampal sequence-based functioning in *concrete* thought and the behavior of the typical

Server person, who also lives primarily in concrete thought. Server thought performs personal actions *and* works with mental sequences. Similarly, Buzsáki & Moser "hypothesize that the mechanisms for representing a path through an environment are similar to those used to represent sequences in memory." The hippocampus contains *time* cells as well as place cells: "Single hippocampal neurons – called time cells – encode moments in temporally structured experiences much as the well-known place cells encode locations in spatially structured experiences" (Eichenbaum, 2013). The hippocampus remembers sequences of events and learning a Server sequence is based upon repetition: "In humans, neurons throughout the hippocampal region replay firing sequences during recall of scenes in film clips. Furthermore, selectively within the hippocampus, neuronal ensembles develop reliable firing sequences as human subjects gradually learn a sequence of scenes in a film." Returning now to Buzsáki & Moser (2013), Server thought organizes actions into plans or recipes that are triggered by the environment. Similarly, "Neuronal representation of travel paths does not consist of long uninterrupted neuronal chains but are often broken up into repeating chunks by prominent landmarks, state changes or reinforcers." The Server person does not naturally think about the future but rather focuses upon the sequence of action that is currently being performed. Likewise, "upcoming locations that are more proximal to the animal are given stronger representation within a given theta cycle, with poorer resolution of locations in the distant future" and "temporally closer events are recalled with more sensory and contextual details than temporally distant events." The Server person naturally acts in a manner that flows smoothly. Similarly, "recollection of an item is facilitated by the presentation or spontaneous recall of another item that occurred close in time to the item just recalled." The Server person enjoys conversing with others about the events of the day. Likewise, "It has been hypothesized that such self-organized cell assembly sequences or neural 'trajectories' underlie the numerous episodes recorded in one's lifetime."

> The posterior hippocampus handles details and is unaffected by emotions.
> The anterior hippocampus handles generalities and interacts with emotions.

We saw previously that the hippocampus has traditionally been regarded as part of the emotional limbic system and that current research has rejected this as inadequate. Consistent with this, what we have discussed so far about the hippocampus is related to facts and sequences and not emotions. However, the anterior (front) hippocampus differs from the posterior (back) hippocampus in two major ways. First, "the pHPC [posterior hippocampus] is activated by retrieving exact local positions of landmarks, whereas the aHPC [anterior hippocampus] is activated by retrieving approximate or relative positions within a global framework; and thinking of local spatial details from past life events, such as wedding seating arrangements, evokes more pHPC activation than thinking of the general location of those events, which evokes aHPC activation." Saying this another way, there are "coarse, global representations in anterior hippocampus and fine-grained, local representations in posterior hippocampus" (Poppenk, et al., 2013). Second, Fanselow & Dong (2009) suggest that "the dorsal or septal pole of the [rat] hippocampus, which corresponds to the human posterior hippocampus, is specifically involved in memory function and the ventral or temporal pole of the [rat] hippocampus, which corresponds to the anterior hippocampus in humans, modulates emotional and affective processes." That is because "Direct reciprocal links between the aHPC and the amygdala, insula, and vmPFC, as well as projections to the nucleus accumbens [related to Exhorter thought], offer the aHPC a privileged interface with motivational processing regions" (Poppenk, et al., 2013). Summarizing, the anterior hippocampus works with generalities and is interconnected with the emotional amygdala, while the posterior hippocampus handles specifics and is not directly affected by emotions.

One can see these two factors interact in the behavior of the typical Server and Perceiver person. As I have already mentioned, the typical Server person lives in the present, focusing upon specific sequences of actions. This type of Server person is also emotionally stable and does not exhibit any emotional highs or lows. However, the Server person becomes emotionally unstable when forced to deal with long-term sequences about which nothing can be done in the present. Thus, it appears that the Server person naturally focuses upon the posterior hippocampus in order to avoid dealing with emotions. A similar trait can be seen in the Perceiver person, who has a tendency to avoid emotions by focusing upon specific facts. This emphasis upon either specific facts or general information is reflected in the size of the hippocampus. Evensmoen (2013) found that "use of a coarse, global representation of the environment during Self-localization and Planning correlated with a larger right hippocampal head [anterior] and smaller right hippocampal tail [posterior]. Hence, involvement of the hippocampal head in a coarse, global environmental representation was not only reflected in the level of activity, but also in its structure... the hippocampal tail was smaller in participants who reported greater use of a coarse, global environmental representation."

I have mentioned that Perceiver thought can either point out specific facts that contradict general theories or come up with general facts that extend Teacher theories. Looking back, it appears that learning to work with facts in the midst of emotional pressure may have also given me the ability to come up with general facts to build Teacher theories. Similarly, our analysis of exemplars suggests that the Server person is capable of high-level thought, and yet the typical Server person behaves more like a human robot. It may be that the Server person can only develop intellectual abilities by gaining the confidence to analyze sequences in the midst of emotions.

Turning now to laterality, there is evidence associating the right hippocampus with spatial Perceiver thought and the left hippocampus with sequential Server thought. Iglói (2010) found "that activation of the right hippocampus predicts the use of an allocentric spatial representation, and activation of the left hippocampus predicts the use of a sequential egocentric representation." When humans navigated a virtual maze, then "the difference between activity in left and right hippocampi in the start alley of the maze predicted the subsequent choice of path between those based on sequence or place memories." Iglói adds that "The left hippocampus has long been implicated in verbal tasks, such as the learning of narrative prose or the learning and retrieval of word lists."

There is also a relationship "between duration of musical practice and grey matter volumes in the anterior part of the left hippocampus, suggesting a specific impact of musical practice on this area. This difference reached 17.8% with a greater grey matter volume for the expert musicians, compared with the nonmusicians" (Groussard, et al., 2014). Two statements can be said about musicians. First, they continually repeat Server sequences of musical notes. Second, they add emotional expression to these Server sequences. This combination is consistent with the left anterior hippocampus.

Basal Ganglia

People often assume that high level rational thought occurs only within the cortex. However, "the concept of basal ganglia function has dramatically changed in the last 30 years, from a purely motor or sensory-motor function to a more complex set of functions that mediate the full range of goal-directed behaviors, including emotions, motivation, and cognition. The change resulted from several lines of inquiry, but at the center was the demonstration that frontal cortical information passing through the basal ganglia returns to all of the frontal cortex, not only to motor cortex" (Haber & Knutson, 2010). In other words, the basal ganglia performs high-level cognition by accessing and processing cortical information from 'next door'.

> Exhorter: dopamine and the ventral basal ganglia.
> Contributor: dorsal basal ganglia (caudate, putamen, globus pallidus, subthalamus).
> Exhorter and Contributor thought manipulate cortical content from a distance.

Basal ganglia research is currently in a state of upheaval. That is the conclusion that I reached after reading about a hundred papers on the basal ganglia, almost all published in the last five years. However, a number of clear findings have emerged and the picture that is forming is consistent with the theory of mental symmetry. My general hypothesis is that the basal ganglia performs Exhorter and Contributor thought, with Exhorter thought being related to dopamine (DA) and the ventral basal ganglia and Contributor thought being related to the dorsal basal ganglia. (Many papers refer to this distinction as ventral striatum versus dorsal striatum.)

I am using the term *ventral basal ganglia* to include the ventral tegmental area (VTA), the ventral striatum (an area that includes the nucleus accumbens but is slightly larger), and ventral pallidum, all areas implicated in reward, motivation, and addiction. In addition, there are three dopamine pathways: The *mesolimbic* pathway transmits dopamine from the VTA to the nucleus accumbens (part of the ventral basal ganglia), the *mesocortical* pathway transmits dopamine from the VTA to the frontal cortex, and the *nigrostriatal* pathway transmits dopamine from the substantia nigra pars compacta to the dorsal striatum (which includes the caudate and putamen). The nigrostriatal pathway is the one which is damaged the most in Parkinson's disease. As Glimcher (2011) summarizes, "Three groups of dopamine secreting neurons send axons along long-distance trajectories that influence brain activity in many areas: the A8 and A10 groups of the ventral tegmental area (VTA) and the A9 group of the substantia nigra pars compacta (Snc)... The A9 cluster connects to the caudate and putamen, and the A8 and A10 axons make contact with the ventral striatum and the fronto-cortical regions beyond."

Dopamine

We will begin by looking at the relationship between dopamine and Exhorter thought. The history of neurological research on dopamine as described by Salamone & Correa (2012) reads like a passage from Thomas Kuhn, with Teacher thought being emotionally driven to come up with a general theory and technical thought eventually being forced by a preponderance of incompatible facts to look for a new paradigm. "Human memory is more efficacious if random facts or events can be woven into the meaningful tapestry of a coherent story. Scientists are no different. An effective university lecture, or a scientific seminar, is often referred to as 'a good story.' So it is with scientific hypotheses and theories. Our brain seems to crave the order and coherence of thought offered by a simple and clear scientific hypothesis, backed up by just enough evidence to make it plausible. The problem is—what if the coherence of the story is being enhanced by overinterpreting some findings, and ignoring others? Gradually, the pieces of the puzzle that do not fit continue to eat away at the whole, eventually rendering the entire story woefully inadequate. One can argue that this kind of evolution has taken place with regards to the DA hypothesis of 'reward'. A 'story' could be constructed, which would proceed as follows: the main symptom of depression is anhedonia, and since DA is a 'reward transmitter' that mediates hedonic reactions, then depression is due to a reduction of DA-regulated experience of pleasure." In simple terms, the original theory was that dopamine equals pleasure. This has been replaced by a new *standard* and *alternative* view of dopamine function, which is now being followed by the realization that dopamine has no single simple function. However, if one examines the various aspects of dopamine function, it appears that they all express core elements of Exhorter thought.

The new *standard* view of dopamine function is summarized by Gepshtein (2014): "The tonic (sustained) release of dopamine establishes background levels of the neurotransmitter. In contrast, the phasic (transient) release of dopamine provides rapid rise and fall of the level of dopamine, which are thought to encode differences between the expected and obtained reward of an action and is associated with synaptic modification and learning."

We will start by describing the function of *tonic* dopamine. Gepshtein suggests that "the motivational role of tonic dopamine is twofold. In the ventral striatam, dopamine determines how vigorously participants perform repeated responses over time. In the dorsal striatum, dopamine determines the speed of single movements according to their different energetic costs." Looking first at the *ventral* striatum, "in the state of high motivational sensitivity (associated with high levels of tonic dopamine in the ventral striatum), participants are willing to perform energetically demanding series of actions to obtain a small amount of reward that would not elicit action if the sensitivity were low" (Gepshtein, et al., 2014). One of the primary traits of the Exhorter person is an excess of *energy*. Exhorter behavior is typically vigorous, expressed through exaggerated word and action. Gepshtein says that there is a connection between the ventral basal ganglia, dopamine, and energy.

Turning now to the dorsal striatum, Gepshtein says that 'dopamine determines the speed of single movements according to their different energetic costs'. Unlike the Exhorter, Contributor behavior tends to be efficient, husbanding energy in order to use it in the most effective manner. This can be seen by examining patients with Parkinson's disease. Gepshtein explains that "motor deficits in PD [Parkinson's disease] patients are associated directly with the degree of dopamine depletion in the dorsal striatum... In PD patients with mild to moderate disease severity, the primary dopamine depletion is in the dorsal striatum... only later in the course of the disease does the degeneration of dopamine pathways affect the ventral striatum." Gepshtein found that "in conditions of low energy cost, the patients performed surprisingly well, in fact similar to prescriptions of an ideal planner and to healthy elderly participants. As energy costs increased, however, the patients' performance dropped markedly below the optimal prescriptions and below the performance of healthy elderly participants." This is "consistent with the notion that at least some aspects of PD manifest as patients' reluctance to make certain movements rather than inability to do so." This tells us that dopamine provides energy for *another* cognitive strategy within the dorsal basal ganglia that plans and executes movement, because Parkinson's patients can still perform in a highly efficient manner, but without dopamine they lack the energy to do so. I have compared the relationship between Exhorter thought and Contributor thought to that of a rider on a horse. The 'rider' is Contributor thought with its detailed plans. However, the Exhorter horse provides the energy that propels the Contributor rider. Without energy from Exhorter thought, Contributor thought go nowhere. One can see this in the behavior of the Contributor person, who can be very lazy when motivation is lacking. In contrast, Exhorter movement tends to be full of energy while lacking in skill.

Motivation is the aspect of dopamine functioning that is emphasized by Berridge's new *alternative* view of dopamine. Mercy and Teacher thought function *emotionally*, whereas drive and motivation play a dominant role in Exhorter thought. The typical Exhorter person is continually pushing, prodding, motivating—and exhorting others, implying that Exhorter thought is a source of drive and motivation. The Exhorter person may even give himself a pep talk when feeling down. Motivation is not the same as emotion. In the words of Berridge, wanting is different than liking. We saw in a previous section that, "pleasure appears most faithfully represented by activity in orbitofrontal cortex, particularly in a mid-anterior subregion. Evidence suggests activity of this mid-anterior zone tracks changes in subjective pleasantness ratings of chocolate and delicious drinks, such as when pleasure intensity is diminished by switching the taster's state from hunger to satiety, and may also encode pleasures of sexual orgasm, drugs, and music" (Berridge & Kringelbach, 2013). Thus, *emotional* labels are stored within the core of Mercy and Teacher thought. In contrast, Berridge explains that "mesolimbic dopamine, probably the most popular brain neurotransmitter candidate for pleasure two decades ago, turns out not to cause pleasure or liking at all. Rather dopamine more selectively mediates a motivational process of incentive salience, which is a mechanism for wanting rewards but not for liking them. When amplified by addictive drugs or by endogenous factors, dopamine helps generate intense levels of wanting, characteristic of drug addiction, eating disorders, and related compulsive pursuits." In addition, "Recent studies have demonstrated existence of an affective keyboard mechanism in the medial shell of Nac [nucleus accumbens] for generating intense dread versus desire... Just as a musical keyboard generates many different notes according to key location, the affective keyboard can generate many mixtures of desire versus fear, each mixture triggered at a different location" (Berridge & Kringelbach, 2013). Notice that this 'keyboard' encodes not emotion but rather desire—both positive and negative.

> Energy and motivation are core aspects of dopamine and Exhorter thought.

Energy and motivation are core aspects of Exhorter thought, and I suggest that the other characteristics of dopamine make the most sense when viewed through the lens of drive and energy. I found the research on dopamine especially difficult to analyze, and it was only after going through several dozen papers that I realized why. Most of the research on dopamine is using technical thought to attempt to analyze something that has nothing to do with technical thought. Descriptions about predictive learning, instrumental appetite behavior and contingent rewards may be technically accurate, but they do not catch the flavor of Exhorter thought. Raw Exhorter thought is Steve Ballmer running around the stage yelling 'developers, developers, developers...' with his armpits dripping sweat. (Look it up on YouTube.) Raw Exhorter thought is Winston Churchill imbibing an endless supply of alcohol (he drank an estimated 42,000 bottles of Pol Roger champagne during his life) (Wallop, 2015) and proclaiming to the British populace that "I have nothing to offer but blood, toil, tears and sweat. We have before us an ordeal of the most grievous kind. We have before us many, many long months of struggle and of suffering. You ask, what is our aim? I can answer in one word: Victory. Victory at all costs—Victory in spite of all terror—Victory, however long and hard the road may be, for without victory there is no survival." (delivered in the House of Commons in Westminster on May 13, 1940). *That* is Exhorter thought, written LARGE in

boldface with many!!! exclamation!!!!!!! marks!!!!! And that kind of Exhorter person would fall asleep after reading one paragraph of the typical scientific paper on dopamine.

With that in mind, let us return to our examination of dopamine. The new *standard* view is that dopamine encodes 'differences between the expected and obtained reward of an action and is associated with synaptic modification and learning'. Bromberg-Martin (2010) explains this in more detail: "DA neurons are excited when a cue indicates an increase in future reward value, inhibited when a cue indicates a decrease in future reward value, and generally have little response to cues that convey no new reward information." This may be technically correct, and I suggest that it describes a primary role that Exhorter thought plays in Contributor-controlled technical thinking. I have often heard my Exhorter brother-in-law complain after cooking some new dish that "It did not turn out as well as I hoped that it would." However, this is not how raw Exhorter thought experiences this trait. The Exhorter person does not just notice an 'increase in future reward value'. Instead, he is sharing with the world his vision of future prosperity. And when he finds himself stuck in a situation that is totally predictable, he will declare in a loud voice that "a rut is a grave with the ends kicked out", or roll his eyes, mumble "booooooringgg", and move on. Many of the papers on dopamine discuss addiction. Raw Exhorter thought is addictive. The Exhorter person often gathers an in-group of followers around him. He shares his vision with them and they are drawn to his energy and excitement. His followers find him not pleasant but addictive, attracted by his vision, excitement, and energy like moths to the flame. When he spills drink on his pants in front of others, then they will rush to the stage with towels to help him to clean up.

Turning to other aspects of dopamine, Bromberg-Martin (2010) says that "DA neuron alerting responses can be triggered by surprising sensory events such as unexpected light flashes and auditory clicks... These alerting responses seem to reflect the degree to which the stimulus is surprising and captures attention; they are reduced if a stimulus occurs at predictable times... they are triggered by any stimulus that merely resembles a motivationally salient cue, even if the resemblance is very slight." The Exhorter person is susceptible to being distracted. If he is giving a motivational speech and someone in the front row is not paying attention, then he may interrupt his speech and tell the disturbing individual to listen—in front of everyone else. Bromberg-Martin states that "Monkeys expressed a strong preference to view informative visual cues that would allow them to predict the size of a future reward, rather than uninformative cues that provided no new information. In parallel, DA neurons were excited by the opportunity to view the informative cues in a manner that was correlated with the animal's behavioral preference." One of the strengths of the Exhorter person is learning lessons from life, by building general Teacher theories upon emotional Mercy experiences. This is *not* a rigorous form of thought. Instead, it could be referred to as 'proof by example'. Bromberg-Martin adds that "DA neurons go beyond simple stimulus reward learning and make predictions based on sophisticated beliefs about the structure of the world. DA neurons can predict rewards correctly even in unconventional environments."

While the theorizing of the typical Exhorter person may use Teacher overgeneralization to construct a massive edifice upon a flimsy factual foundation, it is a quick way of coming up with an initial understanding and is often surprisingly effective.

I am not suggesting that all Exhorter persons yell slogans and spill drinks. Instead, the traits that we have just discussed are most prominent in the Exhorter persons who emphasize conscious Exhorter thought, especially the ones who use their golden tongues to compensate for their lack of mental content. And those Exhorter persons *do* yell slogans and spill drinks—in public and in living color. (It is generally the male Exhorter person who exhibits this over-the-top behavior. In contrast, the natural emotional sensitivity of the female mind usually adds some subtlety to raw Exhorter thought.)

Some say dopamine = desire. Others say dopamine provides error-related feedback.

The new *standard* view says that dopamine cells fire more strongly when the reward is better than expected. As Humphries & Prescott (2009) say, "A currently high-profile theory is that the phasic burst of spikes from dopaminergic neurons is a reward prediction error." Bromberg-Martin says that this is only part of the picture. Instead, "many neurons are sensitive to reward *and* aversive predictions: they respond when rewarding events are more rewarding than predicted and when aversive events are more aversive than predicted." As Bromberg-Martin points out, "It has long been known that stressful and aversive experiences cause large changes in DA concentrations in downstream brain structures, and that behavioral reactions to these experiences are dramatically altered by DA agonists, antagonists, and lesions." In other words, the Exhorter person finds *both* opportunity and disaster exciting and gains energy from crisis. As Bromberg-Martin puts it, "motivational salience-coding DA neurons fit well with theories of dopamine neurons and processing of salient events. These neurons are excited by both rewarding and aversive events and have weaker responses to neutral events, providing an appropriate instructive signal for neural circuitry to learn to detect, predict, and respond to situations of high importance." That describes Exhorter thought, which focuses upon the exciting, ignores the boring, learns from life, and responds in crisis. Bromberg-Martin says that "the Nac [nucleus accumbens] core (but not shell) is crucial for enabling motivation to overcome response costs such as physical effort; for performance of set-shifting tasks requiring cognitive flexibility; and for enabling reward cues to cause an enhancement of general motivation." We see here the core trait of Exhorter thought as a source of energy. When the typical Exhorter person sees that a person's energy is flagging, his typical response is to exhort him to continue with phrases such as "You can make it! Do not give up!!! Hang in there!!"

Bromberg-Martin is also describing another Exhorter trait which is *crisis management*. The Exhorter person shines in times of uncertainty when the next step is unknown, and in periods of transition when a major shift needs to be taken. This mental ability to make transitions is severely impaired in Parkinson's disease, both physically and mentally: "Freezing of gait is a common symptom of Parkinson's disease in which patients experience the feeling that their feet become glued to the floor whilst walking... It is well recognized that a number of specific triggers can either provoke freezing, such as the clinical 'OFF' state [when the dopamine medicine wears off], walking through a narrow doorway and dual-task walking... Freezing behavior in Parkinson's disease is not limited to gait, with a number of studies showing that it also affects other domains, including upper limb movements and speech, suggesting that the mechanism underlying freezing in Parkinson's disease is because of dysfunction across neural regions supporting more general functions" (Shine, et al., 2013).

Exhorter thought is connected with Teacher thought and Mercy thought, and I have suggested that the ventral basal ganglia is associated with Exhorter thought. Haber & Knutson (2010) summarize that "The key structures in this network are the anterior cingulate cortex, the orbital prefrontal cortex, the ventral striatum, the ventral pallidum, and the midbrain dopamine neurons." In other words, the ventral basal ganglia is part of a network that includes primarily dopamine, the orbitofrontal (Teacher and Mercy mental networks) and the anterior cingulate (Contributor value). They describe the cortical input to the ventral striatum (otherwise known as the nucleus accumbens, the region upon which we have been focusing, which receives dopamine from the ventral tegmental area via the mesolimbic pathway): "The best way, therefore, to define the VS [ventral striatum] is by its afferent projections from cortical areas that mediate different aspects of reward and emotional processing, namely the vmPFC, OFC, dACC, and the medial temporal lobe, including the amygdala." Thus, the ventral striatum is defined as the part of the striatum that is connected with various aspects of Teacher and Mercy thought, including mental networks in the orbitofrontal (OFC), self-image and value in medial frontal (vmPFC), Contributor-based value in dACC (anterior cingulate), and the Teacher and Mercy emotional processors (amygdala). In addition, "terminal fields from the vmPFC, OFC, and dACC show a complex interweaving and convergence" in the VS that "could produce a unique combinatorial activation at the specific sites for channeling reward-based incentive drive in selecting between different valued options", which means that the cortical input to the ventral striatum is arranged in a way that makes it possible to process and combine the various aspects of emotion and value.

Dorsal Striatum

Deciphering the role of dopamine is confusing because there are two different viewpoints backed up by two *different* groups of researchers. Comprehending the dorsal striatum is even worse because here the two different viewpoints are backed up by—the *same* group of researchers. In other words, it has recently been discovered that the dorsal striatum is organized in two different ways, and the relationship between these two forms of organization is not yet known. Smith & Graybiel (2014) describe the current predicament: "Given this rapidly changing face of models of striatal organization and function, it is unclear how the neural recordings that we and others have made of the striatum during habit learning relate to underlying mechanisms. Striatal MSNs are divided into the D1-receptor expressing striatonigral (direct) pathway and D2-expressing striatopallidal (indirect) pathway (Alexander et al., 1986; Albin et al., 1989; Graybiel, 1995). Additional compartmentalization occurs through the striosome vs. matrix organization of MSNs, and in the 'matrisome' input-output organization of cortico-basal ganglia circuitry (Graybiel, 1995; Crittenden and Graybiel, 2011)." I include the references in this quote to point out the underlying dilemma. Graybiel, writing in 2014, is not certain how to relate recent findings regarding *habit learning* to research published by Graybiel in 1995 regarding *direct path D1 receptors and indirect path D2 receptors* or research published by Graybiel in 2011 regarding *striosomes and matrix*. And Ann Graybiel is a leading expert on the basal ganglia.

Looking first at the earlier findings, the dorsal striatum is divided into *striosomes* and *matrix*, with the matrix composed of a *direct path* and an *indirect path*. Crittenden & Graybiel (2011) describe the relationship between the striosomes and the rest of the dorsal striatum: "The orbitofrontal, anterior cingulate, and insular cortices preferentially innervate striosomes, whereas projections from the somatosensory, motor, and dissociation cortices terminate mainly in the matrix." This implies that the striosomes are islands of Teacher and Mercy based value, embedded within the matrix of Contributor thought. In the words of Crittenden & Graybiel, "The amygdala, hippocampus, and nucleus accumbens (part of the ventral striatum) are interconnected with the orbitofrontal, anterior cingulate, and insular cortices, supporting the idea that the striosomes are part of a limbic circuit embedded in the sensorimotor and associative striatum." In addition, "The striosome compartment is thought to contain the only striatal neurons that have direct projections to the substantia nigra, pars compacta (SNc), which contains dopamine producing neurons that project back to the entire dorsal striatum" [through the nigrostriatal pathway]. This "striosome-SNc projection would parallel a ventral striatal input to the SNc. The striosomes and ventral striatum are in a position to exert global control over dopamine signaling in the dorsal striatum." Summarizing, striosomes are embedded within the dorsal striatum, which receives its dopamine from the SNc. Striosomes receive input from cortical areas associated with Teacher and Mercy thought, and are the only part of the dorsal striatum that sends projections to the SNc—which also receives projections from the ventral striatum (which was discussed earlier when examining dopamine). I have suggested that Contributor thought is guided by emotional value. This emotional guidance is probably occurring through the striosomes.

> The dorsal striatum is divided into striosomes, direct path, and indirect path. The striatum is *also* divided into motivation, goal-oriented behavior, and habits.

The matrix is divided into a *direct* path and an *indirect* path. Crittenden & Graybiel (2011) summarize: "Medium spiny striatal projection neurons (MSNs) that are part of a circuit that promotes movement express the Drd1 (D1) dopamine receptor, which boosts MSN cell excitability. MSNs that are part of a circuit that suppresses movement express the Drd2 (D2) dopamine receptor, which diminishes excitability of this MSN cell-type.

Thus, dopamine has a pro-movement effect by simultaneously promoting and dis-inhibiting movement through the so-called direct and indirect pathways, respectively." Summarizing, there are D1 dopamine receptors in the direct path and D2 dopamine receptors in the indirect path. Dopamine increases the activity of the direct path while decreasing the activity of the indirect path. However, this idea of the direct path turning movement 'on' and the indirect path turning movement 'off' is now being recognized as simplistic. Wall (2013) observes that "Classical models of the basal ganglia have sug-gested that the direct pathway facilitates, whereas the indirect pathway suppresses, movements and actions, yet their roles are surely more complex than this. Modeling and evidence from reinforcement paradigms suggest that, within specific contexts, the direct pathway may facilitate previously-rewarded actions, whereas the indirect pathway may suppress previously-unrewarded actions."

Observation of personality suggests the following clarifications. First, Exhorter effort is not the same as Contributor cost-benefit. Exhorter effort is a *redoubling* of energy, trying harder and pushing through obstacles. For instance, Rickover, the American Admiral (and Exhorter person) who built the nuclear Navy once remarked that "The shortest distance between two points is a straight line, even if it bisects six admirals." Contribu-tor cost-benefit, in contrast, *reduces* energy expenditure by going around obstacles in or-der to maximize benefit and minimize cost. Consistent with this, Cox (2015) found that "individual differences in learning from positive and negative outcomes are related to striatal dopamine D1R and D2R function, respectively." More specifically, "reductions in dopamine per se can selectively improve negative feedback learning in healthy hu-mans" and "decreased activity of the indirect pathway (or increased D2R stimulation) predisposes to addictive behaviors." Thus, the indirect path adjusts behavior as a result of negative feedback, while shutting down the indirect path causes a person to continue along the current path without making adjustments. When the Exhorter person experi-ences failure, the typical response is to apply *more* energy to the *same* strategy.

Second, Exhorter crisis management is not the same as Contributor choice. Contributor choice decides between options *within* some context that is defined by a certain set of Perceiver facts and Server sequences, as illustrated by *technical* thought. Exhorter crisis management, in contrast, *changes* the context by making Perceiver and Server thought more flexible. In other words, when the Exhorter person does learn from failure, then there will be major learning and not just minor adjustment. This attribute is described in a study by Passamonti (2015) who found that the personality trait of "Openness was positively associated with the functional connectivity between the right substantia ni-gra/ventral tegmental area, the major source of dopaminergic inputs in the brain, and the ipsilateral [same side] dorsolateral prefrontal cortex (DLPFC)." They hypothesize that "increased dopaminergic inputs within the DLPFC reduce the threshold for infor-mation processing in open people and make them highly 'permeable' and receptive to relevant information... Overall, an enhanced functional connectivity within mesocortical networks may explain why open people display a broad range of interests, an active imagination, and high levels of curiosity and creativity." In other words, Exhorter dopamine helps Perceiver persons to emerge from their natural cocoons of conservatism and acquire a sense of curiosity.

Turning now to the newer findings, the dorsal striatum can be divided into two regions, one carrying out *goal-oriented behavior* and the other *habits*. Balleine & O'Doherty (2010) summarize that "Recent behavioral studies in both humans and rodents have found evidence that performance in decision-making tasks depends on two different learning processes; one encoding the relationship between actions and their consequences and a second involving the formation of stimulus–response associations. These learning processes are thought to govern goal-directed and habitual actions, respectively, and have been found to depend on homologous corticostriatal networks in these species. Thus, recent research using comparable behavioral tasks in both humans and rats has implicated homologous regions of cortex (medial prefrontal cortex/medial orbital cortex in humans and prelimbic cortex in rats) and of dorsal striatum (anterior caudate in humans and dorsomedial striatum in rats) in goal-directed action and in the control of habitual actions (posterior lateral putamen in humans and dorsolateral striatum in rats). These learning processes have been argued to be antagonistic or competing because their control over performance appears to be all or none. Nevertheless, evidence has started to accumulate suggesting that they may at times compete and at others cooperate in the selection and subsequent evaluation of actions necessary for normal choice performance."

Wunderlich (2012) had humans perform tasks that *combined* goal-oriented behavior with habits and found that "the computational processes underlying forward planning are expressed in the anterior caudate nucleus as values of individual branching steps in a decision tree. In contrast, values represented in the putamen pertain solely to values learnt during extensive training. During actual choice, both striatal areas show a functional coupling to ventromedial prefrontal cortex, consistent with this region acting as a value comparator. Our findings point towards an architecture of choice in which segregated value systems operate in parallel in the striatum for planning and extensively trained choices, with medial prefrontal cortex integrating their outputs." They noted that "the vmPFC [ventromedial prefrontal cortex] is engaged whenever values are compared, in order to prepare an action, regardless of whether this derives from a planning computation or from extensive training." In other words, the dorsal striatum comes up with plans by *combining* goal-oriented behavior in the caudate with habits in the putamen, and value in the vmPFC determines which of these two strategies will dominate at any given moment. This is consistent with the idea of Contributor thought choosing between various options guided by emotions of value.

As of the beginning of 2015, I have only found one paper that integrates these two concepts of direct-versus-indirect and goal-versus-habit, and what it describes is highly consistent with mental symmetry. Gruber & McDonald (2012) divide the rat striatum into

"(1) a dorsolateral 'motor' sector involved in skilled movements and habits, (2) a dorsomedial 'cognitive' sector involved in allocentric navigation and flexible responding for strategic acquisition of goals, and (3) a ventral 'limbic' sector incorporating the core and shell of the nucleus accumbens in the VS [ventral striatum] that are involved in approach behaviors, arousal, extinction, and response vigor." In other words, the ventral striatum is related to Exhorter energy, motivation, and 'wanting', the dorsomedial striatum (human caudate) is related to Contributor goal-oriented behavior, while the dorsolateral striatum (human putamen) contains skilled movements and habits that can be used as raw material for Contributor thought. They "propose that a ventral emotional network including amygdala and ventral portions of hippocampus, striatum, and medial prefrontal cortex performs triaging of responding based on affective associations so as to avoid unpleasurable stimuli, ignore inconsequential stimuli, and approach pleasurable stimuli" (remember that the rat ventral hippocampus is the equivalent of the human anterior hippocampus, which interacts with the amygdala). In other words, Exhorter thought in the ventral striatum is guided by emotional processing in Teacher and Mercy thought to respond to situations with strong emotions. In contrast, "The DMS is involved in flexible responding using hippocampal-dependent allocentric navigation, switching among cue dimensions for discriminations, and anticipating outcomes." Thus, Contributor thought in the dorsal striatum uses Perceiver facts and Server sequences as a basis for choosing between different options. They add that "In addition to gating responses, this ventral system also appears to invigorate actions as well as provide rich contextual information that aids the model-based control system in complex discriminations and learning." This implies that Exhorter thought provides energy for Contributor thought, gives suggestions to Contributor thought and occurs before Contributor thought. They explain that "The triaging system may allow animals to identify, following little experience, hazards to avoid and opportunities to exploit for benefit. This alone may facilitate survival by providing simple outcome-predictive control over elementary behaviors such as foraging. It may further aid more complex behaviors by unburdening model-based and model-free control from processing or remembering irrelevant information." This is consistent with the Exhorter person acting as the 'instant expert' who is naturally talented at coming up with a quick-and-dirty understanding by focusing upon essential details. They point out that "The intermediate and ventral portions of hippocampus and associated structures innervate both the DMS and VS, and are thought to provide context. Although context is often associated with space, it can also represent temporal ordering in spatial and non-spatial domains." This means that both Exhorter urges and Contributor choice occur within a general *context* provided by Perceiver and Server processing in the hippocampus.

Turning now to the interaction with the direct and indirect path, "Elevated dopamine in the dorsal striatum promotes activation of the direct pathway to invigorate actions mediated by a competition between S-R systems involving the DLS and goal-oriented systems in the DMS. If the subsequent reward outcome is better than expected, a second bout of elevated dopamine causes LTP [long term potentiation] in the direct pathway via D1 receptors and LTD [long-term depression] in the indirect pathway via D2 receptors, thereby increasing the likelihood of repeating the response. If the outcome is lower than expected, then the direct pathway depresses and the indirect pathway potentiates so that the response is more likely to be withheld following future stimulus presentations." In other words, while dopamine in the ventral striatum expresses Exhorter energy and motivation in a general manner, dopamine in the dorsal striatum suggests options to Contributor thought via the direct path and reinforces choices that lead to success. Thus, there are "distinct dopamine circuits mediating: (i) orientation and motivation, (ii) value learning, and (iii) detection of important sensory events." (We saw (iii) earlier in the way that unexpected events grab Exhorter attention.)

Addiction

We will finish our discussion of the basal ganglia by looking at addiction and the formation of habits. Volkow (2011) describes the various aspects: "All drugs that can lead to addiction increase DA in Nac [nucleus accumbens]... Most studies have reported that participants who display the greatest DA increases with the drug also report the most intense 'high' or 'euphoria'. This tells us that drug addiction is related to Exhorter thought with its urges. Drug abuse creates potent mental networks that lurk under the surface, waiting to be triggered: "Some of the most pernicious features of addiction are the overwhelming craving to take drugs that can re-emerge even after years of abstinence, the severely compromised ability of addicted individuals to inhibit drug-seeking once the craving erupts, and the enhanced sensitivity to stress" (Volkow & Baler, 2014). Going further, "The enhanced motivation to procure drugs is a hallmark of addiction. Drug-addicted individuals will go to extreme behaviors to obtain drugs, even at the expense of seriously adverse consequences. Drug seeking and drug taking become their main motivational drives, which displace other activities. Thus, the addicted subject is aroused and motivated when seeking to procure the drug but tends to be withdrawn and apathetic when exposed to non–drug-related activities... cocaine abusers studied shortly after an episode of cocaine binging showed increased metabolic activity in OFC and ACC (also dorsal striatum) that was associated with craving... This suggests that the activation of these prefrontal regions with drug exposure may be specific to addiction and associated with the enhanced desire for the drug. Moreover, in a subsequent study in which we prompted cocaine-addicted subjects to inhibit craving purposefully when exposed to drug cues, we showed that subjects who were successful in inhibiting craving decreased metabolism in medial OFC (processes motivational value of reinforcer) and NAc (predicts reward)" (Volkow, et al., 2011). In other words, addiction is based in *isolated* mental networks that are not integrated with the rest of thought—the type of mental structure that we saw when discussing Piaget's preoperational stage.

This idea of isolated mental networks driving drug addiction is also suggested by Lucantonio (2012): "Cocaine addiction is characterized by poor judgment and maladaptive decision-making. Here we review evidence implicating the orbitofrontal cortex in such behavior. This evidence suggests that cocaine-induced changes in orbitofrontal cortex disrupt the representation of states and transition functions that form the basis of flexible and adaptive 'model-based' behavioral control. By impairing this function, cocaine exposure leads to an overemphasis on less flexible, maladaptive 'model-free' control systems." A mental network that is not satisfied will generate an intense desire. Consistent with this, Lucantanio says that "During early periods of drug abstinence, circuits including the OFC are hypermetabolic [overactive]. This hypermetabolism is correlated with the intensity of spontaneous craving."

Similarly, Meunier (2012) found that "Whether diagnosed as OCD [obsessive-compulsive disorder] or SDI [stimulus dependent individual], patients with higher scores on measures of compulsive symptom severity showed greater reductions of right orbitofrontal connectivity. Functional connections specifically between OFC and dorsal medial pre-motor and cingulate cortex were attenuated in both patient groups." The lack of *connectivity* means that both drug addiction and obsessive-compulsive behavior are characterized by isolated Mercy mental networks.

Smith & Graybiel (2014) have studied habit formation in rats. First, they note that habits emerge as behavior is organized into *chunks* that are carried out *automatically*. They found "a remarkably close DLS [dorsolateral striatum; rat equivalent to human putamen] relationship to the automaticity of a given run. During some runs, particularly early in training, animals would deliberate at the junction of the goal-arms, essentially conducting a 'vicarious trial and error' by using their head to check each one before making a choice. Both the strength of the DLS activity at the start of the run and the strength of the overall DLS chunking pattern were correlated inversely with these deliberative head movements: the DLS pattern was much stronger on trials that lacked this deliberation. This finding suggested that the DLS keeps track of or controls the level of automaticity or decisiveness of behavior at points of choice options." Second, they discovered that habits are under the control of the infralimbic cortex (rat equivalent of medial frontal and/or orbitofrontal). Their "findings suggested a far more central role for the IL cortex in habit acquisition and expression than formerly appreciated." That is because "the IL cortex contributes to more than just habit selection—on-line IL activity during performance is essential for making habits in the first place, as well as for expressing them once they are formed." They describe this transition more simply in a Scientific American article (Graybiel & Smith, 2014): "When the rats were first learning the maze, neurons in the motor-control part of the striatum were active the whole time the rats were running. But as their behavior became more habitual, neuronal activity began to pile up at the beginning and end of the runs and quieted down during most of the time in between. It was as though the entire behavior had become packaged, with the striatal cells noting the beginning and end of each run... As the animals learned a task, activity in the deliberation part of the striatum [DMS] became strong during the middle of the runs, especially when the rats had to decide which way to turn at the top of the T... during the initial learning period we saw very little change in the infralimbic cortex. It was not until the animals had been trained for a long time and the habit became fixed that the infra-limbic activity changed. Strikingly, when it did, a chunking pattern then developed there, too. It was as though the infralimbic cortex was the wise one, waiting until the striatal evaluation system had fully decided that the behavior was a keeper before committing the larger brain to it." They conclude that "even though habits seem nearly automatic, they are actually under continual control by at least one part of the neocortex, and this region has to be online for the habit to be enacted. It is as though the habits are there, ready to be reeled off if the neocortex determines that the circumstances are right. Even if we are not conscious of monitoring our habitual behaviors—after all, that is a large part of their value to us—we have circuits that actively keep track of them on a mo-ment-to-moment basis. We may reach out for the candy dish without 'thinking,' but a surveillance system in the brain is at work, like a flight-monitoring system in an airliner."

Belin (2013) summarizes that "Drug addiction has been conceptualized as the endpoint of a progressive loss of control over drug seeking and taking that becomes compulsive, persisting despite adverse consequences... resulting in explicit urges, or craving, leaving the individual who is addicted to drugs with no alternative choice than to seek and take them" and suggests that "that these incentive habits result from a pathological coupling of drug-influenced motivational states and a rigid stimulus response habit system by which drug-associated stimuli through automatic processes elicit and maintain drug seeking." In other words, free will is replaced by irresistible urges and flexible goal ori-ented-behavior is replaced by inflexible habits.

> Addiction is driven by isolated mental networks in orbitofrontal cortex.
> Addiction replaces flexible goal-oriented behavior with inflexible habits.

Combining this neurological evidence with observation of personality leads to the fol-lowing hypothesis. Normally, Contributor thought is presented with several options within some context, with Exhorter urge emphasizing one of these options. Contributor thought, guided by a knowledge of value, can either accept the recommendation of Ex-horter thought or else choose another option within the context. One sees this trait in the Contributor person, who often views free will as the ability to choose not to do what one feels driven to do, and who may reject the suggestions of others in order to maintain a sense of being in control. This describes *goal-oriented behavior*. Addiction limits Contributor choice from several directions. First, the Exhorter urge becomes so strong that Contributor thought is no longer able to choose other alternatives. Second, flexible behavior that requires choices is replaced by inflexible habits backed up by a mental network within orbitofrontal cortex. Thus, Contributor thought finds itself passively 'along for the ride', carrying out a response that finishes to completion once triggered. Smith & Graybiel (2014) describe this as "the famous 'kerplunk' effect, in which animals are trained well on a complex maze and then an experimenter suddenly moves the re-ward (and end-wall) to a closer position. Well-trained animals continue running right past the reward and contact the wall, as though they had formed a habit of a certain response set that would be carried out in full even if it resulted poorly." Third, because this habit is enforced by an *isolated* mental network based in an *inflexible* habit, the integrity of the mental network will be threatened if it is triggered and not satisfied, explaining why "in late phases of addiction the effects are more likely to be described as 'filling a hole'" (Crittenden & Graybiel, 2011). Thus, Contributor free will has been overwhelmed by the strength of the Exhorter urge, Contributor choice has been sidelined by the establishment of a fixed habit, and normal thought cannot function because behavior is being driven by an isolated mental network.

We saw something similar in a previous chapter when examining technical thought. If technical thought continues to work within some context, then this will lead to the formation of a mental network, which will emotionally imprison the mind within this context. One could say that the person following technical thought eventually becomes addicted to a theory or plan. The problem is not the formation of habits. Whenever a person gains expertise in some field, chunking occurs that organizes repeated routines into habits, making it possible for goal-oriented behavior to function at a higher level by stringing together habitual routines based in mental networks. The problem also is not the addiction itself. As I suggested in a previous chapter, the successful inventor is obsessed—addicted to the achievement of some goal. Rather, I suggest that the underlying problem is the *limited nature* of the obsession. Volkow & Baler open their 2014 paper on addiction by quoting Frankl, the Jewish psychologist who was forced by life in a Nazi concentration camp to explore the internal aspects of human existence: "Between stimulus and response there is a space. In that space is our power to choose our response. In our response lie our growth and our freedom." In other words, everyone constructs a mental 'space' that will turn into a prison in which they will eventually be emotionally trapped. The challenge is to construct a mental prison—an internal space between stimulus and response—that is large enough to sustain life. The drug addict who bypasses physical input to directly stimulate brain mechanisms of desire and pleasure is creating a mental prison that is so small that it does not have room for either the physical body or the mind, because the brain is being stimulated directly without using either the body or the mind to generate motivation and pleasure.

Notice that we have now seen four different kinds of mental networks within orbitofrontal cortex. First, we saw when examining the orbitofrontal cortex that emotional experiences can lead *directly* to the formation of mental networks that combine universality with instability. Second, the medial frontal cortex can give *stability* to mental networks residing within orbitofrontal cortex, leading to feelings of value, conscience, self-image, and social interaction. This may be the brain mechanism behind Platonic forms and exemplars. Third, mental networks within orbitofrontal cortex act as *goals* for Contributor driven goal-oriented behavior in the caudate. Fourth, *habits* in the putamen lead to the formation of mental networks within orbitofrontal cortex.

Subthalamus

We have looked at the direct and indirect paths. There is also a *hyper-direct* path that leads through the subthalamus, which transmits impulses very quickly and can be used to put a brake upon behavior. However, as with the right inferior frontal cortex, researchers are realizing that this part the brain does more than just stop action. Instead, "the subthalamic nucleus (STN) is specifically thought to contribute by acting as a brake on cortico-striatal function during decision conflict, buying time until the right decision can be made" (Cavanagh, et al., 2014).

Part of the subthalamus is sometimes 'therapeutically lesioned' to 'treat' the symptoms of Parkinson's disease. (It is ironic when brain surgery stops the function of a brain region that is thought to have the sole function of stopping behavior.) It was found that "patients with right subthalamotomy had significantly faster Go reaction times with their contra-lesional hand than the unoperated patients and did not differ from the control participants, indicating their speed of response initiation was 'normalized'. However, operated patients made significantly more discrimination errors than unoperated patients and controls, suggesting that subthalamotomy influenced speed-accuracy trade-offs." The authors conclude that "the subthalamic nucleus is involved in response inhibition, in modulating the rate of information accumulation and the response threshold and influencing the balance between speed and accuracy of performance. Accordingly, the subthalamic nucleus can be considered a key component of the cerebral inhibitory network" (Obeso, et al., 2014).

A more sophisticated way of disrupting subthalamus functioning is through deep brain stimulation (DBS). Coulthard (2012) reports that "Most of us take time when we change our minds, or update a decision according to new events. We have shown that the subthalamic nucleus is essential to allow us to slow down and revise response choice. Impaired reasoning following alteration of the subthalamic nucleus firing pattern by DBS stems from a failure to accrue information over time and is associated with an inappropriate speeding of the response when new information should conflict with an already prepared motor programme... Such breakdown in the ability to slow and integrate evidence before making a decision also helps to explain why some patients with subthalamic nucleus DBS clinically manifest abnormal behaviour including impulsivity."

> The subthalamus makes behavior slower and more accurate.
> The Contributor person can act in a manner that is slow and deliberate.

Relating this to personality, some Contributor persons act in a very controlled and deliberate manner. It is as if they are driving through life with their foot on the brake pedal. In contrast, other Contributor persons behave in a manner that the average person would consider to be quite risky. This suggests that the Contributor person has conscious access to the subthalamus and can choose whether or not to function in a manner that is slow and deliberate.

There is literally a direct connection between cautious behavior and self-image: "When control is needed, the mPFC [medial prefrontal cortex] communicates with the STN of the basal ganglia, which acts as a brake on the cortico-striatal system to facilitate a more deliberative response process. The STN receives direct projections from the mPFC, forming a 'hyperdirect' pathway that can rapidly modulate cortico-striatal processing" (Cavanagh, et al., 2011). Cavanagh found that "mPFC activity predicted an increase in the decision threshold during high-conflict trials and that STN DBS reversed this relationship." When one observes cautious Contributor persons, one gains the impression that they are not just acting in a cautious manner but rather that they regard themselves as cautious people. I am not suggesting that the controlling Contributor person is the only individual to act in a cautious manner. However, the controlling Contributor exhibits a deliberate, painstaking stolidness that is far more restrictive and pervasive than normal cautiousness.

Thalamus

Facilitator persons exhibit an unusual combination of traits. They act as if they are observing themselves go through life. They are aware of all modes of thought, but this is a *surface* awareness, implying that they are conscious in a cognitive module that views the rest of the mind from a distance. While they are less aware of mental functioning than the average person, they are more aware of their physical senses. There is a region of the brain, known as the *thalamus*, that is wired in precisely this way. The thalamus is connected to all of the cortex—but from a distance. In addition, processing from the basal ganglia passes through the thalamus on its way back to the cortex (which is why an arrow is shown running from Contributor to Facilitator on the diagram of mental symmetry). Finally, all of the physical senses, except for smell, pass through the thalamus on their way to the cortex.

I have suggested that Facilitator thought adjusts and blends various forms of thought, like a mixing board in a sound studio. Recent research has shown that the thalamus functions in this matter. Saalmann & Kastner (2012) state that "The thalamus is classically viewed as passively relaying information to the cortex. However, there is growing evidence that the thalamus actively regulates information transmission to the cortex and between cortical areas using a variety of mechanisms, including the modulation of response magnitude, firing mode, and synchrony of neurons according to behavioral demands." In other words, the thalamus *adjusts* by 'modulating response magnitude', and it *mixes* by 'synchronizing neurons'. This mixing property is described by Saalmann in another paper (Saalmann, et al., 2012). They found that "The pulvinar [a nucleus in the thalamus] synchronized activity between interconnected cortical areas according to attentional allocation, suggesting not only a critical role for the thalamus in attentional selection, but more generally in regulating information transmission across visual cortex" and they conclude that "Pulvinar control of cortical processing challenges the common conceptualizing of cognitive functions as being restricted to cortex." In other words, it makes sense to regard the thalamus as a legitimate cognitive module capable of supporting conscious thought and not just as a lowly relay station.

The Facilitator person has a natural tendency to emphasize certain aspects of a situation while downplaying other aspects. Similarly, Saalmann (Saalmann, et al., 2012) summarizes that "The limited capacity of the visual system does not permit simultaneous processing of all information from our cluttered environment in detail. Selective attention helps overcome this limitation by preferentially routing behaviorally relevant information across the visual system."

The thalamus is associated with Facilitator thought.
The thalamus adjusts and mixes cortical thought from a distance.
The thalamus lies midway between the internal and the sensory.
The thalamus is controlled by the reticular thalamic nucleus.

I have suggested that Facilitator thought acts as a mental filter which rejects information that is deemed to be counterintuitive, and Kuhn says that a new paradigm causes the scientist to view the physical world through different eyes. Consistent with this, Saalmann & Kastner suggest that "The thalamus may contribute not only to the selection of behaviorally relevant information from the environment, but also to the conscious perception or awareness of visual information."

The Facilitator person tends to be a social chameleon, adjusting behavior to suit the demands of the current environment. The projection from the parafascicular nucleus (another nucleus in the thalamus) to the basal ganglia performs precisely this function. Schoenbaum (2013) summarizes that "Recognizing when the world has changed—and when it has not—is a fundamental yet much ignored component of associative learning... Imagine relocating to Sydney, Australia. While much there might be familiar, one prominent difference is of life-or-death import: the cars come from the right... Optimally, rather than overwriting your original strategy for crossing the street, upon experiencing the strange driving habits in your new hometown, you would form a new 'state' of 'I am in Sydney' and learn new mappings from actions to goals... relevant to that state. Linking these learned policies to the new state would, conveniently, protect the old policies linked to the old state from being overwritten, so that behavior could be modified quickly if the old state were to reappear... Input from a part of the thalamus, the parafascicular nucleus, onto cholinergic interneurons in the posterior compartment of the dorsomedial striatum (pDMS) [goal-oriented behavior in the rat], is critical to the appropriate creation of new states during learning."

The thalamic reticular nucleus (TRN) integrates the various regions within the thalamus: "The TRN forms a thin shell of neurons that covers the lateral and anterior surface of the dorsal thalamus, and it receives input from branches of both thalamo-cortical and cortico-thalamic fibers. The TRN in turn sends its output exclusively to the thalamus and is positioned to provide inhibitory control over thalamo-cortical transmission," and "the TRN has been implicated in playing an important role in selective attention by regulating thalamo-cortical information transmission" (Saalmann & Kastner, 2012). Notice that the TRN controls the cortex *indirectly* through the thalamus, consistent with the idea that Facilitator thought controls the rest of the mind from a distance.

"The TRN has also been linked to internal processing during sleep, where its activity is associated with sleep rhythms and behavior" (Halassa, et al., 2014). Halassa recorded TRN activity in mice and found that "two functional subpopulations of neurons were identified that exhibited opposite modulation by sleep and attentional states." The Facilitator person often talks about a need to 'wake up slowly' and can be incoherent for a while when forced awake suddenly. Halassa concludes that "the subnetwork architecture of TRN may allow for flexible switching between processing of external input and internal constructs in cognitive tasks, facilitating selective thalamo-cortical network engagement." This is consistent with the observation that Facilitator thought appears to operate midway between the external sensory world and the internal world of cognition.

I have mentioned that Facilitator adjusting acquires its stability from solid Perceiver facts and Server sequences (residing in dorsolateral prefrontal cortex). The Facilitator person can also determine 'truth' through consensus by averaging the opinions of important people (using mental networks within orbitofrontal cortex). Consistent with this, "some prefrontal cortices have widespread projections that extend beyond the frontal sector of TRN to sites innervated by sensory and motor cortices. This unique type of projection is found for dorsolateral prefrontal cortex (DLPFC) and posterior orbitofrontal cortex (pOFC), and their associated mediodorsal thalamic nucleus (MD), which have a key role in cognition, emotion and memory. Through these projections, the DLPFC and pOFC may control the passage of signals through the thalamus to shift attention to relevant stimuli and suppress distracters" (Zikopoulos & Barbas, 2012).

The Facilitator person is affected by emotional memories in an unusual way. When talking about personal tragedy, the Facilitator person will describe the situation in objective terms and then be suddenly overcome by emotions and be unable to continue speaking. All communication will stop until the Facilitator person is able to 'pull himself together' and continue talking. Zikopoulos & Barbas found evidence "suggesting that the amygdala may act in concert with the orbitofrontal cortex and its principal thalamic nucleus (MD) to rapidly assess and transfer emotionally significant stimuli to the cortex and veto access to distractions. This robust tripartite circuitry may add another layer to the control of the flow of information for emotions and the ability to attend to relevant signals and ignore the myriad of external and internal stimuli that intrude on our senses, thoughts, and feelings."

Conclusion

When my brother and I began doing research in cognitive styles in the 1980s, we could show that mental symmetry is *consistent* with neurology. It is now possible to make the much stronger statement that neurology is *converging* with mental symmetry. Studying cognitive styles revealed many facets of cognitive functioning. Neurological research is now confirming and clarifying these traits at a detailed level. Scientists want a theory to make predictions. Mental symmetry made a number of predictions about the mind which neurology is now confirming. The traits of the seven cognitive styles were initially published by Lane Friesen (Friesen, 1986) and a detailed description was put online in 2001 and can be retrieved via a snapshot of the website taken by the wayback machine at   http://web.archive.org/web/20010312232753/http://209.87.142.42/y/you.htm. The neurological papers quoted in this chapter were all published after that date.

The correspondence between mental symmetry and neurological research is both detailed and comprehensive. In each region that we have examined, one finds not just a general similarity but a similar *collection* of traits. In other words, the details match. And this correspondence is comprehensive because we have covered all the major regions of the brain and have examined all of the major facets of the theory of mental symmetry.

Several issues still remain.

1) The data regarding *laterality* is still incomplete. In many areas of the brain, it is not yet known exactly what functions are carried out by left and right hemispheres.

2) Neurological research focuses upon *concrete thought* and only touches upon abstract thought. This focus is understandable given the emphasis upon animal research. Studying how rats move through mazes provides useful information, but a rat is only capable of concrete thought—physically moving through real worlds in order to achieve tangible rewards. Mental symmetry makes a number of predictions regarding abstract thought which can only be tested by studying the human brain.

3) Neurology can only examine how the brain *is* working. It cannot observe how the brain could work. Neurology attempts to overcome this by studying the brains of distinctive groups of people, such as trained mathematicians or professional musicians. But even here one notices that the brain is being used in an incompletely programmed manner. In order to gain a deeper understanding of the mind, one must go beyond observation to theory. Using the ancient city analogy, one must add deciphering tablets to archeological excavation. But that means treating an abstract theory of personality, such as mental symmetry, as a legitimate alternative viewpoint to empirical neurological data. And we began this chapter by noting that neurological research is currently regarded as the most reliable method of studying the mind.

The solution, I suggest, is to recognize the relationship between data and theory. One cannot prove a theory. Instead, one can only 'put on' a theory like a pair of glasses and test the clarity and extent of one's vision. A pair of glasses will *always* warp a person's view of reality and cause incongruent data to be overlooked. We have seen repeatedly in this chapter that this principle applies even when building theories upon empirical neurological data. For instance, one gains the impression that those who are studying the medial frontal lobes are examining four *different* regions. Instead, the *same* region is being observed using four different sets of theoretical spectacles. This theoretical myopia is especially prevalent in the study of the basal ganglia. However, this is not an intractable problem because we also saw that in many areas of the brain, outdated spectacles are currently being exchanged for a new and improved set of lenses.

While one cannot use neurological data to *prove* the theory of mental symmetry, this chapter has tried to demonstrate that mental symmetry is a good set of glasses that provides a *clear* view of the *entire* brain. And we have seen in the preceding chapters that mental symmetry can also be used to analyze the thinking of science and religion, as well as normal thought and behavior. I am not aware of any other model of human thought that can make this claim.

That brings us to the final conclusion. We saw when examining science that there is a strange overlap between theoretical mathematics and pragmatic scientific research. For some reason one can make scientific progress either by performing mathematical calculations or by observing the physical world. This chapter suggests that a similar overlap exists between the theory of mental symmetry and pragmatic neurological research. For some reason one can make progress in understanding the mind either by examining personality guided by the theory of mental symmetry or by observing the functioning of the physical brain.

Saying this more generally, science is based in how the world works. The premise of this book is that religion is based in how the mind works. In science there is an overlap between mathematics and research that leads to a concept of incarnation. Similarly, mental symmetry appears to overlap extensively with both observation of the human *mind* and with neurological research on the human *brain*. This overlap is sufficiently extensive to form a concept of incarnation (as well as provide a possible bridging of mind and brain). That is both elegant and frightening, elegant because there is Teacher order-within-complexity, and frightening because this Teacher structure applies to personal identity—and that combination creates a mental concept of God.

Bibliography

Abu-Akel, A. & Shamay-Tsoory, S., 2011. Neuroanatomical and neurochemical bases of theory of mind. *Neuropsychologia,* Volume 49, pp. 2971-2984.

Adlam, L., 2001. Taking Christ to the Rink. *Faith Today,* Jan-Feb.

Alexander, G. & Hines, M., 2002. Sex differences in response to children's toys in nonhuman primates (Cercopithecus aethiops sabaeus). *Evolution and Human Behavior,* Volume 23, pp. 467-479.

Ally, B. H. E. & Donahue, M., 2013. A case of hyperthymesia: rethinking the role of the amygdala in autobiographical memory. *Neurocase.,* 19(2), pp. 166-181.

Ansari, D., Grabner, R. & Koschutnig, K., 2011. Individual differences in mathematical competence modulate brain responses to arithmetic errors: An fMRI study. *Learning and Individual Differences,* Volume 21, pp. 636-643.

Azzi, J., Sirigu, A. & Duhamel, J.-R., 2012. Modulation of value representation by social context in the primate orbitofrontal cortex. *Neuroscience, Psychological and Cognitive Sciences,* 109(6), pp. 2126-2131.

Badre, D. & Wagner, A., 2007. Left ventrolateral prefrontal cortex and the cognitive control of memory. *Neuropsychologia,* Volume 45, pp. 2883-2901.

Baeken, C., De Raedt, R. & Van Schuerbeek, P., 2010. Right prefrontal HF-rTMS attenuates right amygdala processing of negatively valenced emotional stimuli in healthy females. *Brain Behavioral Research,* 214(2), pp. 450-455.

Balleine, B. & O'Doherty, J., 2010. Human and rodent homologies in action control: corticostriatal determinants of goal-directed and habitual action. *Neuropsychopharmacology,* pp. 48-69.

Ball, J., 2013. Revealed: how US and UK spy agencies defeat internet privacy and security. *The Guardian,* 6 Sept.

Barbey, A., Colom, R. & Solomon, J., 2012. An integrative architecture for general intelligence and executive function revealed by lesion mapping. *Brain,* Volume 135, pp. 1154-1164.

Barrett, J., 2000. Exploring the natural foundations of religion. *Trends in Cognitive Sciences,* pp. 29-34.

Barrett, J., 2004. *Why Would Anyone Believe in God?.* Lanhan, MD: Altamira Press.

Baum, S., Martin, R. & Hamilton, C., 2012. Multisensory speech perception without the left superior temporal sulcus. *Neuroimage,* 62(3), pp. 1825-1832.

Beauregard, M., Lévesque, J. & Bourgouin, P., 2001. Neural correlates of conscious self-regulation of emotion. *The Journal of Neuroscience,* Volume 21, pp. 1-6.

Beer, J., Heerey, E. & Keltner, D., 2003. The regulatory function of self-conscious emotion: insights from patients with orbitofrontal damage. *Journal of Personality and Social Psychology,* 85(4), pp. 594-604.

Belin, D., Belin-Rauscent, A. & Murray, J., 2013. Addiction: failure of control over maladaptive incentive habits. *Current Opinion in Neurobiology,* Volume 23, pp. 1-9.

Belyk, M. & Brown, S., 2014. Perception of affective and linguistic prosody: An ALE meta-analysis of neuroimaging studies. *Social Cognitive and Affective Neuroscience,* 9(9), pp. 1395-1403.

Benedict-XVI, 2006. *Address of his Holiness Pope Benedict XVI.* [Online]
Available at:
http://www.vatican.va/holy_father/benedict_xvi/speeches/2006/march/documents/hf_ben-xvi_spe_20060302_roman-clergy_en.html

Bernhardt, B., Smallwood, J. & Tusche, A., 2013. Medial prefrontal and anterior cingulate cortical thickness predicts shared individual differences in self-generated thought and temporal discounting. *NeuroImage,* pp. 290-297.

Berridge, K. & Kringelbach, M., 2013. Neuroscience of affect: brain mechanisms of pleasure and displeasure. *Current Opinions in Neurobiology,* 23(3), pp. 294-303.

Bickart, K., Hollenbeck, M. & Barrett, L., 2012. Intrinsic amygdala--cortical functional connectivity predicts social network size in humans. *The Journal of Neuroscience,* 32(42), pp. 14729-14741.

Bilalić, M., 2010. The Mechanism of the Einstellung (Set) Effect. *Current Directions in Psychological Science,* 19(2), pp. 111-115.

Blumenfeld, R., Parks, C. & Yonelinas, A., 2011. Putting the pieces together: the role of dorsolateral prefrontal cortex in relational memory encoding. *Journal of Cognitive Neuroscience,* 23(1), pp. 257-265.

Boggio, P., Rocha, M. & Oliveira, M., 2010. Noninvasive brain stimulation with high-frequency and low-intensity repetitive transcranial magnetic stimulation treatment for posttraumatic stress disorder. *Journal of Clinical Psychiatry,* 71(8), pp. 992-999.

Bohrn, I., Altmann, U. & Jacobs, A., 2012. Looking at the brains behind figurative language--a quantitative meta-analysis of neuroimaging studies on metaphor, idiom, and irony processing. *Neuropsychologia,* pp. 2669-2683.

Boksem, M., Kostermans, E. & De Cremer, D., 2010. Failing where others have succeeded: medial frontal negativity tracks failure in a social context. *Psychophysiology,* pp. 1-7.

Boorman, E., Behrens, T. & Rushworth, M., 2011. Counterfactual choice and learning in a neural network centered on human lateral frontopolar cortex. *PLOS Biology,* 9(6), pp. 1-13.

Borst, G., Thompson, W. & Kosslyn, S., 2011. Understanding the dorsal and ventral systems of the human cerebral cortex. *American Psychologist,* 66(7), pp. 624-632.

Boyd, G., 2001. *Satan and the Problem of Evil: Constructing a trinitarian warfare theodicy.* Downers Grove: Intervarsity Press.

Britannica, n.d. *Saint Simeon Stylites.* [Online]
Available at: http://www.britannica.com/EBchecked/topic/545077/Saint-Simeon-Stylites

Bromberg-Martin, E., Matsumoto, M. & Hikosaka, O., 2010. Dopamine in motivational control: rewarding, aversive, and alerting. *Neuron Review,* Volume 68, pp. 815-834.

Bruce, S., Buchholz, K. & Brown, W., 2013. Altered emotional interference processing in the amygdala and insula in women with post-traumatic stress disorder. *NeuroImage: Clinical,* Volume 2, pp. 43-49.

Brzezicka, A., Sedek, G. & Marchewka, A., 2011. A role for the right prefrontal and bilateral parietal cortex in four-term transitive reasoning; an fMRI study with abstract linear syllogism tasks. *Acta Neurobiologiae Experimentalis,* Volume 71, pp. 479-495.

Buzsáki, G. & Moser, E., 2013. Memory, navigation and theta rhythm in the hippocampal-entorhinal system. *Nature Neuroscience,* 16(2), pp. 130-138.

Bzdok, D., Langner, R. & Schilbach, L., 2013. Segregation of the human medial prefrontal cortex in social cognition. *Frontiers in Human Neuroscience,* Volume 7.

Bzdok, D., Schilbach, L. & Vogeley, K., 2012. Parsing the neural correlates of moral cognition: ALE meta-analysis on morality, theory of mind, and empathy. *Brain Structure and Function,* pp. 783-796.

Camille, N., Griffiths, C. & Vo, K., 2011. Ventromedial frontal lobe damage disrupts value maximization in humans. *The Journal of Neuroscience,* 31(20), pp. 7527-7532.

Campbell-Meiklejohn, D., Kanai, R. & Bahrami, B., 2012. Structure of orbitofrontal cortex predicts social influence. *Current Biology,* 22(4), pp. 123-124.

Catani, M., Dell'Acqua, F. & Thiebaut de Schotten, M., 2013. A revised limbic system model for memory, emotion and behaviour. *Neuroscience and Biobehavioral Reviews,* Volume 37, pp. 1724-1737.

Catholic Answers Staff, n.d. *How does Nirvana compare with the Christian understanding of heaven?.* [Online]
Available at: http://www.catholic.com/quickquestions/how-does-nirvana-compare-with-the-christian-understanding-of-heaven

Cavanagh, J., Sanguinetti, J. & Allen, J., 2014. The subthalamic nucleus contributes to post-error slowing. *Journal of Cognitive Neuroscience,* 26(11), pp. 2637-2644.

Cavanagh, J., Wiecki, T. & Cohen, M., 2011. Subthalamic nucleus stimulation reverses mediofrontal influence over decision threshold. *Nature Neuroscience,* 14(11), pp. 1462-1469.

Chan, E., 2014. Edmonton teacher fired for breaking 'no zero' grading policy wins appeal. *CTV News,* Aug 30.

Chateauversailles, n.d. *A day in the life of Louis XIV.* [Online]
Available at: http://en.chateauversailles.fr/history/versailles-during-the-centuries/living-at-the-court/a-day-in-the-life-of-louis-xiv

Chaumon, M., Kveraga, K. & Barrett, L., 2013. Visual predictions in the orbitofrontal cortex rely on associative content. *Cerebral Cortex.*

Clos, M., Rottschy, C. & Laird, A., 2014. Comparison of structural covariance with functional connectivity approaches exemplified by an investigation of the left anterior insula. *Neuroimage,* Volume 99, pp. 269-280.

Cloud, J., 2002. Meet the Prophet: How an Evangelist and Conservative Activist Turned Prophecy into a Fiction Juggernaut. *Time*, 1 July.

Cloutier, J., Ambady, M. & Meagher, T., 2012. The neural substrates of person perception: spontaneous use of financial and moral status knowledge. *Neuropsychologia,* Volume 50, pp. 2371-2376.

Corbett, S., 2009. The Holy Grail of the Unconscious. *The New York Times*, 16 Sept.

Costa, A., Oliveri, M. & Barban, F., 2013. The right frontopolar cortex is involved in visual-spatial prospective memory. *PLOS ONE,* 8(2).

Coulthard, E., Bogacz, R. & Javed, S., 2012. Distinct roles of dopamine and subthalamic nucleus in learning and probabilistic decision making. *BRAIN,* pp. 3721-3734.

Cox, S., Frank, M. & Larcher, K., 2015. Striatal D1 and D2 signaling differentially predict learning from positive and negative outcomes. *NeuroImage,* Volume 109, pp. 95-101.

Crittenden, J. & Graybiel, A., 2011. Basal ganglia disorders associated with imbalances in the striatal striosome and matrix compartments. *Frontiers in Neuroanatomy ,* 5(59).

Damasio, A., 1994. *Descartes' Error : Emotion, Reason, and the Human Brain.* New York: Putnam Press.

David, S., 2012. *How Germany lost the WWI arms race.* [Online]
Available at: http://www.bbc.com/news/magazine-17011607

Dictionary.com, n.d. *association cortex. (n.d.). Dictionary.com Unabridged..* [Online]
Available at: http://dictionary.reference.com/browse/association cortex

DiMilta, J., n.d. *Candle Power.* [Online]
Available at: http://www.mysticgoddess.org/candles.htm

Dirac, P., 1938. Lecture delivered on presentation of the JAMES SCOTT prize. *Proceedings of the Royal Society (Edinburgh),* Volume 59, pp. 122-129.

Dirac, P., 1963. The Evolution of the Physicist's Picture of Nature. *Scientific American,* 208(5).

Dyck, M., Loughead, J. & Kellermann, T., 2011. Cognitive versus automatic mechanisms of mood induction differentially activate left and right amygdala. *Neuroimage,* 54(3), pp. 2503-2513.

Eck, D., n.d. *Qur'an and Qur'anic Recitation.* [Online]
Available at: http://www.pluralism.org/resources/tradition/essays/islam6.php

Edison Files, n.d. *The Practical Incandescent Light Bulb.* [Online]
Available at: http://edisonmuseum.org/content3399.html

Edmundson, M., 2007. Defender of the Faith?. *The New York Times*, 9 Sept.

EFF Staff, n.d. *Mass Surveillance Technologies.* [Online]
Available at: https://www.eff.org/issues/mass-surveillance-technologies

Egner, T., 2011. Right ventrolateral prefrontal cortex mediates individual differences in conflict-driven cognitive control. *Journal of Cognitive Neuroscience,* 23(12), pp. 3903-3913.

Eichenbaum, H., 2013. Memory on time. *Trends in Cognitive Science,* 17(2), pp. 81-88.

Einstein, A., 1950. *Out of my Later Years.* New York: Philosophical Library.

Encyclopaedia Judaica, n.d. *Remnant of Israel.* [Online]
Available at:
http://www.jewishvirtuallibrary.org/jsource/judaica/ejud_0002_0017_0_16639.html

Evensmoen, H., Lehn, H. & Xu, J., 2013. The anterior hippocampus supports a coarse, global environmental representation and the posterior hippocampus supports fine-grained, local environmental representations. *Journal of Cognitive Neuroscience,* 25(11), pp. 1908-1925.

Fairclough, N., 1989. *Language and Power.* New York: Longman.

Fairclough, N., n.d. *Critical discourse analysis.* [Online]
Available at: http://semiotics.nured.uowm.gr/pdfs/THEORY_FAIRCLOUGH.pdf

Fanselow, M. & Dong, H.-W., 2009. Are the dorsal and ventral hippocampus functionally distinct structures?. *Neuron Review,* Volume 65, pp. 7-19.

Femando, A., Murray, J. & Milton, A., 2013. The amygdala: securing pleasure and avoiding pain. *Frontiers in Behavioral Neuroscience,* 7(190).

Fleming, S., Huijgen, J. & Dolam, R., 2012. Prefrontal Contributions to Metacognition in Perceptual. *The Journal of Neuroscience,* 32(18), pp. 6117-6125.

Freud, S., 1900. *The standard edition of the complete psychological works of Sigmund Freud.* London: Hogarth Press.

Freud, S., 1930. *The standard edition of the complete psychological works of Sigmund Freud.* London: Hogarth Press.

Freud, S., 1939. *The standard edition of the complete psychological works of Sigmund Freud.* London: Hogarth Press.

Friederici, A., 2012. The cortical language circuit: from auditory perception to sentence comprehension. *Trends in Cognitive Sciences,* 16(5).

Fried, P., Rushmore, R. & Moss, M., 2014. Causal evidence supporting functional dissociation of verbal and spatial working memory in the human dorsolateral prefrontal cortex. *European Jouranl of Neuroscience,* 39(11), pp. 1973-1981.

Friesen, L., 1986. *Cognitive Styles in History: Contributor and Server.* Victoria, BC: Lane Friesen, Inc.

Friesen, L., 1986. *Cognitive Styles in History: Perceiver and Mercy.* Victoria, BC: Lane Friesen, Inc.

Frohlich, T. & Kent, A., 2014. Countries spending the most on the military. *USA Today,* 12 July.

Gao, T., Scholl, B. & McCarthy, G., 2012. Dissociating the detection of intentionality from animacy in the right posterior superior temporal sulcus. *The Journal of Neuroscience,* 32(41), pp. 14276-14280.

Gasquoine, P., 2013. Localization of function in anterior cingulate cortex: from psychosurgery to functional neuroimaging. *Neuroscience Biobehavioral Review,* 37(3), pp. 340-348.

George, A., n.d. *The Place of Man's Deification.* [Online]
Available at: http://www.greekorthodoxchurch.org/theosis_contents.html

Gepshtein, S., Li, X. & Snider, J., 2014. Dopamine function and the efficiency of human movement. *Journal of Cognitive Neuroscience,* 26(3), pp. 645-657.

Gilet, C., n.d. *Cold fusion: A case study for scientific behavior.* [Online]
Available at: http://undsci.berkeley.edu/article/cold_fusion_01

Glimcher, P., 2011. Understanding dopamine and reinforcement learning: the dopamine reward prediction error hypothesis. *PNAS,* 108(42), pp. 15647-15654.

Grabenhorst, F. & Rolls, E., 2011. Value, pleasure and choice in the ventral prefrontal cortex. *Trends in Cognitive Sciences,* 15(2).

Graybiel, A. & Smith, K., 2014. Good habits, bad habits. *Scientific American,* June, pp. 39-43.

Green, A., Fugelsang, J. & Kraemer, D., 2006. Frontopolar cortex mediates abstract integration in analogy. *Brain Research,* pp. 125-137.

Green, A., Kraemer, D. & Fugelsang, J., 2010. Connecting long distance: semantic distance in analogical reasoning modulates frontopolar cortex activity. *Cerebral Cortex,* Volume 20, pp. 70-76.

Groussard, M., Viader, F. & Landeau, B., 2014. The effects of musical practice on structural plasticity: the dynamics of grey matter changes. *Brain and Cognition,* Volume 90, pp. 174-180.

Gruber, A. & McDonald, R., 2012. Context, emotion, and the strategic pursuit of goals: interactions among multiple brain systems controlling motivated behavior. *Frontiers in Behavioral Neuroscience,* 6(50).

Gunaratana, H., 2002. *Mindfulness in plain English.* Boston: Wisdom Publications.

Habermas, J., 1962. *The structural transformation of the public sphere : an inquiry into a category of bourgeois society.* Cambridge: Polity Press.

Haber, S. & Knutson, B., 2010. The reward circuit: linking primate anatomy and human imaging. *Neuropsychopharmacology,* Volume 35, pp. 4-26.

Halassa, M., Chen, Z. & Wimmer, R., 2014. State-dependent architecture of thalamic reticular subnetworks. *Cell,* Volume 158, pp. 808-821.

Hampshire, A., Thompson, R. & Duncan, J., 2010. Selective tuning of the right inferior frontal gyrus during target detection. *Cognitive Affective Behavioral Neuroscience,* 9(1), pp. 103-112.

Hanke, D., 2004. Teleology: The explanation that bedevils biology. In: *Explanations: Styles of explanation in science.* New York: Oxford University Press, pp. 143-155.

Han, Z., Bi, Y. & Chen, J., 2013. Distinct regions of right temporal cortex are associated with biological and human-agent motion: functional magnetic resonance imaging and neuropsychological evidence. *The Journal of Neuroscience,* 33(39), pp. 15442-15453.

Harris, S., Kaplan, J. & Curiel, A., 2009. The neural correlates of religious and non-religious belief. *PLOS ONE,* 4(10).

Hartwright, C., Apperly, I. & Hansen, P., 2014. Representation, control, or reasoning? distinct functions for theory of mind within the medial prefrontal cortex. *Journal of Cognitive Neuroscience,* 26(4), pp. 683-698.

Harvey, F., 1976. Motivational Gifts. *Vision Magazine,* Nov-Dec.Volume 18.

Hassett, J., 2008. Sex differences in rhesus monkey toy preferences parallel those of children. *Hormones and Behavior.*

Hayden, B., Heilbronner, S. & Pearson, J., 2011. Surprise signals in anterior cingulate cortex: neuronal encoding of unsigned reward prediction errors driving adjustment in behavior. *The Journal of Neuroscience,* 31(11), pp. 4178-4187.

Hayward, D., Owen, A. & Koenig, H., 2011. Associations of religious behavior and experiences with extent of regional atrophy in the orbitofrontal cortex during oder adulthood. *Religion Brain Behavior,* 1(2), pp. 103-118.

Heisenberg, W., 1971. *Physics and Beyond: Encounters and conversations.* New York: Harper & Row.

Herbert, B. & Pollatos, O., 2012. The body in the mind: on the relationship between interoception and embodiment. *Topics in Cognitive Science.*

Herbert, C., Ethofer, T. & Anders, S., 2009. Amygdala activation during reading of emotional adjectives--an advantage for pleasant content. *Social Cognitive and Affective Neuroscience,* 4(1), pp. 35-49.

Higgins, T., 1987. Self-discrepancy: a theory relating self and affect. *Psychological Review,* 94(3), pp. 319-340.

Hill, K., 2012. How Target Figured Out A Teen Girl Was Pregnant Before Her Father Did. *Forbes,* 16 Feb.

Holroyd, C. & Yeung, N., 2012. Motivation of extended behaviors by anterior cingulate cortex. *Trends in Cognitive Sciences,* 16(2), pp. 122-128.

Hori, V., 2000. Koan and Kensho in the Rinzai Zen Curriculum. In: *The Koan: Texts and contexts in Zen Buddhism.* Oxford: Oxford University Press, pp. 289-290.

Horr, N., Braun, C. & Volz, K., 2014. Feeling before knowing why: the role of the orbitofrontal cortex in intuitive judgments--an MEG study. *Cognitive Affective Behavioral Neuroscience,* Volume 14, pp. 1271-1285.

Hsu, C.-T., Jacobs, A. & Altmann, U., 2015. The magical activation of left amygdala when reading harry potter: an fMRI study on how descriptions of supra-natural events entertain and enchant. *PLOS ONE,* 10(2).

Hua, H., 2004. *The Chan Handbook: Venerable master Hsuan Hua talks about Chan.* Ukiah, CA: Buddhist Text Translation Society.

Humphries, M. & Prescott, T., 2009. The ventral basal ganglia, a selection mechanism at the crossroads of space, strategy, and reward. *Progress in Neurobiology,* 90(4), pp. 385-417.

Hyde, K., Zatorre, R. & Peretz, I., 2011. Functional MRI evidence of an abnormal neural network for pitch processing in congenital amusia. *Cerebral Cortex,* Volume 21, pp. 292-299.

Iglói, K., Doeller, C. & Berthoz, A., 2010. Lateralized human hippocampal activity predicts navigation based on sequence or place memory. *PNAS,* 107(32), pp. 14466-14471.

Iglói, K., Zaoui, M. & Berthoz, A., 2009. Sequential egocentric strategy is acquired as early as allocentric strategy: parallel acquisition of these two navigation strategies. *Hippocampus,* Volume 19, pp. 1199-1211.

Imamreza, n.d. *The Status of Martyrdom in Islam.* [Online]
Available at: http://www.imamreza.net/eng/imamreza.php?id=5634

Ingalhalikar, M., 2013. Sex differences in the structural connectome of the human brain. *Proceedings of the National Academy of Sciences,* 111(2), pp. 823-828.

Isaacson, W., 2007. *Einstein: His life and universe.* New York: Simon & Schuster.

islamqa, n.d. *Abrogation in the Qur'an.* [Online]
Available at: http://islamqa.info/en/105746

James, W., 1929. *The Varieties of Religious Experience: A study in human nature.* Ann Arbor, Michigan: University of Michigan Library.

Jayaram, V., n.d. *The Definition and Concept of Maya in Hinduism.* [Online]
Available at: http://www.hinduwebsite.com/hinduism/essays/maya.asp

Johnston, B., 2001. Colosseum 'built with loot from sack of Jerusalem temple'. *The Telegraph,* 15 June.

Jung, C., 1963. *Memories, Dreams, Reflections.* New York: Pantheon Books.

Kaller, C., Rahm, B. & Spreer, J., 2011. Dissociable contributions of left and right dorsolateral prefrontal cortex in planning. *Cerebral Cortex,* Volume 21, pp. 307-317.

Kapogiannis, D., Barbey, A. & Su, M., 2009. Cognitive and neural foundations of religious belief. *PNAS,* 106(12), pp. 4876-4881.

Khan, U., 2010. Terrorism and child pornography used to justify surveillance society, says academic. *The Telegraph,* 23 Jan.

Kim, M., Loucks, R. & Palmer, A., 2011. The structural and functional connectivity of the amygdala: from normal emotion to pathological anxiety. *Behavioral Brain Research,* 223(2), pp. 403-410.

Kingslake, B., 1991. *Inner Light: Swedenborg explores the spiritual dimension.* Boston: J. Appleseed & Co..

Knoch, D. & Fehr, E., 2007. Resisting the power of temptations: the right prefrontal cortex and self-control. *Annals of New York Academy of Science,* Volume 1104, pp. 123-134.

Kolb, B. & Whishaw, I., 2005. *An Introduction to Brain & Behavior.* 2nd ed. New York: Worth Publishing.

Kraus, M., Piff, P. & Krltner, D., 2009. Social class, sense of control, and social explanation. *Journal of Personality and Social Psychology,* 97(6), pp. 992-1004.

Kret, M. & De Gelder, B., 2012. A review on sex differences in processing emotional signals. *Neuropsychologia,* Volume 50, pp. 1121-1221.

Krindatch, A., n.d. *The Orthodox Church Today.* [Online]
Available at: http://www.hartfordinstitute.org/research/OrthChurchFullReport.pdf

Kringelbach, M., 2005. The human orbitofrontal cortex: linking reward to hedonic experience. *Nature Reviews/Neuroscience,* Volume 6, pp. 691-702.

Kroger, J., Nystrom, L. & Cohen, J., 2008. Distinct neural substrates for deductive and mathematical processing. *Brain Research,* pp. 86-103.

Krueger, F., Spampinato, M. & Barbey, A., 2009. The frontopolar cortex mediates event knowledge complexity: a parametric functional MRI study. *Neuroreport,* 20(12), pp. 1093-1097.

Kuhn, T. S., 1970. *The Structure of Scientific Revolutions.* Chicago: The University of Chicago Press.

Lahnakoski, J., Glerean, E. & Salmi, J., 2012. Naturalistic fMRI mapping reveals superior temporal sulcus as the hub for the distributed brain network for social perception. *Frontiers in Human Neuroscience,* 6(233).

Lakoff, G. & Johnson, M., 1980. *Metaphors We Live By.* Chicago: University of Chicago Press.

Lakoff, G. & Johnson, M., 1999. *Philosophy in the Flesh.* New York: Basic Books.

Laureiro-Martinez, D., Canessa, N. & Brusoni, S., 2014. Frontopolar cortex and decision-making efficiency: comparing brain activity of experts with different professional background during an exploration-exploitation task. *Frontiers in Human Neuroscience,* Volume 7, pp. 1-10.

Leber, J., 2009. The Pentagon Strives to Tuck in Its Long Logistics 'Tail'. *The New York Times,* 27 July.

Leckman, J., Bloch, M. & King, R., 2012. The diagnosis of tourette syndrome. In: J. Walkup, J. Mink & K. McNaught, eds. *A Family's Guide to Tourette Syndrome.* Bloomington, IN: iUniverse, Inc, pp. 8-23.

Lerch, J., Yiu, A. & Martinez-Canabal, A., 2011. Maze training in mice induces MRI- detectable brain shape changes specific to the type of learning. *NeuroImage,* 54(3), pp. 2086-2095.

Levens, S., Larsen, J. & Bruss, J., 2014. What might have been? the role of the ventromedial prefrontal cortex and lateral orbitofrontal cortex in counterfactual emotions and choice. *Neuropsychologia,* Volume 54, pp. 77-86.

Levy, B. & Wagner, A., 2011. Cognitive control and right ventrolateral prefrontal cortex. *Annals of NY Academy of Sciences,* 1224(1), pp. 40-62.

Levy, S., 1984. *Hackers: heroes of the computer revolution.* Garden City, NY: Anchor Press/Doubleday.

Liebenthal, E., Desai, R. & Ellingson, M., 2010. Cerebral Cortex. *Specialization along the left superior temporal sulcus for auditory categorization,* Volume 20, pp. 2958-2970.

Love, P. & Guthrie, V., 1999. *Understanding and Applying Cognitive Development Theory.* San Francisco: Jossey-Bass.

Lowe, C., Hall, P. & Staines, W., 2014. The effects of continuous theta burst stimulation to the left dorsolateral prefrontal cortex on executive function, food cravings, and snack food consumption. *Psychosomatic Medicine,* Volume 76, pp. 503-511.

Lucantonio, F., Stalnaker, T. & Shaham, Y., 2012. The impact of orbitofrontal dysfunction on cocaine addiction. *Nature Neuroscience,* 15(3), pp. 358-366.

Lyons, I. & Beilock, S., 2011. Mathematics anxiety: separating the math from the anxiety. *Cerebral Cortex.*

Machta, B., 2013. Parameter space compression underlies emergent theories and predictive models. *Science,* Volume 342, pp. 604-607.

Mahoney, M., 1994. *The Mathematical Career of Pierre de Fermat, 1601-1665.* Princeton: Princeton University Press.

Ma, K., 2007. *Cheaters Sometimes Win.* [Online]
Available at: http://www.nerve.com/regulars/lifeswork/stevenortiz Cheaters Sometimes Win KAI MA• APR. 12, 2007

Maloney, E., Waechter, S. & Risko, E., 2012. Reducing the sex difference in math anxiety: the role of spatial processing ability. *Learning and Individual Differences,* Volume 22, pp. 380-384.

Marinkovic, K., Baldwin, S. & Courtney, M., 2011. Right hemisphere has the last laugh: neural dynamics of joke appreciation. *Cognitive Affective Behavioral Neuroscience,* Volume 11, pp. 113-130.

Mashour, G., Walker, E. & Martuza, R., 2005. Psychosurgery: past, present, and future. *Brain Research Reviews,* Volume 48, pp. 409-419.

Maslow, A., 1966. *The Psychology of Science: A renaissance.* New York: Harper & Row.

Mayo Clinic Staff, n.d. *Meditation: A simple, fast way to reduce stress.* [Online]
Available at: http://www.mayoclinic.org/tests-procedures/meditation/in-depth/meditation/art-20045858

McCauley, R., 2011. *Why Religion is Natural and Science is Not.* Oxford: Oxford University Press.

McDonald, W., n.d. *Søren Kierkegaard.* [Online]
Available at: http://plato.stanford.edu/archives/fall2012/entries/kierkegaard/

McDuling, J., 2014. *Elon Musk is the true successor to Steve Jobs.* [Online]
Available at: http://qz.com/275725/elon-musk-is-the-true-successor-to-steve-jobs/

Meteyard, L., Rodriguez Cuadrado, S. & Bahrami, B., 2012. Coming of age: a review of embodiment and the neuroscience of semantics. *Cortex,* 48(7), pp. 788-804.

Metuki, N., Sela, T. & Lavidor, M., 2012. Enhancing cognitive control components of insight problems solving by anodal tDCS of the left dorsolateral prefrontal cortex. *Brain Stimulation,* 5(2), pp. 110-115.

Meunier, D., Ersche, K. & Craig, K., 2012. Brain functional connectivity in stimulant drug dependence and obsessive-compulsive disorder. *NeuroImage,* 59(2), pp. 1461-1468.

Moltke, H. & Hughes, D., 1993. *Moltke on the Art of War.* Novato, CA: Presidio Press.

Morin, A. & Hamper, B., 2012. Self-reflection and the inner voice: activation of the left inferior frontal gyrus during perceptual and conceptual self-referential thinking. *The Open Neuroimaging Journal,* Volume 6, pp. 78-89.

Morin, A. & Uttl, B., 2013. *Inner speech; a window into consciousness.* [Online]
Available at: Neuropsychotherapist.com

Mormann, F., Dubois, J. & Kornblith, S., 2012. A category-specific response to animals in the right human amygdala. *Nature Neuroscience,* 14(10), pp. 1247-1249.

Muscatell, K., Morelli, S. & Falk, E., 2012. Social status modulates neural activity in the mentalizing network. *Neuroimage,* 60(3), pp. 1771-1777.

Newberg, A., 2006. The measurement of regional cerebral blood flow during glossolalia: a preliminary SPECT study. *Neuroimaging,* Volume 148, pp. 67-71.

Nicolle, A., Klein-Flügge, M. & Hunt, L., 2012. An agent independent axis for executed and modeled choice in medial prefrontal cortex. *Neuron,* Volume 75, pp. 1114-1121.

Nieuwland, M., 2011. Establishing propositional truth-value in counterfactual and real-world contexts during sentence comprehension: differential sensitivity of the left and right inferior frontal gyri. *Neuroimage*, 59(4), pp. 3433-3340.

NPR Staff, 2011. *Among the Costs of War: Billions A Year In A.C.?*. [Online]
Available at: http://www.npr.org/2011/06/25/137414737/among-the-costs-of-war-20b-in-air-conditioning

Obeso, I., Wilkinson, L. & Casabona, E., 2014. The subthalamic nucleus and inhibitory control: impact of subthalamotomy in Parkinson's disease. *Brain*, Volume 137, pp. 1470-1480.

Olson, I., McCoy, D. & Klobusicky, E., 2013. Social cognition and the anterior temporal lobes: a review and theoretical framework. *SCAN*, Volume 8, pp. 123-133.

Pachal, P., 2012. *How Kodak Squandered Every Single Digital Opportunity It Had*. [Online]
Available at: http://mashable.com/2012/01/20/kodak-digital-missteps/

Padoa-Schioppa, C. & Assad, J., 2006. Neurons in orbitofrontal cortex encode economic value. *Nature*, pp. 223-226.

Pardini, D., Raine, A. & Erickson, K., 2014. Lower amygdala volume in men is associated with childhood aggression, early psychopathic traits and future violence. *Biological Psychiatry*, 75(1).

Parkinson, C. & Liu, S. W. T., 2014. A common metric for spatial, temporal, and social distance. *The Journal of Neuroscience*, 34(5), pp. 1979-1987.

Passamonti, L., Terracciano, A. & Riccelli, R., 2015. Increased functional connectivity within mesocortical networks in open people. *NeuroImage*, pp. 301-309.

Pearl, J., 1996. *The Art and Science of Cause and Effect*. [Online]
Available at: http://singapore.cs.ucla.edu/LECTURE/lecture_sec1.htm

Philiastides, M., Auksztulewicz, R. & Heekeren, H., 2011. Causal role of dorsolateral prefrontal cortex in human perceptual decision making. *Current Biology*, Volume 21, pp. 980-983.

Piaget, J., 1936. *Origins of Intelligence in the Child*. London: Routledge & Kegan Paul.

Piai, V., Roelofs, A. & Acheson, D., 2013. Attention for speaking: domain-general control from the anterior cingulate. *Frontiers in Human Neuroscience*, 7(832).

Poppenk, J., Evensmoen, H. & Moscovitch, M., 2013. Long-axis specialization of the human hippocampus. *Trends in Cognitive Sciences*, 17(5), pp. 230-240.

Prayercraft, 2009. *On the Jesus Prayer*. [Online]
Available at: http://prayercraft.byethost8.com/JesusPrayer.htm

Qin, P. & Northoff, G., 2011. How is our self related to midline regions and the default-mode network?. *NeuroImage*, Volume 57, pp. 1221-1233.

Quine, W., 1978. *The Web of Belief*. New York: Random House.

Rees, J., 2012. The end of our Kodak moment. *The Telegraph*, 19 Jan.

Rich, T., n.d. *Mashiach: The Messiah*. [Online]
Available at: http://www.jewfaq.org/mashiach.htm

Rolls, E., 2015. Limbic systems for emotion and for memory, but no single limbic system. *ScienceDirect,* Volume 62, pp. 119-157.

Rolls, E. & Grabenhorst, F., 2008. The orbitofrontal cortex and beyond: from affect to decision-making. *Progress in Neurobiology,* Volume 86, pp. 216-244.

Russell, A., 2003. Bush's flying circus leaves out only the kitchen sink. *The Telegraph,* 15 Nov.

Saalmann, Y. & Kastner, S., 2012. Cognitive and perceptual functions of the visual thalamus. *Neuron ,* Volume 71, pp. 209-223.

Saalmann, Y., Pinsk, M. & Wang, L., 2012. Pulvinar regulates information transmission between cortical areas based on attention demands. *Science,* Volume 337, pp. 753-756.

Salamone, J. & Correa, M., 2012. The mysterious motivational functions of mesolimbic dopamine. *Neuron Review,* Volume 76, pp. 470-485.

Samarin, W., 1972. Sociolinguistic vs. Neurophysiological Explanations for Glossolalia: Comment on Goodman's Paper. *Journal for the Scientific Study of Religion,* 11(3), pp. 293-296.

Satomi, M., 1993. *Journey in Search of the Way: The spiritual autobiography of Satomi Myodo.* New York: State University of New York Press.

Schiffer, M., 2003. *Draw the Lightning Down: Benjamin Franklin and Electrical Technology in the Age of Enlightenment.* Berkeley: University of California Press.

Schneier, B., 2014. *Antivirus Companies Should Be More Open About Their Government Malware Discoveries.* [Online]
Available at: http://www.technologyreview.com/view/533136/antivirus-companies-should-be-more-open-about-their-government-malware-discoveries/

Schoenbaum, G., Stainaker, T. & Niv, Y., 2013. How did the chicken cross the road? with her striatal cholinergic interneurons, of course. *Neuron,* Volume 79.

Shackman, A., McMenamin, B. & Maxwell, J., 2009. Right dorsolateral prefrontal cortical activity and behavioral inhibition. *Psychological Science,* 20(12), pp. 1500-1506.

Shanklin, W., 2012. *Steve Jobs' most disruptive trait: his obsession with the customer's experience.* [Online]
Available at: http://www.gizmag.com/steve-jobs-customers-experience/24444/

Sharp, E., n.d. *Gott Mit Uns.* [Online]
Available at: http://ww1centenary.oucs.ox.ac.uk/?p=1638

Shenhav, A., Botvinick, M. & Cohen, J., 2013. The expected value of control: an integrative theory of anterior cingulate cortex. *Neuron,* pp. 217-240.

Shine, J., Matar, E. & Ward, P., 2013. Exploring the cortical and subcortical functional magnetic resonance imaging changes associated with freezing in Parkinson's disease. *BRAIN,* Volume 136, pp. 1204-1215.

Singh, D., 2014. *How feasible is Elon Musk's idea to establish a colony on Mars in the 2020s?.* [Online]
Available at: http://www.quora.com/How-feasible-is-Elon-Musks-idea-to-establish-a-colony-on-Mars-in-the-2020s

SIPRI, 2013. *SIPRI Top 100.* [Online]
Available at: http://www.sipri.org/research/armaments/production/recent-trends-in-arms-industry

Smith, J. & Yong, A., 2010. *Science and the Spirit: A Pentecostal Engagement.* Bloomington: Indiana University Press.

Smith, K. & Graybiel, A., 2014. Investigating habits: strategies, technologies and models. *Frontiers in Behavioral Neuroscience,* 8(39).

Sondhaus, L., 2000. *Franz Conrad Von Hötzendorf: Architect of the apocalypse.* Boston: Humanities Press.

Sowman, P., Crain, S. & Harrison, E., 2012. Reduced activation of left orbitofrontal cortex precedes blocked vocalization: A magnetoencephalographic study. *Journal of Fluency Disorders,* 37(4), pp. 359-365.

Strieber, W., 2015. *Journal.* [Online]
Available at: http://www.unknowncountry.com/journal/anne-lady-autumn

Stuss, D., 2006. New approaches to prefrontal lobe testing. In: B. Miller & J. Cummings, eds. *The Human Frontal Lobes.* 2nd ed. New York: The Guilford Press.

The Great War - Complete BBC Series. 1964. [Film] s.l.: s.n.

Thomas, E., 1986. Defensive About Defense. *Time,* 10 March.

Thompson, C., 2010. *Anatomy of the soul : surprising connections between neuroscience and spiritual practices that can transform your life and relationships.* Carol Stream, IL: SaltRiver.

Toynbee, A., 1947. *A Study of History.* Oxford: Oxford University Press.

Tremlin, T., 2006. *Minds and Gods: The cognitive foundations of religion.* Oxford: Oxford University Press.

Tremlin, T., 2013. Evolutionary religion studies. In: *A New Science of Religion.* New York: Routledge.

Tsujimoto, S. & Postle, B., 2012. The prefrontal cortex and oculomotor delayed response: a reconsideration of the "mnemonic scotoma". *Journal of Cognitive Neuroscience,* 24(3), pp. 627-635.

Vatican Radio, 2013. *Pope Francis leads worldwide Eucharistic Adoration.* [Online]
Available at: http://www.news.va/en/news/pope-francis-leads-worldwide-eucharistic-adoration

Vermorel, H. a. M., 1993. *Sigmund Freud et Rolland Romain.* Paris: Presses Universitaires de France.

Volkow, N. & Baler, R., 2014. Addiction science: uncovering neurobiological complexity. *Neuropharmacology,* Volume 76, pp. 235-249.

Volkow, N., Wang, G.-J. & Fowler, J., 2011. Addiction: beyond dopamine reward circuitry. *PNAS,* 108(37), pp. 15037-15042.

Volle, E., Gonen-Yaacovi, G. & de Lacy Costello, A., 2011. The role of rostral prefrontal cortex in prospective memory: a voxel-based study. *Neuropsychologia,* 49(8), pp. 2185-2198.

Volz, K., Rubsamen, R. & von Cramon, D., 2008. Cortical regions activated by. *Cognitive, Affective, & Behavioral Neuroscience,* 8(3), pp. 318-328.

Wagner, D., Haxby, J. & Heatherton, T., 2012. The representation of self and person knowledge in the medial prefrontal cortex. *Wiley Interdisciplinary Review of Cognitive Science,* 3(4), pp. 451-470.

Wagner, U., N'Diaye, K. & Ethofer, T., 2011. Guilt specific-processing in the prefrontal cortex. *Cerebral Cortex,* 21(11), pp. 2461-2470.

Wall, N., De La Parra, M. & Callaway, E., 2013. Differential innervation of direct-and indirect-pathway striatal projection neurons. *Neuron,* Volume 79, pp. 347-360.

Wallop, H., 2015. Harry Wallop: Churchill's feats impossible to match, beginning with his daily alcohol consumption. *National Post,* 29 Jan.

Wang, J., Conder, J. & Blitzer, D., 2010. Neural represetation of abstract and concrete concepts: a meta-analysis of neuroimaging studies. *Human Brain Mapping,* Volume 31, pp. 1459-1468.

Wang, M., Yang, Y. & Wang, C.-J., 2013. NMDA receptors subserve persistent neuronal firing during working memory in dorsolateral prefrontal cortex. *Neuron,* Volume 77, pp. 736-749.

Watson, C. & Chatterjee, A., 2012. A bilateral frontoparietal network underlies visuospatial analogical reasoning. *Neuroimage,* 59(3), pp. 2831-2838.

Watson, M., 1999. *Merla's Miracle.* s.l.:Catacombs Productions.

Watts, J., 2005. Welcome to the strangest show on earth. *The Guardian,* 1 October.

Weintraub, D., 2014. *Religions and Extraterrestrial Life: How Will We Deal With It?.* s.l.:Cham Springer International Publishing.

Weir, A., 1991. *The Six Wives of Henry VIII.* New York: Grove Weidenfeld.

Weld, T., 1839. *American Slavery As It Is: Testimony of a Thousand Witnesses.* New York: American Anti-slavery Society.

Wellman, J., 2012. *UW Megachurch Study.* [Online]
Available at: http://www.scribd.com/doc/103623517/UW-Megachurch-Study#scribd

Wickware, P., 2001. The numbers game. *Nature,* 412(4-5).

Witteman, J., van IJzendoorn, M. & van de Velde, D., 2011. The nature of hemispheric specialization for linguistic and emotional prosodic perception: a meta-analysis of the lesion literature. *Neuropsychologia,* Volume 49, pp. 3722-3738.

Wolfe, A., 2003. *The Transformation of American Religion: How we actually live our faith.* New York: Free Press.

Wooden, C., 2006. *Pope reflects on Eucharist, makes concrete suggestions for Mass.* [Online]
Available at: http://www.americancatholic.org/Features/BenedictXVI/pope-eucharist.asp

Wright, N. T., 2008. *Surprised by Hope: Rethinking heaven, the resurrection, and the mission of the church.* New York: HarperOne.

Wright, N. T., 2010. *After you believe : why Christian character matters.* New York: HarperOne.

Wright, N. T., 2013. *Paul and the Faithfulness of God.* Minneapolis: Fortress Press.

Wunderlich, K., Dayan, P. & Dolan, R., 2012. Mapping value based planning and extensively trained choice in the human brain. *Nature Neuroscience,* 15(5), pp. 786-791.

Young, C., Wu, S. & Menon, V., 2012. The neurodevelopmental basis of math anxiety. *Psychological Science,* 23(5), pp. 492-501.

Young, H. & Freedman, R., 2012. *Sears and Zemansky's University Physics : With modern physics.* London: Addison-Wesley.

Yü Lu, K., 1964. *The secrets of Chinese meditation; self-cultivation by mind control as taught in the Ch'an Mahāyāna and Taoist schools in China.* London: Rider.

Yu, H., Hu, J. & Hu, L., 2014. The voice of conscience: Neural bases of interpersonal guilt and compensation. *Social Cognitive and Affective Neuroscience,* 9(8), pp. 1150-1158.

Zaki, J., Davis, J. & Ochsner, K., 2012. Overlapping activity in anterior insula during interoception and emotional experience. *NeuroImage,* Volume 62, pp. 493-499.

Zeki, S., Romaya, J. P. & Benincasa, D., 2014. The experience of mathematical beauty and its neural correlates. *Frontiers in Human Neuroscience,* 8(68).

Zhu, L., Jenkins, A. & Set, E., 2014. Damage to dorsolateral prefrontal cortex affects tradeoffs between honesty and self-interest. *Nature Neuroscience,* Volume 17, pp. 1319-1321.

Zikopoulos, B. & Barbas, H., 2012. Pathways for emotions and attention converge on the thalamic reticular nucleus in primates. *The Journal of Neuroscience,* 32(15), pp. 5338-5350.

If a paper has more than three authors, then only the first three are shown here.

Made in the USA
Charleston, SC
20 April 2015